Emerging Methods in Environmental Design and Planning

Hargreaves

Emerging Methods in Environmental Design and Planning

Based on the Proceedings of
The Design Methods Group
First International Conference
Cambridge, Massachusetts
June 1968

edited by Gary T. Moore

First MIT Press
Paperback edition,
August 1973

Set in Linofilm Helvetica by Book
Graphics, Inc.
Printed by Halliday Lithograph Corp.
Bound in the United States of America

ISBN 0 262 13057 2 (hardcover)
ISBN 0 262 63048 6 (paperback)

Library of Congress catalog card number:
71–87290

Completion of this manuscript was made
possible by an enabling grant from
The Graham Foundation for
Advanced Studies in the Fine Arts.

10
Reflections

Preface to the Paperback Edition

"A preface," someone once wrote, "enables a writer to put his afterthoughts foremost." This is even more true for a preface revised three years after the first publication of a book. The present task is a curious and difficult one for me—curious because my active involvement in design and planning methodology came full-circle with the completion of the original hardcover edition of this book, and difficult because I now have only partial knowledge of newer developments in this rapidly expanding area of research. However, the present task does allow me to indicate what lies before you, what the context was for the research reported herein and how it has changed over the intervening years, and to share some reflections on this work, on the advances that have been made, and on new directions explored in recent years.

Context and Organization of the Book

In general, this book is concerned with new methods for solving the problems of the large-scale physical environment. It is based on papers presented at the International Conference of the Design Methods Group held in Cambridge, Massachusetts in June, 1968, and rewritten in 1968–1969. The conference (and the formation in 1966 of the Design Methods Group) stemmed from the realization that traditional methods of designing and planning being taught in schools of architecture, planning, and civil engineering were inadequate for the complexity of problems facing our disciplines. Designers and planners were beginning to recognize problems which had gone unattended for decades, and for which there had been no adequate training programs. Many an architect and planner came to the realization that they, as single individuals, in traditional garb, were incapable of addressing these problems. Some slunk away and hid, preferring to design the occasional highly tailored, overdesigned "estate," or to plan yet another master plan for a few more trees and covered arcades, while others cast aside the robes of tradition, stood naked and open to attack, and began to look for and develop better methods.

The move toward new and improved methods of design and planning began soon after the Second World War, encouraged by this increasing awareness of the complexity of architecture and planning problems and by the realization that certain systematic approaches (systems analysis, operations research, and related procedures) had been tremendously effective in large-scale military problems and might be profitably translated into civilian design and planning areas.

In architecture (as well as in industrial design) the movement received its impetus from the thinking, research, and teaching at the Hochschule für Gestaltung at Ulm, West Germany in the 1950s under the leadership of Horst Rittel and others. Subsequently, this movement was transported to Great Britain, where it benefited greatly from the writings and teachings first of Bruce Archer, Christopher Jones, Edward Matchett, and Sidney Gregory, and more recently also of Thomas Marcus, Geoffrey Broadbent, and others.[1] This early thrust in design methods in Britain was consolidated by the first international meeting of design methodologists in London in 1962[2] followed by the formation of the Design Research Society and further meetings and conference proceedings from Birmingham in 1965,[3] Portsmouth 1967,[4] and Manchester 1971.[5]

In the United States and Canada, the movement toward new methods in architecture received its strongest leads from the teachings of Horst Rittel, who moved to Berkeley in the early 1960s,[6] and from the work of Christopher Alexander and his colleagues (including Marvin Manheim) first at Harvard-MIT and then at Berkeley.[7,8]

The development of new methodology in urban planning and transportation engineering appears to have evolved from ad hoc opportunism at the turn of the century, through comprehensive master planning up to midcentury, to the present concerns with social policy-making and public decision-making. The movement began earlier than in architecture ("satisfactory methods can be arrived at only by applying modern scientific method" was argued as early as 1917) and it has had a longer and somewhat richer history. It has been less dominated by one or two people, although Martin Meyerson and Edward Banfield's classic study of decision-making in

1. The most influential of these early writings was L. Bruce Archer's series, "Systematic Methods for Designers" (1965). (See Bibliography, pp. 369 ff., for this and all subsequent references identified simply by author, title, and (date); new references are given in full.)
2. See J. C. Jones and D. G. Thornley, eds., *Conference on Design Methods* (1963).
3. S. A. Gregory, ed., *The Design Method* (1966).
4. G. Broadbent and A. Ward, eds., *Design Methods in Architecture* (1969).
5. N. Cross, ed., *Design Participation*, London: Academy Publications, 1971.
6. Some of H. Rittel's early lectures are contained in his *The Universe of Design* (1966).
7. C. Alexander, *Notes on the Synthesis of Form* (1964); and C. Alexander and M. L. Manheim, *HIDECS 2* (1962b).
8. See the papers by Rittel, Archer, Jones, Alexander, and Manheim in this volume; some of Marcus' early views are expressed in the paper by his colleague T. Maver.

Chicago in the 1950s signaled a major turning point[9] and the more recent writings of Walter Isard, Britton Harris, Melvin Webber, Marvin Manheim, and many others have had large influences.[10]

Once the beginnings were made, there was considerable interest in the new methods, which rapidly were adopted and further developed in schools of architecture and planning in many countries.

In response to these changes, Marvin Manheim, Martin Krampen, Allen Bernholtz, Serge Bounterline, Robert Frew, Charles Owen, and myself, all of whom happened to be drawn together by Krampen's International Design and Planning Seminars at the University of Waterloo in Ontario, formed the Design Methods Group in 1966. Our purpose was to encourage scientific research, theory, and application of new methods in each of the professions and disciplines involved in environmental design and planning. Our first endeavor was to initiate the monthly *DMG Newsletter,* which I edited from Berkeley and which subsequently was published by Sage Publications in Los Angeles. The *Newsletter* (and now the newer DMG-DRS Publications) contained ongoing and recently completed research on design methods. From the beginning, contributors to these publications represented an extremely broad range of backgrounds and included researchers, educators, practitioners, and students from the professions of industrial design, architecture, civil engineering, and urban and regional planning, and from the disciplines of computer science operations research, systems engineering, and the behavioral and social sciences.

Our next major venture was to sponsor an international conference on design and planning methods. Response was overwhelming. With the help of expert referees, some 36 papers were selected for presentation. Contributors and participants came from the United States, Canada, Great Britain, Argentina, and Australia. After the conference, and largely thanks to the encouragement of Richard Meier and Marvin Manheim, I decided to pursue publication of the proceedings for a wider audience. John Entenza on behalf of the Graham Foundation was gracious enough to financially assist in completion of the manuscript, and The MIT Press offered to publish it. This book, then, contains the papers from that conference, along with additional commentaries invited after the conference. The book includes position papers summarizing the latest work of several internationally known researchers, and introduces the work of a number of younger investigators.

Four papers (those by Bruce Archer, Christopher Alexander and Barry Poyner, Gerald Nadler, and Marvin Manheim) constitute different comprehensive approaches to the overall process of planning and design, and have been brought together in Section 9. Respectively, they represent an analytic systems approach, a structural-behavioral approach (which has evolved into a pattern language approach[11]), a systems engineering approach modified for socio-economic problems, and an evolutionary systems approach stressing the mutability of goals and cycles of prediction, evaluation, and choice.

The remainder of the volume is devoted to presentations and evaluations of specific new methods applicable to problems ranging from architectural building design and urban housing to long-range transportation, water supply, and socio-economic planning. Areas of research and development covered include building layout models, computer-aided design, environmental evaluation, systems engineering, and approaches to behavioral design. Each section of the book begins with a brief introduction and is concluded with a summary and commentary by an acknowledged authority in that area of methodology.

Although some of the papers have been superseded by more advanced work, many are still timely and continue to stimulate research and application. For example, the papers in Section 9 on comprehensive approaches to design and planning methodology form the conceptual basis for many research investigations. On the other hand, a number of interesting directions suggested in other papers have not yet been explored; perhaps readers of this edition will be so inclined.

Many of the papers in the volume are controversial and oppose one another. No attempt was made to select articles which agree with each other. In fact, an effort was made to include contrasting points of view and approaches to environmental problem-solving.

Reactions It has been extremely gratifying personally to see the generally warm reception given the hardcover edition of this book, and to see the demand for a less expensive paperback edition. The hardcover edition is being used as a book

9. M. Meyerson and E. C. Banfield, *Politics, Planning, and the Public Interest* (1965).
10. For example, W. Isard, *Methods of Regional Analysis* (1960); and B. Harris, ed., *Urban Development Models: New Tools for Planning* (1965).
11. See the paper by F. Duffy and J. Torrey in Section 8 of this volume.

of readings in many schools of architecture, planning, and engineering, and I hope that this new paperback edition will finally make it available to a wider audience, especially students who are searching for a personal direction in the field. I am pleased to see that the book received a Design Award from the Type Directors Club of New York, credit which must go to the design, layout, and typography departments of The MIT Press. The book is being translated into Japanese and parts of it into French. Finally, I have received notes, letters, and comments from people in various parts of the world, all of which have been most appreciated.

The book has also been the subject of a large number of reviews. I would like to comment on a few of the interesting questions raised.

William Michelson, a Toronto sociologist, in a review in *Design and Environment,* points out that Section 9, labeled "Major Theories of Design and Planning Methodology," has nothing at all to do with theories in the usual scientific sense. He is quite right. Theories in science are testable statements of functional relationships between variables which both summarize the available data and serve to explain them. The so-called "theories" in Section 9 are not of this sort. They are not testable, except in the sense of practical tests, and they have no connection with data or functional relationships. Rather, inasmuch as the papers in this section represent different philosophies on the overall process of design and planning, this section and its contents might better be termed "Alternative Comprehensive Approaches to Design and Planning." Most of the other papers in the book discuss specific techniques for handling particular aspects of environmental problems; the papers in this section, however, suggest comprehensive approaches to the entire process, each based on different assumptions about what constitutes the structure and critical aspects of environmental problems and the nature of the design and planning process. Thus, for example, Alexander and Poyner argue that the critical aspect of environmental problem-solving is the satisfaction of basic behavioral tendencies and, thus, that the nature of the design process is the determination of tendencies and of possible conflicts between tendencies in different environment-behavior settings.

This line of thinking is pursued also in the Duffy and Torrey paper on the pattern language and in the Ward paper on relational theory. In a different direction, Manheim considers that the most critical aspects of environmental problems are the diversity of opinions of different user and interest groups, including those affected by the project, and thus that problem-solving procedures need to be structured to facilitate explicitly communication among these groups.

It might be thought that one or another of these approaches is more "right" or "better" than the others. It is my view, however, that methodology can only be evaluated in the context of the type of problems to which it is addressed, and thus there can be no absolute "right" or "better." This suggests that what is most needed at the present stage of development is first an analysis of the nature and the context of the problems to which each of these approaches seems best suited and, second, a critical evaluation of the strengths and weaknesses of each of them (and of others, for example Rittel's IBIS system). Yet the articulation of the demands of different problems and contexts and the resultant match of alternative methodologies has yet to be fully addressed. Rittel, however, has made important beginnings in articulating the difference between what he calls "tame" and "wicked" problems and the resultant difference between "first-" and "second-generation" design methods, the latter to deal with the inherently multidimensional and ill-defined nature of "wicked" problems.[12] Thomas Thompson, Donald Grant, and others are attempting to articulate a range of different types of complex, wicked problems and their appropriate strategies.[13]

Another point raised in the Michelson review concerns behavioral evaluation of completed projects. He asks rhetorically, "Why aren't there prizes—valuable and prestigious ones—offered to architects of buildings at least five years old (i.e., old enough to have been broken in and routinized) on the basis of how well these buildings work? Why isn't there a payoff for people who worry about creating designs that achieve their purpose?" He makes the point, and on this I certainly would concur, that the approaches presented in this volume have in common a concern for the satisfaction of meaning-

12. See J.-P. Protzen's interview with Horst Rittel on "The state of the art in design methods," *DMG Fifth Anniversary Report,* Berkeley: Design Methods Group, Department of Architecture, University of California, 1972, pp. 5–10; W. Kunz and H. Rittel, "Issues as elements of information systems" (Abstract), *Ibid.,* pp. 13–15; and W. Kunz and H. Rittel, "Issues as elements of information systems," Berkeley: Institute of Urban and Regional Development, University of California, Working Paper No. 131, 1970.
13. Stimulus statements for the 1973 Joint DRS-DMG Design Activity Conference, London, England. My thanks to Tom Thompson and Donald Grant for information and comments on current work in design methodology.

ful *objectives,* i.e., for *performance,* not esthetics. Our ability to evaluate completed projects vis-à-vis these objectives and in terms of performance, however, is still at a rudimentary level. Some suggestions in project evaluation are made in the papers by Maver and by Silvers, and some sharp comments on evaluation are offered by Brill and Rose, the former of whom has had extensive experience with performance standards at the U.S. National Bureau of Standards. While much work remains to be done, some interesting evaluation techniques have been proposed recently by environmental psychologists and behaviorally oriented architects.[14]

In another review, James M. Addiss, a New York architect and architectural educator, argues in *Progressive Architecture* that the cumulative effect of research on the application of computers to design has been to "flatten out the primary issues and hence distort priorities." He suggests that there is a basic dichotomy between those approaches and techniques which are primarily responses to what can be done with computers, and which thus require, he believes, enormous simplification of the issues involved, and those which attempt to respond to human behavior and the forms required.

R. G. Hopkinton, in the *Journal of the Royal Town Planning Institute,* goes further on this issue, claiming that, as he sees it, most of the papers in this volume are concerned in one way or another with the application of computers to design and are not concerned with the nature and structure of current real, environmental problems.

Though I agree with Addis' distinction between methods which are primarily generated in response to "applications of technology" or, more generally, independent of a problem context, versus those which are developed in response to particular environmental problems, I only share in part his concern that *too many methods* may be of the first type. Similarly, though I agree with Hopkinson's observation that few of the methods proposed herein are usable in their present state in traditional office situations, I feel that this is not a condemnation as much as it is a spur to encourage willing persons to develop further, apply, and modify these methods to fit professional contexts. With regard to both issues, I feel a concern about premature judgment, for I fear we may close our minds on some of the potentially more interesting directions simply because they presently are

abstract or not immediately usable in the profession. Computer technology may be our most valuable asset, and also may be our greatest hindrance. Solving behavioral problems, or at least providing form for behavior, is the ultimate goal of many of the new breed of practitioners and researchers, yet on the one hand we may have lost sight of that goal, and on the other hand we may have adhered so compulsively to it that we may be limiting our ability to see the potential in available technology and in abstract methods. It seems to me that we need a balance between the two poles of pure ideas and problem-oriented approaches and an interaction between the insights of creative thinkers and computer buffs on the one side and the demands of problems and the professions on the other side. We live in a pluralistic society and at a time when absolute value judgments are impossible to make—the creative and egalitarian solution is to recognize and encourage contributions from all directions, to balance the pure ideas of creative minds with the demands of external problem situations, and to integrate and synthesize the best of each.

Finally, the British mathematician and architectural researcher, Lionel March, has offered a very thoughtful review in *Design.* March suggests that despite the weaknesses and narrow scope of some contributions, the papers represent the state of the art at the end of a decade of rapid activity and growth in design methodology. Some of the lines of work, he submits, are played out, while others are highly promising of continuing advances and discoveries. He suggests that the work in design research and methods up to 1970 consisted of three strands: (1) an attempt to understand and make explicit the psychology of the design process (e.g., the papers in Section 3 on thought in design); (2) a concern with the inherent structure of design and planning problems (e.g., Section 4 on problem structure and Section 9 on comprehensive approaches); and (3) an awareness and attempt to harness the powers of the technical achievements of systems engineering, operations research, and computer technology (e.g., Section 2 on computer-aided design, Section 5 on building layout models, and Section 7 on systems engineering). In addition to these lines, a fourth thrust appeared in the late 1960s, a thrust toward behavioral approaches to design (represented, for example in the paper by Alexander and Poyner, and those by Ward, Duffy, and Torrey, and Brolin and Zeisel in Sec-

---

14. For a summary of some recent work on evaluation, see G. T. Moore, "Problems of evaluation: models and techniques of environmental assessment and evaluation," Paper presented at the Association of Collegiate Schools of Architecture Seminars, Yosemite, California, March 1973; to be summarized in the *Journal of Architectural Education,* 1973, Vol. 28, in press.

tion 8). To this I would also add a fifth line of work, the massive development in the late 1960s of advocacy and participatory approaches to both design and planning and community-based decision-making and problem-solving (as suggested implicitly in Manheim's paper and explicitly in the comments of Frieden, Jackson, Morrey, and Peattie in the panel discussion on political processes in design and planning in Section 10).

March concludes with the suggestion that several of the papers point out that the demands of current environmental design and planning problems place both the process of solving them and the implementation of solutions outside the realm of individual effort and into the political arena, where they are more adequately conceptualized as a complex interaction between decision-making, social response, and participation in the design and planning processes. He suggests, therefore, that it may not be design and planning methods we need to study and understand, but the complex nature of the interactive systems of individual people, social groups, economics, and the physical environment. Such considerations are, of course, being explored under the labels of environment-behavior systems, man-environment relations, environmental psychology, and so on.

New Directions A number of new directions in design methods have surfaced in recent years.

Three important developments have been the publication of the first introductory textbook on design methods, Christopher Jones' *Design Methods*,[15] a sourcebook on planning methods, Ira Robinson's *Decision-Making in Planning*,[16] and the first journal explicitly focused on design and planning methods, the *DMG-DRS Journal: Design Research and Methods*.[17] Jones' textbook summarizes many design methods and partially fills the gap between the many short, casual review articles and the few books of technical readings; Robinson's sourcebook collects in one place many new planning methodologies and serves as a useful reference; while the *Journal* replaces the *DMG Newsletter* and provides a regular forum for the dissemination of research on design and planning methods. A comment on the timing and importance of these developments: Richard Meier, in a lecture some years ago at Berkeley, sug-

gested that the development of the scientific aspects of a field was marked by several important stages: first a few people communicating by letters and at informal meetings, a first conference followed by a few more conferences, creation of an organization together with the publication of a newsletter or some other semiformal medium of communication, and then the appearance of the first research journal, and, somewhat later, the first textbook and sourcebook. All of these latter developments have now occurred. Though there is certainly no accepted design methods paradigm, it is interesting that Jones has been able to collect and summarize some 35 specific techniques, including methods for generating problem boundaries, generating ideas, creating patterns among the ideas, and decision-making and convergence towards solutions. His book is being used in introductory courses in design methods in many schools and serves as a useful introduction to the field, though, unfortunately, it does not include critical evaluation of the techniques nor any discussion of planning methods. Furthermore, the techniques described in Jones' book seem most appropriate for problems which have a well-defined problem statement, are linear, and assume that all parties perceive them similarly, all rarities if problems are seen, as March, Manheim, Fleisher, and many others have suggested, in their socio-political context. A second textbook, begun today, would include the many "second-generation" methods which address ill-defined nonlinear problems and their inherent multiple interest groups, and would integrate new design methods with new planning methods.

It is also encouraging that the Design Research Society in Great Britain and the Design Methods Group in the United States and Canada have joined hands and are pursuing an accelerated program of publication and meetings. In its early issues, the *DMG-DRS Journal* concentrated on review articles bringing new readers up-to-date on this still emerging field. In addition, the publishing program of these two groups now includes a monthly Newsletter on each side of the Atlantic (the *DMG Bulletin* and the *DRS Bag,* respectively) and a series of Occasional Papers.

Research activity has increased both in quantity and depth. In the 1960s, con-

15. J. C. Jones, *Design Methods: Seeds of Human Futures,* New York and London: Wiley, 1970.
16. Ira Robinson, ed., *Decision-Making in Urban Planning: An Introduction to New Methodologies,* Beverly Hills, Calif.: Sage Publications, 1972.
17. Published by the Design Methods Group and the Design Research Society, c/o School of Architecture and Environmental Design, California State Polytechnic University, San Luis Obispo, California.

ferences on design research and methods were separated by two to three years. The Environmental Design Research Association conferences (successors, in part, to the first DMG Conference) are now held annually and include a number of sessions devoted to the latest research on design methods. The DMG-DRS is also hoping to sponsor special international meetings every two years. In terms of quantity, current research activity (as measured by numbers of papers on different topics at the design methods sessions of the EDRA Conferences) seems to be moving towards six themes: (1) environmental analysis, performance standards, and evaluation; (2) information systems for storing and retrieving design and planning data; (3) predictive, simulation, and gaming models; (4) computer-aided design; (5) automated space planning, including building layout models; and (6) strategies for design and planning teams involving multiple interest groups.

In terms of the most interesting directions, four strike me as having the most promise. The work of Alexander and his colleagues on the understanding of the structure of design problems, the translation of behavioral findings into form statements, and the development of a pattern language for the description and cataloging of environment-behavior patterns continues to advance at a rapid rate.[18] Alexander was the first recipient of the American Institute of Architect's new Gold Medal for Research in 1972 for his work in developing ways to relate behavior to form.

Manheim's work, together with that of his students and colleagues, has expanded, and is having national impact, especially on transportation planning at the Federal and State levels. Readers of his paper in this volume will note his concern for multiple interest groups in public decision-making. More recently, Manheim's interest and research has concentrated on procedures for incorporating these interest groups in the design and planning process, for resolving value conflicts, and for increasing social choice. Among other things, this work has resulted in a design process manual and a set of procedural guidelines for Federal Highway planning.[19]

As alluded to several times above, Rittel's articulation of the difference between what he calls "tame" and "wicked" problems, and his resultant distinction between "first-" and "second-generation" design methods, is having a powerful impact on current research on design methods. His thinking has also led to a specific application, his development with W. Kunz, J.-P. Protzen, T. Thompson, D. Grant, and others of an Issue Based Information System (IBIS) for design and planning problem-solving. This system stresses the argumentative nature of design problems and the types of information needed at various junctures.[20]

An older line of work on advocacy and participatory planning continues. Development of this approach has been due to awareness of the multiple interest groups affected by most urban problems, each group with their own perception of what constitutes the problem and each with their own value hierarchies, plus a concern not so much for designing *for* people as designing *with* people, i.e., getting various users groups, community groups, and professionals involved together in the design process. Most recently, this approach has led to the development of community games and to the development of approaches and procedures for citizen participation in actual problem-solving sessions. Many new team approaches have been suggested, among which is the modest effort of Charles Burnette, Lynn Simek, and myself to investigate group approaches to improving communication and creativity in design problem-solving.[21]

18. As follow-ups to his paper with B. Poyner in this volume, see especially C. Alexander, S. Ishikawa, and M. Silverstein, *A Pattern Language which Generates Multi-Service Centers,* and C. Alexander, S. Hirshen, S. Ishikawa, C. Coffin, and S. Angel, *Houses Generated by Patterns,* Berkeley: Center for Environmental Structure, 1968 and ca. 1970 (n.d.).
19. See M. L. Manheim, "Reaching decisions about technological projects with social consequences," Cambridge, Mass.: Department of Civil Engineering, Massachusetts Institute of Technology, Professional Paper P70–78, 1970; and U.S. Department of Transportation, Federal Highway Administration, *Report to Congress on Section 109(h), Title 23, United States Code: Guidelines Relating to the Economic, Social, and Environmental Effects of Highway Projects,* Washington, D. C.: U. S. Government Printing Office, 1972.
20. See references in notes 12 and 13.
21. C. H. Burnette, G. T. Moore, and L. Simek, "A role-oriented approach to problem-solving in groups," in W. F. E. Preisser, ed., *Environmental Design Research,* Vol. 1, Stroudsburg, Penna.: Dowden, Hutchinson & Ross, 1973, pp. 173–182. See also the papers on citizen participation and on gaming in Sections 17–18 and Section 27, respectively, of W. J. Mitchell, ed., *Environmental Design: Research and Practice,* Los Angeles: School of Architecture and Urban Planning, University of California, 1972.

All of these recent developments seem
to share at a minimum three sets of
concerns: (1) the introduction of behavioral data into the design and planning
process; (2) a shift from highly regi-
mented methods to an integration of
certain general approaches with one's
own personal style; and (3) a shift from
linear methods to methods which stress
the simultaneity of problem formulation
and solution and the dynamics of the
collaboration among multiple interest
groups.

Finally, it is encouraging to note that
systematic design methods, both first-
and second-generation approaches, are
beginning to have an impact on the
architectural and planning professions.
A number of large firms are beginning
to implement selected methods and procedures into their practices. Several
authors in the present volume (notably
Lavette Teague and Charles Davis) are
active in these efforts. Teague reports,
however, that there is a time-lag of about
five years from the development of techniques to their implementation in practice.

In conclusion, whereas the new methods
emerging in architecture may appear
different from those emerging in urban
planning, I believe that the underlying
assumptions and idea-generation and
decision-making processes are structurally similar. It seems to me, furthermore, that a comparison and open
discussion of their similarities and
differences, their advantages and limitations, and their weaknesses and
potentials vis-à-vis various problem
contexts can be of the greatest benefit
and could perhaps form the next stage
of the development of better methods
for solving our urban and environmental
problems. It is to this continuing effort
that this book is dedicated.

Gary T. Moore
Clark University

Acknowledgments

Beyond the authors, without whose ideas there would have been no reason for a Conference or for a book, many people have actively contributed to make both possible. Without their support and encouragement, neither would have been more than ideas. To these people, I would like to express my sincere gratitude.

The Conference was cosponsored by the School of Architecture of the Boston Architectural Center, the Departments of Architecture and Civil Engineering and the Urban Systems Laboratory of M.I.T., and the Department of Architecture and Laboratory for Computer Graphics of the Harvard Graduate School of Design. My thanks to Sanford Greenfield, Donlyn Lyndon, Charles Miller, Jerzy Soltan, and Howard Fisher for their support. And my special thanks to Dean Lawrence Anderson of the School of Architecture and Planning at M.I.T. Thanks also to Stuart Silverstone and Kenneth Geiser, who handled the many local arrangements.

My thanks to the following members of the Editorial Advisory Board and Staff of the Design Methods Group who reviewed papers and made suggestions for revisions: Donald Appleyard, John Archea, John Eberhard, Jerry Finrow, Howard Fisher, Britton Harris, Alan Hershdorfer, Walter Isard, Christopher Jones, Charles Kowal, Donlyn Lyndon, Gerald McCue, Barry Poyner, Horst Rittel, Charles Rusch, Peter Slann, Martin Starr, Wilbur Steger, Michael Teitz, and Gary Winkel.

Completion of the manuscript was made possible by a grant from the Graham Foundation for Advanced Studies in the Fine Arts. My personal thanks to the Director, John Entenza, for his confidence in this venture.

I would also like to take this opportunity to express my appreciation to several people at the College of Environmental Design, University of California, who have supported the Group and the *DMG Newsletter* since their inception in 1966, especially Gerald McCue, Chairman of the Department of Architecture, Melvin Webber, Chairman of the Center for Planning and Development Research, and Dean William Wheaton. Without their support little of this would have been possible.

Many other people too numerous to mention have contributed ideas, advice, criticism, and assistance on the Conference and this book. To all of them, my sincere thanks.

And my thanks especially to Marvin Manheim, who from the beginning has assisted immeasurably in the formation of the Group, and who provided much of the enthusiasm and coordination for the Conference. Over these years he has been a continual source of guidance, encouragement, and friendship.

G.T.M.

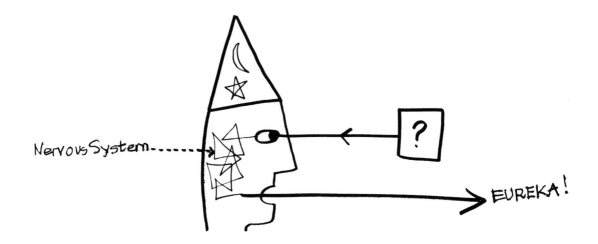

Nervous System

? EUREKA!

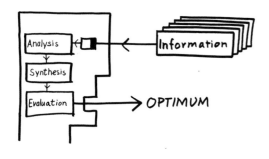

Analysis

Synthesis

Evaluation

Information

OPTIMUM

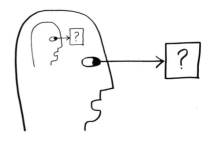

?

1 The State of the Art in Design Methods

J. Christopher Jones

Design Research Laboratory,
Department of Building,
University of Manchester Institute
of Science and Technology
Manchester, England

J. Christopher Jones is Senior Lecturer
in Industrial Design Technology at the
University of Manchester Institute of
Science and Technology and is Vice-
Chairman of the Design Research Society. Previously he was an industrial
designer and ergonomist in the electrical
industry and Chairman of the Industrial
Section of the Ergonomics Research
Society. He has written extensively and
lectured internationally on topics of design methods, human factors, and technological change, and is a coeditor of the
first compendium on design methods,
Conference on Design Methods. Presentation of this paper at the Design Methods
Group Conference was made possible
through the support of Dean Lawrence W.
Anderson and the School of Architecture
and Planning at M.I.T. The author and
Conference Program Committee gratefully acknowledge his assistance. This
paper also appears in Anthony Ward and
Geoffrey H. Broadbent, eds., *Design
Methods in Architecture,* and will appear
in the author's book, *Design Methods.*
It is published here with permission of
John Wiley & Sons.

1. Designer as magician

2. Designer as computer

3. Designer as self-organizing system

It is not easy to see what the new methods of designing the man-made physical environment have in common with each other and with the tradi-tional methods that they are intended to replace. The application of a great variety of techniques, ranging from brainstorming and synectics to decision theory and systems engineering, may appear at first sight to be both contra-dictory and impractical. A second impression is that the apparent diversity may conceal a few new principles of designing that would be of more use to designers than are the methods themselves. A third impression is that the new methods are not concerned with designing as we know it but with the thinking that precedes the making of drawings and designs. It is the aim of this introduction to explore such doubts and questions and to provide a framework that may be helpful to students of design methodology and to practicing designers and planners.

The first question to be answered is, "What do the new methods have in common?" The most obvious answer is that all design methods (such as those which appear in this volume) are attempts to make public the hitherto private thinking of designers, to externalize the design process. In some cases this is done in words, sometimes in mathematical symbols, and nearly always with a diagram representing parts of the design problem and rela-

3

tionships between the parts. Clearly, the underlying aim is to bring designing into the open so that other people can see what is going on and contribute to it information and insights that are outside the individual designer's knowledge and experience.

We can ask ourselves why, at this period in history, have so many people tried to externalize design thinking. Surely the answer is that there is a worldwide dissatisfaction with traditional methods of designing. The high cost of design errors, particularly in the case of complex urban systems, is a strong incentive to externalize design thought; only in this way can it be subjected to criticism and testing before expensive mistakes are made. The sudden appearance, in many parts of the world, of methods of doing this is in itself striking evidence that design problems have grown too big and too complicated to be left to the private judgments of even the most experienced designers. The problem, recognized but not solved, is to devise languages of design in which the complexity and speed of the designer's artistic modes of thought can be combined with scientific doubt and rational explanation.

It is doubtful if any of the design languages that have appeared so far provides an adequate answer to this great problem. Nevertheless, it is likely that these first attempts at bridging the gap between applied art and applied science contain the ingredients out of which effective languages for corporate designing will be constructed. Certainly the business of language construction is the essential step between the piecemeal evolution of manmade things to the present time and the intelligent control that many people now wish to apply to the whole process of technological change. If the intelligence with which we hope to choose the future is itself to be artificial, i.e., composed of computers and computer languages, it becomes even more evident that the invention of languages for designing is an essential step toward gaining control over technological evolution.

Having looked briefly at the common aim of the mixed set of design methods that have appeared so far, we can now discuss the differences between them and their usefulness in practice. A simple way of doing this is to review the new methods from three points of view: (1) that of creativity, (2) that of rationality, and (3) that of control over the design process. Each can be symbolized in a cybernetic picture of the designer. From the creative viewpoint the designer is a black box out of which comes the mysterious creative leap; from the rational viewpoint the designer is a glass box inside which can be discerned a completely explicable rational process; and from the control viewpoint the designer is a self-organizing system capable of finding shortcuts across unknown territory. This last and least familiar viewpoint is the one that leads us most directly to the practical value of design theory and toward the next step in the evolution of usable design methods.

Designers as Black Boxes

An important minority of design theorists, notably Osborn, Gordon, Matchett, and Broadbent, imply that the most valuable part of the design process is that which goes on inside the designer's head and partly out of reach of his conscious control.[1] In making this point, the "creativity" theorists place themselves in opposition to the rationalists of designing and find that many practicing designers agree with them. Despite its "irrational" assumption, the black-box view of designing can be clearly expressed in cybernetic or physiological terms. We can say that the human designer, like other animals, is capable of producing outputs in which he has confidence, and which often succeed, without his being able to say how these outputs were obtained. Expressed in this way we can see that the mysteries of creativity are only a special case of the equally mysterious way in which we produce most of our outputs, or actions, without being able to explain them. The apparently simple action of writing and the even simpler action of reaching for a pencil

1. Alex F. Osborn, *Applied Imagination: Principles and Procedures of Creative Problem Solving*; William J. J. Gordon, *Synectics: The Development of Creative Capacity*; Geoffrey H. Broadbent, "Creativity," in Sidney A. Gregory, ed., *The Design Method,* pp. 111–119; and Edward Matchett, "Control of Thought in Creative Work." Complete references for all footnotes will be found in the bibliography at the end of this volume.

are just as inexplicable as is the composing of a symphony, perhaps more so. (Nobody has yet programmed a computer to produce outputs that are anywhere near as "intelligent" as bodily movement, but we seem to be in sight of composing music automatically.) Most human actions can be explained only if one assumes that they are largely governed by the skilled nervous system without the intervention of conscious thought. The creative view of designing, the view of designer as magician, is a poetic description of that which underlies the action of every human or other animal that has a nervous system.

It is therefore rational to believe that skilled actions are unconsciously controlled and irrational to expect designing to be wholly capable of a rational explanation.

Newman is one of many researchers who have attempted to explain how the nervous system produces its enormously variable output. He suggests that the brain is a network that continually changes its pattern according to the inputs it receives from the outside world.[2] According to this theory, for which there is some physiological evidence, the "leap of insight" which many creative people experience is the result of the network suddenly adopting, after many fruitless attempts, a pattern that is compatible with the inputs that it has recently received.[3] Experimental studies of memory suggest that past experiences are repatterned every time one tries to remember them.[4]

These two hypotheses together lead to the picture of the brain as a semi-automatic device that is capable of resolving incompatibilities between inputs (i.e., capable of solving problems) by assuming a pattern that is compatible not only with the current inputs but also with many previous inputs of which the memory is composed. If we are to believe the psychoanalysts, brain functioning can be both hindered and helped by the persistence of unresolved conflicts from as long ago as early childhood. Certainly the output from the brain is conditioned not only by the current situation but also by situations encountered in the past. This is, of course, a long-winded way of stating the obvious practical fact that nobody can be a good designer without the right experience.

The main conclusions that we can draw about black-box design methods are
1. The output of a designer is governed by inputs received recently from the problem and also by other inputs received from previous problems and experiences.
2. His output can be speeded up, but made more random, by the agreement to relax social inhibitions for a period.
3. His capacity to produce outputs relevant to the problem is dependent upon his being given time to assimilate and to manipulate within himself images representing the structure of the problem as a whole. During a long and seemingly fruitless search for a solution he may suddenly perceive a new way of structuring the problem so that conflicts are resolved. This pleasant experience is the "leap of insight."
4. Intelligent control over the forms in which the problem structure is fed into the human black box is likely to increase the chances of obtaining outputs that are relevant to the design problem.[5]

Designers as Glass Boxes

The majority of design methods are concerned with externalized thought and are therefore based on rational rather than mystical assumptions. The design process is assumed to be entirely explicable, even though practicing designers may be unable to give convincing reasons for all the decisions that they make. The inventors of most systematic design methods do not question

2. A. D. Newman, "Patterns," in Gregory, *The Design Method*, pp. 105–109.
3. For example, see the reports in Jacques Hadamard, *An Essay on the Psychology of Invention in the Mathematical Field*, and in Brewster Ghiselin, ed., *The Creative Process*.
4. Frederic Bartlett, *Remembering*.
5. The reader is referred to Part 2 of this volume, "Thought in Design," for experimental studies of "black-box" processes. Ed.

the idea that a human designer is able to operate with full knowledge of what he is doing and why he is doing it.

The picture of the rational, or systematic, designer is much that of a human computer, a person who operates only on the information that is fed to him and who follows through a planned sequence of analytical, synthetic, and evaluative steps and cycles until he recognizes the best of all possible solutions. This assumption of rationality is, of course, valid in the case of computer optimization of the variables within a familiar design situation, but it also underlies such design methods as morphology, systems engineering, and the decision theory approach, all of which are intended by their inventors for use by the human "computer" in solving much less familiar design problems.[6]

The common characteristics of the glass-box methods are as follows:[7]
1. Objectives, variables, and criteria are fixed in advance.
2. Analysis is completed, or at least attempted, before solutions are sought.
3. Evaluation is largely linguistic and logical (as opposed to experimental).
4. Strategies are fixed in advance; these are predominantly sequential but often include parallel operations, conditional operations, and recycling.

The results of applying these seemingly crippling limitations to human designers are not uniformly bad or uniformly good. For some kinds of design problems, glass-box methods are found to work better than the black-box approach, whereas in other cases they end in confusion from which the designers revert to their accustomed black-box behavior.

Splittable Design Problems

The practical question in the case of glass-box methods is whether the design problem can be split into separate pieces that can be solved in series or in parallel. If a problem can be decomposed, more intelligence can be applied to the solution of each subproblem, and design time can be drastically reduced.

Big design problems are, of course, always decomposed at some point in order to put many designers to work together, but how the splitting is done varies very much from one kind of product to another. Chemical plants, electrical supply networks, telephone systems, and the like can be split from the start into functional subproblems, each of which can be solved in parallel. This is because they are all flow systems in which each function is allocated to a separate physical component that is linked to the others only at predetermined inlets and outlets. There is a one-to-one relationship between functions and physical components. The whole assembly of inputs and outputs can be specified at the start, and each of the components can be designed afterwards on the assumption that if it fits the inputs and outputs it fits the system. Minor departures from the original input and output specification and tradeoffs between components do not unduly disrupt the planned design sequence. In design situations of this sort, glass-box design methods of a rudimentary kind are essential, if project control is to be maintained, and many of the more complicated design methods reviewed here would seem to

6. For a brief discussion of the morphological approach, see the first part of Thomas Maver, "Appraisal in the Building Design Process," in this volume. Other treatments are given by Kenneth W. Norris, "The Morphological Approach to Engineering Design," in J. Christopher Jones and Denis G. Thornley, eds., Conference on Design Methods, pp. 115–140, and by John E. Arnold, "Useful Creative Techniques," in Sidney J. Parnes and Harold F. Harding, eds., A Source Book for Creative Thinking, pp. 252–263. Systems engineering is discussed in this volume in Part 7 and in the paper by Gerald Nadler, "Engineering Research and Design in Socioeconomic Systems." Papers based in part on decision theory include those by Alan Colker and James Leib, Arthur Silvers, Bruce Archer, and Marvin Manheim. Ed.
7. Most papers in this volume represent "glass-box" approaches; examples include papers in Part 5, "Building Layout Models"; Part 7, "Applications of Systems Engineering"; and the paper by Bruce Archer, "An Overview of the Structure of the Design Process." Ed.

have promising applications provided that the main decisions are independent of the physical details of the components.[8]

Unsplittable Design Problems

Many design problems, both large and small, are difficult or impossible to decompose in this way without prejudice to performance, cost, weight, appearance, or other objectives that require many tradeoffs between components. This situation occurs in such products as buildings, cars, machine tools, and the like, in which functions are not allocated to distinct parts but spread, in a complicated and unpredictable way, over a tightly integrated assembly. The traditional answer in such cases is to give to one experienced man, the leading designer, complete responsibility for all the important decisions, whether they concern the general layout or small details of components. A good example is the responsibility of an architect for both the layout of a building and for details of window design that may be critical to the appearance that he aims to achieve. Another example is the chief engineer's responsibility, not only for the performance of a new machine but also for the choice of its critical components. In all such cases the responsible designer uses experience gained from similar design problems to solve the critical subproblems before he fixes the general layout and splits the remaining work among his subordinates. This is, of course, the traditional black-box method.

In problems that are repetitive, such as the design of roads, beams, rotors, circuits, or electric motors, it is sometimes possible to externalize all the designer's experience and to make designing wholly automatic. This is the glass-box method in its pure form. In most cases, and certainly in the ones where the risk of expensive design errors is high, this cannot be done because the necessary experience does not exist. Experience has to be generated artificially by testing and by research as part of the design process. It is in cases like this that neither glass-box methods nor black-box methods suffice and where we seem to be most in need of new design methods and design aids that combine the best of both approaches.

Designers as Self-Organizing Systems

Both black-box and glass-box methods have the effect of widening the area of search for the solution to a design problem. In the case of black-box methods this is done by removing constraints upon the output from the designer's nervous system or by stimulating him to produce a more varied output. In the case of glass-box methods, the output of the nervous system is generalized, in external symbols, to include all the alternatives of which the designer's particular ideas are a special case. The main weakness of both of these approaches is that the designer generates a universe of unfamiliar alternatives too large to explore by the slow process of conscious thought. He cannot make an intuitive, or black-box, choice (for that would reimpose the restrictions of previous experience from which he is trying to escape), neither can he use a high-speed computer to search automatically (for the computer program requires foreknowledge of objectives and criteria of choice that are themselves dependent upon the alternatives that are available). Faced with this dilemma the designer is forced (1) to abandon the new methods, (2) to make an arbitrary or black-box choice of objectives for computer search, or (3) to plod away at the impossible task of consciously evaluating every alternative individually.

The way out of this dilemma is to divide the available design effort into two parts: that which carries out the search for a suitable solution, and that which controls and evaluates the pattern of search (strategy control). If both are done, it is possible to replace blind searching of alternatives by an intelligent search that uses both external criteria and the results of partial search to find

---

8. Decomposition algorithms are presented in Part 4 of this volume. The assumption underlying these methods is that relatively independent subproblems can be isolated by analysis of the requirements of the problem. The systems engineering techniques of Part 7 are based on the assumption that there already exists a one-to-one correspondence between functions and already existing functional components, and thus, decomposition can follow a priori categories. Ed.

shortcuts across the unknown territory.[9] This procedure is possible if the portion of design effort that is reserved for strategy control provides an accurate model of two things: the strategy itself and the external situation that the design is intended to fit.

The purpose of this model of self-plus-situation (or strategy-plus-objective) is to enable each member of the design team to see for himself the degree to which the search actions decided upon do (or do not) produce an acceptable balance between the new design, the situations influenced by the design, and the cost of designing. This is done in two ways, first through the creation of a meta-language which is sufficiently general to describe relationships between a strategy and the design situation, and second through the evaluation, in this meta-language, of a model which will predict the likely results of alternative strategies yet to be undertaken so that the most promising can be selected.

A good example of such a meta-language is provided by Matchett's Fundamental Design Method.[10] In this case the common language in which external objectives and proposed strategies can be described is a tree of primary, secondary, and tertiary objectives coupled with general purpose lists describing some elements common to engineering designs, such as the product life cycle. The model for predicting the effect of any proposed design action upon the objectives is initially the teacher's judgment, and later that of the pupil when he has learned to use the method, that is, when he is able to foresee the external consequences of his intentions and, as a result, to alter his strategy.

The most useful feature of a strategy control method is that it should relate the results of small pieces of search to the ultimate objectives, even if, as is likely, the objectives are in a state of flux. The essential condition for this detailed evaluation to be achieved is that the outcome of each subaction of a design strategy can be compared with the desired consequences of the strategy as a whole. One way of doing this is to estimate the size of the penalty for wrongly guessing the outcome of a given subaction and to compare this with the cost of carrying it out. This trick is embodied in the slogan, "The cost of not knowing must exceed the cost of finding out." Estimating the cost of not knowing requires a model in which one can predict the sensitivity of the ultimate objectives to nonattainment of subobjectives. It can be logically shown that an organism capable of making such a prediction, even roughly, must make a model of itself and is incapable of describing how this model has been constructed.[11]

It is now clear that the major weakness of all methods is the difficulty of controlling strategy in novel design and planning situations and in situations where many people are engaged upon a single project. This being the case, we can see that the next step in design methodology is to evolve some reliable methods for generating and controlling the strategies of design and planning teams.

---

9. "Intelligent search" as defined here is the objective of many computer-aided design systems; see Part 3. Two authors who propose planning methods for "intelligent search" within the assumption that objectives are in a state of flux are Arthur Silvers in "Towards an Economics of Renewal Programming" and Marvin Manheim in "A Design Process Model: Theory and Applications to Transportation Planning." Ed.
10. Matchett, "Control of Thought."
11. Lawrence J. Fogel, Alvin J. Owens, and Michael J. Walsh, *Artificial Intelligence Through Simulated Evolution.*

2 Thought in Design

This selection of papers concerns thought in design, the nature of human thinking and problem-solving in the design process.

Although the psychology of thinking and problem-solving has been investigated since at least the time of Aristotle, it is only since 1950 that experiments have concentrated on understanding the specific characteristics of these processes within design. Some of the first studies are presented here.

The motivation for this research, as Christopher Jones has expressed in his introduction, is "to make public the hitherto private thinking of designers, to externalize the design process, . . . to bring designing into the open so that other people can see what is going on and contribute to it information and insights that are outside the individual designer's knowledge and experience." Augmenting the design process or developing methods to supplement the process presupposes an understanding of the nature of human thought. Some would argue that there has been too much emphasis on developing quantitative methods without first appreciating the qualities and capabilities of the human mind.

The first paper, by Richard Krauss and John Myer, is a careful post hoc analysis of the design process on a specific architectural project. Commissioned to work on a computer system for building design, they found that, without adequate knowledge of what operations were the key to designing, it was virtually impossible to specify characteristics the system should have. They identify key issues and major periods in the design process and two activities that seem to them to be the "essence of design." Based on their analysis, Krauss and Myer offer some suggestions for computer-aided design, a theme which is taken up again in Part 3 of this volume. Their conclusions should perhaps be compared with those of Thomas Heath and with the assumptions underlying the computer systems proposed in Part 3.

From two different points of view, Charles Eastman and Charles Rusch in the next two papers analyze parts of the design process in detail. Eastman reviews the theory and techniques for analyzing problem-solving within the framework of an *information-processing* model of cognition and presents an example protocol and analysis of intuitive processes typical to architectural design. The information-processing model is perhaps best illustrated by the work of Newell, Shaw, and Simon referred to in Eastman's paper and in the bibliography at the end of this volume. Their work was the first attempt to simulate human problem-solving and is closely allied to recent artificial intelligence research. Eastman's study and Thomas Moran's (in the next section) are the first attempts to apply this model to environmental design processes.

Rusch reviews some of the problem-solving literature from a different viewpoint—a *Gestalt* framework—and presents an analysis of the relative effects of productive and reproductive thought and of graphic and nongraphic activity in the design process. His work is derived from theories advanced by Köhler, Wertheimer, and Maier, and is the first interpretation of this school of thought to design processes. It is instructive to compare the points of view in the Eastman and Rusch studies.

To conclude the section, Bernard Kaplan comments on the papers and uncovers and discusses some of the common presuppositions.

In addition to these approaches to thought in design, there are at least four other approaches derived from the psychological literature which have led to fruitful hypotheses and experiments on the design process. One is the *creative problem-solving* approach which combines the work of Guilford on the identification of problem-solving abilities with experiments of Osborn, Parnes, Maltzman, and others on ways to improve these abilities. Our own work at Berkeley a few years ago borrowed from this theory in developing techniques for improving creative problem-solving in architecture. Another line might be called the *genetic-developmental* approach, a dynamic approach differing from any of the foregoing, based on the ideas of Duncker, Piaget, and Werner. Analysis of design processes from this point of view is under way in our present work at Clark University. A third approach is derived from classical *learning theory,* both Hull's stimulus-response and Skinner's operant conditioning models, and is discussed in the volume edited by Kleinmuntz. A final set of approaches is based on *personal awareness* and *group dynamics,* represented on the one hand by Gordon's well-known synectics techniques and on the other hand by personality and clinical psychologists who speak of creativity as a natural consequence of "self-actualization." For these theories the reader is referred to some of the writings of Maslow and Rogers, a good introduction to which may be found in Hayakawa. All are listed in the bibliography at the end of this volume.

2 Design: A Case History

Review of a Designer's Specifications
for a Computer System

Richard I. Krauss and John R. Myer,
with Scott Danielson and Roger
Lewis

Center for Building Research,
Massachusetts Institute of
Technology
Cambridge, Massachusetts

Richard I. Krauss is an Associate in the
architectural firm of Ashley, Myer &
Associates and is Special Assistant to the
Director of the Institute for Applied Technology, National Bureau of Standards,
for whom he is preparing a book on performance specification techniques in the
design process. He received an A.B. from
Harvard College in 1957 and a B. Arch.
from M.I.T. in 1961. John R. Myer is Principal in Ashley, Myer & Associates, is
Associate Professor of Architecture at
M.I.T., and is a member of the City Planning Board of Cambridge and the Board
of Directors of the Boston Society of
Architects. He received a B.Arch. from
M.I.T. in 1952. Scott Danielson and Roger
Lewis are graduate students in the Department of Architecture at M.I.T. The
research on which this paper is based was
carried out in 1968 under grants from the
National Bureau of Standards and the
National Science Foundation to the De-
partments of Architecture and Civil
Engineering at M.I.T. The work was done
under the supervision of Albert G. H.
Dietz, Center for Building Research. The
full report is entitled *Design: A Case
History/A Designer's Specifications for a
Computer System*.

This paper summarizes an extensive study
to determine what operations are key to
the process of design and what characteristics a computer-aided design system
should have to enhance those operations.
All documents and statements in a particular architectural design process were
recorded and analyzed. Three groups of
issues were noted: programming, generation and manipulation of forms, and
examination of technical building systems. The overall process had four major
periods: (1) initial programming, (2) presentation of solutions, characterized by
the designer's attention to all three groups
of issues, (3) determination of the principal
aspects of the final solution, characterized
by concentration on the generation and
manipulation of forms, and (4) design
refinement, also largely manipulation of
forms. Because of its importance, the
third period, called space allocation, was
studied further.

The study indicates that designers carry
out two activities which seem to be the
"essence of design." They make special
forms relating to the pertinent data and
analysis, and they reevaluate the problem
and possible solutions, emphasizing
first one set of criteria then another while
reformulating the problem to correspond.
Both activities are performed in a continuous cycle as the designer tackles
more aspects of the problem. To accommodate these activities, several features
of a computer-aided design system are
specified.

We were asked to react as practicing architects to a proposed format for
putting geometrical data about a building design into computer memory.
The system we were consulted about was the BUILD set of programs developed at M.I.T.[1] We found it difficult to react to these programs because it
was never clear what design operations would be performed or could be
performed on the geometrical descriptions of a building. There has been a
relatively great amount of research on what might be done on the computer
before geometric solutions to design problems are proposed, what goes on
during the programming stages, and what might follow after a tentative solution is selected, for example, the structural and mechanical analyses of a
proposed solution. However, there has been little research but a great deal
of misunderstanding in trying to communicate what conceptual designers do
when proposing or manipulating geometric forms and preliminary solutions.
In order to be able to say what designers use information for, we embarked
on this study. We hoped to find out what operations were key to the process
of creating a form and what characteristics a computer system should have
to enhance those processes.

---

1. Lavette C. Teague and Alan M. Hershdorfer, "BUILD: An Integrated System for Building Design."

We investigated the design process by reconstructing one recent project in our office, the preliminary design phases of a nursery school involving six classrooms for four-, five-, and six-year-olds. The fact that we used only one example gives our conclusions limited validity; we view this study as a rough, early attempt to describe what the design process is.

The Design History

The design history is shown as a bar chart in Figure 1, showing time spent by the designers on the various issues listed on the left-hand side of the chart and showing the main stages and substages or periods of design activity on the upper edge. The issues are presented in words the designers used in narrating what they could recollect from review of field documents, but only part of the tremendous array of issues the designers mentioned has been retained. The issues that seemed to be "associated" in the designers' minds or to have overlapping meaning are grouped to each other. Group A deals with programming issues, Group B refers to the processes of locating functions or manipulating forms and spaces, and Group C to aspects of a final design, to the description of the technical systems any building solution includes.

Vertical divisions occur where client meetings were held, serving to punctuate the design process at the end of each stage. The main activity in these stages is that of presentations 1 through 7. A wide range of issues is touched upon, containing sufficient information so that the client can make decisions.

There are, on the other hand, two periods when the designers' attention was not so spread out and when the major characteristics of the design were determined. These stages we called space allocation and design refinement. Note that although a lot of time was spent during these periods, the major activity reported was that of considering issues in Group B only, the generation and manipulation of spaces and forms. Because it was in the space allocation stage that the outline of the primary features of the final design seemed to be determined, we looked at this stage in some detail.

Space Allocation

Figure 2 shows the series of sketches produced during the crucial space allocation stage. Before this series of sketches began, the designers had a list of functions and of spaces necessary to accommodate each. For example, block playing was alloted 400 sq ft, and a classroom with three separate activities was allotted for teaching 20 ft × 20 ft, for conferring 10 ft × 10 ft, and for "wet" play 10 ft × 20 ft.

Before a first set of geometric solutions could be attempted a number of assumptions were made, such as that the building should have two stories to preserve outdoor play space. A first attempt at a design was made by placing the building mass arbitrarily on the east side of the site. Then the designers reacted to this straw man. They decided that this scheme was wrong for the following reasons: the building mass cast shadows on the major play yard, the outdoor spaces could not partake of the contiguous pleasant space at the interior of the block, and such a siting would be jarring in this residential neighborhood where residences were placed along the street with their major spaces behind. In response to these newly felt needs, they devised scheme C . The other major changes noted from scheme to scheme were the following: the shop moved back in E because the building was still casting shadows across the play yard, and in G the classrooms were brought to the ground floor for the first time where, to minimize shadows, they were placed under a roof pitched to touch the playground.

After reviewing this critical portion of the history we wanted to examine in more detail why and how these changes from scheme to scheme were made. Because it seemed too complex to sort out all the minute changes and movements of building elements, we concentrated on one room only, the music room. What factors caused it to shift location from the north in scheme C to the south in scheme D then back in H and finally around to the inside corner of the L-shaped form in scheme I ?

The reasons the designers mentioned were listed in a flow diagram, as shown in the top line of Figure 3. As can be seen, there were three groups of constraints that affected the shape of the new form: (1) the geometric constraints imposed by the site, (2) the relation of one space to another, proximities of various spaces to the entry and orientation to sun and wind, and (3) most important, the relationships read as a whole, the sequence of spaces and the expressive qualities that come from making one space more prominent than another.

Figure 3 also shows which factors caused the music room to shift location from scheme to scheme. For example, it moved south in *F* to take advantage of a dip in the site which permits it to have a greater volume, to get more sun, to have (still) a distinctive view, and to be near the entry and circulation focus. Note that the designers have dropped one constraint; they no longer consider it necessary for the music room to be near the major play area. They have added other constraints: the music room should have a prominent location and greater volume. In other words, the designers are dropping old concerns and raising new ones, and they even change their minds again as they create forms and react to them.

The variables listed in Figure 3 stem from the narrative of the design history and obviously are far from being defined clearly enough to be worked into a computer-based routine. Hence, we decided to examine one simple variable, the area of the music room, and see how complicated it would be just to evaluate a design and determine if what was proposed was suitable. Figure 4 shows a simplified and somewhat fictitious flow diagram of this dimensional evaluation.

We want to point out one feature that we included to make this suggested procedure feel "natural" to designers. At the onset we can assure that the area of the music room is suitable for the program requirements either by reducing the requirements or by increasing the area available. Now, if we decide to see if we could reduce the program requirements first and then change the design, the resulting form would be different than if we had started by trying to increase the area. Hence, because it appears that the order in which designers select their steps can affect the final solution, one must be allowed to choose the order in which the elements of a problem are evaluated. Indeed, *choosing what to evaluate next* is an important way in which a designer exercises his characteristic judgment.

Figures 3 and 4 merely show the sequential or simultaneous ordering of the variables; they do not show in any detail how the information needed to carry out any step is retrieved. This is shown by Figure 5, using as an example the information necessary to see whether the number of cars (which determines the size of the parking lot) can be reduced. The stored information is at the bottom of a tree diagram and is typical of what good reference libraries might contain. At each branch there is a rule for selecting one source or another: "Use this branch if it is greater than that," and even, "Ask the client or architect to decide."

Two points are particularly important to notice in Figure 5. First, the designer sometimes had to decide which sources to use, and second, not only was his involvement necessary to the retrieval operation, but he received his design insights and his understanding of the problem from such involvement. To take an obvious example, he would not have brought the classrooms to the ground floor, nor would he have pitched the roof to touch the ground if he had not understood the cast of the shadows in relation to the grades of the site and the hours of the school sessions. In other words, a computer-based information retrieval system may be able to save a designer much searching of reference sources, but it should not shield him from the searching process. Rather, it must expose him to much data and involve him in the process of selection.

1. Design history chart

To analyze the design process, an actual
design project, a small nursery school
was charted. The chart records the architects' activities in the midst of the programming stage (including whether to
remodel an existing building). Horizontal
bars on the chart denote the kind of work
done by the architects; vertical bars
denote meetings with the client. Observe
that most major design decisions were
made during the short Space Allocation
stage.
Chart reprinted from *Architectural Forum,*
March, 1968.

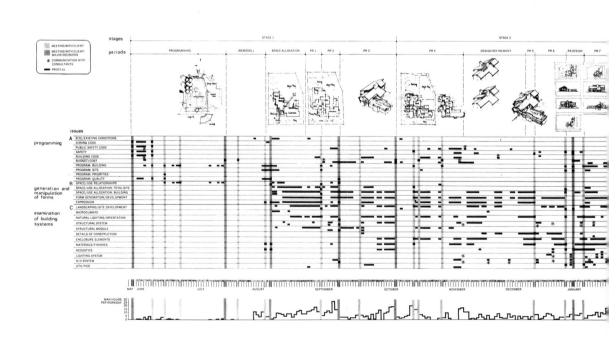

2. Space allocation–schematic history

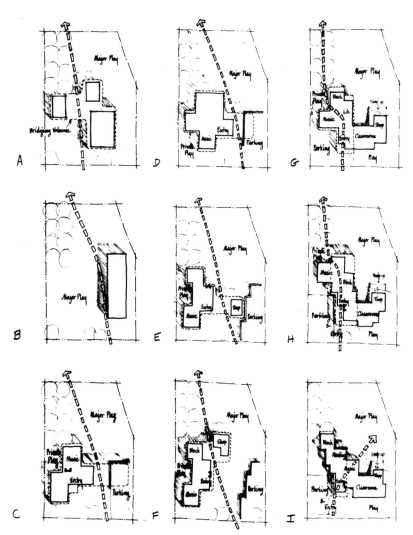

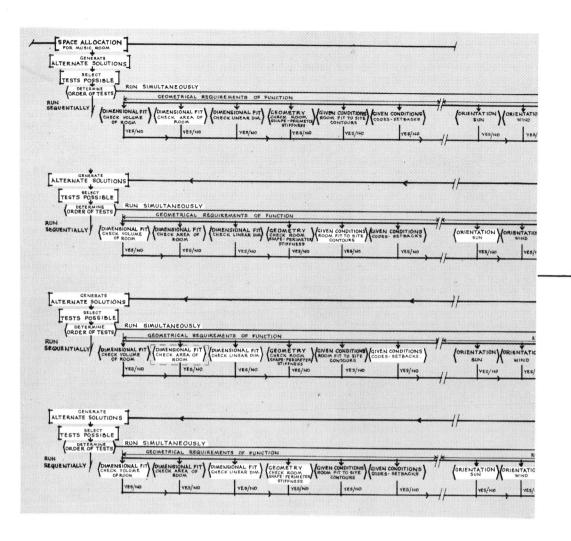

3. Space allocation flow diagram for
determining music room location

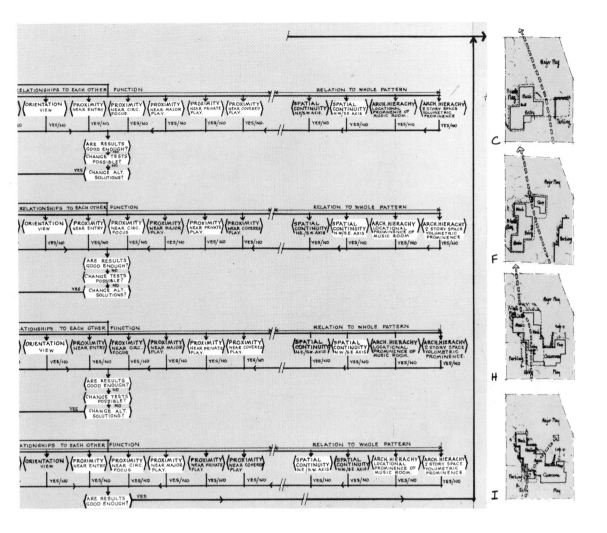

4. Some details of checking the area of the music room

5. Information search for one step in the area check

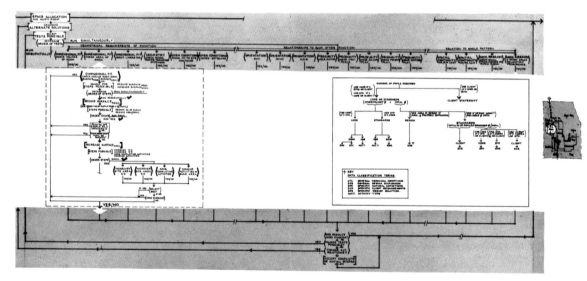

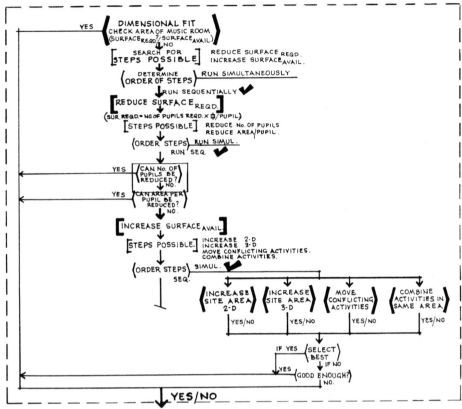

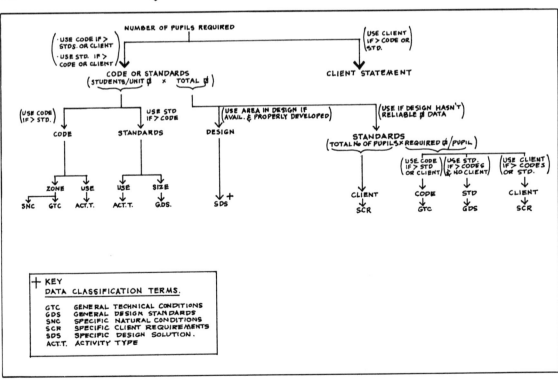

+ KEY
DATA CLASSIFICATION TERMS.

GTC   GENERAL TECHNICAL CONDITIONS
GDS   GENERAL DESIGN STANDARDS
SNC   SPECIFIC NATURAL CONDITIONS
SCR   SPECIFIC CLIENT REQUIREMENTS
SDS   SPECIFIC DESIGN SOLUTION.
ACT.T. ACTIVITY TYPE

Conclusions

At first we had hoped to be able to derive from this study a systematic outline of how designers proceed, but this goal now appears logically impossible. The designer seems to spend a good portion of his time manipulating and generating forms or spaces as his insight dictates. After evolving a program and budget, he starts to play with a whole form (a partial solution) and progressively differentiates it, changing the program as he sees fit. Part of the program comes from possibilities only an investigation of form will reveal. Using the example of the music room, we can say that when it flips to the corner of the L, a new program element is derived. Because of the L shape of scheme *I*, it is now possible to say that the building shall focus around the music room and that the major circulation shall be through it. The program seems to become clearer as various alternative solutions are investigated. In other words, design seems to be a process that is neither replicable nor systematic, and its workings cannot be determined at the outset. The designer's most important role is to exercise subjective judgments about the problem and its geometric solution, and to raise such questions as his reactions and his insight deem necessary.

Implications for
Computer-Aided Design

As mentioned earlier, the motivation for this study was to specify the characteristics of a computer system to assist the building designer. Although we are far from a comprehensive specification, several major implications for such a system arose from this study.

We propose that a computer system that can aid building design activity must have several characteristics.

1. The system should focus on geometric form, permitting its composition and review, and through visual simulation as well as through other modes it should aid in its modification. The system must be graphic and preferably three-dimensional. Its routines must relate back to the geometric form and must show how their output affects physical solutions.

2. The system should permit the designer to select the scale at which he is to operate; to consider part, or whole, or the broader context of the project; and to proceed with operations in the order he judges to be best. It must allow for variables to be investigated in any order.

3. The system should permit the treatment of a large number of variables, most of which become known only after the problem-solving process has begun, many of which are not susceptible to either numerical or discursive definition, and many of which can find definition only in visible form.

4. The system should keep the designer in close contact with the problem-solving process. The system must continuously present the designer with material that will augment his understanding and stimulate his insights.[2]

---

2. Further discussion of this study and its conclusions appears in Ellen P. Berkeley, "Computers for Design and a Design for the Computer."

3 On the Analysis of Intuitive Design Processes

Charles M. Eastman

Department of Computer Science,
Carnegie-Mellon University
Pittsburgh, Pennsylvania

Charles M. Eastman is Associate Professor of Architecture and Director of the Institute of Physical Planning at Carnegie-Mellon University. He received a M.Arch. from the University of California, Berkeley, in 1966. He has been in private architectural practice and in 1966–1967 was Research Architect at the University Facilities Research Center and Lecturer in Environmental Design at the University of Wisconsin. This research was supported by the Advanced Research Projects Agency of the Office of the Secretary of Defense. Part of the work was conducted at the Environmental Design Center of the University of Wisconsin. Their support of this work is acknowledged and appreciated. This paper is an elaboration of issues treated in a more comprehensive report, *Explorations in the Cognitive Processes of Design*.

Intuitive design as carried out by industrial designers, architects, and engineers concerned with the physical environment can be analyzed as a problem-solving task within the framework of an information-processing model of cognition. The theory of such studies and technique for making them are presented, along with an example of the typical data collected. Two major findings about design processes were uncovered by these studies. First, there is a clear correspondence between the kinds of constraints considered by the designer and the types of design representations used—words, numbers, flow diagrams, plans, sections, and perspectives. And second, in terms of problem identification it has been found that designers relying on direct retrieval from past experience or memory are far superior to those who rely on external cues for generating problem constraints. Finally, certain weaknesses and limitations of the efforts made thus far are discussed.

The information-processing model of human problem-solving developed in psychology has been used to gain insight into how people carry out such mental activities as playing games, particularly chess, how they solve geometry and word-algebra problems, and develop proofs in logic. This paper describes some of the results from ongoing studies that apply the information-processing model of cognition to the realm of environmental design.

This paper concerns intuitive design processes. By this is meant the procedures that designers have implicitly derived from their own design experience through case studies in school or from professional experience. If a design methodology can be defined as a formal and explicit procedure taught to a designer, intuitive design can be considered the antithesis of a design methodology.

It is important to understand intuitive design processes for several reasons. As methodologies are proposed, some means for evaluating them against current procedures is required. Just because a methodology is explicit does not mean it is superior to intuition. Little is known about what makes a superior designer or a superior design process. By comparing processes and what they produce we may learn the unique capabilities of the superior

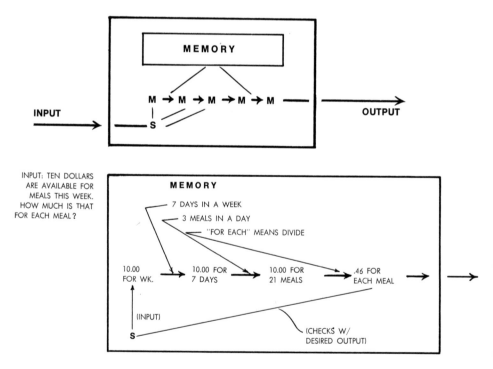

MEMORY

INPUT

OUTPUT

INPUT: TEN DOLLARS
ARE AVAILABLE FOR
MEALS THIS WEEK.
HOW MUCH IS THAT
FOR EACH MEAL?

MEMORY

7 DAYS IN A WEEK

3 MEALS IN A DAY

"FOR EACH" MEANS DIVIDE

10.00
FOR WK.

10.00 FOR
7 DAYS

10.00 FOR
21 MEALS

.46 FOR
EACH MEAL

(INPUT)

S

(CHECKS W/
DESIRED OUTPUT)

1. Model of a problem solver

2. An information-processing model of
problem solving

designer. It may be possible to teach these processes to future designers. Also, the development of computer-aided design systems requires a clear understanding of the operations and processes that a designer uses.

This paper has four parts: First, a technique for analyzing design using psychological problem-solving theory is offered, followed by an example of typical results gained thus far, some of the findings about design uncovered by these studies, and finally, some of the shortcomings and weaknesses of the present efforts.

Background

The psychological premises under which these studies were made have evolved mainly from European psychology, especially Selz.[1] In the United States the approach evolved independently out of information theory as applied to human behavior by Fitts and Miller.[2] My approach builds upon the work of Newell, Shaw, Simon, Hunt, and many others using information-processing concepts to study concept formation and problem-solving.[3] The best descriptions of the psychological model may be found in Miller, Galenter, and Pribram, and in Reitman.[4]

The model that is proposed is shown in Figure 1 and may be described as follows. It is asserted that thinking is information-processing. Man's nervous system seems to process complex information sequentially. Memory is interpreted as allowing independent recall of past inputs and recall of past intermediate processing states. Cognition, or thinking, is a resultant of information from the environment and from memory being brought together in unique sequence.

In this light, a problem situation is unique because a specific response is not directly available. At issue is the selection of appropriate inputs from memory and from the environment and the search for their possibly unique combinatorial sequence. The determinant of a processing sequence has been called a strategy. Little is known concerning the basis of strategies, though it seems that previous experience, the limits of short-term memory, and the organizational structure of memory are strong influences.[5] Processing can be modeled as a series of transformations generating a sequence of information states.

A simple example is shown in Figure 2. As can be seen, information is sequentially combined in a particular order. Notice also that at least two processing sequences could be used to gain the same answer; division could have been carried out after each new input. Out of all combinations of this information, only a very few lead to solutions, and those leading to a solution vary in their efficiency. This example shows that initial inputs give some information concerning the makeup of a response. Some information designating what a solution should be is part of most problems.[6] This type of information is normally called a goal. By studying such a process to determine what information is used to organize a processing sequence and by comparing one person's process with other person's, much can be learned about the different ways in which people solve problems.

1. For a history, see Adriaan D. de Groot, *Thought and Choice in Chess,* or George Humphrey, *Thinking, An Introduction to its Experimental Literature.* De Groot was Selz's student.
2. George Miller, *Language and Communication.*
3. Allen Newell and Herbert A. Simon, "GPS: A Program that Simulates Human Thought," in Edward A. Feigenbaum and Julian Feldman, eds., *Computers and Thought,* pp. 279–296. Earl B. Hunt, *Concept Learning: An Information-Processing Problem.* See also Carl I. Hovland, "Computer Simulation of Thinking."
4. George A. Miller, Eugene Galenter, and Karl Pribram, *Plans and the Structure of Behavior.* Walter R. Reitman, *Cognition and Thought.*
5. Jerome S. Bruner, Jacqueline J. Goodnow, and George A. Austin, *A Study of Thinking.*
6. For an elaboration, see Walter R. Reitman, "Heuristic Design Procedures, Open Constraints, and the Structure of Ill-defined Problems," in Maynard W. Shelly and Glenn L. Bryan, eds., *Human Judgments and Optimality,* pp. 282–315.

Most studies of problem-solving involve giving a subject S a complex task and recording his information-expressing behavior in the form of a protocol. The traditional means to encourage S to express information has been to instruct him to "think out loud." But what is the correspondence in this situation between internal processing and external expressions? The instruction to "think out loud" is sometimes mistakenly interpreted. It does not mean that the analysis of a protocol simply requires an experimenter E to determine what S thinks he is doing when he solves a problem. Rather, the analysis of a problem-solving protocol assumes that verbalization and in our case sketches are simply behavior, to be studied like any other behavior. The expressed behavior requires certain capabilities and specific information which must have been available to S. The capabilities and necessary precedents are studied to determine the sequential organization of processing.

For example, if a room is laid out by a designer who then says, "the lighting is poor," we can assume that certain relationships between the elements of the drawing were considered and from these was made an inference about lighting. If this person later accepts another design that is the same as the earlier one in all respects except that the window is moved, then it may be assumed that his evaluation of lighting included, among other things, the location of the window. By examining other situations in which he considers lighting it may be possible to find out in detail how this particular designer deals with lighting considerations. By analyzing in a similar manner all considerations made by S, significant insight into his problem-solving process is possible.

One task of E in making such a study is to maximize S's external expression of information. The studies of design at Carnegie-Mellon University utilize S's sketches, his talking while solving the problem, and his looking at objects in the room or at his drawings. Eye movements, better recording of the generation of sketches and facial expression will hopefully be included in future studies by utilizing a video tape recorder.

To summarize, the approach elaborated here for analyzing intuitive design follows five steps:
1. The collection of an accurate and detailed protocol.
2. The analysis of the protocol to determine the information expressed by S, the sequence of its expression, and the processes that must have been used to generate each piece of information.
3. The organization of the resulting information to allow an overall description of the transformations from state to state.
4. The determination of consistencies within the problem-solving process.
5. The incorporation of the consistencies into general hypotheses concerning the basic organization of design problem-solving.[7]

An Example Protocol and Analysis

The first studies of design were made by using simple and relatively well-controlled tasks, for example, the design of tableware. As experience in analyzing protocols was gained, more complex tasks were given. In relation to significant design problems, the tasks are still quite simple. The protocols collected vary greatly in complexity. Complexity does not imply sophistication. A protocol may be complex because it does not express the information used in processing. On the other hand, some of the most original information-processing thus far recorded has been very clearly expressed. The example task presented is the most complex yet attempted, but the example protocol is one of the simpler ones collected from this task.

The task is shown in Figure 3. S was asked to redesign a bathroom in a mass-marketed house. The problem was open-ended in that much more information was required to solve the problem than was given. S had to use his own experience and could also ask E for specific facts. S was also given a print of the plan view of the existing design.

---

7. The procedures of protocol analysis presented here are based on the techniques developed by Allen Newell, *On the Analysis of Human Problem-Solving Protocols.*

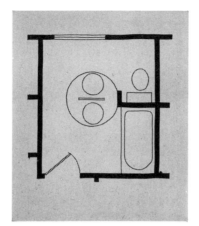

3. Statement of experiment 2

Experiment Number Two

The accompanying plan and photograph represent an existing bathroom plan for one model of a home sold by Pearson Developers in California. This model of house has not sold well. The sales personnel have heard prospective buyers remark on the poor design of the bath. Several comments are remembered: "that sink wastes space"; "I was hoping to find a more luxurious bath." You are hired to remodel the existing baths and propose changes for all future ones. (these should be the same)

The house is the cheapest model of a group of models selling between 23,000 and 35,000. It is two stories with a ranch style exterior. The bath is at the end of a hall serving two bedrooms and guests.

You are to come up with a total design concept. The developer is willing to spend more for the new design—up to fifty dollars. For all other questions, Mr. Eastman will serve as client. He will answer other questions.

4. Problem behavior graph—experiment 2

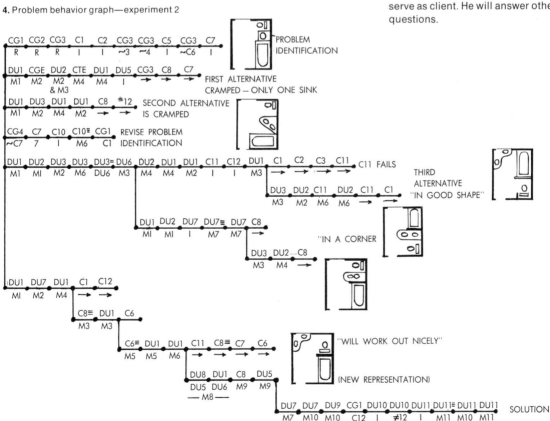

A protocol collected from this task is contained in Appendix A. The S it was collected from is a thirty-year-old industrial designer with approximately seven years' professional experience, who returned to school for advanced study and was considered creative by his colleagues. The protocol gave his verbal and graphic behavior. The series of sketches are reproductions of those made by S, exclusively with a plan view until the very end of the protocol. He made tracings of each of the original fixtures to use as templates for sketching. The graphics presented show the sequential development of the sketches and the movements of the templates. Some of his trials represented considerations of only a second or so. Each sketch or alteration made in relation to his verbal expressions was noted in the protocol text.

The first step in protocol analysis is determination of the information used, its sequence of use, and the operations applied at each state to produce a new state. Ascertaining the information used requires going through all the data collected in the protocol, identifying each piece of information expressed about the problem, and also determining the probable source of that information.

In making such an analysis it has been found useful to look initially for four kinds of information: (1) physical elements which are manipulated (design units), (2) desired relationships between elements and the desired attributes of elements (we call these constraints), and (3) the manipulations made on a design to fulfill the relationships or attributes. Clues to the source of each piece of information are also looked for. They may be S's memory, his perception of the current design, information from the client, or deductions from other information. The notation describing the results of this analysis is shown in the right column of the protocol in the Appendix, opposite the verbal protocol on the left.

Upon completion of this part of the analysis, the sequential organization of the whole protocol should begin to emerge. Where or how was each piece of information gained, how was it used, and what did it produce in the way of new information? These questions should indicate a sequence of processing.[8] The analysis should also allow a complete tabulation of the information used to generate the solution in terms of elements and their desired relations or attributes, and the manipulations carried out on them. For the protocol described, this tabulation is shown in Table 1.

Changes in this S's design can be explained by this information and an appropriate process. Some people have been surprised that a designer's efforts of forty minutes can be tied to so little information. But this is not always the case. It seems to be a matter of the distribution of effort. Another S who was given this problem dealt with over three times as much information but generated fewer schemes and considered fewer combinatorial relations.

The relatively small amount of information considered by this designer defined a small solution space. By counting the number of alternatives considered for each dimension of the design, this S's protocol suggested a search space of 2×10^4 discrete alternatives. As a comparison, de Groot estimates 10^{12} move alternatives considered by the master chess player in a twenty-move game.[9] Other design protocols have had search spaces of up to 10^9 combinations considered in a fifty-minute period. Thus it seems evident that the protocol presented here deals with a rather small search space that was fairly thoroughly explored.

8. The derivation of processing determinants can only regress to levels of processing where cognitive processes can be behaviorally expressed. Beyond this point inputs must be considered as independent variables. Even above this point, inputs with few clues as to their precedents are considered independent variables. Information-retrieval processes are treated in this way in the presented study. For example, see operations 25, 43, and 80 in the protocol analysis presented in the Appendix.
9. Adriaan D. de Groot, "Perception and Memory versus Thought," in Benjamin Kleinmuntz, ed., *Problem Solving: Research, Method, and Theory*, pp. 19–50.

It has been generally found in protocol analyses that the processing at any particular moment is influenced by prior processing, by what information is brought to bear at the moment being considered, and by what operations are available for operating on the current information. It has been found useful to show these influences graphically in what is called a Problem Behavior Graph (PBG). The PBG shown in Figure 4 is simply the concise expression of the previously described analysis and taxonomy. Each node represents an information state. Each line represents a transformation involving specific information and the operations used (both of which are noted). The PBG is coded according to the taxonomy given in Table 1. The PBG is read from left to right, then down. Reiterations of part of the design process show up as branches in the processing sequence. Abandoned lines of thought clearly show through.

Some Results of the Protocol Analysis

The last step of protocol analysis is the determination of the general processing rules implicit within the PBG. In other words, what operations always follow others? What consistencies are expressed that suggest specific processing strategies? To give an indication of the types of answers thus far gained, the major consistencies found in the presented protocol follow.

This *S,* and all others, began design by developing a clearer definition of the problem. He generated operational rules for testing design alternatives that would later be developed, for example, the constraint that the toilet should not be seen by a person using the counter. The field of vision was defined by a 180° field parallel to, but two feet in front of, the bathroom sink. He only commented on a need for privacy, but when designing, this was the operational rule that was applied. Another example was the definition of "no wasted space." The operational definition consisted of a rule "minor areas of clear rectangular floor space must have more than about 45 percent of their perimeter adjacent to the major space." Such constraints were primarily expressed before any form solutions were generated, though new ones were generated throughout design, as was shown in Table 1.

This *S* gained operational constraints by comparing the complaints expressed in the original problem statement—that the bath was "not luxurious," and "wasted space"—to situations in the existing design that could have evoked these comments. He implicitly viewed the problem as one of error correction. This is in contrast to other *S*'s who ignored the complaints and retrieved directly from memory the qualities thought to produce "a good bathroom." Always, the initial task was to retrieve from memory operational tests that would give direction to how the present design should be changed.

Little is known about the organization of memory and the retrieval mechanisms that operate on it. But one approach to the problem was consistently expressed in all protocols. Instead of generating abstract relationships and attributes, then deriving the appropriate object to be considered, the *S*'s always generated a design element and then determined its qualities. This sequence suggests that we may easily think of a kitchen and then define the relationships and attributes of it, but it may be structurally more difficult to think of the relationships and attributes without utilizing the conventional concept. Memory organization would be the delimiting factor. The evidence suggested here is supported by psychological evidence generated both by Kusysgyn and Paivio and by Deese.[10]

The pieces of information that are received, perceived, or retrieved are related during processing to produce a new information state. Each such transformation requires an operation. Four types of operations found were categorized:
1. Logical, including all arithmetic and verbal logic.

10. I. Kusysgyn and A. Paivio, "Transition Probability, Word Order, and Noun Abstractions in the Learning of Adjective-noun Paired Associates," and James Deese, *The Structure of Associations in Language and Thought.*

2. Corroboration and possibly expansion of information from one source by gaining similar information from another source.
3, Application of a manipulation or constraint to the current information state, producing a new form alternative or a test result.
4. Inductive association of a manipulation or sequence of manipulations with a constraint.

An example of the fourth operation was the constraint for visual privacy, directly evoking the creation of a partition. In contrast, the position of the mirror was automatically evoked, or at least there was no evidence of intervening processing. This type of operation well fits the concept of a search heuristic. It also corresponds to Newell, Shaw, and Simon's "table of connections," and to what Minsky calls "heuristic connections."[11] These four operations are those used for analyzing the earlier protocol.

More specific understanding has been gained in studying the manipulative aspect of design. One significant set of rules becomes evident when the sequence in which elements were manipulated and the sequence of manipulations that were made were looked at. Table 2 shows all sequences of design units treated and the corresponding manipulations. These were taken directly from the PBG.

First, it was clear that two different design strategies were involved. In the first strategy the design units were treated in an order called in computer jargon a "stack." Like a deck of cards, a sequence was taken from the top, then replaced in the reverse sequence. In the protocol the order was to work first with counter, then toilet, then tub; then the reverse of these, tub, toilet, and counter. These elements were manipulated in a trial-and-error process, which closely approximated a breadth-first search. By breadth-first is meant a search where all trials of one element are made until all tests relevant to the locating of the element are passed. Then the next element is located. After each trial a test was applied to see if it was satisfactory.

The strategy for dealing with all other elements of the design was quite different. No trial and error was involved. They were directly placed in accordance with search heuristics. Heuristics were used to locate the mirror, medicine cabinet, and towel racks.

Of the operations used, the third type where an S manipulated or applied a constraint to Design Units could be systematized. As can be seen in Table 2, the sequence approximated M1, M2, M3, M4, or "remove the first designated unit," "rotate previous unit 90°," if still unsatisfactory "move it along the same wall to another corner," then repeat these operations on other walls. If all manipulations failed, the next unit was tried. If the design passed all constraint tests while the unit was in a given location, the prior unit was manipulated.

After a general solution was found, Phase Two involved aesthetic touches such as aligning edges, considering symmetry, and locating towel racks. While all earlier work had been done in plan, these operations were done in perspective.

The sum of these manipulation rules, along with those determining the other three types of operations, constitutes a design strategy. They were S's total means for dealing with this problem. Whether such rules represent how this S generally treats this type of problem is not known. It would be valuable to apply a series of similar problems at widely spaced intervals to a single designer to gain some clue to an answer.

The Phase One activities may be combined into a flow chart as shown in Figure 5. Using the same information-retrieval sequence as the S and the

11. Newell and Simon, "GPS"; Marvin Minsky, "Steps towards Artificial Intelligence," in Feigenbaum and Feldman, *Computers and Thought*.

Table 1.
A taxonomy of information for a
bathroom

1. Constraints

Identified Before Trial Sketches
Were Made

Given Information (Constraints Given)
CG1 More luxurious bath
CG2 Total design concept
CG3 Wasting space
CG4 Cost = existing + $50
Retrieved Information
C1 "Looks small"
C2 "Functions okay"
C3 Wasted space between toilet and
washbowl
C4 Wasted space between tub and
washbowl
C5 Round objects are expected to rotate
C6 Blocks of space should have 45% of
perimeter common with larger space
C7 Plumbing on one wall

Identified While Making Trial Sketches

C8 Adequate use space for fixture
C10 No exposed bathtub corners
C11 No sightline to toilet from door
C12 Toilet should not fall within 180°
radius centered toward sink and one
to two feet in front of it
C13 Should have large mirror
C14 Locate towel racks where towels are
used

2. Manipulations

Plan
M1 Remove current unit
M2 Rotate designated unit 90°
M3 Move unit to another corner first on
same wall then on other walls
M4 Add new unit next to previously
manipulated unit
M5 Extend unit around corner
M6 Locate wall next to fixture
M7 Locate over sink
M8 Align spatial metrics
M9 Move unit to align with others

Perspective

M10 Align horizontal edges
M11 Locate along wall

3. Design units

DU1 Counter
DU2 Toilet
DU3 Bathtub
DU4 Mirror
DU5 Sinks (two)
DU6 Tub and wall
DU7 Mirror
DU8 Sink, tub, and mirror
DU9 Window
DU10 Medicine cabinet
DU11 Towel racks

Table 2
Sequence of Design Units and
Manipulations*

Design Units	Manipulations
Phase One	
DU1, DU2, DU2, DU1	M1, M2, M3, M4
DU1, DU3, DU1, DU1,	M1, M2, M4, M2,
DU1, DU2, DU3, DU6, DU2, DU1, DU1, DU1,	M1, M1, M2, M6, M3, M4, M4, M2, M3
DU2, DU2, DU2	M3, M2, M6
DU1, DU2, DU1, DU1, DU7, DU8, DU2	M1, M1, M2, M4, M7, M3, M4
DU1, DU1, DU1	M1, M4, M3,
DU1, DU1	M4, M6
Phase Two	
DU8, DU5, DU1, DU6, DU5, DU7, DU7, DU8	M8, M8, M8, M8, M9, M7, M10, M10
DU10, DU10	M10, M11

* Each row represents a sequence of transformations performed without a major review
of constraints. Underlined manipulations are those directly responding to a search
heuristic.

flow-charted process, the manipulations of this one problem-designer situation can be partially replicated. The state transformations produced by the information-retrieval sequence, the heuristics, and the flow chart in Figure 5 are shown in the PBG of Figure 6. The correspondence between this PBG and the one in Figure 4 indicates the degree to which the S's behavior has been modeled or simulated.[12] The major sequences of alternatives were duplicated.

This protocol and others can be well described in terms of a problem-definition process mixed with a generate-and-test sequence. The tests applied were overwhelmingly of a binary or threshold nature, corresponding to Simon's notion of "satisficing."[13] Only one instance of an attempt to optimize a solution has been found in thirteen protocols concerning three different design tasks.

Findings and Conclusions

The most important general finding from these studies thus far has been the significance of representational languages to problem-solving ability. The processing of information often depends upon some means for representing it. Thus one designer poor in math is not able to deal with cost or other numerical constraints. Less obvious is the difference in the constraints considered by those designers who worked in section versus those who did not. The accessibility to children of sink fixture controls becomes an issue only with the generation of a section representation. Generally, a clear correspondence was found between the kinds of constraints that could be considered and the representations used. One of the strengths of the human problem-solver is his ability to use several representations—words, numbers, flow diagrams, plans, sections, perspectives—to represent, compare, and manipulate information. It would seem that any man-machine system to aid the designer must recognize his reliance on multiple representations. Any methodology must also be able to include within it all information relevant to design or it must allow a designer to work back and forth between representations. It can be argued that most methodologies are in fact new representations that allow explicit comparison of information not previously relatable. Like other representational languages, they augment intuitive design rather than replace it. In this sense engineering is possibly different from architecture, primarily because it is dominated by a particular representation, numerical, versus an iconic one.

Another finding had to do with the problem identification process, which began to yield some understanding. Relying on the limited sample of six subjects doing two problems each, it has been found that those relying on direct retrieval from memory are far superior to those who rely on external cues for generating problem constraints. Also, while most seemed to retrieve constraints from memory randomly, certain S's seemed to have "automatically" organized considerations in memory so that they could be retrieved in a highly structured form. One generated five constraints for the bathtub, then eighteen for the counter and sink, all in order. Other strategies for retrieving constraints such as "imagining yourself functioning in the space" have not been elicited from S's thus far. At some later date, these studies may allow much more to be known about why certain designers are superior in bringing to bear much information to a design problem. We tend to assume that designers utilize all the information mentally available. It can be shown, though, that designers are quite at the mercy of a fallible memory.

A current weakness of our studies is that protocols dealing with several intermixed representations have not been treated adequately. The theory of problem-solving and protocol analysis requires refinement in this area. Also,

12. An implication of the protocol analysis and model presented here is that the design process may be "driven" or controlled by the particular sequence in which design information is retrieved. The model was implicitly formed this way because information retrieval is currently an independent variable.
13. Herbert A. Simon, *Models of Man*, Chapter 14.

5. Block diagram for an administrative process relying on search heuristics

6. Problem behavior graph—simulation 2

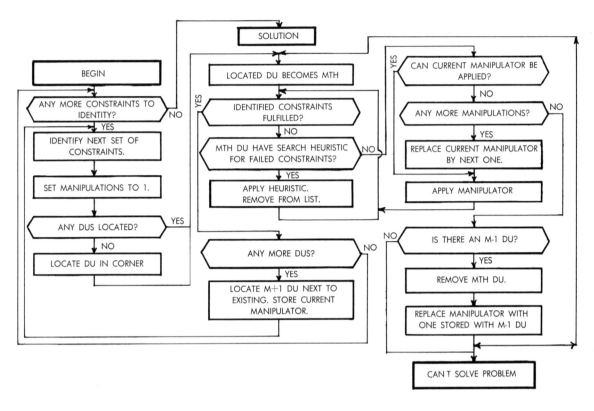

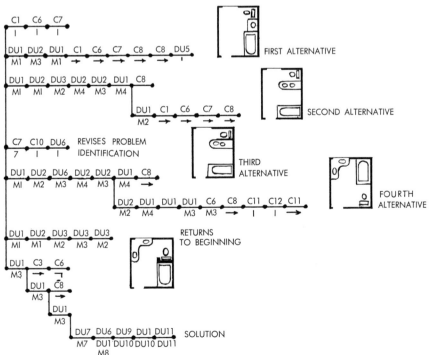

we have only gained a few protocols that clearly show hierarchical processes where one element is designed of smaller elements which in turn become part of a larger design. Surely, this is a central feature of many design problems. Also missing from our studies is an understanding of the many phases that transpire between the receiving of a commission and the production of working drawings. We have looked at only a small portion of the design process.

Larger potential weaknesses may lie in the approach. How deep a penetration these studies will allow into the problem-solving process is an open question. The approach relies on external expression of the information used in design. Currently the density of concept utilization which these studies represent is about one every twelve seconds. Protocol studies in other areas show that processing of familiar information may take place at a rate greater than one concept per second.[14] Studies of design have a long way to go to fill in what's happening in that eleven-seconds gap. Certainly part is spent on the motor activities of drawing or perception. But we still have at least six seconds between each piece of processing that are not accounted for. Whether the approach outlined here will allow understanding of processing at this level of detail may depend on whether external traces of the intervening information can be made available. In eliciting expression of information we are creating some distortion of the design process. This is certainly one issue. Whether the nature of the inputs to design processing are conceptual enough for expression is another issue. At most, one-half the total processing time of short-term memory has been accounted for here. Hopefully the void represented by the other half may slowly be filled in.

This type of a problem-solving analysis, when applied to design, may allow us to understand much more than we know presently about the capabilities of the superior designer. It may give us insights as to what are powerful, and conversely, weak procedural techniques. It may also lead to new methodologies that augment current weaknesses of the human designer. Others are encouraged to explore this approach.

---

14. Allen Newell, personal communication.

Each PA section corresponds to one minute of time.

Legend:
$< >$ implicit activity
[ ] a repeated activity
$\sim$ relates information
$\rightarrow$ applies constraint
$\equiv$ constraint heuristically related to manipulation
GC = general constraint
C = constraint
M = manipulation
DU = design unit

PA1 An objective is "a more luxurious bath," "a total design concept." The list of comments remembered were "wasting space," and some opposite of luxurious. Whoever wants these to be redesigned considers these are the most objectionable.

PA2 One reason that it doesn't have a luxurious quality, I think this would look rather small. In this picture it looks very spacious, but it must have been taken from outside the room in the hall. When you get into this thing you're about four feet to the sink, standing in the door. . . .

PA3 I think I would juggle the drawings here on a piece of paper. It seems that there are no objections with how this thing functions. Left out storage space, but all the necessary utilities, toilet and so forth, have been included. Evidently, they're of a decent size.

PA4 If there are problems of space, and I think there are, in looking at it, it would largely be a case of juggling it around. There is wasted space in this design. In between the toilet and the washbowl and the tub and the washbowl. These are inconvenient little spaces that can hardly be used.

PA5 Something that's sort of superficial, this seems to be a rotating device (the counter). I have an uneasy feeling about it. . . .

PA6 Another thing that wastes space is the toilet facing the wall, which means that you have a block space in here, which, if the toilet were facing this way (into the room), the space would become part of the larger space out here. . . . I think what I would do in this case is start juggling the fixtures and sketch of the room. When such a situation comes up it means many little drawings.

PA7 (Makes tracings of each fixture and of the outline of the room.) I'll assume a washbowl is about that big. . . .

1. Reads GC1.
2. Reads GC2.

3. Reads GC3.
   [GC1]

4. Identifies C1.

5. GC1 $\sim$ C1

6. Identifies C2.
   (Planning strategy)

7. GC3 $\sim$ C3
8. GC3 $\sim$ C4

9. $<$Identifies C5.$>$

10. GC3 $\sim$ C6

11. C6 $\equiv$ M2 $\rightarrow$ DU2

(Generates representation.)

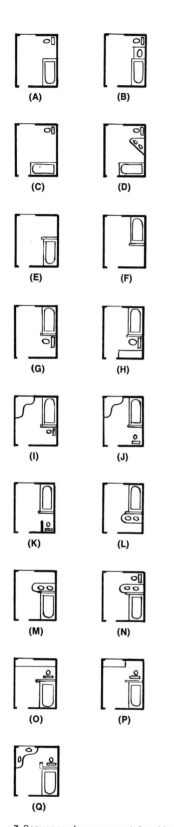

(A) **(B)**

(C) **(D)**

(E) **(F)**

(G) **(H)**

(I) **(J)**

(K) **(L)**

(M) **(N)**

(O) **(P)**

(Q)

7. Sequence of arrangements in subject's protocol

PA8 First I would try and arrange all three, washbowl, tub, and toilet, along this wall, which might be a little crowded. (He makes sketches that sequentially develop as shown in Figure 7.) You have a lot more space . . . open feeling to it. You have one washbowl and it's crowded. It does retain all the plumbing on one wall. . . . (Makes sketches *A* and *B*.) This is going to boil down into making a lot of sketches and thinking most seriously about what exists and criticize and repair it. . . . This thing next to the tub would be crowded.

12. <Identifies C7.>

13. Applies M1 to DU1.
14. Applies M2 and M3 (?) to DU2.
15. C7 ≡ M4. Applies M4 to DU1.
16. <Identifies C8 and DU5.>
17. GC3 → "A lot more space."
18. C8 → DU1 → "It's crowded."
19. C7 → <OK>

[C8 → "crowded"]

PA9 (He rotates the tub, then completes an arrangement as in *C* and *D*.) I'm trying to make an arrangement of toilet, two sinks, and tub, with plumbing on one wall . . . without coming out into the room. Not only to save plumbing, but also to leave a large open space. So far, I feel these arrangements would be cramped.

20. Applies M1 to DU1.
21. Applies M2 to DU3.
22. <Identifies DU5.>
23. Applies M4 and M2 to DU1.
    [C7]
    [C1]

24. C8 → "Cramped"

PA10 I also feel that this tub position, along the wall . . . I feel very strange about it. I think the idea of orienting the toilet toward the middle of the room instead of the corner is going to be a good one. There's something about hiding the toilet back here that I don't like. . . . There's the privacy angle, but there is also the puritanical thing, about the euphemism. It's something you pretend you don't have. . . . Well, it makes me a little uneasy. The word bathroom is a euphemism. . . .

[C6 ≡ M2 → DU2]

25. Associates operation with deep structure memory.

PA11 How much would it cost to run plumbing to both walls? [Expert: The cost would be a 50¢ a linear foot.] . . . I see why I don't like the tub over here. Having the tub with two corners exposed means you have problems with the shower arrangement. It requires an additional wall, or a curved shower rod. Let's see, is there anything wrong with a curved shower rod? I feel that there is. . . .

26. <GC4 ~ C7> <?>
27. <Removes C7 from problem.>
28. Identifies C10.
29. <C10 ≡ M6 and DU6>
    (Planning strategy)

PA12 This method, seeing what I didn't like about the original arrangement, then eliminate what I didn't like. I've already done that. I have a large amount of space in here. Without cutting down on the functions. There are things I don't like about the arrangement yet. I have got more

[C1]
[C2]

central space, but some functions are cramped. I would like to see if I could iron those out without starting to chop up the space again. I suspect that this lack of space was the basis of the objection that it was not luxurious. I don't like the two sinks I have here. So close together...

[C1 → "OK"]
[C8 → "cramped"]

30. GC1 ~ C1
    [C8 → "Sinks too close together"]

PA13 (Draws *E*.) Go back to the bath in the corner. Okay, wall at the end of it. Except that's too close to the original?...

31. Applies M1 to DU1 and DU2.
32. Applies M2 to DU3.
33. Applies M6 to DU3.
    <DU3 and M6 produce DU6.>

PA14 (Draws *F*.) I've put the tub along the same wall but toward the window. It might allow you to put (draws *G* and *H*). . . . I was thinking the toilet could then go on this wall, leaving room for a large vanity along here. Which would work but cut down on the privacy more than somewhat.

34. Applies M3 to DU6.
35. Applies M4 to DU2.
36. Applies M4 to DU1.>
37. <Applies M2 to DU1.>

38. <Identifies C11 and C12.>

PA15 (Erases and draws/.) This arrangement, with the tub in this corner, is the nicest space so far. It's open. I think it solves all the problems, except for this thing of privacy. It has a large space to stand around in to dry. It gives the appearance of space when you walk in. It's adequate but not cavernous. It gives easy access to all the facilities, to the tub and to the toilet, and washbowls.

39. Applies M3 to DU1.

40. C1 → "It's open."
41. C2 and C8 → "It solves all the problems."

42. C11 → "Except privacy."

[C8 → DU3]
[C1]
[C8 → DU3, DU2, DU5)

PA16 I have an uneasy hesitation about the privacy. . . . This is my personal feeling. And I don't want to appear to try and hide the toilet. I have an idea that the client would like the toilet to be hid. I would like to make a compromise.

43. Associates C11 with deep structure memory.

PA17 (Changes drawing as in *J*.) It would appear as if you could do this. I don't quite know how. (Adds wall in *K*.) There is this wall, by the toilet. It only comes out 2 feet, which does not hide the toilet.

44. Applies M3 to DU2.
45. Applies M2 to DU2.
46. <C11 ≡ MG.> Applies M6 to DU2.

PA18 This would be a good thing. . . . This does form a bit of a nook, but it isn't hidden from the door. This semi-enclosure for the toilet, plus this thing about the open plan. I think we're in good shape. . . .

47. C11→ "A good thing."

48. C6 → (?)
49. C1 → "In good shape."
50. Applies M1 to DU1 and DU2.

PA19 There's another possibility of putting sort of a console coming out from this wall (draws *L*.) . . . mirror in here . . . probably a large sink in here and a smaller one here. This would have nice accessibility. I'm not ter-

51. Applies M4 and M2 to DU1.

52. <Identifies DU7.>
53. <DU7 ≡ M7.> Applies to DU7.
54. C8 → "Nice accessibility."

ribly enamored with the design. . . . I feel myself sort of getting into a corner. (Draws *M* and *N*.) This again leaves the toilet . . . in the open.

PA20 Come to think of it, I wonder if the original design with. . . . (Sketches *O*.) Now this seems to be a nice arrangement here. You get these facilities in a small amount of space. But that leaves the toilet here, which is sort of exposed come to think of it.

21 I wonder if this original design, replacing that console. . . . (Draws *P*.) I was thinking of bringing the vanity underneath the window, into this area. But that would leave . . . sort of a nook . . . by the toilet.

PA22 (Draws *Q*.) This one would do it. This one is getting familiar. . . . It would be nice to have an arrangement like this because it gives some privacy to the toilet, the bathtub still has lots of open space. Unfortunately that means putting. . . . if you're going to have the toilet here means you have the washbowls over here, I think, to get the people's backs to the toilet. . . . This will work out nicely. . . . Yeah. That's just fine.

PA23 My objection here was that . . . I dislike rounded corners on these things. It reminds me of artists' pallettes. But it also keeps you from scraping your thighs. I think what I've got right here . . . it's simply a matter of juggling proportions.

PA24 I'd sort of like to have this washbowl right in front of the window. Just have this nice and neat for its length down to here. The length of the counter so it lines up with that wall. Bring the sink down as far as I can so. . . . I think a little space here for shaving cream and stuff like that . . . . make a little more space so you can get two people using washbowls at the same time without being right up against each other. This mirror down to there. There's still some details . . . (draws Figure 8).

PA25 Right now the biggest objection I have is that the mirror. . . . I think, visually, and functionally it would be quite nice to have a large mirror here. Of course, not over the window or wrapping around the corner. I think the large mirror seems to

55. <Current arrangement produces DU8.>

56. Applies M3 to DU8.

57. Applies M4 to DU2.
58. C1 → (?)
59. C12 → "in the open."
60. Returns to beginning. Applies M1 to DU.
61. Applies M4 and M2 to DU1.
62. C1 → (?)

63. C12 → DU2 "Sort of exposed."
64. Applies M3 to DU1.

65. C6 → "Leaves sort of a nook."

66. Applies M5 to DU1.
67. Applies M6 to DU1.

C11 → "Gives some privacy."

69. C8 → DU3 "Bathtub has open space."

70. <C7 → (?)>
71. C12 → (M5 → DU1.)
   (?) → "This will work out nicely."

72. Associates DU1 with deep structure memory.

73. Applies M8 to DU8 and DU5.

74. Applies M8 to DU1 and DU6.

75. C8 ≡ M9. Applies M9 to DU5 until C8 is O.K.

(Generates new representation.)
76. Applies M7 to DU7.

77. Applies M10 to DU7 and DU8.

78. <GC1 ~ C13.> (?)
79. <Identifies DU9.>

conflict with having the medicine cabinet. ... That window doesn't come to the edge either. ... Well, let's put the medicine cabinet mirror in front of this sink. And then optionally you could extend this mirror or any place along this wall. To carry through visually. If it were easier to get a mirror in standard size that doesn't match the window, well, that's the way it goes. ... Yes. Here's a place for the towel rack. I'd forgotten about that. Pretty essential to have a place for towels. Near the bathtub, also along here would probably make sense. Towels in this area. They'd be accessible from both the bathtub and the sinks. ... I think that's it.

80. <Associates DU9 with deep structure memory.>

81. DU10 and C12 conflict.
82. <Abandons C13.>
83. M7 → DU10.

84. Identifies DU11
    DU11 ≡ C14 and M11.

85. Applies C14, M10 and M11 to DU11.
    (Solution ignores C6.)

8. Subject's final sketch

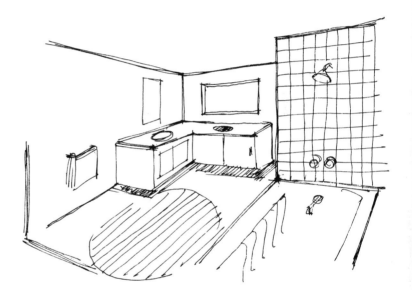

4 The Role of Graphic Activity in the Design Process

A Pilot Study of a Series of Lithographic Bulls by Picasso

I want to develop the ability to do a picture in such a way that no one can ever see how it has been done. To what end? What I want is that my picture should evoke nothing but emotion.
Pablo Picasso

With apologies to Pablo Picasso; not because I see how he did them, but because I tried.

Charles W. Rusch

Department of Architecture, University of California, Berkeley California

Charles W. Rusch is currently Associate Professor of Architecture at the University of California, Los Angeles. At the time this paper was written he was on the faculty at the University of California, Berkeley, and a Fellow of the Center for Advanced Study of the University of Illinois. He received an A.B. in social relations from Harvard College in 1956 and a B.Arch. and M.Arch from the University of California, Berkeley, in 1964 and 1966. He has been in private architectural practice and is a consultant to architectural and building development firms. He is the author of *Reflections on Nonreflective Thought or Why Johnny Can't Think*. This paper is a summary of a larger report, "The Psychological Basis for an Incremental Approach to Architecture."

From a review of the problem-solving section of the psychological literature, several implications are drawn for the process of environmental design. Previous experience is seen as containing the twin components of figural recognition and process recognition. These moments of recognition seem to comprise the substance of the major reorganization or "insight" experience and to be the dominant characteristic of reproductive thought. Productive thought is possible only through inferential reasoning, a process conducted incrementally because of natural limitations of the mind. However, the design process requires an interplay of both productive and reproductive thought. The question studied was the relative effect of these two modes in the design process. Limited results indicate that while decisions derived through incremental activity and reorganization are relatively equal in number, the role of the former is to clarify the form, and the role of the latter is to keep the problem-solver on course toward solution. It is conjectured that these conclusions probably also apply to larger-scale design material. The method of content analysis devised and conducted on the graphic decision elements of the lithographs was based on three criteria of judgment: continuity, clarity, and relevance. It is claimed that, by use of the method presented, the source of the idea content of an artist can be determined by simply studying the graphic output of his work.

A review of the extensive problem-solving literature in psychology for its potential relevance to design problem solving indicates the following:
1. Most of the inquiry is directed toward what Maier calls "reproductive thought" not productive thought.
2. There has been very little study of any sort of graphic material analogous to the graphic output of the designer.

The first of these points is important because of the concern and interest that is expressed in design circles for the "big idea," the grand insight, or the major reorganization of the problem structure. It is these moments that are usually considered most "productive." But it can be argued from the literature available that such moments are actually reproductive and hence subject to the influence of training and previous experience. In fact, it can be argued that only the smallest steps can be considered productive in the sense that they produce knowledge that has never been previously known or experienced in any way.

The second point is important in that one of the primary sources of incremental productive material is felt to exist within the routine graphic activity of the designer. Further, since some designers, such as architects, traditionally keep a record of all their graphic activity, there is a wealth of this material available for the analysis of what designers do, or at least for the determination of the role graphic activity plays in design. Thus, while the "big ideas" or major reorganizations of the problem material get all the credit for problem solution, the minute-by-minute graphic activity (which takes place almost outside of awareness) may be contributing considerably and productively to solution. One of the purposes of this study was to determine how much it is contributing. Another purpose was to learn as much as possible about that graphic activity. How can it be characterized and measured? How does it interplay with insight and reasoning?

Background

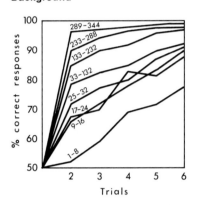

1. Object-quality discrimination in the monkey

There is a widespread tendency to consider all creative work as equivalent to productive thinking, and in a certain general sense it is. However, using Klüver's concept of equivalent stimuli, Maier makes a more restrictive distinction.[1] The equivalent-stimuli concept states simply that if a second situation contains the features (equivalent stimuli) to which the organism has learned to respond in the first situation, then the second situation should call out the learned response. Maier states that solutions which are the result of equivalent stimuli are an extension of the learning process, and any new structural understanding in this case will occur *after* the solution. This type of relation between cognitive activity and solution event he refers to as *reproductive*. On the other hand, a *productive* solution occurs when conceptual restructuring or reorganization of previously isolated experiences immediately precedes the solution. In the latter case, understanding among the relations of the parts of the problem is built up slowly until the solution to the total problem is understood. Two examples, one with monkeys and one with human subjects, illustrate this type of gradual analysis.

In 1949 Harlow conducted a set of experiments, on intelligent monkeys of controlled past experience.[2] Food was placed in one of two food wells, both of which were covered by two equally discriminable stimulus cues. The monkey was given time to search only one well before an opaque screen was dropped between him and the wells. Although the food was shifted in the left-right positions in a predetermined balanced order, it was always accompanied by the same stimulus cue. The experiment continued for 344 problems, over many days. In the first 32 problems, 50 trials were run before the old cues were removed and replaced with new ones. The next 200 problems were run for 6 trials each, and the last 112 problems were run for 9 trials each. Steeper and steeper learning curves indicated that the monkeys seemed gradually to understand that if the wrong stimulus cue was chosen the first time, it would continue to be wrong for some time, i.e., until the cues changed; therefore on the second choice they must pick the other one. The data indicate that the subjects progressively improved in their ability to learn object–quality discrimination problems. The monkeys *learned how to learn* with a minimum of errors. Harlow calls this learning how to learn a particular problem type, a "learning set." As can be seen from Figure 1, when a learning set has been acquired, the curve approaches linearity after Trial 2. Such curves are often described as indicators of insightful learning. However, in this case, something other than insight was going on: the monkeys, by acquiring learning sets, apparently came to understand the problem, not suddenly, but over hundreds of learning trials.

In a set of experiments by Helen Durkin, twenty-eight college graduates were required to form geometric figures from a set of puzzle pieces.[3] To twenty-one subjects she gave preliminary training making squares, while seven started right out on more complex figures. She found that only those with square-making experience solved the more complex figures suddenly. But

1. For the equivalent stimuli concept, see Heinrich Klüver, "Behavior Mechanisms in Monkeys," and for distinctions between learning, reasoning, productive and reproductive thinking, see Norman R. F. Maier, "Reasoning in Humans. III: The Mechanisms of Equivalent Stimuli and of Reasoning."
2. For this important set of experiments see Harry F. Harlow, "The Foundation of Learning Sets."
3. Helen E. Durkin, "Trial-and-Error, Gradual Analysis, and Sudden Reorganization."

subjects without square-making experience were perfectly able to solve the problem by gradual analysis. In the latter case the subjects developed an understanding of the relations between the elements in an orderly stepwise fashion. Background for the steps was supplied largely by inference; the subjects saw the steps clearly one by one, and the picture was changed gradually. On the other hand, in the group with previous experience the background was supplied by this experience; the subjects could see several related factors at once, and the whole picture changed suddenly.

From these experiments it would appear that previous experience in the problem type and/or strategy is an essential prerequisite to large-scale reorganization and to sudden solution. However, large-scale reorganization is not a prerequisite to problem solution. The studies of Harlow and Durkin show that structural understanding may be reached by gradual analysis as well. In these studies, solution was achieved, but without any one major moment of reorganization; structural understanding was instead built up incrementally, step by step, without the benefit of previous experience.

The question remains: Just what constitutes previous experience? What conclusions can be drawn about how it operates to bring on sudden solutions? In the experiments covered so far, the subjects in part responded to two different type of conditions: relational recognition and process recognition. In the case of relational recognition, the subject gets to a point in the problem where the configuration he is visualizing in the problem field is sufficiently similar to a class of previous patterns he has already experienced to cause him to "jump" to that known class. This description is particularly characteristic of Durkin's subjects with previous experience in the problem. type. Similarly, in the case of process recognition the subject reaches a point in the problem where the series of actions he is performing is sufficiently similar to the *way* he has solved previous problems to make him feel he knows how to solve the rest of the present one. Harlow's monkeys in their later trials might be examples of this description, a learning set being a type of process recognition. In either case, reorganization occurs at the point of recognition, and action follows immediately.

The other class of problems remains to be discussed: those problems where the subjects have had no previous experience in the problem type or strategy. Of the experiments covered so far, this would include half of Durkin's subjects, and Harlow's monkeys in their beginning trials. The situation in these problems is quite different from that where previous experience is relevant. The problem-solver can no longer rely on similarity recognition to rescue him from trial-and-error behavior; he must work solely from inferences about the outcome of future actions on his part. These inferences can also be categorized into two types: relational inferences and process inferences. In the former a judgment is made concerning the consequences of some possible new configuration of the problem elements; in the latter the consequences of a series of possible actions are considered. In both cases, because of the limited capacity of the mind,[4] the amount of information carried by the judgments will be small. To solve a problem by inference, the inferences must be made incrementally, and each increment must be checked before passing to the next.

Thus, understanding of the relational structure of a problem can come to the problem-solver in only two ways, by inferential thought which must later be verified in the solution, or by similarity recognition based on previous experience. However, man being the learner he is, all adult human problem-solving situations involve previous experience as a principal input. In particular, no one strategy is an adequate tool by itself for coping with environmental design problems.

---

4. George A. Miller, "The Magic Number Seven, Plus or Minus Two: Some Limits on our Capacity for Processing Information." This article also interrelates work done on cognitive capacity, absolute judgment, and immediate memory.

Graphic Activity

The designer creates with forms through his sketches, and his creation itself is both a form and a collection of forms. So far in this paper I have been dealing with design as a problem-solving process; I shall now focus on the designer's response to his own form-sketches which he makes throughout this process. Conceptual design (the design or creation of physical concepts or abstract physical relations), as currently practiced in the design fields, is ostensibly a graphic process in that it is recorded and developed principally on paper. Several studies dealing with linear form have shown that there is more to this process than one would normally suspect. When changes are made in the form, certain symbolic and artistic operations influence each change in a way quite apart from the problem-solving strategy then operative. One of these operations has been extensively studied in psychology, is in wide use in solving of design problems, but is not generally understood by designers. This is *leveling and sharpening.*

It was upon the principles of perceptual organization that Wulf developed the concepts of leveling and sharpening.[5] He ran tests presenting subjects with a series of simple line drawings and asked them later to remember and redraw them. He found that changes made in the reproductions fell into two categories. Either the figures were strengthened by accentuating certain characteristics of the form (sharpening), or the figures were strengthened by suppressing certain features (leveling). If the change was such as to approximate more and more some well-known structure, he called it *normalizing.* This is shown in Figure 2.

Leveling and Sharpening in Design

What role does leveling and sharpening play in the design process? The sketches done in the course of this work do affect the solution and in a rather unexpected manner. As overlay after overlay of tracing paper is placed on the drawing board, forms are altered to give greater differentiation and a better resolution of the functional requirements of the problem. If the effort is for clarity, then the processes operative have to be leveling, sharpening, and normalization.

Of course, the graphic activity represents only a small part of the information which enters the process. A symbolic, usually verbal, reasoning or logical activity continuously challenges each step for functional correctness. Note that while the entire process can be represented as an interplay between rational and graphic activity, leveling and sharpening is incremental by nature and forces the corresponding rational activity to be also incremental. Reorganizations act to upset this pattern, but their occurrence is beneficial whenever they speed the problem-solver toward solution. When previous experience is not available to him, however, he must fall back on an incremental method.

Many questions remain unanswered. What is the relative effect of leveling and sharpening on solution? Could it be possible that the nature of design problems is such that it is the act of reorganization that really "delivers the goods"? What is the relative effect of incremental leveling and sharpening and of major reorganization on problem direction? Do they both not sometimes lead the problem-solver away from solution? Is one approach any better than the other in this regard? The desire to answer these questions led me to conduct a content analysis of the graphic representations produced during problem-solving.

The Picasso Lithographs

The material selected from this study consists of eleven lithographic bulls created by Picasso in December 1945 through January 1946 and reproduced in Figure 3.[6] Each lithograph represents the completion by the artist of a stage of some period of work, often several days long, within a progression

---

5. For the experiments which led to these concepts, see Friedrich Wülf, "Tendencies in Figural Variation," in Willis D. Ellis, ed., *A Source Book of Gestalt Psychology,* pp. 136–148.
6. Pablo Picasso, *Picasso: Lithographé,* Vol. 1, the complete collection of the lithographs of Picasso.

2. Gestalt principles of leveling, sharpening, and normalizing of graphic material

3. The complete series of eleven lithographs (from *Picasso, Lithographe,* Monte Carlo: A. Sauret, 1949, Vol. I)

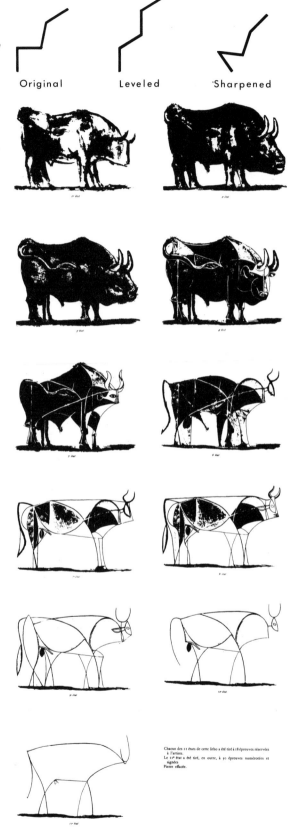

Original   Leveled   Sharpened   Normalized

Table 1 Stimulus Size Hierarchy	A Whole bull	B Major Parts	C Minor Parts	D Graphic Areas	E Line Elements
		Head	horns forehead ears temples eyes cheeks nose mouth		
		Front quarter	neck upper back shoulders		
		Front legs	left knee left ankle left hoof right hoof right ankle right knee right thigh		
		Midsection	ribs testes penis waist back		
		Hind quarter	tail hips		
		Rear legs	thigh right knee right ankle right hoof left hoof left ankle		

4. Final analysis: a composite of stages 5 and 6 (see figure 3). Dashed lines were *removed* from 5 to produce 6; heavy solid lines were *added;* light solid lines were *modified;* double lines were left *unchanged.*

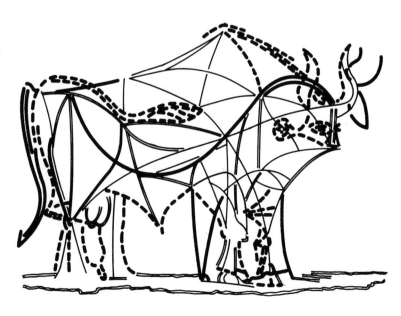

of stages from a concrete or realistic rendition of a bull to a most abstract one. All the lithographs were printed from the same lithographic stone, which was altered by the artist between printings. The content analysis of this study was conducted on the head of the bull and its parts, in the last eight stages only. These stages were felt to most clearly approximate the linear quality of the designer's sketches. In the analysis no special significance was given to Picasso's use of blackened and shaded areas; all areas were considered equal in tonal value.

The material selected, although not the graphic output of design problem-solving, was considered appropriate for a beginning study of the design process for the following reasons:
1. The working method of changing the lithographic stone is similar to, yet more controlled than, a designer's use of tracing paper overlays.
2. The lithographic material was developed sequentially toward a generally understood long-term goal and under the short-term direction of creating stronger forms as is the case with design problems.
3. The lithographic material is considerably simpler and less subject to complicating side explorations than design material. This simplification was considered necessary in a beginning study of a highly complex process.
4. The lithographic material was created by one man, whereas often several designers contribute to the same project. Thus in the lithographs the complexity of the process is further reduced by removing possible individual variations in approach.

Procedure

Each of the last eight lithographs of the bull series by Picasso was conceptually "dissected" into five stimulus size levels: the whole bull, its major parts, its minor parts, its graphic areas, and its line elements. This is shown in Table 1.

Only the elements for the heads of the bulls were analyzed in detail. Judgments were made along the following three criteria and in the following order:
1. Continuity. The change across every stimulus pair of elements (the corresponding elements on consecutive lithographs) was judged to be continuous or discontinuous as shown in Figure 4. All four levels were judged from the bottom of the hierarchy on up. This criterion was used to define reorganization (discontinuous judgments) and leveling and sharpening (continuous or incremental judgments) for those judgments on levels C and above.[7]
2. Clarity. The change across every stimulus pair of elements on the lithographs was judged for the change in clarity of its form. Did the change strengthen or weaken the form? This criterion was used to determine how good the graphic decisions were (level C and above), and also to explain short-term motivation.
3. Relevance. The change across every stimulus pair of elements was compared to the final lithograph and judged for its long-term direction or relevance. Did the change bring the problem-solver closer to his final solution or not? This criterion was used to determine how good the graphic decisions, level C and above, were in terms of reaching the final goal.

These judgments were recorded on seven decision hierarchies and then tabulated for the purpose of comparing the quantitative and qualitative effects on solution of reorganization and leveling and sharpening. The seven decision hierarchies were further inspected across every step-change (every two consecutive lithographs) with the hope of determining decision patterns. From this analysis, pattern criteria were drawn for the determination of the decision direction regarding upper level changes. Did the graphic activity (leveling and sharpening) stimulate the cognitive act (reorganization), or just record it?

---

7. The words "continuous" and "incremental" as used to describe leveling and sharpening are essentially equivalent. In leveling and sharpening the artist makes a change which he thinks will preserve the continuity of the form. In that sense it is a continuous change, at least in his mind. To the observer the change appears to be incremental.

Results

It is with some caution that one approaches the results of this study. The bull heads on the eight lithographs analyzed contain 228 graphic elements. Over 500 judgments were made by the rater along the three criteria. Additional judgments were made identifying patterns among those already made. While these totals seem fairly sizeable, when they are broken apart into the units actually under study, they produce figures often barely large enough to consider.

For example, while all four levels *B* through *E* were studied, the area of statistical concern was principally only levels *B* and *C*. In these two levels there are only sixty graphic elements over the series and no more than nine on any one lithograph. As a result, occasionally the data are reduced to a few elements or judgments which are called upon to provide the answer to some question. Reservations should also be stated about the use of only one rater. Properly, the judgments should be checked against those of other trained but independent raters. It is for these statistical reasons that the data are presented somewhat hesitantly and should be approached with caution. Clearly the study should be seen as only a pilot study which develops a method for achieving conclusive results; the results themselves have not yet been obtained. It is with this thought foremost in mind that the following statements are made.

Turning to Table 2, the continuity judgments on levels *B* and *C* of Table 1 can be considered as indicators of reorganization (R) or of leveling and sharpening (LS). It can be seen that there is little difference between reorganization and leveling and sharpening in the percentage of total decision equivalents shown. Of the total number of graphic decisions made, as many were made continuously or incrementally as were made through major reorganizations.

Table 3 can be read several ways. Reading horizontally, one can see that leveling and sharpening decisions apparently produce stronger forms (H for higher clarity) twice as often as they produce forms low in clarity, while reorganizations produce equal numbers of each. Thus large discontinuous decisions are as likely to produce forms low in clarity as high, while incremental decisions strongly operate to clarify the form. Reading vertically, last column, almost two-thirds of the decisions that are high in clarity were made incrementally, by leveling and sharpening, and of those low in clarity over half were made discontinuously by means of major reorganizations. Finally it should be noted that of the total number of decisions those high in clarity outweigh those low in clarity 55 to 34. These figures would seem to confirm that in this type of material the tendency toward stronger forms is a strong tendency indeed, and a valid one to try to quantify.

However, the clarity issue only prods the artist or problem-solver toward what he should do next. How relevant are his leveling and sharpening decisions to final solution? According to Table 4, they are not very relevant. Again reading vertically, the reorganization decisions show up overwhelmingly more "toward" solution than the incremental ones, leveling and sharpening, and almost all of those judged "away" from the solution were the result of leveling and sharpening. Further, reading horizontally, almost all of the reorganizations were toward solution, while the continuous decisions were equally "toward" or "away." Finally, in Table 4 note that under "Totals" the total number of decisions is overwhelmingly "toward" solution. Again, this seems to confirm relevance as a valid criterion and analytic tool.

While Table 3 gives the comparative effect of the two types of decisions on the form, and Table 4 gives their effect on long-term direction, neither indicates the *combined* effect of these criteria on solution. To put it differently, how many LS and R decisions were both "high" in clarity and "toward" solution? According to Table 5, they work together 30 percent of the time, with discontinuous decisions having a slight edge over the incremental ones.

Studying the judgments for patterns of judgment, one can say that at least 40 percent of the total decisions "come from below," that is, are triggered off

Table 2
Continuity Criterion
(Head of bull only)

Level 1	B	C	B adj.*	C + B adj.	% of Total (106) Decision Equivalents
Decision Type					
LS	4	26	30	56	52.8
R	3	24	23	47	44.4
U	0	3	3	3	2.8
Totals	7	53	53	106	100.0

LS = Leveling and sharpening
R = Reorganization
U = Unchanged

* The figures for level *B* were adjusted equivalent to level *C* to obtain the total effect on solution.

Table 3
Clarity Criterion
(Head of bull only)

Level	B			C			B adj.*			C + B adj.			% of Total (106) Decision Equivalents		
Clarity Decision Type	H	N	L	H	N	L	H	N	L	H	N	L	H	N	L
LS	3	0	1	16	2	8	22	0	8	38	2	16	35.8	1.9	15.1
R	2	0	1	5	2	12	15	0	8	20	2	20	19.0	1.9	19.0
U, O	0	0	0	0	8	0	0	0	0	0	8	0	0.0	7.5	0.0
Totals	5	0	2	21	12	20	37	0	16	58	12	36	54.7	11.3	34.0
		7			53			53			106				100.0

LS = Leveling and sharpening
R = Reorganization
U = Unchanged
O = Omitted
H = Higher clarity
N = No change
L = Lower clarity

* The figures for level *B* were adjusted to level *C* to obtain the total effect on solution.

Table 4
Relevance Criterion
(Head of bull only)

Level	B			C			B adj.*			C + B adj.			% of Total (106) Decision Equivalents		
Decision Type Relevance	T	U	A	T	U	A	T	U	A	T	U	A	T	U	A
LS	2	0	2	12	3	11	16	0	14	28	3	25	26.4	2.8	23.6
R	3	0	0	22	0	2	23	0	0	45	0	2	42.4	0.0	1.9
U	0	0	0	0	3	0	0	0	0	0	3	0	0.0	2.8	0.0
Totals	5	0	2	34	6	13	39	0	14	73	6	27	68.8	5.7	25.5
		7			53			53			106				100.0

LS = Leveling and sharpening
R = Reorganization
U = Unchanged
T = Toward final lithograph
A = Away from final lithograph

* The figures on level *B* were adjusted to level *C* to obtain the total effect on solution.

Table 5
Comparative Effect of Leveling and
Sharpening and Reorganization
(Head of bull only)

Level	B	C	B adj.*	C + B adj.	% of Total (106) Decision Equivalents
Decision Type					
LS	1	4	8	12	11.3
R	2	4	15	19	17.9
Totals	3	8	23	31	29.2

LS = Leveling and sharpening
R = Reorganization

* The figures for level *B* were adjusted to level *C* to obtain the total effect on solution.

by the graphic material. However, the figures here are the least conclusive, and perhaps all that should be said is that graphic decisions can be identified which were first judged to be reorganizations and then later judged to be stimulated by the graphic material itself. The percentage occurrence of this type of decision is probably not very high, but it does seem to happen.

Conclusions

The results of this study can be discussed in two ways. What do the results seem to be saying about the method of analyzing graphic material presented in the study, and what do they seem to be saying about the design process?

The three criteria used in the method, continuity, clarity, and relevance, work together to produce a picture of the design process. The three can be seen as tendencies of artistic behavior peculiar to the type of problem presented in this paper.[8] The first tendency is for the artist to make continuous or non-continuous decisions. That is to say, he "knows" when he puts his pencil to paper whether he is going to modify the form before him or change it completely. The second tendency is that the artist tends to work strongly toward clarifying the form. This tendency toward *Prägnanz* is what leads the artist and creates the discomfort that causes him to want to work on.[9] Finally, there is the tendency to drive toward some long-range goal. The method used seems to quite effectively sort the artistic decisions according to these criteria; at least it does so for one rater and on fairly simple material. Whether the method will prove adequate for other raters working on more complex material remains to be shown.

In addition, the bull study demonstrates that the solution content attributable to continuous or incremental activity can be identified and distinguished quantitatively and qualitatively from that attributable to major reorganization. Further, it demonstrates that to some extent the graphic activity that is part of the design process stimulates reorganization. Instances where this is the case have been identified. Still in question is the exact manner and extent to which incremental activity affects solution. At present, about all that can be said is that major reorganization and leveling and sharpening seem to have about an equal effect on the solution content of problems such as this one where graphic material is used to achieve and represent the conceptual solution.

Perhaps the most interesting conclusion concerns the interplay of leveling and sharpening with reorganization. Leveling and sharpening operates principally as a clarifying agent which leads the problem-solver toward stronger forms. As a result, its stimulus to short-term motivation is probably great. In contrast, reorganization seems to operate primarily as an agent of long-term direction. It acts to direct the incremental activity toward the long-term goal, starting the problem-solver over again in a new "location," if necessary. However, its effect in clarifying the form is equivocal. Similarly, the effect of leveling and sharpening on the long-term goal is equivocal.

While these general remarks can be made in regard to this one problem, it is felt that the relationship between the two activities must vary considerably as the problem and problem-solver are varied. The bull lithographs represent the solution to a problem limited in scale and intent. More than likely, Picasso had a clear idea of what he intended to accomplish. If this was the case, one would expect reorganization to have the pronounced effect it had on long-term direction. One would expect that the clearer the goal is for the problem-solver, the easier it will be for him to decide when a reorganization is relevant. In their selection of problems, most designers are not so fortunate; they usually cannot define the problem in their own terms as an artist can. Confronted with more complex problems with fuzzier goals, the relative roles of reorganization and leveling and sharpening might change, with the latter contributing more to long-term direction than it did in this study.

8. For a more general statement, see Rusch, "On the Use of Levelling and Sharpening as an Analytic Tool in the Study of Artistic Behavior."
9. For this principle see Kurt Koffka, *Principles of Gestalt Psychology,* probably the clearest and most complete statement of the *Gestalt* position.

5 On the Rational Reconstruction of Intuition in the Design Process

Comments on the papers by Eastman and Rusch

Bernard Kaplan

Heinz Werner Institute of
Developmental Psychology,
Clark University
Worcester, Massachusetts

Bernard Kaplan is Professor of Psychology
and a member of the Executive Committee
of the Heinz Werner Institute of Developmental Psychology at Clark University.
He received a Ph.D. in psychology from
Clark in 1953. He has lectured extensively
and was Visiting Professor of Psychology
at the University of Chicago. His major
works include, with Seymour Wapner,
eds., *Perspectives in Psychological
Theory;* with Heinz Werner, *Symbol
Formation: An Organismic-Developmental Approach to Language and the
Expression of Thought.*

At first blush, there seems to be little in common in these two papers; they are quite different in style, in substance, in method, and in scope. A closer examination, however, reveals that the two authors share a common aim: to uncover and render explicit the processes by which superior designers, who rarely follow an explicit "design methodology," produce a superior design. The two authors also share several presuppositions. First, they presuppose that the methods and concepts developed in psychology to deal with prag- matic problem-solving, where the character of the acceptable solution (or range of acceptable solutions) is already known to the investigator, have a direct relevance to the understanding of "problem solution" in the domain of design. Second, they assume that it is possible to render intuitive thinking —involving a heavy dose of what Polanyi has termed "tacit knowledge"— fully explicit and thus to liberate "design" from the stigma of an art and trans- form it into a canonical science. Third, they suppose that it is possible to reconstruct the process of thinking from an examination and collation of external behaviors, e.g., drawings, eye movements, verbalizations. To be sure, there is occasionally an expression of caution and even of commend- able skepticism about the validity of one or another of these presuppositions, but they are all, it seems to me, operative throughout inquiries described in the two papers.

Let me consider, first, the common aim, and, then, the common presuppositions of the two authors. Given the ostensible aim, to explicate the intuitive
processes of superior designers, I am somewhat puzzled by the nature of the
research undertakings. If I were interested in how a superior quarterback
operated, I wouldn't look at a number of third-string quarterbacks. Or, if
I were interested in the functioning of a superior quarterback, I wouldn't
look at Jim Lonborg or Don Drysdale, excellent as these men may be as
pitchers. Yet Eastman, it seems to me, has done something like the first, and
Rusch something like the second.

Eastman does not provide full information with regard to his subjects, but
the little that he does mention scarcely indicates that his sample was drawn
from superior designers. Like psychologists, who presume to study the complexities of thinking by examining the performances of college sophomores
on trivial and simplistic problems, Eastman appears to me to have fallen
victim to a variant of the researcher's dilemma. Although the treasure is to
be found only by searching in the dark alley, he insists on a detailed scrutiny
of the area under the street lamp. Underlying this "strategy," I believe, is
the "assumption of continuity" that once led many psychologists to assert
that they could attain an understanding of the fundamental factors in high-
level human thinking on the basis of detailed studies of the behavior of rats
in mazes.[1] Just as psychologists of old, and indeed many psychologists today, have assumed that man differs from the rat or the ape only in "complexity" (that is, in degree), so Eastman appears to assume that the superior
designer proceeds in the same way as the ordinary designer, differing only
in the values of a fixed set of variables. Without such an underlying assumption, it is difficult to understand how he hoped to elucidate the nature of
intuitive thinking in superior, creative, innovative designers by studying
people who were not known for superior design.

Rusch does not err in this regard. His sole subject is clearly a man of superior
talent, one generally recognized as a genius. Picasso, however, is not a
designer in the strict sense. He is an artist. And although the process of design involves aesthetic considerations to varying degrees, it is not exclusively
an aesthetic enterprise. Doubtless, Picasso's activity is not as far removed
from that of certain designers as Don Drysdale's is from that of Johnny
Unitas, but there is still the question of the legitimacy of inferring the processes of organization and reorganization in the work of superior designers
from those involved in the work of an artist, superb and creative as he may be.
To be sure, Rusch recognizes this issue, but the pertinence of his paper
to his aim is predicated on the assumption that such an extrapolation is
warranted. In addition, of course, there is the question of "size and repre-
sentativeness of the sample." Even granting the assumption that the activity
of a superior designer is akin to that of a superior artist, one would surely
need a representative sample of the modes of procedure of a representative
sample of superior artists in order to draw any general conclusions about the
stages in the process of superior design.

Having briefly discussed the relevance of the papers to the aims of the two
authors, I would like now to turn to those common presuppositions which I
believe one can discern in their inquiries. For convenience, let me designate
these as follows: (1) the presupposition of transposability, (2) the presupposition of uniformity, (3) the presupposition of transparency.

Although Eastman's paper probably reflects the *presupposition of transposability* more overtly than does Rusch's, it seems to me that both authors,
in their amicable allusions to the psychological literature on problem-solving
(almost all of which has had to deal with the attainment of preestablished or

---

1. We shall see that a related "assumption of uniformity," an assumption that all thinking is essentially the same, leads Eastman to regard intuitive thinking as if it were a
diffuse version of explicit thinking and leads to his belief that intuitive thinking can be
decomposed and sequentialized, i.e., rendered discursive.

predetermined solutions to a limited range of problems) show a strong inclination to assume prima facie that the analytic categories and concepts, appropriate (perhaps) for describing the genetic actualization (microgenesis) of solution processes for a limited range of problems, can be directly transposed, without fundamental change, to the description of attempts to deal with quite different kinds of problems, e.g., aesthetic or quasi-aesthetic problems, or moral problems, where "right answers" or "exceptionally good answers" are scarcely specifiable a priori.

The presupposition of transposability, of course, both follows from and leads to a tendency to homogenize all problems and inevitably conduces to the nailing of quite different concrete activities and processes to a Procrustean bed of fixed concepts. One becomes the unwitting victim of vicious abstraction or, in Whitehead's phrase, of "misplaced concreteness." One will recall how the orthodox Gestalt psychologists, whom Rusch is inclined to follow, employed categories, derived primarily for the characterization of certain perceptual phenomena, in the domain of complex problem-solving and creative thinking.[2] All kinds of thought processes were described in terms of "closure" or "good Gestalten" with little real gain in understanding. The world-renowned child psychologist Jean Piaget has done the same thing with his concepts of "assimilation" and "accommodation," transposing these notions from the biological sphere to the psychological and cultural domains, where their application is far less obvious or relevant.[3] I suspect that the same kind of "reduction by translation" is taking place among some practitioners of "information-processing" approaches; I will return to this point later on.

Please do not misunderstand me. I have no desire to urge the outright rejection of this presupposition of transposability. I only wish to suggest that it be scrupulously exposed and scrupulously examined. And I would also like to suggest consideration of the possibility that for practical and quasi-aesthetic disciplines it may be better to develop specific categories and concepts closer to their distinctive "problems" than to extend terminology from some other domain. Too often a new movement, brought to life and sustained by a new technology, takes over the terminology of that technology and translates everything in the world into it. This has, alas too often, led to pretentious ways of saying banal things in the most ponderous jargon, without any noticeable gain in comprehension.

Characteristically, the assumption of transposability goes hand in hand with the *presupposition of uniformity*.[4] This is quite understandable. For this second presupposition pertains to the blurring or dissolution of the boundaries between superficially different mental activities, and when all problems are conceived of as being of essentially the same nature, it is not surprising that mental activities which appear to be prima facie distinct (e.g., thinking, perceiving, imagining) are presumed to be, at a "deeper level," variants of one fundamental process. The nature of this basic process has varied, depending upon a theorist's predilection for the high road or the low. Thus, following Descartes, a number of thinkers have assumed that all mental activity is cogitation or intellection, the products varying in degree of clarity and distinctness. For example, we find Helmholtz asserting that perception is unconscious inference and, more recently, Bruner opting for the same viewpoint. On the other hand, there have been those who have assumed that the fundamental act of mentation is the association of independent elements and have viewed thinking in the rat and in Einstein as essentially a discrete chaining of simple ideas, stimulus-response connections, or "habit mech-

2. The orthodox Gestalt psychologists include Max Wertheimer, Kurt Koffka, and Wolfgang Köhler. See Wolfgang Köhler, *Gestalt Psychology,* and Kurt Koffka, *Principles of Gestalt Psychology.*
3. Jean Piaget, *The Psychology of Intelligence.*
4. One may recognize in these two presuppositions the persistence of beliefs in the unity of subject matter and unity of method so dear to the hearts of the logical positivists and the "unity of science" movement.

anisms." The history of this press toward uniformity is pretty well known.[5] The "unitarian" movement received a considerable boost from Darwinism, and the revolution instigated by Shannon, Wiener, Turing and others appears, in many quarters, to have placed the presupposition beyond dispute.[6]

Yet there have always been those, past and present, who have resisted the press toward uniformity. Against the Cartesian demand for "clear and distinct ideas" Pascal, no mean hand at the mathematical way of thinking, insisted that the heart has its reasons that reason knows not of and, drawing a sharp distinction between geometrical and intuitive modes of thought, maintained the superiority of intuition over the geometrical spirit. During the nineteenth century artists and aestheticians revolted against the pan-scientism and positivism that denied or denigrated the *Erkenntniswert* of art. Shortly after the beginning of this century, both Croce and Bergson inveighed against the attempts to encompass art and life within a set of parochial categories developed for the manipulation and control of inanimate nature.[7] Whatever the differences in detail in their conceptions of "intuition," both these thinkers contrasted intuitive thinking with logical-mathematical thought and argued strongly against the widespread assumption that the former could be reduced to the latter or was, in any way, explicable in terms of the latter. More recently, phenomenologists such as Merleau-Ponty, scientist-philosophers such as Polanyi and others have argued that there are modes of knowing that are essential in human functioning and that cannot be rendered fully explicable or assimilated to the model of discursive reasoning.[8]

As before, let me make clear that I do not urge the rejection of this presupposition of uniformity. I merely want to emphasize that it is a presupposition and that one must be wary of the tendency to transform a presupposition of questionable warrant into an unquestioned dogma. Nor do I wish to argue for the permanent intractability of intuition to some degree of rational reconstruction or impugn the thesis that it is worthwhile to go as far as one can to analyze intuitive processes. What I do object to, however, is the a priori characterization of intuition in terms of concepts developed for fully explicit thinking. In this connection it may be useful to bring up a significant distinction that Scriven once made between derivation and translation. Too often, manifestly distinct activities are simply translated into a common jargon. (We all know of Hobbes' notorious attempt to talk of perceiving, imagining, and thinking in terms of motion and decaying motion.) The illusion is created through a kind of verbal magic that clarity and a more profound understanding of preanalytic differences have somehow been attained, that one is deriving the obvious differences rather than merely dissolving them through a linguistic trick.

I should like to close this brief discussion of the presupposition of uniformity with a quotation from someone whom one might have thought to be in the camp of those who would reduce all mental activities to variants of a single operation or single set of operations. The following is from George Boole's *An Investigation of the Laws of Thought:*

The prejudice which would either banish or make supreme any one department of knowledge or faculty of mind, betrays not only error of judgment, but a defect of that intellectual modesty which is inseparable from a pure devo-

---

5. For details I refer you to Ernst Cassirer, *The Philosophy of the Enlightenment,* and to Elle Halevy, *The Growth of Philosophical Radicalism.*
6. Alan Anderson, ed., *Minds and Machines.*
7. Benedetto Croce, *Aesthetics*; Henri Bergson, *Introduction to Metaphysics,* and *Creative Evolution.*
8. Maurice Merleau-Ponti, *Phenomenology of Perception,* and *The Structure of Behavior*; Michael Polanyi, *Personal Knowledge; Towards a Post-Critical Philosophy* and *The Study of Man.* I would also here like to refer to the three volumes of Ernst Cassirer, *Philosophy of Symbolic Forms*; to Susanne K. Langer, *Philosophy in a New Key, Feeling and Form,* and *Mind: An Essay on Human Feeling*; to Louis A. Reid, *Ways of Knowledge and Experience*; and to Hubert Dreyfus, *Philosophic Issues in Artificial Intelligence.*

tion to truth. It assumes the office of criticizing a constitution of things which no human appointment has established, or can annul. It sets aside the ancient and just conception of truth as one thought manifold. Much of this error, as actually existent among us, seems due to the special and isolated character of scientific thinking—which character it, in its turn, tends to foster.

Let me dilate briefly now on the third assumption that I believe to be operative in the two papers: the *presupposition of transparency*. Once again, this presupposition seems to me to be more apparent in Eastman's paper than in Rusch's. Again, both authors are circumspect about the warrant of this assumption, Rusch perhaps more so than Eastman. But once more, both inquiries reported in the presentations appear to me to rest on the belief that one can establish some kind of one-to-one relationship between the constituent operations of covert thought and the necessarily sequential expressions in overt behavior of the "something going on."

Thus, one finds both authors beginning with the recording of "behaviors" against a time line: verbal remarks, graphic activity, and graphic productions. In Eastman's terminology these behaviors constitute the "information"—or is it the input?—for the investigators.[9] From the designer's or artist's point of view, of course, this material comprises the "output." Although I may be mistaken here, it seems to me that both authors seek to infer the sequence of processes that must have taken place in thought directly from this sequential or parallel (contemporaneous) "output" of the subject. To be sure, to the extent that they posit hypothetical "strategies," "heuristics," and "transformations" (even of such a tame form as "leveling" and "sharpening") that impute some processes in the thinking subject which are not directly manifested in the particularities of behavior, their actual procedures would seem to render my interpretation dubious. Yet it would seem that, even in such cases, these imputed hypothetical processes are either placed in one-to-one correspondence with specific behaviors (e.g., at this point, a leveling tendency operated, at this point a sharpening tendency or operation) or are assumed to be uniquely determinative of a rather limited and finite sequence of behaviors, i.e., it is assumed that one can unequivocally reconstruct the thought process from a sample of surface behavior.

It is true that Eastman recognizes, perhaps more than Rusch, that there may be no easy and unambiguous way of going from input-output analysis to underlying thought processes, without a detailed understanding of the past history and interests of the subject.

Assuming that I have correctly discerned the strategy of the authors, the question arises: "On what grounds can one infer the character of covert processing solely from the output generated by a subject in certain environmental settings?" It seems to me that this is possible only if one identifies thought with external behavior (à la metaphysical and methodological behaviorism) or if one assumes an isomorphism between thought and behavior (an extension of the orthodox, Berlin, Gestalt position). Moreover, one must accept what the phenomenologist Merleau-Ponty has characterized as a "préjuge du monde" and what James, long ago, baptized as the "psychologist's fallacy"—the assumption that the world is given in the same way to everyone: that the input for a subject is the same as the input for the investigator.[10]

One might have expected that Freud and dynamic psychologists would have made the presupposition of transparency problematic, through their demonstration of different, and parallel, levels of "information processing" and their emphasis on the role of desires, wishes, fears, and conflicts in determining

9. I am on uncertain ground here in using Eastman's terminology because it is difficult to ascertain from his ubiquitous use of the phrase "information processing" whether information is distinct from input, equivalent to input, or bears some other kind of relation to input.
10. See Dreyfus, *Philosophic Issues*.

how input is processed (i.e., what "information" in a nontechnical sense is drawn from the environment). Yet one finds that this presupposition has generally persisted in academic psychology along with the kindred "dogma of immaculate perception." In fact, it is only recently, probably under the impact of Chomsky's revolution in linguistics, that the climate of opinion has begun to change.[11]

Although I was not initially asked to comment upon the paper by Krauss and Myer, this paper, presented during a session that I chaired, bears on the issues raised by the papers of Eastman and Rusch and therefore warrants some general comment. As it turned out in the discussion of all the papers, the paper by Krauss and Myer was a "throwing down of the gauntlet" to the Eastman-Moran kind of analysis, suggesting that the concepts now used by certain individuals who regard themselves as belonging to the "information-processing" school are de facto inadequate to deal with the concrete operations designers use in the process of formulating a design.[12] It seems to me that this would be conceded by the Eastman-Moran group, but the real issue is: Can information-processing theory do any better in the future? Is there something, in principle, that precludes the kind of analysis that Eastman-Moran seek to execute? Once again, I think caution is necessary. I have little doubt that the kind of information-processing view adopted by Neisser[13] is superior to that accepted by Eastman and Moran, but whether even an extension of that view will contribute to a better understanding of the processes of creative design, I leave as an open question.

11. Noam Chomsky, *Syntactic Structures.*
12. See also Thomas Moran's paper, "A Model of a Multi-Lingual Designer," in this volume. Ed.
13. Ulrich Neisser, *Cognitive Psychology.*

3 Computer-Aided Design

The application of computers to the design and planning fields has held a peculiar fascination since the early 1960s. Some argue strongly that this fascination is misdirected; that as the pursuit of technological innovation has become an end in itself, it has harmed fields whose real ends are to solve environmental problems. The papers in this section are centered around interactive man-machine systems intended to be direct aids in the solution of environmental problems.

Although the two are sometimes confused, computer-aided design is not just "computer graphics." Computer graphics is the display and perhaps manipulation of visual images on a computer-based display unit, most often a cathode-ray tube. Computer-aided design is dependent on advances in computer graphics but beyond that includes interaction between the designer and the machine and the programming into the machine of specific design capability. Some important computer graphics developments are listed in the bibliography at the end of this volume, including the early three-dimensional rotational techniques of Johnson, machine halftones perspectives by Wylie et al., an interactive programming system by Newman, and the stereoscopic and movie-generation techniques developed by Noll. Applications of computer graphics to architecture are presented in Milne's recent book.

An exciting computer-aided design system, not reported in this volume, was developed by Jacks et al. in 1963–1964 at the General Motors Research Laboratories. DAC-1 accepts as input and reads rough engineering drawings of body assemblies including sketches containing free-form lines, projects the drawings on a cathode-ray tube, enables the designer to make alterations to any part of the design either by alpha-numeric console or light-pen and then to see this alteration from any perspective viewpoint, does engineering calculations or cost estimates on any part of the design in seconds, enables the designer to compare two designs by automatic overlay on the display tube, and finally, produces optical scanning film or hard-copy drawings from any point of view at any state of the process.

The systems described in this section have made other advances particularly important for environmental design and planning applications.

The section begins with a paper by Thomas Heath outlining the algorithmic properties of the design process. It is interesting to compare his argument with the arguments for nonalgorithmic systems in some of the later papers. In the next paper Thomas Moran shows the beginning stages of constructing a man-machine model for simulating the human designer.

Three papers report on operational computer-aided design systems. The first has applications to structural engineering and building design, the second to city planning, and the third to architecture and urban design.

Robert Logcher's STRUDL was the earliest of the three systems to be developed (1966–1967) and is in wide use in the profession, particularly as it doesn't require dynamic display units or programming skill. Basically, STRUDL is a structural information storage and retrieval system which does analyses of any type on any subset of data as requested by the designer while storing or manipulating other parts of the problem. Logcher argues against a fully automated computer design system and sees the most promising approach lying in flexible systems which interact with their users and allow a wide range of design operations and applications.

William Porter, Katherine Lloyd, and Aaron Fleisher's DISCOURSE differs especially from Heath's and Moran's suggestions. The former see a computer-aided system as one which combines the data storage and retrieval capabilities and multiple operations of the computer with the "brooding mind" of the designer. DISCOURSE has a flexible language and data base on which the designer or planner, with little computer experience, can develop operations suited to his particular problem. Thus their system is not algorithmic nor does it attempt to simulate human processes. Rather, it is interactive and differs from the other systems in the source of the intelligence which drives the overall process.

Nicholas Negroponte and Leon Groisser's URBAN5 is a verbal and graphic interactive system which, among other things, allows the designer to work in three dimensions, to move around or through space, and to call for calculations or criteria checks at any time. In fact, after being told what criteria the designer is trying to satisfy the system will keep automatic check to see that these are met at each stage of the process, and if not will inform the designer. URBAN5 adapts to the particular designer, and thus is evolutionary.

In conclusion Michael Noll compares the systems and warns against overindulgence in computer systems as ends in themselves. At best, he says, they are partial means to solving environmental problems.

6 The Algorithmic Nature of the Design Process

Thomas F. Heath

McConnel, Smith & Johnson
Architects and Town Planners
235 New South Head Road
Edgecliff, New South Wales, Australia

Thomas F. Heath is a partner in McConnel, Smith & Johnson and a Lecturer in the Department of Architectural Science at the University of Sydney. He received a B.Arch. from the University of Sydney in 1954, began working with McConnel, Smith & Johnson, and then received a M.Bldg.Sc. in 1966. From 1958 to 1968 he was on the architecture faculties of the University of New South Wales and the New South Wales Institute of Technology. He is the author of *Experimental Aesthetics and Architecture.*

One of the difficulties of studying design and planning methodology lies in defining the goals of such studies and thus in knowing whether or not the goal has been reached or even precisely what the remaining unsolved problems are. In this paper the goal is defined as the construction of an algorithm for the solution of design problems. An algorithm may be defined as a complete and therefore deterministic set of directions for the solution of the problem or for deciding that it cannot be solved. The solution of design problems is defined as the actual process of decision-making which occurs consciously or accidentally in producing a successful design. A skilled design team traces a maze of decisions to a satisfactory solution more quickly than an unskilled one, because experience has taught them to ask the right questions in the right order so as to limit the field as rapidly and as completely as possible. But insofar as this is true of their experience, both the questions and their order can be codified in the form of an algorithm. To this extent the design process is algorithmic. A version of such an algorithm for industrial and commercial building is described.

It is the intention of this paper to explore the relationship between design problems, the design process, and certain characteristics of algorithms. Building design is used as an example. An algorithm in flow chart form will be presented for the design of a particular building type, commercial office buildings. The algorithm is based on the author's observation of the actual process followed in the design of several buildings of this type in his own office. It is thus empirically based, but it has not yet been experimentally tested and is therefore still hypothetical.

The approach proposed and indicated in the algorithm differs from that of some other students in that it attempts to substitute design method for the designer as far as possible rather than to make the computer or design method an aid to more traditional methods of design. From the point of view of the building practitioner and the manufacturing industry at large, quick and reliable results of good quality are more valuable than slower and more problematical methods that may on occasions yield exceptional quality. While there is undoubtedly merit in pursuing both approaches, there is an urgent need for methods which will improve the design quality of the bulk of building production. The rigidity which "a computer program to design buildings" suggests is more apparent than real. The program is, after all, only

1. Theseus and the minotaur—typical maze problem

2. Algorithmic flow chart from the maze problem

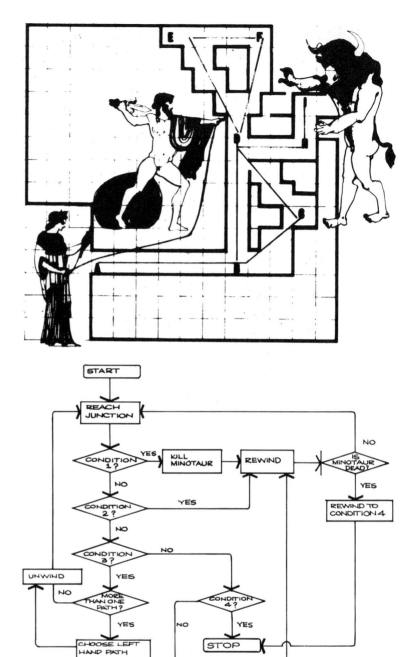

a set of logical relationships, like a generalized equation. The answers it gives will vary both according to the quantities assigned to the "variables" in a given problem—the site, legal restrictions, and so on—and according to the values assigned to the "constants" in the equation. As the existing state of technology will vary, the constants will have to be changed. Or if technological innovation is viewed as forming part of the problem, they may also be changed by deliberation. It is thus quite unlikely that this "rigid" approach would give the same answer, or even similar answers, twice running. It is hoped that the approach and algorithm suggested in this paper is less rigid and will not fall heir to these shortcomings.

Theseus and the Minotaur

Let us first examine the construction of an algorithm for a task of a simple kind, the searching of a maze. In design we may picture ourselves as exploring a maze of alternatives within which, somewhere, lies the solution we seek, hopefully not a minotaur but a beautiful princess. Even this simple problem serves to bring out the point that in such a process of searching we can deal with multiple choices provided that the number of choices is finite (and in practice small) and that we can construct an appropriate empirical or arbitrary rule for making them. The example of a maze is useful also because most of the maps or models of the design process which have been made, either as an aid to the study of methodology or for practical programming, take the form of mazes or networks.

The following example is taken from Trakhtenbrot.[1] Theseus, we recall, had the task of entering the labyrinth or maze in which lived the monstrous minotaur, to kill it. He had the assistance of the princess Ariadne, who gave him a ball of thread, one end of which she held so that he should not become lost. The labyrinth consists of paths, or courses of action and points where a choice must be made. At these points Theseus either has to decide which of a number of courses of action to follow or, in the case of a dead end, retrace his steps.

For the purpose of the search, as diagrammed in Figure 1, the corridors are classified as follows:
1. Those through which Theseus has never passed.
2. Those through which Theseus passed once; these will have Ariadne's thread stretched along them.
3. Those through which Theseus has passed twice and has marked to indicate the fact; he is not allowed under the rules of the game to repass these.

When Theseus comes to a junction he will find one of the following conditions:
1. Minotaur.
2. Loop: at least two other once-passed corridors leading from the junction.
3. At least one never-passed corridor leading from the junction.
4. Ariadne.
5. None of the above.

His strategy will then be:

Condition	Strategy
Minotaur	Stop
Loop	Rewind the thread
One never-passed corridor	Unwind the thread
Ariadne	Stop
None of the above	Rewind the thread

Now we can convert this into a flow chart or model which will represent the algorithm, as shown in Figure 2. The flow chart is different from the maze itself because the maze at points B and D violates the condition of determinism by offering multiple choices. The flow chart thus has to specify a rule

1. Boris A. Trakhtenbrot, *Algorithms and Automatic Computing Machines.*

for making the arbitrary choice as to which of these courses of action to investigate first. In a real life design situation the making of such arbitrary choices is a function of management.

It will of course be clear that such an algorithmic flow chart can be directly transcribed into a computer program in one of the various computer languages. There is no point in pursuing such an exercise here, but we are reminded (if reminder is needed) that in asking the question, "How far is the design process algorithmic?" we are also asking, "How far is it computable?"

Maps of the Design Process

One of the most popular exercises for students of the design process in general and the architectural design process in particular has been the preparation of maps or models setting out its main features from various points of view. It is not intended here to attempt any kind of critical review of these rather numerous cartographic essays but merely to illustrate one or two of them in order to draw attention to certain significant assumptions (it is perhaps too soon to refer to them as objective features) which have become commonly accepted as a result of this work.

Let us look first at a map given in the RIBA *Handbook of Architectural Practice and Management*[2] here shown as Figure 3. The design process is represented in Diagram A as consisting of four parts: assimilation, general study, development, and communication, with feedback loops occurring between parts. However, the authors are evidently dissatisfied with this model as oversimplified or too deterministic, because in Diagram B they give a more complex model which is described as indicating "the sort of unpredictable jumps that are made within the planned progress." This is interesting because it raises the question of just how unpredictable these jumps or revisions are.

Figure 3 can be compared with Figure 4, a familiar type of precedence diagram, taken from the files of a large current job in my own office. This represents a section of the "sketch planning" period, and it is rather explicit about three things: the order in which certain decisions must be taken, the time that will be available for taking them, and the opportunities that will occur for revision. The last may well be described as an attempt to predict unpredictability, but this is of course a feature of all attempts at programming.

There are two features common to these and other maps to which attention must be drawn. The first is that they all acknowledge that the design process can be subdivided into a number of subprocesses, some of them simultaneous and some of them sequential. Thus far they represent the process as a maze, and a maze, as we have seen, can have an algorithm for its solution. Insofar, then, as such models are correct representations of design operations, they tend toward a deterministic or algorithmic model. Nor is this tendency diminished by the second of these common features, the incorporation of feedback loops. Even our handy do-it-yourself algorithm for the minotaur incorporates two or three such loops. So we are not going to drive a wedge between determinism and the design process on this ground.

However, these two models do not say anything about either the conditions that may be found at the various decision points in the maze or the various strategies that may be adopted. Of course, this is not their object. They are concerned only with the temporal relations between decisions and with the bases of decisions only insofar as it can be shown that the making of one decision depends upon another decision having previously been made. The next section of the discussion must therefore concern itself with the bases of decision.

Reasons for Decision

The maps of the design process so far discussed only locate points at which decisions must be made. Starr's "Design Tree" as illustrated in Figure 5 is

2. Royal Institute of British Architects, *Handbook of Architectural Practice and Management,* 1963, Part 3, 210, p. 7, Fig. 1.

3. RIBA map of the design process

4. Precedence diagram

The Process of Design

In the simplest terms, the design process can be seen as a flow system, as in diagram A: a main progression with occasional feedback.

Diagram A

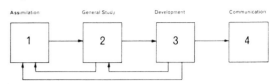

In practice, the mental activity tends to make short flashes from one phase to another according to results achieved and the ideas that are stimulated by the work.

Diagram B shows the sort of unpredictable jumps that are made within the major planned progress.

Diagram B

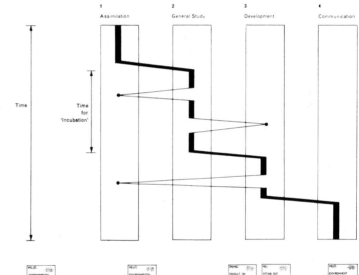

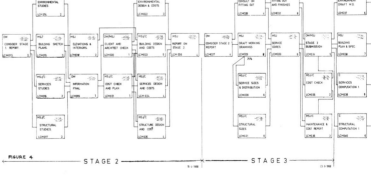

offered as a map of a particular decision.[3] It shows that design decisions cannot be made on the basis of considering every possible alternative; the simple decision represented would involve the consideration of 5184 alternative solutions. Clearly, Starr argues, and I think rightly, we must and do take steps to reduce the number of alternatives actually considered in any more complex design problem, and architectural design problems are certainly that. We must also note in passing that Starr's Tree is a maze.

In fact, Starr's argument is only a particular case of a more general proposition, which is that all restrictions which we introduce on any design problem, including of course what we define as *being* the problem are to some extent arbitrary, and that in all problems, even the simplest, the number of possible courses of action is in fact infinite in the literal mathematical sense. Pye has set us the following enigma: How do you determine what the thing you are going to design "has got to do," what "activity is proper to it," what "it is for," what "its purpose is."[4] The answer he gives, like Starr's and Alexander's in their different ways is "by arbitrarily limiting the problem."[5]

Before struggling a little further with this question of arbitrary limitation it must be made clear that the target of the last paragraph is the inductional or Baconian fallacy, the belief that science is concerned solely with the collection of facts and not with theory, as it tends to crop up in discussions on design method. In science it has long been admitted that the mere collection of facts not only never leads to any useful result but is inherently impossible. But in design as in science we are neither dealing with the formulation of abstract and self-evident concepts nor with the collection of observations, but with a continuous and interacting process of formulation and testing which extends over the whole field, including the objectives to be secured.

To some extent that is a digression. But it helps to emphasize the point that design decisions start with an arbitrary decision or group of decisions about what the problem is. That is, they start by "defining the problem." A number of initial decisions are taken which eliminate the need to examine a very great number of possibilities. Thus it is not uncommon to start an architectural problem with some such statement as "what is required is a 400-bed chest hospital" (a hospital specializing in chest surgery). This process of limiting the field under study can clearly be described not merely colloquially but logically as one of definition.

The statement instanced above is a definition. It defines the problem as lying in a certain class, hospitals, and further reduces the field by adding two species, chest and 400-bed. Also implied in this proposition is that the whole problem is included in the class of buildings as in Figure 6. Thus in the ordinary process of solving design problems we limit the problem (often unconsciously), by accepting, directly or explicitly, certain methods of defining or describing which immensely narrow the field of study, and by accepting indirectly a whole tradition of approaches, attitudes, and methods which give us a great deal of further assistance. Because investigators of design methods are often radicals, they are inclined to talk and to attempt to construct their systems as if this acceptance of traditional definitions of problems were a bad thing: but on the contrary, what is being suggested here is that it is a good and necessary thing, mischievous only if it leads to a general opposition to change or enquiry.

Let us look at the problem of definition in yet another way. At the very beginning of our enquiry we are in a condition of uncertainty. We seek information. We are trying to locate a solution in a field. We are playing a game like Twenty Questions, in which, if we are clever, we can locate a single object among a very large number (1,045,576). Now cleverness in this context is equivalent

3. Martin K. Starr, *Product Design and Decision Theory.*
4. David Pye, *The Nature of Design.*
5. Christopher Alexander, *Notes on the Synthesis of Form.*

5. Design decision tree

6. Defining a problem by class inclusion

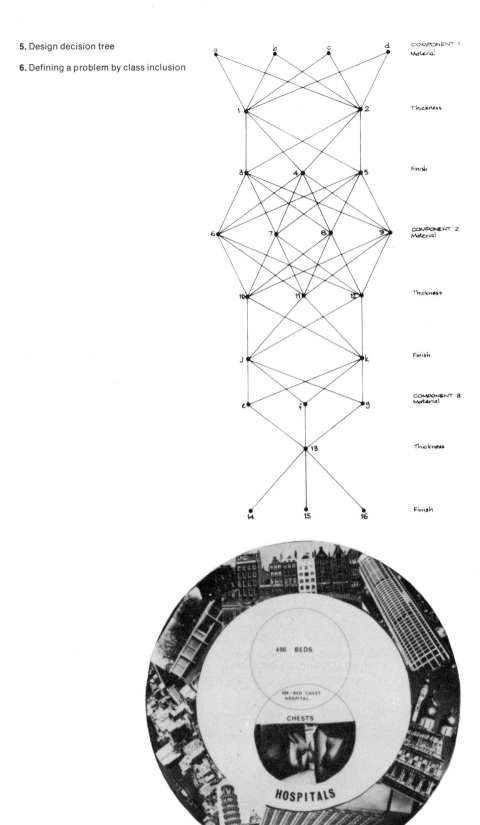

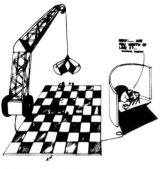

7. Information-theory strategy for solving problems

to economy, to having a sophisticated as opposed to an unsophisticated strategy; that is, referring back to Starr's Tree, *not* considering 5184 alternatives. Now it can be shown (in fact it is a basic proposition of information theory) that the most sophisticated strategy in asking questions is to ask them in such a way as to eliminate exactly half the alternatives each time. A common if elementary illustration is the solution to the problem of locating by questioning a single chessman on an invisible chess board. As we can see from Figure 7, six questions are required. Of course this is an extremely simple instance, but it is clear first that it would be easy to draw up an algorithm for this process, and secondly and conversely, that an algorithm, which by definition presents us with a series of mutually exclusive alternatives, is an efficient device for defining a particular solution in a field.

Now what kinds of questions, in broad outline, can we ask, or what decisions can we make that will decide or define the field for us in the ways discussed? First of all, there are decisions as to ends, the question raised by Pye. From the point of view of the design process such questions are metaphysical, or perhaps I should say metalogical. If they have explanations or can be questioned, the explanations and questions exist as a part of a different system or process, for instance a political organization or the managerial policy of an industrial complex. But secondly there are questions which have, for the purposes of the design process, an empirical answer. This second group includes a wide range of questions from, "What is the rate of interest?" to "What is the thermal conductivity of a brick wall?" It also includes questions that cannot be answered by measurement in the conventional sense but only by asking a skilled person, provided that the reliability of the persons concerned can be checked; many business decisions and such more purely technical activities as wine, cheese, and perfume manufacture depend on decisions of this kind. These first two types of decision may be linked by rational or logical processes. But there is a third possible type of decision: a decision between alternatives where we do not have a sufficient reason to choose one or the other, a situation which may arise either because the facts are not available, or because the alternatives are equally desirable. There is more to say about these arbitrary decisions but it can be deferred during a brief digression on the subject of aesthetic decisions.

A Digression on Aesthetics

It is necessary to digress a little here to try to forestall the tendency of otherwise scientific investigators to go all to pieces when the question of aesthetics is raised. This tendency is largely a consequence of the historically recent but powerful intellectual tradition that defines intellect and art and more especially science and art as inherently contradictory or mutually exclusive. It has either of two unfortunate results: (1) attempts are made to pretend that aesthetic decisions are not involved at all by using some such word as "form" or (2) equally often the attempt to be scientific is simply abandoned at this point. The use of "form" as Alexander uses it is ambiguous, since for instance, a natural object may have form without any aesthetic decisions having been involved and since further, there is a confusion between a "formal" model of the problem and "formal" in the aesthetic usage.

For the argument to continue it is necessary to briefly point out that it is impossible to maintain any kind of discussion of aesthetics or form or appearance or various other paraphrases, unless we admit these matters have some kind of objective or empirical consequences, including psychological effects on people, and unless we further admit the possibility of generalizing about these effects. Now as has already been argued, we do not have to be able to measure such effects or even explain how they occur, provided we have available to us a class of people who can be described as reliable judges of these effects. The ability to submit our problem to such judges and obtain an answer gives an empirical solution to the problem. It is therefore not necessary for us to introduce another class of decisions to accommodate the aesthetic decisions; these are either empirical (where there is a real aesthetic difference) or arbitrary where there is not. In either case we can introduce a decision-making rule. It should be emphasized that I am not here making a statement about the theory of aesthetics, but about design method specifically as defined in my opening paragraph, that is, the process of decision-making which actually occurs in projects. Aesthetic decisions are made, both by individuals and by groups, and as we know from the reputations of certain offices they are made reliably (that is, other expert judges regularly agree with them). Should more objective methods of making such decisions be devised, it might strengthen the argument here, but the absence of such methods does not weaken it.[6]

Arbitrary Decisions

In order to clarify the question of arbitrary decisions it may be helpful to introduce yet another model. This time it is the graphical solution of linear programs. For a solution such as is represented by Figure 8, the problem is converted to a series of constraints which are graphed in terms of the two variables, x_1 and x_2 to define a solution space, a polygon within which all acceptable solutions lie. If we regard the constraints as definitions, then the solution space is the remaining area of uncertainty. In linear programming problems this remaining uncertainty is removed by defining a single variable, generally cost, to be optimized, which makes possible the location of a unique optimum solution.[7]

This model is of course, grossly oversimplified in relation to any design problem. A design problem could have a solution volume or a 4- or n-dimensional space rather than a 2-dimensional area. However, the nature of the space does not in general affect the point being made here. Within this space there will be, except in two extreme cases, an infinite number of solutions that will meet the conditions of the problem. Now since the solution space is defined by *all* the constraints or definitions which we can state explicitly, that is, all the statements about ends and all the empirical statements including any statements about aesthetics, any choices within the solution space will have to be arbitrary unless we can further state a single variable we wish to optimize. Sometimes this will be the case. Cost is a common variable which we may wish to optimize, and in the absence of other stated aims, designers will probably seek to optimize aesthetic quality (although this is difficult because of the lack of quantification). It is by no means necessarily the case that such additional requirements will be imposed, and if they are not and all the constraints have been met, the choice is arbitrary, and some other rule for arbitrary choice needs to be introduced. At least, it can be expected that much time is wasted in design offices attempting to construct empirical justifications for arbitrary decisions of this type, because the notion of making an arbitrary decision is contrary to the ethos of contemporary design. The two exceptions to the case noted above are the case in which by accident the solution space is a point, and the much more probable case in which the solution space is negative, that is, there are no solutions which actually meet the constraints.

Conclusions

Through the investigation of a number of analogies, I have tried in this paper to establish how far and in what respects the design process is likely to be algorithmic. It has been shown that some of the maps of the design process have features that are not inconsistent with an algorithmic model. In particular the following points have been brought out:
1. The process consists of successive dependent decisions.
2. These choices are either empirical or arbitrary; where they are arbitrary it is possible that they can be made to conform to the requirement of determinism by introducing an appropriate rule.
3. Revisions where necessary can be handled by loops provided determinism is not violated.

6. These points are discussed in more detail, with experimental evidence, in my *Experimental Aesthetics and Architecture*.
7. For details of optimization and linear programming not covered here, consult C. West Churchman, Russell L. Ackoff, and E. Leonard Arnoff, *Introduction to Operations Research*, especially pp. 279–387.

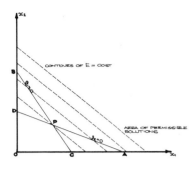

8. Linear programming optimization

9–11. A sketch for an algorithm—commercial and industrial buildings

9. General form of the algorithm, indicating the first 20 routines (expansions for only 2 of the 20 routines are given)

10. Expansion of the fifth routine, indicating the logic of heating and ventilation

11. Expansion of the sixth routine, indicating the logic of acoustics and noise reduction

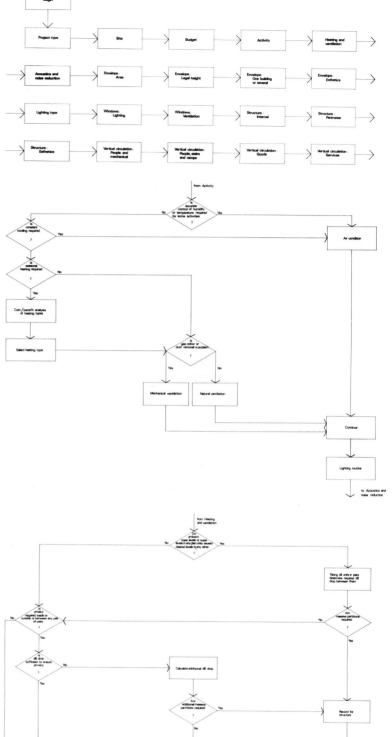

4. The object of the decisions is to eliminate courses of action, not to "invent" them. "Eliminate the impossible, and what remains, however improbable, is the solution."
5. The design process which will reach a satisfactory conclusion with the greatest economy of effort is the one that eliminates the greatest number of possibilities with each decision.

A skilled design team will trace this maze of decisions to a satisfactory solution more quickly than an unskilled one. They will do this because experience has taught them to ask the right questions in the right order so as to limit the field as rapidly and as completely as possible. But insofar as this is true, both their questions and the order in which they are asked can be codified in the form of an algorithm. To this extent the design problem is algorithmic.

A Sketch for an Algorithm: Commercial and Industrial Buildings

On this basis it would seem worth while to undertake the considerable detailed work to construct an algorithm for the design process. A preliminary and experimental section of such an algorithm is shown in Figures 9, 10 and 11. This is not a completely general solution. It is designed for commercial and industrial buildings, but it is submitted that if this problem can be solved, other solutions can be developed from it. It is also a solution only where the restrictions proposed actually apply, for it follows from our argument that the fewer the restrictions or constraints the more arbitrary the solution becomes and the more difficulty we will have both in constructing a model and in solving the problem.

The algorithm here represented consists of a number of sections (or routines) whose order might vary with the particular class of project under consideration. There are thus two levels of structure involved: an order in which certain classes of decisions must be made and an order in which groups of sub-decisions which lead to the general decision in each class must be made. The algorithm commences with a routine concerned with deciding the nature of the project. The assumption is that the commission has just reached an office and the designers need to find out the most fundamental things. That is, is it a building whose purpose is already known or are they being approached to advise on an investment in building where the nature of the building is to depend on the profit motive?

The algorithm continues with a second routine for site selection, again on the assumption that the site may not have been determined. This is followed by a preliminary budget investigation. Although they are not shown in detail, it is implied that other budget investigations of this general structure should be introduced at further points in the investigation. If the prima facie budget requirements can be satisfied, the model continues with an investigation in more detail of the nature of the project, here described as an investigation of activities. It will be clear that (in accordance with the basic theory that states that any algorithm can form a subsection of a larger algorithm and conversely that any subsection of an algorithm can be replaced by a more detailed algorithm) some of the elements of this routine could be greatly expanded.

This is followed by a number of routines which reach decisions concerning the environmental conditions required and the corresponding mechanical services provisions. The routines for heating and ventilation and for acoustics in its noise-reduction aspects are given in some detail. At this point sufficient information is available to make decisions concerning the envelope of the building, and a further group of three routines deals with the area, the height, and whether the space requirements are best provided in the form of one building or several.

At this point the first of a series of aesthetic decision routines appears. Since this cannot be quantified in the present state of our knowledge, this part of the algorithm cannot be computed but only carried out by man–machine interaction. Of course, it must be reemphasized, in certain circumstances one could reach this stage without any envelope restrictions of any significance, but for the type of building to which I am confining this stage of the investigation, this would be most unusual. However, if one did find a situation of this kind it would be permissible and indeed necessary to make a purely formalist aesthetic decision about the general shape of the building.

The next group of three routines investigates lighting and natural ventilation and thus arrives at certain parameters affecting the design of the skin of the building. Some of the quantities introduced here are arbitrary ones taken from Sydney building codes. As with all quantitative parameters or data introduced into such a schema, these might be rendered less arbitrary and more precise by further research, which would change the quantities but not necessarily the logic of the schema.

Similar observations apply to the three routines dealing with "bones," the internal and perimeter structure. Certain assumptions, based on the known state of technology in Sydney now, have been made in stating the range of structural possibilities. These assumptions could be amended by a change in the state of technology: in fact a routine or subroutine might be introduced which could investigate whether some original or innovatory type of structure could perhaps be incorporated in addition to those shown.

Having established a volume and a structure, this algorithm proceeds to knock holes in them, considering the various kinds of vertical movement. The next stage, not illustrated, would be a layout-plann ng stage. A great deal of work has of course been done on systematic methods for layout planning, and while more remains to be done many of the main problems are solved, so that I do not feel called upon to discuss them here.[8] Layout planning would be followed by a routine dealing with the horizontal distribution of services, and at this point it would be possible to establish the constraints for the design of the facades, which for the reasons already discussed would necessarily have to be carried out by man–machine interaction if one were computing the algorithm. This would normally represent the end of sketch planning and the commencement of working drawings, at which point systematic procedures are usually adopted in any case, not forgetting that "God is in the details."

I have presented at this time only a selection of the algorithm and the approach on which it is based, but I would submit that it is sufficient to show a good deal can be done in a purely mechanical way to limit the solution space in certain types of building problems. This holds out the possibility of both reducing errors and obtaining more free time for those decisions which at present are not susceptible to quantification.

---

8. The reader is referred to the entire section on Building Layout Models, Part 5 of this volume. Ed.

7 A Model of a Multilingual Designer

Thomas P. Moran

Department of Computer Science,
Carnegie-Mellon University
Pittsburgh, Pennsylvania

Thomas P. Moran is an Instructor in
Architecture and a Ph.D. candidate in
computer science at Carnegie-Mellon
University. He received a B.Arch. from the
University of Detroit in 1965. He engaged
in interdisciplinary study at Cornell University for two years, has worked for
several architectural and engineering
offices, and has practiced as a computer
applications consultant. His work is supported by the Advanced Research Projects Agency of the Department of Defense.

An information-processing model of an
intuitive designer is outlined, emphasizing the structural aspects of the model.
The primary issue is how the designer
utilizes many kinds of representations or
languages to express different aspects of
his problem and how these representations, in turn, affect his ability to find
design solutions. The model has four
components: an association memory,
representation conventions, interpreted
problem, and design strategy. The association memory is a bank of design-
relevant knowledge in terms of design
concepts. The interpreted problem is a
base language which combines input
problem statements with the concept
definitions in memory. The model is built
to construct for itself different representations of its problem, to operate on these
representations, and to translate the
results back to the interpreted problem.
The model is being formulated as a computer program. A floor plan is used to
illustrate how a model's language is
simulated in the computer program and
how it relates to the overall framework of
the model.

The function of the designer or planner is to effect an intended change of
some part of the human environment. A design problem is given to him in
terms of the present state of the environment and a goal to be achieved.
This goal, however, is not explicitly known; only some of its desired features
are known. It is the designer's role to explicate both the goal and the means
for changing the present state into the goal.

The collection of all the possible states of the environment, including the
present state, constitutes a state space. Each point (or state) in this space
represents a specific configuration of the physical elements of the environment. If the description of such a configuration also includes the abstract
conceptual features by which the designer structures that state of the environment in his mind, then that description is called a form.[1] Many forms
may correspond to any single state, which is to say, any state of the environ-

---

1. A form is conceived here as an abstract relational structure that ties together the
physical pieces of the environment and the abstract concepts which we "see" and
impose on the environment. In this view, form is a complex description of the "real
world" and the designer's conception of it. This is similar to the linguistic notions of
"surface structure" and "deep structure" of a grammar; see Noam Chomsky, *Aspects of
the Theory of Syntax.*

ment may be mentally structured in a variety of ways. It will be seen that the designer works in a space of forms called a problem space.

Within this context, the design process may be viewed as having two aspects. The first is the formulation of the problem, that is, the specification of desirable properties of a solution. This specification provides the criteria for a solution.[2] It is an ambiguous description of the design goal, that is, the criteria may possibly be satisfied by several environmental states or forms. The problem formulation defines the problem space, which is a subset of all conceivable forms including a form for the present state and, hopefully, forms for possible solutions. The second aspect of the design process is the search through the problem space for a solution. The search proceeds by stepping from point to point through the problem space. A step is accomplished by the application of a mental operation (or symbolic transformation) to the current form, transforming it into another form. Operations are selected and executed to achieve a form satisfying the formulated criteria. Both aspects, formulation and search, are active throughout the entire design process, but formulation generally dominates the early stages and search the later stages.[3] Although the early stages of design are the most difficult and the most crucial, the model to be presented here deals primarily with the later stages, that is, it is oriented toward only well-formulated design problems.

There are two obvious but important limitations on the designer. First, the designer cannot afford to search for solutions by building them in real life; rather he must build representations (for example: English sentences, drawings, diagrams, mathematical models) of those solutions. He needs ways to express forms and to manipulate these expressions so that he can simulate their real-life counterparts. These representations are the languages of the designer and the central concern of this paper. (The terms "representation" and "language" are to be taken as synonymous in this paper.) The second limitation is that the designer has only limited symbolic processing powers, that is, he can manipulate only a small number of symbols in his mind at any one time.[4] This forces him to decompose his problem into manageable subproblems that may be dealt with relatively independently.[5] The representations available to a designer influence this decomposition. Any single representation is able to describe only a small portion of all the factors involved in a design problem, that is, it is able to span over only a subspace of the problem space. Such subspaces define corresponding subproblems. For example, the typical architect passes out parts of his problem to structural and to mechanical engineers, each of whom has a language for dealing with his own part. But since no language is available which can represent both structural and mechanical requirements, seldom are these two subproblems dealt with together effectively. A representation is a medium for the applicatation of the operations of design, and thus it tends to guide the search effort

---

2. Design problems are ill-defined in that there is no systematic test for deciding whether a form is acceptable as a solution. See Walter R. Reitman, "Heuristic Decision Procedures, Open Constraints, and the Structure of Ill-defined Problems," in Maynard W. Shelly and Glenn L. Bryan, eds., *Human Judgments and Optimality*, pp. 282–315 for a discussion of this kind of problem.
3. This general picture of the design process is consistent with many theorists of design and problem-solving. For example see Allen Newell, J. C. Shaw, and Herbert A. Simon, "The Processes of Creative Thinking," in Howard E. Gruber, Glenn Terrell, and Michael Wertheimer, eds., *Contemporary Approaches to Creative Thinking*, pp. 63–119; Reitman, "Heuristic Decision Procedure"; Christopher Alexander, *Notes on the Synthesis of Form*; and Marvin L. Manheim, "A Design Process Model: Theory and Applications to Transportation Planning," in this volume.
4. Many of the classical models of economic and social behavior did not take this fact into account. Herbert A. Simon, *Models of Man*. Part IV, p. 198, calls this a basic deficiency of these models and discusses how to account for it by formulating the "principle of bounded rationality." See George A. Miller, "The Magic Number Seven, Plus or Minus Two," for a good summary and data on these psychological limitations.
5. This, of course, is the motivation behind the decomposition models initiated by Alexander. They assume, however, that a problem can be homogenized into a set of uniform elements, an assumption which the model presented here deliberately avoids. (See the entire section on decomposition models, Part 4 of this volume. Ed.)

in the problem space along the subspace spanned by that representation. For example, an architect's floor plan drawings are unlikely to lead to any solutions which are complex along the vertical dimension. It can be seen that a designer with only a limited number of available representations will have access to only a limited region of the problem space.

This paper presents a view of the design process in terms of an information-processing model of the intuitive designer.[6] As such it is expected to exhibit some of the shortcomings and, hopefully, some of the advantages of the intuitive approach. The model is not, strictly speaking, a psychological simulation of the human designer, but its structure closely parallels the way the human, viewed as an information processor, organizes a problem and attempts to find a solution. The purpose is to try to capture in modern, rigorous terms some of the richness of the traditional concepts used in design. The model itself is not a formal design method but rather a framework in which different design methods can be embedded. It is based on the issues of how information is stored, represented, and manipulated in the design process. The model is conceived of as four interrelated components: (1) the association memory, (2) the interpreted problem, (3) the representation conventions, and (4) the design strategy. This paper will deal with the structural rather than the behavioral aspects of this model, that is, primarily the first three components. It will discuss the information handled by the model, the structures in which it is expressed, and the communication channels along which it flows. Design strategies will only be anticipated and not specifically discussed since they are viewed as acting upon the information structure of the model.

The Association Memory

In this model a designer's knowledge of the world may be considered to be stored in a graph of nodes and links. The nodes are "concepts," units of thought. Concepts are usually concrete objects such as door, chair, beam, room, but they may also be more abstract entities such as proportion, axis, module.[7] A concept consists of a name, a list of attributes, and a list of component parts with their interrelations. An attribute has a dimension and a value; it specifies shape, size, color, weight, and material of an object. The dimension (cost, color) specifies a class of values. The value itself may be specific (color: red), a set of specifics (color: red, green, or blue), negative (color: anything but black), over a range (cost: $50 to $100), conditional (weight: if cast iron, then 20 lb/ft), or other. A modified concept is a concept with some of its attribute values delimited such as "4-foot counter," "red door," "big house." The component parts of a concept are themselves modified concepts. These "part-of" relations form one of the types of links (associations) between the concepts in the memory. Another type of link is the "example-of" relation. Figure 1 illustrates a small portion of a simplified, hypothetical memory graph. It shows, for example, that a door frame, a lock, a door panel, or a handle is each part of a door and that a flush door is an example of a door panel, which as part of a door is an example of an exit, which is a part of a room, and so forth. A much more complex and sophisticated memory graph can be stored in a computer-implemented model.[8]

A designer's knowledge also consists of assorted facts and experiences that are not merely conceptual classes but are propositions built up of concepts

6. The model is being formulated as a computer program in LISP 1.5, a list-processing programming language. See Clark Weissman, *LISP 1.5 Primer*.
7. The design protocols of Charles M. Eastman, "On the Analysis of Intuitive Design Processes," in this volume, show a propensity among designers for dealing with concrete rather than abstract conceptual entities. Processes or activities may also be represented as concepts within the general framework to be described. Activities may be considered to be composed of other smaller activities, and processes may be expressed as sequences of activities. Thus an object concept can be defined in terms of its purpose, that is, the activities or functions with which it is associated and its place in those activities.
8. See M. Ross Quillian, "Word Concepts: A Theory and Simulation of Some Basic Semantic Capabilities," pp. 410–430 for an account of his "semantic memory" in which basic English words are encoded. He demonstrates how this memory network accounts for our knowledge of the world.

and predicate relations. Such propositional statements are called *constraints,* since they serve to delimit the problem space. The formulation aspect of the design process produces these constraints by retrieving them from the association memory and by a deductive process on already-retrieved constraints. A constraint is contained in the association memory as a multiple link threaded between all the concepts involved in its statement. A simple example of a constraint expressed as an English sentence is: "the distance between the front of a swinging door and a solid object must be greater than the width of the door."

This constraint would be linked to the concepts swinging door and solid object and would be applicable to any concept occurring as an example of either of these. This constraint in its functional form can be evaluated as being true or false, based on the current state of the design, and thus it can serve as a criterion for a solution. Such a constraint can limit the search in a problem space by ruling out any operation causing a transformation to a state in which the constraint evaluates as "false,"[9] or it may be evaluated after the operation has been performed to test the validity of that operation. (Just when a constraint evaluation is performed is a decision by the strategy component and does not affect the memory structure.)

The association memory has at its disposal a set of "semantic" operators, which perform the functions of storing and retrieving information in the memory. Given any concept, they allow the model to start at the node of that concept and generate its definition (listing its component parts and their interrelations), give specific examples of that concept, and spout useful facts (constraints) concerning that concept. The memory may be viewed as a "generative" structure of design knowledge, that is, it can be used to generate designs. This may be accomplished by using the association links between concepts as production rules in the design process. A production rule is a command of the form: "given a specific pattern or condition, then apply a specific operation associated with that condition." With regard to the association memory, there could be general rules such as "given a problem in the form 'design an X,' transform this to the problem 'design an example of an X'" or "given a problem in the form 'design an X,' transform this to a set of interrelated subproblems each of the form 'design a component of an X.'" For example, at some point in designing a room the subproblem "design an exit" will occur. According to the association memory of Figure 1, this subproblem could be transformed into the more specific subproblem "design a door" by the above production rule. Then all the constraints involving door would be brought into the problem. Next, the subproblem could be transformed into the design of one of the examples of a door, or if a special kind of door needs to be devised, the subproblem would be transformed into the design of each of the parts of a door. Exactly how this process works is governed by the strategy component of the model, but the memory's structure and content give it a rich base to work on.[10]

Building the association memory itself involves a rigorous description of all relevant design knowledge and is not a trivial part of the implementation of this model. How well the memory is constructed will have a great influence on the performance of the model regardless of how sophisticated the design strategy is. This is especially true of many typical design problems which often depend more on the retrieval of the right information than on clever manipulations.

---

9. An early illustration of the use of this tactic is the geometry-theorem proving program of H. Galernter, "Realization of a Geometry-Theorem Proving Machine," in Edward A. Feigenbaum and Julian Feldman, eds., *Computers and Thought,* pp. 134–152. This program uses a diagram language, which by utilizing the constant properties of the diagrams can rule out possible proof steps suggested by the formal axiom language.
10. In fact, with a complete enough memory, a simple "memory-driven" design strategy, utilizing not much more than the illustrated production rules, is conceivable. This would be similar to a syntax-driven computer language translator (except, of course, that a translator is proceeding in the opposite direction). For a survey of such translators, see Jerome Feldman and David Gries, "Translator Writing Systems."

The Interpreted Problem

The language of design problem statements is terse, giving only special conditions and assuming a lot of tacit common knowledge on the part of the designer. Thus a design problem must be interpreted with the aid of a memory of concepts or ideas. "Design a bathroom" is a meaningless problem to one who doesn't possess the concept "bathroom." A designer who does possess this concept will interpret it to mean a room containing a sink, toilet, bathtub, organized according to all the constraints associated with these concepts. Special requirements are reflected in the problem statements "design a bathroom with two sinks" and "design a bathroom in this oddly shaped room" (given a floor plan of the room). Such special requirements cannot be assumed to be in the designer's memory a priori.

The design process can be seen as the translation of a problem statement into a specific proposal, that is, a configuration of concrete, physical objects and the means for constructing this configuration.[11] The model effects this translation by first taking an input problem, such as one of the examples just listed, and formulating an interpreted problem from it. It then transforms this interpreted problem into a solution by applying operations to it to satisfy the binding constraints. The interpreted problem is an operational definition of the problem, that is, it can be processed with available design operations. Since the interpreted problem is by its nature a specific problem, it is built up out of specific instances (design units) of the concepts in the problem statement. It is a relational structuring of design units residing in an immediate memory, which is a work space memory similar in structure to the association memory. It is the central source of problem-specific information showing how the problem is being decomposed into subproblems, which constraints are binding, and the strategy's goals and subgoals. At any point in the design process the interpreted problem reflects the model's current view of the problem—where it has been, where it now stands, and where it wants to go. The interpreted problem, taken together with the problem representations, corresponds to what was defined as a form at the beginning of this paper.

The Representation Conventions

The search for design solutions requires that operations be applied to the current state of the problem until a solution is reached. But how the current state is represented by the designer influences the way he will be able to transform it. A designer thinks of his problem in many different ways, each giving him a different slant on the directions he may take. He does this by constructing different representations, both internal and external, in his head and on paper. An architect, for example, will draw functional relation diagrams and plans, perform strength calculations and cost analyses, visualize his building as tentlike or like a crystalline box, or in some other mental image. In each case he is translating a portion of the information about his problem into another language, operating on it in that other language, and then interpreting the results back into his own problem. It is in this sense that designers are multilingual. Language is being considered here not as a communication device, although this aspect is not to be overlooked since any language used within the model is a valid input/output channel, but rather as a matrix for thought processes.

A language or representation convention may be characterized as a more-or-less formal system made up of a set of symbols and a set of syntactic rules for generating well-formed statements out of these symbols. But a language is useful only if there is a mapping between its symbols and some of the concepts in memory, that is, only if the language may be interpreted by the designer. This mapping may be generated from the information already in the memory. For example, the symbols used in cost analysis, which are simply numeric variables, may be retrieved from memory by referring to the

11. Herbert A. Simon, "The Logic of Heuristic Decision Making." in Nicholas Rescher, ed., *Logic of Decision and Action,* discusses design as a process of translating required changes in the state of the world into a language of actions which will effect those changes.

cost dimension of the attributes of the appropriate concepts. Other symbols must be generated by more complex processes such as the plan or section views of objects which are computed from the three-dimensional descriptions in the shape dimension of the attributes of their concepts. Some symbols, like electrical diagram symbols, are purely conventional and must be explicitly kept in the attributes of their concepts as symbol templates to be copied literally. All concepts, of course, are not expressible in all representations, nor is all the information about any one concept expressible in only one of the representations.

Notice that the association memory and the interpreted problem are themselves a language. In computer terminology they are called a list structure language. (Information is inconceivable without a medium in which to embed it.) In this model this language is unique in that it serves as a base language to which all the other representations refer. This language is general, since all the information used by the model is expressible in it; in fact, it serves as a meta-language for the whole model. For this very reason it is not always conducive to the most efficient processing operations. Hence, other special-purpose representations are required.

The interpreted problem is the locus of information for the strategy component, and all other representations are satellites from it, each mapping directly back to it. Not all the information about the problem is stored in the interpreted problem since it would become cluttered with details and lose its usefulness as the source of control-relevant information. Any piece of information about the problem, however, is directly accessible via the interpreted problem and its mappings to all other representations. This allows the strategy component to control the design process through the interpreted problem. Figure 2 shows the radial pattern of the model's information channels resulting from this control scheme.

A representation is valuable only because of the operations that may be performed on it, for it is from these operations that new information is gained. A design operation is usually associated with a representation and transforms well-formed statements into well-formed statements in that representation. An operation itself may or may not be directly interpretable conceptually, but the change it effects in the representation may be carried back and accepted as a valid transformation in the conceptual language. This indirectness of interpretation is especially true in a formal mathematical model such as linear programming. In this example the design strategy translates part of the problem information into the linear programming language convention, turns control over to the simplex algorithm which optimizes the translated information, and then interprets the resulting optimized solution in terms of the present problem. Other representations, such as the floor plan, require much more direct control by the strategy component since they have only "low level" operations associated with them. (This is the difference between power tools and hand tools.) The important point to note here is that once a concept is mapped into a symbol in a representation, all the properties of that symbol within that representation are attributed to the concept and are interpreted back to it. In a much less formal way, a similar process is going on in the use of analogy.[12] A concept is mapped into another concept and the structure and properties of that second concept are then mapped back and interpreted in terms of the first.

Graphic representations are useful because they allow the designer's visual perceptual processes to operate on them. This entails his scanning the graphic representation, recognizing patterns and building up global relationships which may not be noticeable in less graphic expressions. Scaled

12. George Polya discusses the use of analogy in solving mathematical problems in *How To Solve It,* p. 37. "Analogy is a sort of similarity. Similar objects agree with each other in some respect, analogous objects agree in certain relations of their respective parts."

graphic drawings such as plans and sections also serve as inexpensive two-dimensional simulations of their real-life three-dimensional counterparts. Three-dimensional models are better for this purpose but are more expensive; the translation cost is an important factor in determining the use of representation.

In summary, the many languages a designer utilizes enable him to attack a problem by
1. Expanding his memory capacity and helping to sort information.
2. Bringing disparate pieces of information together under common symbolisms.
3. Allowing perceptual, mathematical, or other kinds of powerful processes to be applied to parts of the problem.
4. Allowing certain aspects of the real-life problem to be simulated and evaluated.
5. Providing convenient frameworks for decomposing the design problem into subproblems and for applying design operations.
6. Guiding and delimiting the search effort through the problem space.

An Example of a Representation

Let us consider a typical problem representation, the floor plan, and see how it may be simulated in a computer-implemented version of the model just described. A floor plan is a scaled allocation of the space in a two-dimensional plane. For the purposes of a computer simulation, "blocks" or rectangular spaces of any dimensions in the plane are seen as a linear graph, the block graph, in which the nodes are the blocks and the links connect contiguous blocks in the plane.[13] Figure 3 shows a simple floor plan of a small room with each block numbered and the block graph which represents it in the computer.

Just as the floor plan will show whether or not certain objects will fit in a two-dimensional plane, as on the floor in a room, so this feature can be incorporated into the floor plan language, if the following rules for structuring blocks in a block graph are imposed: (1) all explicitly empty space in the plan must be represented by special blocks called *nilblocks,* (2) all blocks together must fill the plane, (3) no blocks may overlap.

These rules applied to the block graph of Figure 3 will expand it to the graph in Figure 4 which is a well-formed statement in the floor plan language. The model can execute graph transformations for adding and deleting blocks, and hence the "draw" and "erase" operations associated with floor plans may be simulated.

Since floor plans do not provide complete information about the design units represented, data such as heights of the objects must be referenced in the interpreted problem or in the association memory. But clues to this information may be added by keying the blocks, showing them as solid, shaded, or red, for example. When the strategy component transfers its processing from the interpreted problem to the floor plan, interpretations for these clues are also passed indicating, say, that the shaded blocks refer to walls. In these ways most of the superficial aspects of the use of floor plans may be simulated.

A mechanical processor acting on a block graph can only look at one node at a time. This is like a designer whose eyes can only focus on a half square inch of his drawing: the overall picture is lost. What a designer is actually able to "see" must be accounted for. To do this, the block graph must be scanned, pulling together related blocks into "groups." For example, the

13. This block graph is quite similar to the dual graph floor plan representation of John Grason, "A Dual Linear Graph Representation for Space-Filling Location Problems of the Floor Plan Type" in this volume. His representation, however, is formulated so that it may evolve from a graph of relational requirements, that is, for a new methodology. The block graph, on the other hand, is formulated to simulate the floor plan as it is now used by designers.

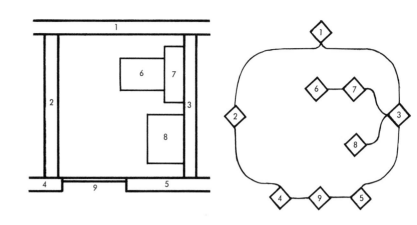

1. A portion of a simple association memory

2. Information flow in the model

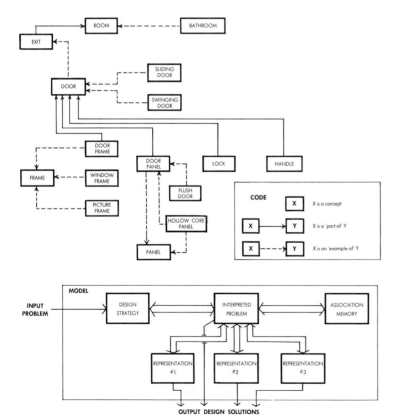

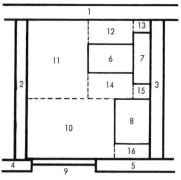

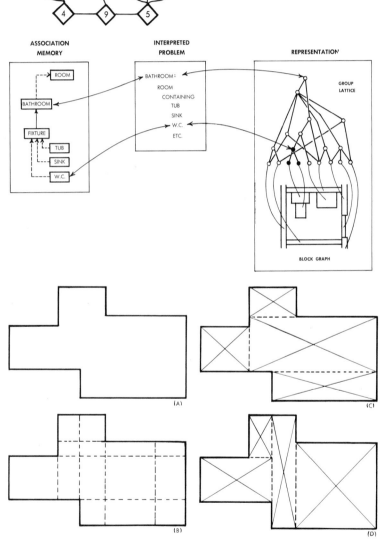

3. A floor plan and its block graph

4. A well-formed floor plan and its block graph

5. Mapping between a concept, its design unit, and one of its representations

6. A floor plan of a room (*a*), its partitioning (*b*), and possible spatial groupings (*c, d*)

blocks labeled 6 and 7 in Figure 4 would be grouped together as a unit representing the design unit "toilet." All the groups thus recognized are assembled into a hierarchical structure called a *group lattice* which is ordered by spatial inclusion, that is, parts within wholes and subspaces within spaces.[14] The groups in this lattice are mapped back to the design units of the interpreted problem. Figure 5 is a sketch of how a design unit (a toilet in this case) in the interpreted problem is mapped to its concept in the association memory and to its representation in the floor plan convention (as a group in the group lattice and as blocks in the block graph). The strategy component of the model deals in terms of design units, and this mapping structure of the model shows how it is able to readily translate the design units back and forth between the model's several languages.

As a part of its floor plan dialect, the model also has a pattern recognizer which examines the empty space in a plan and identifies potentially useful subspaces just as any architectural designer might perceive them. This is done by first partitioning the empty space in a plan into small "atomic" pieces represented by nilblocks as illustrated, for example, in Figure 6. These atomic nilblocks are then reassembled into different groupings, each of which is a potentially useful subspace. The groupings are then labeled and placed into the group lattice where the strategy component may utilize them. The right-hand side of the figure shows some of the possible groupings of the partitioned plan. When the model constructs a floor plan of its problem, this analysis-synthesis process is executed automatically as the designer's ability to "visualize" some of the global aspects of the spaces represented in that plan.

Conclusion

This model is being formulated in order to determine precisely what amounts of knowledge, what form, and what sophistication of strategy are necessary in order to attain certain levels (ultimately, a human level) of performance in the understanding of design problems and in the search for design solutions. A problem space is accessible to a designer only to the extent allowed by his problem representations. This model is a tool for defining the mechanics and characterizing some of the general properties of representation. The first goal is to analyze and simulate some of the commonly used problem representations. It may then be possible to formulate the characteristics and mechanics of representation conventions explicitly enough so that in the future the design process itself may include the subproblem of designing suitable new representations for its own use.

---

14. This algebraic structure has properties which may be usefully interpreted in "viewing" a plan. Christopher Alexander has given a general illustration of structuring the environment in "The City is Not a Tree."

8 ICES STRUDL: An Integrated Approach to a Computer System for Structural Engineering

Robert D. Logcher

Department of Civil Engineering,
Massachusetts Institute of
Technology
Cambridge, Massachusetts

Robert D. Logcher is Associate Professor
of Civil Engineering at M.I.T. and a partner
in Engineering Computer International.
He was born in the Netherlands and received a S.B., S.M., and Sc.D. in civil
engineering from M.I.T. in 1958, 1960, and
1962. He was codeveloper of STRESS, the
first problem-oriented computer language for structural engineering, and was
a member of the group that developed the
ICES Computer System. He is the author
of papers on computers in structural
engineering and on computer system
requirements and is coauthor of several
reports on the ICES System and the subsystems STRESS and STRUDL.

Design in structural engineering is an
iterative process in which the designer
studies aspects of his problem in increasing depth and, usually, with decreasing
alternatives. He calls upon those techniques which he feels are appropriate to
his problem and design stage. Highly
restrained by allied disciplines, he must
also keep up-to-date about changing
design techniques and codes, incorporating new technology as it becomes available. The design process places many
constraints on a computer system. Required computer system characteristics
are discussed, and the Integrated Civil
Engineering System (ICES) is described
as providing the framework for developing subsystems for specific applications.
ICES is a computer system for engineering
design problems. It provides a programming system for incremental development and for finding applications of
problem-oriented languages and a computer environment for their operation.
Characteristics of ICES which illustrate
how it serves for developing application
systems are described. The Structural
Design Language (STRUDL) is an ICES subsystem which attempts to provide the
computer-aided design environment
desired for structural engineering. Its
characteristics are described and its use
illustrated with an example design
problem.

This conference has been convened to discuss environmental design methodology, its goals, its formalism, the tools it requires, and changes in methodology brought about as a consequence of new tools. With structural engineering as a basis, we are fortunate in discussing an old and well estab- lished technical discipline. Yet we are unfortunate in that we cannot report dramatic changes in design methodology. Rather, structural engineers are doing now what they always wanted to do but did not have the time, man- power, or resources to do before.

This paper tries to describe the following: the structural design process and how it is changing, the tools required for this change, and mechanisms for utilizing these tools. In order to illustrate these points, the Integrated Civil Engineering System (ICES) and one of its subsystems, the Structural Design Language (STRUDL), will be used for examples.[1]

The Design Process

The tools we are to discuss here are primarily computer systems, their scope and characteristics. Before the role of the computer in design can be intel-

---

1. Daniel Roos, ed., *ICES System: General Description;* Jane Jordon, ed., *ICES: Pro- grammers Reference Manual;* Robert D. Logcher, Barry B. Flachbart, E. Jack Hall, Conor M. Power, and Robert A. Wells, *ICES STRUDL I: Engineering User's Manual.*

ligently discussed, it is necessary to explore the general nature of the design process itself. Structural design, in the context of this paper, refers to all the work normally done by structural engineers, beginning with the initial concept and ending with implementation in the form of contract drawings and specifications but excluding construction. For purposes of this discussion, design will be divided into four phases: (1) determination of criteria and conceptual design, (2) preliminary analysis and design, (3) rigorous analysis, evaluation, and final design, and (4) documentation.

During the conceptual phase the engineer is perhaps most creative. However, this phase is characterized by an interchange of information and ideas between the structural engineer and others involved, e.g., the architect and utility engineers in the case of a building, or the highway engineer in the case of a bridge. Seldom, if ever, is the engineer free to conceive a design solely on the basis of structural efficiency.

During this phase the design criteria evolve. These vary between structures, depend upon functional considerations, and include requirements related to structural safety, stiffness and vibration, aesthetics, and public acceptance. These criteria may be numerous, are often conflicting, and sometimes abstract. As a result, very few designs can be achieved without compromise. The engineer often selects several alternative designs, each representing a possible solution and warranting further investigation. These may differ greatly in structural configuration, materials used, and the type of further analysis required or appropriate.

During the preliminary design phase the engineer must fully exercise his judgment, intuition, and experience. Except for simple determinate structures, rigorous forms of analysis are usually not appropriate. Sometimes standardized methods of approximate analysis are used, but more often the engineer uses his knowledge of structural behavior to idealize the system and hence simplify analysis. Based on this preliminary analysis, trial sizes and configurations of the individual members are selected, usually in gross rather than detailed form. This permits preliminary cost estimation, evaluation of structural adequacy and efficiency, and comparison of alternatives being considered. The preliminary design and evaluation may actually be more time-consuming than the rigorous analysis which follows. It is also possible that changes in the original concept of the structure will be indicated by these preliminary results.

Rigorous or final analysis will normally be executed for only one or two of the alternative designs previously considered. The degree of rigor varies, depending upon the importance of the structure and the uncertainties in other factors, such as loadings, which affect the accuracy of the final result. It is seldom justified to use the most rigorous analysis possible.

The behavior of the structure, as indicated by the analytical results, must then be compared with the design criteria previously established. In some cases, this may merely be a check against allowable stresses in a standard code. More often, however, this simple device is insufficient and the engineer must use judgment to interpret the analytical results. At this stage it is important that the data indicating the performance of the structure be complete and so organized as to be readily accessible and meaningful to the designer. Following this analysis and evaluation, it is usually necessary to recycle the designing-analysis operation and it may even be necessary to modify the initial concept.

The final documentation phase is primarily one of retrieving and reorganizing the data accumulated during the design process. Although details of the structure are normally added at this point, the procedure should be fairly mechanical if proper consideration has been given to such matters during the earlier phases.

Several general characteristics of the design process are made evident by the outline given above. First, it is probable that the reader will not entirely agree with this representation of the evolution of a design. This in itself is indicative of the inherent flexibility of the engineering approach. No two engineers would go about the same job in the same way. Design is not a fixed procedure. There is no unique solution, but on the other hand there are several paths by which different engineers might reach the same solution.

Design inevitably involves compromise. The structural engineer must interact with other professionals whose point of view and objectives may differ from his own. There are usually multiple criteria for successful design, some of which must be relaxed in order to permit any solution. This need to compromise implies a dynamic quality in the design process and requires a constant interaction between the designer and his problem.

Technological change obviously has a great influence on engineering design. New materials, new construction methods, and new analytical and design techniques are frequently introduced. The design procedure must remain flexible in order to take advantage of these improvements when they occur. With regard to analytical techniques, the design procedure should not be so rigid as to force certain methods on the designer. The competent engineer should not be forced to use simplified, conservative methods intended for less competent practitioners. On the other hand, he should not be forced to use elaborate, time-consuming methods which he knows by experience to be unnecessary for the problem at hand.

Structural design is, of course, an iterative procedure. Direct design is generally not possible. Each phase of the process provides new insight into the problem and generates feedback which affects previous phases. Decisions must therefore be tentatively made and may be considered final only when all criteria are satisfied and all parts of the design consistent. The tools available to the engineer may be considered to be a group of operations which in total and in various combinations provide solutions to all problems in his particular field. Each of these operations is useful at one or more design stages and some may be alternatives at a particular stage. As the design evolves, the engineer creates a subset of the total group which is appropriate for the particular problem. It is important that he have freedom in selecting and ordering this subset and that he exercise good judgment in so doing.

If one analyzes the numerical work in a typical structural design, it is surprising to find how little is actual computation. The major part of the effort is in collecting and organizing the numerical data in preparation for mathematical operations or for display and evaluation. In other words, much of what is normally called design is in reality bookkeeping. Furthermore, the nature and size of the data which are momentarily important constantly change. The efficiency of the total process is greatly affected by that of the data manipulation. A good designer is almost invariably a good bookkeeper.

It is commonly asserted that structural design is creative, but this is an oversimplification and does not imply complete freedom for the engineer. There are too many constraints imposed on the designer which are beyond his control. Design consists of a series of decisions, usually a choice between alternatives, each restricted by the circumstances of the problem. The designer is creative only in the sense that he has a choice at each of these decision points, that he can exercise some ingenuity within the constraints, and that to this extent, the final product reflects his individual preferences and imagination.

In summary, the most characteristic feature of structural design is that it is not a linear process, i.e., it does not consist of a period of conceiving and decision-making, followed by a large quantity of mathematical analysis, followed in turn by implementation. It is rather an iterative series of decisions interspersed with computation tasks of varying size. The exact sequence of operations cannot be predetermined. Therefore, any formalized design procedure must provide a high degree of flexibility to permit the engineer to alter the form and sequence of operations to fit the particular problem. Although certain parts of the process can be mechanized, attempts to completely automate design, in the sense that a final product is created without human intervention, are not likely to succeed except for the most trivial problems.

Because of a lack of consideration of the total process, there has always been a tendency for engineers to become overly engrossed in the details of design. The use of computers can actually aggravate this tendency. The designer can become entranced with the sophisticated analysis made possible by computers and fail to grasp the physical realities of the design problem. In fact, considering engineering design in its entirety, more rigorous analysis is one of the lesser benefits to be gained from computer usage. It is improper and wasteful to use the computer merely for the improvement of computations previously done by hand. The enormous power of the machine should be fully integrated into the design process and not become an appendage thereto. When this is done, the computer may well have a profound effect on the design process itself.

The Effect of the Computer on the Design Process

We see the structural design process primarily as an information-handling problem. Because of this outlook, we can say that the computer can be an ideal tool to assist the engineer. We will discuss the characteristics of this tool, but first we might describe the changes in the design process assuming the existence of a powerful computerized information system.

The structural engineer would have at his fingertips all the information which he has input or generated about his problem, and general design information about his problem area, such as handbooks and catalogues. Also, he has at his disposal a set of procedures to apply to his problem. The tasks he must perform are primarily decision functions: input of basic data, and design criteria, and constraints, sequencing design operations, and evaluating results in order to make decisions on further operations and data changes.

The values of a computer system are embodied in three aspects of his design process. First, he can become engrossed in the nature of his problem rather than its required computation. Second, he can apply only operations pertinent to his problem, operating on it piecewise if appropriate, and applying them in a sequence meaningful to his understanding of the problem. Thirdly, he has at his disposal the most up-to-date and sophisticated techniques available in the problem area, which he may apply even if he is not familiar with all aspects of their algorithms.

The engineer has one more responsibility. He must be aware of and have control over any decision function embodied in the computer system he is using. Generally, decisions are used repeatedly during design so that it would be infeasible to ask the engineer to state such decisions every time they are used. For example, engineering decisions are embodied in code-checking procedures, checking the feasibility of each part of each trial design. These decisions are his interpretation of the meaning and applicability of portions of a code. He must, therefore, accept the task of programming such decision functions, hopefully in his language. In reality, of course, not all engineers are capable of developing their own procedures, but the higher echelon of practitioners is now deeply involved in such functions.

The reader will note that there is no profound change envisioned as a consequence of integrating computers into the design process. This is because the nature of the interdisciplinary communication has not changed. Recognition of conflict and compromise must still be treated. However, it can be expected that more alternatives will be studied and studied in more depth than before, and that, as a result of decreased design and evaluation time, more interactions between disciplines will take place.

Computer System Requirements

We have set down the characteristics of the computer-aided design process and thereby implied some characteristics of the computer system which might be used. By a system, we mean a computer program which has the following characteristics:

1. Contains one or more programming languages which provide users with the facilities to order procedures.

2. Allows for storage and retrieval of a wide variety of data which may be used selectively in procedures.

3. Contains a number of procedures for processing information in the problem area.

4. Provides mechanisms and organization for continued expansion of the scope of the system.

A system, then, contains the basic operations in the problem area, and the engineer, with his language, puts these together to solve his particular problem. The engineer is programming the computer, in a general sense, in languages sufficiently simple that a program can be written for a problem and discarded. These languages we have called Problem Oriented Languages (POL), and they are sufficiently simple to be easily usable by an engineer with no computer knowledge. Figure 1 gives a simple STRUDL example, solving an analysis problem. Figure 2 provides an overview of STRUDL, illustrating the capabilities available to the designer. Note that a number of analysis, design, and input and output procedures are both available to him and interact internally. All procedures may operate on all or a subset of a problem, and any data may be changed at any time by the user. Interaction with other POL's is also illustrated, with information being passed via disk files.

Unfortunately, programming systems currently available from computer manufacturers do not provide the facilities or operating environment in which to develop and use POL systems. None provide for the arbitrary sequencing of input, language translation, the treatment of large and varying amounts and types of data, or for incremental development of POL systems. With previous systems, such as STRESS, these capabilities had to be built into the POL, involving up to 40 percent of the development effort and repeated for each POL.[2] Even then, incremental development was difficult.

Integrated Civil Engineering System

The ICES system, then, represents a pooling of system-programming resources. It provides a framework within which any POL may be developed, expanded, and used. The systems programming needed to support the various POL's is, therefore, done only once and then, of course, in a more general manner than feasible when developed for a single POL.

The ICES user communicates to the computer with a problem-oriented or command-structured language. These commands state or imply the use of procedures developed for operation of the subsystem he is using and supply data to the procedures. Each command is read, translated, and executed sequentially. When the operations for one command are completed, the next command in the input stream is read. This execution process is controlled by the ICES Executive Program (ICEX). ICEX calls upon a translator, the Command Interpreter (COMINT), to translate each input command. COMINT is a universal translator in that the individual commands available to the user are not built within it. Rather, it uses dictionaries and tables (Command Data Blocks) which inform it how to translate each command. Commands, then, can be added at any time by a programmer by adding to the dictionaries and tables. A part of the language definition includes the names of programs which are to be executed for a command. When a command is translated, ICEX will call upon the programs required for that command. These programs operate and modify the problem data base, which is accessible to all programs, and may produce results for the user. Programs return to ICEX when they are finished. The lower left part of Figure 3 illustrates this user environment.

2. Steven J. Fenves, Robert D. Logcher, Samuel P. Mauch, and Kenneth F. Reinschmidt, *STRESS: A User's Manual,* and Fenves, et al., *STRESS: A Reference Manual.*

```
STRUDL 'SHORT' 'EXAMPLE PROBLEM'
UNITS KG M
JOINT COORDINATES
'L1' 0. SUPPORT
'U1' Y 3.75
'U2' 10. 3.75
'L2' 10. S
MEMBER INCIDENCES
1 'L1' 'U1'
2 'U1' 'U2'
3 'U2' 'L2'
UNITS CM
MEMBERS 1 TO 3 PROPERTIES PRISMATIC AX 35.2 IZ 15740.
LOADING 'ONLY' 'WIND AND ROOF WEIGHT'
MEMBER 2 LOAD FORCE Y UNIFORM W -1.
JOINT 'U1' LOAD FORCE X 1000.
TYPE PLANE FRAME XY
LOADING LIST ALL
STIFFNESS ANALYSIS
LIST FORCES REACTIONS DISPLACEMENTS LOADS ALL
FINISH
```

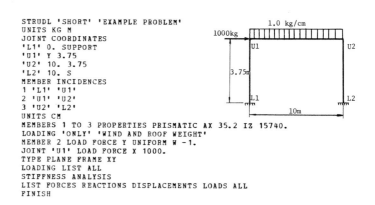

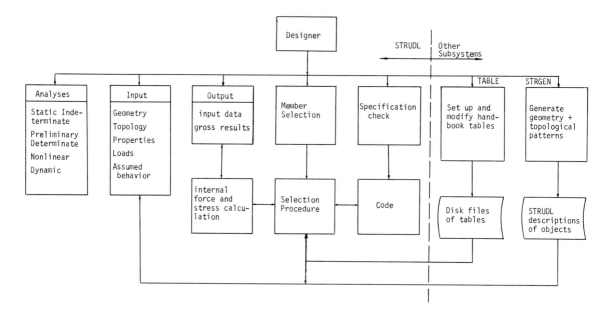

1. Sample STRUDL problem specification

2. Overview of STRUDL

3. Subsystem generation and use

4. Command structure

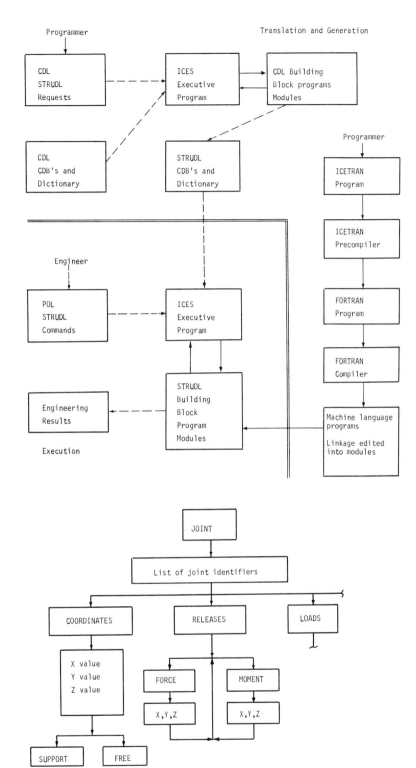

It is the subsystem programmer's task to provide both the programs and command definitions for each of his subsystem commands. ICES provides facilities to assist him in these tasks. First, it provides the Command Definition Language (CDL) for the definition of how COMINT must translate a command. CDL is a command-structured language and as such operates in the same manner as a user language. It uses ICEX, CDL command definitions, and CDL programs as shown at the top of Figure 3. Its primary output is disk files containing the subsystem dictionary and CDB's, which are used during subsystem execution. For program writing, the programmer is provided with ICETRAN (ICES FORTRAN). ICETRAN provides additional capabilities beyond FORTRAN which allow programs to be executed in a random sequence. The ICETRAN language is translated into legal FORTRAN and then compiled with a compiler supplied by the manufacturer. A group of programs may then be linkage-edited into a program load module which may be executed from ICEX. This aspect is shown on the right of Figure 3.

Figure 3, then, shows in macro terms the integrated environment for subsystem generation and execution. For a subsystem, operations can take place at any time in any part of this figure. The only constraint is that for the execution of any command, its definition (and only that one) must have been previously executed with CDL and the load modules required must have been formed and stored on the disk in one of the appropriate load module libraries. We will now discuss in more detail the features of these languages and how they relate to problem execution processing.

The command interpreter reads each command and determines its name to access its CDB. The CDB informs it what data is expected in the command, where to store it in a communications area, and what programs to call. Error and consistency checking are also performed. The basic premise in the command definition and translation is that commands are tree structured. Figure 4 illustrates this structure for a STRUDL command. Branching to different parts of the command is specified in its CDL. COMINT, then, follows through the command translation, down the tree, by branching on the specified conditions. The most common branch is on a modifier word, such as COORDINATES or RELEASES.

CDL is a full programming language, although structured for a specific purpose. It includes such features as subroutines, looping on input and output messages, and even allows recursive calling of its subroutines. Figure 5 provides an illustrative example of some of its features. T1, T2, T3, I1, and I10 are defined variables in the communications area. X, Y, and Z are data identifiers which *may* be included in the user input. If included, the data may be given in a random order. If any data item is not given, the standard value is stored (used in the example for checking by the program STCOOR). Data could also be specified as required. Alphameric information whose existence in the input stream implies data may also be treated. In the EXISTENCE statement, the variable is set equal to the position of the data word in the list if it is found in the input. Although not illustrated, CDL allows for the execution of any number of programs at different points within the translation of a command.

ICETRAN provides language facilities for dynamic data, program structuring, and data management. ICEX provides the programs for handling the operations specified with the language. Its most interesting facility is the dynamic data structuring and dynamic memory allocation. Although a list-processor is provided, we will discuss here only dynamic array data structures. In the system, all available core memory is managed by ICEX. It manages the positions of programs and dynamic data in a data pool. When memory becomes full, it is automatically reorganized, purging unneeded programs, moving data within the core and to secondary storage. When data is accessed in a program, it is automatically retrieved from secondary storage if it had previously been moved there. Thus, a programmer need not be concerned with the location of data but only with its logical structure. Herein lies a large measure of the ICES modularity. By not needing to know where data is stored, a program does not need to know what occurred before it or what will occur after it is finished. The ability to handle movable data rests on the use of a pointer scheme, where a single variable at a known location represents an array. When, and only when, this array contains data, this variable points to its location in the data pool or on the disk.

ICETRAN contains *executable* statements which may be used to manipulate arrays. These statements include DEFINE, DESTROY, RELEASE, and SWITCH. The data structures may be defined at execution time on the basis of the data for the particular problem and may change during execution. By allowing a pointer to point to an array of pointers and by allowing each pointer to be uniquely defined, structuring flexibility is achieved.

The ICETRAN language is basically FORTRAN with added statements. Dynamic array data referencing is similar to FORTRAN, with an array name and subscripts. Figure 6 provides a short programming example, performing the matrix operation $A = A*B$, where A is initially N1 by N2, B is N2 by N3, and the resultant A is N1 by N3. A significant programming feature is that such a program can operate on full arrays and on parts, regardless of the number of subscripts, so long as the parts passed contain the required structure. A program to calculate a segment flexibility matrix can be passed the data for member 1 (along with the length) or for segment 1 of member 2. This facility adds to program modularity.

The normal FORTRAN mechanism for program linkage is the CALL statement. This linkage requires all programs which are called to reside in one load module. In many cases programs, such as error processors, are needed only in pathological cases. Because of the large number of programs in a subsystem and its component procedures, because of the broad utility of some programs in many parts of a subsystem, and because of limited core memory, more flexibility is required. ICETRAN provides the following additional linkage mechanisms: LINK to a program in another module, which returns to the linking program, TRANSFER to a program in another module, LOAD a module, BRANCH to it, and DELETE a loaded module. In addition, ICEX maintains a push-down linkage list which may be manipulated by an ICETRAN program. Whenever control returns to ICEX, it links to the program on top of the list. If the list is empty, ICEX links to COMINT. LINK and TRANSFER operations using the list may also be executed by a program.

The following are a few examples of how STRUDL utilizes dynamic program linkage. For finite element analysis, it is important to combine with general procedures the capability of treating a large and growing set of element formulations. Each formulation requires programs to perform the operations within a procedure which are dependent upon the formulation. Programmers are constantly adding new formulations, and users may use a number of different element types within the solution of a single problem. STRUDL has solved this dynamic problem by using very short control programs for element-dependent phases of procedures and by providing a command with which a programmer can define to STRUDL an element type and the name of the program that may be used for that formulation with each phase-control program. The control programs contain a loop on elements, retrieving for each the element type, searching the dictionary for the program name, and LINKing to the element program. A new element may be used as soon as the program names and programs in load module form have been provided.

Large multiphase procedures such as analyses require a number of load modules for their execution. The push-down linkage list, or program stack, may then be used to control such procedures. For example, for both the stiffness and nonlinear analysis, ICEX links to a compilation phase. This program performs checking and setup operations and, depending upon procedures required for the particular analysis and on the data which need to be treated, the stack is set up. For the nonlinear analysis, an iteration control

```
SYSTEM 'STRUDL' 'PASSWORD'
ADD 'JOINT'
PRESET INTEGER 'I10' EQUAL 1
CALL 'GETID'
MODIFIER 'COOR'
     ID 'X' REAL 'T1' STANDARD -99999.
     ID 'Y' REAL 'T2' STANDARD -99999.
     ID 'Z' REAL 'T3' STANDARD -99999.
     EXISTENCE 'FREE' 'SUPPORT' SET 'I1' STANDARD 0
     EXECUTE 'STCOOR'
OR MODIFIER 'RELEASE'
     .
     .
     .
END MODIFIER
FILE
```

```
     SUBROUTINE MATMPY(A,B,N1,N2,N3)
     DYNAMIC ARRAY A,B,TEMP
     DO 10 I=1,N1
     DESTROY TEMP
     DEFINE TEMP, N3,FULL
     DO 8 K=1,N3
     DO 8 J=1,N2
8    TEMP(K)=TEMP(K)+A(I,J)*B(J,K)
     SWITCH(A(I),TEMP)
10   RELEASE A(I)
     DESTROY TEMP
     RELEASE A
     RELEASE B
     RETURN
     END
```

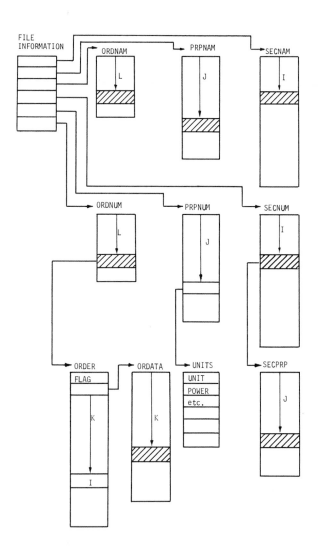

```
STRUDL 'MEMDES' 'EXAMPLE TRUSS CARRYING TRANSVERSE MEMBER LOAD'
UNITS KIPS INCHES DEGREES
CONSTANTS E 30000. ALL
BETA 90. ALL BUT 0.0 'B1'
JOINT COORDINATES $ DEFINE STRUCTURAL GEOMETRY
1 X 0. Y 0. SUPPORT
2 180. S
3 Y 240.
4 180. 240.
MEMBER INCIDENCES
1 1 3
2 2 3
3 1 4
4 2 4
'B1' 1 2
'T1' 3 4
JOINT RELEASES
1,2 MOMENT Z
2 FORCE X
LOADING 'HORZ' 'WIND LOAD FROM LEFT' $ DEFINE INDEPENDENT LOADING CONDITIONS
JOINT 3 LOAD FORCE X 1000.
LOADING 'VERT' 'LIVE LOAD FROM ROADWAY'
JOINT 3,4 LOADS FORCE Y -1500.
LOADING 'CABLE' 'LIVE LOAD FROM LOWER CABLE'
MEMBER 'B1' LOAD FORCE Y CONCENTRATED FR P -800. L 0.5
      $ MAKE PRELIMINARY ANALYSIS FOR HORZ AND VERT LOADINGS
TYPE PLANE TRUSS XY
MEMBER 3 FORCES FX FR 0.5 'HORZ' 833. 'VERT' 100.
LOADING LIST 'HORZ' 'VERT' $ INDICATES ON WHICH TO OPERATE
PRELIMINARY ANALYSIS
INACTIVE MEMBERS ALL BUT 'B1' $ FOR ANALYSIS OF B1 UNDER CABLE LOAD
TYPE PLANE FRAME   $ AS DETERMINATE BEAM
LOADING LIST 'CABLE'
DETERMINATE ANALYSIS
ACTIVE MEMBERS ALL
LOADING COMBINATION 'COMB' 'ROADWAY AND CABLE LOADS'
COMBINE 'COMB' 'VERT' 1.0 CABLE 1.0 $ FORM COMBINATION TO GET DESIGN FORCES
LOADING LIST ALL
LIST FORCES, REACTIONS ALL MEMBERS AND JOINTS $ GET RESULTS TO STUDY
PARAMETER 'CODE' 'AISC' ALL
'KY' 0.9 FOR ALL MEMBERS $ SPECIFY NECESSARY DESIGN PARAMETERS
'KZ' 0.8
'LY' 200. FOR 1,4
'TABLE' 'COLT' FOR 1,4 'B1', 'T1', USE 'DANG' FOR 2,3
MEMBER 1,4 CONSTRAINT
'NOMD' LE 14. $ SPECIFY CONSTRAINTS - HERE NOMINAL DEPTH ONLY
$ SELECT CRITICAL MEMBERS WITH APPROPRIATE PROCEDURE
SELECT MEMBERS 2 TO 4, 'T1' WITH 'TRUSS'
SELECT MEMBER 'B1' WITH 'COLUMN' AT SECTION FR 0.5
TAKE MEMBER 1 SAME AS 4 $ FROM SYMMETRY SELECT NON CRITICAL MEMBER
TAKE MEMBERS 2,3 AS LARGEST OF 2,3 ON BASIC OF 'AX' $ MAKE BOTH DIAG EQUAL
$ TO LARGEST
PRINT MEMBER PROPERTIES
TYPE PLANE TRUSS $ REANALYZE AS INDETERMINATE STRUCTURE - START ITERATION
LOADING LIST 'HORZ' 'VERT' 'COMB' $ DON'T REANALYZE BEAM
STIFFNESS ANALYSIS
LOADING LIST 'HORZ' 'COMB' $ CHECK FOR DESIGN LOADINGS
CHECK MEMBERS 1 TO 4, 'T1', 'B1'
SAVE 'EXTRUSS' $ SAVE PROBLEM FOR FURTHER DESIGN
FINISH
```

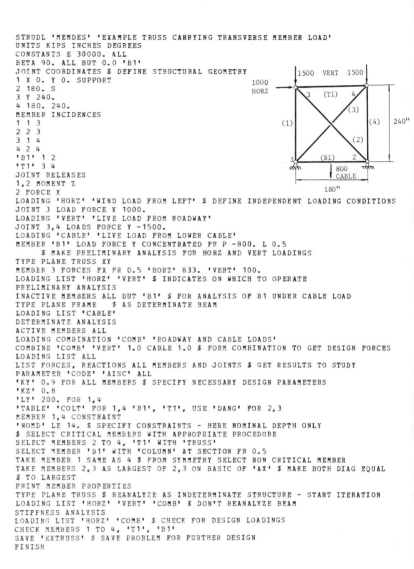

5. CDL example

6. ICETRAN example

7. An example ICES file structure

8. Design example of the use of STRUDL

program is placed on the bottom of the stack. This will be the last program executed, and it will make decisions on what programs to reload onto the stack (depending on whether the process is iterating at a load level or incrementing the load), always putting itself on the bottom. If a fatal error is detected during any of this processing, the stack is emptied and control returned to ICEX.

ICES also provides a truly random access data management (file storage) mechanism. Although it can be used for sequential storage, its flexibility allows a programmer to create files with comparable complexity to any dynamic data structure previously discussed. The structure of a file and sizes of individual records within it may be determined and modified at execution time. Figure 7 illustrates the file structure used in STRUDL for storage of tables of design section properties. The first record in the file contains "file information," including file record identifiers to six basic records which exist in pairs. The SECNAM-SECNUM pair store the name of each row and a record identifier for each row of property data. The PRPNAM-PRPNUM pair store the column name and record identifiers to the dimensional units of each column. Orders, used for sequencing design trials, are also shown. Note that with such a structure it is easy to expand and delete any of the types of information stored in the file. A new row may be added to the file by extending SECNAM, adding the name to the bottom, storing the row of properties in a new record, and adding that record identifier to the bottom of SECNUM.

The system described in Figure 7 is presently a reality. It is being used to develop and operate at least 20 different applications subsystems, both at M.I.T. and elsewhere. In the first few months of its availability, the programs have been obtained from the IBM Program Library by over 400 installations. All indications point to enthusiastic acceptance by programmers and users.

The Structural Design Language

The use of a computer throughout the design process requires convenient access and a powerful applications software system. STRUDL is intended to provide such an environment for structural engineering. The first version of ICES STRUDL in no way attempts to represent a complete structural design tool but rather a framework structured for expansion and continuing development by many different groups. In fact, the first version does not even contain actual design procedures.

Basically, STRUDL is designed as a structural information system. With it a user may store his entire problem in the computer over a long period of time and make investigations on part or all of his problem. As a consequence, he may change, add, or delete any of the information in the machine or make inquiries about any of the information stored in it. This approach allows the user to manipulate his problem in the machine, asking questions about his problem rather than, as with the special program approach, having to extract information from his manually-kept base to insert into the computer for each separate question.

As an information system, STRUDL has no way of knowing what operations are to be performed on its data. This requires that all information be maintained in its most general form, that is, for example, as a three-dimensional problem. Procedures operating on a subset of the general case, such as a plane frame, then extract their required information from the general form. This allows the user to change even the structural type. Conversely, the user need not specify more general information than is needed for the particular conditions and operations he wishes to use for his solution. For a plane frame analysis he need not provide a torsional constant for his members. Consistent with this approach, each of the procedures has been developed in the most general sense feasible. For example, the stiffness analysis has been developed to operate on both planar and space structures, for trusses, frames, finite elements, or any combination of these.

STRUDL provides a range of analytic procedures. The first version provides determinate, preliminary, and indeterminate analyses. The second version supplements these with nonlinear and dynamic analyses and provides treatment of finite elements for continuous (plate and shell) problems in addition to bar structures. Although these analysis procedures are sophisticated and complex beyond the capabilities of most engineers, their basis is sufficiently well understood so that they can be utilized properly as block boxes.

The engineer has a choice from among the analysis procedures available. For some problems less exact analytic procedures are appropriate. The same is true for preliminary phases of complex problems. The preliminary analysis procedure provides him with a mechanism for obtaining, at less expense, an approximate solution, utilizing his experience and knowledge to save computer time. Or he might provide a coarse model of his problem to gain approximate answers. For he may always refine his model and apply any procedure again, any number of times.

As a final example, Figure 8 shows how STRUDL is developing into design and might be utilized for the first phases of a design problem. First, the problem is defined, consisting of a six-member frame with two loading conditions, a vertical load at the top and at the center of the bottom member, and a wind load. The structure behaves primarily as a truss, except for the one-member load. Therefore, the structure is first analyzed as a truss for all loads except the member loads. The one beam is then analyzed for its load, and these results are combined with the results for the rest of the vertical load. The engineer then requests output and proceeds to a preliminary design.

For design, the user first provides any additional design data and constraints applicable to his problem. He then selects what he believes to be critical structural members with preprogrammed design procedures TRUSS and COLUMN and equates a noncritical member to a critical one in a symmetric position. Again, from symmetry, he equates both of two members to the largest of the two if he does not know which will be critical. He then requests output to show how the members have been designed.

Next, the designer requests a more exact analysis in order to check the feasibility of his design. He asks for a code and constraint check for the newly available results against the preliminary design, and saves the problem for further iterations and modifications. With the results he has obtained, he is able to make any decisions necessary to pursue his design problem.

Conclusions

Engineering design has been characterized as an iterative process in which the sequence of operations depends on the nature of the problem and on the experience, knowledge, and imagination of the designer. Because of this inherent variability, a completely automated computer design system, even if possible, would be inappropriate. The most promising approach lies in the development of flexible systems covering a wide range of design operations and applications. In order to provide flexibility, the computer must be used for more than mere computation. It should be viewed as an information storage and retrieval device and as a medium of communication between the designer and his problem. The system should be designed to facilitate this communication by giving the engineer easy access to all pertinent information. In addition, it should provide a variety of design tools, applicable to the different phases of the design process and accessible in any sequence.

The STRUDL system represents an attempt to meet these objectives. It is an open-ended, dynamic system, and its current version includes only a small portion of the potential capability. The system framework has been specifically developed to accommodate an expanding scope of operations.

The ultimate objective is to make the computer an aid throughout the design process. With improvements in hardware, advances in programming techniques, and the education of engineers, this objective will certainly be achieved. Thus the engineer will be able to devote more of his time and effort to decision-making and creativity, the real substance of engineering.

9 DISCOURSE: A Language and System for Computer-Assisted City Design

William Porter, Katherine Lloyd, and Aaron Fleisher

Department of City and Regional Planning, Massachusetts Institute of Technology
Cambridge, Massachusetts

William Porter is Assistant Professor of Architecture and City Planning at M.I.T. He holds a B.A. and B.Arch. from Yale University and received a Ph.D. in City and Regional Planning from M.I.T. in 1969. He has worked for Louis Kahn and more recently for the Joint Center for Urban Studies on the design of Ciudad Guayana, a Venezuelan City. Katherine Lloyd is a Research Associate at M.I.T. She holds an A.B. in economics from Radcliffe. Since 1959 she has been at M.I.T. in the Sloan School of Management, the Instrumentation Laboratory, and the Department of City and Regional Planning working on computer applications in teaching and research. Aaron Fleisher is Professor of Urban and Regional Studies at M.I.T. He received a B.A. in biology from New York University and a Ph.D. in earth sciences from M.I.T. For many years he has been involved in various aspects of quantitative methods and research in design and planning, and has written extensively on these subjects. This paper is drawn from William Porter's Ph.D. thesis under Professors Fleisher and Kevin Lynch as advisors. The DISCOURSE Project has been under the general direction of Professor Fleisher. The computer system design and development work was done by Katherine Lloyd with the assistance of Corrie Menger and Stanley Hoderowski. Part of this paper appears in Murray Milne, ed., *Computer Graphics in Architecture and Design* and is reprinted here with permission.

DISCOURSE is aimed at accommodating and expanding the nonintuitive part of the designer's activities in complex problems of environmental design and planning. Examples of such problems are the design of new towns, the development of design policies for existing communities, and the planning of entire regions. DISCOURSE can handle information about a geographic area and rules about how the information is transformed. The designer can store and retrieve information describing the environment as well as descriptions of market behavior, design or development policies, or rules to predict the effects of environmental change. DISCOURSE has a large vocabulary of building blocks out of which a designer can construct his own special requests. The system allows the designer to build and modify his own techniques of design and his design proposal as he works. He may change the information or alter the constraints; he may try manipulating parts of the environment in different ways; he may try to predict many different effects of his designs; or he may wish to evaluate the design alternatives against many criteria or to compare them with each other. This paper describes the development of DISCOURSE.

Purposes

In this paper we shall describe an experiment in the reduction of the behavior that is called city designing (or city planning), to programmed algorithms.[1] It is an experiment in two respects. There is more than one way to program the same algorithm and to make a system out of several. Call that Experiment 1B. But that job is possible only after you have decided what to program. Therefore, we construe our work also as an experiment in the rationalization of design. That is Experiment 1A. We shall describe Experiment 1A first.

We had proposed to examine processes in city design and planning. We mean by "process" a coherent argument that threads purpose and solution. The solution need not be optimal. It need not even be good. We were less concerned with the qualities of the solution than with the course of reasoning and the succession of operations by which it is obtained. Process must be describable, realizable, transferable, and testable. It can be idiosyncratic, but it can be neither metaphorical nor solipsistic.

---

1. This work began as a design seminar with John Boorn, Christine Boyer, and Hans Bleiker, and was continued by Porter and Boorn. We say with confidence that at no time was there agreement either on the analysis being argued or on the direction the analysis should take. The particular flavor of these remarks, therefore, is ours alone. Nevertheless, we did agree eventually that design could be studied experimentally.

We do not mean process to be synonymous with "principle." It is rather more modest, more occasional, less systematic. We would have preferred to work from principles of design, but they are few and scant of breadth and are not likely to be improved particularly in the near future.

Even so, we had difficulties finding examples that could pass for process. What usually surfaces are the bits and pieces that remain of the problem after it has been reduced to a size that can be grasped by a person and manipulated on a drafting table. Solutions are patched from these pieces by arguments compounded from principles without consequences and preferences kept covert. Order, when it is made, almost always comes ad and post hoc.

One could take the position that if the product were adequately tested, then the nature of the process would become less important. Unworthy solutions generated and discarded are a waste, which may be tolerable provided we could be assured that the procedures for generating solutions would not miss good ones too often. Without principles, such assurances are certainly impossible, and if one would attempt to cover the contingencies by generating many, then the number is likely to be larger than could be reasonably managed.

At this point our inquiry turned. Since it did not appear profitable to look for the processes that would describe design as rational behavior, we thought to ask whether it might be possible to posit processes that would account for the product. The change was substantial. We had begun in the hope that our analysis would help to polish the practice, so that its rationality would become transparent. Now we set the analysis of practice aside in favor of finding a *logical equivalent* to its result.

The equivalence is logical because it would produce the same solution. That it is logical instead of literal releases us from having to account for what the designer does. However potent, his intuitions are obscure and his testimony seldom more than a recital of his choices. These are the outward shows of the designer's sensibilities. Without them no amount of process can make great works. But they are not themselves process. They are too fragile and too arbitrary to sustain the weight of rationality.

Rather than poke in these murky waters, we shift from designing to the design itself. Whatever its faults, it is certainly not contemptible. Frequently it is good, and most important, it is describable. Our problem now is to find a context and a set of explicit procedures that would replicate the design, not to ascribe them to the designer but to provide an objective process for diagnosis.

The process is objective because replication tests its validity. It is process because the argument from problem to solution is explicitly performable. However, neither condition can prevent it from being trivial. It would be easy enough to devise specific procedures to replicate specific products. There would then be as many sets as there were products examined. If these procedures are to have diagnostic value, they must be rather general. We are not sure what "rather general" means. It is not likely that one set of procedures can do for all cases. A successful set ought to be conditional on the type of problem considered and on the specifications within its kind—which strongly suggests that we are hunting for rules by which to generate the procedures that would do the replicating.

Suppose that it is possible to produce such sets of generating rules. Then we could describe the rules of thumb, the devices, manipulations, and simplifications that constitute the skill and wisdom of the designer. We would have described his intelligence. He is simulated, and design, reduced to procedure, becomes conventional. We do not mean it therefore to be inferred that a replicable design is necessarily unworthy, or that the skill and wisdom that produced it are trivial. Conventional wisdom can indeed be wise and a common skill uncommonly subtle.

It is not likely that the replication will always be completely faithful. What remains of the designer after replication can range from random flummery to pure creativity. The simulation can neither account for such events nor detect their quality, a disability endemic among critics of design. The simulation does no worse.

To continue Experiment 1A we began Experiment 1B. How do you program a machine to imitate the designer? You must provide the formalism in which to state the problem and initial conditions, and a language by which to describe an intelligence that could generate the procedures and test their power to replicate. We could not risk any strong prior notions of what this intelligence and these procedures might be like. That would prejudice the experiment. Therefore, the language would have to be rich, for it must be capable of expressing many possibilities.

We proceeded first to program the data structure, and the manipulations and transformations of these data. We could not get as far in programming the intelligence. Then it occurred to us that in the designer we have the presence of brooding mind. If this were added to the combination of data and operations, then we would have a system of computer-aided design, thereby providing yet another example of nature imitating art. The difference between a computer aiding design and one simulating design is only the source of the intelligence that drives the process. Data and operations that suit one would apply as well to the other. We have set aside temporarily the problem of programming an intelligence.

What we have now stands as a computer system that helps the designer by increasing the level of complexity that he can understand and manipulate. It does not replace, it amplifies him. How this is done results from a characteristic of the system that is particular to its history. Our initial intent to make a design simulator led us to devise a language capable of expressing design operations, rather than to program these operations directly. The system therefore contains no commitment to any rationality or to any mode of procedure. It can be bent to the style of the user. It must be bent because it has no style of its own. It is essentially mindless, and having to be made mindful it is more difficult to use. It can do nothing for you, but much with you. The most that we would hope for is a language sufficiently rich and felicitous to express the intent of design graciously. It is not that yet.

Workings of the DISCOURSE System

In order to illustrate the system as it now stands, we shall consider a designer studying the possibilities for urbanization in and around Boston Harbor (Dorchester Bay), shown in Figure 1. The particular zone our designer is working on has been singled out because it comprises a good deal of vacant land, has a so-called "problem area" because its low-income residents are geographically and socially isolated, and it falls within the city limits of Boston. Moreover, building out over the bay, either on fill or otherwise, is a possibility seriously under consideration by state and local agencies because of the shortage of land in the city.

Our designer would be observing this environment, predicting behavior in it, trying out different ideas which may be tested by some of his observations, making tentative changes to the environment, sometimes discarding them, other times holding them until he builds up a design idea. As he is working he will be correcting and improving the description, making new changes, evaluating them from different points of view, all in a continuous stream.[2]

Let's take a look at how some of these activities of the designer are implemented in DISCOURSE.

2. For further description of designers' techniques, see Kevin Lynch, "Quality in City Design," in Laurence B. Holland, ed., *Who Designs America,* especially pp. 141–150.

1 2 3 4 5 6 7 8 9 0 | 2 3 4 5 6 7 8 9 0 | 2 3 4 5 6 7 8 9 0 | 2 3 4 5

2. A portion of the HOOK file

3. A portion of the DATA file

4. Display of SHOW request

```
print wpjul hook
W 1713.3

WPJUL    HOOK      12/30   1713.4

00010    HOOK
00020    5 - LOW/INCOME/RESIDENTS NUMBER * INCOME = 1
00030    6 - MIDDLE/INCOME/RESIDENTS NUMBER * INCOME = 2
00040    7 - HIGH/INCOME/RESIDENTS NUMBER * INCOME = 3
00050    8 - EMPLOYEES REGIONAL LOCAL *
00060    9 - STUDENTS REGIONAL LOCAL *
00070    10 - CONSUMERS REGIONAL LOCAL * BUDGET = 2
00080    11 - RECREATEES LOW/INCOME MIDDLE/INCOME HIGH/INCOME *
00090    12 - LARGE/SPACE PRIVATE/AREA PUBLIC/AREA * COST CAPACITY = 10 10
00100    13 - SMALL/SPACE PRIVATE/AREA PUBLIC/AREA * COST CAPACITY = 15 3
00110    14 - HIGH/STRUCTURE HEIGHT *
00120    15 - PUBLIC/OPEN/SPACE PROGRAMMED NOT/PROGRAMMED * COST = 2
00130    16 - PRIVATE/OPEN/SPACE PROGRAMMED NOT/PROGRAMMED * COST = 3
00140    17 - PATH/1 FLOWS BRIDGE * COST CAPACITY = 60 2
00150    18 - PATH/2 FLOWS TRANSIT/STOP * COST CAPACITY = 120 10
00160    20 - LAND/PLUS/16 AREA *
00170    21 - LAND/PLUS/5 AREA *
00180    22 - TIDAL/FLATS AREA * COST/OF/FILL = 6
00190    23 - LAND/MINUS/3 AREA * COST/OF/FILL = 12
00200    24 - LAND/MINUS/9 AREA * COST/OF/FILL = 18
00210    25 - LAND/MINUS/15 AREA * COST/OF/FILL = 24
00220    30 - ALL/LAND *
00230    31 - SHORE/LINE *
00240    41 - EXISTING/RESIDENTIAL/AREAS *
00250    2 - X * A B C D E F G H I J K L M N = 0 0 0 0 0 '
00260    0 0 0 0 0 0 0 0 0
00270    4 - MISCELLANEOUS INFO1 INFO2 * QUIT
00280    READ/CONSOLE
R 1.750+.500
```

```
2,6 41 5(300) 13(120 0) 12(0 10) 20(160) 8(50 50) 10(150  '
        141 50) 4(0 0) $
2,7 41 5(400) 13(160 0) 21(40) 20(120) 4(0 0) $
2,8 41 5(400) 13(160 0) 21(40) 20(120) 4(0 0) $
2,9 41 5(300) 13(120 0) 21(160) 15(0 40) 11(0 0 0) 4(0 0)   $
```

```
show (low/income/residents)
    4    10
    4     9
    4     8
    3    10
    3     9
    3     8
    3     7
    2     9
    2     8
    2     7
    2     6
    1     9
    1     8
    1     7
    1     6
    0     7
MAKE REQUESTS

show (low/income/residents(number)) at loc 3 9
    400
MAKE REQUESTS
```

The kinds of information a designer will need to describe the environment will vary according to the questions he wishes to ask. Of course he cannot anticipate all the questions he will ask, and this means both that his initial description must be comprehensive and that he must be able to change his description in the future.

To describe the environment initially, in DISCOURSE the designer must decide in how much detail he will look and what the categories of the description will be. He must divide the environment into a grid of "locations."[3] He can select any size grid up to the limits imposed by the size of the computer's core, and the locations of which the grid is composed can stand for any size area. In Figure 1 each location is 400 feet on a side, and there are 805 locations.

The categories or attributes of the description which the designer has decided upon are then recorded in a HOOK file (a file which is "hooked" onto the grid of locations). In Figure 2, a small portion of the HOOK file, the attribute numbers appear at the left of each line. For example, attribute 15 is "public open space." And there are two subcategories: "programmed," that is, designated for some use like a playground, and "not programmed." Additionally there is information that the cost of preparing either "programmed" or "not programmed" land for some use is $2 per sq ft.

The information about the environment is then recorded for each location in the DATA file, a portion of which is shown in Figure 3. For example, in location 2,8 (corresponding to row 2, column 8 of the map of Figure 1), we find the label 41, which denotes that there exists some population in this location; 5(400), that there are 400 low income residents; 13(160 0), 160,000 sq ft of small spaces, for example houses, and of that, none open to the public, for example no speciality shops; 21(40), 40,000 sq ft of land (the average elevation of land in this column is 5 ft above high tide); 20(120), 120,000 sq ft of land (16 ft above high tide); 4(0 0), miscellaneous information, places at each location for the designer to put some special bit of information that might result from some calculation.

The designer works at a console which types the response to requests in anything from a few seconds to a minute depending on how much processing time his request required and how many other people are attempting to share simultaneously the central computer to which his console is connected. The rapid response time allows the designer to see his mistakes, to make other discoveries from his results, and to modify his subsequent ways of working accordingly.

Basic requests and request combination facilities permit the designer to display his information, change it, store the changes, and to create new requests. Two requests, SHOW and MAP are, presently, the only ways to display the data. These are typed out by the teletype console itself. The upper request in Figure 4 shows the locations (row and column number) of the low-income residents. The lower request shows how many are at row 3, column 9. The map, Figure 5, shows the location of all residents by income group and all places where there are schools and large stores.

In order to make a development zone, the designer asks for all unused public open space and all tidal flats next to existing low-income residential areas, the first four requests of Figure 6. He then assigns low income residential use to those locations, the fifth request. If instead he had wished to be more specific in his assignment of low-income residents, he could have added to any location the number of residents which the available land could hold at some density. In order to avoid having to make the many requests necessary

---

3. The present interpretation in DISCOURSE of a geographic area as a grid of locations is not a necessary one, but it is one which has served us for these and many other examples of the designer's ways of working.

5. Display of MAP request—position of income groups, schools, and stores

6. Requests for available development zones

```
map (low/income/residents middle/income/residents '
high/income/residents) with respect to (consumers students)
 MAP COORDINATES ARE MISSING.  DO YOU WISH ENTIRE MAP
yes
```

```
                                      1                   2                   3
            0 1 2 3 4 5 6 7 8 9 0 1 2 3 4 5 6 7 8 9 0 1 2 3 4 5 6 7 8 9 0 1 2 3 4 5
     0    2 . . . . . . 1 . . . . . . . . . . . . . . . . . . . . . . . . . . . . .    0
     1    2 2 . . . .+.+1 1 1 1 . . . . . . . . . . . . . . . . . . . . . . . . . .    1
     2    2 2 . . . .+.+1 1 1 1 . . . . . . . . . . . . . . . . . . . . . . . . . .    2
     3    2 2 . . . . . 1 1 1 1 . . . . . . . . . . . . . . . . . . . . . . . . . .    3
     4    2 2 . . . . .-.-1 1 1 . . . . . . . . . . . . . . . . . . . . . . . . . .    4
     5    2 2 . . . .-. .-. . . . . . . . . . . . . . . . . . . . . . . . . . . . .    5
     6    2 2 . . . . . . . . . . . . . . . . . . . . . . . . . . . . . . . . . . .    6
     7    2 2 . . . . . . . . . . . . . . . . . . . . . . . . . . . . . . . . . . .    7
     8    2 2 3 3 3 . . . . . . . . . . . . . . . . . . . . . . . . . . . . . . . .    8
     9    2 2 3 3 3 3 . . . . . . . . . . . . . . . . . . . . . . . . . . . . . . .    9
    10    2 3 3 3 . 3 3 . . . . . . . . . . . . . . . . . . . . . . . . . . . . . .   10
    11    . . 3 3 . 3 3 . . . . . . . . . . . . . . . . . . . . . . . . . . . . . .   11
    12    . . 3 3 3 3 3 . . . . . . . . . . . . . . . . . . . . . . . . . . . . . .   12
    13    . . 3 3 3 . . . . . . . . . . . . . . . . . . . . . . . . . . . . . . . .   13
    14    . . . . . . . . . . . . . . . . . . . . . . . . . . . . . . . . . . . . .   14
    15    . . . . . . . . . . . . . . . . . . . . . . . . . . . . . . . . . . . . .   15
    16    . . . . . . . . . . . . . . . . . . . . . . . . . . . . . . . . . . . . .   16
    17    2 2 . . . . . . . . . . . . . . . . . . . . . . . . . . . . . . : . . . .   17
    18    2 2 2 . . . . . . . . . . . . . . . . . . . . . . . . . . . . 3 3 . . . . .   18
    19    2 2 2 2 . . . . . . . . . . . . . . . . . . . . . . . . . . 3 3 3 3 . . . .   19
    20    2 2 2 2 . . . . . . . . . . . . . . . . . . . . . . . . . 3 3 3 3 3 3 3 . .   20
    21    2 2 2 2 . . . . . . . . . . . . . . . . . . . . . . . . . 3 3 3 3 3 3 3 . .   21
    22    2 2 2 2 . . . . . . . . . . . . . . . . . . . . . . . . 3 3 3-. 3 3 3 3 . .   22
    23    2 2 2 2 . . . . . . . . . . . . . . . . . . . . . . . . . 3 3 3 3 3 3 3 . .   23

            0 1 2 3 4 5 6 7 8 9 0 1 2 3 4 5 6 7 8 9 0 1 2 3 4 5 6 7 8 9 0 1 2 3 4 5
                                      1                   2                   3
```

```
LEGEND

1 IS ATTRIBUTE   5 - LWINCS
2 IS ATTRIBUTE   6 - MDDLES
3 IS ATTRIBUTE   7 - HGHINS
A IS ATTRIBUTES  5 AND  6
B IS ATTRIBUTES  5 AND  7
C IS ATTRIBUTES  6 AND  7
D IS ATTRIBUTES  5,  6 AND  7
+ IS REF ATTRIBUTE 10 - CNSUMS
- IS REF ATTRIBUTE  9 - SUDENS
* IS REF ATTRIBUTES 10 AND  9
BLANK IS EMPTY LAND
. IS NON-EMPTY LAND
 MAKE REQUESTS
```

```
find (public/open/space(not/programmed)) grt 0
 CALL THIS LIST      45
 MAKE REQUESTS

beside (low/income/residents) find 45
 CALL THIS LIST      46
 MAKE REQUESTS

beside (low/income/residents) find (tidal/flats)
 CALL THIS LIST      47
 MAKE REQUESTS

union 46 47
 CALL THIS LIST      48
 MAKE REQUESTS

put (low/income/residents) in list 48 permanently
 MAKE REQUESTS


put 52 in list 48 temporarily
 MAKE REQUESTS

read/disk assign lir
     2480      (number of people assigned to tidal flats area)
     3840      (number assigned to public open space area)
     6320      (total)
     4300      (number of low income residents elsewhere)
 READ/CONSOLE
```

---

7. Preprogrammed combination request

ASSIGN   LIR   12/30   1709.7

```
00010    C, THIS FILE ADDS LOW INCOME RESIDENTS TO EACH OF THE LOCATIONS
00020    C, IN THE DEVELOPMENT ZONE (52) IN THE FOLLWOING WAY.
00030    C, TWO TIMES THE NUMBER OF THOUSANDS OF SQUARE FEET
00040    C, OF AVAILABLE LAND, IE. EITHER TIDAL FLATS
00050    C, OR PUBLIC OPEN SPACE NOT PROGRAMMED FOR USE.
00060    C, THE DENSITY OF PEOPLE ON NEW LAND IS
00070    C, 87 PERSONS PER ACRE.
00080    C, THE FILE STORES IN (4(1)) AT EACH LOCATION THE
00090    C, NUMBER OF PEOPLE ON FORMER TIDAL FLATS AND
00100    C, IN (X(I)) THE TOTAL OF THOSE.
00110    C, IN (4(2)) THE NUMBER OF PEOPLE ON FORMER
00120    C, UNUSED PUBLIC OPEN SPACE AND IN (X(J)) THE
00130    C, TOTAL OF THOSE.
00140    C, IN (X(K)) THE SUM OF (X(I)) AND (X(J)).
00150    C, AND IN (X(H)) THE FORMER TOTAL NUMBER OF LOW INCOME
00160    C, RESIDENTS.
00170    C, THE FILE PRINTS OUT (X(I)), (X(J)), (X(K)),
00180    C, AND (X(H)) IN THAT ORDER.
00190    START/RCOM
00200    AVAIL2
00210    MAKE (X(H)) = 0
00220    MAKE (X(I)) = 0
00230    MAKE (X(J)) = 0
00240    FOR (X(A)) = EACH (5)
00250    PLACE5 $ CALCULATE (X(H)) = (X(H)) PLUS (5(1)) AT LOC (X(A))
00260    NEXT (X(A))
00270    GO BACK TO PLACE5
00280    PUT 5 IN LIST 52 PERMAN
00290    INTERSECTION (TIDAL/FLATS) (52)
00300    AVAIL2
00310    FOR (X(A)) = EACH (53)
00320    PLACE6 $ CALCULATE (4(1)) AT LOC (X(A)) = (22(1)) '
00330    AT LOC (X(A)) MULTBY 2
00340    CALCULATE (X(I)) = (X(I)) PLUS (4(1)) AT LOC (X(A))
00350    CALCULATE (5(1)) AT LOC (X(A)) = (5(1)) AT LOC '
00360    (X(A)) PLUS (4(1)) AT LOC (X(A))
00370    NEXT (X(A))
00380    GO BACK TO PLACE6
00390    INTERSECTION (15) (52)
00400    AVAIL2
00410    FOR (X(A)) = EACH (54)
00420    PLACE7 $ CALCULATE (4(2)) AT LOC (X(A)) = (15(2)) '
00430    AT LOC (X(A)) MULTBY 2
00440    CALCULATE (X(J)) = (X(J)) PLUS (4(2)) AT LOC (X(A))
00450    CALCULATE (5(1)) AT LOC (X(A)) = (5(1)) AT LOC (X(A)) '
00460    PLUS (4(2))  AT LOC (X(A))
00470    NEXT (X(A))
00480    GO BACK TO PLACE7
00490    CALCULATE (X(K)) = (X(I)) PLUS (X(J))
00500    SHOW (X(I))
00510    SHOW (X(J))
00520    SHOW (X(K))
00530    SHOW (X(H))
00540    DELETE (22) FROM LIST 52
00550    CHANGE (15(2)) TO 0 ON LIST 52
00560    READ/CONSOLE
```
R 2.350+.650

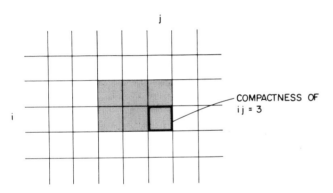

COMPACTNESS OF
i j = 3

"COMPACTNESS" OF THE WHOLE GROUP = 3.67

```
read/disk wpcom1 rcom
 READ/CONSOLE/RETURN
read 1 variable
v1 = 5
 MAKE REQUESTS
return/to/disk
       16.00    (number of locations with low income residents)
        5.13    (compactness index for low income residents)
 READ/CONSOLE

read/disk wpcom1 rcom
 READ/CONSOLE/RETURN
read 1 variable
v1 = 6
 MAKE REQUESTS
return/to/disk
       45.00    (number of locations with middle income residents)
        5.16    (compactness index for middle income residents)
 READ/CONSOLE

read/disk wpcom1 rcom
 READ/CONSOLE/RETURN
read 1 variable
v1 = 7
 MAKE REQUESTS
return/to/disk
       59.00    (number of locations with high income residents)
        5.46    (compactness index for high income residents)
 READ/CONSOLE
```

for such an assignment, the designer can preprogram his requests so that he can call them with a single "combination request," the last request of Figure 6. The sixth request assigns to the development zone the list number which his preprogrammed request requires. Figure 7 shows the designer's preprogrammed "combination request" which allowed him to make the assignment at that density and to find how many residents had actually been placed according to his assignment rule.

Combination requests can also be constructed to make new basic requests. For example, Figure 8 shows a graphic representation of a "compactness index"; Figure 9 is an illustration of its use. The three types of residences being measured in Figure 9 have fairly simple "compactness indexes," with the higher-income residences having the most compact pattern. Among other combination requests which have been written are those that calculate average income in a zone of the designer's choosing, the most central point in a zone, and special-development zones which conform to certain criteria.

Where Do We Stand?

We have, of course, found that DISCOURSE is not as good as we hoped. It is a good approximation, and we are confident that we know how to improve it. We are less confident that it or any similar systems can be improved and kept simple simultaneously.

DISCOURSE is intended as a problem-oriented language, which is to say that it should be usable without extended instruction or practice. This intention we implemented by preprogramming the data structure and such operations as we thought would most felicitously express the particularities of design. It is clear that the numbers of possible operations and of their combinations are far larger than even a large machine could hold—if the programming resources were available in the first place. Therefore, we were led to the use of combination request files, a device that permits the designer to do a little of his own programming. DISCOURSE makes it much easier for him to do the job, but program he must. We do not think that this is a basic deficit in the system. It is, instead, the result of how we think it best to assist the designer. As a designer works he creates new ways of working, of analyzing and of generating environmental forms. The techniques he uses toward the finish of a design exercise may be entirely different than those he used at the be- ginning. No programmer can anticipate all the requests that a designer will want to make. The making of combination request files can be improved. However, we are persuaded that any "user-oriented language" intended to express a rich variety of ideas must, at some point, involve the user in some of the programming.

Combination request files can of course be written at any point in the process of design. They might, for example, be written initially, as a set of prerequi- sites by which to monitor and evaluate the products of design. And since these files can be saved, they are transferable to other users and their accu- mulation can become the collected wisdom of designers.

DISCOURSE is a verbal system. It performs verbal manipulations on verbal materials. Its graphics are intended only for the purposes of presentation, not analysis. There exists now no computer system that is as good in general visual analysis as the human eye. That may well change. We shall reconsider our purposes then.

Computers appear to be purely verbal devices, even when they are working at pattern recognition, and their uses in design depend almost entirely on the description of design as a verbal process. To be sure, machines can be used to make pictures. But it is the eye that does the visual analysis. The machine usually enters in a relatively trivial way. We do not say that computer graphics is easy. We do say that there is normally no visual intelligence built into com- puter graphics. That is contributed from the outside.

Does it follow then, that the increased use of computers in design traces the shift in design from a visual to a verbal mode of argument? That shift would be a radical one affecting the man and his education as well as the product. Now is none too soon to reconsider both.

Appendix
The Computer System

The design of the first-phase computer system for DISCOURSE was intended to satisfy several criteria which we felt were important for the designer. The system had to handle large amounts of information about the environment and had to respond rapidly to the designer's requests, to afford a conversational mode of working. The internal procedures of the computer were not the responsibility of the designer, but the language was to be as close to his "designese" as possible. Programming the functions used by the designer, adding new programs, and modifying old ones all were to be easy. In order to get a sense of how well the system performs we will look briefly at the data structure and the functions written on that structure, and at the operation of the system as a whole.

Data Structure and Functions

The list-processing language of AED was chosen because it seemed to afford great flexibility in structuring the data. Data that are not uniform can be described well. The size and distribution of the items need not be carefully predicted. There are many possibilities for representing relationships. Dynamic modification is easy. A "list" of members may be thought of as a "string" of beads or a "chain" of data, hence the interchangeability of the words "list," "string," and "chain." And, since a "bead" can occur at the crossing points of several strings it can appropriately be called a "node."

The data in DISCOURSE I can be pictured as strung together on chains with each data bead a member of two chains, one of which is accessed from a LOCATION dictionary (row and column of the grid) and the other from an ATTRIBUTE dictionary (category of the designer's legend, e.g., "public/open/space"). This concept is pictured in Figure 10. The various requests which the designer is able to make are implemented by procedures which look along these chains in various ways. For example, "intersection (public/open/space) (path L)," (the upper two arrows of Figure 11), is implemented by following along the "public open space" chain until the first member is encountered, then looking down the location chain at that member to see if "path L" occurs. If it does the program makes a new list, say list 45 (the third arrow of Figure 11), with that location as its first member. In any event it follows the "public open space" chain until it meets the next member; there again it looks down the location chain for "path L." If it occurs, that location too is added as a member of list 45. The program continues this procedure until returning to its starting point, at which time the machine stops and prints "call that list 45." The designer might like to place "public information centers" at all these places. He would type "put (public/information/centers) on list 45." The program then follows list 45, making every member a new member of the "public information center" chain (the bottom arrow of Figure 11). Figure 11 therefore shows a picture of the entire location chain satisfying the requests on this example. The designer could then type on the console "clear" which would take away the temporary list 45 he made in the process of deciding where to put the information centers. His description of the environment would now be altered to include his "design changes." If he asked where the information centers were, the new locations would be included. During this process the designer would not have to worry about where (in the computer) things were; he can call them by name.

The data structure can accommodate two other kinds of information in addition to places and attributes of places. They are numerical or nominal values of attributes at places (CHARVARS) and of attributes regardless of place (CHARCONS). These permit the designer to determine, for example, that there are 250 square feet of public information center at location 1,1 (a CHARVAR); and he can establish a cost per square foot which would be true in any location (a CHARCON). And both CHARVARS and CHARCONS can be named and are addressable by their names.

10. Location chain

11. Nodes on a location chain

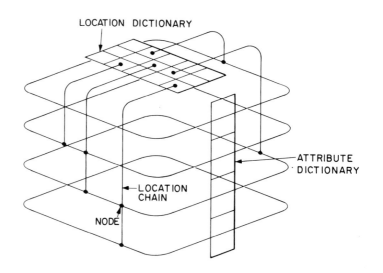

LOCATION DICTIONARY

ATTRIBUTE DICTIONARY

LOCATION CHAIN

NODE

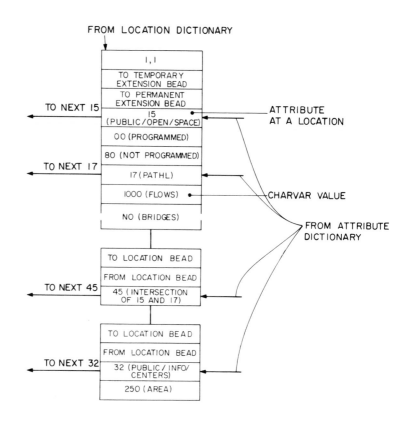

NODES ON A LOCATION CHAIN

12. Components of the computer system

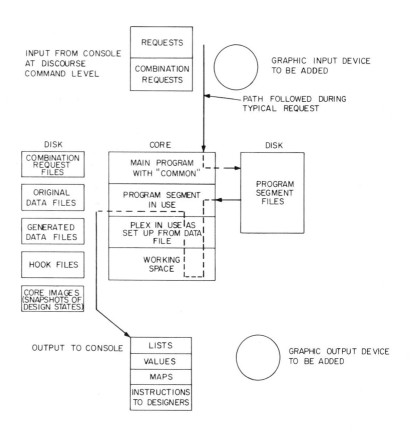

COMPONENTS OF THE COMPUTER SYSTEM

The Compatible Time Sharing System at the Massachusetts Institute of Technology, CTSS, affords rapid interaction at relatively low cost for what appears to the user as a machine fully dedicated to him. Without the availability of CTSS, DISCOURSE could never have been implemented as it was.

To start up the DISCOURSE system, illustrated in Figure 12, the designer first enters CTSS and calls for the main program of the DISCOURSE system to be loaded into the computer's core. He then requests the data file he had previously made and indicates which parts of the file he wants to work with. Those parts are loaded into core as a network of lists called a plex. He does the same for the legend he wants. At this point he can make his requests. The appropriate program segment is loaded into core and the request carried out. The designer can also call a combination request he has previously programmed (see for example Figure 7) in which case the combination request file is read as if it were the console. Once a designer has arrived at a point he would like to stop, he can store his design alternative. Later he can either load it back into core to continue working on it, or load it and several other design alternatives into core one after the other in order to compare them in some way.

At present the programs are stored in segments that are loaded into core only when needed. This means that more programs can be added without taking up additional space in core. The data in DISCOURSE I are not segmented and must be resident in core at all times. In DISCOURSE II[4] the data will be segmented and, coupled with other improvements, the amount of data which can be handled will be increased several fold.

---

4. DISCOURSE II is being developed under the direction of Wren McMains.

10 URBAN5:
A Machine
That Discusses
Urban Design

Nicholas Negroponte and
Leon Groisser

International Business Machines
Cambridge Scientific Center and
Department of Architecture,
Massachusetts Institute of
Technology
Cambridge, Massachusetts

Nicholas Negroponte is Assistant Pro-
fessor of Architecture teaching computer-
aided urban design at M.I.T. and a faculty
member of the Joint Center for Urban
Studies of Harvard University and M.I.T.
He received a B.Arch. and M.Arch. from
M.I.T. in 1965 and 1966. From 1966 to 1968
he worked with the IBM Cambridge
Scientific Center, where he developed
URBAN5. He is presently working in M.I.T.'s
Urban Systems Laboratory and Project
MAC's Artificial Intelligence Laboratory.
Leon Groisser is also Assistant Professor
of Architecture at M.I.T. He received a B.S.
in civil engineering from M.I.T. in 1948, a
B.A. from Middlebury College in 1949, and
an M.B.A. from Columbia University in
1950, and is completing his doctoral
dissertation in civil engineering at M.I.T.
Until 1960 he worked privately in industry
and taught at Tufts University. This paper
reports on work done under the direction
of the authors through the joint sponsor-
ship of Dean Lawrence B. Anderson
(M.I.T. School of Architecture and Planning), Dean Gordon S. Brown (M.I.T.
School of Engineering), and Norman
Rasmussen (IBM Cambridge Scientific
Center). This paper is also part of *The
Architecture Machine* by Nicholas Negroponte.

URBAN5 is said to discuss urban design
because it does not do urban design and
because it works with such abstractions
that it can only simulate urban problems.
It is not a tool; it is a toy. It was developed
to study the desirability and feasibility of
conversing with a machine about environmental design projects. The user is
assumed to have no previous computer-
programming knowledge. He specifies
design criteria in English and generates
physical form with computer-graphics
techniques. The system responds with
states of compatibility or conflict to which
the user responds, and so on. A conversation proceeds. The computer is used as
an objective mirror of the designer's
design criteria and form decisions; the
responses are reflected from a larger
information base than the user's personal
experience.

The system changes over time. The more
a designer uses URBAN5, the more URBAN5
transforms itself to be compatible and
congenial with that designer. Eventually
the system will have overlaid upon itself
a version of some machine that is in fact
a machine in the image of the particular
user. A complete description of the
system is given.

Before URBAN5 was started, four assumptions were made: (1) the user would
be an architect or urban designer, (2) urban design is based on physical form,
(3) the design process is not algorithmic, (4) urban environments are equi-
libria resolved from many basic, primarily qualitative relationships.[1] The first
assumption alone generated the spirit of the system, as we further assumed
that the architect–urban designer user would have no previous experience
with computers, let alone having ever talked to one. Thus URBAN5's first
task was to be capable of communicating with an architect or urban designer
in languages he understood. To do this, the authors of the system chose two
languages: English (entered from a typewriter) and a graphical language
(using a cathode ray tube and light pen). The adopted hardware is shown in
Figure 1.

The concern to create a graphical language made it evident that URBAN5
would have to handle some (if not all) problems in terms of their suitable
abstractions. In other words, the system committed itself to work under
synthetic conditions and not to attempt to canvass real-world problems. The

1. The objectives and early work are discussed fully in Nicholas Negroponte and Leon
Groisser, *URBAN 5: An On-Line Urban Design Partner,* and in a paper by the same title
in *Ekistics.*

URBAN5

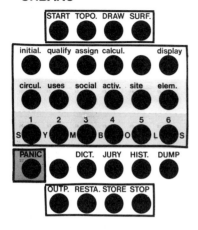

1. URBAN5 system: cathode ray tube, light pen, modes, and keyboard

2. Modes

3. Display of qualifications

4. Consistency mechanism

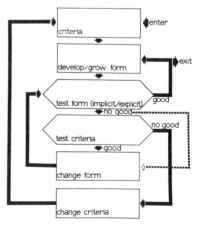

graphical system is exemplary of such abstracting; the geometry selected was the cube, in this case ten-foot cubes. This building block system abridged urban design to such an extent that URBAN5 had to recognize it was only simulating a design environment. The hypothesis was that this graphical abstraction provides a method of simulating the graphics of urban design, furnishes the necessary "frictionless vacuum" environment in which to work, and provides the full range of basic design interrelationships.

This original graphical abstraction, in some cases, has distorted concerns, but the simplification has permitted advances that would have been thwarted by any attempt to furnish the "comprehensive" architect-machine graphical language. Critics have often misunderstood URBAN5's ten-foot cube; it is only a launching vehicle. For example, in Newtonian mechanics, an experiment will commence with the assumed absence of friction. The experimental results bear information relevant only to the abstract problem; if an engine were designed with only such information, it would indeed run badly in the real world. Similarly, URBAN5 cannot handle real design problems; it is a research toy and playing with it has been a learning experience.

The ten-foot cube has few architectural or urban design impositions and has many research conveniences. It generated a language of nouns (the cubes, pointed to be detecting a displayed dot) and verbs (text appearing on the right side of the cathode ray screen). In this vernacular, the designer can pile up these blocks in three dimensions. He can give them qualities and the machine can give them qualities. He can talk about them. He can play with them. But all this occurs within a context, and a context is defined by a *mode*.

Concept of Modes

When the user pushes one or more buttons, shown in Figure 2, which appear to his left, he signals the machine that there will be a major change in context or activity, a change in mode. Associated with each mode is a string of machine-defined or user-defined text (verbs) that appears as a menu of "light buttons" on the right side of the screen. Each mode has its own set of light buttons which denote related operations. The detection of one light button with the light pen will change this menu of words, making endless the potential number of operations per context.

The graphical modes permit the handling of the ground plane, the ten-foot cubes, and their surfaces. TOPO displays a site plan, for example, which appears as a grid of altitudes that the designer can manipulate with his light pen in order to create a warped surface that approximates his topography. DRAW, a separate mode, allows the manipulation of (1) view (orthographic, perspective), (2) viewing plane (scale, rotation, translation), and (3) physical elements (solids, voids, roofs, people, trees, vehicles). In DRAW mode, when two cubes are placed tangent to each other, the adjoining surfaces are automatically removed, thus forming one continuous volume the surface of which is inherently part of an external membrane. Therefore, to further qualify external surfaces or add internal surfaces, the designer must enter a new context, SURFACE mode. In SURFACE mode, any of the six surfaces of the cube can be ascribed one of four characteristics (again abstracted and simplified): solid (defining a major activity boundary), partition (a subdivision of a common usage), transparent, or absent. Each of these surface traits can be assigned with or without the attribute of "access."

The next three rows of buttons are interdependent modes that require multiple button-pushing. The combination of an operation from the first row with a context from the second with a set of symbols from the third yields a mode. At first these modes are primarily empty receptacles for the designer to employ to define his own light buttons. For example, the user may QUALIFY in the context of ACTIVITIES and press symbol button number 1. At this point a cursor will appear on the right of the screen below the last word in the list of light buttons. He can then type a word for future use in some operation; for example, f-o-o-t-b-a-l-l. As soon as he finishes typing "football," a list of "generics" appears on the screen. These generics are a function of the context, in this case ACTIVITIES, and they allow the designer to define his word by detecting the relevant qualifying words. In this example, the generics describe age groups, times of day, noise levels, participation, and other activity characteristics that have a built-in meaning to the machine. Later, this user-made light button can be employed as a verb (footballizing a space) in an operation of ASSIGNMENT or CALCULATION.

Beyond assigning and calculating with symbols, generalized verbs can perform calculations and simulations within some context. For example, in CIRCULATION mode, a designer can have the machine simulate pedestrian travel between two points on the site. An X, the pedestrian, will prance across the screen trying to get from one point to the next, searching for a reasonable or at least feasible path. The machine will report the pedestrian's distance and time of travel or else the impossibility of the trip (through lack of enough elements with access). Similar simulations exist in the context of ELEMENTS for the path of the sun and for growth patterns.

The next row of buttons, the therapeutic ones, are instructional modes which are intended to make the designer-machine interface as conversational and personal as possible, permitting the user to express himself in privacy. The PANIC button, for example, summons instructions on the usage of other modes, directions on how to proceed, and an accounting mechanism that can be interrogated for computer time spent in dollars (often affording cause for greater panic). The therapeutic modes were inconsistently designed. In truth, PANIC should never be depressed for reasons of total distress. In a true dialogue, the machine should sense the designer's panic long before the button is pushed. PANIC, in fact, was erroneously designed as an alarm monologue rather than a teaching dialogue.

The remaining modes, the bottom row of buttons in Figure 2, are primarily procedural ones that act in a janitorial fashion. STORE mode, as an example, permits design studies to reside on either short-term or long-term storage devices, to be given arbitrary names, and to be recalled in a few hundredths of a second (recalled by either name or time of creation).

Within these modes there is no predetermined sequence of usage, there is no presupposed chain of events. URBAN5 has one central "attention" mechanism that either listens to or hears from the designer, always giving him the opportunity to change his mind or restate a situation at any time. However, the reader should notice that the context, which is so important to intelligent behavior, is explicitly stated by the human designer and not, in URBAN5, implicitly discerned by the machine.

Handling of Qualities

URBAN5 handles qualities either explicitly or implicitly. Beyond the traits of solid and void, each ten-foot cube (whether solid or void) has preallocated receptacles for ten characteristics that refer to aspects of: sunlight, outdoor access, visual privacy, acoustical privacy, usability, direct access, climate control, natural light, flexibility, and structural feasibility, all shown at the right in Figure 3. These qualities are implicitly ascribed to elements. In other words, without the user's permission, intervention, or even awareness, URBAN5 automatically assigns the absence or presence of these features using a predefined geometry for each quality. (This geometry can be changed by the user at a later date when he is more familiar with the workings of the system.) This means that when a ten-foot cube is added (making a solid) or removed (making a void), URBAN5 tacitly rearranges local and, if necessary, global characteristics. For example, the addition of an element not only casts shadows on other solids and voids but might obstruct another element's natural light or visual privacy.

Implicit qualities are occasionally reported to the designer (depending on their importance), but in most cases the designer must explicitly interrogate the cube to find its qualitative status. URBAN5 is more prone to divulge implicitly ascribed qualities when the neighboring influences are significant.

Certain characteristics are strongly communicative and their presence is directly transposable to neighboring elements or members of the same space (natural light, acoustical privacy). Other qualifications are less communicative (visual privacy, direct sunlight), and their influence is particularly local and is apt not to be posted.

Explicit qualities are assigned by the designer; they are the symbols that he has previously defined with the context-dependent generics. Each element can carry four symbols within any context. The designer can assign these symbols to a single element or enter a "flooding operation" to fill an entire "use space," defined by solid walls, with the given symbol. For example, a single cube might be part of a set of "school" elements that are at the same time "a place to vote" elements which are still further part of a subset of "eating" and "auditorium" activities. In other words, a multiplicity of explicitly assigned symbols can exist for each cube. These traits are then cross-coupled with the implicit qualities of the space.

It is important to notice that the implicit and explicit assignment of attributes are sequential events. The machine ascribes certain qualities in response to the adding or subtracting of cubes by the user. In effect, it gives an answer, even though it is not explicitly voiced. On the other hand, cross-coupling qualities, relating implicit qualities to explicit qualities is a temporal event. This interaction forms the architect-machine search for consistency and equilibrium, a temporary state of no conflicts and no incompatibilities.

Consistency Mechanisms

URBAN5 searches for two types of consistency. It searches for incompatibilities and conflicts following the flow chart of Figure 4. An "incompatibility" or "error message" is a remark about an incongruity between the designer's action and a predefined requisite imbedded in the machine. An incompatibility can cause the machine to signal the user (by ringing a bell and displaying the message on the top of the screen) but allow the action, or it can cause the machine to refuse to act in cases where the violation is severe. For example, a cube might be placed floating in midair as shown in Figure 5. The machine would indeed draw the cube but simultaneously display the message that it was "not structurally possible at this time." However, if a vertical surface is assigned the attribute of "access" (explicitly by the user) when there is no horizontal surface on one or both sides, URBAN5 refuses to make the qualification and alerts the designer of the problem. Although incompatibilities are simple relationships, their oversight can be embarrassing or disastrous.

A *conflict* is an inconsistency discerned by the machine relating criteria specified by the designer to forms generated by the designer. A conflict is thus generated when there is an inconsistency between what the designer has said and what he has done. To state a constraint, the designer must enter INITIALize mode, describe a context, and push the "speak" button on the typewriter console. At this point he can type a criterion to the machine using the English language.[2] The machine relies heavily upon the context of the designer's activities to interpret the sentence. If it understands, URBAN5 asks, "How important is this criterion?" The designer's reply defines to the machine how frequently it must survey the project in search for consistency between criteria and form. Also, the reply establishes a range of satisfaction for the machine to employ; that is, it governs the relative enforcement of not-so-important constraints and the to-be-strictly-observed ones.

When URBAN5 finds an inconsistency between what has been said (linguistically) and what has been done (graphically), it states that a conflict has occurred, it quotes the designer's statement of criterion, and it displays the present status of the situation. This is illustrated in Figure 6. From here, the designer can take one of four courses: (1) he can change the form to be compatible with the criterion, (2) he can alter the criterion to be compatible with

---

2. URBAN5's English translation system uses a parching routine implemented by Paul Mockapetris during the summer of 1967.

5. Display of incompatibility and error message

6. Display of conflict, criterion, and present status

7. Background activity

8. The man-machine monitor

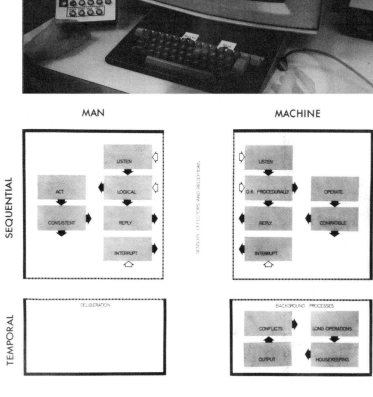

the form (now that he has learned that the issue may not be so important), (3) he can postpone the issue, or (4) he can ignore the conflict (much to the chagrin of URBAN5).

This sort of interplay between form and criteria, designer and machine, begins to suggest a dialogue. The statements of criteria are deliberations on the designer's behalf, issues he feels to be relevant. Discernments of inconsistency are noted temporally during the machine's background work.

Background Activities

Background work is perpetually executed within the machine devoted to service the specific designer. This kind of work did not appear relevant in the beginning of URBAN5. About half way through the system's development, it became clear that URBAN5 had to function in parallel to the user in order to support the growing concern in dialoguing.

While the designer deliberates, URBAN5 engages in five temporal tasks in the following order of priority: (1) it checks for conflicts (as described in the previous section), (2) it does long operations, (3) it takes care of output procedures, (4) it does housekeeping, (5) it plays.

When the designer presses a button, types in a message, or uses the light pen, he is interrupting one of these five operations by demanding the machine's attention elsewhere. As soon as the machine finishes serving him, it returns to the unfinished or newly created background work. This is illustrated in Figure 7.

Long operations are user-requested design tasks that require more than just a few seconds of machine time. To expedite the designer's sequence of actions, URBAN5, when it recognizes a lengthy job, places the operation in the temporal zone to be processed when operationally convenient. The system suggests that the designer continue, and the outcome will be reported later. Naturally, if the operation is critical to a next step (or if the designer is going off for a cup of coffee anyway), he can intervene and demand that the task be undertaken sequentially, thus tying up the machine until completion of the long operation.

Output procedures are specific long operations that take particularly great amounts of computer time due to the slowness of many output devices such as plotters, printers, card punches, and the like. A complex drawing can take three minutes to plot and is accordingly ascribed a low priority.

For example, when URBAN5 is plotting a site plan in the background and the designer interrupts it, the machine stops drawing and tends to the foreground command. After answering the designer, if his command has meanwhile generated a new long operation of higher priority than plotting, URBAN5 starts the new job. Only when it finishes does the machine return to the previously stated site plan.

Housekeeping chores are in the nature of a physical check-up. Leftover memory, messy files, and disorderly data structures are cleaned up. As background work, housekeeping procedures are of low priority until untidiness becomes an ailment that warrants full devotion. Finally, if the house is tidy, the machine can play.

Playing is learning. URBAN5 was never sufficiently sophisticated to actually frolic; instead it bovinely printed garbage.

The Ubiquitous Monitor

Within URBAN5 resides a monitor, a general eavesdropping mechanism that observes the designer's actions, as in Figure 8. The monitor records the rate of interrupts, the sequence of contexts, the time spent per mode, and the relevance of sequential acts. This barrage of statistics not only supplies the designer with a history of his own actions but affords the machine some material from which to gather personal manifestations and innuendoes to be applied later in an attempt at congenially conversing with the designer.

The monitor endeavors to transform a conversation into a dialogue, two monologues into one dialogue. The monitor controls both the temporal zone and the interrupting mechanism; both are functions of what and how the designer is doing. For example, if the designer is interrupting the machine only one or two times per minute, the monitor, knowing the designer's familiarity with the system, presumes that the designer is either deliberating (in which case the monitor might notify the criteria mechanisms to relax and not interrupt the designer's thought), floundering (in which case the monitor attempts to clarify the system's protocol, or devoting his attention elsewhere (in which case the monitor accepts the distraction and continues with its own work). At the other extreme, if the designer is interrupting URBAN5 forty times per minute, the monitor accelerates its own speed. It speeds up the conflict mechanisms and may barrage the designer with statements of inconsistency and incompatibility.

URBAN5's monitor is concerned with context. A designer working in circulation mode does not want to be confused with petty structural problems. A structural consideration must be extremely critical for the monitor to allow its intervention in, for example, the context of circulation. URBAN5's monitor is primarily a timer with the purpose of making the machine's interruptions opportune and in rhythm with the designer's particular design temperament. For example, "the length of delay in a person's response tells his interlocutor (man or machine) information he might otherwise miss. It is information that can be sensed on a nonverbal and nonvisual level."[3] In URBAN5, the monitor is such a nonverbal and nonvisual mechanism. Its implementation is crude. However, its relevance cannot be overstated and must not be understated if evolution is to ensue.

Inklings of Evolution and Adaptability

URBAN5 was designed to be a self-teaching system. At first it was assumed that the user, whether architect or urban designer, would have had no previous programming experience. Later, it was further assumed that he had not even read an instruction manual. Thus URBAN5 would have to teach its own language (learn through teaching, change through learning, and adapt through changing).

URBAN5 greets a designer with only the start button illuminated. When it is depressed, the first question from the machine is whether it is the first time you are using the machine. (The hardware had to be shared in the experiment, and the system could not assume the same users.) If it is indeed your first time, the machine presents an unsolicited page of text that describes how to proceed, how to use the hardware, and what to do when you get stuck. Also, each time you enter a mode for the first time or use an operation for the first time, the monitor automatically calls forth a set of instructions. In each case, as the designer is told, he must reinterrupt the machine with his original request to have the operation actually executed and the text removed.[4]

However, even the text of these instructions might employ a language that is new or unclear to the designer. In this case, the designer may point out an unintelligible word with his light pen, and the machine will display a new paragraph defining that word. The interrogation of word meanings can continue, definition within definition. However, all words are not internally defined; when simple terms are reached, the designer is referred to a dictionary.

The word-learning role works both ways. For example, a designer might state a criterion in the following conversation:

---

3. Warren M. Brodey and Nilo J. Lindgren, "Human Enhancement Through Evolutionary Technology."
4. This interchange is well illustrated in a 16mm movie available through the M.I.T. Department of Architecture.

Designer:
"All studios must have outdoor access."
URBAN5:
"I am sorry I do not understand."
Designer:
"All studios must have access to the outdoors."
URBAN5:
"I am sorry I do not understand."
Designer:
"A one-room residential unit must have outdoor access."
URBAN5:
"Now I understand. Furthermore, from now on, whenever you say studios, I will assume you mean one-room residential units."

At this point, not only is the criterion entered into the general conflict structure, but the new word "studios" is recorded in the translation mechanism that belongs to this particular designer. Another designer would have to undergo a similar session with his machine to define "studios," possibly with another meaning.

When symbols are defined by the designer, they too are registered in his personal machine lexicon. In just these examples of word-building, the designer is beginning to construct his own machine partner out of the aboriginal framework of URBAN5. This transformation occurs in the machine; the user is allowed to penetrate the surface of URBAN5, getting deeper and deeper into its assumptions and definitions. The user can even change algorithms without actually programming in a computer language or knowing where the routine resides.

This pseudoevolution is implemented in the following manner. The virgin system resides on a disk and the user's consciously and subconsciously composed system resides on a magnetic tape. When a designer arrives at the display terminal, he meets a generalized computer system that asks his name. Having identified the designer, URBAN5 automatically dumps the contents of the designer's magnetic tape onto URBAN5's disk; thus overlaying the general system with the personal edition of this designer. At this point, the machine appears to the designer as his particular (possibly evolved) designer partner. At the termination of a design "sitting" the designer's magnetic tape is recreated, incorporating any changes or inklings of evolution, and URBAN5's disk is restored to anonymity.

At the first man-machine encounter, the designer's tape is empty; he converses with the unaborted nucleus of the system. As he converses with the machine more and more frequently, the contents of his tape become more significant. As time passes, URBAN5 in fact shrinks, letting certain operations self-destruct themselves through obsolescence. To allow for the user-created machine, unused procedures are discarded. If the designer requests a procedure that has been previously removed, the system will require some time to fetch the routine from a library and reincorporate it into the system.

In theory, after some time the designer's system would bear little semblance to the original URBAN5. The authors of URBAN5 might not recognize the transformed version. URBAN5 will have nursed the user deeper and deeper into the system, first teaching him, then learning from him, and eventually carrying on a dialogue with him. The progression that URBAN5 suggests is one which proceeds from a *rigid* system (for the designer to easily understand), to a *flexible* system (volatile enough to allow different tacks), to an *adaptable* system (where the machine loses flexibility but gains adaptability through evolution). In other words, URBAN5 suggests a true dialogue, suggests an evolutionary system, suggests an intelligent system, but in itself is none of these.

11 Computer-Aided Design Systems

Comments on the papers by Heath, Moran, Logcher; Porter, Lloyd, and Fleisher; and Negroponte and Groisser.

A. Michael Noll

Bell Telephone Laboratories
Murray Hill, New Jersey

A. Michael Noll is on the research staff of the Bell Telephone Laboratories, where he has developed computer-aided systems in the visual and performing arts. He holds degrees in mathematics and electrical engineering and presently is completing his doctoral dissertation in electrical engineering at the Polytechnic Institute of Brooklyn. He has written several papers on man–machine systems

To many people, computers seem to be ever increasing their control over decisions and tasks formerly performed by man and thereby in effect enslaving man, their creator. But to many other people the computer is only another manifestation of the progress of technology, with its capability of freeing man from drudgery and thereby extending his intellectual powers. The actual role of the computer in our society, whether it should be cursed or blessed, will probably never be adequately settled for many people just as there are still those who longingly look back to the supposed simplicity of the days before the atomic age or even the machine age. However, technological progress, be it to the ultimate good or ultimate destruction of man, apparently cannot be stopped without even more assuredly destroying man or his insatiable curiosity.

The articles in this section of the book all pertain to the use of computers in design and to a lesser extent in planning. Although there is wide disparity among the authors as to the exact roles and tasks to assign the computer, there is complete agreement that the computer is of considerable assistance to the designer. Since this tacit assumption is unchallenged by any of the authors, as a word of warning about the potential dangers of giving too much control to the machine, the reader is referred to the writings of the father of cybernetics, Norbert Wiener.[1]

Digital computers are electronic devices that are capable of performing a prearranged or programmed set of mathematical operations. By coding information as a series of bits, they are able to store and fetch large quantities of facts and figures and manipulate this data with astonishing speed and accuracy. Thus the computer is a vast information source coupled with the capability of almost instantaneously manipulating or displaying this information in a form easily assimilated by man. The simple fact that the computer must be programmed by a set of instructions forces the design process into an algorithmic procedure which might be programmed. In their articles, Heath and Moran have explored the degree to which the design process can be considered algorithmical and have dealt with the constraints thereby imposed.

Structural engineering involves lengthy calculations for which the great calculating power of the computer is most appropriate. In this manner the computer allows the structural designer to investigate and evaluate many alternative structural designs. The programming language STRUDL in the structural-design system described by Logcher has deliberately and painstakingly been designed so that computer expertise is not required to use it.

The vast potentialities of the computer's data storage capabilities are particularly applicable to urban planning problems as described in the article by Porter, Lloyd, and Fleisher. Although the computer can store and manipulate vast quantities of information, man is able to grasp the interrelationships and significance of only a few pieces of information. The efficiency of such cognition is strongly dependent upon the methods used to display and present the pieces. Computer-generated displays with possibilities for interaction on the part of the designer are of considerable use here, although the actual efficiency of different means of data presentation have not yet been thoroughly studied in a truly scientific manner.

An extremely sophisticated computer graphics system with interactive facilities formed the basis of URBAN5 as described by Negroponte and Groisser. In my opinion, this system touches upon the truly creative aspects of urban design, and although it might have become something of a toy, URBAN5 and its descendants probably represent the prime direction of future research into computer-aided design. As has been suggested for art, the designs of the future might well be arrived at through a creative partnership between man and machine.[2]

A workshop and discussion period on computer-aided design systems was held at the Design Methods Group Conference. Some interesting concepts and questions arose both from the panel and from the audience, and the remainder of my comment is a summary of this workshop.[3]

The first question from the audience immediately touched upon a particular point which usually comes up at the end of most discussions, namely, will the designer or planner have to become a computer programmer in order to use the machine to help him solve environmental problems? The panel answered the question by pointing out that special-purpose programming languages were available or were being developed for architectural design and planning problems. These languages could be particularly suited to the terminology of their users or might even be similar to conversational English. However, some panelists felt that conversational English would be difficult

1. Norbert Wiener, *Cybernetics: Or Control and Communication in the Animal and The Machine.*
2. A. Michael Noll, ''The Digital Computer As A Creative Medium.''
3. The members of the panel included John Boorn, Aaron Fleisher, Leon Groisser, Thomas Heath, Alan Hershdorfer, Katherine Lloyd, Nicholas Negroponte, William Porter, and A. Michael Noll as Chairman.

to implement because of our present lack of knowledge about context and other grammatical problems. Although some people thought that the particular programming language was not important, there was general agreement that the language would impose constraints upon the user and that these constraints would dictate the available possibilities. Thus, the user must decide what service or function he desires from the computer and use the most appropriate language. That the architect will not become a programmer was a general conclusion of the panel although many of the panelists were themselves architects turned programmers! What I think will happen here is that the early research into computer-aided design will be done by architects with a programming background (or programmers with an architectural background), and the computer-aided design systems that result will be used by people with no programming knowledge. It is all too easy to forget that DISCOURSE, URBAN5, and most other computer-aided design systems are really still in the research stage and therefore have many undesirable traits that will be removed in due time. This conclusion is augmented by the fact that these systems have not yet been used on a practical design project. However, such purely mathematical problems as determining stress are being solved in many architectural and engineering firms with the widely-distributed programming package STRESS.

It was felt that the computer-aided design system should adapt itself to the user. For example, the cute messages to the user of URBAN5 would become annoying if one were to use the system for any long time. Obviously, programs which "learn" the requirements and idiosyncrasies of the user and modify the program accordingly are required, but research into such self-adaptive programs is presently only in its earliest stages.

A point that arose from the concept of programming languages which would be easy to use was that the people to be affected by city planning and architectural environments could be given the opportunity for a stronger role and perhaps even the opportunity to do some of the designing themselves. Although the architect would still have to direct the overall strategy, the resultant design would probably be more readily accepted by the people most affected. However, all of this would imply efficient communication channels between the community and the designer or computer, but it nevertheless is an interesting concept.

The closing discussion centered around the working architect or planner who needs something now. This nicely brought things back to the question of what is available in special-purpose languages and can the designer who is not a programmer use them. Much of the work in computer-aided design is certainly "researchy" in nature. There are many unsolved problems requiring extensive research, and much "icing" needs to be added before these systems will be available to every architect in any size firm and to every planning agency. But, then again this was a research conference, and although it is important for the practitioner to be aware of current research, he will have to be patient until the results of the research are generally available. However, he is most certainly welcome to join the research bandwagon if he is really that impatient.

4 Identification of Problem Structure

One of the first tasks confronting the design or planning team is the transformation of a vaguely defined area of concern into a clearly articulated problem. Because of the complexity of problems and the desire to formulate them in ways which will not bias their final solution, methods have been suggested for objectively identifying their underlying structure. One method was suggested by Alexander who proposed the identification of misfits between function and form in the present environment and from misfits the derivation of requirements that any new solution must satisfy. By identifying the relationships between the various requirements, the overall problem, perhaps unmanageably large, would be structured so that relatively independent subproblems could be solved one at a time and their solutions combined. Alexander and Manheim developed several computer programs which would decompose the network of relationships between requirements into subproblems and which would define the hierarchical order in which solutions would be combined.

For those not familiar with the method, Charles Owen in his paper in this section gives an intuitive introduction to the theory of decomposition and introduces the necessary graph-theoretic definitions, notation, and basic concepts. More detailed treatments are listed in the bibliography.

The papers in this section present new techniques and computer programs for the identification of problem structure.

Charles Davis and Michael Kennedy suggest a method for structuring problems based on analysis of the relative influences between subproblems. They describe a computer program, EPS, which analyzes and structures these influences. Contrasted to the early programs of Alexander and Manheim, which could only operate on binary information, EPS allows four weights of relationship between requirements.

Murray Milne describes a program, CLUSTR, which structures problems on the basis of identifying most highly interconnected subproblems and groups of subproblems. In addition, his efforts have led to a more-nearly-conversational input-output format and man-machine interaction. Milne also suggests a new technique, a multilayered input matrix, which would allow the designer to specify to the computer additional information about the problem.

Owen proposes an additional new method. The relative importance of requirements is determined by a computer program, DCMPOS, from an analysis of interrelations with other requirements, and a mathematical scanning device selects and structures clusters of requirements. The algorithm is described in detail. Charles Kowal in closing the section reviews the papers and points out some limitations.

Other programs, not reviewed in this volume, have been developed by Bierstone and Bernholtz, Frew, and by Brams. Whereas Alexander and Manheim's early programs left the designer with a certain amount of hand calculations, Bierstone and Bernholtz's was the first to provide automatically an overall structure to problems. Brams's program is the only one which operates on the specification of the direction of relationships. He demonstrates an interesting application to international affairs.

The best application of these methods to environmental problems is a case study done by Koenig et al. on educational facilities for visually handicapped children. His group also executed revisions to parts of the underlying theory.

12 EPS: **A Computer Program for the Evaluation of Problem Structure**

Charles F. Davis and
Michael D. Kennedy

School of Architecture
University of Kentucky
Lexington, Kentucky

Charles F. Davis is Assistant Professor of
Architecture at the University of Kentucky
and a partner in Davis, Kennedy Consul-
tants, a firm applying computers to environmental problems. He received a
B.Arch. from Auburn University in 1962
and an M.Arch. from M.I.T. in 1966. He
has worked for architectural and planning
firms and as a research associate for the
Kentucky Department of Highways.
Michael D. Kennedy is also an Assistant
Professor of Architecture and Assistant
to the Dean of the University of Kentucky
School of Architecture. He received a
B.S. in engineering physics from the
University of Tennessee in 1963, and has
worked primarily in computer science.

This paper represents an attempt to re-
examine what it means to solve a design
or planning problem. One paradigm calls
for analysis leading to an explicit formulation of the problem in terms of misfits or
requirements. The problem is represented
as a linear graph, the nodes representing
the requirements and the links between
nodes representing some form of inter-
connection between pairs of requirements. Programming efforts to decompose linear graphs into manageable
subproblems have all assumed that final
problem solution was the synthesis of
the solutions to the smaller subproblems.

An alternative approach is suggested.
This approach deals at first with subsets
of requirements which tend to influence
a solution to a greater extent than do
others. A measure of the influence is the
structural distance and number of paths
between any two requirements. Present
procedures admit four weights of link
between nodes. From such a representation the degree of connection between all
pairs of nodes is determined and the linkage values rescaled. The resultant linear
graph is then decomposed into subsets.
Each cycle admits links of value equal to
or greater than a computed threshold,
thus producing a path through the problem which coincides with a movement
from gross to fine tuning.

EPS is a computer program for the evaluation of problem structure. It processes a problem formulated as a network or linear graph, consisting of
vertexes or nodes and nondirected links connecting specific pairs of vertexes. The vertexes represent requirements or criteria of the problem, and
the links represent the existence of explicit relationships between pairs of
criteria. It is understood that the criteria are (1) equal in scope or significance,
(2) specific and detailed, and (3) as independent as possible. An explicit
relationship is a causal relationship, that is, a relationship exists if the form
responses of the two criteria are either in conflict or coincidence. A problem
is defined and structured by analysis of the interrelationships between
criteria.[1]

Of the several types of computer programs presently available for accomplishing this task, the first set, HIDECS, by Alexander and Manheim[2] decom-

---

1. See Serge Chermayeff and Christopher Alexander, *Community and Privacy: Toward
a New Architecture of Humanism*; and especially Alexander, *Notes on the Synthesis
of Form*.
2. Christopher Alexander and Marvin L. Manheim, *HIDECS 2: A Computer Program for
the Hierarchical Decomposition of a Set with an Associated Linear Graph*; and Alexander, *HIDECS 3: Four Computer Programs for the Hierarchical Decomposition of
Systems Which Have an Associated Linear Graph*.

poses the problem hierarchically into subsets of related requirements, either as a tree of disjoint subsets, or as a semilattice which allows overlap of subsets. In the HIDECS–RECOMP program by Bierstone and Bernholtz, the hierarchic semilattice structure is retained.[3] The differences between the tree and semilattice structures are shown in Figure 1.

The nature of urban systems more closely parallels the semilattice structure than the tree. In the lowest level of both, the subsets are relatively undifferentiated in the degree to which they may affect the final form. This is also true of the requirements. In the design process associated with these two decomposition structures the designer begins at the lowest level and is free to concentrate over time on each subset of requirements and develop formal solutions to each. Often these partial solutions are represented by diagrams. It is after the decomposition procedure then that the designer's real task begins. He must now bring the partial solutions together. When he encounters conflicts between these solutions he may work with all the requirements involved at the point of conflict as if they constituted a subproblem. This procedure may be possible at the lowest structural levels. At the higher levels it may become impossibly complex. Alternatively the designer may go back to the lower level and re-solve the individual subproblems. However, in this instance, he may only discover that a new set of misfits has sprung up between two of the conflicting subsolutions. A reduction in the arbitrariness and difficulty of organizing a total solution has been achieved through a reduction in the number of elements to be organized at any one point in time. However, the complexity of the elements has been increased substantially; *they* are now the subproblems. Adjustment remains difficult.

An Alternative Approach

In response, one wonders if it is not possible to determine what are those parts of the problem which have the most far-reaching implications within the problem structure. Let us call these the dominant sets of attributes. As an example of what a dominant set of attributes might be, consider the design of an office building. Often the amount of space required per floor, the optimum dimensions of that space, the total space required, and the vertical transportation requirements as a set have more to do with the organization of an office building than many other equally important requirements or criteria. This is true because many other attributes of the form vary directly with respect to this set. When this is the case these criteria may be said to constitute a dominant set of attributes.

If it should be possible to determine these sets, the designer could concentrate on them in the early stages of design. He would be assured that he is dealing with those elements that potentially could transform the problem into a state of rough adjustment. Subsequently, if successively less far-reaching sets of criteria and links were added, the designer would be able to achieve some close tolerance of adjustment through iteration of the design process. The output of each level would be one diagram of the partial solution to the total problem. The diagram would respond to those requirements with which the designer or designers had dealt. Figure 2 may make this more clear.

Such a process is analogous to tuning a television set. One first tunes the set to the approximate channel location and then makes fine tuning adjustments. One could reverse the process or tune the set using the fine tuner exclusively but at the expense of unnecessary time and effort.

Development of EPS

The underlying assumptions in the development of EPS were (1) that determining a path through a problem which enables a sequence of progressively finer tunings was both possible and desirable; and (2) that such a path would minimize backtracking. In attempting to determine a path through the problem which coincides with the movement from gross adjustments to fine tuning, two major questions needed answers: what constitutes sets of dominant attributes and how are they to be recognized? Dominant sets have

---

3. Edward Bierstone and Allen Bernholtz, *HIDECS-RECOMP Procedure.*

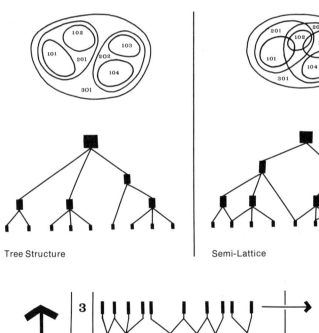

1. Comparison of tree and semi-lattice structures

2. Illustration of successive refinement in a design process

Tree Structure   Semi-Lattice

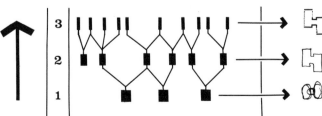

Design Process   Design Output

3. Linear graph showing various connections between *A* and *B*

4. A linear graph representing a problem

5. Two examples of conductance between nodes *A* and *C*

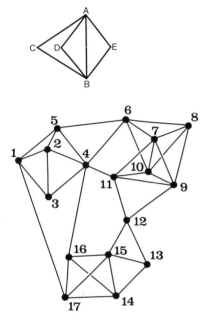

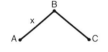

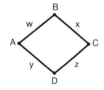

been defined as those parts of the problem which have the most far-reaching implications within the problem structure. The individual requirements of the problem affect the solution to an equal degree. On this basis they are equal. However, it does not follow that the same is true for pairs of requirements. The set consisting of requirements A, B, and link L_{AB} is not necessarily equal in value to the set C, D, L_{CD}. The value of the pairs is not equal to the sum of their values. The value of a pair depends upon the relationship between the elements.

The original question is now transformed into: what determines the degree to which a pair of requirements (vertexes) affects the problem structure (the graph), and how does one measure it?

Let us analyze this question first graphically and then mathematically. Consider Figure 3. Which pair plays a dominant role? Observe that nodes C, D, and E vary directly with respect to the pair A, B. Now consider A, C: B alone varies directly with this pair. Any other vertex, say D, varies with respect to this pair, directly to A and indirectly to C through B. Elements D and E are one link more removed from C than B. Hence, it may be said that the pair A, B are a dominant attribute. This means that if in an attempted solution A and B as a pair are not correctly solved, then the solution to requirements C, D, and E is most probably out of adjustment.

It should now be clear that (1) the weight of a pair of requirements depends on its position within the graph, and (2) what should be measured is the degree to which a pair of vertexes is related to the other vertexes. Thus, a link should be weighted according to the degree of interconnectedness of its end vertexes. In fact, it matters little whether a pair of vertexes is explicitly connected or not. Even in Figure 3, A and B had not been stated by the designer to be related, one could see that they were in fact closely related since A varies with respect to B through three other vertexes. Such indirect relationships may be termed implicit links.

More generally notice in Figure 4, representing a problem structure as a linear graph, that each node is connected to every other node by means of a number of paths. A change at any one node will theoretically effect changes throughout the graph. The mathematical problem is how to measure the relationship between nodes not explicitly connected. There are two principles which a mathematical model would have to recognize: (1) the greater the distance (linkwise) between nodes the weaker the relationship, (2) the greater the number of paths connecting two nodes the stronger the relationship.

The solution lies in an analogy between an electrical circuit and the linear graph of a problem. If one had a voltmeter and a set of nodes connected by conductors he could apply a voltage at one node and then measure the voltage drop at every other node to determine the conductance. Even though two nodes are not connected directly, there would be a flow of current between them. In an analogous manner information flows throughout the linear graph. Consider the two circuits in Figure 5, with conductances *w*, *x*, *y*, and *z*.

On the left of Figure 5 the conductance between A and C is given by the formula

$$C_{ac} = \frac{1}{\dfrac{1}{x} + \dfrac{1}{y}}$$

because A, B, C, are in series. On the right, the conductance between A and C is given by the formula

$$C_{ac} = \frac{1}{\dfrac{1}{w} + \dfrac{1}{x}} + \frac{1}{\dfrac{1}{x} + \dfrac{1}{z}}$$

because A is connected to C through two circuits in parallel consisting of A, B, C in series and A, D, C in series.

The appropriateness of this analogy may be open to debate. It does, however, produce useful results and some beneficial by-products. It gives us the basis on which to determine the dominant sets of attributes. The higher the conductance between nodes, the greater the total connection between them and, therefore, the more the pair affects the total structure of the problems. By setting appropriate thresholds we can decompose the graph using a one-step decomposition program a number of times.[4] At each pass the threshold is lowered and more pairs are considered, until at the final level all pairs that meet the minimum threshold of acceptability are considered. A secondary benefit is that it is possible for the designer to evaluate his problem description by analyzing the changes in linkage value that were made. Direct relationships that were omitted may be added before decomposition is accomplished. Another benefit is that the technique allows the designer to specify weights of links on the basis of the strength of the correlations of the variation of the two end nodes. For example, given three criteria for an office building, A the number of elevators, B height of the building, and C number of cars parked, criteria A and B would have a higher degree of connectedness than B and C, or A and C. Finally, it is possible to relate the decomposition technique to statistical methods such as correlation matrixes, factor analysis, and regression analysis. This potential opens up avenues for the statistical derivation of many of the linkage values between pairs of requirements.

Space does not allow us at this point to explain in detail how EPS works. Such information is available in the program documentation.[5] In closing let me reiterate the two principles I have presented.
1. It is possible to improve our present abilities to deal with complex problems, through a process which allows the designer to bring into rough adjustment the most significant aspects of the problem before proceeding to deal with the lesser ones.
2. An electric circuit, used as a model of the linear graph, gives an accurate assessment of the more significant aspects of the problem.

---

4. Charles F. Davis, *EVAPROBST3*.
5. Charles Davis and Michael Kennedy, *EPS: Program Documentation*.

13 CLUSTER: A Structure-Finding Algorithm

Murray Milne

Department of Architecture
Yale University
New Haven, Connecticut

Murray Milne is currently Associate Professor of Architecture at the University of California, Los Angeles. At the time this paper was written he was on the faculty at Yale University. He received a B.S. and an M.S. in industrial engineering from the University of Michigan in 1959 and 1961 and an M.Arch. from the University of California, Berkeley, in 1965. He was employed in the Behavioral Science Group at North American Aviation and has also taught at the University of Oregon. He is the editor of *Computer Graphics in Architecture and Design*.

CLUSTER is a computer program mainly intended for teaching problem-solving in environmental design. CLUSTER identifies all perfectly interconnected subsets in any network of design or planning elements and combines them into tightly interconnected subproblems. It gives information about decomposition and recomposition. The advantages of CLUSTER over previous linear graph programs are: (1) It is capable of uncovering the semilattice structure of problems, that is, the structure in which elements appear in more than one subproblem. (2) It is deterministic and consistent in that it will produce repeatable results and will not require random numbers or probabilistic thresholds. (3) It is capable of a more-nearly-conversational mode input, output, and on-line interaction. (4) The conjunctive elements are identified at every step in the recomposition. (5) With the help of a multilayered matrix, CLUSTER will utilize more of the information that is available during the interaction phase. (6) Finally, CLUSTER is compatible as far as possible with all other similar programs and may be segmented so that parts can be coupled with other programs.

The design process is a complex and fascinating thing. In spite of its inexactitude, it is capable of yielding valid and highly sophisticated results. When an architect or urban planner attacks a problem using what might be called an intuitive design process, he is never explicitly aware of the total structure of his problem. He proceeds toward a solution by evaluating or comparing his present position in the problem domain according to a set of goals or desired conditions (which are usually not explicitly stated and which occasionally change over time). The differences that he detects give him information about how the design should be modified. This process repeats in a step-by-step linear way until the designer can detect no significant differences between his current goals and his present position in the problem domain, or until he is obliged to terminate prematurely under the pressure of a deadline.

Because of the limited capacity of the human's immediate memory, the designer is forced to approximate the structure within the problem domain as a recursive incremental linear system.[1] He can deal with only a small amount of additional information at each step in the process. Unfortunately, in a de-

1. See George A. Miller, "The Magic Number Seven, Plus or Minus Two," and Murray Milne, "The Design Process."

cision-making process of this type, the designer will occasionally forget information, or will make incorrect decisions, or will find himself caught in an infinite loop, repeating the same series of steps over and over.

At the beginning of a design problem the designer should be able to articulate the goals or requirements or intended modes of behavior which an acceptable design solution must accommodate. Whatever form they take, they become the elements of his problem. The designer can also decide which of these elements interact with one another, that is, whether or not the solution of one element will effect the solution of another element. This matrix of elements, some of which are linked, can be conceived of as a three-dimensional network, a model of the design problem mapped into the problem space.

It would seem reasonable that if the networklike structure of a design problem could be made visible, the designer should be able to see decision-making strategies which are more efficient and perhaps more reliable than the less systematic intuitive design process. This assumption might not hold in cases where the goals of the design problem can be met by an existing prototypical solution. In this case the designer's task is to compare the problem elements with the relevant existing prototypes. Here an intuitive decision-making strategy might succeed in identifying an adequate solution in less time than a more rigorous systematic method.

In theory the most challenging and meaningful design problem is one which contains a number of elements which are tightly interconnected with each other.[2] In this case the solution of one element will have an effect on the solutions to all the other elements with which it interacts. On the other hand, the solution of one element will have little or no direct effect on the solution to other elements with which it does not interact. Therefore, within the network of problem elements it would be desirable to identify all the most highly interconnected subsets or subproblems.

A *simplex* is a set of elements, each of which interacts with all others. Admittedly, some of the most meaningful design problems, although highly interconnected, may not be perfect simplexes. However, it can be shown that a subset of this type is in fact made up of two or more simplexes.

CLUSTER is a computer program which first identifies all the simplexes in the network of problem elements and then selects and combines the appropriate simplexes in order to produce the most highly interconnected subsets.[3] These combined subsets can be seen as growing from clusters of simplexes.

A number of computer programs have previously been written for particular application to this aspect of environmental design.[4] Although CLUSTER is a new program incorporating many unique features, it can be thought of as a second generation descendant of these earlier programs.

Input Format

To demonstrate CLUSTER, data have been reanalyzed from a small project done by former students at the University of Oregon. The problem dealt with the design of study carrels for university libraries. There were only eighteen design elements or requirements in this project, although CLUSTER is now able to handle up to one hundred elements. The example requirement list is shown in Figure 1.

In order to make CLUSTER compatible with previously developed algorithms, the interaction matrix is input in the same format as that used in the HIDEC

---

2. Christopher Alexander, *Notes on the Synthesis of Form.*
3. CLUSTER is written in FORTRAN IV and is presently operational on Yale's IBM 7040-7094 DCS and 360 CYTOS Interactive System for use with a standard IBM 2741 typewriter terminal.
4. See Christopher Alexander and Marvin L. Manheim, *HIDECS 2,* and Alexander, *HIDECS 3;* and Edward Bierstone and Allen Bernholtz, *HIDECS-RECOMP Procedure.*

series of programs. A number of options are available as to the types of information the program computes and prints out. The user can select any of these options by simply inserting any of the commands of Figure 2, in plain English, in the front of the data deck or by typing them in if he is using an on-line terminal.

Because the program requires a symmetrical matrix, all initially one-way interactions will be made two-way unless the program is instructed to drop them out.

Decomposition Strategy: Simplex Subsets

The program contains an algorithm which finds all of the simplexes in a symmetrical binary matrix.[5] The program is instructed to establish the minimum allowable number of elements in a simplex as any number equal to three or greater. A given element may appear in more than one simplex. The program will also identify any elements which are not contained in at least one simplex, if this condition exists. Simplex information is output as shown in Figure 3.

Recomposition Strategy: Coherency

The program then finds the coherency between all subsets (i.e., simplexes and/or clusters) according to an empirical formula, currently established as the following:

$$C_{ij} = \frac{NM}{NT^2 - NT}$$

NM = twice the actual number of links between all elements in the inclusive disjunction of subset i and subset j.
NT = actual number of elements in disjunction of subset i and subset j.
$NT^2 - NT$ = twice the maximum theoretical number of links in the disjunction of subset i and subset j.

The program computes and prints out, if desired, a table of all coherency factors. It then searches this table to find the highest coherency value. It identifies the two subsets involved, combines them into one subset, and gives this new subset an identification number. The two old subsets are removed from the table, the new subset is added in, and coherency values are recomputed for this new list of subsets. This process repeats until one final set remains. This output is shown in Figure 4.

Although the recombination strategy may resemble a binary tree in its form, it is in fact a semilattice because many elements are common to more than one of the original simplexes, and therefore overlap is built in automatically at every level as shown in Figure 5.[6] In fact, the pair of subsets which have the greatest amount of overlap should have the highest coherency factor.

Conversational Mode Output

CLUSTER prints out all subset information in plain English thus avoiding the time-consuming task of translating the element numbers into their written statements. This function is performed by a subprogram called TEXT. It is intended that all relevant information about the structure and content of any simplex or cluster will be contained on one print-out sheet as shown in Figure 6 and that the designer can use this as a work sheet to record his notes, conclusions, and a description of the solution.

Content Analysis: Conjunctive Elements

At every point where two subproblems are combined, the program prints out the design elements contained in every subproblem below this point. These are called the *conjunctive elements* because they are contained in the conjunction of all the inferior subsets. Figure 6 shows the elements in Subset 1001 which are conjunctive to Subsets 16 and 17.

5. In network analysis this type of matrix is also known as an undirected adjacency or vertex graph. A simplex is a subset, all of whose elements are linked (interact) with each other; it is also known as a complete graph in network analysis or a universal graph in graph theory. See Robert G. Busacker and Thomas L. Saaty, *Finite Graphs and Their Networks*; or Oystein Ore, *Graphs and Their Uses*.
6. For a discussion of the relevance of semilattice structures to environmental design see Christopher Alexander, "The City is Not a Tree."

```
001 STUDENT LIKES TO LEAN ON WORK SURFACE
002 STUDENT LIKES TO SPREAD OUT MATERIALS WITHIN REACH AND VIEW
003 REORGANIZATION OF MATERIALS IS AN UNDESIRABLE DISRUPTION
      OF STUDY
004 STUDENT LIKES TO KNOW HIS MATERIALS ARE SECURE IN HIS ABSENCE
005 STUDENT LIKES ADEQUATE BOOK STORAGE WITHIN REACH AND VIEW
006 STUDENT LIKES A PLACE TO ACCUMULATE SMALL ITEMS
007 STUDENT LIKES ORGANIZED STORAGE OF LOOSE LEAF MATERIALS
008 STUDY PROCESS GENERATES WASTE
009 BULK STORAGE NEEDED FOR SPECIAL STUDY EQUIPMENT
010 STUDENT SOMETIMES USES A TYPEWRITER
011 A VARIETY OF COMFORTABLE POSITIONS IS NECESSARY FOR WRITING,
      TYPING, RELAXED READING
012 STUDENT LIKES TO COME AND GO AT WILL
013 STUDENT LIKES A CONTROLLED VISUAL CONTACT WITH AN INTERESTING
      EXTERNAL ENVIRONMENT
014 STUDENT LIKES THE OPTION OF VISUAL PRIVACY
015 PERSONAL CONTROL OF AUDITORY ENVIRONMENT IS ESSENTIAL
016 STUDENT WOULD LIKE TO MODIFY TEMPERATURE AND AIR MOVEMENT
017 FEELING OF CONFINEMENT IS UNDESIRABLE
018 STUDENT SHOULD HAVE THE OPTION OF CONTROLLING ILLUMINATION
```

```
ELIMINATE ONE WAY LINKS
PRINT FIRST COHERENCE TABLE ONLY
PRINT ONE WAY INTERACTIONS
PUNCH SYMMETRICAL MATRIX
PRINT DEBUGGING INFO
PUNCH CONJUNCTIVE ELEMENTS
PUNCH SIMPLEXES
PRINT MATRIX
PRINT ALL COHERENCE FACTORS
PRINT ANALYSIS OF SUBSET STRUCTURE
```

```
THE SIMPLEX LIST

        THE FIRST NUMBER IDENTIFIES THE SIMPLEX,

SECOND GIVES NO. OF ELEMENTS IN THAT SIMPLEX

SIMPLEX (  1,  7) =    1   2   3   5  10  11  18
SIMPLEX (  2,  5) =    2   3   5   6   7  10
SIMPLEX (  3,  6) =    2   3   5   6  10  18
SIMPLEX (  4,  5) =    2   5   7  10  17
SIMPLEX (  5,  6) =    2   5  10  11  17  18
SIMPLEX (  6,  5) =    3   4   5   6   7
SIMPLEX (  7,  3) =    3   4   9
SIMPLEX (  8,  4) =    3   4  12  14
SIMPLEX (  9,  4) =    3   4  13  14
SIMPLEX ( 10,  5) =    3   6   7   8  10
SIMPLEX ( 11,  3) =    3   9  10
SIMPLEX ( 12,  5) =    3  10  11  13  18
SIMPLEX ( 13,  2) =    3  11  13  14  18
SIMPLEX ( 14,  4) =    3  12  14  18
SIMPLEX ( 15,  3) =    9  10  17
SIMPLEX ( 16,  7) =   10  11  13  15  16  17  18
SIMPLEX ( 17,  7) =   11  13  14  15  16  17  18
SIMPLEX ( 18,  5) =   12  14  15  17  18
```

1. Eighteen requirements for the design
of a study carrel

2. User input-output options

3. Output from a SIMPLEX decomposition

ADD SUBSET   17 TO SUBSET   16 AND CALL THE RESULTING SUBSET 1001
          THE CONJUNCTIVE ELEMENTS ARE   11 13 15 16 17 18

ADD SUBSET   3 TO SUBSET   2 AND CALL THE RESULTING SUBSET 1002
          THE CONJUNCTIVE ELEMENTS ARE   2   3   5   6 10

ADD SUBSET   13 TO SUBSET   12 AND CALL THE RESULTING SUBSET 1003
          THE CONJUNCTIVE ELEMENTS ARE   3 11 13 18

ADD SUBSET   5 TO SUBSET   1 AND CALL THE RESULTING SUBSET 1004
          THE CONJUNCTIVE ELEMENTS ARE   2   5 10 11 18

ADD SUBSET   4 TO SUBSET   8 AND CALL THE RESULTING SUBSET 1005
          THE CONJUNCTIVE ELEMENTS ARE   3   4 14

ADD SUBSET   4 TO SUBSET 1002 AND CALL THE RESULTING SUBSET 2001
          THE CONJUNCTIVE ELEMENTS ARE   2   5 10

ADD SUBSET 1001 TO SUBSET 1003 AND CALL THE RESULTING SUBSET 2002
          THE CONJUNCTIVE ELEMENTS ARE   11 13 18

ADD SUBSET   14 TO SUBSET 1005 AND CALL THE RESULTING SUBSET 2003
          THE CONJUNCTIVE ELEMENTS ARE   3 14

ADD SUBSET   15 TO SUBSET   6 AND CALL THE RESULTING SUBSET 1006
          THE CONJUNCTIVE ELEMENTS ARE   3   6   7

ADD SUBSET   11 TO SUBSET   7 AND CALL THE RESULTING SUBSET 1007
          THE CONJUNCTIVE ELEMENTS ARE   3   9

ADD SUBSET 2001 TO SUBSET 1004 AND CALL THE RESULTING SUBSET 3001
          THE CONJUNCTIVE ELEMENTS ARE   2   5 10

ADD SUBSET   13 TO SUBSET 2002 AND CALL THE RESULTING SUBSET 3002
          THE CONJUNCTIVE ELEMENTS ARE   18

ADD SUBSET 1007 TO SUBSET 1006 AND CALL THE RESULTING SUBSET 2004
          THE CONJUNCTIVE ELEMENTS ARE   3

ADD SUBSET 3002 TO SUBSET 2003 AND CALL THE RESULTING SUBSET 4001
          THERE ARE NO CONJUNCTIVE ELEMENTS

ADD SUBSET   15 TO SUBSET 3001 AND CALL THE RESULTING SUBSET 4002
          THE CONJUNCTIVE ELEMENTS ARE   10

ADD SUBSET 2004 TO SUBSET 4002 AND CALL THE RESULTING SUBSET 5001
          THERE ARE NO CONJUNCTIVE ELEMENTS

ADD SUBSET 4001 TO SUBSET 5001 AND CALL THE RESULTING SUBSET 6001
          THERE ARE NO CONJUNCTIVE ELEMENTS

4. Output from recomposition strategy

5. Recomposition semilattice hierarchy

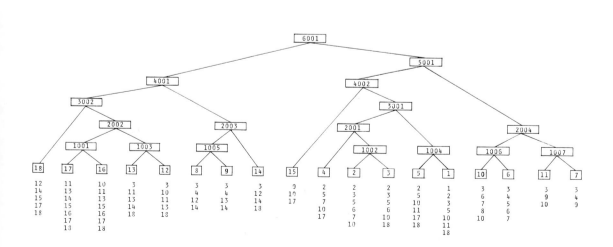

THESE ELEMENTS ARE CONJUNCTIVE TO BOTH SUBSET   16 AND SUBSET   17

11 A VARIETY OF COMFORTABLE POSITIONS IS NECESSARY FOR WRITING, TYPING, RELAXED READING

13 STUDENT LIKES A CONTROLLED VISUAL CONTACT WITH AN INTERESTING EXTERNAL ENVIRONMENT

15 PERSONAL CONTROL OF AUDITORY ENVIRONMENT IS ESSENTIAL

16 STUDENT WOULD LIKE TO MODIFY TEMPERATURE AND AIR MOVEMENT

17 FEELING OF CONFINEMENT IS UNDESIRABLE

18 STUDENT SHOULD HAVE THE OPTION OF CONTROLLING ILLUMINATION

6. Conjunctive elements

7. Conjunctive elements as an organizing principle

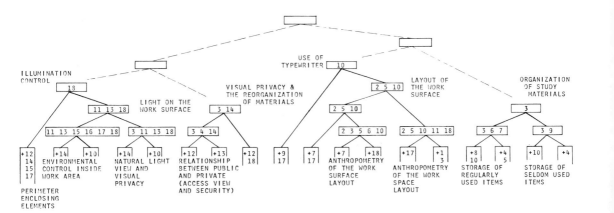

These conjunctive elements give the designer a valuable clue as to the main organizing principle that binds the subproblems together. Figure 7 shows how the conjunctive elements might be interpreted by the designer at each point in the recombination structure for the example of study carrels. Thus the designer can scan up and down the recomposition structure, reading the conjunctive elements, and can stop at the point at which the informational content of the conjunctive elements represents the most meaningful design problem. If he can solve this problem, he need only check the solution against every subproblem below this point, and he can then begin to combine this solution with the appropriate clusters above this point. This is a great time-saver because it means that the designer will not have to solve all the first level subproblems but can concentrate on only the most meaningful clusters, many of which will be found higher up the recomposition structure.

Future Development:
Multilayered Matrix

The process of making interaction decisions is not only time-consuming but also does not make full use of all the information that is potentially available. Certainly in terms of information theory more than one bit of information could be recovered from the designer's decision that two elements interact. For instance, he could probably tell in what domain the interaction lies: Is it in the domain of physical form at the scale of hardware or furniture, or at the scale of a single space, or at the scale of a building, or at the city, urban, or regional scale? Or does it lie in such nonform domains as communication systems, or in the legal-political domain, or in the education-propaganda domain? Each designer should be able to identify the different domains which are appropriate for the problem he is attempting to solve.

Each of these domains can be seen as a layer superimposed on the two-dimensional matrix. Although it is presently not operational, CLUSTER will soon be able to accept a multilayer matrix. Because each layer will contain many interactions, it should be possible to identify all the simplexes which lie exclusively in each domain. When all the simplexes are identified for each layer, all the domains can be collapsed into one layer. Because some interactions will lie in more than one domain, there will be a good deal of cross-connection between the various layers. Thus when the coherency is computed using the collapsed matrix, the strategy for combining clusters within and between domains will be made evident.

The concept of the multilayered matrix should give the designer valuable information about the nature of the solution of any given subproblem. The designer knows what kind of solution to anticipate for subproblems which lie exclusively in one domain, and further he knows that a subproblem which crosses between domains is telling him something about how the previously solved single-domain subproblems relate to one another.

Application

CLUSTER was written mainly for use as a teaching tool.[7] Its purpose is to illustrate to architecture students how the informational content of a design problem can be described in terms of simplexes (completely interconnected subsets) and how these subsets can be used to grow clusters of ever larger subsets. This information can be used to illustrate the networklike structure of a design problem. It is possible that this program may be of some use to researchers or to practicing architects, engineers, or planners, although it must be emphasized that this procedure is time-consuming and costly and therefore would probably prove uneconomical for all but the most non-prototypical design problems.

---

7. The use of this type of program as a teaching tool is discussed by Murray Milne and Charles Rusch, "The Death of the Beaux Arts: The Cal-Oregon Experiment in Design Education."

14 DCMPOS: An Algorithm for the Decomposition of Nondirected Graphs

Charles L. Owen

Institute of Design
Illinois Institute of Technology
Chicago, Illinois

Charles L. Owen is Assistant Professor in the Institute of Design at Illinois Institute of Technology and a consultant to the Missile and Space Systems Division of the McDonnell Douglas Corporation. He received a B.S. in chemistry from Purdue University in 1956, studied city planning at Johns Hopkins University, received an M.S. in product design from I.I.T. in 1965, and is a Ph.D. candidate in information science at the University of Chicago. He has been head of the Physics Department of the U.S. Naval Preparatory School, and a Project Engineer at the I.I.T. Research Institute. He is the author of *Case Studies in Design Methods*.

The model for a decomposition routine is introduced. The algorithm proposed decomposes a graph into subgraphs with high internal link connectivity, either by partitioning the graph or by decomposing it nondisjunctively into intersecting subgraphs. The new model borrows from the characteristics of molecular structure. Links are given weights according to their membership in three-link circuits, establishing a correlation between link weight and structural importance. From the weights of links, vertex weights are calculated, assigning prominence to those vertexes most closely associated with vertex clusters. Vertexes are scanned in order and formed into nucleus clusters about which successive vertexes agglomerate. To eliminate links not contributing to the identification of subgraph clusters, several devices are incorporated, most notably a cutting function which snips away low-value links by stages. Finally, a user-controlled connectivity function allows variable levels of restriction to be set on internal subgraph connectivity, permitting the investigator to adapt the decomposition process to the nature of the graph and the needs of the real-world source from which it was abstracted. Basic concepts for the model are discussed and illustrated. Details are given of the partitioning process and of the supplementary steps necessary for nondisjunctive decomposition.

In the last few years experimental work in the representation of the structure of a design problem as a network or graph has been undertaken, resulting in a program completed in 1967 called VTCON2 (an acronym for Variable Threshold Condensation). VTCON2 developed a semilattice structure from a description of the connectivity of a given graph and a trial decomposition. It produced a hierarchical structure by first reconsidering the distribution of vertexes in the subgraphs of the trial decomposition, then condensing the resulting new subgraphs through successively higher levels of fewer but larger subgraphs until a level was reached at which the entire graph was reassembled. For the original decomposition, computer programs of the HIDECS series were used[1] or trial decompositions made by hand.

During the past year it became evident that changes to the VTCON system were desirable because: (1) uses outside the original intention suggested the value

1. See Christopher Alexander and Marvin L. Manheim, *HIDECS 2*; also, Alexander, *HIDECS 3*. The programs most used for the generation of trial decompositions were HIDECS 2 and the EQCLA version of HIDECS 3.
2. Since its inception as a problem-structuring program, VTCON 2 has also been used to study curriculum organization, group communication relationships, and architectural space allocation. The special requirements of these studies suggested the generalization of the program with control options for many previously fixed features.

of a more general, flexible approach;[2] (2) the programs used for trial decompositions generally were not adapted to third generation computers, and
(3) trial decompositions sufficiently close to optimal were not as easily
generated by hand as had been expected. For these reasons, development
was begun of a third version of VTCON to contain more control features for
the user and its own decomposition subroutine. The algorithm for this decomposition subroutine, DCMPOS, is the subject of this paper.

Definitions

The terms of graph theory to be used in this discussion are defined as follows:
Graph. A figure consisting of vertexes and links.
Vertex. A point in a graph.
Link. A line segment connecting two vertexes of a graph and passing through
no other vertexes.
Circuit. A closed loop of links beginning and ending at the same vertex and
passing through no vertex more than once.
Connected graph. A graph in which a link exists between any two vertexes;
no vertex or group of vertexes is disconnected from the remaining vertexes.
Nondirected graph. A graph in which no order is specified for vertexes con-
nected by links (in other words, no direction is given to the links).
Complete graph. A graph which contains all possible internal links.
Subgraph. A component graph less than or equal to the original graph and
containing only links and vertexes from the original graph.
Disjoint subgraphs. Subgraphs which have no common vertexes.
Link density. The ratio of the actual internal links of a graph to its possible
internal links. A complete graph has a link density of 1.00.
Connection ratio. The ratio of actual internal links of a graph to possible
internal links for any vertex of a graph. If all vertexes have connection ratios
of 1.00, the graph is a complete graph.
Relation. A relation is defined for a collection of entities if for every pair (x, y)
the statement "x is in Relation R to y" (xRy) can be shown to be true or false.
In this case R is a binary relation and can be any mathematical (e.g., "is
greater than") or nonmathematical (e.g., "is the cousin of") statement which
can be tested logically.
Decomposition. The breakdown of a graph into component subgraphs.
These subgraphs may or may not be disjoint.
Partition. A decomposition of a graph in which the subgraphs formed are
disjoint.
Block. Each of two or more subgraphs of the decomposition of a graph. If
the decomposition is a partition, any vertex of the graph will be contained
in one and only one block.

Objectives

The goal of flexibility suggests that a decomposition algorithm should be
capable of producing either a partition or the overlapped organization associated with general decomposition. The discussion which follows is directed
toward partitions.

From an intuitive consideration of the problem of classification or organization generally, it would seem that entities are grouped together which have
some feature in common or have more features in common than they individually share with entities in other groups. A collection of books may be
categorized by subject matter, publisher, year published, or any of many
other organizing principles. Some of the organizations are easily made because of the clarity of the organizing principle, e.g., categorization by year
published. Others, like that of categorization by subject matter, are often
much more difficult. The book with broad coverage of many topics may
relate to several categories, but if the organizing principle restricts it to a
single one, it must be placed in that one with which it is most strongly
identified.

In the general partitioning problem the situation is analogous. From graph
theory we see that a relation (principle) creates a graph by establishing
links between pairs of vertexes. A partition may already be determined by the
relation, or the structure may require additional treatment for the creation of

a partition. The graph of the book collection determined by the relation "published in the same year as" has a natural partition. A graph for the book collection established by the relation "contains the same subject matter as" may be, on the other hand, a connected graph requiring the disconnection of additional links for its partition. (See Figure 1.) Graphs to be considered here are assumed to be of the second class, complex and requiring link disconnection. Choosing the links to be disconnected or, conversely, deciding which vertexes should remain together is the job of the partitioning algorithm. Its operations are directed by a partitioning rule defined to meet the objectives of the investigator. From the many possible partitioning objectives which could be selected, the requirement placed on DCMPOS is that it partition a graph into subgraphs having the largest number of vertexes for a given connectivity description. It should find within the graph the largest subgraph having a degree of connectivity at least corresponding to the given control value, and it should find from the remaining vertexes and links the next largest subgraph meeting the requirement and continue until all vertexes are accounted for. By defining the partition objectives in this way, control can be exercised over the size of subgraphs and the degree of connectedness within them. The investigator, knowing the nature of the graph and the intent of the decomposition, thus is able to induce partitions with high or low subgraph connectivity by varying an input parameter.

Preliminary Concepts

The factors the decomposition process must reckon with can be realized from an attempt at partitioning by eye. The complexity and the vertex arrangement of the graph are attributes immediately affecting such an analysis. The analyst can see, for example, that both graphs on the bottom of Figure 2 are contained in the upper graph. Unfortunately, most graphs of interest are not small enough to be partitioned by eye. It would appear that a device analogous to human perception which would aid in the recognition of clusters would be of great benefit. In fact, a concept of this or some other kind must be applied to avoid the problem of generating too many possible partitions to be evaluated in any reasonable length of time, even with the use of high-speed electronic computers.[3] Two important capabilities of human perception are worth considering for such a device: first, the ability to detect groupings or clusters, and second, the ability to direct attention in an ordered manner.

Detection of Clusters

In recognizing a cluster of vertexes, the human perceiver notes not only that a vertex is connected to other vertexes, but that the vertexes of the cluster are more densely connected among themselves than to other vertexes. Therefore, cluster recognition requires establishing a difference between the vertex connected to individual vertexes and the vertex connected to vertexes which are themselves interconnected, as in Figure 3. The eye recognizes the difference at once, but the machine, considering links sequentially, sees no immediate difference between the links incident on A and those incident on B.

An answer to this problem is suggested by the structural model of the molecule, a model in which the links contain more than simple connection information. For the sake of analogy, a molecule can be thought of as a graph in which the vertexes are occupied by atoms (or ions) and the links are replaced by interatomic bonds. The forces of the bonds between atoms position the atoms and do much to reveal the nature of the molecule's organization by their strengths and the distances through which they act.

---

3. The number of partitions, $P(n)$, possible for a graph of n vertexes can be calculated recursively:

$$P(n) = \sum_{r=0}^{n-1} \frac{(n-1)!}{r!\,(n-r-1)!} \times P(r) \text{ where } P(0) = 1$$

The problem of simple generation/evaluation schemes can be appreciated when $P(n)$ for even small values of n is calculated: $P(5) = 52$; $P(10) = 115{,}975$; $P(25) = 4.6 \times 10^{18}$; $P(50) = 1.9 \times 10^{47}$. It is interesting to realize that even if it were able to generate and evaluate one partition per microsecond, a computer would require more than 10^{33} years to consider all the possible partitions for a fifty vertex graph.

1. Natural and imposed partitions on graphs

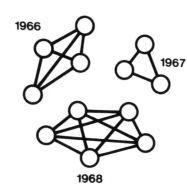

1966

1967

1968

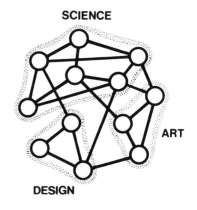

SCIENCE

ART

DESIGN

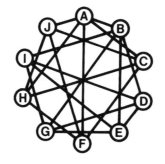

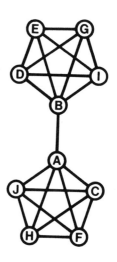

2. Arrangement as a factor in visual analysis

3. Cluster unrevealed by links incident on *A* or *B* alone

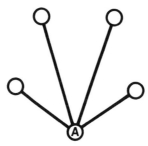

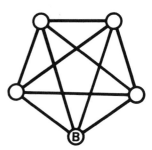

An analogous self-organizing principle is inherent in the structure of the graph. Consider a three-link circuit, a triangle, the smallest complete subgraph containing more than binary information. Because it relates more than two vertexes, it can be used to reveal clusters by identifying links that are important to the structure either because they are members of potential subgraphs or because they connect potential subgraphs. This information-gathering property is illustrated in Figure 4. Wherever a three-vertex circuit appears in a graph, a weight of 1 is added to each of its component links. Following this strategy, AB = 0 in graph (AB) because no three-vertex circuit exists; in (CDE) each link has the weight 1 because the graph is itself a three-vertex circuit. In (FGHI) each link is a member of two three-vertex circuits, and in (JKLMN) each link is a member of three such circuits. In a complete graph, containing all possible links, all link weights are equal and are a function of the number of vertexes in the graph. Where w^v is the weight of any link in a complete graph of v vertexes, $w^v = v - 2$. More generally, the weight of the ith link in any graph can be expressed as the number of three-vertex circuits which contain it, c_i; as $w_i = c_i$.

The usefulness of this device is apparent in Figure 5 where the question of how a partition should treat vertex A can be immediately resolved from the weights of the links incident on A alone.

Ordering the Search

The ability to conduct an ordered search is the second basic concept to be developed for the algorithm. This is necessary both to reduce search time and to improve the probability of finding an optimal partition. Translated into the needs of an algorithm, it must be a device for placing the vertexes in an order for consideration that will enhance the probability of finding large subgraphs quickly. In hindsight, if the optimal partition were already known, it could be recreated much more easily and quickly a second time by considering the vertexes in the order of their already-known membership in subgraphs. The objective of this device is to approach that order by placing high on the list those vertexes which will tend to be nuclei around which clusters will form. To achieve this a weight W is computed for each vertex:

$$W_i = \frac{1}{l_i} \sum_{j=1}^{l_i} w_j$$

where l_i is the number of links incident on the ith vertex and w_j is the weight of the jth link. This vertex weight has the general property of assigning precedence on the basis of membership in large, dense clusters or important connective positions. The graph of Figure 6 illustrates the discrimination of vertexes under this system. G and H have the highest weights by their connective relationship between the two large center clusters; F, I, J, and L follow by membership in the dense five-vertex clusters. K is next followed by N, O, and P in the four-vertex cluster, and C is a connective. A, B, D, and E are least in importance. Suppose G is used to start a subgraph block and each vertex following in order by weight is either (1) allowed to join a block if connected to all the present members, or (2) required to form a new subgraph block otherwise. The following partition is generated in one pass: {(GHFIC), (JKL), (NOPM), (AB), (DE)}. This partition has the desired property of containing the largest subgraphs.

As will be seen, perception of clusters and ordering of search are not sufficient, unaided, to decompose the general graph, but with the help of some additional devices to reduce the "noise" of extraneous links and circumvent indeterminate cases they can be employed with a high probability of producing an optimal partition.

The Partitioning Process

To describe the connectivity within a graph or subgraph two concepts are used: *link density* to define connectivity for the entire graph or subgraph, and *connection ratio (c.r.)* to define connectivity at the individual vertex. To establish a flexible foundation for the partitioning operation, the concept of a *threshold partition* is introduced. This is a partition in which all subgraph

4. Link weights by counting three-link circuits

5. The partition around *A* decided by using link weights

6. A partition determined by vertex and link weights

7. Graphs meeting different connection ratio requirements

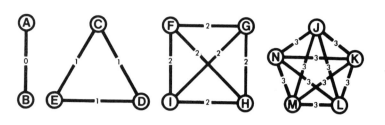

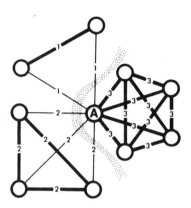

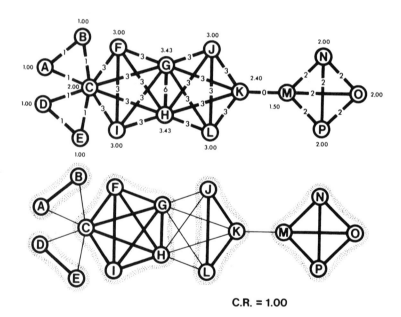

C.R. = 1.00

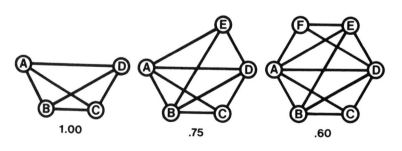

1.00   **.75**   **.60**

blocks contain only those vertexes that are connected to other vertexes in the subgraph by at least the number of links determined from an externally supplied minimum connection ratio.

The equivalence relation R which partitions the graph now can be defined as, "meets the ith subgraph threshold requirement with," where size of the subgraph blocks decreases monotonically as i, indexing the order of block formation, increases. As the logical value of xRy for any pair of vertexes x and y is not known except in terms of those vertexes already processed, the partitioning operation is recursive. Subgraph blocks are built up with successive entries assigned on the basis of those already present. The blocks are constructed in such a way that the subgraph or subgraphs with the largest number of vertexes for the given connection ratio are found first, followed by those of successively smaller size until only singleton vertexes, if existent, remain.

As was implied earlier, the threshold concept applied to subgraph clusters permits the investigator to study the graph's structure under varying degrees of restriction. Both the link density and the amount of order (the degree to which vertexes cluster) in a graph affect its behavior under partitioning. Dense graphs respond better to higher threshold requirements; sparse graphs require lower values. Highly ordered graphs are much less sensitive than are those less well ordered. Finally, the system of real-world values for which the graph is an abstraction exerts its own requirements on the nature of the partition. To control the partitioning process, a connection ratio is specified, establishing a threshold for the number of links a vertex must have to other vertexes in its subgraph. The effect of lowering the threshold is seen in Figure 7. As the connection ratio decreases from 1.00 to .75 the threshold for a new vertex to be added to the original four-vertex subgraph decreases from four out of four to three out of four and the new vertex E is added. Decreasing the connection ratio to .60 reduces the threshold to three out of five and the new vertex F is added. Notice that all vertexes have at least the minimum number of links specified by the connection ratio.

Before discussing the actual decomposition algorithm, three corrective devices must be introduced to deal with special problems which arise when weighted vertexes are locally not in optimal order, either because they have equal weights and therefore random order, or because their weights are biased from the effect of extraneous links. The basic process to be modified is the simple partitioning system previously used in Figure 6. It may be stated as follows.
1. Weight all links by finding three-vertex circuits.
2. Compute vertex weights from incident-link weights.
3. Consider vertexes in descending order by weight.
4. Starting with the first vertex, construct subgraph blocks by finding the first block where the vertex under consideration is connected to vertexes already present by at least the number of links computed as a threshold from the connection ratio.

The example of Figure 8 illustrates the first problem. Because all vertexes have equal weights, ordering is simply alphabetic. With a connection ratio of 1.00, the following partition is generated: {(AB), (CD), (EF), (GH), (IJ), (KL)}. The difficulty occurs because there is no discrimination among the vertexes and because the only condition for membership in a subgraph is connection to the threshold number of vertexes. Starting with A in the first block, B joins A because they are connected; C starts a new block because it is not connected to both A and B, and so on. The corrective device is a second "strong-link" condition: that the vertex under consideration be connected by its most heavily weighted link to a member of the subgraph block. Using both conditions, the partition generated is {(AFGL), (BCHI), (DEJK)}, the optimal partition.

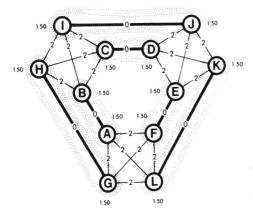

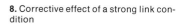

8. Corrective effect of a strong link condition

9. Corrective effect of a multiple pass condition

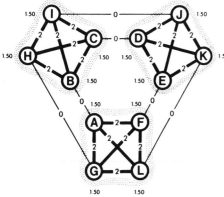

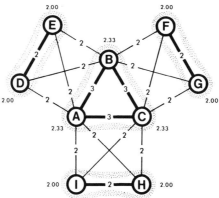

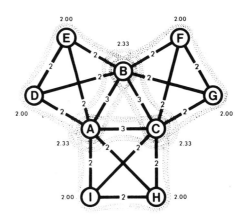

The second problem arises when two or more clusters share some of their vertexes. In Figure 9, with either the original partitioning condition or both conditions, the partition generated is: {(ABC), (DE), (FG), (HI)}. The corrective device is a second decomposition pass (or multiple decomposition passes) in which the strong-link condition is dropped and a vertex is permitted to join as many blocks of the first pass partition as it can under the threshold limitation. With this procedure, the original nuclei blocks attract additional vertexes to become: {(ABC), (DEAB), (FGBC), (HIAC)}. This is no longer a "partition," because the blocks intersect in common vertexes, but it has the property of identifying all three large subgraphs.

"Noise" from extraneous vertexes and links only nominally associated with nucleus vertexes creates the third problem. Vertexes J, K and L in Figure 10 effectively prevent the discovery of the four-vertex subgraphs in the strong-link first decomposition pass, and the blocks are not augmented in subsequent decomposition passes. The partition produced is: {(ABC), (DEJ), (FGK), (HIL)}. To resolve this problem a cutting function is introduced which snips away low-weight links to isolate or reveal cluster nuclei. Links with weights less than or equal to the cutting function k are removed, changing the weights of the vertexes and, consequently, the order of vertex consideration. Applied in a series of higher-level cutting passes, the cutting function permits the now secondary decomposition passes to develop several decompositions for comparison and subgraph selection:

$$k_i = \max \left[k_{i-1} + 1, \min (w_j) \right]$$
$$\text{where } j = 1, 2, \ldots, n$$

with n = the number of weighted links remaining at the beginning of the ith pass

$$i = 1, 2, \ldots, r-1$$
$$\text{and } k_{i-1} = 0$$

with $r = i$ when $k_i \geq \max (w_j)$
when $i = 1$.

With $k_i = 1$ in Figure 10 the links connecting J, K, and L to the rest of the graph have been cut and the remaining link weights recalculated. This and the restriction that disconnected vertexes not be considered in the strong-link first decomposition pass produce the subgraphs (ABC), (DE), (FG), and (HI). In the second decomposition pass additional vertexes are attracted, producing the subgraphs (ABC), (DEAB), (FGBC), and (HIAC). Comparison can then be made of subgraphs, the selected removed, and the entire process repeated for the remaining vertexes until, as a final step, the singletons J, K and L are accepted as individual subgraphs and the partition is completed.

The Algorithm

The complete partitioning process can now be stated as an algorithm:

1. Weight all links: $w_i = c_i$

2. Weight all vertexes: $W_i = \dfrac{1}{l_i} \displaystyle\sum_{j=1}^{l_i} w_j$

3. Sort vertexes into descending order by weight.

4. Apply a strong-link decomposition pass. Construct subgraph blocks by considering the vertexes in order. A vertex may join a block under these conditions:
(a) If it is connected in the original uncut graph to the vertexes of the block by at least the threshold number of links calculated from the given connection ratio.
(b) If it is connected to vertexes present by its strongest link, determined by using the link values of the current graph structure under the cutting passes. If a vertex does not meet the conditions for entry with any of the blocks already created, permit it to start a new subgraph block. Ignore disconnected vertexes.

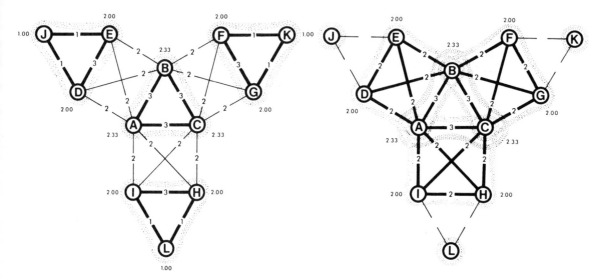

10. Corrective effect of "snipping away"
low-weight links

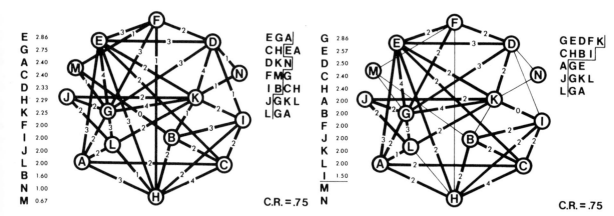

E	2.86		E	2.86
G	2.75		G	2.57
A	2.40		E	2.50
C	2.40		C	2.40
D	2.33		H	2.40
H	2.29		A	2.00
K	2.25		B	2.00
F	2.00		F	2.00
I	2.00		J	2.00
J	2.00		K	2.00
L	2.00		L	2.00
B	1.60		I	1.50
N	1.00		M	
M	0.67		N	

Left list:
EGA
CHEA
DKN
FMG
IBCH
JGKL
LGA

C.R. = .75

Right list:
GEDFK
CHBI
AGE
JGKL
LGA

C.R. = .75

11. First passes: $k = 0$ (left), $k = 1$ (right)

5. Apply follow-up decomposition passes. Augment already-formed sub-graph blocks by reconsidering all vertexes in order (including disconnected vertexes last) and allowing a vertex to join any block in which it meets condition (a) of Step 4. Continue passes until no further additions are made in a single pass.[4]

6. Compare the subgraphs found in the present series of decomposition passes with those saved from previous passes. Save all subgraphs that are not identical to previously saved subgraphs.

7. Compute the value of the cutting function k_i for a possible ith cutting pass: $k_i = \max [k_{i-1} + 1, \min (w_j)]$, $(k_{i-1} = 0$ if no cuts have yet been made). Compare k_i with $\max (w_j)$ for the $j = 1, 2, \ldots, n$ uncut links. If $k_i \geq \max (w_j)$, go to Step 8; otherwise, apply a cutting pass, cutting all links with weights less than or equal to k_i and return to Step 1.

8. When the test of Step 7 indicates the conclusion of a cutting pass series, select according to the following rules the largest previously unselected subgraph (or subgraphs if there are more than one of the same size) from the list compiled in Step 6. Ignore all subgraphs which intersect previously selected subgraphs.
(a) If only one largest subgraph exists, select it.
(b) If more than one largest subgraph exists, select all which have no intersections with others of the selection group.
(c) If intersections exist, but all subgraphs do not intersect all others, select the combination which has the greatest number of nonintersecting members.
(d) If all subgraphs intersect all others or if more than one combination of nonintersecting subgraphs exists with the same number of members, select the subgraph with the highest link density or the combination of subgraphs with the highest average link density.
(e) If link densities are the same for the subgraphs or combinations, select the subgraph or combination with the lowest vertex weight sum (except in the case of a pass where selection is being made among doubletons; select the doubleton or combination of doubletons with the highest vertex weight sum in this case).
(f) If vertex weight sums are the same for the subgraphs or combinations, select the subgraph or combination which was first discovered in the decomposition passes.

9. Remove the selected subgraph (or subgraphs) from the graph and make it a block of the final partition. If it is larger than previously established subgraph blocks, remove them from the partition and restore their subgraphs to the graph.

10. Examine the remaining vertexes in the graph. If only disconnected singleton or doubleton subgraphs remain, go to Step 11. If larger structures are still present, replace all cut links between remaining vertexes and return to Step 1.

11. Complete the partition with the addition of remaining singleton and doubleton subgraph blocks.

Figures 11 through 13 demonstrate the algorithm's application. The example graph has 14 vertexes, 37 links, a link density of .4066, and is to be partitioned for a connection ratio of .75. Its state in Figure 11a, along with the additional information shown, represents the progress of the algorithm through Step 6. Links have been weighted and the vertex weights calculated from them and listed to the left of the graph. On the right, the subgraph blocks are shown as constructed by the passes of Step 4 (left of the divider) and Step 5. Starting

---

4. Occasionally in Steps 4 and 5 a vertex added to a subgraph block may, because it is not connected to a particular vertex in the subgraph, create a situation in which the earlier assigned vertex is no longer connected to enough vertexes to be above the required threshold. When this occurs, the earlier assigned vertex is removed.

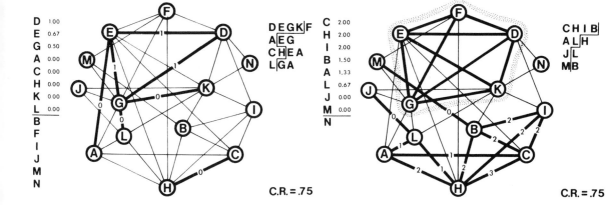

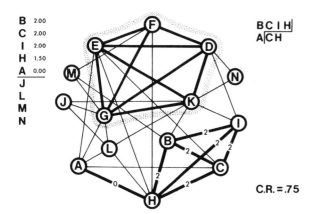

C.R. = .75

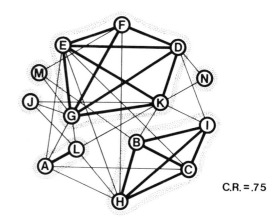

C.R. = .75

C.R. = .75

C.R. = .75

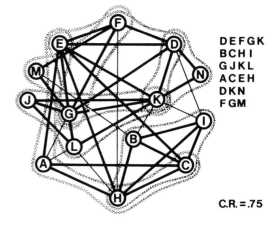

DEFGK
BCHI
GJKL
ACEH
DKN
FGM

C.R. = .75

12. End of first series, $k = 2$ (left); new series, $k = 0$ (right)

13. End of second series, $k = 1$ (left); final partition (right)

14. Nondisjunctive decomposition

with E in the first subgraph block, the Step 4 strong-link pass added G to E because it is connected to E by its strongest link. A joined the same block because it is connected to both E and G and has its strongest link to E. C did not meet the threshold requirement of the first condition with the (EGA) block because it does not have the three links required. (The threshold in this case is three; the minimum number of actual internal links which will meet the given connection ratio of .75 when the number of possible internal links is three.) Also C does not have its strongest link to the block; it therefore started a new block.

In similar fashion the pass continued through the remaining vertexes. In the first Step 5 decomposition pass, E was able to join one additional block, G joined three new blocks, A two, and so on. When the pass was complete (no additions occurred in further Step 5 passes), the following subgraphs were identified for retention: (EGA), (CHEA), (DKN), (FMG), (IBCH), (JGKL), and (LGA).

In Figure 11b a cutting pass with $k_1 = 1$ has been applied following the test of Step 7. The light lines in the graph indicate the links with weights less than or equal to 1 which have been cut. Weights for the remaining links have been recalculated, vertexes reweighted and reordered, and decomposition passes applied again through Step 6. The reordering produced by the cutting pass reveals a larger subgraph (GEDFK) which lacks one link for completeness, but meets the requirements defined by the .75 connection ratio. A second cutting pass required by Step 7 produces the graph structure and accompanying information in Figure 12a. Only eight vertexes have links remaining, and of these only three have weights greater than zero. No subgraphs different from those previously discovered were revealed by the decomposition passes, and no further cuts are required by Step 7.

In succession, Steps 8, 9, and 10 select the largest subgraph so far identified, (GEDFK), remove it from the graph, and initiate a repetition of the entire process for the remaining vertexes and links. The results are shown in Figure 12b, again with the process completed through Step 6. Except for those links that were connected to vertexes in the removed subgraph, all links in the original graph structure have been restored. Although three new subgraphs, (ALH), (JL) and (MB), were found in the decomposition passes, the largest subgraph found, (CHIB), is not new. In Figure 13a the only possible cutting pass, $k_1 = 1$, has been applied, again yielding (CHIB) as the largest subgraph. Since (CHEA) and (JGKL), the other previously found four-vertex subgraphs, both intersect (GEDFK), (CHIB) is selected and removed as the next block of the partition. Because the three-vertex chain (JLA) still remains, Step 10 requires an additional repetition of the process. The decomposition passes generate the subgraph blocks (AL) and (JL) from which (AL) is selected in Step 8, and the partition is completed in Step 11 with the addition of (AL) and the singleton blocks (J), (M), and (N). The partitioned graph in its final form appears in Figure 13b.

Some additional comments on the partitioning process are necessary to explain the actions of Steps 7 through 10. First, the complexity of the expression for the cutting function in Step 7 results from forcing a continual increase on the value of the function. The more consistent approach, which would follow from the natural cutting function choice, $k_i = \min(w_j)$, requires considerably more computation time. Most of the algorithm's activities are organized within the cutting pass loops. If the minimum weight criterion is used alone, the number of cutting passes increases significantly. The compromise, forcing an increase in cutting function value for each pass, saves time with almost no loss in accuracy.

A second comment concerns the necessity of removing subgraphs from the graph sequentially. The procedure has much the same function as the cutting passes, the reduction of extraneous information affecting vertex weights and vertex ordering. While not as important for partitions made with high connection ratios, it becomes critical as the connection ratio is reduced. A complete subgraph cluster has link weights at least equal to the number of cluster vertexes minus two. Such a subgraph cluster remains intact until the value of the cutting function reaches the level of that minimum link weight, making discovery of the subgraph highly probable. As the link density of the subgraph cluster decreases, however, variation in the link weights increases as the permissible connection ratio is lowered. Concurrently, the effect of outside links is felt more appreciably. The sequential removal of subgraphs reduces this effect by restricting the source of influence to only those vertexes yet to be partitioned.

Nondisjunctive Decomposition

Because all subgraphs discovered in the partitioning process are retained, it is possible with little additional effort to obtain decompositions in which subgraph intersections are permitted. As with partitions, the criteria for the construction of these decompositions are dependent on the goals of the investigation. An acceptable decomposition containing all subgraphs found under the partitioning process which are not proper subgraphs of others will usually contain considerably more subgraphs and have much more overlap than a decomposition containing only the minimum number of subgraphs necessary to cover all vertexes. The criteria chosen for the nondisjunctive algorithm below produce a decomposition consistent in objectives with the partition previously described, and somewhere in between the extremes of coverage above.

To make the decomposition, select from the list of subgraphs compiled for the partition the largest subgraphs meeting the requirement that each successive selection cover vertexes not previously covered. For the new algorithm, make the following additions to the steps of the partitioning algorithm:

12. From the list of Step 6, select and remove the largest subgraph (or, where more than one of the same size exists, the combination meeting the criteria of 13*b* through 13*g*) for the first block of the nondisjunctive decomposition.

13. Select and remove according to the following rules the largest remaining subgraph (or subgraphs) covering previously uncovered vertexes. Ignore all subgraphs which are proper subgraphs of those previously selected.
(a) If only one largest subgraph exists, select it.
(b) If more than one largest subgraph exists, select all which independently cover previously uncovered vertexes.
(c) If the same previously uncovered vertex or vertexes are covered by more than one subgraph, select the subgraph which covers additional previously uncovered vertexes.
(d) If the subgraphs covering the same previously uncovered vertex or vertexes cover the same number of additional previously uncovered vertexes, select the subgraph with which the vertex or vertexes have the greatest number of links.
(e) If the number of links is the same from the vertex or vertexes to the covering subgraphs, select the subgraph which has the highest link density.
(f) If the link densities are the same for the covering subgraphs, select the subgraph with the lowest vertex weight sum.
(g) If the vertex weight sums are the same for the covering subgraphs, select the subgraph which was first discovered in the partitioning process.

14. Examine the remaining graph structure. If all vertexes are covered, the decomposition is complete; otherwise return to Step 13.

In Figure 14, the graph of the partitioning example has been nondisjunctively decomposed. The subgraphs outlined in the graph and listed on the right were selected from the compilation made for the partition. With (DEFGK) first, the next three subgraphs—(BCHI), (GJKL), and (ACEH)—covered all but two vertexes. From the three-vertex subgraphs, (DKN) and (FGM) covered the remaining M and N vertexes to complete the decomposition. Remaining subgraphs from the compilation are either proper subgraphs of others or contain only vertexes that have already been covered.

15 Difficulties with Network Models in Problem Formulation

Comments on the papers by Davis and Kennedy, Milne, and Owen

Charles D. Kowal

Department of Architecture
Case Western Reserve University
Cleveland, Ohio

At the time this commentary was written, Charles D. Kowal was a Lecturer in Architecture at Case Western Reserve University, teaching in the Departments of Architecture and Psychology. He is conducting educational and behavioral research projects. He holds degrees in architecture and presently is completing his doctoral dissertation in psychology at the University of Maine.

We are interested in design methods because of their influence on achieved solutions to design and planning problems. Attempts to clarify this influence, or the relationship between design methods employed and design solutions achieved, have been made by using computer-based, topological network models to aid in the formulation of problems.

HIDECS 2, the earliest model and computer program proposed for architecture and transportation engineering was criticized for several reasons:
1. Occasional anomalous output was produced because decomposition took place as a series of binary steps. This decomposition technique did not allow for consideration of the system as a whole, but only as a part of the sub-system.
2. The decomposition procedure was based on strict assumptions about the system. These assumptions were so rigid that it was difficult to find real-world problems that the model and program adequately represented.
3. The program output was in the form of a tree rather than a semilattice. This is to say, an element appeared in only one subgraph or one part of a system, whereas in a semilattice, an element may appear in many parts of a system. It was argued that this factor was inconsistent with problem struc-

ture in the real world and would lead to inappropriate design solutions.[1]

To compensate for these weaknesses, four new computer programs were produced, HIDECS 3. Although all four addressed themselves to the first two criticisms, only two preserved a semilattice structure. The final output of all of the programs was in the form of subsets of the lowest level of a hierarchy. This left the designer without any way to recompose the subgraphs into a hierarchical structure as the earlier HIDECS 2 program had done. Furthermore, there was no efficient way to combine output from the two series of programs.

It is within this framework that the research discussed in the above papers in this section has been conducted. I shall comment on the three papers individually.

In the introduction to their paper, Davis and Kennedy argue that it ought to be possible to determine the parts of a problem that are the most dominant, and thus those which also have the "most far-reaching implications." The authors have arrived at this point by discussing what they feel are failures of the existing techniques for combining partial solutions into a complete solution. An example of such an existing technique is seen in the use of "overlaying" for highway route location as shown by Manheim.[2] In this example each requirement (represented graphically) is combined or averaged with the other requirements of that particular subgraph. The diagrams for each subgraph are combined until a complete solution is achieved. The main advantage of such a technique is that it allows the designer to deal with a large number of requirements sequentially, thereby reducing, at a given moment, the amount of requirements to be organized. This, of course, puts heavy emphasis on how the groups or subgraphs are derived from the problem. Arbitrary grouping, or grouping not based on the problem structure, is one of the difficulties that the HIDECS programs attempted to avoid. This brings us back to EPS and a difficulty that I believe it has not solved.

For instance, Davis and Kennedy's Figure 2 shows a diagram which contains the dominant sets of attributes, levels of the program, and sketches of the information of that level. As the program reran, the designer would obtain more dominant sets in the output. The first output group, or level, would be translated into a fairly rough sketch representing the particular dominant set group. As the designer went to the second step, he would refine the diagram a little more, and then when he obtained all the attributes in the output, he would again refine and produce a finished version of the design. However, if the results produced in level 1 happened to number approximately fifty sets of pairs, which would mean one hundred requirements, how does the designer deal with such a large number of elements? Such a situation is likely when one considers the number of requirements generated in a large urban planning problem. How does the designer organize the requirements into a workable number for consideration at any one point in time without arbitrary grouping? If our existing techniques for combining partial solutions is inadequate, what may the designer substitute in the above example? These are some of the questions that are not clearly answered in this paper, but questions that the designer will very likely pose.

In choosing pairs of nodes as a unit for determining a path through the problem, Davis and Kennedy have made an assumption that doesn't seem to be correct, namely that "individual requirements of the problem affect the solution to an equal degree." This assumption is similar to the one made by

1. An illustration of a tree and a lattice in architecture is given by Allen Bernholtz and Edward Bierstone, "Computer-Augmented Design: A Case History in Architecture," also in Martin Krampen and Peter Seitz, eds., *Design and Planning 2*, pp. 41–51. For discussion of further limitations of HIDECS 2, see Christopher Alexander, *HIDECS 3*.
2. Marvin L. Manheim, "Problem Solving Processes in Planning and Design," also in Krampen and Seitz, *Design and Planning* 2, pp. 35–38. The technique is discussed more fully in Christopher Alexander and Marvin L. Manheim, *The Use of Diagrams in Highway Route Location*.

Alexander, which, for computational purposes, held that all requirements were of roughly equal scope and significance. Davis and Kennedy use this assumption to argue that pairs of requirements allow greater differentiation of the system's properties than individual requirements. But individual requirements do not have an equal effect upon the design solution. For example, if requirement A is connected to many other requirements and requirement B is connected to only one other requirement, requirement A is likely to affect many more aspects of the design solution than requirement B. This situation is likely to occur whenever we have requirements that are highly interactive with each other, such as in most architecture or urban planning problems.

Davis and Kennedy have mentioned that one of the advantages of EPS is that it allows specification of initial link values by the designer. This would allow the designer to instruct the program to give special consideration to certain pairs of requirements. The designer does this by weighting a link, or interaction between requirements, with a number corresponding to the strength of linkage that he desires (from weak to strong). It is not clear, however, what the criteria are that the designer should use in specifying the weighted linkages. Consider the example given by Davis and Kennedy of three office building criteria. If we agree that requirements "A, number of elevators" and "B, height of the building" have a higher degree of connectedness than "C, number of cars parked" and A, or C and B, then we could weight the link between AB. But should that link receive an "average," "strong," or "very strong," weight? What is the rational basis for weighting some links between criteria and not others? We are left without an answer to these questions.

Even more questions are apparent. For example, how does the designer easily determine the higher degree of connectedness for the link between two requirements before the problem has been run on the computer? What is the effect of poor weighting by the designer on the design solution?

I am skeptical about the advantage to the designer of weighting links between requirements. In this instance, it seems that it is more a source for bias by the designer than a source for additional useful information about the problem.

Milne's program has utilized a different technique for dealing with the network of requirements than that of Davis and Kennedy. EPS tried to find the more dominant aspects of the problem by determining the sets of requirements (in pairs) that had the least separation distance (number of links) between the two requirements and the highest conjugate connectivity (number of requirements common to both). CLUSTER, however, tries to find the more dominant, or more important, aspects of the problem by identifying all the complete subgraphs of the problem. The program then recombines the subgraphs to produce output with overlap. It might be argued that decomposition into complete subgraphs is somewhat restrictive, because it does not allow for slight variations from a complete subgraph. For example, a subgraph of five requirements (ABCDE) that is complete but for two links (between AE and CD) would yield the following four complete subgraphs when decomposed: (ABC), (ABD), (BCE), and (BDE). This subgraph is 80 percent complete, and it might therefore be argued that we should like to consider it as an "almost-complete" subgraph of the order five, instead of as four subgraphs of the order three. CLUSTER handles this problem by taking the subgraphs produced by the decomposition and recombining them as the output occurs. This automatic recombination is useful as it enables the designer to work with fewer and more appropriate subgraphs. The particular two-step process (decomposition and recomposition), while useful for determining complete subgraphs from a graph that is relatively incomplete, may be somewhat inefficient for problems where relatively complete subgraphs exist in fairly large numbers. I say *may* be inefficient, because no run times for the program are indicated in the paper. If the run times are very large, it might be more desirable to try to directly solve for incomplete subgraphs that we wish to treat as complete, instead of first breaking them down into their complete subgraph components, and then recombining them.

A multilayered matrix would seem to be initially useful to the designer as an organizing tool when he specifies the requirements of the design problem. The designer could, for instance, begin this specification at one scale and then proceed to the next associated scale, until he has covered all domains of the problem. The use of a multilayered matrix and the scale construct, however, does not change the basic relationships between requirements and their links or interactions. A network, for instance may be represented by one matrix, containing all of the network's elements, or by several layers of matrixes, each containing part of the network's elements. The latter changes only the grouping of requirements but does not change the original con-figuration of the network. Thus, the links or interactions between require-ments will remain constant regardless of matrix multiplicity. Operationally, the multilayered matrix permits the designer to group his input data and allows a partial display in the output of all complete subgraphs from a par-ticular level of matrix. Milne suggests that the levels be used for designat-ing scales—hardware, space, building, and city scales, for instance. Given a program able to accept a multilayered matrix, however, it is just as possible to generate intrascale levels or matrixes as it is to generate interscale levels. This is to say, the designer might use each level of the matrix for a separate space rather than a separate scale. For example, Matrix A might be kitchen area, Matrix B bedrooms, and Matrix C living area. The use of the scale or domain construct represents, then, an ordering or bias of the requirements of the problem by the designer. Where this ordering corresponds to the sub-system structure of the problem, a bias will not present any difficulty. A de-signer doesn't usually begin, however, with a neatly organized network of the requirements of the problem. The ordering used in this case might not correspond to the problem's structure, and will be likely to present difficul-ties. Furthermore, when all of the domains are collapsed into a matrix of a single layer, we get a matrix containing all of the network's elements. Al-though there is a "good deal of cross-connectedness" or links between the various complete subgraphs, I do not see the strategy becoming apparent, as Milne does, for "combining subsets within and between domains. . . ." Although the idea of a multilayered matrix has a little plausibility, I am skeptical that it will yield useful results to the designer.

DCMPOS is similar to CLUSTER in that it also produces complete subgraphs of requirements on the output of the program. Both programs have adopted a strategy that emphasizes the identification of the largest complete subgraphs of a problem. Because these subgraphs are generally adjacent to other sub-graphs of the problem, overlap in the output is easily generated by both programs. The general similarity of the two strategies is not completely sur-prising, as is suggested by the limitations of the HIDECS 2 and HIDECS 3 programs.

Although the strategy of identification of tightly or completely connected groups of requirements appears to be logically without problem, it may pro-duce a small difficulty. Previous programs, and the ones commented on here, have tended to decompose complete subgraphs directly into their individual requirements. A complete subgraph of four requirements, then, would be decomposed into four separate subgraphs of one requirement each. DCMPOS and the entire VTCON system have dealt only with problems that are fairly small in size (roughly 12–50 requirements) and whose complete subgraphs are not very large. The design resolution of the resulting complete subgraphs has not been beyond the capabilities of the designer to deal with the re-quirements simultaneously. This is fine for small problems but may not be adequate for problems that produce a complete subgraph of a size com-parable to those now being run with HIDECS. This puts the designer in the position where he may be expected to aggregate a substantial number of requirements simultaneously. The complete subgraph could, however, be broken down into a number of small complete subgraphs of a given size. The number and size of these subgraphs could also be adjusted to allow for the designer's abilities. Neither program (DCMPOS or CLUSTER) currently provides for this kind of situation. This may be because the situation never arose before with a design problem. Larger order problems than those illustrated in DCMPOS are not uncommon for architecture and planning. Indeed, this increase in the size of the problem increases the likelihood that a large complete subgraph may be produced. It must also be mentioned that such a condition could exist as a result of poor requirement wording and interaction decisions by the designer.

As the reader can see, there are many different approaches possible when dealing with a network model of a design problem. There has been no attempt on the part of the authors to evaluate the comparative value of the programs available. It is difficult, therefore, to say clearly which program is superior or even if any one of them produces consistent results. It would be valuable, however, for the designer to know what technique provided the most usefulness in the design process. Nonetheless, each program seems to have some value and some improvement over the earlier programs. Davis and Kennnedy's method, for example, of staging the output from the group of the most dominant sets to the group of all sets could offer (if refined) a good way of getting into the problem through successive approximations. This could be particularly useful for large planning problems such as the designer frequently faces today. Milne and Owen have both attempted to identify the complete and semicomplete subgraphs of a problem. Both programs have allowed for lattice output in trying to display as accurately as possible the interrelationships of parts of the problem structure.

It should be obvious that the use of computer-based network analysis models is a fairly recent development in design methodology. Because of some unrefined aspects of the earlier programs, the technique has drawn criticism that has centered mainly around the specifying of requirements and the design resolution of subsets of requirements. As the reader can observe, these are areas that have been conspicuously ignored in the papers of this section. This, of course, is not entirely without reason on the part of the authors, for the model and our current technology lend themselves to further development in the algorithmic area more easily than in the areas of problem specification and graphic delineation. Clearly, however, these latter are the areas that make the model useful in design, where subsequent improvement of technique will have a benefit to the designer. Thus, at present the designer and educator is faced with the evaluative problem not of whether the model is useful, but how useful is it in design.

The use of a network analysis model has had some consequences for the designer: it has clearly shown design as a process and not just as a result, it has stimulated research into design methods, and it is strongly suggestive that further work and research with this technique be directed toward the areas of indicating design requirements, translation of subgroups of requirements into subsolutions, and the aggregation of subsolutions into a complete solution.

5 Building Layout Models

In architecture and building design, one of the most articulated subproblems is the physical layout of spaces. Because a successful layout must satisfy a multitude of conflicting requirements, it is the point at which many students for the first time realize the inadequacy of traditional methods and look for more powerful techniques.

One of the earliest and best known layout models in the United States was the CRAFT Computerized Relative Allocation of Facilities Technique described in the first paper of this section by Paul Lew and Peter Brown. Like most techniques developed primarily for business or industrial applications, CRAFT requires many modifications for architectural application, some of which these authors have accomplished and now discuss.

Although using building layout only as an example, Thomas Maver in his paper in Section 6 of this volume, reviews some of the early work in the United Kingdom and criticizes the reductionism of these models from the multitude of factors which *should* determine the layout for a building to a small number of quantifiable variables. For readers new to this area of research, the first part of Brown and Lew's paper and the midsection of Maver's may serve as an introduction.

There are two classes of models commonly used for building layout, "location" models and "allocation" models. The former are models for the location *of* spaces within a shell, the latter for allocation of activities, machines, people, or whatever, *to* spaces. The first three papers in this section concentrate on location models, whereas the study by Alan Colker and James Leib combines both location and allocation models.

Lavette Teague presents a greatly improved technique for computer representation of spaces and spatial relationships—the first which in addition to proximity relationships allows explicit consideration of size, shape (including three-dimensional shape), and proportions of spaces in determining building layout.

John Grason offers a new technique for subdivision of the old and limiting "frequency × distance" function to a combination of contiguity and/or communication between spaces. He also introduces ways of dealing with the relative sizes of spaces, remote communication, and orientation requirements.

Both the Teague and Grason models and algorithms go well beyond other efforts to date. In his commentary on Grason's paper, Horst Rittel points out some pos-sible procedural and computational limitations and suggests alternate heuristic approaches.

The Colker and Leib study is a good example of a more comprehensive approach based on simulation techniques rather than either the optimization or heuristic approaches adopted in the other papers. They modify and combine several existing models in order to translate curriculum and study characteristics into an efficient school space layout. Their study, together with the Judy and Levine study they quote, is among the most advanced in the field.

Paul Roberts in his commentary discusses different theories for combining multiple goals in any type of analysis problem. Although addressing himself ostensibly to the Colker and Leib study, the first part of his commentary applies to many of the papers in this volume.

We have yet to see any body of work showing the interaction between building layout models and other building system models, for example, work combining layout models with constraints generated by mechanical and electrical systems as well as with structural loads. Logcher's STRUDL system discussed in Part 3 handled this kind of combination. Mechanical, structural, and material benefit-cost models could also be related to advantage to layout models. Another fruitful interaction would be between layout models and recent circulation-simulation programs, such as those of Campion and of Hutchinson listed in the bibliography.

A final word of introduction. The layout models described in this section, although primarily for architectural applications, could be adopted (as Brown and Lew point out) for urban design, for the location of facilities in neighborhoods, cultural facilities in an urban center, or (as Teague suggests) for land-use planning.

16 Evaluation and Modification of CRAFT for an Architectural Methodology

I. Paul Lew and Peter H. Brown

School of Architecture
Columbia University
New York, New York

I. Paul Lew is currently a member of the New York engineering firm of Zetlin, De Simone, Chaplin, and Associates. At the time this paper was written he was a graduate student at Columbia University. He received a B.S. in civil engineering from Tulane University in 1967 and an M.S. in architectural technology from Columbia University in 1968, and worked with several consulting engineering and architecture firms. Peter H. Brown is a graduate student at Columbia University. He received a B.Arch. from Cornell University in 1967 and an M.S. in urban design from Columbia in 1968, and has worked for several architectural firms including Skidmore, Owings, and Merrill.

This paper analyzes the basic methodology governing the CRAFT computer program for spatial allocation within the context of architectural building layout analysis. CRAFT works on the principle of minimizing a total "energy cost" function based on the frequency of trips between spaces and the cost per trip. An initial cost function is calculated for a reasonable layout, then cost functions for all possible exchanges of pairs of spaces are calculated and the new layout of minimum cost selected. The procedure continues until no further reduction is indicated. CRAFT is criticized on three main points: (1) it allows consideration of economic constraints only, (2) areas of spaces must be input as fixed quantities, no variation is possible, and (3) it alters the configurations of spaces without consideration of usability of the new shape. Two phases of modification have been completed and a third proposed. The capacity of the program has been increased. A variable-area methodology has been designed and is illustrated. And finally a hierarchic system is proposed for analyzing and improving the layout of subspaces while doing the same for entire units of spaces.

Most spatial allocation models for architectural building layout analysis are designed without consideration of limitations set by area or square foot requirements for different spaces. Traditional allocation models using optimizing procedures might implicitly handle area requirements if locations were defined at every intersection of a modular grid, thereby achieving an equal area association with each location. In so doing, area requirements would have to be broken down to the least common denominator to be usable in optimizing techniques. Such an approach is not feasible within present computing capabilities.[1]

A much more promising approach to layout allocation problems is by heuristic techniques. In this class of methodology CRAFT (Computerized Relative Allocation of Facilities Technique) is the most advanced program now fully operational.[2] But modifications are necessary to better adapt it to specifically architectural applications.

One series of modifications is the subject matter of this paper. It was our

1. Elwood S. Buffa, *Modern Production Management*, p. 417.
2. See Gordon C. Armour, Elwood S. Buffa, and Thomas E. Vollmann, "Allocating Facilities with CRAFT."

objective to modify CRAFT to do the following:
1. To take account of wide variations of flow paths.
2. To allow for different material handling systems.
3. To meet requirements of certain departments for certain locations.
4. To take account of the different floor area requirements of apartments.
5. To minimize the material-handling costs.

CRAFT: **A Sample Problem**

To clarify CRAFT's operation a four-department model involving food prep-aration and serving will be illustrated. First, these activities are broken down for the model as storage, cooking, food preparation, and serving. Area allot-ments were based on a 3 ft by 3 ft module and were fixed as 2 modules, 3 modules, 4 modules, and excess to fill out rectangular layouts. The block layout is bounded by a 3 module by 4 module area as shown in Table 1.

Next an internal transportation-cost matrix is generated. Two inputs are needed for this: a frequency matrix (FREQ of Table 1) showing the number of trips between activities over a specific period of time, and a cost-per-unit-distance-per-trip matrix (PREF of Table 2) indicating in basic form a prefer-ability index which represents in this model energy dissipation. The prefer-ability index reflects that the "energy cost" of carrying heavy articles from storage to food preparation is high, while the direct transport between cook-ing and serving will be lower. To simplify the example only integers have been used in these two matrixes.

By multiplying on a one-to-one basis each component of the two matrixes FREQ and PREF, a cost-per-unit-distance is established, as shown in TRANS of Table 3. This new matrix remains constant throughout the analysis. There-fore, any reductions in cost of this system will be dependent on the changes of distances between activities. Mathematically this operation is described by:

$$TRANS_{ij} = FREQ_{ij} \times PREF_{ij}$$

for $i = 1, 2 \ldots, m$ and $j = 1, 2, \ldots, n$.

Next an initial-distance matrix is established. This matrix DIST is based on the centroidal distances between departments; by necessity it is symmetrical about the main diagonal.

By multiplying the i,j component of the TRANS matrix with its corresponding component in the DIST matrix the cost component for transportation between each set of departments can be found. By summing up all the components, the total cost of transportation over the entire system will be established as shown in Table 4. Mathematically this would be described by:

$$TSYS \times \sum_{i-1}^{5} \sum_{j-1}^{5} TRANS_{ij} \times DIST_{ij}$$

TSYS, the initial cost of distribution for the entire system, is the beginning of the decision-making process of CRAFT. In order to minimize TSYS the program now decides what departments are possible candidates for exchange. To be a candidate for a two- or three-way exchange the departments must meet at least one of the following criteria: (1) they must be the same size, (2) they must have a common border, and/or (3) they must both border on a third department. The initial layout generates a list of possible exchanges or strategies as shown in Table 5. The difference in cost of the entire system due to each possible strategy is computed. The greatest cost reduction strategy replaces the initial layout, and the process continues until no further cost reduction is indicated. At this point the new relative location pattern and the associated cost information are printed out. From this evaluation strategy, arrangement 11 of Table 5 is seen to produce the greatest cost reduction.

The new "cost" of transportation over the entire system equals the original system's cost minus the cost reduction of the accepted strategy. In the case

Table 1. CRAFT—Initial Block Layout (input)

1	1	5
2	2	4
3	3	4
3	3	4

Table 2. Internal Transportation-Cost Matrix (input)

FREQ = Number of Trips

Department from	Department to				
	1	2	3	4	5
1 Storage	0	2	5	1	0
2 Food preparation	3	4	0	4	0
3 Cooking	1	0	4	2	0
4 Serving	2	1	4	0	0
5 Excess	0	0	0	0	0

PREF = Cost Index

Department from	Department to				
	1	2	3	4	5
1 Storage	0	2	3	1	0
2 Food preparation	1	2	0	2	0
3 Cooking	1	0	2	2	0
4 Serving	2	2	1	0	0
5 Excess	0	0	0	0	0

Table 3. Cost-per-Unit-Distance Matrix (computed). Initial Distance Matrix (input)

TRANS (5,5)

Department from	Department to				
	1	2	3	4	5
1	0.0	4.0	15.0	2.0	0.0
2	2.0	0.0	8.0	4.0	0.0
3	3.0	8.0	0.0	8.0	0.0
4	4.0	2.0	4.0	0.0	0.0
5	0.0	0.0	0.0	0.0	0.0

DIST (5,5) Distances in terms of modules between Activities

Department from	Department to				
	1	2	3	4	5
1	0.0	1.0	2.5	2.5	1.5
2	1.0	0.0	1.5	1.8	1.8
3	2.5	1.5	0.0	1.6	2.9
4	2.5	1.8	1.6	0.0	2.0
5	1.5	1.8	2.9	2.0	0.0

Table 4. Total Systems Cost Matrix (computed)

$$
\begin{bmatrix}
0 \times 0.0 & + & 4 \times 1.0 & + & 15 \times 2.5 & + & 2 \times 2.5 & + & 0 \times 1.5 \\
+ \ 2 \times 1.0 & + & 0 \times 0.0 & + & 8 \times 1.5 & + & 4 \times 1.8 & + & 0 \times 1.5 \\
+ \ 3 \times 2.5 & + & 8 \times 1.5 & + & 0 \times 0.0 & + & 8 \times 1.6 & + & 0 \times 2.5 \\
+ \ 4 \times 2.5 & + & 2 \times 1.8 & + & 4 \times 1.6 & + & 0 \times 0.0 & + & 0 \times 2.0 \\
+ \ 0 \times 1.5 & + & 0 \times 1.8 & + & 0 \times 2.9 & + & 0 \times 2.0 & + & 0 \times 0.0
\end{bmatrix}
=
\begin{bmatrix}
+ & 0.0 & + & 4.0 & + & 37.5 & + & 5.0 & + & 0.0 \\
+ & 2.0 & + & 0.0 & + & 12.0 & + & 7.2 & + & 0.0 \\
+ & 7.5 & + & 12.0 & + & 0.0 & + & 14.4 & + & 0.0 \\
+ & 10.0 & + & 3.6 & + & 6.4 & + & 0.0 & + & 0.0 \\
+ & 0.0 & + & 0.0 & + & 0.0 & + & 0.0 & + & 0.0
\end{bmatrix}
= 121.6
$$

Table 5. Strategies and Resultant Arrangements

List of Strategies

Strategy	Move A Dept.	Move B Dept.	Move C Dept.	Criteria
1	1	2		1
2	3	2		2
3	4	5		2
4	1	5		2
5	1	5	4	3
6	1	2	3	3
7	1	2	4	3
8	2	3	4	3
9	2	5	4	3
10	3	5	4	3
11	2	5	1	3

Arrangement	ΔTc	Arrangement	ΔTc	Arrangement	ΔTc
1: [2 2 5 / 1 1 4 / 3 3 4 / 3 3 4]	+2.0	5: [4 4 4 / 2 2 1 / 3 3 1 / 3 3 5]	+5.2	8: [4 4 5 / 4 1 1 / 3 3 2 / 3 3 2]	+6.4
2: [1 1 5 / 3 3 4 / 3 3 4 / 2 2 4]	+6.3	6: [1 1 5 / 4 4 4 / 2 3 3 / 2 3 3]	+7.0	9: [1 1 4 / 5 4 4 / 3 3 2 / 3 3 2]	−7.6
3: [2 2 4 / 1 1 4 / 3 3 4 / 3 3 4]	+6.0	7: [3 3 4 / 2 2 5 / 3 3 4 / 1 1 4]	+3.5	10: [2 2 3 / 1 1 3 / 5 4 3 / 4 4 3]	+6.2
4: [5 1 1 / 2 2 4 / 3 3 4 / 3 3 4]	−3.5			11: [5 2 2 / 1 1 4 / 3 3 4 / 3 3 4]	+16.8

of the example the initial "cost" is 121.6 units and the greatest cost reduction (due to strategy 11) is 16.8 so that the cost of the new layout is 104.8. This layout now becomes the initial layout for a new set of strategies. The process continues until no further cost reduction is indicated. The final layout of a CRAFT analysis for another problem, involving eight departments, has been illustrated in Figure 1.

Evaluation

With this background of the operation of CRAFT, it is possible to evaluate the methodology within an architectural building design context. The basic presupposition of the program is that the goal of design is to minimize the "cost" (or "sacrifice") required for interaction and thereby maximize the tendency for interaction. Accepting this presupposition does not in itself lead deductively to the development of valid parameters to measure interaction *except at the economic level.* Assuming that a broader set of parameters (including social ones) could be established, CRAFT would provide the designer with a valuable building-evaluation tool.

However, even accepting the validity of CRAFT as an evaluation procedure does not answer the question of how it can be used in design and planning methodology. Two additional major obstacles lie in its path. First, in any architectural design process, area requirements have a range of acceptable values. At present CRAFT will only accept one value for each area. With only a one-module difference in size, a possible means of exchange and the only means of major locational shifts has been eliminated. The second obstacle is just as critical. In the process of making exchanges, CRAFT has the ability to alter the configuration of a department without consideration of the usability of the new shape. The program has no internal structuring device, and therefore unworkable configurations can result.

Other shortcomings of the program are related to the capacity of the present program and not to the design procedure itself. Only forty departments can be handled within a 30 by 30 modular grid layout. With these obstacles the present status of CRAFT for an architectural methodology is limited; its potential, however, is great.

Potentially, CRAFT could be particularly effective in the design of hospitals where efficiency of movement is essential. It has already been used in the designing of public schools.[3] Of course, CRAFT's greatest use has been in laying out factories and offices where partitions are minimal and topological considerations dominate. Most architectural designs have more stringent requirements than this and will have to wait until the previously mentioned two major drawbacks have been corrected.

It is essential to note in relation to CRAFT that to obtain meaningful results the original layout must be reasonable. If this is so, CRAFT will produce small improvements that can lead to new insight regarding the proper allocation pattern.

Modifications to CRAFT

The problems that have been discussed in the last section are now under study at Columbia University. The first area of study was an attempt to broaden the scope of the CRAFT program and to minimize the extent of the problems created by its procedure.

Capacity

Basically, the first study consisted of increasing the *capacity* of the program. By increasing the number of departments CRAFT is able to handle it is possible to break down departments into smaller components with an interconnecting structure. Furthermore, by increasing the program's capacity, problems of much broader dimensions such as exist in urban design and planning can be handled.

---

3. Louis J. Kishkunas and Donald H. Peckenpaugh, *A Comprehensive Concept for Vocational Educational Facilities*, pp. 9–29. See also Alan Colker and James Leib, "A Comprehensive Approach to Vocational Education Facility Planning," in this volume.

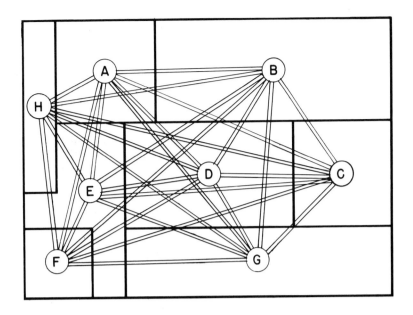

1. Final layout using the basic CRAFT program

2. ARCOS—step function of cost to changes in area

Table 6. Initial layout—variable area method

Table 7. AREXC—Possible Location and Area Exchanges

Table 8. Final layout—variable area method

Table 9. Hierarchical decomposition layout technique

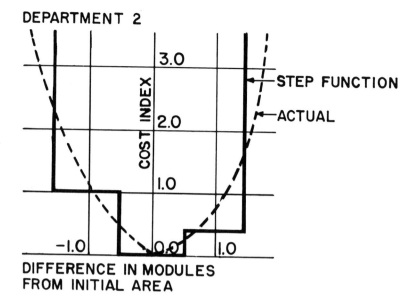

DEPARTMENT 2

STEP FUNCTION

ACTUAL

COST INDEX

DIFFERENCE IN MODULES FROM INITIAL AREA

Table 6

1	1	1
2	2	3

Table 7

	1	2	3
1	−1	+1	
2	−1		+1
3		+1	−1
4	+1	−1	

−1 Minus One Area Module
+1 Plus One Area Module

Table 8

1	1	3
2	2	3

Best Exchange 2
Total Final
Cost = 8.4

Table 9

Initial Layout

1	1	3	3	12	12
2	2	3	3	12	12
4	4	5	5	10	10
4	4	5	5	10	10
6	6	6	7	11	11
6	6	7	7	12	11
9	9	7	7	11	11
9	9	8	8	11	11

——— Level A
——— Level B

Level "A" Shift

2	2	5
1	1	4
3	3	4
3	3	4

Level "B" Shift

5	5	5	4
5	4	4	4

The second study was the development of a *variable area methodology.* Most research has been centered here. The procedure that is now being added to CRAFT is based on two basic assumptions about area requirements: first, that there is an optimum area for each separate department, and second, that each department has a range of area allotments with higher costs (economic or any other equivalent scale) than the optimum area. The department area allotments may or may not be able to reach an optimum, depending on the limitations of the overall layout area and the complexity of the problem.

Area allocations must be multiples of the basic modules of the grid established to describe the layout. Therefore costs can only be described by increments of one module of area at a time, that is, by a step functional relation with area allotments. The variable area method will be illustrated by a simplified three-department problem, shown in Table 6. Remembering the evaluation procedure of the basic program, it is clear that under the conditions of initial layout and the TRANS matrix, the incremental function of cost to changes in area (ARCOS) just described for which department 2 has been illustrated in Figure 2, a whole new series of exchanges becomes possible.

In the food preparation example given at the beginning of the paper, the optimum cost was described as zero because only differences were sought. This is not the case if total evaluation is sought. A list of possible location and area exchanges (AREXC) is therefore established as shown in Table 7, whereby the smaller department increases in area (+1 module) and exchanges location with the larger department which has decreased in area (−1 module). In this particular example the best exchange was number 2 and the best layout was as shown in Table 8. In actual operation the best exchange would be evaluated by a combination of distribution and area costs. Through the addition of a variable-area technique the CRAFT methodology is brought into closer agreement with the flexibility of an actual design process.

Hierarchical Decomposition

The last study is in the initial formulation stage at the time of writing. It is just as critical to the program's performance as the variable area method, but much more difficult to make operational. This study consists of applying *hierarchical decomposition techniques* (as discussed in Part 4 of this volume) to the major departments. In this way, entire departments will exchange with departments of the same order while their subdepartments seek optimum interior arrangement within the department's boundary, briefly hinted at in Figure 6. This phase essentially requires the innovation of a CRAFT–within–CRAFT.

Redefining the original model according to these criteria would require the partitioning of the TRANS matrix according to its subunits. Once this step is complete, not only will external distribution be included as criteria but the internal distribution pattern will be just as meaningful. Orientation of subunits of different departments, such as mechanical areas, can be promoted; this was not possible under the homogeneous department composition.

It is expected that once these modifications are complete CRAFT will become a more valuable tool in the architectural building design process. It will still be dependent on the architect's ability to structure the initial input to achieve significant results. CRAFT will not stand by itself and can only complement the unifying nature of intuitive design processes. It is this ability of CRAFT to work within the present architectural framework that leads to its promise of greater acceptance and success.

17 Network Models of Configurations of Rectangular Parallelepipeds

Lavette C. Teague, Jr.

Skidmore, Owings and Merrill
Architects and Planners
Chicago, Illinois

Lavette C. Teague, Jr., heads the computer group at Skidmore, Owings, and Merrill in Chicago and is a research affiliate in the Department of Civil Engineering at M.I.T. He received a B.Arch. in 1957, and an S.M. and Ph.D. in civil engineering in 1965 and 1968, all from M.I.T. He has worked for Synergetics in Raleigh, North Carolina, and the Rust Engineering Company, Birmingham, Alabama. His publications include papers on architectural systems analysis and computer-aided structural and architectural design. This paper is based on his doctoral dissertation, "The Representation of Spatial Relationships in a Computer System for Building Design." Research was supervised by Professor Alan Hershdorfer, and partial support was provided by the 1966 Arnold W. Bruner Scholarship of the New York Chapter of the American Institute of Architects and by the National Science Foundation.

A model for the representation of spatial relationships which is responsive to changes that occur during the course of the design process is essential to a system for building design. Theoretical models based on graphs representing adjacencies have been used for problems in building layout synthesis. However, a network representation of squared rectangles developed by Tutte is more appealing because geometrical as well as topological information can be contained. This representation and the ways in which it can be generalized to configurations of rectangles are reviewed. The representation is extended to three dimensions as a theoretical basis for architectural applications and thus computer implementation. From the point of view of theory, the ability to interpret configurations of rectangular spaces as a network makes the results of network theory available for application to analysis and synthesis of spatial relationships in building design. As the basis for computer representation of spatial relationships, the network approach is applicable to the modeling of building systems other than the system of spaces which motivated this study. These results will contribute to a more nearly unified theoretical framework for analysis and synthesis of building systems to aid the building designer.

For architects, spaces are fundamental constituents of buildings. They become the places for human activity, the major elements of architectural form. In the words of Le Corbusier:

Architecture is the masterly, correct and magnificent play of masses brought together in light. Our eyes are made to see forms in light; light and shade reveal these forms; cubes, cones, spheres, cylinders or pyramids are the great primary forms which light reveals to advantage; the image of these is distinct and tangible within us and without ambiguity.[1]

Thus these primary forms, so vividly perceived, are the elemental volumes in terms of which architecture is conceived. So, too, can architectural space be analyzed, in terms of relationships among simple constituent elements. This emphasis on the arrangement and perception of space makes the identification, analysis, and organization of spatial relationships a key problem for the designer.

Systems of Spatial Relationships

Central to the study of these relationships is the discipline of architectural geometry. In geometric terms a space is a volume, idealized as a connected three-dimensional region of three-dimensional Euclidean space. A collec-

---

1. Charles E. Jeanneret-Gris (Le Corbusier), *Vers une Architecture,* translated by F. Etchells, *Towards a New Architecture,* p. 31.

tion of spaces may be regarded as a system within which relationships among spaces may be defined and studied.

In the most direct sense a set of spaces is defined completely once the points belonging to each space are specified, whether explicitly in terms of their coordinates or implicitly in terms of their boundaries. From these data, points can be classified as interior or boundary points; a space can be classified as a polyhedron, a cone, an ellipsoid, etc.; the volume and surface area of a space can be calculated; and other properties and characteristics of the individual spaces can be determined.

Similarly, relationships between and among spaces, such as distance and adjacency, and the properties of these relationships can be defined and determined. These relationships and properties of spaces are inherently geometric and topological. They are thus inevitably related to the geometric and topological information about every other building system.

Among the properties of space that are of interest to the building designer are the following: convexity, shape, size (volume and surface areas), proportions, location in the building or on the site, and orientation with respect to the earth. Relevant relationships among spaces include: distance, adjacency, direction from one to another, whether spaces contain certain specified lines, curves, planes, surfaces, or spaces, and pattern relationships such as symmetries in arrangement.

In addition to these fundamental geometric and topological properties and relationships which are characteristic of spaces considered as an independent system, the building designer is concerned with other relationships involving spaces. These relationships require information about elements of other building systems. For example, relationships of visual or acoustical openness and privacy between spaces are determined by the optical and acoustical properties of the materials of the intervening surfaces as well as by the location of the spaces themselves.

Models of Spatial Relationships

The representation of the spaces in a building as a system entails a model which exhibits the properties and relationships of importance to the designer. The usefulness of the model depends on how well it embodies the relationships and to what extent it facilitates the designer's understanding of the real-world system being modeled. Also important is the ease with which the model can be manipulated for the design operations of analysis, evaluation, and synthesis. For, as just pointed out, the spatial relationships can always be determined from the fundamental space-defining data.

The designer of a building models a configuration of spaces so that he can study spatial relationships. Building systems are now being represented and manipulated by use of computers. Indeed, as Gray has written:
The aim of computer aided design is to create in the computer a model of the design problem . . . This model may now be tested against the specification and will generally be modified until the design goal is achieved . . . several users of the design system may wish to access and transform the model, for instance to display views and projections of it, or check on how it interfaces with a parallel project.[2]

Of particular practical significance are models for configurations of rectangular parallelepipeds. Because of the preference for rectangular geometry in building practice, a large percentage of the buildings that are constructed consist of rectangular spaces. A system for computer-aided building design can take advantage of this fact to achieve efficiencies which exploit the specialized properties of rectangular geometry. It can still employ more general though possibly less efficient geometric representations when they are required by a particular design problem.

---

2. J. C. Grey, "Compound Data Structure for Computer Aided Design," *Proceedings of the ACM 22nd National Conference,* 1967, p. 355.

Mathematical models known as graphs and networks provide useful representations of relationships of all kinds. There have been a number of instances in which plane configurations were represented by graphs based on the relationship of adjacency between spaces. Such a representation contains only topological information.

However, spatial arrangements in buildings must be geometrically as well as topologically feasible. They must obey constraints on the size, shape, and proportions of spaces as well as adjacency constraints. Moreover, relationships of "nearness" instead of adjacency must often be defined and measured by distance or travel time rather than in terms such as the number of intermediate spaces.

Tutte's Network Representation

It is possible to represent a two-dimensional arrangement of rectangular spaces in a more compact way which embodies both geometric and topological information. This is a network representation invented by Brooks, Smith, Stone, and Tutte for the purpose of solving the problem of the dissection of a rectangle into squares.[3] Because Tutte has published additional discussion of the representation, it will be referred to here as the "Tutte representation."[4]

The original paper, published in 1940, presents and proves the general theory of such networks and gives methods for the synthesis of squared rectangles. The concluding section mentions possible generalizations of the representation to rectangulations of rectangles, polygons with angles of $\pi/2$ and $3\pi/2$ degrees (configurations of adjacent rectangles), triangulations of triangles, and squared cylinders and tori. Near the end of the paper is the statement: "As yet, however, there is no satisfactory analogue in three dimensions. The problem is less urgent, because *there is no perfect cube (or parallelepiped)*." A proof follows that in any dissection of a rectangular parallelepiped into a finite number of cubes, two of the cubes are equal. Such a proof may well have discouraged further work on a three-dimensional representation.

The network representation of Tutte is presented here, along with the modifications required to generalize it to arrangements of arbitrary rectangles. Restrictions are introduced where necessary to retain architecturally significant relationships.

Figure 1 shows the construction of Tutte's network representation for the rectangle also shown.

Perhaps the most straightforward way to visualize the construction of the network is to draw the diagonal of each rectangle from its lower left corner to its upper right corner. These are the *arcs* of the network. Assign to each diagonal a *flow* equal to the vertical dimension of the rectangle. If the lefthand sides of two or more rectangles form a continuous vertical, move the corresponding diagonals until their left-hand ends coincide. This common point is a node of the network. Assign it a number, the *potential,* equal to the x coordinate of the vertical it represents. The result is the network shown in Figure 1. Just as the diagonal vector which spans each rectangle is composed of two orthogonal components (sides of the rectangle), the arc which represents the rectangle has a flow (the vertical dimension) and a *potential difference* (the horizontal dimension).

A network can also be constructed in which the nodes represent continuous horizontals and in which the node potentials are y coordinates. The arc flows then represent x dimensions. Such a network is shown in Figure 2 and is called the *conjugate* of the network of Figure 1. In fact, the conjugate network shown in Figure 2 is the representation used as the example in the original paper.

3. R. L. Brooks, C. A. Smith, A. H. Stone, and W. T. Tutte, "The Dissection of Rectangles into Squares."
4. W. T. Tutte, "Squared Rectangles."

1. Construction of the network

2. Conjugate network

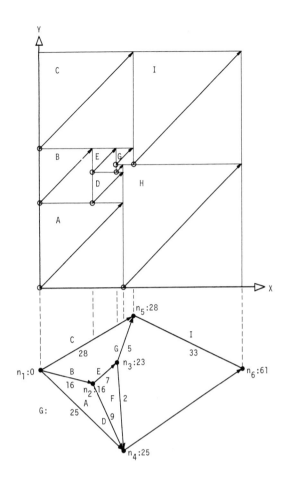

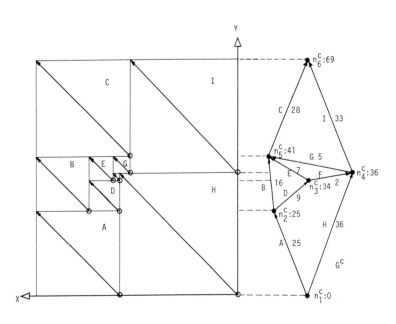

165 Network Models of Configurations of Rectangular Parallelepipeds

Generalization to Rectangulations of Rectangles

The network representation of a squared rectangle can be generalized to the case of a rectangle composed of other rectangles. Such a network may be constructed by following a procedure similar to that described above. Figure 3 shows an example.

An element is now a rectangle instead of a square. In addition, the arcs incident out of each node must be ordered.

The network may now have multiple arcs. The ordering of the arcs at each node is necessary to distinguish among symmetries in the arrangement of the rectangles, especially in the case of multiple arcs, as an examination of Figure 4 will indicate.

Construction of the Three-Dimensional Representation

A rectangular parallelepiped comprising rectangular parallelepipeds may also be represented by a network, if the concept of flow is generalized further. Figure 5 shows such a network.

The construction of the three-dimensional network may be visualized as follows.

Using an orientation convention which associates with each of the vertical faces of a parallelepiped one of the directions north, south, east, or west, draw the diagonal of each parallelepiped from its *origin* (the southwest lower corner) to its northwest upper corner. These diagonals will be the arcs of the network. Assign to each diagonal a flow with two components: the first representing the y dimension of the parallelepiped and the second representing the z dimension of the parallelepiped. If the west faces of two or more parallelepipeds form a continuous (xz) plane, move the corresponding diagonals until their origins coincide. Begin with the diagonal of the space whose origin is at the southernmost lower corner of the plane. Take next the diagonals of spaces with origins immediately above that of the first space, from bottom to top. Then move across the plane to the space whose origin has the next smallest y coordinate, followed by the spaces directly above it, and so on, until all the arcs have been collected at the origin of the first space. That point is a node of the network; its potential is the x coordinate of the plane. The upper ends of the diagonals are brought together at the nodes corresponding to the east faces of the spaces in a similar fashion. The result is the network shown in Figure 5. Each arc comprises a space. Its potential difference is the x dimension; its flow consists of two components representing the y and z dimensions and thus the area as well.

The arcs incident upon each node are ordered, just as in the two-dimensional case, but the ordering must now be two-dimensional, rather than one-dimensional. The flow now has two components instead of only one. However, the flow is not an ordinary vector, because it cannot be combined with another flow in accordance with the ordinary rules for vector addition. As a result, determining the coordinates of the origins of spaces which correspond to interior arcs of the network is somewhat more complicated than in the two-dimensional case.[5] By analogy to the two-dimensional case, it is also possible to represent the configuration by either of two conjugate networks. In one of these the node potentials represent y coordinates, and the components of the arc flows represent x and z dimensions. In the other the node potentials represent z coordinates, and the components of the arc flows represent x and y dimensions.

Applications

Preceding sections described a network representation of both two- and three-dimensional configurations of rectangular spaces. Such representations can serve as the basis for a computer data structure for use in a building design system. However, the implementation of the data structure is not discussed here.[6] Because of the centrality of geometric information to building

---

5. A more detailed discussion may be found in Section 6.3 of Teague, "The Representation of Spatial Relationships in a Computer System for Building Design."
6. Ibid, Chapter 7.

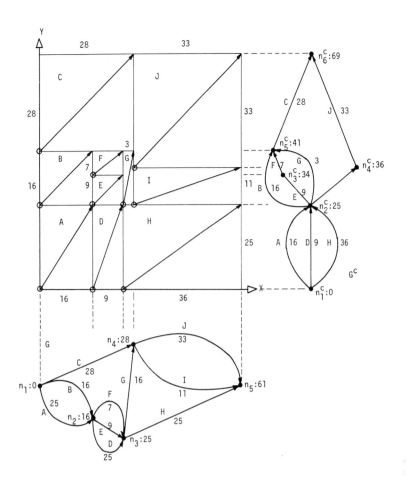

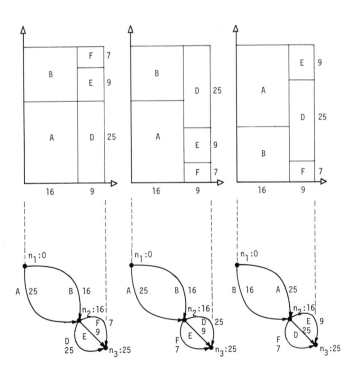

167   Network Models of Configurations of Rectangular Parallelepipeds

5. Construction of the three-dimensional
network

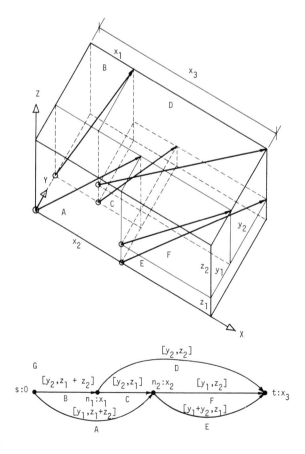

design, such a data structure may be used to organize the general information base for a design problem. There are also possible applications to special-purpose data structures for particular design tasks.

Among these applications are data structures for graphical display of rectangularly subdivided planes, the representation of structural loading patterns comprising rectangular distributed loads, and the use of the network in finite-element methods of structural analysis. Similar applications to other building systems containing rectangular elements can also be expected. Applications to urban land-use mapping within a grid are also anticipated.

Many transportation techniques for analysis and simulation of circulation systems use a network model. Such network models can be extracted from the network representing spatial relationships

The network also provides an approach to spatial synthesis based on a representation and theoretical model which includes such geometric constraints as fit, shape, and proportion. It arose, after all, in response to a problem of spatial synthesis: how to construct a rectangle composed of square elements with no two of the squares the same size. The synthesis of such networks and thus of the corresponding rectangles is not simple. Many of the examples of perfect rectangles presented have been discovered through heuristic techniques for combinations of known rectangles or alterations to known rectangles. Some use has also been made of computers to make an exhaustive search of the combinatorially possible networks corresponding to rectangles of given order.

Even in two dimensions the architectural problem of spatial synthesis is one of greater generality than that of constructing a squared rectangle. There are more combinations to be considered, and even with a greater number of constraints the problem is likely to be more difficult. In three dimensions a clear procedure for network synthesis needs to be worked out. Although the synthesis of networks is a new and difficult field, from a theoretical point of view the network approach to spatial synthesis in architecture seems promising.

18 A Dual Linear Graph Representation for Space-Filling Location Problems of the Floor Plan Type

John Grason

Department of Electrical Engineering
Carnegie-Mellon University
Pittsburgh, Pennsylvania

John Grason is Assistant Professor of Electrical Engineering at Carnegie-Mellon University. He received a B.S. in electrical engineering from Lehigh University in 1964, an M.S. in electrical engineering from the Carnegie Institute of Technology in 1965, and a Ph.D in electrical engineering (systems and communication science) from Carnegie-Mellon in 1969. He has worked with the General Motors Corporation, the Bell Telephone Laboratories, and the RCA Laboratories. Portions of the present work were supported by the National Science Foundation and the Advanced Research Projects Agency of the U.S. Department of Defense and were done under the guidance of Herbert Simon. Much of the initial work was done in 1967 at the RCA Laboratories in Princeton under the guidance of Saul Amarel.

A formal class of space-filling location problems of the floor plan type is introduced. A problem representation is defined as the manner in which information pertinent to the solution of a problem is organized. It is proposed that a dual graph representation is superior to the grid mapping representations currently in use for computer solution of floor plan layout problems. This contention is supported by showing that the dual graph functions well as both a "requirement diagram" and a "form diagram" in that it allows direct mapping of a primary set of design constraints into independent form realizations. Formal properties of the dual graph representation are presented, including some theorems on physical realizability. An example design problem is presented to illustrate several design activities which can be used to solve a design problem using this representation. Finally, a brief discussion of the treatment of area constraints using the dual graph representation is given.

In this paper a *space-filling location problem* is defined as a problem which has the goal of the placement of a set of subspaces in a particular larger space, subject both to a class of location requirements and to the constraint that the subspaces must entirely fill the larger space. In any problem the manner in which the information pertinent to the solution of that problem is organized is important. This manner of information organization can be called the problem representation, and this paper presents such a representation for a class of space-filling location problems of the floor plan type.

A Class of Space-Filling Location Problems

A rigidly defined but nevertheless reasonably general class of floor plans can be specified in the following way:

A building consists of a set of contiguous rooms which completely fill the simply connected area enclosed by the *walls* of the building. All buildings and all rooms are rectangles. Buildings are by convention oriented with their walls parallel to the axes of a north-south rectangular coordinate system. Thus it is possible to divide the space outside a building into four rectangular outside spaces, as shown in Figure 1. A *space* is defined to be either a room or one of the four outside spaces. Any two contiguous spaces may have at most one door joining them, and the existence of a door is indicated by a double-headed arrow intersecting the wall segment separating the two spaces. A typical floor plan of this class is also shown in Figure 1.

The convention that rooms and buildings be rectangles need not seriously limit the generality of the class of floor plans. As long as right-angled wall intersections are adhered to, irregular buildings can be filled out to rectangular shape by using "patios," and irregular room shapes can be formed by treating compound spaces as single rooms, as shown in Figure 2.

A floor plan of this class may be completely described by using three primary concepts basic to architecture, *contiguity, communication,* and *physical dimensions.* In keeping with these primary concepts, only three basic types of constraints are necessary to specify design problems for this class of floor plans: (1) Contiguity, space A is contiguous to space B on the north, south, east, west, or unspecified side. (2) Communication, there exists a door between them. (3) Physical dimensions, the length of the wall segment is specified in metric units.

The first two types of constraints will be called the *location constraints.* Since the location constraints and the length constraints are capable of totally specifying a floor plan within the class, all higher order constraints, such as area, proximity, and remote communication must be definable in terms of this basic set. In this paper such definitions are stated in a natural-language form of a simple predicate calculus.

The Representation

In order for a diagram (or representation) to be useful in design, it must be simultaneously both a requirement diagram and a form diagram. This can be interpreted as stating that the diagram must contain information about the design requirements only in terms of the forms that are to satisfy them. Most current attempts at computer-implemented floor plan layout rely on some sort of modularized grid representation with arrangements optimized by either sequential "best placements" or random perturbations and hill climbing.[1] However some researchers have recognized that such a representation does not allow for the highly desirable mapping of design requirements directly and exclusively into form components. In particular, location constraints and physical dimension constraints cannot be treated independently. Thus, attention has been turned to an independent topological specification using a dual linear graph of the floor plan.[2] (Recall that a linear graph is simply a collection of nodes connected by lines called edges.) The following paragraphs set the basis for a dual graph approach to floor plan layout that has been worked out in some detail by this author.

Setting aside doors for the moment, a floor plan of the class discussed here can be drawn in the form of a linear graph, as shown in Figure 2. In keeping with the terminology of floor plans, this will be called the *floor plan graph,* and its edges, nodes, and regions will be referred to as *wall segments, corners,* and *spaces,* respectively. The *dual graph* of this floor plan graph, or any graph, is obtained by placing a node inside each space and constructing edges to join the nodes of contiguous spaces. By convention, edges crossing north-south wall segments will be colored, dotted, and directed from west to east, while edges crossing east-west wall segments will be colored, slashed, and directed from south to north. Dimensioning is accomplished by labeling these edges with a number equal to the length of the wall segments that they cross. Such a dual graph for the floor plan graph of Figure 2 is shown in Figure 3.

To distinguish it from the floor plan graph, the local structures of the dual graph will be referred to as nodes, edges, and regions. The utility and appro-

1. For example see David Parsons, "Planning by the Numbers"; Bertram Whitehead and Mohamed Z. Elders, "An Approach to the Optimum Layout of Single-Storey Buildings"; and Elwood S. Buffa, Gordon C. Armour, and Thomas E. Vollmann, "Allocating Facilities with CRAFT."
2. See P. H. Levin, "Use of Graphs to Decide the Optimum Layout of Buildings"; and Vince Casalaina and Horst Rittel, "Generating Floorplans from Adjacency Matrices."

1. Examples of the defined class of floor plans

2. Examples of nonrectangular spaces and the floor plan graph

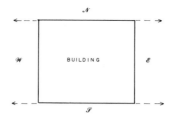

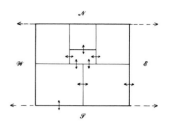

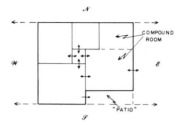

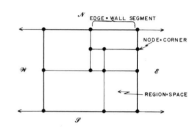

3. A floor plan graph with its corresponding dual graph

4. Obtaining a floor plan graph from its dual graph

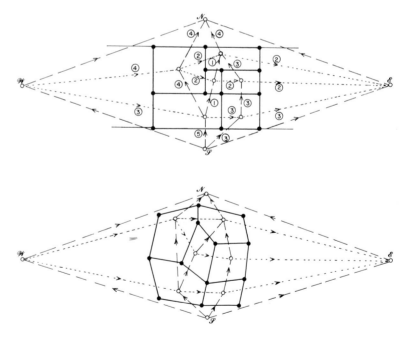

priateness of this dual graph representation for floor plan problems is discussed in the next two sections.

The general idea of the use of the dual graph representation in the solution
of design problems is to start with the nondimensioned outline of the building, as specified by the four directed, slashed edges SE, SW, EN, and WN in
Figure 3, and then gradually fill in the rest of the structure, node by node and
edge by edge, in response to the design constraints. The two fundamental
form components of the floor plan graph, wall segments and spaces, map
directly into the edges and nodes respectively of the dual graph. Thus, in
terms of these local structures, the three basic constraint types now take the
following form:

1. Contiguity. "Space A is contiguous to space B on the north, south, east,
west, or unspecified side" becomes "construct an appropriately directed
edge between node A and node B," where contiguity on an unspecified side
can be indicated by using a nondirected edge, i.e., a solid line.
2. Communication. The addition of a door to the constructed edge, indicated
by a slash intersecting the edge.
3. Length. "Wall segment X is L units long" becomes "assign a weight L to
edge X."

As was stated earlier, a simple predicate calculus can be used to construct
higher-order constraints from this basic set. Some examples follow:
4. Direct accessibility. "Space A is directly accessible from space B" becomes "either space A communicates with space B or space A and space B
both communicate with the same 'corridor' (a special class of space)."
5. Easy accessibility. "Space A is easily accessible from space B" becomes
"either space A communicates with space B or space A and space B both
communicate with a third space (not necessarily a corridor) by way of wall
segments corresponding to edges both dotted and slashed.
6. Room size. "Room A is L units long by W units wide" becomes eventually
"the sum of the weights of the slashed edges directed away from node A
is L; the sum of the weights of the slashed edges directed into node A is L;
the sum of the weights of the dotted edges directed away from node A is W;
and the sum of the weights of the dotted edges directed into node A is W."

Notice that the desired goal of mapping design requirements directly into
form realizations has been achieved through the use of the dual graph
representation. Notice further that the form realizations satisfy only the design requirements which generated them and nothing else.

In order to be useful, the dual graph representation should be capable of
completely specifying a floor plan of the class under consideration. This is
indeed the case, since it can be shown that if one takes the dual of a well-
formed completed dual graph, he obtains the floor plan graph. An example of
this step for the dual graph of the floor plan of Figure 3 is shown in Figure 4.
Next, it can be shown that the wall segments of the floor plan graph can be
appropriately straightened and rectangularized to form a floor plan.

A nested hierarchy of structures can be treated, considering the dual graph
of a rectangular building as itself a node in a larger graph, or considering a
room node as representing a rectangular space which is to be further subdivided using dual-graph techniques. Various attributes other than doors can
be assigned to the edges, such as windows and facilities for the distribution
of utilities.

Finally, through the use of uncolored, undirected edges and/or unweighted
edges, a partially completed dual graph is capable of simultaneously representing a large set of potential floor plans without actually enumerating them,
because the attributes of these edges can eventually be assigned in a variety
of ways. Furthermore, since the addition and removal of constraints is
equivalent to the addition and removal of independent local structures, no

gross upheavals of the entire representation are necessitated when design updating is desired.

Properties of the Representation

The following are properties of the dual graph considered important for the design process. Because of space limitations, proofs of nonobvious properties will not be included in this paper.

Structures

Using standard linear graph notation, the local structures of the dual graph are called *nodes, edges,* and *regions.* A sequence of edges, joined end to end, is called a *chain.* A chain that closes on itself and forms the boundary of a region is called a *circuit.*

Planarity

Since the floor plan graph is planar, a partially or completely specified dual graph must also be planar. That is, none of the edges of a dual graph may cross one another.

Well-Formed Room Nodes

Since a rectangular room has four walls, it is necessary in a completed dual graph that a node corresponding to a room have connected to it at least one each of the four edge types, slashed directed outward, dotted directed outward, slashed directed inward, and dotted directed inward, taken in clockwise order as shown in Figure 5. If the physical dimensions of the room are known, then for a node the sum of the weights of the slashed-inward edges must equal the sum of the weights of the slashed-outward edges, and this must equal the length of the room. A similar condition holds for the dotted edges.

Any partially completed room node must not have its edges and/or weights arranged in such a way that these conditions cannot be satisfied when the node is completed.

Well-Formed Terminal Regions

The regions of a completed dual graph, called *terminal regions,* can be of only five types. These five well-formed terminal regions are shown in Figure 5. Their floor plan counterparts (corners) can be found in appropriate parts of Figure 3.

The Turn Concept

Consider again the room node shown in Figure 5. Imagine that by convention all slashed edges of a dual graph would be oriented in the north-south fashion shown, and all dotted edges east-west. Then one can envisage making $0°$, $\pm 90°$, or $\pm 180°$ turns as he passes from edge to edge across a node. The appropriate turn matrix is shown in Table 1. The decision as to whether an "about face" turn is a $+$ or a $-180°$ turn is important and depends on the relative clockwise positioning of the involved edges about the node in question.

Two definitions are necessary at this point. A sequence of turns along a chain in which a $+180°$ turn is followed immediately by an arbitrary number (including none) of $+90°$ turns followed immediately by a $+180°$ turn will be called a $+180° (+90°) +180°$ *turn sequence*; the converse, in which a $-180°$ turn is followed immediately by an arbitrary number (including none) of $-90°$ turns followed immediately by a $-180°$ turn, will be called a $-180° (90°)$ $-180°$ *turn sequence.* A partially or entirely completed dual graph will be termed *physically realizable* if it is possible to construct a two-dimensional layout of nonoverlapping rectangles corresponding to the nodes of that dual graph which satisfy the contiguity relationships specified by the edges of that graph.

Theorems Pertaining to Realizability

There are three theorems pertinent to the realizability of a cell configuration. *Theorem 1.* A chain of unweighted edges of a dual graph is physically realizable if and only if it contains no $\pm 180° (\pm 90°) \pm 180°$ turn sequences. *Theorem 2.* A circuit of unweighted edges of a dual graph is physically realizable if and only if it contains no $\pm 180° (\pm 90°) \pm 180°$ turn sequences and the sum of its turns, taken in the clockwise direction, is $-360°$. *Theorem 3.* Any nonterminal region of a dual graph surrounded by a phys-

Table 1
Turn Matrix

First Edge \ Second Edge	Tip of Slashed	Tail of Slashed	Tip of Dotted	Tail of Dotted
Tip of Slashed	±180°	0°	+90°	−90°
Tail of Slashed	0°	±180°	−90°	+90°
Tip of Dotted	−90°	+90°	±180°	0°
Tail of Dotted	+90°	−90°	0°	±180°

Table 2
Design Constraints for an Example Building Design Problem

A rectangular house is to be designed containing four rectangular rooms (the living room L, the bedroom S, the kitchen K, and the bathroom B) and possibly a rectangular corridor C.

Location Constraints
(L1) K is contiguous to E.
(L2) S is contiguous to N.
(L3) S communicates with B.
(L4) K is contiguous to B.
(L5) "Street" is equivalent to N or S.
(L6) L is contiguous to "street."
(L7) S is directly accessible from "street" by way of "front door (FD)" which opens onto "street."
(L8) L is easily accessible from "street."
(L9) K is easily accessible from "street."

Dimension Constraints
(D1) Measuring size in area, L is larger than S which is larger than K, which is larger than B.
(D2) The allowable room sizes are, in arbitrary metric units, 6 x 3, 4 x 3, 3 x 3, 2 x 3, and 1 x 3.
(D3) C, if it exists, is 1 unit wide and any number of units in length.

Contradiction Constraints
(C1) "Front door (FD)" cannot open into S.
(C2) The long side of C cannot be contiguous to an outside space.
(C3) B cannot be not contiguous to an outside space.

5. Well-defined local dual graph structures

At least one of each edge type, arranged in the proper order. Sum of weights of same colored edges flowing into and out of a node must be equal.

ROOM NODE

TERMINAL REGIONS

6. Two early snapshots of example design problem

Undimensioned outline of the building is specified, and constraint L1 is satisfied.

Constraints L1 through L5 have been satisfied. It has been decided to try street = S first.

7. Two intermediate snapshots of example design problem

All location constraints now satisfied, with some deduced edges included.

Starting to introduce the dimension constraints while filling in non-specified edges.

8. One solution to the example design problem

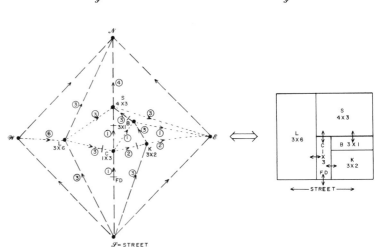

ically realizable circuit can be filled in with well-formed terminal regions by the addition of appropriately directed edges, and without the introduction of additional nodes.

An Example Design Problem

The properties of the dual graph relate mainly to the "well formedness" of partially completed dual graph structures in terms of physical realizability. In carrying out a building design using this representation, these properties are extremely useful in predicting the potential success or failure of partially completed dual graphs, and in deducing certain physical relationships that are implicit in the constraints.

The author is currently implementing computer routines related to the solution of the limited class of floor plan design problems described in this paper. In these routines the information describing a partially completed dual graph is organized in terms of a special hierarchy of graph substructures. This special organization, not described here, allows the writing of highly efficient routines for checking graph planarity and generating alternative graph topologies in the course of the solution of a design problem.

To illustrate how these computer routines could be applied to a typical design problem of this class, an example is given. The design constraints (typified by Theorems 1, 2, and 3 in the preceding section) are shown in Table 2, and five "snapshots" of the dual graph representation as the design process progresses are shown in Figures 6 through 8.

Corresponding to the three classes of constraints specified in Table 2 three types of design activities are involved in the solution of this problem. The design activity for location constraints is applied first, as shown in Figure 6 and the left half of Figure 7. It adds structures to the dual graph which satisfy the various location constraints, and at the same time it checks for planarity of the graph, well formedness of space nodes, and physical realizability of chains and circuits. If the satisfaction of a particular constraint causes one of these properties to be violated, then it is known that the problem is over-constrained and no solution will exist. At this point some decision would have to be made as to which constraints could be relaxed to resolve the difficulty. A discussion of this topic is not within the range of this paper.

At the conclusion of the location design activity, as in the left half of Figure 7, the dual graph represents a partially specified topology of the floor plan. The task is now to fill in the rest of the edges of the dual graph in conformance with the topological rules of physical realizability in such a way that the dimension constraints are also satisfied within the generated topology. This is done by the *dimension design activity* which tries various well-chosen combinations of edge assignments and edge weights, as in the right half of Figure 7, until either a set of design solutions is produced or until it is shown that the problem is overconstrained and no solution exists. It is important to note here that the dual graph formalization allows *all* alternative design solutions that satisfy the set of design constraints to be systematically generated.

A third design activity for *contradiction-constraints* is called into action, whenever it is needed, to insure that none of the contradiction constraints are violated.

One solution to this design problem is shown in Figure 8, right.

An Observation About Area Constraints

Within the context of a computer implementation, constraints of contiguity, communication, and length have the desirable property that they can be mapped independently and exclusively into form realizations in the dual graph. However, an architectural designer using this program would like to have the capability to specify area constraints as well. While area can tentatively be assigned independently as an abstract attribute of a space node of the dual graph, eventually the area constraints must interact with the graph topology as weights must eventually be assigned to the various edges. This creates special problems.

One approach to area constraints, that of allowing a choice from a finite vocabulary of room sizes, was presented in the example problem. However, it seems that a designer would much rather speak in terms of a range of areas and perhaps a maximum length-to-width ratio of a room. The difference between these two classes of constraints is mainly one of degree, for a range of areas and a maximum length-to-width ratio merely specify a large vocabulary of room sizes. Nevertheless, this change of degree greatly enlarges the solution search space, and if the latter class of area constraints is used, a suitable heuristic search strategy must be developed. It is interesting to note that while in the modularized grid representation this search is essentially one of varying topologies within a context of fixed areas, in the dual graph representation the search takes on a flavor of varying area assignments within a context of a partially fixed topology.

19 Theories of Cell Configurations

Comments on the paper by Grason

Horst Rittel

Department of Architecture
University of California
Berkeley, California

Horst Rittel is Associate Professor of the
Science of Design at the University of
California, Berkeley. He was born in
Berlin and studied mathematics and
theoretical physics at the Universities of
Göttingen and Münster. From 1958 to
1963 he was tenure Lecturer in Design
Methodology and Operations Research at
the Hochschule für Gestaltung in Ulm.
Since 1963 he has been at Berkeley,
where he introduced the first courses and
research in design methodology.

If something like a theory of architecture will ever be developed, then one of
its first chapters will deal with the theory of cell configurations, and its first
paragraphs will introduce relationships exactly like those which are the
subject matter of Grason's paper. Since I am most interested in such a theory
I welcome the opportunity to comment on this paper.

The system of concepts put forth by Grason is promising. His introduction
of directed, colored, and weighted graphs as means of describing the dual
of a planar floor plan offers much more detail and distinction than previous
models based on undirected, unkeyed, and unweighted graphs. Hitherto,
orientation could be described only for exterior rooms (by making them
adjacent to dummy-rooms, called "North," "East," "South," "West"). The
system presented here not only allows one to describe orientations among
rooms within the building, but also the length of wall segments in common to
adjacent rooms by weighting the links in the dual. For example, "the kitchen
is (or ought to be) west of the bathroom, and they have (or ought to have)
seven feet of wall in common."

The central issue of the paper is the following: Given a set of rooms, together
with adjacency, orientation, and metric constraints, find a planar rectilinear

179

cell configuration that fulfills these constraints, provided that they are not contradictory. Then the first problem is to determine whether the constraints are contradictory. The author mentions that there are three theorems pertinent to this problem of realizability of a cell configuration. It would be most interesting to learn more about these theorems and their practical implications, since here seems to lie an area of major difficulties concerning the problem of algorithmic efficiency.

There are many theorems in topology and graph theory which suggest algorithms that must yield a certain result—if you only try long enough, perhaps years. Let us simplify the present problem and consider a system of undirected, unweighted, and unkeyed (no dots or slashes) relationships between nodes representing cells. Then a necessary condition for the existence of a planar configuration fulfilling these relations is the existence of a *planar* dual graph (i.e., one where no links between the nodes representing rooms intersect each other). A theorem of topology[1] tells us that such a graph cannot exist if the system of constraints generates a dual graph containing a subgraph of either of the following types: (1) there are two sets of three nodes each, every node of each set being connected to every node of the other set, and (2) there are five nodes, all of them connected with each other. These relationships are illustrated in the top and middle of Figure 1.

Given a matrix of adjacency requirements of nontrivial size, the check for such subgraphs may necessitate a major procedure. Even if there are only twenty cells, the number of checking operations may run into several thousands. In addition, as indicated at the bottom of Figure 1, many more operations may become necessary in order to guarantee the existence of a planar dual.

It would be interesting to see how much effort it will require to test for the existence of a feasible floor plan in the much more detailed and elaborate system of the author. It may be possible to find heuristic shortcuts which drastically reduce such efforts. But they have to be developed first before the practicality of the system as a floor plan generator can be assessed.[2]

Another, more serious question, refers to the postulated identity of "requirement diagram" and "form diagram." If they were identical, then one would be implied by the other: not only would "form" truly follow "function," but every form would correspond to exactly one system of requirements. Certainly, to every floor plan corresponds exactly one dual graph and its equivalent matrix description. But unfortunately it is not the other way around. A given system of constraints ("requirements") allows either a very great manifold of graph interpretations or none at all. The probability that a constraint system allows for exactly *one* floor plan is negligibly small. In any practical case one would start off with a matrix of desired relationships between rooms and then want to translate them into a dual. If a dual exists, it will almost certainly not be a well-formed graph in the author's sense because the matrix of desired adjacencies will be notoriously saturated. There will be many links which are undirectional; one does not bother to specify that the pantry must be south of the kitchen but just that it must be next to it. The multitude of orientations of *interior* walls will remain unspecified, reducing the completeness of the graph even more. Consequently, you get rapidly very, very great numbers of possible duals. Completing the graph step by step, e.g., by working from one room to the next, making arbitrary decisions about the undecided parameters, does not provide a straightforward strategy toward a solution. The greater the number of rooms, the more intimately they are to be connected, and the greater the number of arbitrary decisions already made, the greater

1. Planar graphs

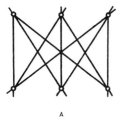

A

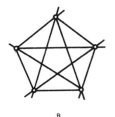

B

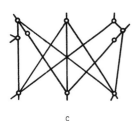

C

1. Kuratowski's Theorem (1930). For an introduction to graph theory and topology, see Oystein Ore, *Graphs and Their Uses*; Bradford H. Arnold, *Intuitive Concepts in Elementary Topology*; Claude Bergé, *Theory of Graphs and their Applications*; and Edwin F. Beckenbach, ed., *Applied Combinatorial Mathematics*.
2. Another approach would be to skip the feasibility test and to start constructing the dual from one "corner" proceeding by trial and error. But for reasons discussed later, this is likely to become even more tedious.

the probability of a dead end. One has to make major revisions because the remaining constraints cannot be fulfilled. This corresponds to the architect's juggling with bubble diagrams in his search for reasonable spatial arrangements.

Some related remarks. It is unlikely that the length of a wall segment plays a major role in this phase of building design. The length of a wall may be interesting but not the length of a wall segment. (The length of a wall is of course the sum of the length of segments, but that again increases the search space tremendously.) Further, in the system suggested by Grason (as in the system suggested by Lew and Brown) the details of the shape of a room are assumed to be specified as requirements ahead of time. But in practice, compound rectangular floor plans (like L-shaped rooms) are not necessarily required to be this way but result as leftovers in the attempt to satisfy adjacency and metrical constraints. The same is true for corridors, courts, and the like. You do not require them, usually; they just result for reasons of configuration. Consequently in every practical case—let's again say of only twenty rooms—tremendous combinatorial possibilities arise.

This multitude of combinatorial possibilities makes the intended computerization of the model difficult because computers are notoriously bad and slow in recognizing topological features. For example, in order to figure out whether a point lies within or outside a triangle requires the computation of three determinants. But we can see it at a glance. In addition, computers are not good in dealing with arbitrariness: it takes elaborate programs, for example, to "pick a point in a domain, not too close to a boundary." In some experiments with a much simpler model than that suggested by Grason it was found that a program generating planar adjacency graphs from "unsaturated" constraint lists, using random generators to cope with arbitrariness, when applied to only forty rooms already requires the full capacity of large computing machines.[3] It is a question whether this kind of manipulation of spatial configurations can be profitably delegated to computing machines, at least at the present time. There is rich evidence that our eyes are extremely good in identifying intersecting lines in a graph and in "seeing" ways of eliminating these intersections at a glance. Simple graphic devices allow the fast manipulation of adjacency graphs for forty to sixty rooms.[4]

But computerization of these processes is only of secondary importance. The main issues are still the better understanding of the theory of spatial configurations and of our reasoning in manipulating them. Here seems to lie the significance of investigations like those discussed in this section.

3. Vince Casalaina and Horst Rittel, "Generating Floor Plans from Adjacency Matrices."
4. Some experiments with a peg board, some golf tees, and colored rubber strings were made in a number of seminars at Ulm and Berkeley. They indicated that alternative feasible duals can be developed very quickly even for unusual constraint sets.

20 A Comprehensive Approach to Vocational Education Facility Planning

Alan Colker and James Leib

CONSAD Research Corporation
5600 Forward Avenue
Pittsburgh, Pennsylvania

Alan Colker is Project Director at the
CONSAD Research Corporation. He received a B.S. in industrial management
and an M.S. in industrial administration
from the Carnegie Institute of Technology
in 1953 and 1954. He was an industrial
engineer for the Pittsburgh Plate Glass
Company and for the Operations Research
Group of the U.S. Steel Corporation,
where he helped develop the GASP Simulation Language. James Leib is also a
member of the CONSAD Research Corporation. He received an A.B. in mathematics from Washington and Jefferson
College in 1963 and an M.S. in industrial
engineering and operations research
from the University of Pittsburgh in 1968.
He has been on the actuarial staff of John
Hancock and has been an industrial
engineer for U.S. Steel. This work was
performed as part of "A Comprehensive
Concept for Vocational Education Facilities," a project supported by the Bureau
of Technical Education and Continuing
Education of the Pennsylvania Department of Public Instruction and the Pittsburgh Board of Public Education.

This paper reports on the application of
mathematical modeling techniques in the
evaluation of architectural plans and
equipment needs within the context of a
vocational education curriculum. A model
system is developed which translates
curriculum and student characteristics
into an efficient space layout. This translation is performed by a series of models.
The first is a classroom simulation model.
Its purpose is to simulate student activities in a given classroom situation with
respect to the effects of alternative mixes
of teaching equipment. The second model
is a business cluster model. Its function is
to aggregate the equipment needs of a
group of related classes over time in
order to provide a useful means of evaluating overall equipment utilization.
Finally, a space layout model is used as
an architectural planning tool. The findings of this exploratory study indicate that
there may be many benefits to be derived
from the development of a more in-depth
system. The prototype system described
is capable of producing logical and satisfactory results in specific areas. However,
additional research directed toward a
more generalized modeling system is
needed.

Today's rapidly changing business environment is creating many new demands on the vocationally trained high school graduate. Foremost among
these demands is that he have the type of multidisciplined background that
will assure individual flexibility and successful adaptation to future changes.
This burden of accommodating these demands has fallen upon our high
school administrators and faculty members. This is evidenced by widespread
activity in the areas of high school facility planning and curriculum design,
two areas which had been left relatively unattended for far too long.

The contents of this paper are directed toward providing a brief insight to the
potential application of mathematical modeling techniques in evaluation of
architectural plans and equipment needs within the context of curriculum
design. In order to provide the required degree of realism, it is essential that
any such modeling effort be responsive to curriculum changes and to student
needs, both academic and socioeconomic. It should also be capable of re-
flecting the effects of alternative spending policies on the evaluation criteria.

Three different types of models are described in this paper. The first is a
"classroom simulation model." Its purpose is to simulate student activities
in a given classroom situation with respect to the effects of alternative mixes

of teaching equipment. The second model is a "business cluster model."
Its function is to aggregate the equipment needs of a group of related classes
over time in order to provide a useful means of evaluating overall equipment
utilization. Finally, the "space layout model," as its name implies, is an architectural planning tool. The interrelationships and linkages among the models
are schematically illustrated in Figure 1.

Classroom Simulation Model

The classroom model[1] has been designed to simulate the activities of one
particular type of course, characterized as one in which participating students are instructed in the use of a set of various types of equipment, for
example, office machines, woodworking equipment, and metal working
equipment. The student need follow no rigorous sequence in learning to use
the various machines. Thus the course lends itself quite well to a rotational
scheme (or course plan) whereby each student initially takes a position at
some available machine and then periodically rotates to another type of
equipment until a satisfactory degree of proficiency has been achieved on
each.

With this understanding, let us consider the planning role of the course
instructor. He must determine the time required to achieve reasonable proficiency levels and formulate some definite rotational scheme so that all
available types of machines are learned and all individual machines are
efficiently used. The achievement of these objectives may be severely
hampered by inadequate course planning or inaccurate equipment mix.

In formulating his overall course plan, the instructor can take into account
only certain known or controllable parameters such as number of students,
available equipment, and average time requirements. The problem is further
complicated by the introduction of certain uncontrollable or random variables
such as absenteeism, individual differences in aptitude, and equipment
breakdown. The objective of the classroom model is to evaluate the service
provided by, and the utilization level of, a given equipment mix within the
constraints imposed by all the other parameters.

The model itself is a dynamic simulation of the classroom activities during a
fixed period of time (normally one semester). The instructor's course plan is
submitted to the model as a set of one or more distinct rotational sequences
which the students are to follow. In addition, the model is also told the number of students assigned to each sequence and the expected time required
(class-days) for an average student to gain average proficiency on each type
of equipment. Other model inputs are: (1) the equipment mix number of
different types of machines and number of available machines of each type,
(2) course duration (class-days), (3) machine breakdown parameters, and
(4) absence parameters.

The model contains a scheduling algorithm which logically advances students through the planned coursework. Absences, equipment breakdowns,
and student aptitudes are randomly generated internally, and the original
course plan (rotational sequence) is constantly realigned as these factors
affect activity patterns.

The classroom simulation is an event type GASP[2] model in which each event
normally occurs once each day. The events comprehended in the model
include the following: daily absences, equipment repair, equipment breakdown, classroom activity and assignment of students to machines, and re-

1. Details of this model are given in Donn A. Carter, Alan Colker, and James S. Leib,
"Simulation Model for Vocational Educational Facility Planning." Another model is
given in Richard W. Judy and Jack B. Levine, *A New Tool for Educational Administration: Educational Efficiency Through Simulation Analysis.* For general discussions of
simulation techniques, see Daniel Teichroew and John F. Lubin, "Computer Simulation: Discussion of the Technique and Comparison of Languages," and Thomas H.
Naylor, Joseph L. Balinfy, Donald F. Burdick, and Kong Chu, *Computer Simulation
Techniques.*
2. Philip J. Kiviat and Alan Colker, *GASP: A General Activity Simulation Program.*

1. Educational space planning process

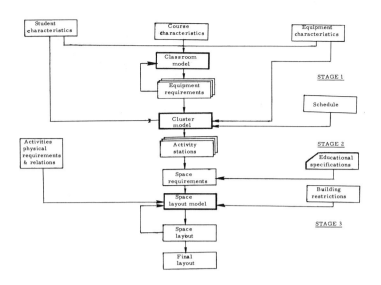

2. Classroom model

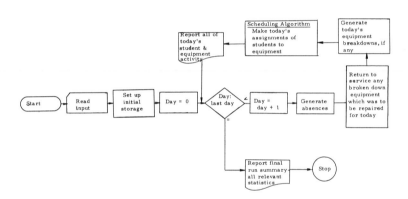

Table 1
Estimated Equipment Needs for Desired
Levels of Service

Machine Type[a]	Maximum Weekly Requests	Mean Weekly Requests	Standard Deviation	Required Number of Machines For Varying Service Level		
				90%	95%	99%
1	3	0.87	0.86	2	2	3
2	3	0.38	0.65	1	1	2
3	4	0.85	0.96	2	2	3
4	3	0.88	0.89	2	2	3
5	8	2.30	2.27	5	6	8
6	18	6.75	3.99	12	13	16
7	9	2.86	1.58	5	5	7
8	8	3.00	1.89	5	6	7
9	8	2.27	1.76	5	5	6
10	49	38.68	3.85	44	45	48
11	8	2.16	1.56	4	5	6
12	7	1.98	1.61	4	5	6
13	5	2.13	1.30	4	4	5
14	2	0.85	0.82	2	2	3
15	8	2.57	1.70	5	5	7
16	5	1.27	1.15	3	3	4
17	5	1.52	1.02	3	3	4

[a] See Table 2 for names of machines.

porting daily activity. Figure 2 illustrates the logical relationship among these events.

The simulation is initiated by reading the prescribed input data into the computer. The data may be real, drawn from classroom records, or it may be fabricated by the analyst in order to determine the relative changes to the system brought about by a set of hypothetical parameter changes. Then, within the framework of the model logic, a continuous record of equipment utilization and service levels is maintained in memory for summary analysis. The model output, which is reported on a daily basis and also accumulated for a final summary report, comprehends the following important information:
1. Distribution of daily equipment requirements by types of machine.
2. Percent of student requirements satisfied, by equipment type.
3. Equipment utilization levels, by type.
4. Individual student progress as of the end of the simulated time interval.
5. Statistical projections of equipment requirements, by type, necessary to provide various degrees of service to the students.

Given these output data, the instructor can critically examine the implications of his course plan and equipment mix. He can compare the actual equipment mix with the computer's projections, the simulation equipment utilization with what he considers to be a normal level, and simulated student progress with the results he hopes to obtain. A detailed case study of the application of this model to an office machines course at Pittsburgh's Schenley High School will more clearly illustrate the utility of the model's output. It is presented later in this paper.

Business Cluster Model

The classroom model provides a means of measuring the equipment utilization and service levels in a single classroom situation. However, regardless of the optimality of results achieved in individual classrooms, poor coordination of overall class scheduling may result in poor equipment utilization and serviceability on a school-wide basis. The objective of the cluster model is to measure the school-wide serviceability and utilization of a given equipment mix within the constraint imposed by a suggested master schedule of classes.

The model, as it now stands, is quite artificial. Ideally, the outputs of a set of different classroom models should provide the inputs of the cluster model. Since these models are not available, daily demand patterns are synthetically generated for a cluster of classes that are known to have related equipment and facility needs. Thus the model presented is purely for illustrative purposes, and its ultimate implementation is still in the conceptual stage.

The inputs to this model are a set of mathematical representations of the equipment demand patterns of all classes included in the cluster. The model then proceeds to aggregate these demands over time and to collect various statistics related to aggregate demand. At the conclusion of the model run, a final summary report is generated. The report includes such useful information as (1) aggregate distribution of weekly requirements by type of machine, (2) mean and maximum daily requirements by type as well as the standard deviations about the mean, and (3) projections of the number of machines of each type required to provide various levels of service within the constraint of the given master schedule. (For instance, the 90 percent service level means that student requests for that type of machine will be satisfied 90 percent of the time). Table 1 illustrates the type of data obtained from this model.

The model summary data quickly points out those time intervals during the term in which serious conflicts occur. Given this information, the reason for the conflict can be traced down and some corrective action employed. This action may simply imply a revision to the course plans of one or more classes, or it may require revision of the master schedule. Once the change has been made the model can be run again to measure the effectiveness of the new strategy and to look for additional improvements.

Space Layout Model

The previous two models have provided the means of objectively evaluating course planning, class scheduling, and equipment requirements. Even with the improvements resulting from these models, student activities may still be severely hampered by an inefficient space layout. It is obvious that related activity areas should be adjacent in a vocational school to eliminate unnecessary student movement and simulate the real-world relationships among certain activities.

The space layout model has been designed to determine the spatial arrangement of a one-floor building. The program used is a modification of the CRAFT program,[3] which was originally designed for the layout of industrial facilities. The objective of the model is to determine an efficient space layout that will tend to minimize both student movement between activities and construction or remodeling costs. In order for the model to function, some measure of the desirability of locating course spaces adjacent to one another must be provided. This information is input in the form of an "adjacency matrix" which describes the relative attraction (with respect to physical adjacency) of each activity area to every other activity area. Clearly, the key to successful application of the model lies in the planner's ability to provide a reasonably good set of adjacency indexes.

Given the adjacency matrix, the other model inputs include: (1) some initial layout described in matrix form, (2) prescribed boundary constraints, and (3) definition of any indicated locations.

The model logic heuristically reduces the nearly infinite set of possible layouts by iteratively stepping from the current solution to a better one until no better alternative can be found. The worth of a given solution is evaluated in terms of the sum of the products of adjacency indexes and distance in feet between all area pairs. The program attempts to minimize this sum, thus maximizing the total attractiveness.

The output of this model is a graphic illustration of the final layout. Figure 3 depicts the output. Each activity is coded numerically. Area perimeter numbers are printed and the lines drawn in by the authors. Each number indicates a course area of approximately 100 sq ft. In Figure 4 the computer printout is transformed into a schematic layout, and the actual course names are shown. The impact of attractiveness on space layout can be analyzed and evaluated by making a series of runs using alternative attractiveness assumptions.

A Case Study

The following case study represents the application of the Classroom Model in simulating an actual high school course devoted to teaching students the use of office machines. The course itself is part of the vocational education curriculum at Schenley High School in Pittsburgh, Pennsylvania. All data input to the model were obtained from conversation with the course instructor and from official school records. This course was planned to familiarize business education students with the fifteen different types of equipment and activities shown in Table 2. The right-hand column indicates the amount of time, in weeks, that the instructor believed was required for average students to gain familiarity with the equipment.

The course was set up on a rotational sequence; that is, the first two students started with the first machine type, the next two students with the second type, and so forth. In the simulation, the hypothetical students could move on to the next type of machine at the end of one or two weeks or could stay with a machine until they demonstrated adequate competence. A student could break the rotational sequence if he followed an especially slow student or was delayed by equipment breakdown.

---

3. "CRAFT: Computerized Relative Allocation of Facilities Techniques," IBM Share Program #3391.

3. Output from space layout model

4. Schematic space layout

```
      1  2  3  4  5  6  7  8  9 10 11 12 13 14 15 16 17 18 19 20 21 22 23 24 25 26 27 28 29 30
 1 | 4  4  4  4  4  4 |23 23 23 23 23 |21 21 21 |24 24 24 24 24 24 24 24 24 | 9  9  9  9  9  9  9|
 2 | 4              4 |23           23 21     21 24                    24 |                      9|
 3 | 4  4  4  4       |23 23 23 23 23 21 24 24 24 24 24 24 24 24 | 9  9  9  9  9  9  9|
 4 | 2  2  2 |4  4  4 |3  3  3 |7  7 21     21 22 22 22 22 22 22 22 |14 14 14 14 |11 11 11 11 11 11|
 5 | 2  2  2  2  2 |3  3  3 |7  7 21 21 21 22 22 22 |22 14 |14 11 |11 11 11 11 11 11|
 6 | 2          2 |3     3 |3 |7  7  7  7  7  7  7 22 22 |22 14 |14 11 |11 11 11 11|
 7 | 2          2 |3 |7  7  7  7  7  7  7  7 22 |22 22 22 |22 14 |11 11 11 11 11|13 13 13 13 13|
 8 | 2  2  2  2  2 |3 |3 18 18 18 18 18 18 18 |7  7 22 22 22 |22 14 14 14 14 |13 13 13 13 13|
 9 | 2  2  2  2  2 |3  3 |18 18 | 18 18 18 | 6  6  6  6 |15 15 15 15 15 |13 |13|
10 |19 19 19 19 19 |1  1  1  1 |18 | 18 18 18 18 18 18 | 6 | 6 15 | 15 13 | 13|
11 |19          19 |1 | 1 18 18 | 8  8  8  8 | 8  6 | 6 |15 15 15 15 15 |13 |13|
12 |19          19 |1 | 1  1 18 18 | 8 | 8  6 | 6 |12 12 12 |15 15 |13 13 13 13 13 13|
13 |19          19 |1 | 1 18 18 | 8 | 8  8  6  6 |12 |12 10 10 |16 16 16 16 16|
14 |19          19 |1  1  1 | 1 18 18 | 8  8  8 | 5  5  5  5 |12 | 12 10 10 |16|
15 |19 19 19 19 19 |1 |40 |20 20 20 20 20 | 5  5  5  5  5 | 5 |12 |12 10 10 |16|
16 |17 17 17 17 17 17 17 |20 20 | 20 | 5 | 5 37 37 37 |12 12 12 | 10 10 |16 16 16 16 16|
17 |17          17 | 17 20 | 20 | 5 37 | 10 10 10 10 10 |27 27 27 27 27|
18 |17          17 | 17 20 | 20 | 5  5  5  5  5 37 | 37 10 10 10 10 10 |27|
19 |17          17 | 17 20 |37 37 37 37 37 37 | 37 29 29 29 29 29 |27|
20 |17          17 | 17 20 20 20 20 20 20 37 37 37 37 37 37 37 | 29 | 29 27 |27|
21 |17          17 | 17 17 31 31 31 31 31 30 30 30 30 |37 37 | 29 29 29 29 29 |27 27 27 27 27|
22 |17          17 | 17 31 | 31 30 | 30 29 29 29 29 |28 28 28 28 28 28 28 28|
23 |17 17 17 17 17 17 17 17 17 | 17 31 | 31 30 | 30 29 | 29 28 |28|
24 |33 33 33 33 |34 34 34 34 31 | 31 30 | 30 29 | 29 28 28 |28|
25 |33          33 34 | 34 31 31 31 31 31 31 30 30 30 30 30 29 29 29 29 29 28 28 28 28 |28|
26 |33 33 33 33 |34 34 | 34 39 39 39 39 |32 32 |25 25 25 25 25 25 |26 26 26 26 26 |28|
27 |38 38 38 |35 35 |34 34 34 |39 39 39 39 |32 32 |25 | 25 26 | 26 26 |28|
28 |38       38 |35 35 35 36 36 36 36 36 36 |32 32 |25 | 25 26 | 26 26 |28|
29 |38       38 |35 |35 36 | 36 32 32 |25 | 25 26 | 26 26 |28|
30 |38       38 |35 35 35 36 36 36 36 36 36 |32 32 |25 25 25 25 25 25 |26 26 26 26 26 |28 28 28 28 28|
```

FIGURE 3

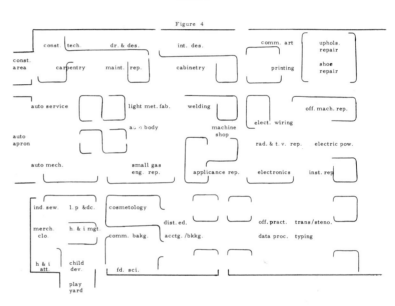

Figure 4

const. tech. | dr. & des. | int. des. | comm. art | uphols. repair
const. area | carpentry | maint. rep. | cabinetry | printing | shoe repair
auto service | light met. fab. | welding | off. mach. rep.
auto body | machine shop | elect. wiring
auto apron | rad. & t. v. rep. | electric pow.
auto mech. | small gas eng. rep. | applicance rep. | electronics | inst. rep
ind. sew. | l. p &dc. | cosmetology
merch. clo. | h. & i mgt. | dist. ed. | off. pract. | trans/steno.
comm. bakg. | acctg. /bkkg. | data proc. | typing
h & i att. | child dev. | fd. sci.
play yard

Table 2
Business Machines and Learning Time in Vocational Education Curriculum of Schenley High School

Machine Type	No. of Machines	Name of Machine	Time Required to Learn (weeks)
1	4	Electric Typewriter	2
2	4	Transcriber	2
3	4	IBM Selectric-Key Punch Simulator	2
4	2	IBM Card Punch and Verifier	2
5	1	Ditto Duplicator—Spirit	1
6	1	Stencil Duplicator	1
7	2	Full Keyboard Adding-Listing Machine	1
8	1	Statistical Typewriter	1
9	2	Friden Rotary Calculator Marchant Rotary Calculator Monroe Rotary Calculator	2
10	2	Burroughs 10-Key Multiplier National 10-Key Adding-Listing Monroe Adding-Listing	2
11	2	A. B. Dick Offset Duplicator	2
12	2	Teacher Helpers	1
13	2	Olivetti Print Calculator Victor Print Calculator	2
14	1	Comptometer, Key Driven	2
15	1	Check Protector	1

5. Student reference table

6. Distribution of student time

STUDENT NO.	SPEED RATING	SEQUENCE NO.	INITIAL TYPE IN SEQ.	CURRENT TYPE IN SEQ.	REMAINING TOT. DAYS REQUIRED.	COMPLETION DATE
1	5	1	1	99999	7	
2	3	2	1	*****	0	126.0
3	2	1	2	*****	0	124.0
4	2	2	2	*****	0	128.0
5	2	1	3	*****	0	128.0
6	4	2	3	99999	4	
7	3	1	4	*****	0	127.0
8	3	2	4	99999	2	
9	1	1	5	*****	0	118.0
10	3	2	6	99999	4	
11	2	1	7	*****	0	123.0
12	4	2	8	99999	4	
13	1	1	9	*****	0	121.0
14	2	2	9	*****	0	128.0
15	3	1	10	99999	3	
16	1	2	10	*****	0	124.0
17	4	1	11	99999	1	
18	4	2	11	*****	0	130.0
19	3	1	14	99999	4	
20	2	2	15	*****	0	127.0
21	2	1	12	15	5	
22	3	2	12	99999	1	
23	3	1	13	12	10	
24	5	2	13	99999	3	

STUDENT NO.	DAYS ACTIVE	DAYS ABSENT	DAYS IDLE DURING TERM	POST-COMP. IDLE DAYS	TOT. DAYS IDLE
1	124	6	0	0	0
2	125	5	0	4	4
3	121	8	1	6	7
4	117	7	6	2	8
5	120	7	3	2	5
6	122	6	2	0	2
7	124	6	0	3	3
8	117	10	3	0	3
9	119	10	1	12	13
10	116	14	0	0	0
11	122	8	0	7	7
12	122	8	0	0	0
13	118	4	8	9	17
14	115	6	9	2	11
15	117	8	5	0	5
16	113	7	10	6	16
17	120	10	0	0	0
18	125	3	2	0	2
19	118	4	8	0	8
20	119	8	3	3	6
21	111	12	7	0	7
22	120	9	1	0	1
23	113	12	5	0	5
24	126	3	1	0	1
TOTALS =ALL STUDENTS	2854	181	75	56	131

7. Machine performance

MACHINE TYPE	MACHINE NO.	DAYS AVAILABLE	DAYS ACTIVE	DAYS IDLE	DAYS DELAYED	MACHINE EFFICIENCY	NO. OF REQUESTS	TOTAL WAIT. DAYS
1	1	130	124	6	0	95.38%		
1	2	130	83	47	0	63.85%		
1	3	130	6	124	0	4.62%		
1	4	130	0	130	0	0.00%		
TOTALS TYPE 1		520	213	307	0	40.96%	213	2
2	5	130	125	5	0	96.15%		
2	6	130	86	44	0	66.15%		
2	7	130	9	121	0	6.92%		
2	8	130	2	128	0	1.54%		
TOTALS TYPE 2		520	222	298	0	42.69%	222	2
3	9	130	121	9	0	93.08%		
3	10	130	86	44	0	66.05%		
3	11	130	14	116	0	10.07%		
3	12	130	5	125	0	3.85%		
3		520	226	294	0	43.46%	226	2
4	13	130	129	1	0	99.23%		
4	14	130	107	23	0	82.31%		
TOTALS TYPE 4		260	238	24	0	90.77%	297	56
5	15	130	113	17	0	86.92%		
TOTALS TYPE 5		130	113	17	0	86.92%	157	42
6	16	130	108	22	0	83.08%		
TOTALS TYPE 6		130	108	22	0	83.08%	150	26
7	17	130	94	36	0	72.31%		
7	18	130	21	109	0	16.15%		
7		260	115	145	0	44.23%	116	1
8	9	130	113	17	0	86.92%		
8		130	113	17	0	86.92%	178	61
9	20	130	124	6	0	95.38%		
9	21	130	82	48	0	63.08%		

8. Histogram of daily requests for machine type 4

9. Distribution of student primary requests

```
NO. OF   75
DAYS
                  64
OBSERVED          XXX
          60      XXX
                  XXX
                  XXX
                  XXX
                  XXX
          45      XXX
                  XXX
                  XXX
                  XXX
                  XXX
                  XXX
          30      XXX
                  XXX 25
               22XXXXXX
             XXXXXXXXX 18
             XXXXXXXXXXX
          15 XXXXXXXXXXX
             XXXXXXXXXXX
             XXXXXXXXXXX
              1XXXXXXXXXXXX
             XXXXXXXXXXXXXX
        --------------------------------------
          0  1  2  3  4  5  6  7  8  9  *9

          NO. OF REQUESTS PER DAY

MEAN=2.28      STANDARD DEVIATION= 0.93
```

REQUIRED NO. OF MACHINES FOR DESIRED SERVICE LEVEL

MACH. TYPE	NO. OF MACHINES	MIN. DAILY REQ.	MAX. DAILY REQ.	MEAN DAILY REQ.	STD. DEV.	90 PER CENT	95 PER CENT	99 PER CENT
1	4	0	3	1.64	0.65	2	3	3
2	4	0	4	1.71	0.70	3	3	3
3	4	0	4	1.74	0.84	3	3	3
4	2	0	4	2.28	0.93	3	4	4
5	1	0	3	1.21	0.67	2	2	3
6	1	0	3	1.15	0.70	2	2	3
7	2	0	3	0.89	0.67	2	2	2
8	1	0	3	1.37	0.79	2	3	3
9	4	0	3	1.68	0.72	3	3	3
10	5	0	3	1.66	0.76	3	3	3
11	2	0	4	1.82	0.74	3	3	4
12	2	0	3	1.68	0.63	2	3	3
13	4	0	3	1.67	0.60	2	3	3
14	1	0	3	1.06	0.66	2	2	3
15	1	0	2	0.98	0.63	2	2	2
TOTALS-ALL TYPES	36	0	4			36	41	46

Several selected output reports of this particular run are displayed in Figures 5 through 8. Each of these reports captures information or statistics that will aid in course-planning. For the most part, the report headings are self-explanatory, but the following comments are also offered.

Figure 5 represents student status as of the end of a 130-day simulated period of time. The column headed SPEED RATING is essentially an aptitude indicator, where the value 3 is considered normal, or average. In the column headed CURRENT TYPE IN SEQ., the value 99999 implies that the student has at least been exposed to all the equipment types being taught, but has not completed the course. The appearance of ***** in the same column implies course completion.

In Figure 6, the column headed TOTAL WAIT DAYS contains for each type of equipment the total number of days that students had to wait to use the machine because it was for one reason or another unavailable. Figure 7 is a histogram of the daily distribution of student requests for one particular machine type (type 4). The actual number of machines required should be at least as great or greater than the mean daily requirement. Figure 8 is a composite of all the histograms produced, in tabular form. This is perhaps the single most important report with respect to estimating equipment requirements.

The three columns at the right in Figure 8 indicate recommended equipment mixes for certain desired levels of service to the students. For example, if student requests for machine type 10, adding-listing machines, are to be satisfied 90 percent of the time, there should be three machines available. Service levels can be set by educators as they gain experience with the process. It is interesting to note that at the 90 percent service level only two less machines are required than the total number that the instructor is actually using. However, the machine mix by type is considerably different, suggesting that the school may have overinvested in some types and underinvested in others.

Summary

Although the modeling system described is of an exploratory nature, the results of initial runs are indicative of the potential benefits to be gained from the development of a more in-depth system. Additional work is necessary in the development of a generalized classroom model in order to accommodate at least a majority of the situations that will be encountered. Additional effort should also be expended in researching improved (and more educationally oriented) measures of location attraction for input to the space layout model.

21 The Treatment of Multiple Goals in Systems Models

Comments on the paper by Colker and Leib

Paul O. Roberts, Jr.

Transport Research Program
Harvard University
Cambridge, Massachusetts

Paul O. Roberts, Jr., is Supervisor of the Transportation Policy Planning Research Project and Visiting Associate Professor of Transportation and Logistics in the Graduate School of Business Administration at Harvard University. He received a Ph.D. in civil engineering from Northwestern University in 1966. He has supervised several other projects for the U.S. Bureau of Public Roads and the U.S. Agency for International Development, and he was Research Director of the Harvard Transport Program.

Let me begin by making a point which seems to underlie a basic pitfall of design and design methods in general. That is that you can not optimize if you have more than one goal. You are out of luck if you find yourself in this position because there is no theoretical "way out." However, there are several things that you can do. Perhaps it is worth while to briefly indicate the avenues that are open.

1. First you can *combine goals* by assigning to them *weights* which reflect the rate of tradeoff of one against the other. This allows them to be combined in the same objective function. Now, with only one statement of goals or objectives, you can optimize. This approach has the virtue that it will work for a relatively large number of factors which enter into the statement of the overall goal. It may be difficult to find appropriate weightings, however, or the functional form of the objective statement may become difficult to work with.

2. A second way you can work with more than one goal is to treat them as *constraints*. This involves accepting a fixed upper or lower level of that goal used as a constraint and optimizing while holding that level constant. Then, if you want, you can do parametric analysis to determine the range over

which the results are of interest. The basic problem with this approach is that it may be necessary to try a number of levels of this goal as well as others. This may defeat the original purpose of the analysis. The answer could be virtually lost in a forest of results.

3. A third approach to working with more than one goal is to search for a *pareto optimum*. This means that you have one solution with an associated value for the first goal. You then look for ways you can improve the values of other goals without affecting the value of the first goal. If you can move one of the others without affecting the first in an adverse way, then you do so. Successive moves of each goal will eventually produce a pareto optimal solution. The real world appears to function largely in this way. A group will refuse to cooperate in a new solution unless it benefits by so doing.

4. A fourth way that multiple goals can be dealt with is to trace the *tradeoffs* between goals. If you have "more" of one goal you typically have "less" of another goal. If you explicitly trace out the tradeoffs between goals and present the results so that the full implications are apparent to the decision-maker, he can then deal directly with the problem. This is perhaps the principal problem of the analyst.

5. A fifth way is to *satisfice* in some way. In doing this you admit that no goal is the ultimate goal. It might be useful in some cases to work out a goal matrix in which alternatives are arrayed against goals. By searching through this, one can pick out those alternatives that seem to have the best values for each of the goals that are deemed important. In some cases there may be dominance or near dominance of one alternative over the others. By this I mean that the values for all goals for one alternative are better than all goals for any of the other alternatives.

6. Finally, *feasibility-seeking systems* may be of interest for some kinds of problems and *improvement algorithms* are important for others. In complicated problems, if you could just get one feasible solution (one bridge which will stand up) you would buy it. By contrast, in cases where it is fairly easy to find a feasible solution, then what you are looking for is an improvement to that solution. It is this kind of problem that the paper by Colker and Leib describes. It seems to me that the general word of wisdom which I would give to designers and planners is that we need to be seeking more of these latter two kinds of algorithms rather than overly concerning ourselves with optimization.[1]

Though the paper by Colker and Leib is entitled "A Comprehensive Approach to Vocational Education Facility Planning," it appears to me that it is not comprehensive. It may be useful, but not comprehensive. The authors approached the problem using a three-point breakdown. First, the class-lesson plan is treated, then these are organized into a master-plan schedule, and finally the space is physically planned in support of this master plan.

I said you could not optimize with multiple goals and in this case the authors did not. They realized that they had a difficult problem so they *simulated* instead of optimizing.[2] They ran into problems because of the scale of the problem with which they were dealing. In this case they were working with a public system which has relatively clear, easy goals in the abstract and at the highest level. But at the detail in which they were forced to work— scheduling equipment, laying out classrooms—goals get rather fuzzy. It is no longer clear what contributes to the larger goal. At the detail level there is a fuzziness associated with this larger goal. It's easier to work with a series of smaller goals that you want to achieve. The result, however, is multiple

---

1. Further discussion and an example of the use of these models in urban planning is given in Paul O. Roberts, "Multi-Viewpoint Evaluation of Transportation Projects and Systems."
2. A good example of simulation in planning is presented in David Kresge, "A Simulation Model for Development Planning."

goals that are still fuzzy and difficult to deal with. The authors ran head-on into this.

The way they attacked this problem was the way that any rational person would attack it. They tried to work on the problem at its smallest level using mainly a classroom model and aggregating between the classroom model and the master-schedule level. They ran into problems principally because they were unable to perform all the aggregations that they had to accomplish at this level. It was impossible to go through the entire school system and to detail every single course that used special equipment and also the courses that, though they did not use special equipment, used some of the same instructors in the time that was involved. So the problem in taking this kind of an approach is that all of the design work that is needed at the very smallest level in the sequence just cannot be done by hand adequately.

One thing that could be done is to model the subprocesses, scheduling the individual classes by using some sort of goal-seeking subsystems that would be a part of the larger complex of the school. Each subsystem has its own operating rules and goals. The solutions are then aggregated back together. This might have produced a more satisfying solution overall.

The classroom-simulation model is similar to a job-shop simulation or an equipment-schedule simulation. These sorts of processes are fairly well known, and some standard solutions could be employed. In this case they might have been useful. The business cluster model would be useful if the statistics could be aggregated, but the authors have not really solved this scheduling problem. The problem at the heart of this business cluster model is solving the overall school scheduling of classrooms and available facilities.

In the space layout model the one thing that concerned me was the tradeoff of cost versus adjacency. I am sure that it was treated somewhere in the study, but I could not find it in the paper. It is not clear that the adjacency variables are in the same costs term as space variables. Total cost in this case is budget-constrained, in fact, the education system as a whole is budget-constrained and has very little to do with the student use of space anyway. It is common in public systems to ration capital and to spend less money than is really needed for highest efficiency. The effect of this is to make the people who use the systems pay a higher use-cost over the long run. I do not mean to imply that this is either good or bad, just a typical public action. Also, there is not any feedback in this model.

The thing that bothers me most about the study is that too much time is spent making an efficient allocation of machines. The larger objective should be education, not machine selection. However, the models do allow you to examine the tradeoffs between the amount of money spent on machines and the course selection. The real design problem here and in this kind of problem in general is how to organize institutions so that the appropriate learning experience can be acquired at some given cost. I think the authors have made a good start in this area, but it obviously needs much more work.

6 Evaluation Systems

One of the characteristics of a science is that it entertains methods of self-evaluation and methods for determining its own progress and what constitutes an advance. Notions of "inquiry," "understanding," "explanation," and "development," although always open to debate, have bases of general agreement. Platt argues that one method of internal evaluation, the method of "strong inference," accounts for the fact that fields like molecular biology and high-energy physics are moving forward orders of magnitude faster than others.

There are no equivalent evaluation systems for the emerging environmental sciences. Three needs are noted. First, at present there is no generally agreed upon method for evaluating existing environments to decide, out of the apparent chaos, what is going wrong and which are the most crucial problems. Second, only a beginning has been made toward evaluating alternative proposals by predicting and simulating impacts and consequences *before* implementation. Where there are beginnings, they are generally confined to predicting regional growth or the allocation of economic activity under different sets of constraints or evaluating alternatives among cost-benefit criteria. In architecture there are no techniques for predicting or simulating consequences, as an example, for simulating social interactions as a result of different housing patterns. And third—perhaps most of all—there is no paradigm for testing and evaluating architecture or planning projects *after* completion to determine whether they have been successful or, more precisely, which parts have been successful and bear repetition and which parts have not been successful and require additional research.

The concepts of "performance specification" and "design specification" introduced by Jones in 1963 and the idea of "requirements" introduced by Alexander in 1964 were the earliest suggestions for testable design units for the first and third of these needs. In this volume Alexander and Poyner introduce the further concepts of "tendencies," "relations," and "patterns." Requirements and tendencies are hypotheses about human behavior, argued to be crucial to the determination of form, and testable by experiment. Performance specifications are verbal statements about the desired performance of some piece of the environment and may be tested by comparing a specific environmental configuration with the specification of its desired performance. Finally, design specifications, relations, and patterns are statements of geometry and are testable in that a particular environmental configuration and the behavior within it may be tested against the desired performance specifications or set of tenden-cies. As these concepts have the form of hypotheses, they may be evaluated and falsified experimentally or by traditional observational, interview, and statistical methods.

The two papers in this section follow different tactics. The first presents a general framework for the building design process, and the second describes an economic model for urban renewal. But implicitly both papers suggest general evaluation systems for environmental design and planning.

Thomas Maver, influenced by Markus, introduces the concept "design morphology," the chronological sequence of operations in a design project which advance from the abstract and general to the concrete and particular, and uses it in much the same way that Nadler and Archer in later papers use "strategy," "operational model," and "plan-of-work." The reader may find it instructive to compare these concepts. Maver proposes evaluation techniques based on a number of cost and performance variables. Although working from a single client in an architectural situation, his suggestions could be extended to the corporate client or community if one assumes or can construct a unified point of view among a group of people. In a paper delivered at the Conference but unavailable for publication, Horst Rittel presented a technique for collapsing the diverging interests and values of multiple clients or of members of low-income communities.

Addressing the problem of providing better housing for low-income urban communities, Arthur Silvers develops a dynamic programming model for evaluation of urban renewal alternatives. He proposes methodology for determining which buildings to treat in any annual period and for determining what series of treatments to apply to a building over time. His paper is the first in this volume to consider a wide variety of decision-makers.

In conclusion, Michael Brill and Sharon Rose discuss both papers with regard to the measurement concepts employed, point out limitations in both analyses, and refer to recent approaches to evaluation.

Other researchers have made forays into evaluation systems. In a paper in this volume Marvin Manheim describes a process for predicting impacts and evaluating consequences of transportation proposals. Work at the United States National Bureau of Standards has been concerned with measuring the performance of buildings. And papers have appeared by Hill, Ellis, Falk, and Wachs on the measurement of community values, social consequences of urban freeways, and evaluation. See the bibliography.

22 Appraisal in the Building Design Process

Thomas W. Maver

Building Performance Research Unit
University of Strathclyde
Glasgow, Scotland

Thomas W. Maver is an operations research member of the Building Performance Research Unit of the University of Strathclyde. He was born in Scotland and received a B.Sc. in mechanical engineering and a Ph.D in operations research from the University of Glasgow in 1955 and 1960. Before joining Strathclyde, he was a Research Fellow at the Building Services Research Unit of the University of Glasgow. Ideas put forward in parts of this paper are as much those of the Director and members of the Building Performance Research Unit as they are of the author. Their support and unselfishness are gratefully acknowledged. Preparation of the paper and the author's attendance at the DMG Conference were made possible by the Unit and by IBM (U.K.) Ltd.

The design process is distinguished as an interactive and cyclic activity involving analysis, synthesis, appraisal, and decision, applicable at a number of stages in a sequential design morphology. The process takes place within a framework of a cost-benefit model and against a background of nonspecific and disparate objective functions. Taking spatial environment as illustrative of a decision area, the paper deals with the limitations of attempts to generate design syntheses and suggests that the designer's intuitive synthesis should be accepted as a first approximation, explicitly appraised on a variety of counts, modified, reappraised, modified again, and so on, until convergence on an optimum solution is achieved. Degree of attainment is measured in a number of cost and performance levels for which the designer can elicit the client's approbation. An example of such an appraisal is given. Finally, it is suggested that this mechanism may lead to mathematical formulation of the relationship between design and performance variables and the emergence of true performance specifications.

Decision-making in building design, as in many other fields of design and planning, is concerned with narrowing the field of search, in the universe of possible design solutions, for that design which optimizes the return on the client's investment.

The first of the designer's difficulties is that the client is seldom, if ever, able to make an explicit statement of the objective function in terms of which the level of return can be measured; at best the client will be in a position to state what features of the built environment will promote the attainment of his objectives and what features will inhibit their attainment. The second of the designer's difficulties is that the universe of possible design solutions is constrained from the outset by the client's inability to make an investment of an amount which would allow optimum solutions.

The problem can thus be seen to be that of recognizing, weighting, correlating, and manipulating the host of interdependent variables which affect the built environment in a manner which is sufficiently rational and explicit to promote joint decision-making on those levels of performance which together comprise the optimum design solution.

1. Framework for design management

2. Conceptual cost-benefit model

Design process →

2   Feasibility

3   Outline proposals

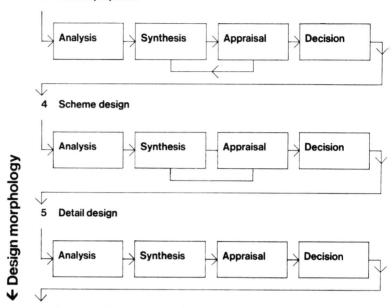

4   Scheme design

5   Detail design

← **Design morphology**

6   Production information

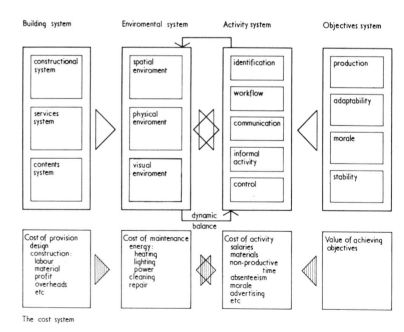

This paper sets out to provide a decision-making mechanism, based on the iterative explicit appraisal of design syntheses, within a cost-benefit framework.

Framework For Design Decision-Making

A number of commentators have suggested frameworks for the management of design decision-making which, although differing in terminology, all embody the concept of vertical and horizontal dimensions. Markus, dealing with the management of architectural design, refers to the vertical dimension as the *design morphology* and describes it as "a chronological sequence advancing from the abstract and general to the concrete and particular."[1] The Royal Institute of British Architects' "Plan of Work" is in fact a building design morphology comprising the following stages:

1. Inception
2. Feasibility
3. Outline proposals
4. Scheme design
5. Detail design
6. Production information
7. Bills of quantities
8. Tender action
9. Project planning
10. Operation on site
11. Completion
12. Feedback

Stages 2–5 are concerned with "design" as we understand it and subsequent stages are concerned with implementing the design as accurately, cheaply, and quickly as possible (stages 6, 7–8, and 9–11, respectively). The characteristic of a morphology is that the stages are sequential and not iterative; return from a later stage to an earlier stage is recognized as failure in the management of the design activity.

The horizontal dimension, referred to by Markus as the *design process,* is, however, iterative and cyclic in character and comprises four steps, analysis, synthesis, appraisal, and decision, defined as follows:

Analysis. Clarification of goals, identification of problems, nature of difficulties, exploring relationships, producing order from random data.
Synthesis. Creation of part-solutions, combination of part-solutions.
Appraisal. Evaluation, application of checks and tests, application of criteria, constraints and limits, consistency testing,
Decision. Selection of "best" solution from a set, advancement to next morphological stage.

The total framework of the management of design thus comprises a vertical dimension of design morphology and a horizontal dimension of design process linked operationally as shown in Figure 1. It is of value to have not only a management framework, as already described, but also an objective framework. To embody the philosophy of cost-benefit in design decision-making, the Building Performance Research Unit has developed a conceptual model of the relationships between the building and the users. Figure 2 demonstrates the interaction between four conceptually separate systems. The building system gives rise to an environmental system just as the objectives system gives rise to the activity system. At the center of the diagram the animate/inanimate interface, the two-way arrow represents the fact that the environment modifies the activity at the same time as the activity modifies the environment.

For each of the four conceptual systems there are associated costs. It is in terms of these costs, or alternative measures of system provision and performance, that a design is optimized.

The Approach

Since spatial environment is a major decision-taking area in the design of all building types, it will be taken as a suitable vehicle for the development of the proposed approach. The *spatial environment* in buildings may be said to be the number, size, and type of individual spatial elements and the relative disposition of these elements in three dimensions within the building en-

1. Thomas A. Markus, "The Role of Building Performance Measurement and Appraisal in Design Method."

3. Approach of Whitehead and Eldars
showing the relationship matrix and the
location matrix

Number of element

		Ante space nurse's station				Scrub up		Theatre no. 1						Theatre no. 2						Sink-room		
		1	2	3	4	5	6	7	8	9	10	11	12	13	14	15	16	17	18	19	20	21
Ante space nurse's station	1																					
	2	1000																				
	3	1000	1000																			
	4	1000	1000	1000																		
Scrub up	5	23	23	23	23																	
	6	23	23	23	23	1000																
Theatre no. 1	7	5	5	5	5	10	10															
	8	5	5	5	5	10	10	1000														
	9	5	5	5	5	10	10	1000	1000													
	10	5	5	5	5	10	10	1000	1000	1000												
	11	5	5	5	5	10	10	1000	1000	1000	1000											
	12	5	5	5	5	10	10	1000	1000	1000	1000	1000										
Theatre no. 2	13	5	5	5	5	10	10	1	1	1	1	1	1									
	14	5	5	5	5	10	10	1	1	1	1	1	1	1000								
	15	5	5	5	5	10	10	1	1	1	1	1	1	1000	1000							
	16	5	5	5	5	10	10	1	1	1	1	1	1	1000	1000	1000						
	17	5	5	5	5	10	10	1	1	1	1	1	1	1000	1000	1000	1000					
	18	5	5	5	5	10	10	1	1	1	1	1	1	1000	1000	1000	1000	1000				
Sink room	19	2	2	2	2	4	4	6	6	6	6	6	6	6	6	6	6	6	6			
	20	2	2	2	2	4	4	6	6	6	6	6	6	6	6	6	6	6	6	1000		
	21	2	2	2	2	4	4	6	6	6	6	6	6	6	6	6	6	6	6	1000	1000	
Sterilising room	22	1	1	1	1	3	3	6	6	6	6	6	6	6	6	6	6	6	6	16	16	16
	23	1	1	1	1	3	3	6	6	6	6	6	6	6	6	6	6	6	6	16	16	16
	24	1	1	1	1	3	3	6	6	6	6	6	6	6	6	6	6	6	6	16	16	16
Small theatre	25	1	1	1	1	9	9	1	1	1	1	1	1	1	1	1	1	1	1	3	3	3
	26	1	1	1	1	9	9	1	1	1	1	1	1	1	1	1	1	1	1	3	3	3

Annotations on the matrix:

- Area 600 sq ft i.e. 6 elements
- i.e. This figure represents number of standard journeys between elements 6 and 8
- Dummy relationship
- (rows 23, 24) — 1000, 1000
- (rows 25, 26) — 2, 2

Number of standard journeys between each two elements

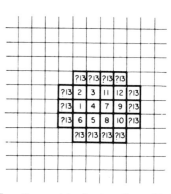

Locations matrix showing all possible locations of element 13.

velope. More simply put, the spatial environment comprises the accommodation schedule and layout.

What then are the difficulties of a design team attempting to progress through the design morphology of the spatial environment in, say, a school? While the team may be able to elicit some statement from the education authorities with reference to the activity and objectives systems, this will be neither specific nor readily translatable into a cost function. The design process, therefore, must be one of obtaining at each stage of the morphology a balance between the cost investment on the inanimate variables and some measure of performance on the animate variables in a form sufficiently explicit to determine the degree of client approval.

Research workers in the United Kingdom concerned with spatial environment have, almost to a man, been brave enough to apply their efforts to the synthesis step in the design process. Some consideration of their methodology and results is necessary to the development of the arguments in this paper.

The earliest work was an attempt to apply the transportation technique of linear programming to the location of rooms in a building.[2] The objective function to be minimized was the product of number of journeys and journey distance. It is possible to formulate such a problem in linear programming terms only if the number and distance of journeys are considered between each room and a single fixed station; such a formulation optimizes the location of each room with respect to the fixed station but not with respect to each other.

To deal with the traffic patterns between every room in every location clearly is a mammoth problem, outside the bounds of formal mathematical analysis. Realizing this, Whitehead and Eldars developed a heuristic program which, using the number of "standard" journeys as a measure of association between spatial elements, placed the elements consecutively on a two-dimensional grid, as shown in Figure 3.[3] The first element to be placed was that with the highest association with all other elements; the second was that having the highest association with the first; the third was that having the highest association with the first and second, and so on. Each new element will take up a position somewhere on the periphery of the elements already placed; the exact location is that which yields the least sum of the products of the association and the distance between the new element and each of the elements already placed. This program will produce a layout and an envelope in two dimensions only.

Other research workers have employed variations on this theme. Beaumont, in what he describes as a $2 \times n$ hierarchical decomposition, starts by breaking the total space into two parts in a way that minimizes the association between the two; these are then placed on a grid.[4] Each part is itself broken into two and the subparts located. The hierarchical breakdown continues until the individual elements are themselves located. The advantage claimed for this method is that it more closely follows the intuitive design morphology of increasing specificity and allows interruption at each stage to manually adjust the partial solution. There is provision in Beaumont's program for taking daylight requirements into account by making inadmissible those layouts that do not permit a predetermined proportional disposition of external wall.

It is clear that the determination of an optimum layout on the basis of a single variable, say traffic movement, by formal mathematical analysis, e.g., linear

2. Lynn Mosley, "A Rational Design Theory for Planning Buildings based on the Analysis and Solution of Circulation Problems"; L. Bruce Archer, "Planning Accommodation for Hospitals and the Transportation Problem Technique."
3. Bertram Whitehead and Mohamed Z. Eldars, "The Planning of Single-Storey Layouts."
4. Michael J. Beaumont, "Computer-Aided Techniques for Synthesis of Layout and Form with Respect to Circulation."

programming, is not feasible unless the problem is simplified by assumption beyond the bounds of realism. The alternative, a series of heuristic algorithms such as those proposed by Whitehead and Eldars, and Beaumont generate a solution, but the proximity of the solution to an optimum is dependent on the relevance of the heuristics adopted and is therefore impossible to judge. If it is desired to take account of additional variables, the relevance of the heuristics adopted becomes increasingly dubious, as does the complexity of the program, until a stage is reached when the solution generated may be further from a true optimum than a solution intuitively arrived at by the most simple-minded architect. The difficulty of putting forward valid heuristics, as has already been seen, is due to the lack of knowledge of the functional relationship between the variables and, if they are not all measured in cost terms, lack of knowledge of their relative importance.

The approach proposed here embodies the philosophy that if a number of variables are to be manipulated simultaneously, a design synthesis cannot be generated as effectively as by an architect using his intuition. It *is* possible, however, to get such a synthesis by using an intuitive synthesis as a first approximation and then explicitly appraising it in a way that promotes iterative modification towards an optimum solution. The iterative method of successive approximations is well tried in algebra, and there would appear to be no fundamental reason why it should not apply to the simulation of design solutions. It does depend, however, on two conditions: one is that all possible solutions should exist along the single dimension (of good-bad), the other is that each appraisal should be carried out in sufficient detail to suggest the appropriate modification for convergence on the optimum solution.

Souder's work on traffic movement in hospitals illustrates this approach for a single variable and provides a useful comparison with the approach of Whitehead and Eldars.[5] Using a performance criterion similar to that of Whitehead and Eldars (that is, a product of number of journeys and journey distance), Souder input a design solution and had the computer simulate the traffic movement associated with the solution. The output gave a level of performance, measured in total journey time, and gave details of the usage of lifts, stairs, and corridors. This secondary detailed output allowed conclusions about the best way of modifying the design for a better level of performance.

The drawbacks to Souder's program as it stands are threefold: (1) it deals with only one variable, (2) there is no way of telling when the synthesis/appraisal recycle has produced a near-optimum solution, and (3) while a level of performance is output, there is no comparable level of cost investment.

The proposed approach, then, is to develop a series of appraisal programs: a cost appraisal dealing with the cost of provision and maintenance of the inanimate side of the conceptual model and a performance appraisal for each of the variables on the animate side. At any stage of the design morphology, say scheme design, Figure 1, an intuitive synthesis is put forward and appraisals made. The designer then has, as primary output, a cost figure and a performance level for each variable; as secondary output he has sufficient detail of each appraisal to assist him in the modification of the synthesis if this should be considered desirable. The desirability of modifying the synthesis may be discussed with the client, since only the client is able to weigh intuitively the balance of performance levels on a variety of variables. This balancing cannot be done other than by reference to basic cost and performance criteria. The cost criterion may be simple enough, for example, the client's predetermined upper limit for capital and running costs. The performance criteria may be of quite disparate form, a statutory minimum (e.g., 2 percent daylight factor) or a recommended maximum (e.g., no more than 100 ft between classrooms and lavatories).

5. James J. Souder et al., *Planning for Hospitals: A Systems Approach Using Computer-Aided Techniques.*

There are some performance criteria, particularly those directly dependent on the spatial environment (for example, traffic movement) which are more difficult to state. For these cases it may be possible to use heuristic programming to generate a criterion, as in the total journey distance solution of Whitehead and Eldars.

In any event the design process, as envisaged, is concerned with proceeding round the synthesis/appraisal cycle until client and designer are satisfied that the cost investment results in performance levels which optimize the allocation of the client's resources. Even if the client is not consulted on every cycle, his approbation should be sought at the end of the cycling process and before progressing to the next stage of the morphology.

The Mechanism: An Example from the Design of Schools

In the school design problem the process would be as follows: On the basis of an analysis of the user requirements, the architect would put forward a design synthesis. This first approximation would then be subjected to a battery of appraisals. The appraisals on the inanimate side of the conceptual model would be in cost terms and the appraisals on the animate side would be in performance terms most appropriate to each variable. The cost appraisals might comprise the cost of provision of outside walls, internal partitions, floor area, service runs, as well as the cost of maintaining the fabric, plus heating and lighting. The performance appraisals might comprise the number of alternative curricula possible, the level of daylighting, the volume of traffic movement, the departmental propinquity, the integration of social and educational space, and the potential for growth.

The Building Performance Research Unit is at an early stage in the production of computer programs for design appraisal. The main effort is being centered on cost appraisal and those appraisals which have direct relevance to the spatial environment in schools. As an example it may be appropriate to take the difficult problem of flexibility with regard to curriculum change.

Data may be gathered to provide a frequency histogram of numbers of pupils engaged in the same activity for a variety of curricula. If these data are re-plotted with the number of pupils on the y axis and with the column width representing the number of periods (in a 40-period week) in which each number of pupils meet, the resulting format is as shown in Figure 4. Now assuming for the moment a building system with partitions fixed at points on a 3 foot module, there are a very large number of schedules of accommodation possible, some of which will satisfy both curriculum A and curriculum B. One such schedule (1) is the envelope of the two curriculums. An alternative solution, however, is to employ a building system incorporating demountable partitions in which case the schedule may be dramatically reduced (2). If a large number of different curriculums are under consideration, the sequential appraisals of schedule 1 and schedule 2 could be in terms of the number of curriculum structures which were, say, 90 percent satisfied. The parallel cost appraisals will of course exhibit a marked difference: for schedule 1 the space cost will be high and the partition cost low; for schedule 2 the space cost will be low and the partition cost high.

Now schedule 1 and schedule 2 would of course be embodied in two consecutive design syntheses of specificity appropriate to the stage reached in the design morphology. Whatever the stage might be, some information would be available regarding the acoustic properties of the boundaries. The parallel and simultaneous appraisal of these two syntheses with regard to acoustic environment would show a deterioration in performance level, and this could lead to a modified synthesis in which certain noise-producing classrooms are articulated from the others and scheduled separately. The subsequent appraisals would show a change in cost, a change in acoustic performance, and perhaps a change in departmental propinquity.

This simplified example illustrates how a series of simultaneous appraisals leads to synthesis modification and how the designer, in consultation with the client, can assess the overall satisfaction with the design in terms of cost and performance levels. To be effective, such an iterative process must be fast. The Building Performance Research Unit is investigating the potential of on-line analogue input devices to promote rapid synthesis or appraisal recycling.

It is my firmly held belief that the mechanism described will have value, not only as a design tool for specific buildings but, by varying the parameters systematically, as a means of determining the functional relationship between design and performance variables. Systematic variation of the design parameters on each cycle will generate data for a range of simulated designs that can be used in the formulation of mathematical relationships such as an analysis of covariance. In the best of all possible worlds, continued investigation of the building-user interaction by such a mechanism could result in the eventual emergence of true "performance specifications" in building design.

4. Scheduling of accommodation

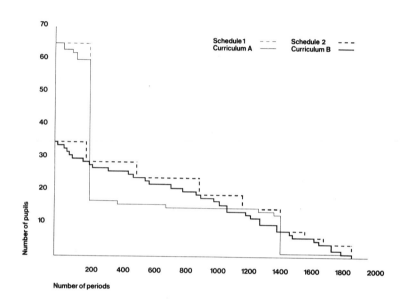

23 Toward an Economics of Renewal Programming

Arthur Silvers

CONSAD Research Corporation
5600 Forward Avenue
Pittsburgh, Pennsylvania

When this paper was written, Arthur
Silvers was a member of the CONSAD
Research Corporation, where he managed
projects in urban and regional development. He holds a degree in economic
development planning from the New
School for Social Research and is completing doctoral requirements in regional
science at the University of Pennsylvania.
He has served as Assistant City Economist
in Philadelphia's Economic Development
Unit and as a planner for the Lower East
Side New York Mobilization for Youth and
for the New York City Planning Commission. He is now a member of the faculty in the Department of Urban Planning
and Policy Development at Rutgers University.

The purpose of this paper is to develop a
rationale and methodology for evaluating
and optimizing an urban renewal plan.
The creation of an annually staged renewal plan is taken to depend upon requirements such as the attainment of a
set of building condition standards and
occupancy density standards, annual
costs for alternative technologies of
rehabilitation, code enforcement, and
construction, budget availability, and
priorities of decision-makers. The initial
tasks of the renewal planning process are
then (1) evaluating alternatives providing
quality housing for target area households, (2) determining a minimum cost
renewal strategy over time for each candidate building in the plan area such that
an optimal alternative is selected for
application over an optimal life span, and
(3) selecting candidate buildings for
inclusion in the renewal plan according
to cost-benefit criteria, such that the
priorities of decision-makers are maximized subject to annual budget availability. Thus the buildings for inclusion in the
renewal plans and a time-dimensional
renewal sequence to be used for each
building, are determined through economic analysis as input to the urban
renewal planning process.

Awareness of scarcity is an important stimulus to resourcefulness; it encourages innovation and efficiency.[1] Planners, architects, and economists
who have been concerned with the problem of housing in the slums of the
nation's big cities have been greatly aware of scarcity—the lack of funds for
rehabilitation, construction, and code enforcement both in city-wide urban
renewal programs and in locally sponsored housing programs. And they
have responded by being resourceful. Many innovations have been proposed; some have been implemented. But too many plans, often developed
with the participation and hopes of slum residents, have never seen the light
of day because of the persistent inability to meet the limited financing capabilities of the community. Too often, instead of providing better housing, the
community planning effort has merely discouraged community residents
and has made the task of gaining constructive community participation even
more difficult than before.

This paper is concerned with efficiency in planning. Its purpose is to develop
techniques to be used together with design innovations for making better use
of scarce resources toward the goal of providing better housing for low-
income urban communities.

1. John Friedmann, "Planning as Innovation: The Chilean Case."

The problems to be discussed are: (1) The method for determining which buildings to treat when renewal budgets are limited, and the related problem of equitably distributing the renewed units, (2) The method for determining which renewal treatments to apply to a building over time and for determining the economic life span.

To begin with, we note five important factors that bound the scope and the structure of the renewal plan and require that a method for planning a renewal program explicitly consider them: renewal costs per building, durability or physical life of each renewal treatment, time preferences or the discount rate, desired building condition standards, and budget availabilities.[2]

Next, we define certain terms to be used in the discussion: The term *renewal* is used together with *renewal treatment* and *renewal alternative* to denote actions that transform a building from substandard condition to the desired condition standard. *Code enforcement* and *rehabilitation* are types of renewal treatments to be applied to existing buildings. However, in order to assure that renewal program performance measures are stated in terms of the number of households in the community receiving benefits (social welfare is people-oriented, not building-oriented), construction is defined to be the action that improves the condition of a building by acquiring, demolishing, and replacing it with an equal number of housing units (of course, new construction may provide one building with enough units to offset those of several demolished buildings). Finally, we define two classes of renewal actions common to all types of treatments: *initial costs* to replace deteriorated building components at a point in time, and *maintenance costs* to hold the condition of the components constant over time. Since the "initial costs" are for replacement of components, the quality of initial investments can determine a new deterioration rate, thereby determining the structure of annual maintenance costs over time. This effect can be used to distinguish among the various renewal alternatives: type and cost of initial investment, the accompanying decay function, and the resulting maintenance cost structure.

Optimal Treatment Plan, Economic Life Span, and Renewal Cost

Our objective is to select a building that is presently in a given state of deterioration and upgrade (renew) it to a desired condition standard by applying the most economical renewal alternative. How economical an alternative is depends on its cost structure over time in comparison to other renewal alternatives. The most economical is the one that achieves all objectives at the lowest total cost over a predetermined time period.

From replacement theory, we learn that the total discounted cost C of maintaining and renewing a physical facility over an infinite period of time can be calculated as a function of the life span of a renewal cycle, i.e., the number of years following a renewal treatment before the facility has to be renewed again.[3] The length of the life cycle will be a constant n number of years, and the same type of treatment will be applied over and over again if the length of the life cycle is optimal (in the sense that no other life span could result in still lower costs). The least-cost life span n^* for a given type of renewal treatment may be found simply by inserting various values of n into the equation for the total discounted cost over an infinite period until the lowest such cost C^* is obtained:

$$C^* = \frac{A + \sum_{t=1}^{n} \frac{M_t}{(1+r)^{t-1}}}{1 - \frac{1}{1+r}^{n^*}} \tag{1}$$

where A is initial cost, M_t is maintenance costs in time period t, and r is the discount rate.

2. Richard U. Ratcliff, "Housing Standards and Housing Research," reprinted in William L. C. Wheaton, Grace Miligram, and Margy E. Meyerson, eds., *Urban Housing*.
3. C. West Churchman, Russell L. Ackoff, and E. Leonard Arnoff, *Introduction to Operations Research*.

By finding the value of C^* for each type of renewal alternative (construction, rehabilitation), both the least-cost type of renewal treatment, the optimal life span, and the annual cost may be determined.

As convenient as Equation (1) appears, however, many problems prevent its use. It does not apply to situations where the renewal time horizon is limited because, among other considerations, the first and the last renewal cycles will not necessarily have the same optimal life span as the intervening cycles. The first application of renewal treatment upgrades a building from an existing condition to a higher condition standard, while further renewal treatments are applied to the building as maintained at the condition standard. We therefore expect initial renewal costs for the first renewal cycle to differ from initial renewal costs for later cycles, resulting in differences in average annual costs and in optimal life spans. The application of Equation (1) for determining the optimal renewal alternative for the last cycle is beset by the problem that the end of the planning period will ordinarily occur prior to the full economic life span of the last cycle. Truncating treatment life at this point results in a higher annual average cost for the last cycle than for intervening cycles, and an alternative treatment might do the job at less cost.

Selecting the Optimal Renewal Sequence for Each Building

We now attack the problem of assembling for each building in the plan area a sequence of actions which minimizes the total renewal costs over the planning period. There are three general types of decisions to be made at this stage:
1. Should the building be purchased or can the renewal objective be attained through code enforcement?
2. Assuming a decision was made to purchase, what type of initial renewal treatment from among the various types of rehabilitation and replacement construction should the building receive?
3. Given that a renewal treatment was made in the previous year, should the initial treatment be terminated this year and the treatment repeated or replaced with some other renewal alternative, should the previous year's investment be continued through maintenance outlays this year, or should the building be sold and maintained through code enforcement?

Utilizing a single computational technique, these three types of decisions can simultaneously be resolved to yield the lowest total cost over the planning period. We can illustrate both the decision problem and the computational method with the schematic diagram, Figure 1. It covers three stages and utilizes the following illustrative set of costs properly discounted where applicable:

Purchase price P	$10
Demolition and replacement construction A_1	$ 7
Maintenance costs $M_1(t)$	$ 1 + \$1\,(t-1)$
Rehabilitation (A_2, first cycle)	$ 5
Rehabilitation (A_2, add t cycles)	$ 4
Maintenance costs $M_2(t)$	$ 2 + \$1\,(t-1)$
Code Enforcement (initial costs)	$15
Code Enforcement (annual costs)	$ 4

where $t=1$ is the first year following initial costs for the respective renewal treatment.

For the three-stage planning period, the optimal policy is to purchase the building, rehabilitate in the first year, and maintain during the second, at a total cost of $17. For a five-stage problem covering four years, the building should be purchased and either replaced by new construction and maintained for the rest of the planning period or rehabilitated and maintained for two cycles of two years each, initial costs occurring in the first year of the cycle and maintenance in the second. Either policy will cost $23 for the planning period. The reader may check this himself by using the cost rules above.

Where there are many renewal alternatives, many years to the planning period, and many buildings in the plan area, a complete enumeration of all

1. Tree diagram of costs of renewal alternatives

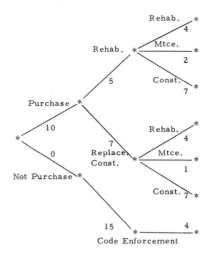

2. Dynamic programming format of tree diagram

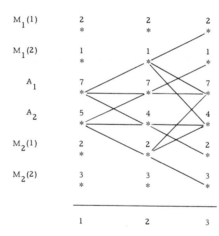

3. Minimum cost sequence at each stage of a six-stage renewal program

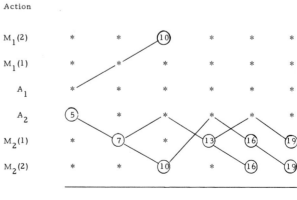

alternative renewal sequences can be an arduous, if not impossible, task. Fortunately, by utilizing a dynamic programming framework these questions can be simultaneously resolved so that the lowest total cost is obtained over the planning period.[4] (See Appendix for formal statement of the problem.) This framework also provides a ready means for exploring some of the economic considerations of the design problem, including the determination of optimal life spans for renewal treatment and condition for cycling of renewal treatments.

Let us return to the decision tree, somewhat simplified in form, to demonstrate more closely the nature of the dynamic program. Figure 2 shows a rectangular coordinate system, with the vertical coordinates corresponding to the elements of the action set and the horizontal coordinates corresponding to the stage numbers of the planning period. The cost of each policy alternative in each stage is written at the appropriate location in the field. Thus, the initial cost of replacement construction A_1 is \$7, maintenance cost in the year following construction $M_1(1)$ is \$1, for second year following construction $M_1(2)$ is \$2, etc. The initial cost for rehabilitation A_2 in the first stage is \$5, and \$4 thereafter. Maintenance cost in the year following rehabilitation $M_2(1)$ is \$2, and so on. The lines connect a renewal action that may occur in a given stage to an admissible action alternative that may follow from it in the following stage. Notice that the two initial cost actions can follow *any* action that could occur in the preceding stage, while a maintenance cost action can follow but one action of the preceding stage.

Figure 3 shows the optimal action sequence for planning periods containing anywhere from one to six stages. The encircled numbers at each stage give the minimum cost sequence for a planning period ending in that stage, while the connecting lines trace the optimal sequence of actions up to the encircled terminal action. Notice that for planning periods of three or more stages the optimal sequence is not unique. The three-stage planning period has two optimal solutions: either construction followed by two maintenance periods or rehabilitation followed by two maintenance periods. For a six-stage planning period only rehabilitation is optimal. It may occur in cycles of two or three stages in length, in the combinations shown.

The solutions show that where the planning period is equal to or greater than the economic life span of the action having lowest average annual costs ($\min_i \min_n C_i(n)/n$), then that action is to be selected and applied in cycles of n stages each. In this example the action having minimum average annual costs, with life span also optimized, is rehabilitation, which has average annual costs of \$3 if applied in cycles of either two or three stages each.

Renewal Programming with Limited Annual Budgets

When the optimal renewal treatment plan for each candidate building in the target area has been determined, the selection of buildings for inclusion in the renewal program can be undertaken. We shall examine two design environments: (1) where renewal budgets are adequate; and (2) where renewal budgets are inadequate to upgrade all buildings in the plan area (neighborhood, city, metro region, or other).

The first case is straightforward. If funds were available to finance the entire renewal program, whatever the size, the decision-maker would simply ask that all design requirements be fully satisfied in the most efficient way. Under this set of rules, all housing units in the plan area would be renewed to the building condition standard (where the standard might include all sorts of structural, safety, health, amenity, and other functional requirements) at lowest cost. This can be done by determining the most economic renewal treatment for each building, as discussed in the preceding section. Since funds are available for all buildings in the target area, the optimal renewal

4. See Stuart Dreyfus, "Dynamic Programming," in Russell L. Ackoff, ed., *Progress in Operations Research.* For a more extensive treatment, see Dreyfus, *Dynamic Programming and the Calculus of Variations,* and George Hadley, *Nonlinear and Dynamic Programming.*

plan for the area is simply the optimal renewal plan for each building taken separately, and the total cost of the area plan is minimized as the sum of the minimized renewal cost for each building.

The second case is that funds are not unlimited. Local renewal programs are usually financed through federal funds which, as urban planners are well aware, are not always equal to the need. Under these conditions progress toward goal achievement can be made by compromising either the required building standards or by relaxing the requirement that every building in the plan area be renewed. These two sets of requirements are interdependent when funds are limited. If some of the building condition requirements are relaxed, funds will be released to renew additional buildings, or if fewer buildings are renewed, higher standards can be attained on those that are renewed. Let us assume, however, that standards are taken as given.

The formulation of the problem of selecting buildings, renewable at a known optimal cost, for inclusion in the area renewal plan will then depend upon values held by decision-makers. Should priority be given to renewing buildings presently in worst condition? Or should available funds be used to upgrade the condition of occupied housing for the maximum number of households?

If priorities are building-oriented, e.g., worst buildings first, then the optimal renewal program is determined by selecting buildings in descending order of condition for inclusion in the area program until the budget is depleted.[5] The better buildings in the area will of course be excluded from renewal treatment. In addition, since the worst buildings will be the costliest to renew, a given budget can be used to treat fewer area buildings and therefore reach fewer area households.

If, however, decision-makers place greater emphasis upon providing standard quality housing for a maximum number of area households, then a building will be included according to its contribution to the objective relative to other candidate buildings. The decision of whether to renew a candidate building will depend both upon the benefits obtained, i.e., the number of additional area households that would benefit by gaining standard quality housing, and the costs to renew that building. The economics of this decision may be understood directly from the structure of the problem. To see this, we state the problem in formal terms as follows:

$$\max g = \sum_{j=1}^{u} B_j X_j,$$

subject to

$$\sum_j C_{jt} X_j \leq Q_t, \quad t = 1, \ldots, T;$$

where $0 \leq X_j \leq 1$, X_j is an integer, B_j is the number of housing units in the jth building among a total of u buildings, and C_{jt} is the renewal cost for that building during time period t, remembering that this cost and the associated renewal treatment (rehabilitation, replacement construction, code enforcement) has already been determined according to the methodology discussed earlier. The Q_t are the renewal budgets for the tth year of the T year planning period. The X_j are the variables to be solved for and are restricted to values of either zero or one. They indicate whether the jth building is to be included ($X_j = 1$) or not ($X_j = 0$), such that Equation (1), the total number of housing units in the area, is maximized while not violating the requirement that the sum of renewal costs in any year not exceed the budget for that year. Costs and benefits for each period should be weighted by a discount term that appropriately reflects the greater utility for earlier rather than late net benefits.[6]

This problem may be restated in an alternative form, more fruitful for understanding the economic factors involved in the selection decision.

---

5. Actually, the problem is somewhat more complicated since many annual budgets over the time span of the program must be considered. Methodology for dealing with this problem will be discussed later in this paper.
6. See Roland McKean, *Efficiency in Government Through Systems Analysis.*

It can be shown that each problem of the type in Equation (2) possesses a specific companion or dual problem.[7] For purposes of exposition we shall assume that the original or primal problem is not constrained to produce integer values for the X_j. The price paid for the modification will be small; although the X_j can now take on fractional values, implying that only a percentage of a renewal treatment be applied to the building, the number of fractional X_j that appear in the solution can never exceed the number of time periods in which the budget restraint is binding.[8] The dual of the modified primal problem will read:

$$\min z = \sum_{t=1}^{T} Q_t P_t + \sum_{j=1}^{u} Y_j$$

subject to $\qquad\qquad\qquad\qquad\qquad\qquad\qquad\qquad\qquad\qquad$ (3)

$$\sum_t C_{jt} P_t + Y_j \geq B_j; j = 1, \ldots, u,$$

$$Y_j, P_t \geq 0.$$

In this problem, we solve for two sets of unknowns, the P_t and the Y_j. The explanation of the meaning of these variables will reveal that the dual problem establishes economic criteria for the selection of buildings for renewal.

We shall focus first upon the meaning of the inequalities in Equation (3) which establishes cost and benefit criteria for each of the buildings in the target area. Let all candidate buildings be ranked in decreasing order of desirability based upon a consideration of both costs and benefits. Then the least desirable building that is included in the area renewal plan will just exhaust an annual budget constraining the program. The variable X for this building as determined in the primal problem will take on a fractional value between zero and one. By a theorem in linear programming, it can be shown that inequality for this marginally included building will be an exact equality,[9] with zero value of Y_j:

$$\sum_t C_{jt} P_t = B_j \qquad\qquad\qquad\qquad\qquad\qquad\qquad\qquad\qquad (4)$$

or, the total weighted costs for renewing marginally included buildings must just equal the benefits gained from renewal, where benefits are measured in terms of number of standard quality housing units made available to area households. These weights or shadow prices (the P_t), may be identified as the physical productivity of the last available dollar of the budget in period t, which indicates the number of additional housing units that could be renewed if the budget in period t were increased by one dollar.

Let us make a simplifying assumption that only the budget for the first planning period will be limited. In this case, P_2 through P_t will take on zero values, and Equation (4) becomes:

$$C_{j1} P_1 = B_{j1}$$

or $P_1 = \dfrac{B_j}{C_j}$ for any j such that $0 < X_j < 1.$ $\qquad\qquad\qquad\qquad (5)$

This equation states that buildings are to be selected for inclusion in the area renewal plan according to a cost-benefit rationale: the last building to be included in the renewal program must have a benefit-cost ratio equal to the marginal productivity of the limited budget. In addition, all other buildings included in the renewal program must have higher benefit-cost ratios, such that net benefits will have a positive value of Y_j.

7. Refer to any of the standard texts on linear programming, including Saul Gass, *Linear Programming*, and George Hadley, *Linear Programming*, for an explanation of duality in linear programming. However, a more rigorous and more general explanation can be found in the excellent discussion of Kuhn-Tucker Theory in Hadley, *Nonlinear and Dynamic Programming*, chapter 6.
8. This useful observation is explained at length in Martin Weingartner, *Mathematical Programming and the Analysis of Capital Budgeting Problems*.
9. If an activity is included in the solution to the primal ($X_j = 0$) the corresponding jth restraint in the dual will be a strict equality (slack variable of the jth restraint will be zero). See Hadley, *Linear Programming*.

The meaning of the Y_j's can be gleaned from the fact that they will be positive when the requirements in the primal problem Equation (2) are satisfied such that $X_j = 1$. The Y_j are interpreted as the scarcity rent accruing to building j in an amount equal to the benefit from renewing that building.

It is interesting to note that scarcity rents will be higher for buildings in better condition, which as a result require lower renewal costs. Undoubtedly, this result would also be recognized in the private real estate market, and would be reflected by higher acquisition prices for the better buildings. This would tend to equalize the renewal costs for buildings in different physical condition.

The restraint of Equation (3) can be interpreted as requiring that the value of resources stemming from their scarcity, including the scarcity value of funds ($\Sigma Q_i P_i$) and of "quality" buildings (ΣY_j), be minimized. This will require that as many as possible of the buildings that still meet the cost-benefit criteria be included in the program, implying that resources must be used to their full capacity.

Observations

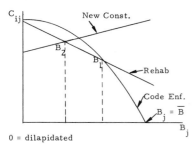

0 = dilapidated

4. Costs of renewal alternatives as a function of building condition

If we relate the cost of the various renewal alternatives to building condition, as shown in Figure 4, and assume that the objective is to maximize the number of standard quality dwelling units for area residents, we may observe the following:

1. So long as the condition of substandard buildings in a slum area covers the entire range from "most dilapidated" to "least substandard," some code enforcement will always be a part of the renewal program. The reason for this is that since the cost of code enforcement approaches zero as building condition approaches the standard, a condition that does not exist for any of the other renewal alternatives, there will exist a number of buildings for which code enforcement will be the least costly alternative.

2. The very worst buildings will never be renewed unless they can be replaced with new construction at lower costs than through rehabilitation, or unless scale economies exist for renewing larger buildings with many dwelling units.

The explanation of the first part of statement 2 is that both increasing acquisition costs and decreasing restoration costs determine the cost of rehabilitation as building condition improves, while only increasing acquisition costs affect construction costs as building condition improves. Therefore, the possibility that buildings in worst condition would not be the costliest to renew stems from the possibility that such buildings would be the least expensive to acquire and demolish for new construction and from the possibility that rehabilitation of such buildings would be costlier than new construction, as seen in Figure 4.

The second part of statement 2 is explained by the fact that if the ratio of benefits to costs is independent of the number of units in a building, then buildings in poorer condition will always have lower benefit/cost ratios.

Appendix

The formal dynamic program can be written with the following definitions:

$F_i(t)$ is the total cost of a T-stage renewal treatment sequence over the first t stages, using renewal treatment i in stage t.

$F_i(t-1|i(t))$ is the optimal cost of the first $t-1$ stages of a T-stage renewal treatment sequence that could occur given renewal treatment i in stage t.

$C_i(t)$ is the cost of renewal treatment i in stage t.

We find the minimum total cost sequence of renewal treatments over T-stage period for a given building by applying the following recurrence relation beginning with $t = 0$ and ending with $t = T$. Note that t is used here to refer to a decision that occurs at some time in the planning period, and these stages need not occur in annual increments. Then:

$$F_i(t) = \min_i (c_i(t) + F_i(t-1|i(t))); \quad t = 0, \ldots, T;$$

with boundary conditions $C_i(0) = 0$
and $F_i(0-1|i(0)) = 0$.

24 Some Thoughts on Measurement on Problem-Solving

Comments on the papers by Maver and Silvers

Michael Brill and Sharon Rose

Building Research Division,
National Bureau of Standards
Washington, D.C.

Michael Brill is currently Associate Pro-
fessor of Building Technology in the
School of Architecture and Environmental
Design, State University of New York,
Buffalo. At the time this commentary was
written, he was Senior Systems Architect
with the Building Research Division of the
Institute for Applied Technology, National
Bureau of Standards. Sharon Rose is
Senior Systems Analyst with the Com-
puter Center of Howard University in
Washington and a consultant to several
government agencies, including the
Institute for Applied Technology.

The two papers presented here demonstrate the painful dilemma the researcher has when he wishes to more clearly understand human relationships to shelter. Maver's paper, "Appraisal in the Building Design Process,"
attempts to combine objective and subjective measurements, to combine the
physically quantifiable and cost measurements with the "value of achieving
objectives." The inclusion of this parameter renders the process nonquantifiable and subject to manipulation by official and unofficial decision-makers
and, thereby, of marginal utility. Silver's paper, "Toward an Economics of
Renewal Programming" approaches internal rigor by deliberately excluding
a wide range of real-world factors affecting renewal. Cost parameters alone
remain for consideration. These exclusions and simplifications allow the
findings to be applied immediately in decision-making but, by being insensi-
tive to anything but cost prevent the decisions from being comprehensive.

The dilemma, simply stated, is this: Where the researcher wishes to reflect
the complexity of the human condition, we do not have the metrics available
to render the work rational enough for utilization by public decision-makers.
And where the researcher constructs his work so that implementation is
possible, he is forced to simplify and reduce the variables often to the point
where man is perceived as one-dimensional.

Techniques are becoming available to resolve this traditional dilemma, and criticisms can be leveled at both these papers for not exploring them.[1] Further, to deliberately eschew complexity in order to make problem-solving easier may not do the job it is intended to do. To simplify problems, to exclude certain variables or make limiting assumptions, reduces and often impoverishes the range of solutions possible. There is somehow a lack of richness, a meagerness of nuance in solutions arrived at through a process of reduction in problem definition and methodology.

There is also an implicit assumption in this process of simplification that "If we can solve this simplified problem, we can add more variables later and then model the real world." This assumes that difficulty is a linear function as you add variables. In fact, there is a takeoff point, a quantum jump in difficulty and complexity that occurs in environmental problem-solving which may render the "Let's start with simple problems" vision unworkable. *It is only in the context of these cautionary statements that the two papers are examined.*

The first paper is one of few which deal with the economic component of renewal and is an important addition to a meager literature. The faults we find with it are not inherent in the methodology, and the techniques the author has developed are capable of growth and amplification. The author hints at this in his title, using the qualifier "toward."

The first section presents the working assumptions and definitions, and it is here that the simplification process begins. We believe it is unnecessary. The five factors related to "the most appropriate renewal treatment" could be expanded to include a factor for social stability (a value for how much each building and present occupants add to the social stability of the renewal area), a factor for aesthetics (how handsome, unusual, or historical each building in the renewal area is), and so on. These factors could certainly be as rigorously determined as the author's factor, the "desired condition standard."

The definitions of renewal alternatives, particularly "construction," do not preclude, but also do not suggest, the possibility of utilizing vacant land in the renewal area as a phasing device or surge tank. Such a device has been the hallmark of a number of innovative plans which combine renewal with new construction.

The assumption that "building condition can be described by a single index which has its own 'well-behaved' (monotonically increasing) deterioration rate over time" is a mathematical convenience which is supportable neither by mathematics nor in terms of the actual behavior of housing. One of the biggest building problems is the radically different rates at which building components deteriorate; buildings themselves seem not to deteriorate in a "well-behaved" way. We know that building deterioration is heavily affected by the attitudes of its users, and vice versa. It might have been possible to be more sophisticated about deterioration, as ultimately that is what renewal is all about. The author does not develop or define the measures of the "given state of deterioration" or the "desired condition standard."

Equation (1), which finds the optimum total cost for a building's renewal over time, is quite elegant. Two immediate apologies follow, because of the difficulties of applying the equation to cases where there is a finite time horizon. Neither apology is accepted, because the current literature does deal with solutions to precisely this problem, common to many optimum-seeking finite-time problems.[2]

1. See Alan G. Wilson, "Morphology and Modularity," in Fritz Zwicky and Wilson, eds., *New Methods of Thought and Procedure: Contributions to a Symposium on Methodologies.* For a less esoteric approach, see Martin L. Ernst, *Operations Research for Public Systems.*
2. For treatment of delayed renewal processes, see William Feller, *An Introduction to Probability Theory and Its Applications,* especially pp. 293–296.

As this paper expands its concern to many renewal alternatives, many years, and many buildings from this first one-building equation, dynamic programming is utilized to simplify an "arduous, if not impossible, task." However, such techniques only function within a framework of infinite resources, and it is questionable whether we would ever be in a position fortunate enough to utilize dynamic programming. Silvers turns then to linear programming to optimize within the constraint of resource scarcity, the prevalent real-world condition.

As the author rightly points out, the duality principle of linear programming shows that the minimum cost and maximum benefit solutions are equivalent. But his solution of the primal (optional dollar cost) problem *as stated* forces him to infer a definition of benefits in terms of "scarcity rent." He then reaches the frightening "rich-get-richer" conclusion that buildings in better condition are the ones to be chosen for renewal treatment. We suggest that an *initial* consideration of benefits accrued from renewal in a real world (social) context would lead to a different objective function.

We think it is safe to assert that people who live in better housing lead better lives. Granting that "quality of life" is far from quantifiable, it still seems reasonable to assume that the social benefits of renewal are at least as great as what people are willing to spend (in terms of temporary disruption of their lives) to obtain them. Thus, the cost equation should include a term for the dollar cost of this disruption, as in the New York City "Instant Rehabilitation" experiment sponsored by the United States Department of Housing and Urban Development.

From a rigorous operations research point of view it is also clear that this additional term is necessary in order that the objective function be the sum of *oppositely directed costs,* which are in some manner "balanced" by the set of values that form the optional solution. By not including such a term, where renewal areas make use of these equations, there would be a forced polarization of building quality over time.

Buildings in good condition are constantly brought to an even higher standard, but once a building has an accelerated period of deterioration in a cycle, it is marked for the junkheap, as it will not be selected for renewal unless there is an increase in funds available or a reduction in the size of the renewal area with funds constant.

None of these additional functions are precluded by the work the author presents, and their inclusion would strengthen and enrich this economic tool so it could deal with the real complexities of urban renewal.

The concerns of the second paper are considerably broader than of the previous paper. It does attempt to connect human objectives in some way to the process of appraising designs and their cost implications. However, the author makes some assumptions about the design process which may not be true and, further, accepts as permanently "intuitive" in this process some factors which others have begun to quantify.

The design morphology is modeled as sequential; thus to "return from a later stage to an earlier stage is recognized as failure in the management of the design activity." In an ideal world, this ought to be the case, but the design and construction process operates quite differently. For instance stage 5, detail design, strongly affects and is affected by stage 10, operation on site, while stage 3, outline proposals (we believe this to be the program or brief) affects and is affected by the final stage, feedback. Happily, the act of manipulating forms can enrich the program by perceiving relationships not previously conceived of and forces an iterative cycle in the design morphology.[3]

---

3. This is documented by Richard Krauss and John Myer in "Design: A Case History" in this volume.

The "conceptual cost-benefit model" (Maver's Figure 2) shows the author's vision of the interaction between the "animate and inanimate" parts of the model and implies a dynamic balance. This dynamic balance must recognize in some way that it is human objectives that generate the need for buildings and that the process is one-way in its first cycle. Further, the benefit side of this model lacks rigor or even a hint of how it might be made rigorous. The "value of achieving objectives" ought to be equal to that portion of the hardware which supports such achievement.

But how do you trace such value? This model has all the problems of cost-benefit analysis and is rationally unresolvable as stated, since the author ultimately invokes the intuition of the client. Rittel has said, "Tell me what you want to prove, and unfortunately, I can construct a cost benefit analysis to prove it."[4] This is not any improvement on how we operate now.

As the author progresses through examination of the work of others (Souder, Whitehead, and Eldars), he proposes a series of appraisal programs to overcome the obvious deficiencies in each and arrives at the concept of appraising an intuitively-arrived-at design synthesis in terms of "a cost figure and a performance level of each variable." It is the client whose intuition is to weigh performance levels, as the designer searches for "optimum design."

This can only happen if certain conditions are met, and some of them cannot be met. First, it is assumed that in designing, when the client "rejects" certain aspects of a scheme and asks the designer to "go back to the drawing board," all the nonrejected portions can be held as fixed while the designer seeks formal solutions to the rejected components. This is often not so.

It is also important that the designer and client agree explicitly on the boundaries of the system being designed and appraised in terms of cost. Seldom does this happen. As an example of how the issue of boundaries is critical in the design process, our own work has been concerned with the design of federal office buildings, and we perceive them as only one element in a federal information-processing system consisting of buildings, men, machines, energy, and rules whose job it is to transact abstractions, to process information. We analyze the total system costs over 40 years and find that the first cost of the building is 2 percent of the total, operating costs and maintenance is 6 percent, while the cost of people (in salaries) is 92 percent. With this understanding of the boundaries of the system, it is obvious that all attempts to reduce the first cost of the building, including durability trade-offs, can have only marginal results, while trying to improve the productivity of the people (perhaps even by raising the cost of the building through quality increases) may be a major cost-efficiency opportunity. Unless designer and client agree explicitly as to boundaries, such opportunities slip by.

The author is proposing a system in which the "program brief" is fixed, and that may be a constraint. He is proposing appraisal of the designer's intuitive first cut with subsequent appraisals based on the client's intuitive metering of performance levels. The costs of hardware and operation can be measured, as they are now. Although the speed and rigor gained by automatic data processing are real, they do not make the design process more effective.

The problems of both papers revolve around measurement: one paper simplifies its vision of the world to accommodate the measurement systems available while the other does not really have the measurements to examine the complexities of a real-world design process.

Man's physical, psychological, and social responses are the measures of performance of his environment, and the research community's attitude as to what constitutes "acceptable" measurement systems must change to give support, credence, and utility to these newer measures.

4. Horst Rittel, *Measuring the Performance of Buildings.*

7 Applications of Systems Engineering

The papers in this section discuss a general problem-solving approach developed for industry, the government, and the military, which is now being applied to social and urban-planning problems. Systems analysis and systems engineering have been developed in response to the general agreement on the need for systematic approaches to large complex problems and the widespread recognition that major social problems cannot be solved by looking at each problem separately when there are in fact systems of interacting problems.

The first paper, by Joseph Stafford, Richard de Neufville, and James Hester, addresses the need for a systematic approach. The paradigm for systems analysis is presented and applied to the analysis of urban water supply needs over a twenty-year period and to the evaluation of alternative systems for fulfilling those needs.

The second paper, by Paul Nutt, David Gustafson, and Gerald Nadler, addresses the problem of providing a framework for considering social and urban-planning problems. The investigators have attacked the problem of providing regional health care, including prevention, diagnosis, and treatment within the interacting fields of medicine, nursing, social work, mental health, alcoholism, and heart, stroke, and cancer care. The theoretical part of their paper is expanded in another paper by Nadler in Part 9 of this volume.

In conclusion, Daniel Brand discusses the approaches in the two papers and alludes to similar approaches for urban housing and transportation. By way of contrast, in a paper in the next section Ward challenges the basic assumptions and approach of systems analysis.

What is the relation between "systems engineering" and "operations research"? There is often confusion about these terms and disciplines. They share many of the same presuppositions and ways of looking at problems, and they share many of the same mathematical techniques. Operations research as an overall process is primarily interested in making procedural changes, while systems engineering is primarily interested in making physical or equipment changes. For environmental design and planning, the two obviously go hand-in-hand; procedural changes imply changes in the physical environment, and physical changes necessitate changes in operation. The important thing for designers and planners to keep in mind is that the approaches and specific models of both fields may be useful for certain environmental problems. Two such problems, for example, are discussed in this section. In addition, the reader is referred to a set of applications of system engineering to other urban problems given in articles by Steinmetz et al., listed in the bibliography.

25 Systems Analysis: The Analysis of the Expansion of a Water Supply System

Joseph Stafford, Richard de Neufville, and James Hester

Departments of Civil Engineering and City and Regional Planning, Massachusetts Institute of Technology Cambridge, Massachusetts

Joseph Stafford is Assistant Professor of Civil Engineering at M.I.T. He received a B.S., M.S., and Ph.D. in agricultural economics in 1961, 1962, and 1965 from Purdue University. He has been with the Office of the Joint Chiefs of Staff, Headquarters of the Military Traffic Management and Terminal Service, and the U.S. Army Transportation Corps. Richard de Neufville is also an Assistant Professor of Civil Engineering at M.I.T. He received an S.B. and S.M. in 1961 and a Ph.D. in 1965 in civil engineering systems from M.I.T. From 1965 to 1966 he was a White House Fellow, serving as an Assistant to the Secretary of Defense and a Staff Member of the President's Office of Science and Technology and the Department of Housing and Urban Development. James Hester is a doctoral candidate in city and regional planning at M.I.T. He received a S.B. and S.M. in aeronautics and astronautics in 1965 and 1966 from M.I.T. He has worked with the NASA Manned Spaceflight Center, the Avco Everett Research Laboratory, and the Ford Motor Company Transportation Research and Planning Office.

This paper concerns the problem of expanding the capacity of New York City's primary water distribution system. Students in a project course first estimated the range of magnitude and spatial distribution of demands for water in the city by disaggregating the users into ten groups, residents and employees in each of the five boroughs of New York, and projecting the growth of each group and its per capita demand. Six major alternative ways of meeting the projected increases in demand were then evaluated on the basis of pressure distribution, cost, reliability, and flexibility. Computer routines, developed to aid in the demand projections and network analysis, greatly expanded the range of alternatives which could be examined in detail and, most important, permitted an analysis of the sensitivity of the design to changes in demand and to variations in pipe resistances. Specifically, they were used to calculate the pressure distributions that would exist if different projected demands were met by alternative networks. The program recommended involves reconditioning and expansion of the existing tunnels plus the optional construction of a new tunnel to Queens in 1985. The previously proposed design was based entirely on construction of new tunnels. The solution proposes to reduce costs by two-thirds while meeting the range of projected demands.

This paper is a report on a student project in Engineering Systems Analysis conducted in the spring of 1968 in the Department of Civil Engineering at M.I.T.[1] In order to gain experience in the use of systems analysis techniques on real, unstructured problems, we addressed the problem of expanding the capacity of New York City's primary water distribution system. This particular problem demonstrated the need for sensitivity analysis and sequential decisions when working with imperfect information and an uncertain future, showed the difficulties in establishing good design criteria for the comparison of alternatives, and illustrated the utility of computer routines as a design aid.

The New York City problem was selected because of its relevance and timeliness (the city was examining the question of whether to approve the project) and because preliminary analyses and the accompanying data were available.[2] This background enabled us to bypass much of the time-con-

---

1. The student members of the team were S. Disman, P. Flanagan, B-A. Genest, M. Gernand, P. Hoxie, Y. Ichikawa, and A. Munds.
2. "Report of the Board of Water Supply of the City of New York to the Board of Estimate on the Third City Tunnel: First Stage in the Boroughs of the Bronx, Manhattan, and Queens," unpublished report, Board of Water Supply, New York, 1966; and "Final Evaluation of the Report on the Third City Tunnel," unpublished report, Parson-Jordan Corporation, New York, 1967.

1. New York City primary water distribution system

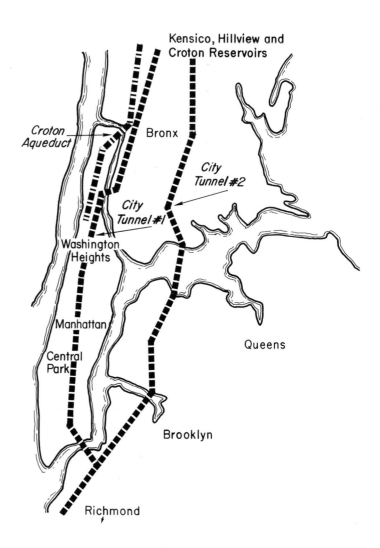

2. Demand projections for water in New York City

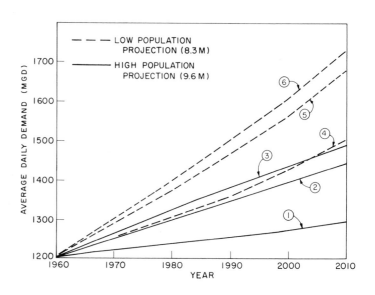

suming task of collecting data and to proceed directly with a design analysis.

Description of the Problem

Over 90 percent of New York City's water needs are carried by the primary water distribution system which connects the Croton, Hill View, and Kensico reservoirs north of New York City to sets of secondary water mains located throughout the city. The present system consists of two tunnels ranging from 11 to 17 feet in diameter and the smaller Croton aqueduct, as illustrated in Figure 1. A few public and private wells round out the system, whose present status is summarized as follows:

1. The Croton aqueduct, built in 1891, can supply between 200 and 300 million gallons daily (mgd) to low-pressure areas in Manhattan and the Bronx. It is reported to be in poor condition but not yet beyond repair.
2. City tunnel No. 1, completed in 1917, is 18 miles long, 15 feet in diameter, and located in bedrock 200 to 750 feet deep. Its capacity is about 500 to 600 mgd, which is delivered to all boroughs but primarily to the western areas in the Bronx and to Manhattan. Tests made in 1962 suggest that this tunnel is showing signs of age with the most seriously degraded section between Washington Heights and Central Park.
3. City tunnel No. 2, finished in 1936, is 20 miles long and 17 feet in diameter and is also a deep tunnel. Its capacity ranges between 700 and 800 mgd. Apart from some leakage and a few difficulties with some of the control equipment, this tunnel is in good condition.
4. The municipal well fields are limited in extent and are not normally relied on except in Richmond County. There are no plans to use them permanently unless emergencies develop.
5. Private wells are used by two water companies in Queens; they now supply about 60 mgd. The private and municipal systems are interconnected and the city might eventually have to assume the responsibility for supplying the water needs now met by the private companies.

With the exception of the water taken from wells, all of the water transported by the primary system originates in the upland watersheds north of New York City. An adequate upland water supply can be assumed, and this analysis was confined to the primary distribution of that water from the reservoirs north of the city, through the main tunnels to the secondary distribution mains. The details of final distribution through the approximately 6000 miles of secondary mains were not considered, principally because of lack of information. Thus the pressure at the exits to the primary system was taken as a proxy for the ultimate measure of effectiveness of the water distribution system, that is, for the adequacy of the pressure at the end of the secondary system, where the water is in use.

The basic problem in the primary distribution system is that the tunnel walls are gradually deteriorating, so that their ability to supply water decreases, while the use of water within the city is increasing. The result is a continual reduction in pressure at the uptake shafts. Even under the most optimistic assumptions the existing facilities will not be adequate for 1985 demands.

In the system current in 1968 all energy was supplied by gravity. The elevations at the intakes at the Hillview and Croton reservoirs are greater than the elevations at the top of any of the uptakes where the primary and secondary systems join. Loss of pressure depends on the amount of energy required to move a volume of water through a pipe of given resistance and is measured in terms of head of water (in feet). Greater head losses are caused both by increased flow and greater resistance within the pipes. If, as a result of drawing more water from the existing system, the pressure becomes unsatisfactory, then the head can be increased either by adding more energy to the system or by reducing the energy loss. Viewed from this perspective the design alternatives are:
1. Add energy by supplementing the gravity system with pumps.
2. Add new tunnels to reduce the flow and thus the head loss in the existing tunnels.

3. Equations used by the network analyzer

4. Network of alternatives 1 through 5

$$F_j = \sum_{i=1}^{n} \frac{H_i - H_j}{R_{ij}^{0.54} \, | H_i - H_j |\, 0.46} + C_j = O_{j=1,\ldots,n}$$

F_j = sum of the flows into node
C_j = net consumption or input at node
H_i = head at node i
L_{ij} = length of the pipe i to j
D_{ij} = diameter of the pipe between i and j
C_{ij} = Hazen-Williams coefficient of roughness

R_{ij} = resistance in the pipe or tunnel from i to $j = \dfrac{850260 \, L_{ij}}{(C_{ij}^{1.85})\,(D_{ij}^{4.87})}$

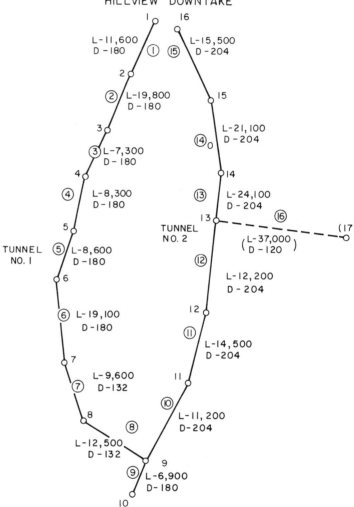

HILLVIEW   DOWNTAKE

RICHMOND DOWNTAKE

NODES	2,3,14,15	– BRONX
"	4,5,6,7,8	– MANHATTAN
"	12,13,(17)	– QUEENS
"	9,11	– BROOKLYN
	10	– RICHMOND

NOTE:
1,2,... – NODE NO.
①,②,... – PIPE NO.
L-PIPE LENGTH (FT)
D-PIPE DIAMETER (IN)

3. Enlarge or smooth the existing tunnels to reduce their resistance.
4. Combinations of (1), (2), and (3).

The primary criteria for evaluating specific alternatives within these classes are system cost and deficiencies in the water pressure at the point of delivery. However, since the risk of complete failure at some point in the tunnel must be considered and since the expansion of the system will help meet the needs of New York over the next fifty years (long as compared to the periods over which good projections can be made), the reliability and flexibility of the system design have been added as secondary measures of effectiveness.

Analysis: Projection of Demand

In order to compare alternative network designs, it was necessary to project the magnitude and spatial distribution of future demand for water, calculate the head distribution for each alternative which would result in meeting these flow demands, and estimate the construction costs of each system.

Changes in the amount of water required depend on changes both in the number of users and in their individual rate of usage. In addition, the design flow must take seasonal and hourly peaking into account. All three factors were considered, and a program was written to facilitate analysis of the sensitivity of flow requirements to alternative assumptions. The resulting aggregate predictions of demand are shown in Figure 2. As can be seen, six different sets of assumptions resulted in only three basically different estimates of demand for the design year 2010. The low-level demand is based on very slow growth in population from 8.1 million in 1967 to 8.3 million in 2010. The high-level demand is based on population growth to 9.6 million by 2010 plus 15 percent increase in per capita usage. These population projections are near the extremes predicted in other studies of New York City. Most studies predict either no population growth or possibly a slight decline.

The medium-level demand can be based either on a population increase to 9.6 million and no increase in per capita usage or on no increase in population and 15 percent increase in per capita usage. That is, per capita usage and population are equally important variables for predicting flow requirements. We recognized this fact but were unable to analyze either factor in depth. We did, however, identify the range of uncertainty which is applicable to the design problem and did recommend that per capita usage projections receive more attention.

In the analysis, we broke with tradition in water system planning and treated demand as a function of employment as well as of resident population. We found that it was unrealistic to treat Manhattan, with an enormous non-resident work force, on the same basis as Richmond, which is primarily residential. Instead of estimating per capita consumption at 155 gallons a day, as is now done, our investigations indicated that it would be better to estimate use on the basis of 120 gallons per resident plus 80 gallons per employee.

To account for the hourly peak in daily demand, we used a peaking factor of 1.5 in the analysis of all systems except those with storage tanks, for which we used a peaking factor of 1.2. These are the generally accepted factors and were not seriously challenged.

The spatial distribution of demand which was needed for the network analysis was estimated by first projecting the growth in population, employees, and per capita demand for each of the city's 5 boroughs, then estimating how much of each borough's demand went to each uptake. A more accurate estimate of the spatial distribution would have required (1) a detailed investigation of the secondary distribution system (about 6000 miles of mains ranging in size from 6 ft to $1\frac{1}{2}$ in), and (2) a larger computer so that an exact simulation of the system could be performed. The sensitivity of the pressure distribution in the network to moderate shifts in the distribution of demand was briefly checked and found to be small, so it is not felt that more accurate estimates of the distribution would change the basic results of this study.

5. Maximum drops in the present system for 1985–2010

6. Head drops for demand in 2010 with a smooth or enlarged city tunnel #1

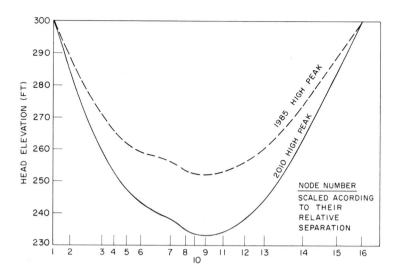

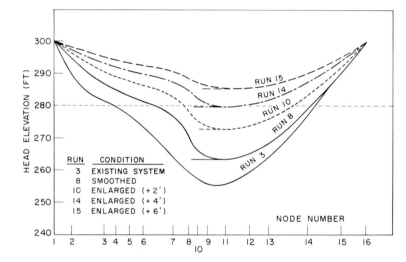

Network Analysis

The response of each of the alternative networks to the projected demands derived above was calculated using a hydraulic network analyzer programmed for the IBM 1130 computer. The program, based on a technique developed by Shamir and Howard, uses the Newton-Raphson iteration method to improve the estimated solutions by balancing the discrepancies in the estimated head at each uptake until an arbitrarily specified tolerance is reached.[3] The model uses Hazen-Williams equations, as shown in Figure 3, to calculate the head lost along each link of the network from the flow in each link. In the form used for this project the network analyzer determines the pressure distribution required to obtain specified outflows from a network.

The schematic of New York's existing system in Figure 4 illustrates how the networks were described for input into the analyzer. The network topography was specified to the program by numbering the uptakes, hereafter referred to as nodes and pipes, then listing the two nodes which each pipe connects. Each pipe in the network was described in terms of its length, diameter, and roughness or Hazen-Williams coefficient. The net flow into or out of each node had to be specified. The head at one node, usually taken to be one of the reservoirs, had to be given as a reference pressure level in the system, since the Hazen-Williams equation only determines the pressure drop and is independent of the absolute pressure levels.

The use of this analyzer program instead of conventional hand techniques easily allowed us to examine over forty networks in the course of analyzing six basic alternative designs. Using the IBM 1130, which is a small and fairly slow machine, the computations for each analysis took about 15 minutes each.

Alternatives

After discarding some of the more exotic alternatives such as nuclear desalinization, which cost too much or were otherwise impractical, we analyzed six distinctly different primary distribution networks. These were:
1. The present system, the base case.
2. The present system with some large storage tanks to reduce the volume of flow and consequently the pressure drops at times of peak demand.
3. The present system with a branch tunnel (37,000 feet long, 120 inches in diameter) to the rapidly growing area in Queens.
4. The new system of tunnels proposed in the earlier study.
5. An enlargement of 4 feet for city tunnel No. 1 in the present system.
6. An enlargement of 4 feet for city tunnel No. 1 plus a branch tunnel into Queens.
The performance of each of these alternatives was predicted for several different demand conditions both in the design year 2010 and in an intermediate year 1985.

It was assumed that a minimum head of approximately 280 feet would be needed at each node in order to allow for pressure losses in the secondary distribution system and for the changes in ground elevation throughout the city. Using this criterion, it was estimated that the present system would be inadequate to meet the peak demands which could arise in 1985, shown in Figure 5, and that by 2010 the head at Richmond would be below 240 feet, the base of the storage tanks.

Much of the energy lost in the present system is caused by deterioration and increased resistance, especially in the older city tunnel No. 1. The loss could be reduced by cleaning and smoothing the tunnel surfaces and could be further reduced by enlarging the tunnels. The effects of such reconditioning are shown in Figure 6. This analysis led to the conclusion that repair of the existing facilities constituted an attractive alternative.

Widening city tunnel No. 1 by four feet substantially eliminates the head loss as we can see in Figure 7. It was determined it would be possible to enlarge

3. Uri Shamir and Charles D. Howard, "Water Distribution Systems Analysis."

7. Maximum head drops for 1985 and 2010
with city tunnel # 1 enlarged by 4 feet

8. Comparison of alternatives

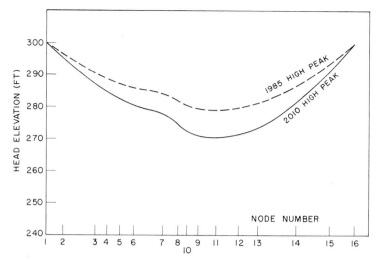

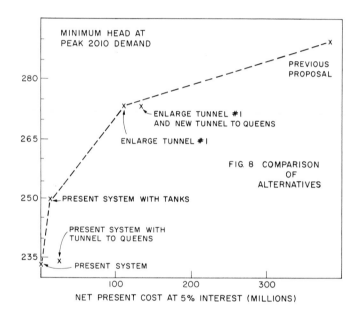

FIG. 8 COMPARISON
OF
ALTERNATIVES

and recondition city tunnel No. 1 if winter demands were diverted to a re-conditioned Croton system. As the operation would require careful staging, the network analyzer was used to check the feasibility of each stage.

Each of the other alternatives was similarly evaluated: the minimum heads were recorded for peak-flow requirements using high-, medium-, and low-demand predictions for 1985 and 2010. The results are summarized in Figure 8, a cost-effectiveness plot of the alternatives using minimum head under maximum flow requirements as the measure of effectiveness and net present value of all construction outlays as a measure of cost. From this chart it appears that major increases in system effectiveness can be attained from relatively small outlays. The design that had been previously proposed to the city, which would cost three to four times as much, achieved only a small increase in effectiveness above that obtained by enlarging the old city tunnel No. 1.

Clearly, minimum head in the primary system under peak loads is not the only plausible measure of effectiveness; ultimately the pressure at the point of use governs. The value of a branch tunnel to Queens lies, for example, in its effect on pressure in the secondary system at a distance from the present primary system. Other criteria include minimization of risk of failure, in-sensitivity of system performance to likely changes in flow requirement, and flexibility for adapting the system to unknown future demands.

After considering these additional evaluation criteria, the team recom-mended that the City of New York take these measures:
1. Recondition the Croton Water Supply System by 1975.
2. Recondition City Tunnel No. 1 and enlarge it to a diameter of 19 feet, to be completed by no later than 1985.
3. Study the option of constructing a seven-mile tunnel ten feet in diameter from City Tunnel No. 2 to Flushing, Queens. This option would be exercised if the demand conditions in 1985 made it desirable to improve the pressure of water delivered to Queens County.
4. Examine the use of large storage tanks to alleviate the problem of short-term (hourly) fluctuations in the demand for water.

26 Systems Engineering as Applied to Planning Processes:

An Example from the Wisconsin Regional Medical Program

Paul C. Nutt, David H. Gustafson, and Gerald Nadler

Department of Industrial Engineering
University of Wisconsin
Madison, Wisconsin

Paul C. Nutt is Program Coordinator for the Wisconsin Regional Medical Program (WRMP) and a Ph.D. candidate in industrial engineering at the University of Wisconsin. He received a B.S. and M.S. in industrial engineering from the University of Michigan in 1962 and 1963 and has been an industrial engineer and project engineer on several medical center projects. David H. Gustafson is an Assistant Professor of Mechanical Engineering at Wisconsin and a member of the Planning Committee of WRMP. He received a B.S., M.S., and Ph.D. in industrial engineering from Michigan in 1962, 1963, and 1966. He was a research and teaching fellow at Michigan and a project engineer and advisor on several medical center projects. Gerald Nadler is Professor of Industrial Engineering at Wisconsin and Chairman of WRMP. He received a Ph.D. in industrial engineering in 1949 from Purdue University. He has had extensive industrial and management experience and was Chairman of the Human and Organizational Factors Area at Washington University, St. Louis, and Chairman of the Industrial Engineering Division of the University of Wisconsin.

This paper concurrently describes systems engineering and its application to planning processes. The systems engineer has three types of expertise which are useful to large-scale organizations: an overall planning strategy which permits innovation and interrelation, an interdisciplinary viewpoint, and techniques for allocating resources. The program discussed represents all phases of medicine, nursing, administration, and social work. The planning committee identifies needed subprograms, designs a communications system, and reviews physical planning proposals. It has prepared a pyramid model to represent potential programs, has developed measures of effectiveness for programs, and has provided a means of coordinating programs to make best use of existing resources and to discover needs for new resources. Some of the techniques discussed in the paper include a computerized representation of the pyramid model for rapid storage and retrieval of information, a cost-benefit method for setting priorities on programs, and a project selection model using multidimensional scaling.

Systems or industrial engineering, as employed in the planning process of the Wisconsin Regional Medical Program (WRMP) discussed in this paper, treats the arrangement of health-care resources for cooperative use and the geographical enhancement of health-care requirements as a complex system that needs to be designed. Systems engineering makes available a number of concepts that are quite useful in such an undertaking: (1) a systems design strategy that focuses on function determination and ideal systems development as a means of achieving innovative designs with minimum data collection, (2) an interdisciplinary framework that brings various professions together in utilizing this strategy and making the needed decisions, and (3) tools and techniques that can be used in optimally allocating resources required by the master plan and its components.

Levels of Planning

Three levels of planning can be identified for large-scale complex systems as shown in Table 1: conceptual, strategic, and operational. In conceptual planning, goals and objectives are developed, and a mechanism is provided to improve them by continuous assessment of the strengths and weaknesses of the plans from other levels and operational systems. In strategic planning, long- and short-term functional components are determined to achieve the objectives established in conceptual planning. In operational planning, the specific systems (projects) are developed to implement the functional components determined at the strategic level. These levels are related in WRMP by a planning staff serving all three levels. Information flow among these levels is continuous; for example, questions about objectives and policies at the operational level are fed back to the conceptual level, and decisions of the conceptual level are fed forward to the other planning levels and operational programs.

Planning is quite critical in any large-scale complex system but especially so in an effort such as embodied in WRMP. The need to foster cooperative arrangements among institutions, agencies, and professions and to involve the entire region requires that many professionals be effectively utilized and that projects optimize potential benefit for the citizens of the region at any point in time. The three levels correspond to different sizes of systems, with conceptual planning for the overall WRMP system, strategic planning for the four systems related to heart, cancer, stroke, and resources, and operational planning for the specific systems within each of the four at the strategic level.

Conceptual Planning

Conceptual planning in WRMP is accomplished through a multidisciplinary planning committee composed of twelve professionals whose common tie is a knowledge and interest in health. The disciplines include medicine, nursing, engineering, law, economics, social work, and hospital administration.

The systems design strategy employed is called the IDEALS concept.[1] The IDEALS concept is a design strategy and organized program applicable to contemplated and present systems, through which are formulated the most effective systems for achieving necessary functions.

This concept embodies three fundamental ideas: (1) a universally applicable definition of a system of any size, that a system is described by seven elements (function, inputs, outputs, sequence, environment, physical catalysts, and human agents) whose precise conditions are specified in four dimensions (physical, rate, control, and state). (2) a ten-step design strategy that starts with function determination and ideal systems development. This causes the design of more innovative systems, the amount of data collection is minimized, future changes are built into the systems design, skilled and professional people are utilized more effectively in the final system, and less time is spent in the system design efforts; and (3) a program to organize and involve professionals and all others in systems design, thereby minimizing the difficulty in implementing proposed systems or programs.

A planning committee developed the goals and objectives of WRMP and expanded them into functional components that could be effectively used by the strategic and operational planning levels. The selected goal was to reduce the incidence, duration, prevalence, and mortality of heart disease, cancer, and stroke, and to improve the quality of the life for sufferers from these three major diseases.

Because the design strategy requires that necessary functions be identified before attempting to design systems, the planning committee developed a pyramid model describing successive levels of functional components as shown in Figure 1. The functional components of health care activities were identified as mental health care, alcoholism health care, heart, stroke, and cancer care, alcoholism, and other diseases. The functional components were identified as prevention, diagnosis, treatment, and posttreatment health care. Successive levels were identified by asking at each level, "What are the functional components of (a component at the previous level)?" An interesting result is that levels 9 through 12 in Figure 1 were common functional components at the end of all the other channels, and that these levels were the resources needed for achieving the results of the whole program.

Table 1
Planning Levels of the Wisconsin Regional Medical Program

Conceptual Planning (Overall System)

Goal Development
Objective Determination
Program Assessment

Strategic Planning (Four Systems: Heart, Stroke, Cancer, Resources)

Project Selection
Time Phasing

Operational Planning (Specific Systems Within Each of the Strategic Systems)

Project Development
Proposal Preparation

1. A summary of this design strategy is given in Gerald Nadler, "Engineering Research and Design in Socioeconomic Systems" later in this volume. See also Nadler, *Work Systems Design: The IDEALS Concept.*

1. Wisconsin Regional Medical Program
health care activities for citizens in region

2. Planning organization of the Wisconsin
Regional Medical Program

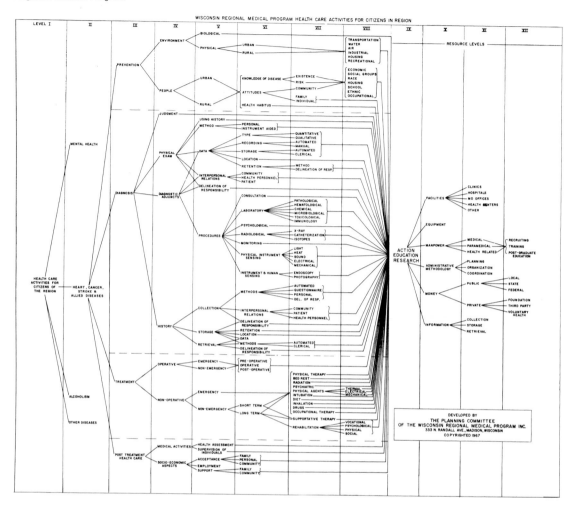

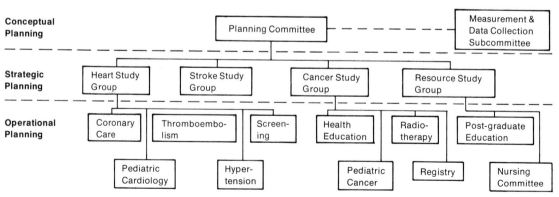

The whole model thus represents an almost exhaustive listing of the functions for which systems need to be designed. For example, starting at levels 10, 11, or 12, it is possible to identify over 15,000 possible systems for all of WRMP. This changes easily to over 60,000 at the strategic planning level where each of the four systems in heart, stroke, cancer, and resources would use the same model. Reading from right to left on the chart, a specific system might be one for *recruiting paramedical manpower* for an *action* program in *automated methods* in *collection* of *histories* in *diagnosis* of *heart diseases* in *health care activities* of citizens of the region. The pyramid model is programmed for computer processing to permit easy checking for other systems (or channels) that might be incorporated in a specific system design proposal. Without such a model, the work of planning would be much more difficult as the number of alternate systems or programs could overwhelm most groups of people.

The planning committee next prepared guideline criteria to be used in the strategic and operational planning of projects. The guidelines emphasize the provision of benefits to the citizens of Wisconsin in the shortest period of time, thus giving higher priority to service or action programs rather than research or educational programs. The development of a specific program or system follows the system design strategy presented earlier, thus a defined need must be identified first (function determination), and then existing potentials to meet that need (ideal systems) are determined before selecting the needs with greatest potential as the basis for systems (project proposals) design.

Strategic Planning

Strategic planning requires in-depth knowledge of specific advances made and individuals engaged in specific aspects of health care. The planning committee delegated this responsibility to four study groups: heart disease, cancer, stroke, and resources. Each study group has the responsibility for the following:
1. Develop comprehensive programs and systems, including a timetable for short-term and long-term projects.
2. Delegate specific programs or systems to an appropriate operational planning group to design the remaining system elements (inputs, outputs, sequence, environment, equipment, and human agents.
3. Review the program once developed to assure adequate medical methodology.
4. Evaluate progress of operational programs.

In all program developments the model is reviewed, with or without computer assistance, to assure comprehensiveness. Proposals, programs, or systems are reviewed to find possible parallels in the model. If a proposal from outside the organization is well developed, the proposer is encouraged to integrate his work within the committee to further expand and strengthen his core concept. When an outside or internal proposal requires specialized knowledge to prepare adequately a regional medical system, the committee appoints an ad hoc subcommittee for this purpose.

Operational Planning

Table 2
System Elements Considered by Committee

1. Function
2. Inputs (patients, medicines, history of patient)
3. Outputs (results of converting inputs to achieve function)
4. Sequence (the order of converting the inputs to outputs)
5. Environment (physical and attitudinal)
6. Facilities and equipment
7. Human agents (people who aid the change from inputs to outputs)

Operational planning is accomplished by an ad hoc subcommittee. Once a specific program or system is selected by a study group, those individuals considered to be potential collaborators and/or experts in the program area develop it for a funding request. These programs, which emanate from an expressed need defined by a study group, frequently take a noncategorical cast. For example, multiphasic screening emanated from the heart study group and health education from the cancer study group. To adequately develop broad programs such as these, the project and/or subcommittee may be transferred to the more general resource group which provides overall guidance.

Figure 2 depicts the present operational planning committees. Two of these, the post graduate education and nursing committees are expected to define programs over an extended period of time in these areas. Table 2 describes

Table 3
Minimum Limitations for Medical Center
System Design

Inputs

1. Human
Educational: All existing programs and level of student numbers maintained as minimum; entering class of 160 medical students.
Patients: State, student health, inpatient, outpatient.

2. Informational
Library, etc

3. Physical
Animal Care, etc.

Outputs

Approval and accreditation bodies.
Specialty boards.
Licensure.

Sequence

Must have interdisciplinary service.
Must have interdisciplinary research.
Must have interdisciplinary education.
Must have affiliated institutions and program services.
Must provide flexibility for education programs (content and required years).

Environment

Opportunities for academic freedom.
Time to pursue academic interests.

Facilities and Equipment

Flexibility in building to permit future programs of reduced or increased education.

4. Partial systems pyramid for executive committee responsibilities

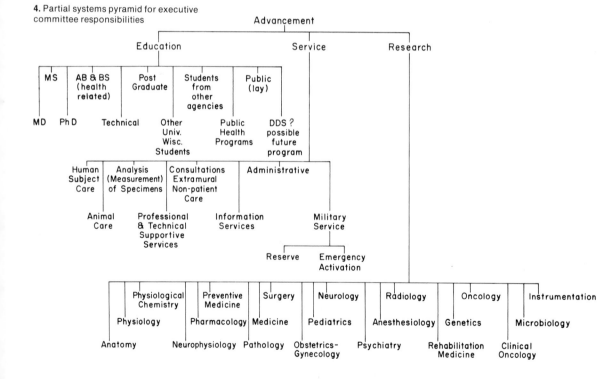

Criteria for Evaluating Proposals

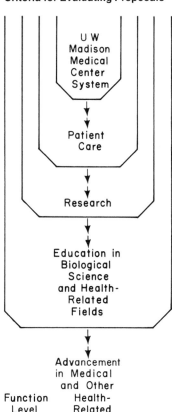

3. Function determination for the medical center system

Data Collection

Early in the development of WRMP the planning committee prepared a list of criteria for evaluating proposals for funding programs or systems. An extensive research project has developed into a model to describe the relative value and minimum acceptable level of a proposal as it relates to WRMP.

The goal of this research project was to develop a reliable and efficient methodology for establishing priorities on proposed and potential research projects. While there has been some previous investigation into this general area of research and development project selection, very little of it has been applicable to the regional medical program. This research hoped to fill the gap between theory and practice by focusing on the question, "Is the allocation of research funds optimal?" or "Where are we obtaining maximum return on the government investment?" A successful solution to this problem will be of tremendous value to all grant-giving agencies in both federal and private organizations.

After the specification of the criteria, measures were developed that would permit quantification of the degree to which projects met each of these criteria. The criteria were weighted in terms of relative importance in project selection. This information is now in the process of being fit into a predictive model of linear form:

$$E = e_0 + e_1 x_1 + e_2 x_2 + \cdots + e_N x_N$$

where each x_i represents the extent to which the ith criterion has been satisfied and each e_i represents the increase in value corresponding to one unit increase in x_i. This model will be used as a tool to give additional information to the decision-makers who must decide whether or not a project will be supported for further development and in the final stages will be supported for funding.

The effectiveness of the methodology will be evaluated by several means: (1) the performance of the methodology will be compared with the decision by the committee members, (2) the recommendations of the model will be compared with the decision of the committee to determine which received a higher percentage of subsequent funding, and (3) the committee's ranking of the proposal will be compared with that developed by the staff, using the methodology to determine if the two approaches are consistent.

Contrary to the way almost all other regional medical programs operate, WRMP data collection is kept to a minimum. The object of the most important data collection project thus far is to develop a means for determining what health data are being collected for the Wisconsin region, the scope of each data collection project, the type of analyses done on the data, and the quality of the data collection process.

The regional medical program did not want to collect large amounts of health data if the data were already being collected by other agencies. However, at this time there is no inventory of health data or information about what health data are currently collected. The study attempted to answer the questions stated in the last paragraph to allow the regional medical program and any other health agencies to assess the advisability of beginning a data collection program in light of the available data and their quality. The methodology employed was to survey a large segment of the institutions that would conceivably be collecting data for Wisconsin. For this purpose a survey instrument was developed which involved personal interviews with representatives from other organizations also collecting this type of data.

The results of this survey included responses to approximately seventy survey questions concerning availability, type, and quality of data collection projects for each organization. A linear model was developed to aggregate the value of the various data, resulting in one number which was an indicator of overall quality. The approach used here was similar to that used for determining the value or the potential benefits of various research proposals as described above. The data collection is completed, and the results are now in the process of being coded on computer cards for immediate retrieval by system users. This information system will permit a representative of any interested organization to determine the availability of health data. The system can respond to the measures of quality mentioned previously. The user then can obtain from the files of the regional medical program a copy of the data collection instrument used by the organizations selected.

This project in its current form is a pilot study to determine two things: (1) Can an inventory of health resource data be effectively and efficiently devised? and (2) Will this inventory of experience provide sufficient usage to warrant continued up-dating and modifications? At this point the answer to the first question appears to be affirmative. The second will be evaluated in the coming year.

Systems Engineering Framework for a $120 Million Medical Center

The Medical Center at the University of Wisconsin campus in Madison is going to be relocated on the western part of the campus with a facility estimated to cost around $120 million. The three basic ideas of the IDEALS Concept (systems definition, design strategy, and involvement of all personnel, including professionals) are guiding the project. The three levels of planning are located in the Medical Center Executive Committee (conceptual), a planning task force (strategic), and twenty-two planning committees (operational).

Following the IDEALS design strategy presented later in this volume, the Executive Committee determined the function of the medical center, shown in Figure 3, and the minimum number of limitations for guiding all remaining systems design, Table 3. Then, because of the very large size of the system, they developed functional components by constructing a system pyramid model, a portion of which is shown in Figure 4. This enabled the individual planning committees to take portions of the pyramid for the system they were to design. For example, one committee was assigned the responsibility of designing the system for achieving the function of "technical education for advancement in medical and other health related fields."

The task force established the committees based on the functional components in the system pyramid. Each committee is proceeding (some with greater urgency or priority than others) to design ideal systems for achieving the necessary functions. Several computer programs are available to handle parts of the specific designs: relationships, location and area configurations, project control, and so forth.

Conclusion

These experiences portray the advantages of using systems engineering in the design and planning of large-scale complex systems. Having everyone use the same definition of a system and the same strategy provides a consistency in approach by all those involved, greatly facilitating communications and assuring a better system solution.

27 Systems Engineering: Definitions, Working Hypotheses, and Examples

Comments on the papers by Stafford, de Neufville, and Hester; Nutt, Gustafson, and Nadler

Daniel Brand

Peat, Marwick, Livingston & Co.
4800 Tower Building
Prudential Center,
Boston, Massachusetts

Daniel Brand is a partner and Director of the Traffic Research Group of Peat, Marwick, Livingston & Co., supervising projects in transportation and land-use planning and transportation technology development. He is a member of several transportation and planning societies and has presented papers in publications and meetings of the Highway Research Board, Operations Research Society of America, and the American Institute of Planners.

Charles Hitch has defined systems analysis as "explicit, quantitative analysis, which is designed to maximize or at least increase the value of the objectives achieved by an organization, minus the values of the resources it uses."[1] Systems engineering is much the same, with perhaps a flavor of familiarity with the data or the mechanisms of the system being engineered. For example, "Systems engineering is a formal awareness of the interactions between the parts of a system."[2] Semantic problems in the definition of these two terms abound. It is probably best not to take the jargon too seriously but to concentrate instead on understanding the essence of the common definition.

Furthermore, defining terms does not always tell how to "do it." A procedure or model must be based on a working hypothesis that something follows from something and results in the desired output. For example, a working hypothesis for forecasting automobile trips in urban areas is that the trips are an economic commodity, the frequency and length of which increase with decreasing cost and decrease with an increase in substitute transportation. With such a hypothesis, a model can easily be developed and the right

1. Charles J. Hitch, "Program Budgeting."
2. Jay W. Forrester, *Industrial Dynamics*, p. 5.

variables inserted to achieve the desired output; namely, automobile trips. Conformity, although not necessarily unanimity, can be obtained on the procedure after the working hypothesis is formulated.

Perhaps we have not specifically realized that one of the problems in systems engineering is that the definitions available or accepted do not lead to working hypotheses. There is great divergence in the way that systems engineering is practiced, as is evidenced by the two preceding papers. Perhaps it is necessary to concentrate on working definitions rather than on proliferation of names.

Avoiding definitional problems for the moment, the one almost classic working hypothesis for systems analysis, at least in the context of the planning applications treated in the present volume, is a four-step procedure:
1. Enumerate objectives for the system.
2. Generate alternative systems.
3. Evaluate alternative systems.
4. Select a final system.

It must almost be taken on faith that this hypothesis produces results. It leads to a procedure that is used with varying degrees of success and is varyingly embellished with terms and definitions. Some embellishments are profound and incisive, others are tedious and insignificant.

The first paper, by Stafford, de Neufville, and Hester, is an example of the former. The paper describes a relatively simple systems analysis used as a classroom problem. The students were asked to address themselves to a "real, unstructured problem," that of expanding the capacity of New York City's primary water distribution system. Unfortunately, the uninitiated might never recognize it as systems analysis, for the paper might well have been written in 1868 before the new "catch" words were invented.

Closer inspection of the paper reveals a clear and powerful example of systems analysis. One might only fault the authors on not describing, at the beginning of the paper, their plan of attack. However, they have a clear and precise model, and it gives good results. Its steps are as follows:
1. Define the existing system, e.g., the primary tunnels and wells.
2. Define the objectives or measures of effectiveness, e.g., pressure at the end of the primary system.
3. Relate a measure of effectiveness to the technology of the system, e.g., head losses, pipe sizes, smoothness.
4. Generate alternative improvements, e.g., the six primary distribution network proposals.
5. Evaluate alternatives, e.g., evaluation of the cost/effectiveness of each alternative to satisfy the given water demands.
6. Select the final system, e.g., the four-step recommended program.

The alternatives generated in the first paper were technological in nature; that is, only hardware variables were changed. In the evaluation of alternatives the assumption was made that the demand for the commodity being delivered (water) did not vary with its cost. This is certainly not an objectionable assumption for this classroom analysis. In New York City the demand for water is relatively inelastic over the ranges of cost which (we assume) the consumer would perceive under any of the proposed alternatives. However, the ease of the analysis, using this assumption, contrasts with the difficulties encountered in evaluating other types of urban public works programs, for example, transportation and housing, for which the provision of alternative facilities changes the demand (in the broadest sense) for these facilities. In evaluating transportation alternatives it is relatively simple to calculate the capacity of the facilities or the speed losses at increasing levels of flow (analogous to head losses). The uncertainty and difficulty are in predicting the changing demand (including link flows, activity distributions, and the entire set of social and economic consequences). The authors avoided this difficult part of evaluation by the example they chose.

Where the first paper did not define its approach in advance, the second paper, by Nutt, Gustafson, and Nadler, is guilty of defining too many terms at the outset and not making a plausible case for their significance to the analysis at hand. Three levels of planning are defined in the paper: conceptual (goals, development, and program evaluation), strategic (project selection and scheduling), and operational (project development). This is not an uncommon model. The paper goes on to define how the model is applied in the context of many institutions and individuals getting together and planning a large medical center.

The method which the authors employ to get people to work together on multidisciplinary planning committees is the IDEALS concept. Unfortunately, the description of this concept includes several apparently arbitrary definitions of systems, design strategies, and programs. From these systems, strategies, and programs are said to come: "design of more innovative systems, the amount of data collection is minimized, future changes are built into the systems design, skilled and professional people are utilized more effectively in the final system, and less time is spent in the systems design . . . minimizing the difficulty in implementing proposed systems or programs."

One wishes the paper had concentrated on explaining how this was accomplished.

One has to assume that each field of application develops its own planning process and that it would not be fun if we were not allowed to be creative, even if our creativity is sometimes muddled. The field of systems engineering is presently muddling in at least two cases dealing with "common" information totals, such as social and economic criteria. The first case is the prediction of consequences of alternative programs (e.g., health care, transportation, education) in terms of common social and economic variables. In this case users of program budgeting for large organizations are attempting to develop a framework for the problem. The second case is the conversion of program elements to specific physical elements such as facilities and equipment. Hitch describes how, in the Department of Defense, "we developed a 'torque converter' for translating the five-year program into the budget format, and vice versa."[3] We have another "torque converter" presented in the paper by Nutt, Gustafson, and Nadler, who state that in the system pyramid model "An interesting result is that levels 9 through 12 of Figure 1 were common functional components at the end of all the other channels, and that these levels were the resources needed for achieving the results of the whole program." If it were only made clear *how* all the complicated programmatic strands were brought together, twisted, and brought out again in line item form, we would have been able to learn much.

A final item of interest in the second paper is the proposed project selection procedure. This procedure is not new, but, as the authors say, it may be new to regional medical programs.[4] The procedure takes the form of a linear model:

$$E = e_0 + e_1 x_1 + e_2 x_2 + \cdots + e_N x_N,$$

where

x_i = the extent to which the ith criterion has been satisfied by the alternative program, and

e_i = increase in value corresponding to a unit increase in x_i.

---

3. Hitch, "Program Budgeting."
4. In transportation the method has been proposed and applied in William Jessiman, Daniel Brand, Alfred Tumminia, and C. Roger Brussee, "A Rational Decision-Making Technique for Transportation Planning."

Unfortunately, the authors call the model "predictive." While it is a model, it should not be used for prediction. The problem should be restricted to forecasting x_i, namely, the consequences of the alternative programs in terms of the common social and economic criteria set out in advance to assess the different programs. In addition, there are serious problems in estimating parameters for such a model as well as problems in the structure of the model. Since the values of the e_i are the weights or relative importance of criteria in project selection, they should be subjectively set by the decision-maker rather than estimated by some least squares method. A weight e_0 on no criterion at all is hardly logical. Also, in any real application, x_i has to be measured against a nonlinear utility scale in order that e_i may be a constant term.

To use the model, which some have called a weighted sum technique, to improve our understanding of decisions would be better than to apply it in a mechanical way. For example, systems engineers can see how decisions change (how utility totals differ), with different e_i's representing the value judgments of different interest groups and actors in the community. Experiments of this sort lead to determining how the interests of the community may best be served. It is such thoughtful understanding of the mechanisms and interactions of our systems, using such models, that characterizes systems engineering at its best.

8 Approaches to the Form/Behavior Relationship

The following papers address themselves to designing and planning for individual differences and values and propose approaches suited to form and behavior considerations. In comparison to many of the earlier papers whose theoretical foundations were in various fields of applied science and mathematics, the contributors to this section derive their approaches and insights primarily from the behavioral sciences. For example, Brolin and Zeisel attribute their viewpoint to the structural-functionalist school in anthropology and sociology, and Ward gains many of his insights from the psychological and psychiatric literature.

Rather than imposing values and needs on users, Brent Brolin and John Zeisel argue that we must identify the social patterns of the group and design to allow those patterns to exist and grow. The major part of their paper is devoted to describing a research framework for collecting and interpreting behavioral information, especially information about living patterns and values of people who are in different cultures and subcultures from the designer's own. Their distinction between "physical slum" and "social slum" is an important distinction for urban designers and planners to keep in mind.

It is perhaps instructive in this regard to compare Silver's paper in Part 6 of this volume with Brolin and Zeisel's. Both methods are aimed at urban low-cost housing, but Silver's is an economics-based analysis. Convergence between these two extremes has been suggested. Both methods are necessary. One without the other could lead to technically adequate and economically optimal but socially disastrous mass housing, or conversely, socially adequate housing that is economically and politically infeasible. A quantitative approach which has been suggested for uncovering and insuring the continuation of latent community structure is Ellis's measure of "residential linkage" applied to the location of transportation routes, but the same approach could be used for renewal, housing, and other applications.

The next two papers by Anthony Ward and by Francis Duffy and John Torrey have their foundations in theories advanced in conjunction with Alexander and Poyner. Alexander's doctoral dissertation, published in 1964, had a profound impact on design methodology, especially in architecture. A series of papers and reports by Alexander and various colleagues and by other researchers, such as Koenig et al., appeared between 1964 and 1967 and hinted at new thinking, but no major theoretical statement appeared. Then in 1967 Alexander and Poyner de-veloped a new theory which is published in Part 9 of this volume. Ward's and Duffy and Torrey's papers are built on these foundations. The reader may wish to read Alexander and Poyner's paper in conjunction with the papers in this section.

Ward challenges the assumptions and viewpoint both of systems analysis and of the relational theory of Alexander and Poyner and argues for a more in-depth encounter between designer and user. Working from recent findings in conflict and frustration theory, he proposes that environments be planned to remove sources of frustration and conflict between form and behavior. His argument is illustrated with examples from the design of workshops for prisoners and for the blind.

Ward identifies what he considers a critical dilemma in design and planning methods: If humans are objectified into user populations, solutions are built whereby individual differences, and perhaps values, are lost. Alternatively, if populations are not objectified, it is difficult to achieve cumulative improvement in the environment. One may notice the same argument in several behavioral science fields today, between those who rely on large samples and statistical analysis and those who rely on the one-to-one "clinical" situation. Each is wary of the other's methods. But Charles Rusch suggests in his commentary in this section that this dilemma is perhaps being resolved in anthropology and sociology and, we might add, in psychology in the intensive work of Piaget, Werner, and their students. Much can be gained from experiences in these fields.

In the third paper, Duffy and Torrey present a progress report and evaluation of the pattern theory developed by Alexander and his colleagues. They define and describe patterns, develop the structure of a language of patterns, and show how it applies to the building-design situation. One part of their paper is devoted to a discussion of the pattern theory in relation to other major theories of design and planning methods, several of which are represented by papers in this volume. Problems and some potentials of the pattern theory are illustrated by two examples.

In conclusion, Rusch discusses some of the basic tenets of form/behavior approaches with regard to influences on human behavior brought about by planned changes in the environment.

28 Social Research and Design:
Applications to Mass Housing

Brent C. Brolin and John Zeisel

Brolin Zeisel
Urban Research and Design
New York, New York

Brent C. Brolin is a partner, with John Zeisel, in the New York firm of Brolin Zeisel Urban Research and Design and is a Visiting Critic in the Department of City Planning at Yale University. He received a B.A. in art history and an M.Arch. from Yale in 1962 and 1968. He has worked as a planner and architect in New York and Jamaica and as a research consultant for rehabilitation in Harlem. John Zeisel, a Visiting Critic in the School of Architecture at Columbia, received a B.A. in Oriental studies from Columbia in 1965 and is now completing his Ph. D. dissertation in sociology. He has been a data analyst and Assistant Project Director in the Bureau of Applied Social Research at Columbia and is now Research Editor for *Design and Environment.* This paper appeared after the Conference in *Architectural Forum,* and is adapted here with permission. Copyright 1968 by Urban America, Inc.

Technically adequate mass housing is often socially inadequate. An important reason for many failures in large-scale urban design and planning is that the product does not fit the way people live. The designer or planner, unable to intuit the needs of a group with which he is unfamiliar, often imposes his own values and needs on those for whom he builds. To prevent this, he must be able to identify social patterns necessary to the group and incorporate them into the design process.

This paper demonstrates one method for doing research on the social patterns of a group so that the information can be applied in designing a physical environment to fit the needs of that group. A research framework was developed to collect design-related sociological information. The framework, based on the structural-functionalist approach to sociology, describes significant social relationships which the designer has often disrupted by erecting or leaving out physical barriers. The starting point was a study by Herbert Gans of the inhabitants of one area. The specific information applicable to mass housing design was translated into physical-form requirements for the designer to meet. As an example of the process, one environment was designed which met these requirements.

Since the beginning of the Industrial Revolution, mass housing has been designed for the worker, not by the worker, and has had a dehumanizing and degrading effect in imposing new ways of life on its tenants.[1] This is in sharp contrast to unplanned housing built by the inhabitants themselves, changing over a long period of time, and serving social functions not apparent to architects who are not of that culture. Urban redevelopment and new town programs are often based on what the designer considers adequate for himself. Often when he consciously tries to build for those different from himself, he unconsciously imposes his own values.

Modern architecture asserted the principle of functional design, but the architect's concept of function has usually been limited to manifest functions: kitchens for cooking, stores for buying, streets for driving. He does not usually take into account the latent functions: for example, driving a car as a means of demonstrating a certain status as well as a means of transportation.[2]

1. See Karl Polanyi, *The Great Transformation.*
2. For a more complete discussion of manifest and latent social functions, see Robert K. Merton, *Social Theory and Social Structure,* especially pp. 51 and 63.

In building for cultures other than their own, architects have introduced, along with modern sanitary standards, Western middle-class assumptions of privacy, comfort, forms of sociability, and community living. Yet middle-class norms have often proved inappropriate. Here are three examples: The Brazilian government built apartment buildings in Pedregulhos for the inhabitants of the shantytown around Rio de Janeiro and then destroyed their primitive shacks. Several months later the tenants of the project rebuilt their shacks and moved back. Second, a modern low-income community was built by the Hungarian government in Budapest for families from a physically deteriorated district in the city. Many of these people sold their new apartments to middle-class families from the old district and, exchanging apartments, moved back to their old but familiar physical slum. The third example is that of Kingston, Jamaica, where in the summer of 1966 riots reportedly "were partly prompted by resistance to public housing proposed to replace familiar 'slums.'"[3]

Although the cause of these violent reactions is complex and demands investigation, the situation is partly encouraged by mass housing that is socially inadequate, though technically adequate.

Unfamiliar Cultures

When a person moves from the country or from a small urban neighborhood into urban mass housing, one way of life is cut off for him and another begins. His new environment is often incompatible or hostile to his regular way of life. When traditional living patterns are denied him, it is always with the implication that they are wrong or inappropriate and that he must now imitate the new way of life around him. But if left to his own choice, the urban migrant often seeks to retain his cultural identity.

It is easy to document the many socially exclusive towns which grew up across the country in the nineteenth century; it is more difficult to find examples of the successful integration of different cultures within a single city. The assimilation of ethnic groups was a challenge that the American city met with neither grace nor efficiency.[4] In addition, cultural integration may not be felt possible, or desirable, by all minority groups. Instead of asking if America has lost its power of integration, we should ask whether America ever had that power.

For moral as well as for practical reasons it is vitally important to respect the different customs of groups within our own society, and within urbanizing societies throughout the world. The social parameters of housing are as important as the legal, economic, and physical parameters. The architect and planner need detailed information about the living patterns of people of different cultures or of rural cultures in transition to urban life. This information can be provided by analyzing the latent social structure and living patterns as they relate to the architectural environment. The architect must then be able to translate this information into a form useful in three-dimensional design and planning.

Observations of Latent Social Structure

For the study which is the subject of this paper, we have drawn freely from Herbert Gans's *The Urban Villagers*, an insightful description of working-class Italian life in the old West End of Boston, now torn down by urban renewal. This group was chosen because of the availability of substantial information, but our method could be applied to any ethnic group, or to groups homogeneous by class or age.

Since the old West End has been torn down, we had little knowledge of the people's surroundings, though considerable of their behavior. To demonstrate the method of using specific research for design and to place our study in a relevant physical context, we chose an existing site in the North End of Boston. This area is physically, ethnically, and demographically similar to the old West End.

3. The *New York Times*, Sept. 11, 1966, p. 39.
4. Irving Kristol, "The Negro Today is like the Immigrant Yesterday."

Gans lived in the West End and studied it over a period of months. Since his observations were not intended for architects, we translated them into specific guidelines. From these guidelines we designed housing which might have replaced the physically substandard housing in the neighborhood Gans studied without destroying the healthy, low-income community.

Some samples of Gans's original observations and our architectural requirements that arose from them follow:
Observation: "Food preparation serves as an example of the woman's skill as a housewife and mother. When company is present, it enables her to display her skills to relatives and peers."
Requirement: Area for cooking visible from the place where women visitors gather.
Observation: ". . . the normal tendency is for men and women to split up, the men in one room and the women in another."
Requirement: Privacy between men's and women's social gathering areas.
Observation: While the teen-age groups were sexually segregated, girls' groups in the West End met near the corners where the boys hung out."
Requirement: Adolescent girls' areas visible from boys' areas.

We then grouped together the requirements that referred to activities taking place in the same physical area: apartments, groups of apartments, areas of informal social activity, and commercial areas. The architectural designs followed from this grouping are illustrated in Figures 1–3. On each of the drawings there is a set of observations as well as the requirements met by the drawing.

Relevance of Observations

At first we picked those of Gans's comments we felt could help the architect meet the social needs of that community. We began with over 200 observations of behavior, most of which described an activity taking place in a physical setting. But many of these, although telling us how the West Enders behaved, were not necessarily helpful to the architect. For example, "Girls from about age ten are expected to help with the household tasks . . . Adolescents and young adults are frequent moviegoers." Whether young girls help around the house does not tell us about the preferred apartment layout or the size of rooms. Nor does the second observation, as it stands, guide the architect's work; he knows no better than he did before whether the movie theater should be in the center of the area or in its outskirts, or whether the movies downtown are just as good. He must know who else is involved in moviegoing. If he knew, for instance, that when going to the movies, teenagers were seen and wanted to be seen by other young people from the neighborhood—but avoided adults—he would know that the social significance of this activity is related to its physical location in the area. The theater should be visible to teen-agers doing other things, and it should not be easily visible from areas of adult activity.

Another type of observation tells us more about physical location: "The peer group meets regularly in the kitchens and living rooms of innumerable West End apartments." But here, too, we do not know what factors, physical or otherwise, make these rooms more desirable than others. Further, we do not know which peer groups meet regularly in the kitchens and living rooms.

In sum, the observations we found to be useful to the architect possessed the following attributes:
1. A primary actor and his activity.
2. The significant others in the situation.
3. The relationship between the primary actor and the significant others.

In the example of moviegoing, the teen-agers who go are the prime actors, the significant others are nonmoviegoing teen-agers and adults. The relationship in the teen-agers' case calls for visual and auditory connection, and in the adults' case for visual and auditory separation. The field observer, by

1. Mass Housing: Schematic Layout of Building Unit

OBSERVATIONS AND REQUIREMENTS

1 OBS: Cooking is a way for a woman to demonstrate her skill as a mother and housewife, especially to relatives and other women who visit.
REQ: Area for cooking visible to where women gather.

2 OBS: Owning many modern kitchen appliances is important for the standing of the family.
REQ: Area for using kitchen appliances visible from where women gather socially.

3 OBS: The adolescent is away from home a lot. When he is home, he often fights with his parents.
REQ: (A) Separation of adolescents' area from adult area.
(B) Direct access to exit from adolescent area.

4 OBS: When there are guests, the men separate from the women by going into the living room. Men and women often stay apart the entire evening. Even at the kitchen table, men will stay at one end and women at the other.
REQ: Privacy between men's and women's social gathering areas.

5 OBS: West End working-class men expect to have little to do with child-rearing.
REQ: Children's areas separate from men's gathering areas.

6 OBS: West Enders have a different sense of privacy than middle-class families. They do not mind the crowded tenements if they do not have to climb many stairs.
REQ: Maximum connection between apartments.

7 OBS: West Enders enjoy staying up late and socializing loudly.
REQ: Connection between apartments.

8 OBS: Visual contact between apartments is often the basis for "neighboring."
REQ: Visual contact between apartments.

9 OBS: Neighbors help each other in emergencies.
REQ: Ready access from apartment to apartment.

10 OBS: Unmarried men make frequent visits to relatives' apartments. These visits allow them the small amount of contact with children that is required of them.
REQ: Apartments for single people not isolated from other apartments.

11 OBS: Friendships between different peer-groups are often based on living together and sharing facilities.
REQ: Common facilities for groups of apartments.

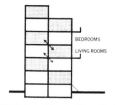

BEDROOMS

LIVING ROOMS

NOTE: Typical floor is either all bedrooms or all living-kitchen areas. Any bedroom area is thus either above or below another apartment's living-kitchen area.

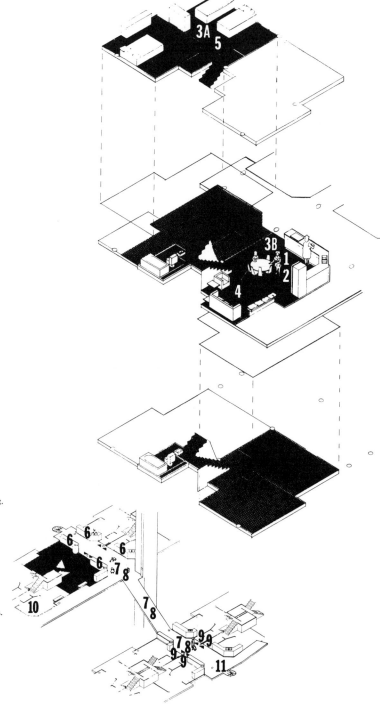

2. Perspective through Interior Street

OBSERVATIONS AND REQUIREMENTS

12 OBS: After they are ten years old, boys
are generally unsupervised while
outside, and enjoy the freedom to roam
the neighborhood.
REQ: Many places for pedestrian movement.

13 OBS: Groups of teen-agers of different
sexes spend a lot of time "hanging
around" or looking for something to
do. Often they do this with adults
or teen-agers of the opposite sex.
REQ: (A) Connection between boys' group
and peer groups of other statuses.
(B) Connection between boys' and
girls' outside areas and apartments.

14 OBS: Teen-agers gather on corners near
small stores.
REQ: Areas for informal congregating
outside and around commercial areas.

15 OBS: Although boys meet with boys, and
girls with girls, the girls meet near the
corners where the boys hang out.
REQ: Adolescent girls' areas visible to
boys' areas.

16 OBS: Young teen-age girls take care of
younger children on the streets.
REQ: Adolescent girls' areas near
children's play areas.

17 OBS: Both men and women use dress as a
means of self-expression, spending
much money on clothes.
REQ: General visibility among pedestrian,
apartment, commercial, and
recreational areas.

18 OBS: Men wash their cars on the streets
as often as once a week. For men, the
car is important as a means of
expressing their identity.
REQ: Visibility for areas related to
automobiles.

19 OBS: Bars and luncheonettes are places to
exchange news and gossip, as well as
message centers for regular customers.
REQ: (A) Commercial area connected to
living areas.
(B) Commercial area visible from
street and other commercial areas.

20 OBS: Women socialize while shopping.
REQ: Commercial areas visible to and
from streets.

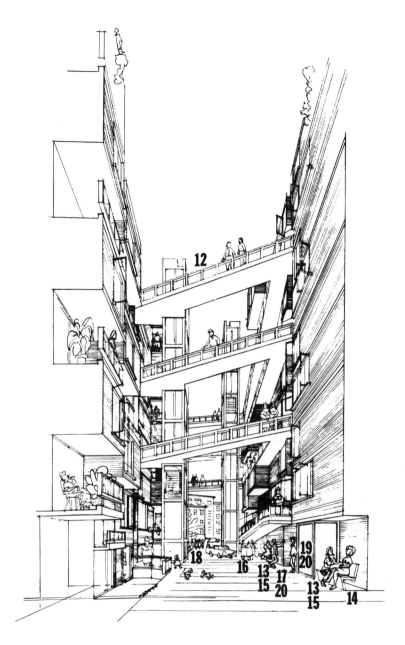

3. Site Plan

OBSERVATIONS AND REQUIREMENTS

12 OBS: After they are ten years old, boys are generally unsupervised while outside, and enjoy the freedom to roam the neighborhood.

    REQ: Many places for pedestrian movement.

13 OBS: Groups of teen-agers of different sexes spend a lot of time "hanging around" or looking for something to do. Often they do this with adults or teen-agers of the opposite sex.

    REQ: (A) Connection between boys' group and peer groups of other statuses. (B) Connection between boys' and girls' outside areas and apartments.

14 OBS: Teen-agers gather on corners near small stores.

    REQ: Areas for informal congregating outside and around commercial areas.

15 OBS: Although boys meet with boys, and girls with girls, the girls meet near the corners where the boys hang out.

    REQ: Adolescent girls' areas visible to boys' areas.

16 OBS: Young teen-age girls take care of younger children on the streets.

    REQ: Adolescent girls' areas near children's play areas.

17 OBS: Both men and women use dress as a means of self-expression, spending much money on clothes.

    REQ: General visibility among pedestrian, apartment, commercial, and recreational areas.

18 OBS: Men wash their cars on the streets as often as once a week. For men, the car is important as a means of expressing their identity.

    REQ: Visibility for areas related to automobiles.

19 OBS: Bars and luncheonettes are places to exchange news and gossip, as well as message centers for regular customers.

    REQ: (A) Commercial area connected to living areas. (B) Commercial area visible from street and other commercial areas.

20 OBS: Women socialize while shopping.

    REQ: Commercial areas visible to and from streets.

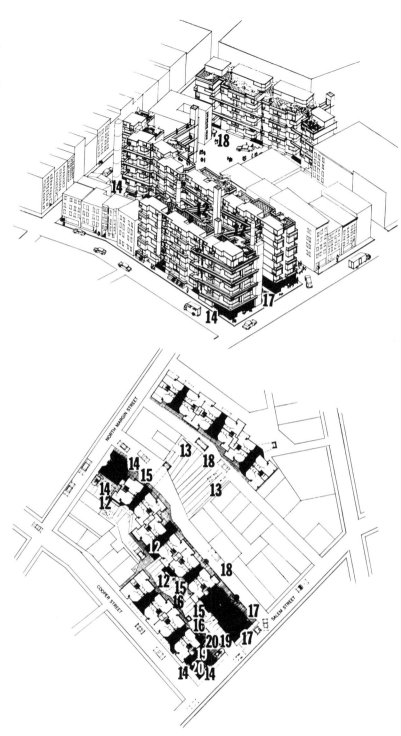

asking: "Who is doing what, including or excluding whom?" will most likely encompass all the necessary sociological components in his observations.

Furthermore, in spelling out the means of inclusion or exclusion we get the requirement to be fulfilled by the new physical form. This is the link between social behavior and physical form by which we can specify how an area in which a given activity takes place should be connected to or separated from another area. From the three examples already given the following inclusion or exclusion relationships emerge:
1. The area for cooking must include women visitors.
2. The men's and women's social gathering areas must exclude those of the other sex.
3. The adolescent girls' areas must include (visually) the boys' areas.

If we see the design process in large part as putting up or leaving out different kinds of environmental barriers, we can help the designer meet the people's needs by defining where these barriers are socially desirable and where they would be socially harmful.

The Existing Environment

The design requirements we have discussed are implied by patterns of social behavior. We must also see the social implications of the existing physical environment that is to be replaced. Although a simple description is necessary of apartment layouts, relationship among spaces, size of rooms, where the stores are, where the playground is and so on, this is not sufficient. Two things must be established: (1) Is the existing physical form compatible with the prevalent social patterns? and (2) What social patterns does the physical form make difficult or easy?

Some indicators of incompatibility between the existing physical form and social needs are: windows painted black, doors nailed shut, ramps built over stairs. Playgrounds, balconies, and park benches may be totally unused, and other facilities may be falsely used: children playing in the street instead of a nearby park, dinner cooked on the fire escape, the car parked in the living room. If these changes in form or use have not been made, and if there have been little destruction, much use, relatively low turnover, and conscious efforts to beautify, one can assume that the environment is physically compatible to the social needs.

Avoiding Mistakes

To find out what behavioral patterns the physical form allows, we translate an observation of the existing physical environment into the requirement it seems to fulfill. If that aspect is compatible, the requirement is one to be fulfilled by new designs, while the requirements reflected in incompatible form are clearly to be avoided. By taking into account both the social implications of the environment and the indicators of conflict, we can avoid present mistakes.

The field observer could apply the method we have described in the following ways:

1. Looking at behavior. The observer sees that boys play ball in the street. Looking for the significant others in the situation, he finds that girls of the same age often sit around watching the boys, while adults stop to look and comment. The primary actors, the boys, are related visually to two groups of significant others, the girls and the adults. This observation is translated into the requirement: boys' play areas should be visibly connected to where the girls "hang out" and to where adults are. If other observations indicate a similar requirement, the designer might build a playground near the shopping area or subway station, as well as near the stoops where young girls get together.

2. Looking at the environment. A playground with basketball courts is far from both the busy life of the street and from the door stoops and shops where the teen-age girls congregate. By asking, "Who can play in the play-

ground?'' we translate this simple observation into a social pattern: boys, mostly teen-agers, can play basketball there. While other boys, both younger and older, may be included, both adults and girls of the same age are excluded. Since this playground is rarely used by anyone, it is evident that we should avoid the separation of the boys' play area from that of the girls and from "where the (adult) action is." Thus this approach, too, leads to the requirement: The boys' play area should be visibly connected to these other places. Of course, this observation alone would not be enough to make final judgment. By repeated observations, informal interviewing, and counting how often people do certain activities, we can validate findings.

Appropriateness of the Method

Although it should be augmented with survey techniques, this observational method is very different. Most people will answer questions about a proposed plan in terms of what they have experienced or what they want. When the respondent is a potential buyer in a housing market, it is important to know his preferences. But this often has little to do with the latent behavior that is integral to the social stability of a group. We therefore distinguish his conscious wants from unconscious needs.

This approach is appropriate for both new and redeveloped urban areas. It may be applied to people already living in cities and to rural in-migrants. Its value in the latter case should be clear. When people move from the country to the city or from primitive to more modern housing, their patterns of living undergo strain. Taking these patterns into account when planning new housing will not limit behavior, but by accommodating familiar life styles and providing alternatives will make the transition easier for them.

In urban redevelopment it has been argued that when the architect tries to reinforce the social structure, he reinforces the pathology of the slum. The distinction between a physical and social slum must be clarified. A physical slum refers to an area with a large percentage of substandard housing. A social slum, on the other hand, might be characterized by a loosely connected social structure, anomic inhabitants, and a social pathology reflected in crime, suicide, drug addiction, and other deviant behavior. Often these two go together, but often they do not. City planners, as they did in the West End, often tear down a physical slum and at the same time tear apart a healthy climate in which social pathologies are relatively low and people take an active part and interest in the community. Applying the approach of this paper may not enable the architect to revive this healthy social atmosphere, but it may help him avoid contributing to its decline.

We must be aware that living patterns will stay the same or change regardless of the physical environment. If the designer tries to limit behavior when change is imminent or to force change when the inhabitants neither want it nor are ready for it, he can cause potentially harmful conflict. This conflict can have several consequences: the physical environment may be altered, misused, or not used at all, and the people may suffer social and psychological stress. To stop this we would have the designer understand the social behavior of those who are to live in his buildings and try to avoid putting up barriers to their way of life. True, the living patterns of those for whom we design will eventually change, but even so, many existing social patterns will remain. If the Italian community of Gans's research becomes more middle-class it will still retain many of its present social customs. In any case, to design now in a way that we know will not fit existing life styles is to make the hypothetical misfit of the future a reality of the present.

Anthony Ward

School of Architecture
Portsmouth College of Technology
Portsmouth, England

Anthony Ward is currently Assistant Professor of Architecture at the University
of California, Berkeley. At the time this
paper was written, he was a Research
Fellow in Design Methods at the Portsmouth College of Technology. He was
born in England, graduated from the
Birmingham School of Architecture in
1965, worked in private practice, and then
joined the Ministry of Public Buildings
and Works. He has directed research on
prisons, workshops for the blind, mental
hospitals, and old people's communities.
In 1967 he organized the Portsmouth
Symposium on Design Methods in Architecture and has edited its proceedings,
Design Methods in Architecture.

The present state of design methods particularly in Great Britain is discussed in
terms of the normal sequence of analysis,
synthesis, and evaluation. This sequence
is compared to the evolutionary scheme
used by Alexander, Poyner, and others in
which the prime aim is a "natural selection" of forms and which consists of
evaluation first and then analysis and
synthesis. The emphasis is on the initial
evaluation of misfits and conflicts in the
present environment. How the designer's
model of the environment influences the
form and appropriateness of his solutions
is discussed. Next, a model of behavior
to be used in the stage of initial evaluation is presented. This model is comprised
of approach-avoidance conflict situations
and field theory analysis patterns incorporating dyadic relationship theories.
Two recent case studies are presented.
Originally based on the evolutionary
relational theory of Alexander and Poyner,
they were of such an order as to drastically
alter the theoretical presuppositions of
their work. The model previously described is equated with learning theory.
The case studies involve research and
design of a workshop for the blind and a
prison workshop, neither of which was to
act therapeutically. They indicate how the
physical environment can function as an
antilearning system leading to regression
and atrophy for the human organism.
Additional hypotheses about environmental contingencies are discussed.

During the last two years, I have been engaged in the study of two design
problems which have led me to believe that in trying to create a better environment we are actually making the one we have much worse. Design
method, with its frequently accepted analysis, synthesis, and evaluation
cycle is only one aspect of a much broader movement toward a system of
evolutionary design. This movement lays a great emphasis upon a scientific-
objective approach to design, which it is hoped will lead to cumulative improvements and a healthy environment.

In this paper I will try to show that the terms "objective" and "improvement"
are mutually exclusive. The kinds of "rightness" and "wrongness" with
which I will be concerned are not those which Alexander calls "fit" and
"misfit" between design variables, but are to do with basic ethical or value
issues.[1]

**Evolutionary Design, Systems
Analysis, and Values**

Unfortunately, design method techniques, culled from operations research
and systems analysis, do not make value judgments for us. The role of value
judgments in design methods has become obscured by the numerous tech-

1. Christopher Alexander, *Notes on the Synthesis of Form*.

1. A model of diadic interpersonal relationships

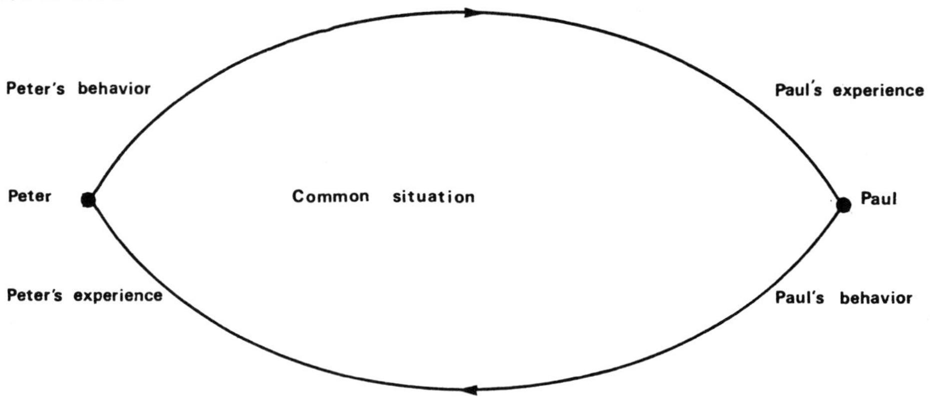

Peter's behavior

Paul's experience

Peter

Common situation

Paul

Peter's experience

Paul's behavior

niques and mechanisms which architects and planners have accepted. The classic design method cycle of analysis, synthesis, and then evaluation, which seems to include all other subdivisions that various designers attribute to their activities, is permeated implicitly with value judgment. Sometimes the sequence changes, sometimes the stages merge into each other, and sometimes complex combinations are used. One such variation places its emphasis upon the "natural selection" or evolution of design forms from an analysis and evaluation of existing situations.

In the evolutionary approach to design, best represented by Alexander and Poyner, formal qualities in existing situations are evaluated and abstracted, and used as the basic geometry of new solutions.[2] The choice of qualities for abstraction is determined by observing the behavior of people in existing situations, abstracting the physical qualities, and using the abstractions to produce new solutions to new problems. This approach differs from current practice in that it attempts to be scientifically objective. The evolutionists maintain that there are ways of objectively evaluating what already exists and that any value judgments can be safely relegated to the synthesis stage in the design process. But this is a tautology. These values are applied at the very beginning of the process, and the subjective choice of evaluative criteria implicitly predetermines the formal context of the solution. Any "objective" analysis is built upon a framework of criteria or standards against which designed changes can be measured, and these criteria are often derived from social and cultural pressures and traditions. The choice of an "objective" method, with all its chosen criteria and standards of evaluation, is itself based upon personal value constructs (as evidenced by the fact that it was a choice), so that a person will often choose mechanisms that seem appropriate to his view of the world.

There is ample evidence for instance, that when objective analysis techniques are applied to the human condition, they create difficulties. This is not to say that they are not relevant to certain aspects of the design problem, but those aspects do not include the analysis of human needs or tendencies.

The question facing the designer is thus very simple: What kind of attitude do we want people to have toward their existence? The answer is not so simple. Whereas the concept of social ethics is firmly entrenched in current social sciences, there are often instances where the "social good" directly opposes the values of the individual.

Suppose, for instance, that we are designing an environment for someone who is insane. How do we know if he is truly mad? How do we know what madness is? Even accepting the social science definition of madness as "deviation in behavior from a group norm,"[3] who is to say that the "group," i.e., society, is not mad too? As Laing has pointed out, this problem is beginning to trouble an increasing number of psychiatrists.[4] He quotes the example of an actual patient who thought he was Napoleon, when, in a lie-detector test, he said he was not Napoleon, the machine registered a lie. Laing's solution to the problem is one which involves the process of insanity. He describes madness as the "degree of conjunction or disjunction between two persons, where one is sane by common consent." His main work has been with schizophrenics, and he has found some kinds of schizophrenia which seem to evolve from personal relationships. His studies have led him to produce a model of dyadic relationships, shown in Figure 1, which seems to describe the dynamics at work in the schizophrenic situation.

In a common situation between two people, Peter and Paul, each behaves toward the other on the basis of his experience of the other, which is in turn a function of the other's behavior toward him. But each person must, in perceiving the other's behavior, interpret it, and this is done on the basis of

2. See Christopher Alexander and Barry Poyner, "The Atoms of Environmental Structure," in this volume, Part 9.
3. Leslie T. Wilkins, *Social Deviance.*
4. See Ronald D. Laing, *The Politics of Experience,* and *The Divided Self.*

experience. An act which Peter construes as harsh may seem gentle to Paul. But each can only perceive himself through the behavior of the other which in turn is based upon a perception of himself through the other's interpretation of his behavior and so on. When we objectify another, that is, when we treat him as an object in a class *A* of objects which will behave consistently, we implicitly objectify ourselves as objects in a class of non-*A* objects. We thus behave consistently and so lead the other to reaffirm our self-classification. A spiral is established which can be overcome only through a deep and personal discourse in which each is prepared to render himself vulnerable to the other. The designer who designs for a mass client has no such opportunity for discourse. His objective classification sticks. *His users become objects in solution.* The objectification of people in Figure 2 speaks for itself and is concomitant with the classification systems currently used in much of design analysis.

Take for instance, the application of systems analysis to a design problem. A system can be anything the designer wishes it to be. It can be the pedestrian flow at a traffic junction, the movement of people in congested entrances, the organization of a group of elevators, or the flow of trains in a railway system. Often these variables are expressed as density of traffic flow or of population and are graphically expressed by varying thicknesses of line on a diagram, which become road widths in the final solution. Systems analysis separates out these supposedly independent components and attempts to define them by changing the input variables, as shown in Figure 3. What goes on within the system can be gauged by varying the input and observing the change in output.

For example, a problem of traffic congestion would be approached by changing the density of flow and observing the resultant changes in the form of the flow. From this an abstract model can be developed which generalizes this relationship and which can be applied to the design of new traffic flow situations. Even in more complicated examples, where the output of one system becomes the input to another system, the fundamental linear quality of the organization is not even remotely comparable to the dynamics of human experience. No number of iterations can ever overcome this basic structural limitation. We are left with no concept of meaning about the traffic situation for the people involved, unless we begin to interject our own experience, which is contrary to the objective-scientific approach espoused by systems analysts and the evolutionary theorists.

In addition, it is characteristic of all inputs to a system that they must be uniform and stable. They must be consistent. If they are not inherently so, they must be made consistent by the application of statistics and other generalizing techniques. In a design this is done with physiological behavioral data. For instance, the ranges of human dimensions used in the design of chairs is averaged and established as a uniform whole by the application of standard deviation and other statistical techniques. As shown in Figure 4, any midgets or giants are automatically excluded from the analysis to facilitate the design data manipulation.

Although this is an obvious example of which most tall or tiny people will have had direct experience, its fundamental philosophy is one that is applied at all levels of designing. Consider the locational design of a pedestrian route across a busy road. As shown in Figure 5, a survey is made to establish the existing random crossing points. The average point or standard range of deviations is established, and the crossing is located within this range. A prediction is made about how the introduction of a crossing will affect total movement. This prediction is established from past (generalized) experience, and the crossing is finally located. But you will still find many instances where the crossing is ignored because it is too far from an intended route, particularly for blind or infirm people for whom a difference of twenty yards can seem a very great distance. When this happens, barriers are often erected to make the deviants conform to the group behavior, so as to further facilitate

2. Above, a Chicago slum, 1944. Below, the same neighborhood rebuilt in the 1950's under the auspices of the U.S. Urban Renewal Authority, the Chicago Housing Authority, and others. Federal Street was rerouted to run adjacent to the railroad tracks, allowing room for a parkway between the street and the eight housing units.

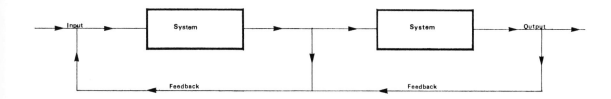

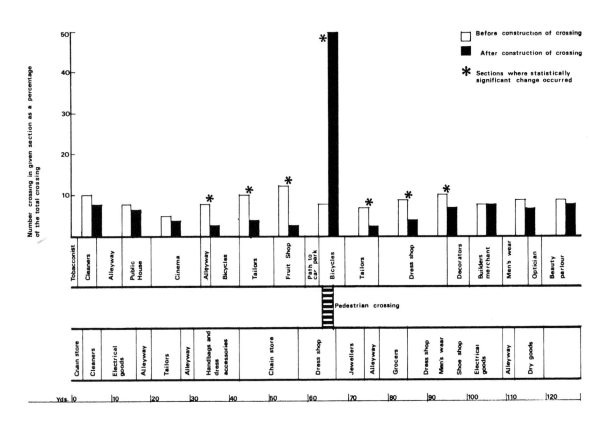

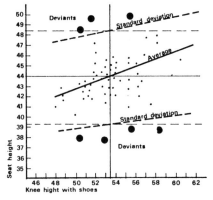

3. Systems analysis input-output model

4. Graph of survey to locate pedestrian route across a busy road

5. Statistical objectification

the development of a total solution. People are made to behave in the same way.

To restate my argument against objectification and for the explicit recognition of value and meaning, consider again a situation from common human experience. By far the largest proportion of recent psychiatric patients complain of a "lack of identity," or "feeling not to exist," or "thing-less," or "alienation." It is now becoming more accepted that a substantial majority of society feels alienated and that traditional psychiatric treatments are totally unable to cope with this problem. In fact, many of them, for example aversion therapy and behavioral therapy, *cause the problem.* The American psychologist Carl Rogers has said explicitly that when he tries to interpret the patient's behavior on the basis of an objective abstraction, the abstraction gets in the way.[5] He finds that an objective attitude toward the patient's ills actually increases the patient's feeling of alienation. This phenomenon occurs in a peculiar way, brilliantly analyzed by Laing.

All these examples are merely symptoms of a much broader attitude toward the design of a physical environment, an attitude which is having a detrimental effect upon the general population.

So here is the problem—the dilemma—as I see it: If we objectify user populations we establish a system whereby the people we are designing for become objects with no conception of their own freedom. Alternatively, if we do not objectify populations we can never achieve a cumulative improvement in the environment.

When we attempt to be objective, the "group structure" we establish inevitably becomes more cohesive, leaving the person with even less identity or at least with an identity that can have meaning for him only in the group situation. He becomes dependent upon the group for his existence. He sees himself more as an object, as a thing. It is my contention that this kind of problem is increased by current methods of design analysis and that increased dependency of people on the environment is a direct result of such methods. Moreover, this kind of dependency can sometimes be dangerous. When it occurs we may need to change the physical environment in order to establish an awareness of individuality within the person, even though this may sometimes mean that we have to refuse to concur with his tendencies.

This, of course, has serious implications. If we cannot agree upon a basic system of values there can be no cumulative improvement in the environment, because we cannot first agree upon what constitutes an improvement. Nor is this something that can be arrived at rationally, because basically my values are felt first and reasoned afterwards. They are the result of a lifetime of experiences unique to me, and it is impossible to communicate experiences, for in communication we establish not the original experience but a totally new one of "trying to communicate," which like all "objective" analyses of the human condition is twice removed from situational reality.

Conflict and Frustration Theories

A recent survey of children's attitudes to their environment threw up some interesting insights, not the least of which was evidenced in the comments of a twelve-year-old girl: "I am told that I am a member of the younger generation; that our task is to create a better world; to correct all of the mistakes that you have made. How can you expect me to do this, if you try to make me like yourself?"

These words cast some insight into two of the problems with which I have recently been involved, the design of workshops for the blind and prison workshops.[6] The treatment of blind workers and prisoners is not always the

5. Carl R. Rogers, *On Becoming a Person.*
6. These problems are reported in my *The Organization of Prison Workshops* and in Neville Longbone, "The Physical Organization of Sheltered Workshops for the Blind," in Ward and Geoffrey Broadbent, eds., *Design Methods in Architecture.*

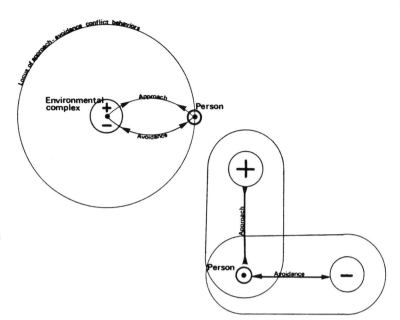

6. Approach-avoidance conflict behaviors
Left
Environmental complex with both attractive and repellent qualities
Right
Environment which has attractive and repellent qualities spatially or temporally separated

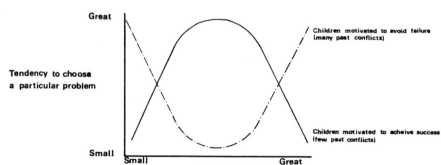

7. Graph showing the relationship between conflict and motivation

Great

Tendency to choose a particular problem

Children motivated to avoid failure (many past conflicts)

Children motivated to acheive success (few past conflicts)

Small

Small — Great

Psychic complexity of task
(Perceived difference between known and unknown problems)

straightforward "resocializing" process that we are led to believe. One of the things you very soon discover when you are confronted with a design problem of such criticality is that there is no such thing as *the* blind worker or *the* prisoner. There are as many kinds of blind workers as there are blind workers, and the same is true of prisoners. If we accept that each person has a potential for unique reaction to his environment, it is inevitable that a "standard" solution will lead to difficulties.

Take the problem of mobility for blind people. Some blind people are more mobile than others, that is, they have a greater capacity for orientating themselves in relation to their physical environment. However, their capacity to do so may vary from environment to environment and from time to time. What may be a complicated environment for a person today may seem quite negotiable tomorrow.

The two workshop examples were identical in one respect: they were both stagnant. Their stated function was to reintegrate people into society, but in this they were unsuccessful. The uniform complexity of the workshop geometries tended to even out the reaction potentials of the users. Thus, those blind people who had originally been of above-average mobility quickly atrophied, while those who were of below-average mobility actually regressed and were less mobile after their introduction to the workshop than they had been before. The blind workshops of Great Britain are therefore becoming gradually filled with a residual population who cannot cope with the special system within which they work. A similar situation exists to some extent in the prison system, with respect to the difficulty of creating a solution where the first-offenders do not automatically become institutionalized into the inmate subculture.

In both these examples the cohesive quality of the subculture and the individual's subjection to it are critical. The problem in both cases is to find ways of organizing the person's environment so that he can begin to accept his own independence. There are several experiments providing clues to how this can be done. Among these, the work of Lewin, Rosenzweig, and Amsel and Hancock in the analysis of conflict and frustration theories are significant.[7]

If a person conceives a task as being too difficult, even though he may have a great desire to overcome it, he is said to be feeling conflict. This is particularly so when his fear of the situation is as intense as his ongoing feelings. A conflict situation is not one which is simply disturbing but one where the person consciously tries to avoid the experience while still being attracted by it. A simple example of a conflict situation is the one in which a young boy is attracted by a girl, but is too self-conscious to actually approach her. This need not necessarily be a conflict; rather, if he can conceptualize his capacity to overcome his reticence, he is experiencing a frustration.

The conflict situation is by definition insurmountable but can be eliminated by the separation of the attractive and repugnant qualities of the object perceived as a goal by the person or by raising his self-esteem in relation to this goal. This is schematized in Figure 6. A typical example could be the relocation of a highway which has to be crossed by children going to and from a candy store. This could be expressed as an abstract relation: "no traffic route between the home and store."

If the person continuingly experiences conflict, there is every possibility that his whole perspective can be affected, leading to a total breakdown of his concept of "self." It is this conflict limit that the designer must try to define:

---

7. See Kurt Lewin, "Frustration and Regression: An Experiment with Young Children," and *Principles of Topological Psychology*; Saul Rosenzweig, "An Outline of Frustration Theory," in J. McV. Hunt, ed., *Personality and Behavior Disorders*; and Abram Amsel and William Hancock, "Motivation Properties of Frustration. III: Relation of Frustration Effect to Antecedent Goal Factors."

the point at which stress becomes distress.[8] This point, which has been called the frustration threshold, may vary from person to person, from time to time, and from situation to situation, depending upon the experience of the person. Two kinds of motivation are recognized in psychology, motivation to achieve success and motivation to avoid failure. There is, for instance, strong evidence that when a person never experiences conflict (as opposed to frustration), his motivation to avoid failure decreases while his motivation to achieve success increases.[9] In other words, he begins to be adventurous and curious. It is also known that his capacity to exercise accurate choice relative to his own store of experiences increases. Children who have been consistently conflicted in problem-solving situations tend to play safe. They choose problems that are either much too easy (which they have already done several times) or much too difficult. Either way they cannot lose, in that there is no sense of defeat in the event of failure. Their whole attitude becomes defensive. On the other hand, children who have never been allowed to experience conflict choose problems slightly beyond the complexity to which they are already accustomed, thus increasing their store of complex experiences at a self-determined rate. They determine their own "progress" far more accurately.[10] Figure 7 shows a graph of the relationship between motivation and task complexity for frustrated children and conflicted children.

It is not the abstract complexity of the task which is significant in such situations but rather the perceived complexity, i.e., the psychic distance between known and unknown. A chosen goal becomes more attractive in the event of failure than an enforced goal, which becomes less attractive.[11] Hence, motivation can affect choice, while motivation can be improved, given choice. But choice is the very thing which is eliminated by systems analysts. They tend to penalize creative endeavor.

In both the psychoanalytic and design contexts, the problem is to help the person to pinpoint his own experimental standpoint; his frustration threshold. If this can be done, if the degree of physical complexity relative to his individual needs can be accurately ascertained, then the person begins to develop an increasing self-confidence and an increasing capacity to exercise wise choice. He also becomes more curious and more capable of organizing his own environment with respect to his own needs.

A typical example of the range of formal characteristics which are needed to satisfy individual needs can be seen in the different reactions of blind people to distance, with regard to self-orientation. Experiments which simulate this difference have been conducted with blindfolded sighted people and have been adequately described by Longbone.[12] Individuals trying to walk a straight line in a totally open situation vary considerably in the degree of veer; some (untrained) subjects may veer as much as 5 yards over a 20-yard distance while trained subjects may veer as little as 2 or 3 yards. In physical terms such variation obviously has significant implications. It means, for instance, that form cues must be provided at smaller intervals for untrained than for trained blind people. If this is not done, the untrained come to rely upon the trained for any new experiences. They become dependent. Even

8. Current work on conflict theory in psychology tends to be clouded by the lack of accurate definitions of terms used. Thus, when Berlyne and Piaget talk about conflict as being necessary, they are really referring to a state in which the differing responses to form have not reached a level of criticality and hence are still ongoing. This is what I have taken to be frustration. The point is also made by Yates. See Daniel E. Berlyne, "Conflict and Arousal," Jean Piaget, *The Construction of Reality in the Child,* and Aubrey Yates, *Frustration and Conflict.*
9. John W. Atkinson and George H. Litwin, "Achievement Motivation and Test Anxiety Concerned as Motive to Approach Success and Motive to Avoid Failure" and Heinz Heckhausen, *The Anatomy of Achievement Motivation.*
10. Piaget, *The Construction of Reality in the Child.*
11. Leon Festinger, "Self-Confidence and Selective Exposure to Information," in Festinger, *Conflict, Decision, and Dissonance.*
12. Longbone, "Workshops for the Blind." For the original source, see Bryant J. Cratty and Harriet G. Williams, *Perceptual Thresholds and Non-Visual Locomotion.*

further, those blind people with perhaps an originally high degree of mobility have no opportunity to exercise their capacity and hence come to identify more closely with their less capable colleagues, as illustrated in Figure 8. In both instances, the structure of the subculture is made more cohesive.

A Prison Workshop

In 1966 I began investigations into workshop design problems, for the blind and for prisoners. I will discuss a prison workshop here. The analysis techniques used were those originally developed by Alexander and Poyner[13] which have subsequently been modified in the light of our findings.

To begin with, it is first necessary to get a "feel" for the problem. This is done by visiting as many examples of the building type as possible, by talking to a broad spectrum of users, and observing their behavior. This comparative analysis is unstructured, but out of it arise what appear to be central issues which are interconnected. These issues are then checked in an extension of the comparative technique, and hypotheses are made about their effects in as yet unseen situations. Physical characteristics, normally in the form of abstract geometric patterns, are thus isolated and stored in a general "library" of forms. Each formal pattern implies a predicted set of values and behaviors of the user. The problem is to try to make the "library" exhaustive. Areas of overlap will be found which are common to all users, and these of course can be generalized. It is from this basic overlap that the prototype relations and final form are organized. Figure 9 shows part of the library of conflicts, tendencies, relations or patterns, and partial solution for prison workshops.

This diagram represents the synthesis of relations which center about the problems of supervision of prisoners in prison workshops. The analysis process upon which it is based is strictly "problem-oriented," i.e. the environment is only changed when it can be demonstrated to be causing a problem. The problem may at first be only "felt" intuitively and its component parts ill-defined. In the diagram shown here, the "conflict" is the problem, and the tendencies are its motivated components. The tendencies and conflict are developed together, so that their respective definitions are closely interwoven. Once the conflict has been specified, a relation is suggested which incorporates the *converse* physical qualities to those found in the conflict. The relation is in the form of a brief statement, together with a diagram. The form shown here is from a group of five relations, each derived from five different conflicts or problems based upon motivational factors, i.e., "staff try to avoid annoying inmates." These conflicts differ from person to person. Only certain staff feel this way, and only certain prisoners resent being supervised. The proposal is only made for these people. It does not govern the general role of supervision in a prison, but only that of a particular workshop where these people will work. Other relations would be necessary with different staff and prisoners. To generalize this solution would be to extend into the whole prison the problems upon which it is based, i.e., to perpetuate the tendency to institutionalization.

The designed building is then treated as a working model, within which the difference in needs is made explicit. Often, however, insufficient overlap can be found to precipitate a basic solution, and when this happens more exhaustive abstract research is necessary. Since the needs of users will vary from locality to locality, the library must be supplemented with data particular to a given site.

The solution produced as a building is seen only as a base from which the user and the designer can achieve a "better fitting" environment. Thus, there will be found to be areas of overlap and areas of separation between population needs and the building. These are found directly from the forms causing difficulty. The areas of separation are then grouped so as to avoid incongruence as much as possible.

13. Alexander and Poyner, "The Atoms of Environmental Structure."

8. Dependence of untrained blind persons on trained blind persons

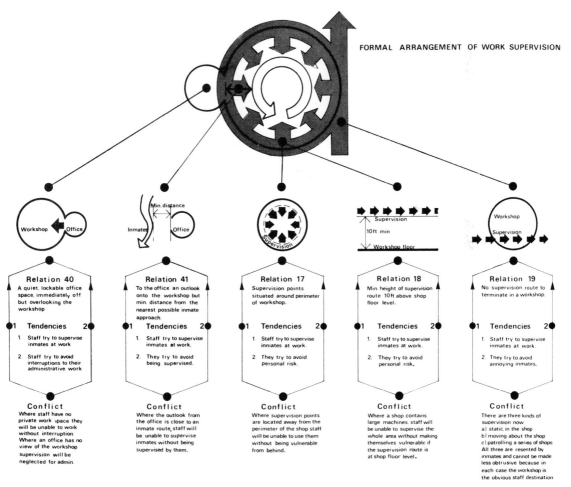

FORMAL ARRANGEMENT OF WORK SUPERVISION

Relation 40

A quiet, lockable office space, immediately off but overlooking the workshop

Tendencies

1. Staff try to supervise inmates at work

2. Staff try to avoid interruptions to their administrative work

Conflict

Where staff have no private work space they will be unable to work without interruption Where an office has no view of the workshop supervision will be neglected for admin.

Relation 41

To the office, an outlook onto the workshop but min. distance from the nearest possible inmate approach.

Tendencies

1. Staff try to supervise inmates at work.

2. They try to avoid being supervised.

Conflict

Where the outlook from the office is close to an inmate route, staff will be unable to supervise inmates without being supervised by them.

Relation 17

Supervision points situated around perimeter of workshop.

Tendencies

1. Staff try to supervise inmates at work.

2. They try to avoid personal risk.

Conflict

Where supervision points are located away from the perimeter of the shop staff will be unable to use them without being vulnerable from behind.

Relation 18

Min. height of supervision route 10ft above shop floor level.

Tendencies

1. Staff try to supervise inmates at work.

2. They try to avoid personal risk.

Conflict

Where a shop contains large machines, staff will be unable to supervise the whole area without making themselves vulnerable if the supervision route is at shop floor level.

Relation 19

No supervision route to terminate in a workshop.

Tendencies

1. Staff try to supervise inmates at work.

2. They try to avoid annoying inmates.

Conflict

There are three kinds of supervision now
a) static, in the shop
b) moving about the shop
c) patrolling a series of shops
All three are resented by inmates and cannot be made less obtrusive because in each case the workshop is the obvious staff destination

9. Partial library of forms for a prison workshop

However, it is never possible to determine complete isolation between elements, nor is it desirable. The essence of a good solution is that it should form a continuum, since any abrupt change in complexity creates an insurmountable barrier for the user. The areas of overlap are therefore used to bridge this obstacle. They are usually made of both familiar and unfamiliar forms, in much the same way that Dembar and Earl conceptualize their "pacer."[14] In this way, the work area of the individual is always extending his capacity to a point which is uncritical. He begins to monitor his own development and modify his own environment. In prison workshops, for instance, he will eventually emerge into the "open environment" with complete self-confidence, not "integrated" in the common sense but able to accept the world on his own terms. Even where this does not happen, the increased independence of the individual leads automatically to a breakdown of the subculture. Once this happens, the designer becomes superfluous. This, in my opinion, should be the ultimate goal in design methods.

Conclusion

Reducing the omnipotence of the designer qua designer is one goal which current methods of analysis will never realize. The present semantic breakdown between "research" (supposedly pure) and "development" (to do with buildings), combined with the existing work-fee structure completely inhibit the kind of dedication by architects and planners to real-world situations which is necessary for improvement. In my mind, research and education in architecture and planning must begin to face this problem. However, the relationship outlined between choice and motivation creates a difficult obstacle in the development of effective misfit solutions, and I must confess that I have no specific answer to this problem save that of direct contact between myself and the people for whom I am designing. We assume that emotional contact will in some way warp our objective perspective and confuse our design reasoning. Yet emotional contact *can* be used to help the designer zone into crucial problem areas. As Rogers says, "I have found that my total organismic sensing is more trustworthy than my intellect."[15] It is a disturbing thought that most current research in architecture and planning is founded upon the intellectual need for academic respectability.

---

14. William N. Dembar and Robert W. Earl, "Analysis of Exploratory, Manipulative, and Curiosity Behavior."
15. Rogers, *On Becoming a Person*.

30 A Progress Report on the Pattern Language

Francis Duffy and John Torrey

Department of Architecture
University of California
Berkeley, California

Francis Duffy currently is a doctoral
candidate in architecture at Princeton
University. At the time this paper was
written he was a graduate student at
Berkeley. He was born and educated in
England, received the A.A. Diploma
(Honors) from the Architectural Association School in London in 1964, and then
an M.Arch. from Berkeley in 1968. He was
an architect for the National Building
Agency in London, where he helped prepare *Generic Plans,* and was editor of
Arena, Architectural Association Journal.
Since 1967 he has been a Harkness Fellow
in the United States. John Torrey is a
member of the Seattle office of Okamoto
Liskamm, Architects and Planners. He
received a B.S. in economics from the
University of Pennsylvania in 1960 and
an M.Arch. from Berkeley in 1968, and
was associated with the Center for Environmental Structure.

This paper is a progress report on the
development of a pattern language, a
design method proposed by Alexander
and his associates based upon generic
solutions to isolable environmental
problems. The paper is concerned especially with overall schemes of order, with
the relative influence of patterns on the
total design, and with variability caused
by local conditions. Patterns are defined
and an attempt is made to point out some
fundamental assumptions. Comparisons
are made to other design methods. An
unbiased assessment is attempted of
some theoretical and practical problems.
After a discussion of what seems to be
most promising about the approach,
some suggestions are made for further
development. To give the reader an idea
of problems in using the method, two sets
of examples by the authors are illustrated.

In a field of such new and rapid development as design methodology, it is not
surprising that confusion is caused both by new developments and by unstable terminologies. Moreover, there is always a grave risk that new ideas
be confused with old. Alexander's work has been beset by such misunder-
standings. This paper is an attempt by two relative outsiders to explain simply
what is meant by "patterns" and "pattern language."[1] But more than that, it
is an assessment of the promise and utility of the "pattern" and "pattern
language" ideas.

The Idea of a Pattern

Buildings are so full of detail that it is difficult to believe that they consist of
anything that is not entirely dependent on local and accidental circumstances. On further study similiarities are detected. An example is the almost
universal system of connections between entry, receptionist, and waiting
area in offices. It seems that this is a type of solution that turns up again and
again but each time with slightly different variations.

---

1. The basic theoretical statement plus two examples of relations and patterns are
presented in Christopher Alexander and Barry Poyner, "The Atoms of Environmental
Structure" in Part 9 of this volume. For later work, see Alexander, Sara Ishikawa, and
Murray Silverstein, *A Pattern Language Which Generates Multi-Service Centers.*

Many who are interested in design methodology are happy to ignore the fact that typologies of solutions exist. They prefer to believe that the best results will come from a completely fresh approach to each local problem in each local situation. Each solution will then be derived uniquely from the analysis. Only then will the fit between the analysis and solution be exact.

The idea of a pattern is an attempt to combine a high level of functional analysis with the advantages of the typological approach. A *pattern* may be defined as a typical arrangement in space of physical objects (or parts) which allow behavioral tendencies or forces to coexist in a context without conflict. To find what is critical in human activities it is necessary to introduce the ideas of "tendencies" and "conflict." *Tendencies* are observable human drives towards satisfying needs, and need according to Malinowski is a "system of conditions in the human organism, in the cultural setting, and in the relation of both to the natural environment, which are sufficient and necessary for the survival of group and organism."[2] Similar to tendencies, and sometimes acting counter to them, are nonhuman forces, such as the natural forces of wind and rain, the structural forces of tension and compression, and the economic forces of supply and demand, i.e., reflections in the financial system of the tendencies of groups. *Conflicts* occur when tendencies or forces come into apparent opposition. Conflict and the resolution of conflict are central to the idea of patterns. However some situations are better expressed than others in these terms. Where there is no conflict, a "standard" is more appropriate than a pattern. The context is whatever environment is necessary for tendencies to come into conflict, and parts are the named components of context and pattern.

Underlying the definition of pattern is the ideal of human freedom. At present the environment is fragmented. Since all tendencies are assumed ultimately to be good, and since there is no reason to suspect that the resources of nature are inadequate, this fragmentation is suspected to be the sole cause of all conflicts. That tendencies and forces come into conflict is the effect and not the cause of the inadequacies of our physical environment. So our goal should be to rearrange the environment until all tendencies, all forces can coexist without coming into conflict. Human life will not be entirely free until the physical environment permits it to be so. Only then will the physical environment be seen to have a healthy organic unfragmented unity. This is the basic philosophy of patterns.

The Idea of a Pattern Language

But patterns alone are not enough. However sharp they may be as individual tools, however precisely they delineate solutions to each local conflict, they will remain disparate reference material unless a means can be found of coordinating them into unified designs. Coordination implies: (1) Combining appropriate patterns in a design to solve a local set of problems, not only adequately but with the greatest possible elegance and economy; (2) Collecting all newly discovered or newly invented patterns; (3) Retrieving from this store patterns appropriate to the problem in hand, or if not obviously appropriate, patterns which are analogous; and (4) Communicating patterns to others.

Natural languages perform similar tasks admirably for words. A language collects words that express simple ideas, retrieves them when appropriate, combines them with other words into sentences to express more complex ideas, and shares these words with others. The pattern language does not share the powerful and complex phenomenon of the meaning of the words themselves. It is as if we had a language of bricklaying: the bricks (or patterns) have no particular significance beyond their existence; yet there is an analogy in that there is a grammar of rules for combining bricks into walls.

The pattern language is claimed to be a set of rules for combining patterns. Moreover it is claimed that lesser rules can deal with the problems of col-

---

2. Bronislaw Malinowski, *A Scientific Theory of Culture.* p. 90.

lection, retrieval, and communication of patterns.[3] Patterns may have no significance beyond themselves, but they must be capable of being exchanged and understood.

What progress has been made toward developing these rules? A considerable amount of time has been spent discussing retrieval and combination, but unfortunately no final set of rules has yet been worked out. However, before we take stock of the situation in detail, we should consider the pattern language in comparison to the achievements and promise of other design methodologies.

The Pattern Language in Relation to Other Design Methods

The idea of a pattern language seems to be parallel to some recent ideas on design methods and in opposition to others; however some opposition is more apparent than real.

1. *The "black-box" approach.* Black box is a term to describe work which is concerned with manipulating the inputs and outputs of the design process rather than with the process itself. The Building Research Station study of decision-making in the planning process is of this nature, and so are techniques such as synectics or brainstorming.[4] Since patterns claim to be an aid to the design process rather than a substitute, and since the method of combining patterns is still unclear, any knowledge gained in this area is likely to be of direct use in developing the language.

2. *Analytical procedures.* A real quarrel seems inevitable with proponents, such as Archer, of extremely analytical design procedures.[5] The basis of this and other similar methods is to break problems down to their constituent parts. Only then may design begin. The pattern language depends upon a far closer and, it may be argued, more realistic relation between the components of the analysis and design solutions than any overall analytical procedure permits.

3. *Goals, criteria, values.* Design methods based on "operations research" incorporate the idea of weighting. Goals are set, criteria formulated, and relative values or weights given to each criterion. Criteria are used not only to find the best way to reach a goal but also to evaluate solutions after they have been completed. There is no doubt of the practical application of such methods. Ehrenkrantz's work is an excellent example: first he establishes user requirements, then studies technologies that seem appropriate, examines possible tradeoffs, and finally, on the basis of the user requirements, prepares performance specifications.[6] Alternative solutions can then be evaluated on the relatively simple basis of cost. The differences to the pattern language should be noted. First performance specifications are more abstract and less spatial than patterns. Secondly any approach based on the idea of the compromise of values or tradeoffs is antithetical to the pattern language which attempts in each situation to achieve the best of all possible worlds by resolving all conflicts.

4. *Alternatives.* More sophisticated adherents of the "goals, criteria, values" method are becoming increasingly interested in a dialectical process of deciding the relative importance of values. Churchman argues for a variation on advocacy planning, "counterplanning," a technique of confronting any plan of action with an alternative which deliberately adheres to the same overall goals and constraints but which is informed by a different value

3. Alexander, Ishikawa, and Silverstein. *A Pattern Language.*
4. See the work in progress by the Urban Planning Division, Building Research Station, Garston, Herts, England: "Decision Making in Urban Design" under P. H. Levin, early reports of which include Levin, "Design Process in Planning," and "Decision-Making in Urban Design."
5. See L. Bruce Archer, "An Overview to the Structure of the Design Process," in Part 9 of this volume.
6. For a general introduction to Ehrenkrantz' method and a review of his major project to date, see James Benet et al., *SCSD: The Project and the Schools.*

system or *Weltanschauung*.[7] A third and better plan is likely to be developed, superior to either of the original plans because it incorporates a fuller value system. Such a process is based upon the assumption not only that local values are necessarily incomplete but that they may be broadened and reconciled.

The pattern language differs in that it does not proceed in a gradualistic way and in that it is based on the assumption that arguments about values are unnecessary. However, in the long view it might be said that there are some striking similarities between patterns and counterplanning. Both are monistic, both are based on a desire to provide man with the greatest possible freedom, to permit all possible behaviors. In the short view, counterplanners are content to let limited value systems broaden and reconcile themselves in the field in a piecemeal fashion, while pattern adherents work, as it were, in the laboratory, basing their work on the most thorough empirical research and attempting to resolve each local conflict without resort to compromise, before the pattern is given to the world. Patterns are the approach of the isolated scholar; counterplanning of the politically committed team. Both approaches aim to set people free to design for themselves what they really want.

Problems of the Pattern Language

1. *The Problem of Stability.* We live in a world of incomplete and biased sets of values. No data from the social sciences can possibly determine norms because contradiction is always possible and change is certain. Pattern-makers are, therefore, faced with severe problems when deciding how far patterns should be stretched—whether they should be tailored precisely for a local situation or generalized to cope with all possible uses. The danger is not so much that either approach is impossible but that the patterns are likely to be unstable, hovering somewhere between the two extremes. An example is the relation of bank officers and public. In all banks there are officers who should be accessible to the public. This relationship is a pattern. In California banks the officers are extremely accessible, separated only by a change in floor surface from the public; the officers in British banks are less accessible and are often to be found in private rooms on upper floors. The reason is probably that less loan and mortgage business is conducted in British banks. Nevertheless the moral is clear: how generalized can a pattern of accessibility to bank officers be while preserving some precision for specific situations?

2. *The problem of variability.* The other side of the problem of stability is the problem of variability. It has been suggested that patterns may cope with varied situations by incorporating variables within themselves. To solve one conflict in several contexts may necessitate a whole range of variations on one basic pattern. Contexts themselves may be classified into categories; this may make pattern variation an easier task. Nevertheless sufficient difficulties remain to recall the problem of the rag trade: given a style of dress, a particular material, and all the shapes and sizes of all possible women, how does one decide to make only a limited range of sizes? How does one decide how many variations should be incorporated in a pattern range?

3. *The problem of values.* Although patterns within themselves avoid the problem of compromise, it can be argued that, willy nilly, each pattern will have built into it the consequences of a value system. It is impossible to be entirely objective, to cut oneself free from past experiences and tradition. Not only is each pattern culture-based so that it is difficult to transmit patterns from one culture to another, but it is difficult even to hand over a pattern to one's closest collaborator because any pattern is liable to be viewed differently. The question is to discover exactly how much the applicability of patterns is affected in practice by the real and important value differences between societies and between individuals. This is a serious responsibility.

4. *The problem of cost and resources.* The example of three different architects' offices in the Appendix brings up the problem of what effect different

---

7. C. West Churchman, *Challenge to Reason*.

costs and resources have upon the use of patterns. Some architects' offices can afford more than a minimum amenity while others cannot. Not only is it clear that the same basic patterns can be expressed in a variety of different ways but also that a considerable part of the design process is taken up with juggling designs to fit the constraints imposed by local resources and cost conditions.

5. *Problems of combining patterns.* Individual patterns must be brought together, somehow or other, into design for buildings. Clearly, combinations are always theoretically possible, but it is difficult to understand the practical mechanism of the combinatorial process. Once understood, the use of patterns would be open to those who would not ordinarily claim to be designers, and perhaps even to machines. But we do not understand the process, and we are not even able to present in a convincing visual manner the effects of combinations. Three potential solutions to the combinatorial problem are proposed:

Linkages. Patterns are elemental relations of built form which solve conflicts. Each independent pattern has its own context. When patterns are brought together (for example, the patterns for tellers and officers in a bank), contexts are combined and further patterns are conceived which are appropriate to the enlarged context, e.g., circulation for customers between tellers and officers. Alexander, Ishikawa, and Silverstein represent this phenomenon visually by symbols of linkages which join independent patterns together and suggest others.[8] But these linkages seem to be derived after-the-fact and are not likely to be a reliable guide for other problems. It is indicative of the intractable nature of this problem that earlier attempts at mechanically recording such linkages had to be abandoned. The major practical difficulty is the labor of anticipating for any one pattern all likely combinations and linkages.

Orders of magnitude. Patterns may be classified by the effect they are likely to have on a total design problem. Alexander uses the image of a box, i.e., the solution space, with patterns represented as colored clouds floating within it. The point is that some patterns influence the whole solution, while others influence only a corner. Some patterns interrelate with others; some do not. Unfortunately, to make this image do some work requires detailed study of the effect of each pattern in all the various building types and local situations in which it may be used.

Formal and geometrical schemes. In contrast to these organic approaches, a counter argument has stressed the significance of form in design, the designers often rely upon remembered formal schemes or upon geometry. Such schemes are modified by the demands of local contexts and may be assumed to be modified similarly by patterns. Nevertheless from the start an overall skeleton is provided which makes testing of alternatives and the development of detail possible. The obvious danger is that such schemes impose unworkable and irrelevant rigidities on design at too early a stage.

In regard to the last point, it is difficult to find historical precedent for a completely formal point of view. Even medieval or renaissance churches, which are often mistakenly discussed as purely formal devices, were shaped to some extent by "patterns" which concerned down-to-earth requirements of liturgy and participation. But not everything about a church is down-to-earth; we cannot talk of an exact "fit" between form and function. Indeed there seems to be a considerable area of "slack" or absence of "fit." The nature of this "slack" is intensely interesting and extremely relevant to our enquiry. We may explain it in cultural terms, if we choose to abandon Alexander's strictly functional point of view. Lévi-Strauss insists that man imposes intellectual structures upon reality in order to control reality.[9] He uses

8. Alexander, Ishikawa, and Silverstein, *A Pattern Language.*
9. Claude Lévi-Strauss, *Tristes Tropiques,* Chapter 17, and *Structural Anthropology,* Chapter 8.

the beautiful examples of native body-painting and, even better, of village plans to demonstrate deliberate encoding of cultural messages in the formal elements of a way of life. Could it be that even our modern buildings have the task of reinforcing our conceptions of ourselves as well as fulfilling our simpler needs?

This kind of speculation does not invalidate Alexander's empiricism but suggests a higher level of intellectual imagery than he is presently willing to accept. In much the same way, Lévi-Strauss's structuralism was developed on the solid empirical foundations laid by such functional anthropologists as Malinowski.[10]

The use of patterns in the two banks in the Appendix is a small attempt to demonstrate that overall schemes do have a role in design, if only to provide a developing framework which permits the testing of alternative combinations of patterns until the framework and the patterns become united. Clearly, this inquiry must be taken much further to substantiate the argument we have begun to develop here.

6. *Problems of integrating nonpattern material.* Unless it is assumed that designers will eventually use only patterns, the problem of incorporating nonpattern material into both the language and individual designs will be perennial. How badly will such material disrupt a design method based entirely upon patterns? On the other hand, if patterns can never be used in their entirety and must always be diluted with other material, why is it necessary to be precise in their formulation?

Points for Patterns

Despite these serious problems, the pattern language, even at this early stage of development, may give to the designer advantages that we believe no other methodology can promise.

1. *Fact and image.* Patterns are founded upon the analysis of real forces but simultaneously transmit notions of possible solutions. No other design method has hit upon such a way of capturing the essential dimensions of design solutions and tying them down so precisely to the forces that generate them. Perhaps the pattern language approximates the way the designer's mind itself stores ideas for solving problems. Certainly patterns do not contradict but, in fact complement the best skills of the traditional designer. The usually loose relationship between building form and human behavior lends support to any methodology based upon generic types. Any attempt to argue that each local building problem is unique and needs an entirely original solution is bound to lead to unnecessary and repetitive design work, because building problems are generally not unique, nor are building solutions. Both problems and solutions can be classified usefully into types. Patterns, however, lack the disadvantages of coarser typologies because individually they are small enough units, because they are based on single problems, and because together they can be combined to solve any scale of design programs.

2. *New solutions.* Each pattern is based on analysis, and in the present muddled state of design this, in itself, is a sufficient guarantee of original solutions to small problems. But the real promise of originality lies in the fact that patterns are made to be added to one another to form whole designs which will contradict the simplistic building forms that are common today.

3. *No compromise.* The approach of manipulating physical form to permit tendencies to interact without compromise encourages a more thorough search of the range of possibilities. The argument that patterns are based on a behaviorist assumption that tendencies are mechanical and that the pattern language is a form of totalitarian straitjacket is misconceived. Of course, patterns are based on probabilities but they are not deterministic;

---

10. Malinowski, *A Scientific Theory of Culture.*

they are open to contradiction and they are capable of being developed. To accuse those who use observed regularities in behavior as a basis for design of manipulation or social engineering is absurd.

4. *Interdisciplinary format for the social sciences.* Patterns cannot exist without data, and data unrelated to design problems are difficult to use. The designer uses data and ideas about physical solutions simultaneously and does not want them to be presented to him separately. Patterns serve his needs. The pattern language is a format for material from a wide range of fields, sociology, psychology, anthropology, and many others. The designer is certain to begin to take an active interest in the contributions of these fields to design. There is some hope that as design grows more rational the special role of the professional designer will be eroded and more ordinary men and women will feel free to design for themselves.

5. *Refutability.* Patterns are like hypotheses; they are based upon empirical evidence and may be tested and refuted. Deciding whether a pattern is suitable is a rational process rather than a matter of sales talk or mystique. The pattern language contains a principle of growth, for as contexts and forces change, old patterns will become vulnerable and new patterns will have to replace them.

6. *Design time.* One of the most important social arguments for patterns is that they save the designer the wasteful labor of working out each new design solution from the beginning. Patterns provide everyone with the accumulated experience of all designers.

What Remains to Be Done

Much work has still to be done before the pattern language can become an indispensable tool to designers. The purpose of these concluding notes is to point out some urgent lines of enquiry which promise improvement.

1. *Combination.* It has still not been shown that there corresponds to any problem only one solution. The bank examples are intended to make this point. It seems very difficult to eliminate entirely the possibility that many design decisions, even using patterns, will be based to some extent on a less than complete understanding of all that is involved. The pattern language might guard against and profit from these inadequacies by using Churchman's dialectical method of counterplanning to seek a better course of action and to avoid as far as possible decisions made on the basis of incomplete knowledge and values. Combination brings up the problem of using patterns with the greatest economy, in a way which eliminates superfluity. Much study is needed here.

2. *Collection.* Local conditions determine the exact form a pattern will take. But the pattern may still be integral in different conditions, if a way is found of building in ranges of variability and yet preserving its essential nature. The consequence of this idea for pattern collection is that it is not sufficient to identify a pattern in one local condition of conflict; the real problem is to try to generalize that pattern to cope with as many local conditions as it can before it breaks down or turns into something else.

3. *Retrieval.* The matter of retrieving patterns from storage has already received considerable attention. One way of looking at the problem is to consider the dialogue between the Center for Environmental Structure and the user. This perspective, at least, brings into focus what the Center does and does not control: It has control over the patterns issued and the order in which they are issued. But it has no control over the designer's stimuli, local conditions, the designer's skill, the number of patterns the designer chooses to use, what new ideas or patterns the designer chooses to use, or at what stage in the design process the designer asks for help. The example of three different architects' offices shows the important effect of local conditions; the bank examples are intended to show the consequences of different stimuli. Empirical studies are needed to throw light upon this fundamental

problem. At present it seems clear that the designer generally makes use of a broad stream of thought which may be modified but is nevertheless more or less continuous from beginning to end of design. Interweaving in and out of this broad stream are many other lines of inquiry, for example, into local conditions and into patterns. Some of these inquiries are made once, others recur. Through this process the design is slowly built. If only a model could be made of this mental process, the three main preoccupations of this paper —overall schemes of order, the relative influence of patterns on the total design, and variability caused by local conditions—might fall into place and instead of being separate notions might interweave and complement each other.

4. *Communication.* It is not true that the problem of communicating patterns to users and critics has been solved. All attempts so far have floundered on the rock of precision, being either too general or too limited. It is tempting to hope that a method of diagramming patterns can be invented which will be accurate but quick, combinable yet clearly distinct, descriptive yet liberating. On the other hand, this vision may turn out to be a chimera. More down to earth, mixed methods may serve the purpose equally well. Work is urgently needed here.

This report reveals considerable areas of doubt in the pattern language as well as considerable promise. Far-reaching claims are made, but serious gaps are apparent in the framework of ideas. We learn, for example, that a pattern is based on a precise idea of conflict, but we lack any overall model of the kinds of conflict that may occur. We become persuaded of the importance of adjusting the physical environment to permit tendencies free play but remain uncomfortably aware that other sorts of adjustments— legislative, regulatory, even fiscal—might have the same effect. What edge is there to the effect of physical measures?

Until more solid foundations are constructed it would be wiser to be more humble in public claims but more ambitious in private attempts to construct what promises to be a most hopeful and all-embracing design methodology, a pattern language.

Appendix
Case Studies in the Use of the Pattern Language

To demonstrate the way in which patterns are generated, how the same set of patterns are combined, and how individual patterns vary when they are applied in different circumstances, two case studies in the use of the pattern language are illustrated.

Patterns for Architects' Offices

From the September 1966 *Progressive Architecture* special issue on architects' offices, three offices were chosen for their immense range in size and circumstances. Although dimensions and program, especially the maximum number of staff, were fully respected, no limit was set to rearrangement within the structural shells.

Office A, the smallest office, is to contain 6 architectural staff in an area of 675 sq ft, i.e., about 113 sq ft per person. The shell, which is the third floor loft of a 4-story building, is long and narrow, the critical dimension being 15 ft. Office B is 2 stories with street frontage in a converted tailor's shop. Critical dimension is the 19 ft width. It is to contain a maximum of 12 architectural staff in an area of 1634 sq ft, i.e., 136 sq ft per person. The third office, C, is much bigger, being 6392 sq ft, i.e., 213 sq ft per person since the maximum staff is said to be 30. There is sufficient space in this third story loft of a converted warehouse that no dimension is really critical.

Eight problems, conflicting tendencies, and typical patterns from the complete study of twenty are summarized below. Notice that the verbal statement of the pattern has two parts: an "if" clause states the context, and one or more "then" clauses state the physical pattern.

These examples of pattern combination are intended to show that while patterns are often designed as isolated elements, they are nonetheless considered as clumps of patterns or whole series of patterns coming together in the design process. Patterns combine in an additive manner, first one pattern or set of patterns and then that set in combination with another set. It is difficult, and perhaps unnecessary, to show patterns combining in ideal situations. While individual patterns can be represented diagrammatically as having a certain form and geometry, real situations indicate the ranges of variability for individual patterns and relationships between them. The successful combination of patterns, even after they have been fully differentiated and articulated is seen to remain the greatest and most difficult part of the design process.[11]

It must be emphasized that these examples merely summarize the patterns and do not attempt to present them in full detail together with all the behavior evidence which is essential to the design process as it actually occurs and essential to full pattern presentation.[12]

Patterns for Banks

After the problem of combining patterns in different circumstances had been investigated in the case study just presented, an attempt was made to discover if patterns could be combined in the same circumstance in different ways. It was thought that such an experiment might reveal that overall formal schemes play an important part in the combination of patterns.

As a second case study, two alternative designs for the same bank on the same site were prepared to explore this point. One was deliberately designed on the principle of a centralized public forum, the other on the idea of a forum which wraps around the two street frontages of the corner site. At the beginning of the experiment there seemed to be no reason to choose either alternative over the other except for formal, nonpattern reasons.

Both banks occupy a corner site 104 ft by 99 ft. A 12-foot column grid, based on similar existing bank buildings, was assumed. The western street was assumed to be busier than the southern; the other two sides of the square are built up. Six officers and their four assistants have to be accommodated as well as seven tellers, three specialist tellers, and eleven clerks. Based upon the existing bank the following space standards were adopted:

Entrance and forum space	2230 sq ft	34%
Officers' area	1230 sq ft	19%
Tellers' area	580 sq ft	9%
Clerical area	1150 sq ft	18%
Vault and access	430 sq ft	6%
Staff lounge and storage	900 sq ft	14%

The length of the tellers' counter was set at 75 ft or $7\frac{1}{2}$ ft per person. Public writing shelf provided was said to be about 30 ft.

Figures 4 and 5 show how the same patterns are used and approximately the same standards met in two different situations. Again, this example merely summarizes patterns and does not present fully supported statements. Also, the exercise is somewhat inconclusive. It is clear that both overall bank configurations are workable alternatives, and since there is nothing in the pattern language to suggest that each problem has only one unique solution, it may be argued that both solution ideas were nothing but intuitive leaps to workable but alternative combinations of patterns. Such an argument by-passes but does not disprove the possibility that overall formal schemes may help coordinate shapeless pattern material.

11. Other completed examples of patterns include: H. Field et al., *Problems of Pediatric Hospital Design*; Sim Van der Ryn and Murray Silverstein, *Dorms at Berkeley: An Environmental Analysis*; Ronald Walkey, "A Transportation Network for Cities"; Theodore Goldberg, "Design for a Teenage Center," and "The Automobile"; and Anthony Ward, the *Organisation of Prison Workshops*.
12. For the form of complete patterns, see Alexander and Poyner, *The Atoms of Environmental Structure,* Appendix A, the example of patterns for a house entrance.

Numbers	Topic	Problem	Tendencies conflicting
1	Entrance to architect's office—transparent	Visitors feel that they are not welcome when they approach the office.	1. Visitor feels uncomfortable about entering an alien professional world. 2. "Architects" fear complete exposure to public realm.
3	Entrance—position of reception desk in relation to entrance	Office has to control entrance of visitors.	1. Visitors want a route. 2. Some visitors want to come into office unobserved. 3. Visitors want to prepare "face." 4. Receptionist wants to observe visitor as soon as he enters and be unobserved. 5. Receptionist wants another direction to face.
5	Staff and path to drawing office	In many offices there is nowhere for the staff to get together. There is nowhere to go (except at the work table), nowhere to sit, nowhere to prepare coffee, snacks, etc.	1. Staff tend not to meet each other except when they are actually collaborating on a problem. 2. Staff tend to learn more from each other if they meet informally away from workplace. 3. Staff tend to get jaded, need breaks, light relief.
6	Partners and contact with staff	Partners must keep in contact with staff yet want a place of their own in the office.	1. Partners tend to make special "places" for themselves in the office. 2. Staff tend to lose contact with partners.
8	Two workplaces	People want to work in groups as well as work as separate individuals	1. People tend to want relief from a single task. 2. People tend to want to work in groups—realize that it's more efficient for certain kinds of arch. problems.
9	Conference room	Not all meetings can be held in the drawing office.	1. Need for meetings with limited outside contact. 2. Need for staff and partners to keep in touch (see pattern 6).
12	Group proximity	Group work is impossible without proximity.	1. Tendency for groups that are geographically separate to act separately. 2. Tendency for proximity interchange to increase sentiments of solidarity.
13	Privacy and access with the group	Solitary work is often necessary within a working group—the problem of interruptions becomes critical.	1. Tendency to want solitude. 2. Tendency to want contact within group.

1. Patterns and transformations for architects' offices

Pattern	A	B	C
If: Entrance to any architect's office. Then: Entrance facade has transparent surfaces on either side of *door* and/or door can be transparent also.			
If: Entrance to any architect's office that maintains a reception desk. Then: Visitor faces wall as he enters, then turns right angle. Receptionist nearest to entrance has clear view of entry; can turn in 2 directions faces visitor, no way ino office except by R desk.			
If: Any architect's office. Then: Kitchen near receptionist, breakplace in center of office where all circulation joins & BETW. All workplaces and entrance, library niche can be used as breakplace but should be opposite BP if have both, breakplace near R & K.			
If: Office where partners and staff are in danger of being separated. Then: Common circulation for each and staff and partners work together in teams in drawing office.			
If: Any architect's office. Then: Library is equipped with carrels for individual study & is large enough to store books and materials. Open on one side of main circulation route. Space large enough for 1/3 maximum office staff at any time.			
If: Any architect's office. Then: Conference room just off main circulation route, entrance not through workplace, receptionist can give easy directions to it, distractions controllable to and from workplace.			
If: Any architect's office. Then: Cluster workplace tables in work groups for any size job. Semi transparent screens drop from ceiling grid enable any group to totally enclose itself.			
If: Any architect's office. Then: Option for closure on at least 2 sides of each workplace. Use existing walls or screens.			

2. Combination of patterns
Local condition—
Example A: Small office
Local condition—
Example B: Medium office

The Architects' offices examples show that local conditions (three existing structural shells in this case) affect the order in which patterns are used and that individual patterns vary where applied in different circumstances.

1. Entrance facade has transparent surfaces on either side of *door* and/or door can be transparent also.

2. A part of the display area in waiting space explains architect's design approach.

3. Visitor faces wall as he enters. Then turns right angle. Receptionist nearest to entrance has clear view of entry; can turn in 2 directions faces visitor, no way into office except by R desk.

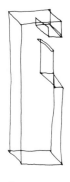   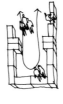 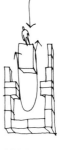 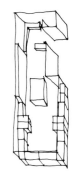

A 1,3 1,3,8 1,3,8,6 1,3,8,6,9 1,3,8,6,9 +

  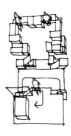  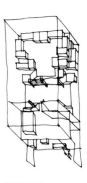

B 6,13 6,13,9 6,13,9,8 6,13,9,8 +

4. Route from waiting area to conference room includes whole view of office.

5. Kitchen near receptionist, breakplace in center of office where all circulation joins and between all workplaces and entrance, library niche can be used as breakplace but should be opposite BP if have both, breakplace near R & K.

6. Common circulation for each and staff and partners work together in teams in drawing office.

7. Central location for library shelves on main circulation route.

8. Library is equipped with carrels for individual study and is large enough to store books and materials. Open on one side of main circulation route. Space large enough for 1/3 maximum office staff at any time.

9. Conference room just off main circulation route, entrance not through workplace, receptionist can give easy directions to it, distractions controllable to and from workplace.

10. Destroy all non-current drawings; use microfilm and store in library provision for scanning in ind. study space in library.

11. Common circulation for partners and staff; partners and staff work together in teams in office (see pattern 6).

12. Cluster workplace tables in work groups, for any size job. Semi transparent screens drop from ceiling grid enable any group to totally enclose itself.

13. Option for closure on at least 2 sides of each workplace. Use existing walls or screens.

14. Provide two surfaces as shown.

15. Provide for slide out surface as shown.

16. Provide for quick reference (technical) books as shown.

17. Provide adjustable drawing surface as shown.

18. Provide for a 4′ minimum back up space as shown.

19. Provide for range of acceptable work-place layouts—workplaces rearrangeable.

20. Provide flat file (4′ × 5′ × 4′) under layout surfaces whenever 2 layout tables come together. One layout table must belong to partner.

0   5   15   30

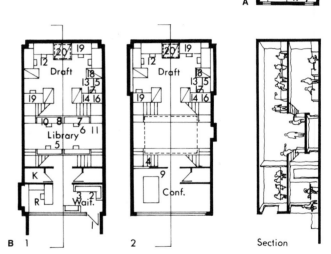

B   1   2   Section

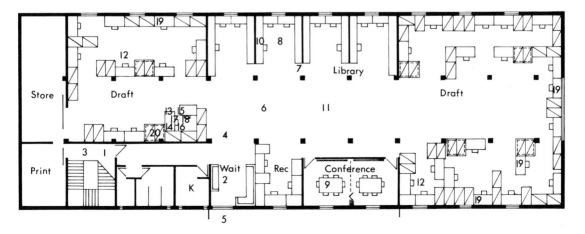

Numbers	Topic	Problem	Tendencies conflicting
3	Entrances to banks	Banks are anxious that people should feel at ease when coming off the street.	1. Banks want people to feel free to stand around without interception by receptionists or other checking devices. 2. People want to locate quickly the part of the bank they are looking for.
4	Bank forums	Banks want to guide but not propel people towards their services.	1. Banks want people to feel free to enter. 2. People demonstrate the desire to hesitate a little before launching into their business.
6	Writing out and calculations by customers	Banks want to permit people to write out checks etc. but don't want blocked circulation.	1. People write out checks etc. after they have entered the bank. 2. Banks don't want such people blocking free circulation.
8	Internal circulation	Banks permit the public to enter freely but want to limit their access to certain sections of the bank.	1. Public circulates freely unless checked. 2. Bank staff wish to go about their business without distraction from unauthorised public.
9	Bank officers and the public	Banks want to attract the public to their officers but control access.	1. Banks want public to feel free to talk to its officers. 2. Public may either miss altogether or inundate officers.
10	Tellers and the public	Banks want to attract the public to their tellers and yet ensure security.	1. Banks want public to feel easy and friendly when dealing with tellers. 2. Banks want to protect their tellers and cash.
13	Contact between officers	Bank officers need to be separate from each other and yet keep in contact.	1. Bank officers deal with limited ranges of decisions and may wish to pass a problem to a colleague quickly and without fuss. 2. Public wants privacy in dealings with bank officers.
14	Tellers and administration	Tellers need to be in contact with both the public and bank administration.	1. Tellers deal with public. 2. Tellers seek records, statements, etc. from administration constantly. 3. Administration supervises tellers.

4. Patterns and transformations for banks

	A	B
1. Public enters the bank without check. 2. Entrance point permits an overview of all bank services. 3. All bank services are clearly marked and distinct from one another.		
1. Public enters bank without check. 2. Waiting or hesitating space is provided both immediately outside and inside the bank. 3. Exhibits may be used to mask hesitation.		
1. Writing space is provided near the entrance but in a position out of the main flow of circulation and which does not impede vision.		
1. Clearly defined circulation for public. 2. Entirely separate circulation for staff.		
1. Clear visual link between public and officers. 2. Distinct separation between officers area and public forum. 3. Guides stationed on border to sanction access to officers.		
1. 4' 6" high continuous bench 2' wide separates public and tellers. 2. Tellers can control moveable and lockable cash boxes.		
1. Bank officers are open to each other as well as to the public. 2. Sufficient separation between officers to ensure private individual dealings.		
1. Tellers are sandwiched between public and administration.		

5. Combination of patterns

Example A: Formal scheme

Example B: Formal scheme

The Bank examples show that the same patterns combine in the same circumstances (1 structural shell) in different ways. Two different formal schemes (two variations of pattern 8) influence the way in which shapeless pattern material can be organized in the design process.

1. Banks on corners or on other conspicuous sites (at a certain frequency). Sidewalk and entrance to bank is designed to permit loitering.

2. Public may glimpse bank activities from outside but are not permitted to register any great detail.
Certain bank activities are screened from the public eye.

3. Public enters the bank without check. Entrance point permits an overview of all bank services.
All bank services are clearly marked and distinct from one another.

4. Public enters bank without check. Waiting or hesitating space is provided both immediately outside and inside the bank.
Exhibits may be used to mask hesitation.

5. Counter design permits variation·in number of tellers. Space provided for lines of 6 but no more.
Customer at entrance point can survey all lines equally easily and select the shortest.

6. Writing space is provided near the entrance but in a position out of the main flow of circulation and which does not impede vision.

7. More than enough space and height is provided in the public part of the bank. Materials are chosen which connotate richness.
A limit is set to both space extravagance and richness in accordance with public notation of what is fitting.

8. Clearly defined circulation for public. Entirely separate circulation for staff.

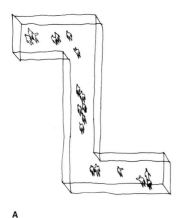

A

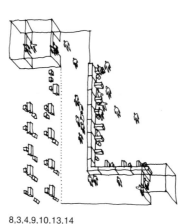

8,3,4,9,10,13,14

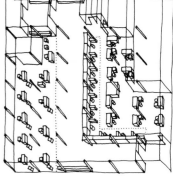

8,3,4,9,10,13,14+

B

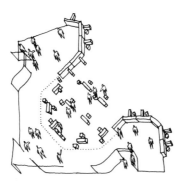

8,3,4,9,10,13,14

8,3,4,9,10,13,14+

9. Clear visual link between public and officers.
Distinct separation between officers area and public forum.
Guides stationed on border to sanction access to officers.

10. 4'6" high continuous bench 2' wide separates public and tellers.
Tellers can control moveable and lockable cash boxes.

11. Security is achieved by appropriate low barriers and also by overall openness and visibility.

12. Vault is near entrance. Vault is easily visible at night from outside the bank for police checks.

13. Bank officers are open to each other as well as to the public.
Sufficient separation between officers to ensure private individual dealings.

14. Tellers are sandwiched between public and administration.

15. Officers may be separated from administration but no request for a piece of information whether requested by telephone or secretary should be the cause of delay.

16. Officers are arranged in rank order. Space and equipment is sufficient to indicate that officers are of managerial status.

17. A hidden rest area is provided where staff can go occasionally to relax or eat lunch or exchange informal conversation.

6. Final configurations—banks

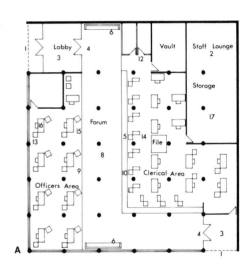

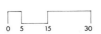

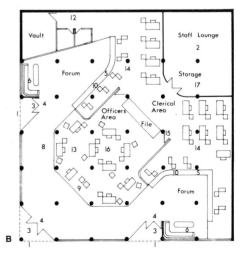

31 On the Relation of Form to Behavior

Comments on the papers by Brolin and Zeisel, Ward, and Duffy and Torrey

Charles W. Rusch

Department of Architecture
University of California
Berkeley, California

Charles W. Rusch was a Fellow at the Center for Advanced Study at the University of Illinois when this commentary was written. The support of the Center, both for the time to prepare this commentary and for the financial support to attend the DMG Conference, is gratefully acknowledged.

There is a kind of fantasy which surrounds the world of design research into which I slip occasionally when I read a collection of papers such as the previous three by Brolin and Zeisel, Ward, Duffy and Torrey. It is a fantasy whose mother is Utopian Planning and whose father is the Manifest Destiny of Physical Determinancy. It is usually triggered by a catchy phrase like "therapeutic environment," or "the realization of the ideal of human freedom," or "the education of attention," and slowly I feel myself filling with a heady sense of omnipotence. My hands are drawn inexplicably toward a control panel and I begin to manipulate the variables of BEHAVIORAL DESIGN. I notice as I turn down the knobs marked "conflict" that the red ink rises in the Human Freedom tube. "It seems to be working," I think to myself. When I reach over the partition and move the seats closer in the model of the group therapy room, the "Mental Health" needle begins to swing from "crusty" over toward "mildly pleasant." I draw a baseball diamond in the dust under the teen-agers' balconies, and the "Excitement" button begins flashing in the urban ghetto.

The fantasy picks up speed and I find myself moving through a landscape. I pass a sign marked, "Relax: Designed Environment Ahead." But before I have time to relax, I feel the tension draining out of me, my brow unfurls, a smile begins to work on the corners of my mouth. I seem to be following a clearly marked dashed line which appears to be on the Edge of a District. I notice that the texture gradient on the far side of the hash-marks is of a higher density, and I am comforted. I move smoothly along through a conflict-free environment, my perceptual attention being guided easily from

Landmark to Node to Landmark, my heightened hypereducated visual awareness never bored, never overloaded by the unfolding sequence of spatial variety and the interacting rhythm of illumination gradients and simultaneous color contrasts.

It is a litter-free environment where supergraphics has replaced the billboard, and Smokey-the-Bear has retired to the controlled microclimate of the Land of Sky-Blue Waters. All the banks look like banks, the libraries like libraries, the hot-dog stands like hot-dogs, and the residential areas like Italian hill villages. A glance at any building is sufficient to understand immediately not only the hierarchy of its internal functions but the percentages of its budget which were devoted to structure, heating, and air conditioning. All this information, of course, flows rapidly in and out of my attention as the latter is triggered by perceptual cues; my train of thought is never interrupted nor are my interactions and conversations with other people.

At last, with never a moment's disorientation, I arrive at my destination, some sort of high-level conference. There are, of course, exactly eight people present, the content of our conversation flows easily, and communication is good. Apparently the seats in our Conversation Unit are perfectly spaced, and the lighting level is correct. I notice that as two participants begin what could become a heated exchange, their seats slide out slightly from the rest of the group, and the light level is raised several footcandles.

High-level thoughts course through my mind. "Life is good." "Human freedom is a profound idea." "Therapy by design," I like that . . . "therapy by DESIGN!" Suddenly, the fantasy breaks, the jackhammer under my study window tears simultaneously into the pavement and my mood. I surface for air from the bottom of my think-tank.

If one is willing to probe not too deeply into the finer levels of architectural theory, the conclusion can be reached rather quickly that there are, after all, only three basically different aspects to the architectural design problem:
1. Structural and environmental control, or structure and mechanics, or what Norberg-Schulz[1] calls "physical control."
2. Functional or behavioral satisfaction, or the study of the interaction between form and overt behavioral response. Norberg-Schulz breaks this category into two parts: functional frame and social milieu, but the two seem to be collapsing today, and are becoming the same problem.
3. Affect and signification, or what the designed environment means, what emotions it evokes in people—connotative response as opposed to overt behavioral response. Norberg-Schulz calls this category cultural symbolization: how the forms act symbolically within our culture. This category includes the realm of aesthetic response, but that can only be part of it because there are many levels of meaning in experience.

Of these three subproblems, we are so much in command of the first, physical control, that it generally seems uninteresting to architects, and they usually turn it over to engineers to handle. That is not to say, however, that its potential excitement has been exhausted; witness the work of Nervi, Fuller, Otto, and Ehrenkrantz. The third problem of affect and signification has barely been scratched today except in the traditional tacit design-studio sense, and in the beginning attempt by Robert Venturi and Chuck Moore to use the historical meanings of forms with an explicit connotative intent. Thus it seems that the major interest and effort in architecture today falls within subproblem two, functional and behavioral control. What used to be just considerations of circulation, proximity relations, and space utilization, now includes ergonomics, proxemics, and countless studies of such subjects as path-choosing, large and small group dynamics, the various subcultural life-styles of the dorm and the ghetto, and many, many more.

It is possible to get a sense of how far we have come in the last two thousand years of architectural theory when you compare the above three aspects of the architectural problem to Vitruvius's categories of "firmness, commodity, and delight." Furthermore, if the intent of architectural theory is to clarify for us our present actions and future intentions, then the differentiation of the global term "commodity" into "functional and behavioral satis-

1. Christian Norberg-Schulz, *Intentions in Architecture*.

faction'' seems to have yielded us little in the way of clarification. It has been my experience that much confusion underlies our understanding of the form/behavior relation. Let us explore this confusion.

First of all, what are our intentions in trying to understand the relation of form to behavior? Is it our intention to try to control behavior by the manipulation of environmental form? Are we trying to change people's behavior, subliminally, outside of their awareness? Are we trying to control behavior *within* their awareness and consent? Can an environment be ''therapeutic'' in the sense that it helps to cure sickness or bring happiness, and is it our intention to design such environments?

By way of answering these questions, let us first dismiss the idea that we can ever design an environment which will be in any significant way ''therapeutic,'' nor should we claim that the users of a design are ''happier,'' ''get along better,'' or ''are better adjusted,'' *because of the design.* There is nothing we can say about someone's internal state of satisfaction or health which can be causally related to his interaction with the physical environment. What we *can* observe, measure, predict, and make claims about is overt behavioral response to objects and relationships in the physical environment. Thus, by means of ergonomics, proxemics, and such techniques we can claim the ability to reduce by design a person's conflict with the objects or people in his environment (and the ability to measure that reduction by observing his overt behavior), but we cannot claim to reduce any internal conflicts he may also have. In other words, environmental design cannot buy happiness any more than money can.

''But,'' you say, ''like money, it helps,'' and of course as designers we all believe that it does, but now we are speaking of personal belief, which is hardly the material for predictive models or behavioral research. Even within the realm of personal belief, my own assumptions about the therapeutic benefits of design are cautious. Along with Tony Ward, I believe that careful design of the functional relations of one's environment can do much in the way of reducing the number of frustrations one encounters in a day, but the effect of frustration reduction upon mental health can only be conjectural.

Second, let us lay to rest the hope that we shall someday make meaningful correlations between the environmental variables and a person's mood or state of well-being. Research that attempts to relate texture gradients along a section of highway to subjective responses to questions like ''How did you like that last stretch of highway?'' is doomed either to failure or triviality. Thoughts and moods are largely the result of internal need and tension states, and the environment is turned on and off at will. We perceptually structure our environment much more than it structures us. This is not to say that we cannot obtain subjective impressions or images of designed objects or environments; we can and have, but we cannot say that these impressions have anything to do with mood or well-being. In other words, a well-designed plaza or workspace or landscape might in one case serve to reinforce a good mood (but not change it), and in another case have no effect on, or even reinforce, a bad mood. If state of well-being is largely internal in origin, then we cannot expect to find any predictable significant effect of the environment upon it.

Third, let us dismiss the idea that we can control a person's attention by the manipulation of perceptual cues. It is as impossible to make someone attend to some object or quality in the environment as it is to make a horse drink water. Sartre argues convincingly that at any one moment in time we can attend to either the exterior perceptual world or the inner conceptual world, but never both at the same time.[2] What a person attends to at any one moment is up to that person and has little to do with his physical environment itself (unless it is threatening in some way, which is hardly a worthwhile design

---

2. Jean-Paul Sartre, *The Psychology of the Imagination*, pp. 123–156.

goal). The classic example of a dominant internal attention is the absent-minded professor, who is so inwardly turned on to his own thoughts that he almost never allows the physical environment to intrude. So the designer who thinks he can lead people's attention around by sophisticated manipulations of the environment is just fooling himself and wasting his time; control of attention is the prerogative of the individual and not amenable to design.

Oddly enough, responses that are amenable to design manipulation are those which take place *outside* of one's awareness, and I believe this area to portend the most fruitful joint effort between sociologist and designer. Thus by minutely observing people choosing paths we can come to some conclusions about their behavioral path-choosing tendencies. Then, should we desire, we could design a system of paths to serve, but not change, those tendencies. In that sense, we would be leading people through the environment by manipulating perceptual cues, but in this case the behavior is outside of their awareness and within very restricted limits. If we try to go beyond those limits, the individual will shift into environmental awareness and take corrective action. So in effect this power of control is given to us under the conditions of tacit consent, and if that consent is removed so is our power of control.

However, you might be able to think of examples where the individual himself is unaware of the limits of his consent, in which case "subliminal" control of behavior would become a reality, and the individual could then be led around by manipulating his behavioral tendencies by design. I can think of this possibly occurring in small group dynamics, for example. Of course, the more people become aware of such possibilities the harder such acts of control will be to accomplish, since they rely upon tacit consent.

Fourth, if control of behavior is possible on this basis, then on moral grounds we should reject its use and limit ourselves to serving or satisfying behavior rather than controlling it. The state of the art being what it is today, however, I think concern over the possibility of control of behavior by design is perhaps premature.

Turning finally to the papers by Brolin and Zeisel, Ward, and Duffy and Torrey, I think there is little disagreement among them. Despite Ward's title of "Notes on a Therapeutic Environment," his proposal is basically one of *serving* behavioral tendencies and conflict reduction, as are both of the others. The Brolin and Zeisel paper concentrates primarily on the translation of social research into useful design statements and proposals. Significantly, the sociologist they found most useful is Gans[3] who operates from just the intense personal observation base Ward so strongly recommends. Other examples of similar work would be that of the anthropologists Hall and Lewis,[4] particularly the latter, whose histories of Mexican and Puerto Rican life styles should prove a rich source of behavioral tendencies for those interested in designing for "the culture of poverty." Duffy and Torrey, on the other hand, describe a much neater method of translating the observed behavioral information and its physical design requirements into prototypical form and variations than the other authors, who were far too cursory on this phase of the problem.[5]

What seems like a disagreement erupts with Ward's "dilemma" and ultimate rejection of objectivity, but what he is calling for is not a return to the personalized base of intuitive design but an objectivity with a finer screen. It takes several sieves to sort gravel into more than two sizes of rocks. The finer the screen, the finer discriminations it can make between sizes of

3. Herbert J. Gans, *The Urban Villagers.*
4. Edward T. Hall, *The Hidden Dimension,* and Oscar Lewis, *The Children of Sánchez* and *La Vida.*
5. For a clearly stated example of the pattern language in use, see Christopher Alexander, Sara Ishikawa, and Murray Silverstein *A Pattern Language Which Generates Multi-Service Centers.*

pebbles. All the authors in this section recommend not relying exclusively upon the "old" sociological tools of survey questionnaire and interview techniques; they call for the additional information of the keen observer. Some American sociologists and anthropologists are already providing such information.

With the resolution of Ward's dilemma by the modern sociologist, I find the authors on a common philosophical and research base, their slight differences in approach complementing one another rather than conflicting, and all attacking real issues in the realm of functional and behavioral satisfaction.

Epilogue

Lest the ending be unduly happy, however, I must tell you briefly about another fantasy of mine. It is a nightmarish kind of tale, triggered by words like "population explosion" or "urban crisis," and I find myself slipping down into the dark dank domicile of the Dire Predictors, that species of Giant Spiders who dwell in the land of the REAL WORLD. It is an exhausting fantasy which finds me continuously flailing away at the webbing of these spiders some of which, incredible as it may seem, are larger than automobiles.

I am trying to free my friends, the Dwarfs, who are caught in the spiders' webs, trussed around and around until they can barely move or breathe. Fortunately, I am protected by a magic spell of invisibility as long as I wear my college ring. My sword, which I have named "Academic Clarity" is honed razor sharp by years of research and study, before The Fall.

But it seems that for every strand I cut, two pop back in its place; the battle is exhausting. My foes are all around me; giant beasts with names like "Bad Taste," "Litter," "Traffic Snarls," "Air Pollution," "Budgetary Constraint," "Billboard Lobby," "Dollar Drain," and on and on. My friends, the Dwarfs, are tied high in the webs, which I must climb to free them. Over there is "Good Design," over here "Human Freedom," there "Integration," here "Gun Control."

Occasionally, I hack my way through the tangle to free my friend "Systems Analysis," but no sooner is he free than the tangle gets worse than ever, and he is bound up once again. Once I got close enough to a giant spider named "Over Population" to run Academic Clarity, with a fantastic thrust, into his innards, but instead of expiring with a sigh, he exploded like a lanced boil, and I found myself covered with a mess of half-digested webbing such as I had never seen before. Another time I was cutting through to free a Dwarf named Ralph Nader, but he was so bound up by red webbing from a Spider named "Bureaucratic Red Tape" that I could neither reach him nor hear him.

And so the fantasy goes. I, on the one hand, am cutting a path through the webbing to free my friends, only to have the path closed behind me, on the other hand, in a worse tangle than before, by those Giant Spiders the Dire Predictors.[6]

6. For the original version of this tale, see J. R. R. Tolkien, *The Hobbit* (New York: Ballantine Books, 1966), pp. 140–166.

9 Major Comprehensive Approaches to Design and Planning

One of the important outcomes of the development of design and planning methodology has been the emergence of several major theories. In architecture, as the field has developed toward a science allied more with the behavioral sciences than with the arts, many of its members have left behind, perhaps prematurely, the postwar philosophies of CIAM, the "New Humanism," Corbusier, Kahn, and Team 10. Those were primarily philosophies of goals, of form, or of the end-product of the design process, and only to a limited extent were they theories of the process of designing itself. Planning, in emerging from ad hoc opportunism at the turn of the century to an official status in metropolitan and federal agencies and a greater alliance with the social, economic, and political sciences, has had parallel philosophies of form but, being perhaps less encumbered by dogma, has had a slightly more extensive history of process and methodology.

Both of these fields, along with industrial design and, more recently, landscape architecture and urban design, have cherished, pursued, and transferred to generations of designers and planners their own classical models of process, seldom explicit but always unquestioningly held and followed. But these classical models have come under heavy attack for being unable to handle the environmental crises facing their respective fields.

As has been the case in the natural sciences, dissatisfaction with traditional approaches has led to the development of new theories. Although several of the new theories have received wide acceptance and attracted enduring groups of adherents and although they have been sufficiently open-ended to suggest all sorts of questions for other researchers to resolve, we hesitate to refer to any of them as "paradigms," a term used by Kuhn and others in the natural sciences to refer to the scientific revolutions brought on by such geniuses as Newton, Lavoisier, and Einstein. At the present time in environmental design and planning, no theory seems to command the surity of its followers nor hold such supremacy as to be considered a new paradigm. As a science, design and planning methodology is still in a preparadigmatic stage. Indeed the question may be asked (and is asked in this section) whether in a world of continually and rapidly changing values any one theory of the process of design and planning need survive beyond a few years. The mettle of the theory may lie in its heuristic value for solving current problems while supporting further research and theory. As our views of environmental problems become broader and deeper, so must our theories of how to solve them.

Nevertheless there are several major theories worth the attention of serious students of the field. There is a general feeling that these theories are competitive, that if you believe in one you can't believe in any other, that there is only one best way to solve environmental problems. Reflection reveals, however, that many of the current theories do not compete. Various observers have noted that a theory of planning aimed, for example, at solving a problem with well-defined goals may be very different from a theory aimed at a problem where the goals are ill-defined and goals and solution emerge simultaneously. Similarly, a theory for a problem demanding small, successive changes in the allocation of resources may be different from a theory for introducing major physical innovations. Problems in each of these realms exist. Many theories are needed, not just one.

Since the existing major theories seem to have more in common than in difference and since insights and specific methods associated with each seem to have value for all, a comparative analysis is suggested and may be of the greatest value.

Four major theories are presented in this section, each of which pertains to several areas—industrial design, architecture and urban design, engineering, and urban and regional planning. Furthermore, this collection of general theories gives alternative frameworks by which to interpret and understand many of the specific methods in the rest of the volume.

At the Conference the commentary was intended for only one paper, but because it questions whether it is possible to describe general problem-solving processes, it may be read in relation to all the papers in this section.

For references and further comparison, the energetic reader will find gateways to other principal theories in section A9 of the bibliography at the end of the volume.

32 An Overview of the Structure of the Design Process

L. Bruce Archer

Industrial Design (Engineering)
Research Unit
Royal College of Art
London, England

L. Bruce Archer is Head of the Industrial Design (Engineering) Research Unit of the Royal College of Art. He was born in England and trained as a mechanical engineering designer at the Northampton Polytechnic Institute in London. He spent many years in industry as an engineering designer before beginning teaching and research into design methods. He was a Guest Professor at the Hochschule für Gestaltung at Ulm in 1960–1961, then returned to London to set up and head the Research Unit at the Royal College. He received the Kaufmann International Design Award in 1964. He has written and lectured internationally on design subjects. His major work is *Systematic Method for Designers*. The present paper is based on his *The Structure of Design Processes*, to which the reader is referred. Parts of this paper also appear in Anthony Ward and Geoffrey Broadbent, eds., *Design Methods in Architecture*, and are reprinted with permission. Anthony Ward's assistance in editing this paper is gratefully acknowledged by the editor.

A logical model of the design process is developed and a terminology and notation are adopted which are intended to be compatible with the neighboring disciplines of management science and operations research and upon which case study analyses might be based. Many of the concepts and techniques presented are derived from these disciplines. The nature of the act of designing is discussed, and the range of techniques and disciplines which might be employed at various stages in design are referred to in general terms. There is no suggestion that all design should be conducted according to a given formula, only that the logic of design may be perceived better against the background of a common framework. Laws that are thought to connect phenomena common to most design problems are indicated. A systematic model of the design process and its operational counterpart are outlined and extended to include the overall design program. Rating scales and merit curves are proposed and the rated-objective merit-index technique is discussed. It is hoped that the model, terminology, and notation presented will facilitate the accumulation of the case-study data and the derivation of the more precise laws upon which an emergent science of design must be based.

This thesis attempts to set up a framework within which the set of skills, sensibilities, and intellectual disciplines that constitute the art of design might logically be related to form the basis of a science of design. No attempt is made to distinguish between architectural, urban, engineering, and industrial design. Indeed, it is an essential element in the philosophy underlying this thesis that the logical nature of the act of designing is largely independent of the character of the thing designed. By the same token, no attempt is made here to define "good design." The argument presented is concerned with the theory of navigating toward a chosen destination rather than with the identity or merit of the destination itself.

The Nature of the Act of Designing
Man sets different values on different conditions. Those values may vary from time to time.[1] When a man discerns that there is a discrepancy between a condition as it is and the condition as he would like it to be, he experiences discontent. Should the feeling of discontent be sufficiently strong, he takes action calculated to change the condition so that it more nearly approximates what he desires. The condition giving rise to desire is here described as a

---

1. The unavoidability of reference to a value system in defining objectives is well argued on p. 29 of Irwin D. J. Bross, *Design for Decision*. The terms used in the present paper also owe a great deal to those used in Horst Rittel, *The Universe of Design*.

property (of the environment); the attainment of a state of satisfaction in response to that property is described as a *goal-directed activity*.

When the action appropriate to the correction of a particular unsatisfactory condition is not apparent, a problem exists, which may be concerned with the identification of the nature of the improvement required or with the identification of the means for achieving it, or both.

The presence of the unsolved problem, acting as a barrier to the achievement of the goal, is itself an undesirable condition, requiring action to remove it. The problem-solving activity is thus itself a goal-directed activity.[2]

Design may be defined as "to conceive the idea for and prepare a description of a proposed system, artifact, or aggregation of artifacts." The condition in which the designer would like to be is that in which he can offer an adequate description of the proposed system or artifact. The activity of getting into this condition is a goal-directed activity, and where (as is usual) the nature of the design idea and its development is not immediately apparent, a problem exists. The activity of designing is thus a goal-directed activity and normally a goal-directed problem-solving activity.[3] The properties which are required to be exhibited by the proposed artifact are defined by the goals or objectives of the problem. The details of the design are the designer's conclusions as to the means by which those properties may be provided.

1. A goal nominates a property, indicates the direction in which changes would be for the better, and identifies a threshold between acceptable and unacceptable states.

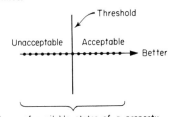

Range of available states of a property

In a goal-directed problem-solving activity, all the properties required to be present in the end result may be thought of as having existed, in varying degrees, in the prior, unsatisfactory situation. The goals of the activity are thus to cause those properties to be present to a satisfactory degree, or to as high a degree as possible. Each goal thus nominates a property, indicates the direction in which changes would be for the "good," and identifies a threshold between "good enough" and "not good enough," as shown in Figure 1.

Since the properties referred to may be of many different kinds, and since they may be subject to different scales and units of measurement, it is convenient to introduce a convention or form of notation[4] by which they may be more uniformly expressed:

G signifies a goal or objective
P signifies a property or condition
G(y) signifies a particular degree of fulfillment of a goal
P(x) signifies a particular state of a property of a goal
P(u) signifies the ideal state of *P* in respect to a given goal
P(l) signifies a minimum acceptable state of *P*
P(m) signifies a maximum acceptable state of *P*
P(v) signifies a state of *P* which represents total lack of fulfillment of a goal

It is clear that the degree *y* of fulfillment of a goal *G* is a dependent variable, controlled by the state *x* of the property *P* exhibited in the solution,[5] that is:

$G(y) = f[P(x)]$.

P(x) is expressed according to whatever scale is most appropriate to the property concerned (dimensions are expressed in inches or centimeters,

2. See David W. Miller and Martin K. Starr, *Executive Decisions and Operations Research.*
3. Russell L. Ackoff, *Scientific Method: Optimizing Applied Research Decisions,* describes design problems as falling into the general class of developmental problems, which he defines similarly.
4. Somewhat similar definitions and notation are used in separate chapters by Russell L. Ackoff and C. West Churchman in Ackoff, ed., *Progress in Operations Research,* Vol. 1. See also R. Duncan Luce and Howard Raiffa, *Games and Decisions,* considered by some to be the best work on value theory.
5. Nonmathematicians are often greatly put off by mathematical notation. Any reader who shares this feeling is invited to try the trick of reading out in the mind's ear the full verbal equivalent of each cipher, thus: "The degree *y* of satisfaction of objective *G* is some function *f* of the state *x* of property *P.*"

2a. The degree of fulfillment of a goal is a dependent variable, governed by the state of its associated property.

2b. A given design may fulfill two simultaneous goals to the same or differing degrees.

2c. The degrees to which two alternative designs fulfill two simultaneous goals can be compared with the ideal degree of fulfillment.

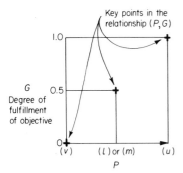

Key points in the relationship (P, G)

G
Degree of fulfillment of objective

States of a property

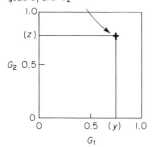

Degree $\left[G_1(y), G_2(z)\right]$ of fulfillment by design i of two simultaneous goals G_1 and G_2

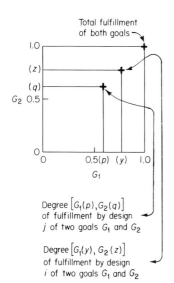

Total fulfillment of both goals

Degree $\left[G_1(p), G_2(q)\right]$ of fulfillment by design j of two goals G_1 and G_2

Degree $\left[G_1(y), G_2(z)\right]$ of fulfillment by design i of two goals G_1 and G_2

weight in pounds or kilograms, time in seconds, minutes, and hours). According to the conventions adopted here, $G(y)$ is always expressed on the scale:

$G(y) = 0$ (zero) when there is total lack of fulfillment of the objective
$G(y) = 0.5$ when the related property is at the threshold between fulfilling and not fulfilling the objective
$G(y) = 1.0$ (unity) when there is total fulfillment of the objective.

Moreover, according to this convention, the key states of a property P defined above are always related to the key values of degree of fulfillment of its related objective G in the following way, as also when in the left side of Figure 2.

when $P(x) = P(u)$ then $G(y) = 1.0$
when $P(x) = P(m)$
or $P(x) = P(l)$ $\left.\right\}$ then $G(y) = 0.5$
when $P(x) = P(v)$ then $G(y) = 0$

The states of these properties may vary continuously along scales based on some agreed unit or interval. Such scales are known as *ratio scales* or *interval scales*.[6] Not all properties can be expressed on interval scales. Beauty, convenience, and importance are examples; there are no units with which ratio scales could be constructed. However, in such cases it is usually possible to compare designs and to list them in descending order of merit, according to the property concerned. This constitutes an *ordinal scale*, and the act of constructing the list is called *ranking*.[7]

Few problems are concerned only with the fulfillment of a single objective. Any solution will fulfill various objectives in varying degrees. In order to find some way of illustrating the interdependence of the degrees to which a given design will fulfill two or more coexisting objectives, some further notation must be introduced:

G_n signifies a given goal
P_n signifies a given property
i signifies a given design
j signifies an alternative design
$P(w)$ signifies a particular state of a property (alternative to x)
$G(z)$ signifies a particular degree of fulfillment of goal (alternative to y)

Thus a given design i will exhibit state x of property P_1 and state w of property P_2, fulfilling objective G_1 to degree y and objective G_2 to degree z. This can be illustrated according to the convention of coordinates as shown in the center of Figure 2. The performance of two or more designs in respect of two coexisting objectives may be indicated in a similar manner, shown on the right of Figure 2.

Two goals coexisting in a problem may be referring (though in different ways) to the same property in the desired end result. For example, the bed of a machine tool may be required to be extremely stiff not only to maintain the alignment of slides and spindles but also to prevent the transfer of working loads to weak structural members. The property of stiffness serves two objectives. In this case the better states of the property lie in the same direction, greater stiffness. These two objectives may be described as *cooperating objectives*. On the other hand, two coexisting objectives may refer to the same property but seek opposite ideal states. For example, a piece of equip-

---

6. Stanley S. Stevens in "On the Theory of Scales of Measurement," recognizes ratio scales (having a nonarbitrary zero and a constant unit of measurement), interval scales (having an arbitrary origin and a unit assumed to be constant), ordinal scales (having an order but no unit of measurement), and nominal scales (having identities but neither order nor measurement). See also Clyde H. Coombs, "Psychological Scaling Without a Unit of Measurement."

7. The rankable, rather than the quantifiable, basis of perceptual and aesthetic criteria is argued by Eric H. Gombrich, *Art and Illusion*. Techniques for ranking and testing the validity of rankings are well described in M. J. Maroney, *Facts from Figures*.

ment might need to be as light as possible in order to be portable but as heavy as possible in order to be stable in use. Such objectives may be referred to as *opposing objectives*. Or again, two objectives may refer to different properties in the end product (say, durability and cost) but these properties may themselves be interdependent, so that the fulfillment of the objectives, too, becomes effectively interdependent. Some objectives may, of course, be only distantly connected. These relations are diagrammed in Figure 3.

Where objectives are dependent, the locus of the points of coincidental states of a property or properties will mark out a curve of feasible mutual states, as shown on the left side of Figure 4. The limiting states of the properties concerned may be similarly set out. The spaces marked off by these limits indicate the field of mutually acceptable degrees of fulfillment of the coexisting objectives. Any solution whose mutual states of the associated properties lie within this field is an acceptable solution, shown in the center of Figure 4. Where objectives are dependent, the curve of feasible mutual states may be superimposed on the fields of limiting states, as shown on the right.[8] In some cases a section of the curve of feasible mutual states of the properties concerned will lie within the field of mutually acceptable degrees of fulfillment of the objectives. In these cases, feasible and acceptable solutions are available. In other cases there might be no solution which is both feasible and acceptable. The only escape from such a situation is either to move one or both of the limits of acceptability or to introduce some inventive step to change the interrelationship of the objectives. The former course of action constitutes a change in the performance requirements of a design (that is, in solution by negotiation), while the latter constitutes an act of invention (that is, solution by innovation).

Where, as in most problems, there are many more than two objectives, these can be taken pair by pair and expressed in the terms described. In aggregate the interaction of fields of acceptability will constitute an n-dimensional domain of acceptability. This domain may be discontinuous; that is to say, there may be more than one acceptability-space, each bounded by limiting states for various properties, implying that there is more than one distinctive class of acceptable solutions. Similarly, the interdependence of the curves of feasible mutual states will constitute an n-dimensional hypersurface or realm of feasibility. An important prerequisite for an ultimate solution is that at least a portion of the realm of feasibility should intersect the domain of acceptability, producing an arena within which a solution must be found. A 3-dimensional arena is shown in Figure 5.

Thus the act of designing consists in:
1. Agreeing on objectives.
2. Identifying the properties or conditions required by the objectives to be exhibited in and the end result.
3. Determining the relationships between varying states of the properties and the varying degrees of fulfillment of their respective objectives.
4. Establishing the limiting and ideal states of the properties and hence the domain of acceptability implied by the objectives.
5. Identifying the laws controlling the interdependence, if any, of the properties.
6. Ensuring that the interdependence of the properties constitutes a realm of feasibility and that this lies at least in part in the domain of acceptability.
7. Selecting an optimum solution within the arena thus delineated.

The Systematic Model

Where two phenomena are causally related, that is to say, where one phenomenon is caused to occur or to change its state by the introduction or

8. This invokes the techniques of linear programming. See S. Vajda, *An Introduction to Linear Programming and the Theory of Games,* George B. Dantzig, *Linear Programming and Extensions.* See also the AIDA technique (Analysis of Interconnected Decision Areas), referred to in the Travistock Institute's *Interdependence and Uncertainty,* p. 27.

Co-operating goals

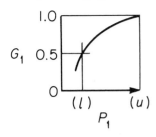

G_1 P_1

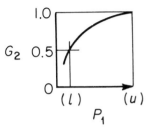

G_2 P_1

Opposing goals

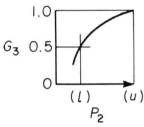

G_3 P_2

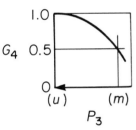

G_4 P_3

3. Two goals referring to the same (or interdependent) properties and pointing to the same ideal states may be referred to as cooperating goals. Two goals referring to the same (or independent) properties and pointing to opposite ideal states may be described as opposing goals.

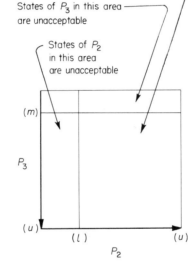

Curve of the functional relationship between (P_2, P_3)

P_3 P_2

States of P_2 and P_3 in this area are acceptable from the points of view of both sets of criteria

States of P_3 in this area are unacceptable

States of P_2 in this area are unacceptable

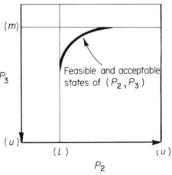

P_3 P_2

Feasible and acceptable states of (P_2, P_3)

4a. Where two properties are interdependent, the locus of the points of coincidental states of the properties determines a curve of feasible mutual states.
4b. The spaces marked off by the limiting states of the properties indicate the field of mutually acceptable states.
4c. The superimposition of the fields of acceptable states of a property upon curves of feasible states determines the range of feasible and acceptable states.

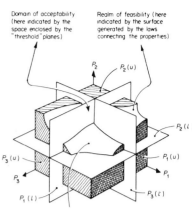

Domain of acceptability (here indicated by the space enclosed by the "threshold" planes)

Realm of feasibility (here indicated by the surface generated by the laws connecting the properties)

Arena for a solution (here indicated by that part of the realm of feasibility which is cut off by the domain of acceptability)

5. The interdependence of the states of the properties constitutes an *n*-dimensional hypersurface or realm of feasibility. The product of the erection of limiting states of the properties is an *n*-dimensional space or domain of acceptability. The superimposition of the domain of acceptability on the realm of feasibility determines the arena within which a solution is to be selected.

change of state of another phenomenon, these two are said to form a *system*.[9] A spring balance, for example, is such a system, since adding a load to the pan causes the spring to compress an appropriate amount. In systems terminology, the causal phenomenon is described as the *input* and the resulting effect is termed the *output*. Where information about, or energy produced by, the output of a system is used to adjust the input (for the purpose of controlling the output), this cycle is called *feedback*.[10] For example, in the case of the spring balance, if the user watches the indicator and controls the amount of, say, sugar poured into the pan until the indicator reaches a desired point, this watch-and-control activity is an example of feedback. This feedback system is shown in Figure 6. Feedback can be exercised through human perception and control, or it can be automated. Thermostats in heating systems and speed governors in engines are examples of automatic feedback.

In many cases, systems are influenced by more than one input and may have more than one output. For example, an electric motor is a system in which the input of electrical energy at a certain voltage and a certain amperage will produce mechanical energy with a particular speed and power. Varying either or both the inputs will result in a variation in either or both the outputs (unless the input variations are self-compensating). A factor which could or does take up one or more of a variety of states is called a variable. Often, certain of the inputs are under the control of an operator or decision-maker (for example, a designer may be able to choose the depth of a beam to be incorporated in a structure), while others are governed by circumstances outside the operator's control (for example, the designer will have no control over the tensile strength of the beam material). The former are described as *decision variables* and the latter as *context variables*.[11] They are shown in Figure 7. Similarly, outputs may consist of those which the decision-maker wishes to control (for example a designer may wish to ensure that a structural beam is capable of bearing a given load) and those to which he is indifferent (for example, the volume of metal in the beam). The former are here described as *relevant outputs* and the latter as *incidental outputs*. These also are shown in Figure 7.

The incidental output of one system, however, might be the context variable of another. For example, the volume of metal which was only an incidental output from a structural system might be a context variable in another system, say, costing or building operations. Where two systems are being handled simultaneously, these two systems can be said to form a larger, or *complex system*. Where one system in a complex of systems produces outputs which affect another in the same complex, it is convenient to regard the decision variable in the first as being also a decision variable in the second. Figure 8 illustrates a complex system.

A design problem or any other sort of problem can be expressed in systems terms.[12] Problem-solving activities were described earlier as being directed toward the provision of certain properties, or certain states of certain properties, in the end result. The problem is thus a system, with the decision variables as input and the properties as output. The laws determining the ways in which given properties vary under the influence of different decisions constitute the external or general laws within which a problem must be solved.

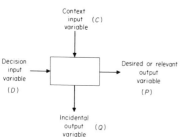

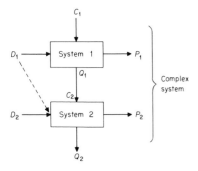

6. The feedback concept in systems theory and the spring balance in systems terms.

7. Some input variables (*C*) may be outside the control of the decision-maker, and some variables (*D*) may be within his control. Some output variables (*P*) will be those which the decision-maker wishes to control, and others (*Q*) may be merely incidental.

8. An incidental output from one system may be a context variable in another. A decision variable in a system that partly controls another system may be regarded as being a decision variable in the second system also.

9. For an admirably clear statement of the systems idea, see W. Ross Ashby, *Introduction to Cybernetics.* See also Kenneth E. Boulding, "General Systems Theory: Skeleton of Science," and Gordon Pask, *An Approach to Cybernetics.*
10. Norbert Wiener's exposition in *Cybernetics* of the concept of feedback as a principle of control, common to machines, animals, and human beings, formed the basis of modern systems theory.
11. Ackoff and Churchman in Ackoff, *Progress in Operations Research.*
12. This is demonstrated for general problems by Ackoff, *Scientific Method,* and by Miller and Starr, *Executive Decisions.* For design problems it is demonstrated by Hugh M. Bowen in a series of articles "Rational Design."

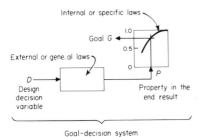

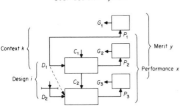

The way in which varying states of a property relate to varying degrees of fulfillment of a goal also constitutes a system, with the property as input and the degree of fulfillment of goal as output. The laws connecting states of properties with degrees of fulfillment of objectives constitute the internal or specific laws of a problem. A complete *goal-decision system* as shown in Figure 9 is therefore a linked pair of systems, where the decision variables control a property and the property controls an objective. In a complex of goal-decision systems, where a decision variable may directly or indirectly control a number of properties, there may be some ambiguity as to how the goal-decision systems should be conceived. For the purposes of this argument, a goal-decision system is constructed so that it contains one and only one objective, so that the system can be identified with, and named after, the objective it contains.

In a complex of goal-decision systems the aim is to select a set of states for the decision variables such that the resulting set of states of the properties satisfy their respective objectives, or that the degree of fulfillment of objectives is optimized.

9. Where a decision variable controls a property and the property controls a degree of fulfillment of a goal, the whole is said to form a goal-decision system. A design problem may be expressed in systems terms.

10. A set of states *i* for the decision variables constitutes a design.

A set of states *x* for the properties constitutes a performance.

A set of states y for the degree of fulfillment of goals constitutes the merit of a performance.

A set of states *k* for the context variables constitutes the context.

The distinctions as to whether an input variable is a decision variable or a context variable, whether or not certain states of a decision variable are accessible to the decision-maker, and whether or not a decision variable is also a property, are all part of the definition of the problem rather than part of the real problem to be handled.[13]

A set of states selected for the decision variables in a particular case constitutes a design proposal or design. If the proposal were to be implemented, the consequence would be a set of states of the properties which might be called the outcome. Strictly speaking, the product as a piece of hardware does not appear until it has been embodied by the set of goal-directed activities to which the problem-solving activities relate. However, since the problem-solving activities are conducted with the end product in mind, these distinctions are difficult to make. The set of states of the properties arising from a proposal will be referred to as its *performance,* and the set of degrees of fulfillment of the objectives appropriate to a particular performance will be referred to as the *merit* of this performance.[14] This is diagrammed in Figure 10 and may be expressed in notation as follows:

Design $i \longrightarrow$ Performance $x \longrightarrow$ Merit y

Design $i \qquad = \{D_1(i), D_2(i) \dots D_n(i)\}$
Performance $x \qquad = \{P_1(x), P_2(x) \dots P_n(x)\}$
Merit $y \qquad = \{G_1(y), G_2(y) \dots G_n(y)\}$

$\{D_1(i), D_2(i) \dots D_n(i)\}$ signifies a set of states *i* for a set of decision variables $D_1, D_2 \dots D_n.$

$\{P_1(x), P_2(x) \dots P_n(x)\}$ signifies a set of states *x* for a set of properties $P_1, P_2 \dots P_n.$

$\{G_1(y), G_2(y) \dots G_n(y)\}$ signifies a set of states y for a set of objectives $G_1, G_2 \dots G_n.$

Similarly, the set of states of the context variables which apply in a given case constitutes the *context* of the problem. It is the combined effects of the proposal and the context which determines the outcome, or performance.

Context $k \longrightarrow$ Performance $x \longrightarrow$ Merit y
Design $i \longrightarrow$

Context $k = \{C_1(k), C_2(k) \dots C_n(k)\}$
$\{C_1(k), C_2(k) \dots C_n(k)\}$ signifies a set of states *k* for a set of context variables $C_1, C_2 \dots C_n.$

---

13. This distinction between the situation in the real world and the problem-solver's mental concept of what might be done is studied in Ackoff, *Scientific Method,* p. 372 ff.
14. The term "set," as used here, and the notation which follows are in accordance with the conventions of the theory of sets. See Irving Adler, *The New Mathematics,* or Paul R. Halmos, *Naive Set Theory.*

The set of criteria against which performance is measured can be described as the *performance specification*.[15] A performance specification will lay down the properties which the outcome is required to constitute and will indicate the way in which various states of these properties will be regarded as being more or less satisfactory. In other words, it lists the properties and defines the goal/property relationships of Figure 11.

$\{(G_1 = fP_1), (G_2 = fP_2) \ldots (G_n = fP_n)\}$ signifies a performance specification relating to properties $P_1, P_2 \ldots P_n$.

For example, the performance specification for a chair may lay down that it must accommodate people of a prescribed range of statures and build, withstand certain structural tests, sell at less than a certain price, and earn a profit at a certain rate on investment. The design resource will be the set of materials, processes, shapes, finishes, and so on, which the designer has at his discretion. The context will be the characteristics of materials, prices of commodities, and other imponderables which will affect the result, but over which the designer has no control. The design will be the set of decisions (materials, processes, shapes, finishes) that he actually chose. The performance of the design would be range of statures and build of people that the chair (if embodied) would actually accommodate, the tests it would meet, the price at which it would sell, and the profit it would earn. And the merit of this performance would be the degree to which it approached the ideals indicated in the performance specification.

The Rated-Objective Merit-Index Technique

In a particular design problem it may be possible to produce several feasible and acceptable designs. Although it is quite possible for two different designs to exhibit an identical performance, it is more usual for alternative designs to fulfill the given objectives in differing degrees.

Design j ⟶ Performance w ⟶ Merit z
Design (or proposal) $j = \{D_1(j), D_2(j) \ldots D_n(j)\}$
Performance w $\quad = \{P_1(w), P_2(w) \ldots P_n(w)\}$
Merit z $\quad = \{G_1(z), G_2(z) \ldots G_n(z)\}$
where $D_n(j)$ signifies an alternative state j of decision variable D_n (state j being an alternative to state i).

It is also likely that attainment of a satisfactory performance in respect of some objectives will be regarded as more important than the attainment of a satisfactory performance in respect of others. That is to say, the objectives themselves have an order of importance. In a diagram of performance the relative merit of alternative designs may be more readily discerned if the goal-fulfillment scales are arranged in order of importance and the merits of the individual performances are indicated on them as in Figure 12. It is likely that in the case of any two competing designs each will score well on a different set of goals. In general, a solution which scores well on high-ranking goals is to be preferred over one which scores well only on low-ranking ones. On the diagram, comparison is simplified if the points indicating merit for a particular performance are joined. Overall merit can then be evaluated by comparing the resulting merit curves.

In two merit curves a tendency to lie above is better than a tendency to lie below, since according to the conventions adopted the direction called good always points upwards. Similarly, a tendency to a positive slope (northeast to southwest) is better than a tendency to a negative slope (northwest to southeast), since the higher scores should be in the higher-ranking goals. Again, a convex curve (intermediate values tending upwards) is better than a concave curve (intermediate values tending downwards) since the intermediate values score better in the convex curve. These three relations may be seen in Figure 12.

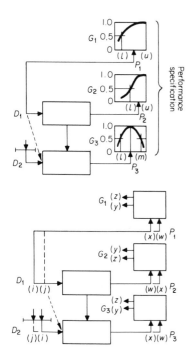

11. A performance specification lists the properties required and defines the relationships between states of the properties and degrees of fulfillment of goal.

Design i might give rise to performances x of merit y.

Design j might give rise to performance w of merit z.

15. Performance specifications (or P-specs) are discussed in J. Christopher Jones, "A Method of Systematic Design."

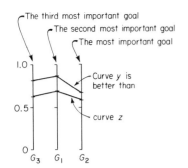

The third most important goal
The second most important goal
The most important goal

Curve y is better than

curve z

G_3 G_1 G_2

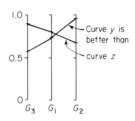

Curve y is better than

curve z

G_3 G_1 G_2

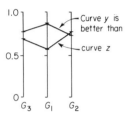

Curve y is better than

curve z

G_3 G_1 G_2

12. A tendency for a merit curve to lie above its fellows is better than a tendency to lie below.
A tendency to a positive slope is better than a tendency to a negative slope.
A tendency to a convex curve is better than a tendency to a concave curve.

Curve y consists only in the points on the G scales (i.e., curve y is the set of points $\left[r_{G_n}, G_n(y) \right]$)

The ideal performance would fulfull every goal completely

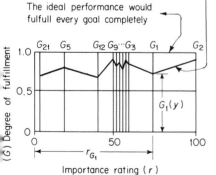

(G) Degree of fulfillment

G_{21} G_5 G_{12} $G_9 \cdots G_3$ G_1 G_2

$G_1(y)$

r_{G_1}

Importance rating (r)

13. A merit curve consists in the points defined by the degrees of fulfillment of goal and the importance rating of each goal. The goal fulfillment scales may be arranged according to a scale of importance.

However, the analysis of these curves is hampered by the fact that in real-world design problems the notational difference in importance between the goal ranked first and the goal ranked second may be regarded by the arbiters as very much greater (or less) than the difference in importance between the goal ranked second and the goal ranked third. Hence a rating scale, such as that employed for the rating of merit in respect of nonquantifiable properties, may also be employed for the rating of importance.

It is convenient to begin by rating the importance of goals on a scale of 0 to 100. Thus, in a project with, say, 40 goals, that which is regarded as over-whelmingly the most important might be rated at 100, the next most important at 75, and most of the others between 60 and 50. A very minor goal might be rated at 5. Two or more goals may take the same rating, where necessary, and the scale may be extended or modified as convenient.

The comparative evaluation of merit curves then becomes simpler, as illustrated in Figure 13. Each curve is fully described by the location of the points on it. The importance scale becomes the horizontal axis, and the merit scale becomes the vertical axis.

r signifies an importance rating (where r is any factor appropriate)
r_{G_n} signifies the importance rating of objective G_n

$\{(r_{G_1}, G_1(y)), (r_{G_2}, G_2(y)) \ldots (r_{G_n}, G_n(y))\}$
  signifies the merit curve y for a set of objectives $G_1, G_2 \ldots G_n$

An ideal overall performance would be one in which each goal is completely fulfilled, that is to say, where

$G_1(y) = 1, G_2(y) = 1 \ldots G_n(y) = 1.$

Hence: curve of ideal performance =

$(r_{G_1}, 1), (r_{G_2}, 1) \ldots (r_{G_n}, 1)$

The relative merits of the performance of two or more designs may be expressed in terms of their departure from the ideal performance. All the criteria for merit comparison are satisfied when the overall *index of merit* of a design is calculated as the ratio of the sum of the degrees of fulfillment of the individual goals, each weighted by its importance rating, to the sum of the ideal degree of fulfillment of objectives, weighted by their importance weighting, namely:

$$M_{iy}(t) = \frac{\Sigma r_{G_n} \cdot G_n(y)}{\Sigma r_{G_n}}$$

where
M signifies an index of merit,
M_{iy} signifies an index of merit M relating to a performance y arising from a proposal i (where i and y are identifying letters or numbers for particular proposals and performances respectively),
$M_{iy}(t)$ signifies a particular value t for an index or merit M_{iy} (where t is a number lying between zero and unity).

In this formulation, overall merit in respect of any given number of goals is rated on the scale zero-to-unity in exactly the same way as degree of fulfill-ment of a goal is measured. That is to say, when the index is 1.0 the performance is ideal; when the index is 0.5 the merit of the performance is at the threshold between acceptability and unacceptability. The technique of employing this index of merit for the evaluation of performance will be described here as the *rated-objective merit-index technique* (ro-mi).

Clearly, the validity of the rated-objective merit index hangs upon the validity of the importance ratings by which the degrees of fulfillment of individual objectives are weighted. Equally clearly, the importance ratings assigned to objectives are human judgments and prey to all the fallibilities of human judgment. However, the presence of human values in a problem is inherent in the concept of problem-solving as a goal-directed activity.[16]

The occurrence of an incorrect assignment of an importance rating at the commencement of a project need not be a disastrous event. It is open to the arbiter or arbiters in a problem to manipulate the importance ratings in any way they wish and to revise their true aims and interests as the consequences of their decisions emerge or as fresh information becomes available. For example, if it is desired that good fulfillment of a lower-ranking goal should be capable of outweighing a less-good fulfillment between their respective ratings, then small intervals between ratings may be chosen. Thus where the rank of G_1 is greater than the rank of G_2 but

$r_{G_2} \cdot G_2(y)$ is to be permitted to exceed $r_{G_1} \cdot G_1(y)$

then r_{G_1} might be assigned 100
and r_{G_2} might be assigned 99;
therefore, when $G_1(y) = 0.5$
and $\qquad\qquad G_2(y) = 0.6$
then $r_{G_1} \cdot G_1(y) \qquad = 50.0$
and $r_{G_2} \cdot G_2(y) \qquad = 59.4$

Alternatively, if it is desired that even the maximum fulfillment of a lower-ranking goal should never be capable of outweighing even the most marginal fulfillment of a higher-ranking one, then large intervals between ratings may be chosen. Thus where the rank of G_1 is greater than the rank of G_2 and

$r_{G_2} \cdot G_2(y)$ must not exceed the threshold value $r_{G_1} \cdot G_1(y)$

then r_{G_1} might be assigned 100
and r_{G_2} might be assigned 50;
therefore, when $G_1(y) = 0.5$
and $\qquad\qquad G_2(y) = 1.0$
then $r_{G_1} \cdot G_1(y) \qquad = 50.0$
and $r_{G_2} \cdot G_2(y) \qquad = 50.0$

In addition to selecting appropriate importance ratings for the objectives in a project, arbiters must also ensure that the correct values are chosen for the key values of the properties P identified by the objectives, particularly in respect of the limits of acceptability $P(l)$ or $P(m)$. According to the conventions adopted in the ro-mi technique a design is totally unacceptable if it falls below the limit of acceptability in respect of any objective. If, in order to obtain a solution at all, arbiters are compelled to accept a design falling below the threshold previously adopted in respect of a certain objective, the decision to accept the design is equivalent to deciding to shift the level of acceptability in respect of that objective.

The combination of the ro-mi technique thus defined with the systematic model just described provides a further formulation of the nature of the design act, as follows:
1. Agreeing on goals.
2. Rating goals.
3. Identifying the properties required to be exhibited in the end result.
4. Determining the relationships between the varying states of the property and the varying degrees of fulfillment of their respective goals.
5. Establishing the limiting states of the properties and hence the domain of acceptability implied by the goals.
6. Identifying the decision variables available to the designer and the scope of the resources as defined by their limiting states and interrelationships.

---

16. The point that the selection of goals necessarily involves a more or less arbitrary decision based upon an individual's set of values is clearly argued by Miller and Starr, *Executive Decisions*. The repeatability of subjective measurement is demonstrated by Stevens, "Scales of Measurement," by Ernest Adams and Samuel Messick, "An Axiomatic Formulation and Generalization of Successive Intervals Scaling," and by Coombs, "Psychological Scaling."

7. Formulating a model of the goal-decision systems present, linking the decision variables with the properties and the properties with the goals.
8. Ensuring that the interdependence of the properties constitutes a realm of feasibility and that this lies at least in part in the domain of acceptability.
9. Proposing one or more sets of states for the decision variables, within the scope of the resources; establishing the predicted performances, that is to say, the resulting sets of states of the properties, and ensuring that at least one performance lies within the arena defined by Step 8.
10. Evaluating the merit of the predicted overall performances.
11. Selecting the optimum solution.
12. Communicating the design description.

The diagrammatic form of the systematic model employed in this argument so far (for example, the combination of Figures 10 and 11) becomes excessively complicated when more than four or five properties are involved. A more flexible model is provided when the variables are displayed in the form of a matrix, as in Figure 15. In the course of formulating a problem and developing a solution the matrix is gradually filled out, in interplay with the real-world situation and with the analogues adopted, as will next be described.[17] The matrix form lends itself to automatic computation and replication. In the remainder of this text, the diagrammatic form of the systematic model will be retained as a conceptual model, but the matrix form will be regarded as the effective form.

The systematic model developed previously is an effective means for setting out the logical structure of a problem, but it does nothing in itself to establish what the solution might be. That is to say, it is not an operational model.

The Operational Model

In any given system the ways in which the outputs vary in response to changes in the inputs will be governed by appropriate laws. It is frequently difficult to discern the laws operating in a particular case or, if the general form of the law is known, it is often hard to predict an outcome. A system in which the precise connection between input and output variation is unknown is referred to as a *black box*.[18]

One means for determining the effect of various inputs on the output of a black box is to employ as a model another system which is known to behave in a similar way.[19] For example, scale models of river and tidal basins have been used to predict the silting effects of proposed pier-building operations. Architects' and engineers' drawings are graphic models of the structures they represent. Models may also be employed where the laws governing a system are known. The mathematical formulas in engineers' handbooks, for example, are abstract models for predictable systems.

A model which behaves in a way analogous to the way in which a real-world object or system behaves is known as an *analogue*.[20] No analogue behaves in every way like the real object or system it represents; if it did it would be described as a *prototype* rather than an analogue. Prototypes are useful in determining the overall effect of many design decisions. On the other hand, they can be expensive to build and modify and may be ineffectual as a means for indicating the possible results of alternative configurations. In general, analogues are selected because they are economical to set up and easy to adjust in exploring alternative solutions. Drawings, nomographs, and mathematical formulas make effective design analogues.

17. The relationship between a real-world system, a logical model of the structure of that system, and an analogue used to imitate the behavior of the system is examined in Ackoff, *Scientific Method,* beginning on p. 372.
18. The "black box" idea is well described in Eric Duckworth, *A Guide to Operational Research,* and is discussed more briefly in J. Christopher Jones, "The State of the Art in Design Methods," in this volume.
19. Stafford Beer, *Cybernetics and Management,* argues that in black box situations the use of models is the only alternative to systematic meddling with the real-world system.
20. See Duckworth, *Operational Research,* and Rittel, *Universe of Design.*

It has already been observed that the systematic model employed in this argument so far is not an operational analogue, since it cannot of itself produce predictions about the solutions to the problem it represents. However, if the systematic model is used in conjunction with one or more analogues it becomes operational. The designer can employ the systematic model to represent the logical relationships between the parts of the real-world problem.[21] He can also use it to evaluate the overall effect of the various system outputs, while using various analogues to determine the outputs that would result from various design proposals. Because no analogue is complete and perfect, it is usually necessary to employ different analogues for different systems or for different parts or aspects of a given system, so that typically the overall operational model consists of one or more systematic models with a number of analogues, as in Figure 14. For example, a plan drawing might be employed to determine the layout of the rooms in a building, vector diagrams to work out the distribution of structural loads, and a block model to predict overall appearance.

Since, in terms of the systematic model, some systems receive as inputs the outputs of other systems, it is usually necessary to operate on their respective analogues in sequence. Sometimes, however, a system of systems may form a closed loop, with every subsystem depending on inputs from another subsystem. In such cases, it may be desirable to allot trial values to one or more of the input variables, and then to proceed around the cycle, perhaps more than once, adjusting the trial values until mutually acceptable results are obtained. Closed loops may enclose the whole or only a part of the systematic model of a real-world problem. In the course of cycling the loop the designer's perception of his real-world problem and his concept of the design solution grow. In a sense, the design process is thus a dialogue between the real-world model and the operational model, as diagrammed in Figure 16.

On the basis of this operational model, the act of designing can be thought of as comprising a reiterative subroutine applied to different parts of the overall problem in turn, recycling where necessary as the problem becomes clearer and as the effects of trial values are discerned.

14. Typically, an overall operational model takes the form of one or more systematic models together with a number of analogues.
Mathematical, graphical, or physical analogues may be employed to predict the effect of given inputs.
Taken together, the systematic model and one or more analogues constitute an operational model of the real-world problem.

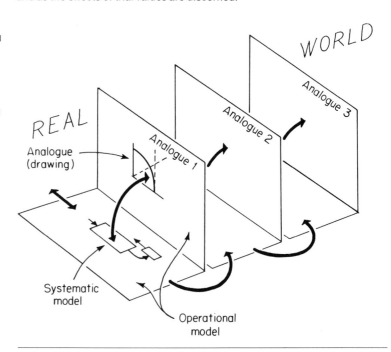

21. The general case, as distinct from the special case of the design problem, is set out in Ashby, *Cybernetics*.

A more detailed formulation of the movements of a designer between his problem and the operational model, as defined so far, may therefore be outlined.[22] The step numbers correspond to the circled numbers in Figure 16 and the column numbers on the right correspond to the columns of the matrix in Figure 15.

1. Appraise the overall problem in the light of the systematic model and partial solutions, if any, as discerned so far.

2. Select the next subproblem most intimately related to subproblems handled so far, or the next most dominant subproblem which promises to yield to analysis.

3. Identify the arbiters entitled to nominate goals in this subproblem.

4. In consultation with the arbiters, identify the goals in this subproblem.
col. 1

5. Identify the property defined by each goal.
col. 2

6. By agreement between arbiters, assign importance ratings to the goals.
col. 3

7. In consultation with the arbiters, determine the limiting states of the properties which are to be equivalent to the ideal and threshold degrees of fulfillment of their respective goals.
cols. 4–5

8. Establish the relationships (internal or specific laws) connecting varying states of the properties with varying degrees of fulfillment of their respective goals.
col. 6

9. Establish the domain of acceptability defined by the superimposition of the limiting states of the properties. If necessary, in order to gain a positive domain of acceptability, negotiate changes at 7, and repeat.
cols. 4–5

10. Identify the relationship (external or general laws) governing any interdependence existing between the states of properties identified at 5.
cols. 4–5

11. Establish the realm of feasibility defined by the compatible ranges of states of the properties. If necessary, in order to obtain a positive realm of feasibility, take an inventive step creating new relationships at 10, and repeat.
cols. 4–5

12. Establish the arena within which a performance must be found, as defined by the superimposition of the domain of acceptability and the realm of feasibility. If necessary, in order to obtain a positive arena for performance, negotiate changes at 7, and/or create new relationships at 10, and repeat.
cols. 4–5

13. Identify the context variables which contribute to governing the goal-decision systems under examination, including those context variables which arise from subproblems already handled.
col. 7

14. Identify the decision variables governing the states of the properties.
col. 8

15. Erect a new systematic model, or improve the existing one, of the goal-decision systems connecting the decision variables with the properties, and the properties with the goals, in the subproblem.

16. Identify the laws connecting the varying states of the decision variables and context variables (inputs) with the varying states of the properties (outputs) in the goal-decision systems identified at 15.
col. 9

17. Establish the ranges of states of the individual context variables which apply to the case in hand.
col. 10

---

22. This formulation is based mainly upon the examination of case studies at the Royal College. It is substantially in accordance with patterns observed by Morris Asimow, *Introduction to Design*; Bowen, "Rational Design"; Jones, "Systematic Design"; R. J. McCrory, "The Design Method: A Scientific Approach to Valid Design"; Edward Matchett, "The Controlled Evolution of Engineering Design"; Rittel, *Universe of Design*; and Martin K. Starr, *Product Design and Decision Theory*.

18. Establish the context defined by the superimposition of the prevailing states of the context variables.

col. 10

19. Establish the ranges of states available in the individual decision variables.

cols. 11–12

20. Identify the laws governing any interdependence existing between the states of the decision variables at 14.

cols. 11–12

21. Establish the scope of the design resource defined by the compatible ranges of states of the decision variables. If necessary, in order to obtain a positive scope of design resources, negotiate changes at 19, and repeat.

cols. 11–12

22. Erect one or more analogues to represent laws identified at 10, 16, and 20.

23. Identify the decision-makers entitled to select states of the decision variables in the subproblem.

24. By agreement among the decision-makers and using the analogues erected at 22 for the laws at 20, select a self-compatible set (design i) of states for the decision variables.

col. 13

25. Using analogues erected at 22 for the laws at 16, determine the resultant set (performance x) of states of the properties.

col. 14

26. Establish whether performance x lies within the arena for performance defined at 12. If not, repeat from 24. If no solution is obtainable, create new relationships between the properties at 10 (inventive step) or rework subproblems giving rise to context variables at 13 (reappraisal), or negotiate new limiting values for the properties at 7 (restatement), and repeat.

cols. 4–5

27. Evaluate merit y of overall performance x in respect of all objectives handled so far (rated-objective merit-index M_{iy}).

cols. 15–19

28. Repeat from 24 (alternative design j) as often as necessary or as often as time and money will permit, until the merit z of overall performance w is as high as possible (ro-mi M_{jz}).

29. Identify and validate any critical assumptions or approximations made during the course of the solution of the subproblem.

30. Repeat from step 1 until the overall problem is resolved.

This formulation is quite general. It describes problem-solving behavior in terms which include, but are not limited to, the needs of the activity of arriving at a configuration for a proposed artifact. The application of problem-solving behavior to the specific class of problems called design is developed next.

Systematic model of a multiobjective goal-decision system

Item	Performance specification						Decision resource			Proposal		
G_n	$G_n = \int P_n$	r_{o_n}	$G_n(y) = \int (P_n(l), P_n(u), P_n(x))$				$P_n = \int(C_n, D_n)$		$C_n(k)$	$D_n(i) \subset \{D_n(g), \ldots, D_n(h)\}$		
$n_n =$	n_D	$r =$	$l =$	$u =$	$f =$		$n_c =$	$n_D =$	$f =$	$k =$	$g =$	$n =$	$i =$
1	2	3	4	5	6		7	8	9	10	11	12	13
					1 ___ .5 ___ 0 ___ 1 ___ .5 ___ 0 ___								

Evaluation of proposal			Merit so far		
$P_n(x) = \int (C_n(k), D(i))$	$G_n(y) = \int P_n(x)$	$M_{lp}(t) = \dfrac{\sum (r_{o_n}\, G_n(y))}{\sum r_{o_n}}$			
$x =$	$y =$	$r_o\; G_n(y) =$	$\sum (r_{o_n}\; G_n(y)) =$	$\sum r_o =$	$t =$
14	15	16	17	18	19

15. The variables in a systematic model of a goal-decision system may be displayed in the form of a matrix in which, in interplay between the real world and various analogues, the problem may be formulated and a solution developed.

16. Illustration of a characteristic pattern of movements of a designer between the real world, his structured concept of that problem, and the analogues he uses in resolving it (for key, see text).

The design process is a dialogue between the real world and the operational model.

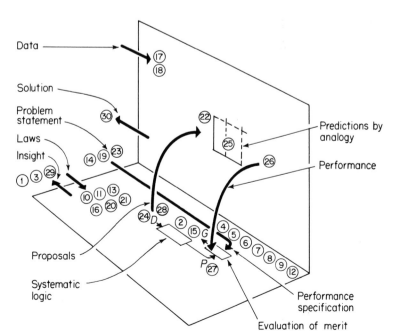

The Design Program

The great majority of design tasks are carried out by designers on behalf of employers or clients. The nomination of some of the objectives and the acceptance or nonacceptance of some of the standards of performance lie within the discretion of the employer or client rather than in the discretion of the designer. The community, represented by government and other agencies, has its own intersecting sets of objectives, some of which will impinge upon the design project, and in most circumstances it will impose certain overriding requirements and limitations on the design through laws, regulations, and standards.[23] The user and the community may also exercise a form of control through the machinery of the marketplace.[24]

A high proportion of design tasks are regarded by the clients as investments calculated to yield a prescribed return. For example, a developer commissioning an architect to design a building is concerned that there be a high enough probability of the architect's producing within given limits of time and cost a design, with a high enough probability of being erected within given limits of construction time and cost, and with a high enough probability of commanding a profitable rent or sale price.[25]

In general, the movement of capital through the money market results in higher yields being demanded on investments to which the higher risks are attached.[26] Hence, where a developer has to raise capital for a project, he has much to gain from first showing evidence of the degree of risk attached to, and the extent of returns expected from the venture. Even where the developer has adequate resources of his own, he will normally put only a given proportion of his capital at high risk or invest a given proportion of income in new development. If, over a period of time, a developer undertakes a number of projects, he will normally expect some of them to fail. Consequently, those projects which succeed must, in the long run, offset the losses of those which fail.

In virtually all cases, therefore, a development project will go through an exploratory phase in which feasibility, cost, risk, and probable yield are estimated.[27] Usually this exploratory phase is conducted on a limited budget, rounded off with a formal report, sometimes extended to the preparation of sketch designs and/or models, and almost always submitted to investment analysis before authority is given for the project to proceed to detailed design stages.

With certain exceptions, the bulk of the cost of an investment in a design development project resides in the cost of tooling and manufacture, with a lesser but still large investment in marketing. Once the design is completed, but before funds are finally committed in these directions, it is usual for a further study to be made of production and marketing prospects and costs.

The design act must therefore be seen within the context of a more extensive process which includes the realization of the design proposals as well as the formulation of them. The overall process will be referred to here as a development program, which will normally contain the following phases, with reappraisal and the opportunity to withdraw at the end of each phase:

---

23. An interesting description of the relations between the participants in a problem-solving activity, using sociological and communications theory models, is given in Travistock Institute, *Interdependence and Uncertainty*.
24. See Richard A. Tybout, ed., *Economics of Research and Development*, for a collection of histories and theoretical papers, many of which relate to these aspects of the design function.
25. See the preface to Robert Schlaifer, *Probability and Statistics for Business Decisions*.
26. Or alternatively, at any given yield, capital will tend to flow to those investments which offer the least risk. See National Economic Development Council, *Investment Appraisal*.
27. The presentation of business activities in this sort of problem-solving format can be seen in Adrian M. McDonough, *Information Economics and Management Systems*.

1. Policy formulation
2. Preliminary research
3. Sketch designs
4. Detailed design
5. Prototype construction
6. Marketing appraisal
7. Production design
8. Production planning
9. Tooling
10. Production and sale

In the light of such a program the primitive concept of a systematic model of the design activity set out in the midsection of this paper can be seen to be more an outline for a specific phase than a model of a complete design development project. A design project is, in fact, a sequence of design problems, each aspect of the problem and each component of the product becoming a new design problem to be resolved in the context of what has been decided so far.[28]

Reverting to the operational model of the design process referred to above, the design program may be thought of as coexisting with the systematic model and the analogues, but on a third plane as shown in Figure 17. Thus the systematic model describes the logical relationships of the parts of the problem and permits evaluation of predicted performance, the analogues simulate the behavior of systems in the problem and predict the consequences of proposed decisions, while the design program indicates the sequential relationships necessary to resolve the problem.

The design program (and indeed the entire product development program) can be made even more effective as a control over the design and/or product development activity if the conventions of critical path methods are adopted.[29] According to this convention every activity which must be carried out in order to implement the program is indicated by an arrow. An activity takes* place over time, and maximum and minimum time allowances for that activity can be laid down. Every event which terminates an activity is indicated by a box or circle at the end of its associated arrow. An event occurs at an instant in time, and earliest and latest permissible dates for the event can be laid down. Two or more activities may have to be completed before an event can take place. The critical path is that set of sequential activities which, added together, determines the minimum time span of the whole operation.

The design process may therefore be thought of as having the three main components shown in Figure 18.
1. The advance through the project and through time, indicated by the design program and accomplished with the aid of various analogues.
2. The branching of the problem into its logical parts, independent of time, indicated by the systematic model.
3. The cyclical movement through the subproblems, occupying man-hours but perhaps coexisting in time, connecting the real world, the systematic model, various analogues, and the design program as described by the 30-step reiterative operational model.

Examination of case studies indicates that a characteristic program in the consumer goods and light industrial products field is as follows:

---

28. F. de P. Hanika, *New Thinking in Management,* describes management problems generally as examples of programmed problem-solving.
29. A lucid explanation and attractive approach to critical path methods is contained in Albert Battersby, *Network Analysis for Planning and Scheduling.* See also K. Lockyer, *Critical Path Analysis.* A model design program in network form is given in Archer, *Systematic Method for Designers.*

Phase 1. Policy formulation	Establish objectives. Outline timetable and budget.
Phase 2. Preliminary research	Identify problem boundaries. Establish the existing state of the art (library research). Outline performance specification (specification 1). Identify probable critical problem areas.
Phase 3. Feasibility study (sketch design)	Conduct information generating experiments. Resolve critical problems. Propose overall solutions (sketch design 1). Estimate work content of phases 4 and 5 and probability of success.
Phase 4. Design development	Expand performance specification (specification 2). Develop detailed design (design 2). Prepare design documentation.
Phase 5. Prototypedevelopment	Construct prototype (prototype 1). Evaluate technical performance of prototypes. Conduct user trials.
Phase 6. Trading study	Appraise market potential. Appraise marketing/production problem. Revise objectives and budget. Finalize performance specification (specification 3).
Phase 7. Production development	Develop production design (design 3). Execute production design documentation. Construct pre-production prototypes (prototype 2). Conduct technical, user, and market field tests.
Phase 8. Production planning	Prepare marketing plans. Prepare production plans. Design jigs and tools.
Phase 9. Tooling	Construct jigs and tools. Construct trial batch of products (prototype 3). Test trial batch. Install marketing machinery and production control.
Phase 10. Production and sale	Initiate marketing effort. Commence production and sale. Feed-back market and user information.

Taking the model Plan of Work published by the Royal Institute of British Architects[30] as a basis, the equivalent program for a building would be as follows:

Stage A. Inception	Set up client organization for briefing. Consider requirements. Appoint architect.
Stage B. Feasibility	Carry out study of user requirements. Carry out study of site conditions. Examine planning, design, and cost feasibility.
Stage C. Outline proposals	Develop brief further. Complete study of user requirements. Carry out study of technical problems. Carry out study of planning, design, and cost problems.
Stage D. Scheme design	Finalize brief. Full design of project by architect. Preliminary design by engineer. Prepare cost plan. Prepare full explanatory report. Submit proposal for all approvals.
Stage E. Detail design	Complete designs for every component of building. Complete cost-checking of designs.

---

30. See "Plan of Work" reprinted from the RIBA *Handbook of Architectural Practice and Management*.

Stage F. Production information	Prepare final production drawings.
	Prepare schedules.
	Prepare specifications.
Stage G. Bills of quantities	Prepare bills of quantities.
	Prepare tender documents.
Stage H. Tender action	Dispatch tender documents.
	Examine tenders and select tenderers.
	Let contracts.
	Notify unsuccessful tenderers.
Stage J. Project planning	Arrange effective communications system.
	Agree on project program.
Stage K. Operations on site	Provide design and construction information.
	Implement construction program.
	Install and effect budgetary control.
	Install and effect quality control.
Stage L. Completion	Inspect completed construction.
	Specify rectification of defects.
	Make good defects.
	Complete contracts and settle accounts.
	Relinquish possession to owner.
Stage M. Feedback	Analyze job records.
	Inspect completed building.
	Study building in use.

Clearly, the 30-step reiterative operational model presented in the text and in Figure 16 applies to every subproblem at every step of this design program. As shown in Figure 19, the essence of this thesis is that the structure of the design process consists in applying a reiterative problem-solving operational model to a specific complex of goal-decision systems in accordance with the design program.

Conclusion

Traditionally, the designer has worked intuitively for the most part, studying his brief, scanning the evidence, ruminating upon implications, and sketching ideas without exercising much conscious control over the activity of design decision-making itself. In many classes of design problems this procedure is likely to remain entirely adequate. In textile, clothing, jewelry, some ceramics, much interior, and most furniture design, for example, it would seem that circumstances would seldom warrant the expenditure of much time and effort on intellectually justifying propositions which can be rapidly tested in practice.

There are some areas, however, where it is becoming less and less possible to depend wholly upon intuition in choosing a route through the problem or in making design decisions. For example, the design of complex buildings such as hospitals involves such a large number of interacting variables and requires so many detailed subproblem solutions that the architect cannot trust his intuition to tell him which is the best order in which to deal with them or whether he has covered all the ground. Similarly, there are some mechanical and systems engineering problems (not always relating to big or complex structures) which involve complex overlays of the areas of acceptability in objectives and limited intersections of the curves of feasibility. Then the chances of selecting intuitively a design idea that will turn out to be both feasible and acceptable are remote. The increasing standards of performance of designs and the increasing variety of materials and processes to construct them with are tending to increase the frequency of these difficult cases.

There is evidence, moreover, that even where problems are to be handled intuitively, a designer (or other problem-solver) is better able to ruminate on his particular problem when he is in possession of "structural" concepts of the logic of the general class of problems into which his problem falls and of

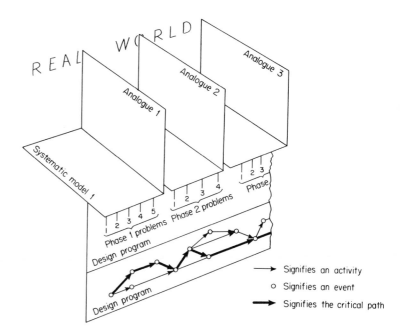

REAL WORLD

Analogue 1
Analogue 2
Analogue 3

Systematic model 1

1 2 3 4 5
Phase 1 problems
Design program

1 2 3 4
Phase 2 problems

1 2 3
Phase

Design program

→ Signifies an activity

○ Signifies an event

▬► Signifies the critical path

17. While the systematic models describe the logical relationships of the parts of a problem and the analogues simulate the probable consequences of proposed solutions, the program indicates the sequential relationships of the activities required to resolve it.

The design program may be displayed using the conventions of critical path methods.

18. The design process may be thought of as having three main components: the advance through the project and through time, as indicated by the design program; the branching of the problem into its logical parts, as indicated by the systematic model; and the cyclical problem-solving process, described by the reiterative routine.

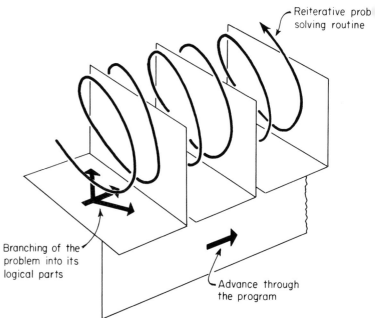

Reiterative prob solving routine

Branching of the problem into its logical parts

Advance through the program

19. Design procedure consists in applying a reiterative problem-solving routine to a complex of goal-decision systems in accordance with a project program.

The expediency of continuing, and of alternative courses of action, must usually be appraised at each stage.

Real world (in which the goals and resources are determined by a coalition of participants and arbiters)

Hierarchical recomposition of overall systematical model (for guidance as to interrelatedness of subproblems)

Reiterative problem-solving routine

Set of analogues (for seeking and testing subproblem solutions)

REAL WORLD

Pay-off matrix for program reappraisal at each stage

Project program (expressed as a network of the activities to be undertaken)

Set of systematic models (for setting out the logic of the relations between performance required and decisions to be made)

the general program of events through which his activity is likely to pass than when he has no such structural concept.

It is important to distinguish between technique and policy. A problem-solver may choose to follow a policy of planning or one of expediency. Whichever he chooses, as he comes to each decision point, he can employ the techniques of rational decision-making or the techniques of intuition.

It is also important to distinguish between the manner of forming an intent and the manner of pursuing it. The objectives in a design project may be selected by reasoning or intuition. The standards set may be high or low. But however they are arrived at, questions as to the merits and demerits of the objectives and standards selected must rest ultimately on question as to the value systems of the people involved or of the society in which they operate. Some such questions stand beyond the reach of analytical reasoning. The pursuit of these objectives, on the other hand, can always be evaluated as efficient or inefficient, effective or ineffective, and safe or risky.

Thus the polarities of reason versus intuition occur at all three levels: in the selection of objectives, in the organization of the design activity, and in the making of decisions. All combinations and degrees of these polarities are found in design practice.

In general, careful reasoning at any or all levels tends to slow down the design activity and make it more costly, especially during the earlier stages. On the other hand, it also tends to diminish risk. Intuitive methods are therefore appropriate where the risk and/or consequences of failure are acceptably low, and rational methods are appropriate where risk and/or penalties are high and must be minimized. The principles developed in this thesis are intended to apply to both intuitive and rational methods and at all three levels —design, planning, and execution. The technique and terminology presented are intended to be compatible with the neighboring disciplines of cybernetics, management science, and operations research. Indeed, the argument set out here can be considered as the application of these disciplines to the design activity.

Although some of the techniques are far from fully developed, there is at least a principle, established in management science, operations research, or conventional design practice, which can be applied to each of the steps in the design process. It remains, therefore, to accumulate sufficient case studies on the application of these techniques to design problems to provide a valid science of design.

It has been repeatedly argued here that the exercise of value judgments in the nomination and rating of objectives is and must remain a human responsibility outside the logic of the problem itself. The development of automatic problem-solving techniques would not, therefore, affect the importance or human control of value systems. Indeed, they might well cause the exercise of value judgment to become a vastly more important part of the designer's role.

The other area where the role of the designer has hitherto been regarded as vital is in the creative act of conceiving design ideas or solutions-in-principle. Given adequate data, however, it is possible, at least in principle, to employ automatic search techniques for finding feasible and/or optimal solutions within the problem constraints. This is particularly practicable in the case of probabilistic and deterministic systems, that is to say, in problems where the laws governing the relationships between decision variables and output properties are known or capable of imitation by models.

Even in the case of problems where no laws can be discerned in the connection between the decision variables and the outcomes, it is at least theoretically possible to generate random decisions automatically, to build prototypes of the system, and to compare outcomes until an acceptable solution is reached. The capacity to postulate new ideas is therefore not an indispensible part of the human role, although in the present state of the science of design it is an extremely important one.

For maximum efficiency, a comprehensive design method would be conducted with a mixture of rational and intuitive techniques appropriate to the nature of the objectives, the quality of the data, the character of the problems, and the certainty required in the end result.

It cannot be emphasized too strongly that this paper is not advocating the slavish pursuit of the principles and routines set out here, in the manner of a step-by-step recipe for designing. On the contrary, the matters contained here are seen as providing, at best, the same sort of guidance as that provided by semantics, accidence, syntax, and the principles of composition for the preparation of literary works. In other words, they are an attempt to make explicit the practices which discerning people seem to be adopting.

33 The Atoms of Environmental Structure

Christopher Alexander and
Barry Poyner

Center for Environmental Structure
2701 Shasta Road
Berkeley, California, and
Department of Architecture
University of Aston
Birmingham, England

Christopher Alexander is Associate Professor of Architecture at the University of California and Director of the Center for Environmental Structure in Berkeley. He was born in Austria and educated in England. He received an M.A. in mathematics in 1956 and a B.A. in architecture in 1958 from Cambridge University and a Ph.D. in architecture from Harvard in 1963. He has lectured, consulted, and published extensively in several fields. His major work is *Notes on the Synthesis of Form*. Barry Poyner is on the research staff of Scientific Control Systems Ltd. in London and is a Research Fellow at the University of Aston. He was born and educated in England, receiving the Dip.Arch. in 1960 from the Birmingham School of Architecture. He has been associated with the Directorate of Works of the British War Office and the Development Group of the Ministry of Public Buildings and Works in London. The present work was done in association with John Redpath and Ian Moore of the Offices Development Group, Ministry of Public Buildings and Works, London, in 1966–1967. The first part of the paper was printed under the same title by the Center for Planning and Development Research of the University of California and subsequently by the Ministry.

This paper is about design programming. The atoms of environmental structure are relations, the simplest geometry which can be functionally right.or wrong in the design of any man-made object or environment. They are statements about the physical organization which is required if the design is to function well. A list of required relations replaces the design program or brief and the first stages of sketch design. The argument of the paper has four parts. First, the idea of need should be replaced with its operational counterpart, tendency. Second, a single need, when operationally defined, makes no demands on the physical environment, and the environment requires a specific geometry only to resolve conflicts between tendencies. Third, once a conflict between tendencies is clearly stated, it is possible to define the geometrical relation required to prevent the conflict and to insist that this relation be present in any context where the conflict might occur. Finally, the environment needs no geometrical organization beyond that which it gets from combinations or relations so defined. Two appendices follow, the first illustrating specific tendencies, conflicts, and relations for the entrance to an office and the second illustrating tendencies, conflicts, and patterns for the entrance to a suburban house.

At present, there are two things wrong with design programs. First of all, even if you state clearly what a building has to do, there is still no way of finding out what the building must be like to do it. The geometry of the building is still a matter for the designer's intuition; the program does not help. Second, even if you state clearly what the building has to do, there is no way of finding if this is what the building ought to do. It is possible to make up an arbitrary program for a building. There is, at present, no way of being sure that programs are not arbitrary; there is no way of testing what the program says.

As far as this second point goes, most designers would maintain that no program can ever be made nonarbitrary. They would say that the rightness or wrongness of a program is not a factual matter but a moral one; it is not a question of fact but a question of value. These people argue in the same way about the physical environment itself. They say that the environment cannot be right or wrong in any objective sense but that it can only be judged according to criteria, or goals, or policies, or values, which have themselves been arbitrarily chosen.

We believe this point of view is mistaken. We believe that it is possible to define design in such a way that the rightness or wrongness of a building is clearly a question of fact, not a question of value. We also believe that if design is defined in this way, a statement of what a building ought to do can yield physical conclusions about the geometry of the building directly. We believe, in other words, that it is possible to write a program which is both objectively correct and which yields the actual physical geometry of a building.

What Is a Need?

Let us begin with the kind of programs which people write today. It is widely recognized that any serious attempt to make the environment work must begin with a statement of user needs. Christopher Jones calls them performance specifications; Bruce Archer calls them design goals; in engineering they are often called design criteria; at the Building Research Station they are called user requirements; at the Ministry of Public Building and Works they have been called activities; they are often simply called requirements or needs. Whatever word is used, the main idea is always this: Before starting to design a building, the designer must define its purpose in detail. This detailed definition of purpose, goals, requirements, or needs can then be used as a checklist. A proposed design can be evaluated by checking it against the checklist.

But how do we decide that something really is a need? The simplest answer, obviously, is "Ask the client." But people are notoriously unable to assess their own needs. Suppose then, that we try to assess people's needs by watching them. We still cannot be sure we know what people really need. We cannot decide what is "really" needed, either by asking questions, or by outside observation, because the concept of need is not well defined. The word need has a variety of meanings. When it is said that people need air to breathe, it means that they will die within a few minutes if they do not get it. When someone says, "I need a drink," it means he thinks he will feel better after he has had one. When it is said that people "need" an art museum the meaning is almost wholly obscure. The statement that a person needs something has no well-defined meaning. We cannot decide whether such a statement is true or false.

We shall, therefore, replace the idea of need by the idea of what people are trying to do. We shall, in effect, accept something as a need if we can show that the people concerned, when given the opportunity, actively try to satisfy the need. This implies that every need, if valid, is an active force. We call this active force which underlies the need a *tendency*. A tendency, therefore, is an operational version of a need. If someone says that a certain need exists, we cannot test the statement, because we do not know what it really claims. If someone says that a certain tendency exists, we can begin to test the statement.

Here is an example. Suppose we say, "People working in an office need a view." This is a statement of need. It can be interpreted in many ways. Does it mean "It would be nice if people in offices had views"? Does it mean "People say they want a view from their offices"? Does it mean "People will pay money to get a view from their offices"? There are so many ways of interpreting it that the statement is almost useless. We do not know what it really says.

But if we replace it by the statement, "People working in offices try to get a view from their offices," this is a statement of fact. It may be false, it may be true, but it can be tested. It is a statement of a tendency. If observation shows that people in an office actively try to get those desks which command a view, it is clearly reasonable to say that they need the view. If, on the other hand, people make no effort to get a view even when they get the chance, we shall naturally begin to doubt the need.

Every statement of a tendency is a hypothesis, an attempt to condense a large number of observations by means of a general statement. In this sense, a statement of a tendency is like any scientific theory. Since a statement of a tendency is a way of interpreting observations, we must try as hard as possible to rule out alternative hypotheses. Suppose we have observed that people in offices try to get desks near the window when they get the chance. It is possible to infer from this that they are trying to get a view. But we might equally well infer the existence of other tendencies. They could be trying to get more light, or better ventilation, or direct sunlight. Or they may be trying to get something far more complicated; they may want to be in a position from which they see the light on the faces of their companions instead of seeing them in silhouette against the window.

In order to be confident that people really seek a view, we must make observations which allow us to rule out such alternative interpretations one by one. For example, suppose we construct an office in which light levels are uniform throughout, because windows are supplemented by artificial light. Do people still try to work near the window in such an office? If they do, we can rule out the possibility that they are merely trying to get more light. Ruling out all the alternative interpretations we can think of is a laborious and expensive task. Furthermore, in order to make the hypothesis more accurate, we must try to specify what kind of people seek a view from their offices, during what parts of their work they seek it most, what aspects of "view" they are really looking for, and so on. Again, this is a laborious and expensive task. It is like the task of forming any scientific hypothesis or theory. A good theory cannot be invented overnight; it can be created only by refinement over many years and by many independent, different observers.

It is, therefore, vitally important that we do not exaggerate the pseudo-scientific aspect of the concept of tendency. Since a tendency is a hypothesis, no tendency can be stated in any absolute or final form. The ideal of perfect objectivity is an illusion, and therefore there is no justification for accepting only those tendencies whose existence has been "objectively demonstrated." Other tendencies, though they may be speculative, are often more significant from the human point of view. It would be extremely dangerous to ignore such tendencies just because we have no data to "support" them. Provided they are stated clearly, so that they can be shown wrong by someone willing to undertake the necessary experiments, it is as important to include these tendencies in the program as it is to include those tendencies that we are sure about.

Conflicts

Now we face the central problem of design: Given a statement of what people need, how can we find a physical environment which meets those needs?

In order to answer this question we must first define clearly just what we mean by meeting needs. This is not as easy as it seems. So long as we are using the word needs, the idea of meeting them seems fairly obvious. However, once we replace the idea of need by the idea of tendency and try to translate the idea of meeting needs into the new language, we shall see that its meaning is not really clear at all.

The idea of needs is passive. But the idea of tendencies is highly active. It emphasizes the fact that, given the opportunity, people will try to satisfy needs for themselves. When we try to interpret the idea of meeting needs in the light of this new emphasis, we see that it is highly ambiguous. To what extent are people expected to meet needs for themselves, and to what extent is the environment expected to do it for them?

Take for example a simple situation, a man sitting in a chair. He has various needs. He needs to shift his position every now and then, to maintain the circulation in his buttocks and thighs. If he is trying to read, he needs enough light to read by. If he sits in his chair long enough, he will need food or refreshment. He needs ventilation. Under normal circumstances he is perfectly able to meet these needs for himself. But if we define a good environment as one which meets needs, we should logically be forced to design an environment which meets these needs for him. This conjures up an image of

a man lying in an armchair, food being fed him mechanically, a window opening automatically when the room becomes too hot, a light being switched on
automatically as evening comes, and pads in the chair massaging his buttocks to keep the pressure from building up too much in any one place.

The image is absurd. It is absurd because the man is perfectly capable of
meeting these needs for himself. Indeed, not only is he capable of meeting
them for himself, but for his own well-being it is almost certain that he should
meet them for himself. Man is an adapting organism. A man who is no longer
meeting his needs is no longer adapting. The daily, hourly, process of adapting is the process of life itself; an organism which is no longer adapting is
no longer alive.

It is, therefore, clear that a good environment is not so much one that meets
needs as one that allows men to meet needs for themselves. If we define a
need as a tendency, as something which people are trying to do, then we
must assume that they will do it whenever they get the chance. The only job
which the environment has is to make sure they get this chance.

Now at first sight it may seem that the argument leads to a dead end. Go
back to the example of the man sitting in a chair. Under normal conditions
each one of the tendencies which arises in this situation can take care of
itself. The man can do everything for himself. There is no problem in the
situation. The environment does not require redesign. If needs are defined
as tendencies, and if tendencies are capable of taking care of themselves,
then why does the environment *ever* require design by designers? Why
cannot people be left to adapt to the environment and to shape their own
environment as they wish, with the help of bricklayers, carpenters, elec-
tricians, and others. If tendencies are active forces, then people will presumably take action whenever the environment is not satisfactory and will
meet their own needs for themselves. Why does the environment need
design? Why should designers ever take a hand at all?

The answer is this. Under certain conditions, tendencies conflict. In a *conflict* situation, the tendencies cannot take care of themselves, because one is
pulling in one direction, and the other is pulling in the opposite direction.
Under these circumstances, the environment does need design; it must be
rearranged in such a way that the tendencies no longer conflict.

Let us go back once more to the man sitting in a chair. There are certain
chairs, made of canvas slung between wire supports, in which you cannot
move about at will, because your body always sinks to the lowest position
and is held there by the canvas. After sitting in one of these chairs for a few
minutes you begin to feel uncomfortable; the pressure on certain parts of
the body builds up, but you cannot move slightly to reduce this pressure.
You try to shift positions but you cannot. At first sight it might seem that
this is not so. Indeed, the tendency to try to reduce the pressure on your
body has a simple outlet. You can simply get up and walk about. The trouble
is, of course, that in many cases there will be another tendency operating
which makes you want to stay sitting where you are. It is the conflict between
your tendency to stay where you are and your tendency to shift position
which makes a problem. In a properly designed chair this conflict does not
occur.

We may, therefore, replace the simple-minded definition of a good environment as one that meets needs, by the following definition: a good environment is one in which no two tendencies conflict.

Of course, the conflicts that occur in buildings and cities can be much more
complicated than the one we have just described. There can be conflicts
between tendencies within a single person, between one person and a
tendency of a group, or between a tendency in a person and some larger
tendency that is part of a mass phenomenon. But the principle is always the

same. Provided that all the tendencies can operate freely and are not brought into conflict with other tendencies, the environment in which they are occurring is a good one. It follows then that the environment only requires design in order to prevent conflicts occurring. If we wish to specify the pattern an environment ought to have, we must begin by identifying all conflicts between tendencies which might possibly occur in the environment.

In summary: Until we have managed to see design problems in terms of conflict between tendencies, there is nothing for the designer to do. So long as we see nothing but isolated tendencies we must assume that they will take care of themselves. We have only succeeded in stating a design problem in a constructive way at that moment when we have stated it as a conflict of tendencies. Since the tendencies in conflict may often be hidden, to state the problem is a difficult process which requires a deliberate and inventive search for conflicts.

Relations

We design the environment, then, to prevent conflict. We must now start talking about the features of buildings which can help us do this. The features that cause and prevent individual conflicts are not bricks, or doors, or roofs; they are geometrical relationships between such concrete pieces. We shall call them *relations*.

Before describing how we invent a new one, let us look at some examples of well-known relations. Here are five typical relations from a supermarket:
1. Check-out counters are *near* the exit doors.
2. The stack of baskets and trolleys is *inside* the entrance and directly *in front* of it.
3. Meat and dairy refrigerators are *at the back* of the store, and all other goods on display are *between* these refrigerators and the check-out counters.
4. Display shelving has a *tapering* cross section, narrow at the top and wider at the bottom.
5. The store is glass-fronted, with aisles running from *front to back at right angles* to the street.

These relations have become widely copied and typical of supermarkets because each of them prevents some specific conflict. Here are the five relations, followed in each case by the conflicts.

Check-out near exit doors. This relation prevents a conflict between the following tendencies:
1. Management has to keep all goods on the sales side of the check-outs.
2. Management is trying to use every square foot of selling space.

Baskets or trolleys inside the entrance and directly in front of it.
1. Management tries to encourage shoppers to use baskets, so that they are not reluctant to pick up extra goods.
2. Shoppers tend to move as fast as possible for the goods and are therefore likely to miss the baskets.

Meat and dairy products at the back of the store and all other goods between these counters and the check-outs.
1. Management tries to get every shopper to walk past as many goods as possible.
2. Shoppers visit meat and dairy sections almost every time they go to the supermarket.

Display shelving with tapering cross section so goods near the ground are clearly visible to shoppers.
1. People tend to walk around a supermarket without bending down constantly to look for goods.
2. People want to be able to find the goods they are looking for without having to ask.

Glass fronts, aisles running back from the street and at right angles to it.
1. Management is trying to give passersby a view of the entire inside of the supermarket, to draw them in.
2. If the supermarket is on a street most of the passersby are walking past the front.

A *relation,* then, is a geometrical arrangement that prevents a conflict. No relation can be regarded as necessary to a building unless it prevents a conflict that will otherwise occur in that building. A well-designed building is one which contains enough relations to eliminate conflicts within.

So far we have discussed only known relations, those which exist already. How do we invent a new relation? Obviously, we start by stating a conflict. But how do we invent a relation that prevents the conflict? The key is this: tendencies are never inherently in conflict; they are brought into conflict only by the conditions under which they occur. In order to solve the conflict we must invent an arrangement where these conditions do not exist. For example, where a public path turns the corner of a building, people often collide. The following tendencies conflict: (1) People are trying to see anyone approaching them some distance ahead, so that they can avoid bumping into them without slowing down, and (2) going round a corner, people try to take the shortest path. At the blind corner the first tendency makes people walk well clear of the corner, the second makes them hug the corner. At a blind corner the tendencies conflict.

Before we can invent an arrangement that prevents this conflict, we must find out exactly what makes these tendencies conflict. In our example there are several aspects of blind corners to blame: the fact that the corner is solid, the corner is square, and the ground is unobstructed around the corner. To eliminate the conflict we must get rid of one or more of these features. If we make the corner transparent, people will be able to see far enough ahead through it. If we round the corner with a gradual curve, people will be able to see round the corner. If we place a low obstruction at the corner, like a flower tub, people will have to walk around it and will see each other over it.

It is plain from the example that there are certain arrangements causing the conflict and certain "opposite" arrangements preventing the conflict. These two classes of arrangement are mutually exclusive. Our task, given any conflict, is to define the class of arrangements that prevents the conflict. This is always difficult. In theory the class is infinite; even in practice it is very large. We must, therefore, define an abstract geometric property shared by all arrangements in the class and by no others. This is what we mean by a relation. A relation is a precise geometric definition of the class of arrangements preventing a given conflict. It must be so worded as to *include* all the arrangements that prevent the conflict and *exclude* all those which cause it.

Let us continue our example. We have described certain arrangements that cause a conflict at corners and others that prevent it. Those preventing it include: a corner made of transparent materials, a rounded corner, a tub of flowers so placed that people have to walk clear of the corner. What is the property common to all these good arrangements, which the bad arrangements lack? Roughly speaking, it is this: If we define a path around the corner at a distance of one foot out from all walls and objects which project from the ground, and if we examine all chords on this path which are less than fifteen feet long, we shall find that none of these chords is, at eye level, obstructed by anything opaque.

The conflict in this example happens to be a simple one. However, even when the conflicting tendencies are much larger in scale, or more subtle, the logic is the same. We state the conflict, give examples of arrangements causing and preventing it, and then try to abstract the relation that defines the latter class.

Two minor points remain. First, conflicting tendencies occur under specific conditions. The relation required to prevent the conflict is required only under these specific conditions. The conditions under which the conflicting tendencies occur must be stated as part of the relation. Thus, the final form of a relation will always be: "If such and such conditions hold, then the following relation is required." Second, the actual process of inventing a relation will not follow the process of finding conflicts and defining relations in strict sequence, as it has been presented here. In practice, the statement of tendencies, the statement of conflict, and the statement of relation all develop together.

Let us summarize what we have done. We have described a process which has two steps: (1) identifying a conflict, and (2) deriving a relation from it. This process for obtaining a relation is objective in the sense that each of its steps is based on a hypothesis that can be tested. The two hypotheses are: (1) under certain specific conditions such and such conflicting tendencies occur, and (2) under these conditions the relation is both necessary and sufficient to prevent the conflict. If we cannot show that either of these hypotheses is false, we must then assume that any building where the conflict can occur must contain the relation specified.

In order to create a building in which no tendencies conflict, the designer must try to predict all the conflicts that could possibly occur in it, define the geometric relations that prevent these conflicts, and combine these relations to form a cohesive whole.

The Scientific Attitude to Relations

The point of view we have presented is impartial. This is its beauty. Because it is impartial, it makes possible a sane, constructive, and evolutionary attitude to design. It creates the opportunity for cumulative improvement of design ideas. Everything hinges on one simple question: What does a designer do when faced with a relation which someone else has written?

The traditional point of view about design says that the rightness and wrongness of a relation is a question of value. A designer with this point of view will claim that a relation can be judged only by subjectively chosen criteria or values. Since people value things differently we can never be certain that one designer will accept another designer's opinion and there is, therefore, no basis for universal agreement.

Our point of view is different. We believe that all values can be replaced by one basic value: Everything desirable in life can be described in terms of freedom of people's underlying tendencies. Anything undesirable in life—whether social, economic, or psychological—can always be described as an unresolved conflict between underlying tendencies. Life can fulfill itself only when people's tendencies are running free. The environment should give free rein to all tendencies; conflicts between people's tendencies must be eliminated. In terms of this view, the rightness or wrongness of a relation is a question of fact.

As we have said, each relation is based on two hypotheses: (1) the conflicting tendencies do occur as stated, under the condition specified, and (2) the relation proposed is both necessary and sufficient to prevent conflict between these tendencies. Faced with a relation stated in this form, the designer must either accept it or show that there is a flaw in one of the hypotheses. Whatever he does, he cannot merely reject the relation because he does not like it. The body of known relations must, therefore, grow and improve. Design, if understood as the invention and development of relations, is no longer merely a collection of isolated and disconnected efforts. It becomes a cumulative scientific effort.*

---

* Since the first version of this paper was written, the theoretical framework has been developing. For example, the term "relation" has been supplanted by the term "pattern," as the latter gives a more accurate picture of the fact that the entities are spatial and are conditional on context. Several workers in Berkeley have been developing the idea of a pattern language as a system that gives the grammar of the combinatory process. See Francis Duffy and John Torrey, "A Progress Report on the Pattern Language," in this volume.

Appendix A
Relations for an Office Entrance

The relations presented in the original study[1] prescribed the organization of an office entrance situated on a busy city street. It was assumed that the building was built right up to the sidewalk, so that the entrance opened directly onto the street. It was also assumed that there was a receptionist in the entrance. The relations dealt with the arrangement of pavement, entrance doors, elevators, reception desk, and seats for visitors. In each case, the statement of the relation was accompanied by a written explanation and a diagram to show how the relation was incorporated into the whole entrance structure shown in Figure 5.

For the purpose of this extract, four examples from the original twenty-two relations have been chosen. Relations 1, 2, and 3 have been chosen because they illustrate the way in which relations can be combined. Relations 2 and 3 interlock neatly with the general structure defined by Relation 1. The overlapping and interweaving of relations is characteristic of relational design, and it makes possible the creation of compact and economic forms. Relation 4 is included because it illustrates particularly clearly the idea of conflict.

Relation 1.

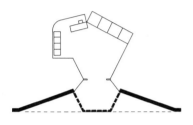

1. Diagram of the relation for projection of entrance

The parts of the building on the ground floor, adjacent to the entrance, must be set back to allow the entrance to project.

The following tendencies conflict:
1. Some people coming to the building will be unfamiliar with its location. They will know roughly where it is and on which side of the street, but because the street is busy, they will tend to cross to the correct side at an intersection well before reaching the building. But the building is built right up to the sidewalk, so they will approach it at an acute angle and may have difficulty seeing the entrance.
2. On a busy sidewalk people try to work out their route some distance ahead, to preposition themselves to take the shortest path.[2]

Some arrangements which cause this conflict are as follows: If the entrance doors are recessed and there is no projection at the entrance, people will tend to move to the outside edge of the sidewalk to see along the building more clearly. If they do this, they cannot preposition themselves to take the shortest path into the entrance because they will have to bob and weave their way across the path of other pedestrians. A projecting canopy will not necessarily be associated with the entrance. If there is a low projection, like a step, people will not see it because it will be obscured by other pedestrians.

Arrangements which may prevent the conflict are these: Some projections, for example, a classical portico with columns, a projecting lobby, or a revolving door, can be seen by people approaching the entrance at an acute angle. Such projections are roughly single-story height. In the example in Figure 1, the building is built right up to the sidewalk, so the entrance cannot project onto it. To gain a projection, the parts of the ground floor on either side of the entrance must be set back.

A covered linear recessed space, at the side of the entrance doors, about two feet deep and roughly parallel to the street.

Relation 2.

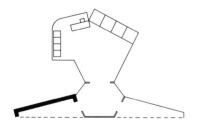

2. Diagram of recessed space relation

Where the building entrance opens directly onto the sidewalk, the following tendencies conflict:
1. When it begins to rain heavily, people in the street take shelter in the entrance for awhile. They try to stand out of the way of others going in and out.
2. While sheltering in an entrance, people tend to stand in a line facing the street. It is characteristic of human behavior that people in crowds avoid standing face to face.

1. This study was conducted by Barry Poyner in 1966. The complete study is available from the Ministry of Public Buildings and Works, London.
2. See Tyrus Porter, "A Study of Path-Choosing Behavior," in particular the study of the Kaiser Center lobby.

Arrangements which cause this conflict are these: If the only cover is in front of the entrance doors or on a direct path in and out of the entrance, and if many people try to shelter, the entrance gets blocked. Even where there is a covered space at the side of the doors, if the doors are set back so that this space runs in at right angles to the pavement from a narrow opening, people will not use it; they will tend to form a line across the opening facing the street, again blocking the entrance.

Arrangements which may prevent the conflict will have some covered space at the side of the entrance doors, so that people can shelter without blocking the doorway. The space must also be recessed to avoid being on any direct path in or out of the entrance. But if it is deeply recessed or not parallel to the street, it is wasted, because people tend to stand in a line facing the street, watching for the rain to lessen. The space must therefore be a shallow linear recess, roughly parallel to the street. A depth of two feet should be sufficient to allow a single line of people to shelter. Note: the length of this space will depend on how busy the pavement is, whether there is a bus stop near by, and how much other shelter is available. A convenient relative length is shown in Figure 2.

Relation 3.

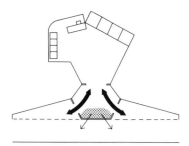

3. Diagram of the relation for a direct view of the street

Space immediately inside the entrance, close to the doors and clear of all entry and exit paths, with a direct view of the street.

When it is cold and windy, people who are waiting to be picked up by car will want more shelter than the covered entrance provides. The following tendencies conflict:
1. People tend to wait at a point overlooking the street; they will want to know the moment the car they are expecting arrives.
2. People who are waiting try to keep out of the way of those going in and out.

Arrangements which cause this conflict: If the only windows near the entrance doors are in the entrance doors themselves, those who are waiting will tend to crowd around the doors. Even if there is another window near the doors, if the space just inside is close to any path in or out of the entrance, then again people will get in the way. In both these arrangements, people cannot stand by the window and at the same time keep out of the way.

Arrangements which may prevent the conflict: If the entrance lobby is large and surrounded by glass, the conflict will not occur. Indeed any entrance with a space overlooking the street and near the entrance doors will prevent the conflict, provided the space is clear of movement. Figure 3 shows one solution.

Relation 4.

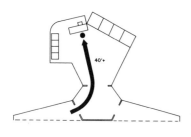

4. Diagram of distance relation

The shortest path from outside the entrance doors to the reception desk is not less than forty feet.

Visitors arrive at the building after finding their way along a busy street. The street is noisy, and they have been jostled along the pavement. The following tendencies conflict:
1. Visitors try to move directly, without hesitation, from the entrance doors to the reception desk.
2. Visitors need a minute or two in which to reorient their thoughts before arriving at the reception desk.

Arrangements which cause this conflict: An entrance which has the receptionist just inside the door, particularly if there is no entryway to protect from drafts.

Arrangements which may prevent the conflict: If the receptionist is placed well away from the entrance doors, or if there are one or more lobbies between the street and reception, the conflict does not occur. The essential property of these arrangements is that the visitor must cross a quiet space after leaving the street, before arriving at the reception point; forty feet seems to be about the minimum length of such a space. See Figure 4.

Porter made observations of an entrance to a department store in Berkeley.[3] A number of display cases separate the store front from the street, forming an arcade between street and store. He found that most people entering the store chose a path through the arcade rather than the direct path between the pavement and door to the store. He suggests, also, that people will choose to use a transition space to reorient themselves, on entering a space which is radically different from the one they have just left.

5. One possible arrangement containing the twenty-two relations for an office entrance

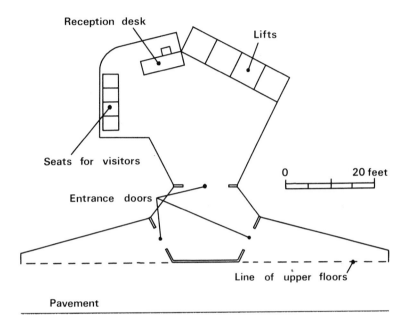

3. *Ibid.*, the study of Hink's Arcade, Berkeley.

Appendix B
Patterns for the Entrance to a
Suburban House

This appendix[4] describes four of the twenty-six relations or patterns[5] that must be present in the entrance to a single-family house standing on its own private lot on a suburban street. Each pattern is a geometric relationship between specified physical elements. Each pattern is necessary, in the sense that a predictable conflict will occur and recur during the life of the house if it is missing.

The twenty-six patterns do not form a perfectly self-contained complex. The circumstances which surround any one particular kind of housing may require only some of these twenty-six or they may require extra ones. The twenty-six patterns must be thought of as a kit of parts to be put together differently in different conditions.

It is therefore important to specify the precise conditions or context under which each individual pattern is necessary. Given knowledge of the circumstances which surround a particular building, it is possible to decide exactly which of the twenty-six it must contain. This detailed specification of conditions will accompany the discussion of each pattern. In general, it can be said that the patterns all apply to the entrance of a single detached suburban house, containing a single family, with or without children; it is assumed that the family owns at least one car and that its way of life is some version of that commonly found in a middle-income suburb in the United States and, more recently, in England. It is assumed that the house stands on a street carrying fairly light traffic, that the house contains a kitchen and some kind of living room, and that these rooms contain windows. These elements are not being questioned. Whether the street should have sidewalks, whether the kitchen should be closed or open, whether there should be one living room or two, whether windows should have built-in curtains, or whether any of these elements should exist at all—none of these questions is being asked.

This does not mean that streets, kitchens, living rooms, windows are right as we now know them. Above all, it does not mean that one-family suburban houses are a good idea. They are very likely not. But discussion of these elements would be fruitless without deep analysis of the relationships which define them. The problem has been deliberately restricted to avoid the dangers of unlimited expansion.

This has an obvious consequence. The twenty-six patterns defined here apply only to certain houses whose other defining patterns are those normal for suburban houses in 1968. As soon as the patterns now defining suburban houses—relatively quiet streets, windows, kitchens, living rooms—are changed, the entrance patterns presented here will have to be reexamined. It is impossible to predict how many of them will be stable under the impact of such changes. However, many will still be required. To this extent the twenty-six patterns form an isolable, independent complex.

Four of the twenty-six patterns are presented. Each has the same format: first a verbal statement of the topic, the context, and the relations which the pattern specifies; second, a description of the problem and conflicting tendencies; third, a description of the kinds of arrangement which cause the conflict and the logic of the solution.

Pattern 1.

Finding house numbers from a moving car.

If: Free-standing house on a street where cars move at speeds between 5 miles per hour and 30 miles per hour.

---

4. This study was begun by Christopher Alexander in 1966 and revised and extended for this presentation. The original twenty-six patterns for a suburban house are available from the Center for Environmental Structure, Berkeley.
5. The theoretical framework developed in Berkeley from the concept of "relation" to that of "pattern." The distinctions are briefly made here and in Francis Duffy and John Torrey, "A Progress Report on the Pattern Language," in this volume. This appendix is an example of patterns. See also Alexander, Sara Ishikawa, and Murray Silverstein, *A Pattern Language Which Generates Multi-Service Centers*.

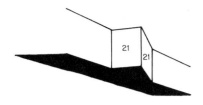

6. Diagram of the pattern of house signs

Then: Two house signs, each at about 45 degrees to the street, facing up and down the street; sign letters 12 inches high, or down to 6 inches if the house is one of a regular sequence of houses all visibly numbered with house signs following this rule. House signs must be 5 feet to 10 feet from the ground and as far forward on the lot as possible.

The problem is that house numbers are hard to see from a moving car, especially for the driver. Many signs have too-small numbers, are parallel to the road (on the house face or garden gate), or they are low enough to be obscured by parked cars or high enough to make the driver crane his neck forward (anything higher than 10 feet may have this effect if the car is near).

The following tendencies conflict:
1. The driver is trying to maintain a reasonable speed on the road, say 25–30 mph.
2. He is trying to identify a house without getting out of his car.
3. He is trying to see the number far enough ahead so that he can slow down and if necessary turn into the driveway.
4. He is trying to keep his eye on the road.

Arrangements that cause this conflict, in addition to numbers that are too small and signs placed too high or too low, include a sign placed at right angles to the street, since this cannot be read from the part of the street in front of the house; a sign more than 10 degrees off the driver's path when close enough to be read;[6] a sign facing only one way.

This conflict may be resolved as follows: At 30 miles per hour, under average road conditions, the safe stopping distance is 245 feet. Furthermore, it will take about 2 seconds to read the number, or 88 feet at 30 mph.[7] The sign must therefore be legible 333 feet from the house. For 99 percent of all drivers to be able to read them, the numbers must be 12 inches high to be legible at 333 feet.[8] Further, so that these numbers are legible from either direction and from the front, they must be placed at an angle to the street, say between 45 and 70 degrees, one facing each direction. The sign must also be as close to the street as possible, so as not to violate the 10 degrees limit. If there is any private land between the sign, and those parts of the street from which the sign is supposed to be visible, trees or outhouses may be put up there in the course of the years and obscure the sign. The sign must therefore be on the property line which divides the street from private property.

At present houses containing this pattern are very rare. However, as soon as the pattern becomes widely accepted, a new factor will come into play: drivers will read house numbers in sequence and slow down as they approach the one they want. Under these conditions it will not be necessary to see the number quite so far ahead, and the numbers may be reduced by half.

Pattern 2.

Letting people inside the house know who is coming to the door.

If: Entrance to any dwelling.

Then: The area outside the main door at least 200 square feet enclosed by walls on three sides and shielded from the street. Kitchen windows and living room windows open onto this area, but not visible from the street. Parking places within or immediately adjacent to this area, and all parts within this area surfaced in noisy material like gravel or wood.

The problem is that people like to know who is coming before they hear the doorbell. In the United States, where almost everybody has a phone, it has become a common courtesy to call ahead; people like to know who's coming in advance. Knocking on doors before you enter is a widely accepted habit

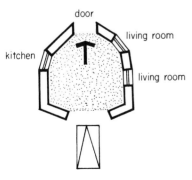

7. Diagram of the pattern of paths leading to the front door

6. R. L. Moore and A. W. Christie, "Research on Traffic Signs."
7. *Ibid.,* especially p. 113 and the formula on p. 117.
8. J. B. Davey, "The Vision of a Group of Drivers."

throughout the Western world. It gives the person inside a chance to adjust himself, mentally, for the coming encounter. In many countries a visitor has to pass through a court before he reaches the house, and while he is in this court he can be seen and heard. However, if the living room or kitchen windows overlook the area in front of the house, they may be exposed directly to the street, which is also undesirable.

The following tendencies conflict:
1. People like to hear visitors coming before the doorbell rings.
2. Visitors tend to take the shortest path off the street, the path to the door is usually within range of street noise, and the noise of arrival is therefore often unnoticed.
3. People tend to "live" away from the street, or if they do live on the street side they tend to keep windows closed.
4. People do not want the inside of the house to be visible from the street.

Some arrangements that cause this conflict are windows that look out on the front but are visible from the street, thus forcing people to curtain them and to live away from them; or a path to the front door that does not pass windows of living areas.

The area in front of the door must be so laid out that the path to the door is visible from windows but the street itself is not. This means that there must be some kind of obstruction placed near the street end of the path. The area must be acoustically shielded from the street; otherwise arrival noises are indistinguishable from street noises. But arrival sounds, like a car engine and footsteps, must be heard, so the car must be brought into the area by the door, and the area must be paved in resonant materials.

Pattern 3.

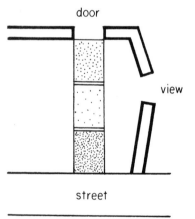

8. Diagram of the change of levels pattern

Transition between street and house in an urban area.

If: Any dwelling in an urban area.

Then: The surface of the paths between street and door and between parking places and door must have at least two changes of level and be made of more than two materials. If possible, there should be some change of view, like an opening into the back garden. The floor of kitchen and living room should be at least one step lower than the floor immediately inside the main door.

The problem is that if the house is too closely associated with the street, people who come into the house find it difficult to lose the "closedness" and tension that are appropriate to street behavior and public encounters, and are thereby prevented from relaxing, or from opening up sufficiently to interact with people in maximum contact.

The following tendencies conflict:
1. On the street people adopt a mask of "street behavior"; the momentum of this mask tends to persist until wiped clean.[9]
2. Arriving home, people search for an inner sanctum where they can relax completely.

Arrangements which cause the conflict are any kind of environmental continuity between street and house, for instance, where the sidewalk continues

9. Evidence for this tendency comes from the report by Serge Bouterline and Robert Weiss, *The Seattle World's Fair.* The authors noticed that many exhibits failed to hold people; they drifted in, then drifted out again within a short time. However, in one exhibit the viewers had to cross a huge, deep-pile, bright orange carpet on the way in. Although the exhibit was not better than other exhibits, they stayed. The authors concluded that people were, in general, under the influence of their own "street and crowd behavior" and that while under this influence they could not relax enough to make contact with the exhibits. But the bright carpet presented them with such a strong contrast that it broke the mood of their outside behavior, in effect "wiped them clean," with the result that they could then become absorbed in the exhibit.

unbroken up to the front door, or where the inside of the house is at the same level as the street or has the same view as from the street.

Arrangements which may prevent the conflict are changes of view, surface materials, and level. A step down into a living room helps destroy the street mask by creating a strong sense of stability and arrival.

Pattern 4.

rooms

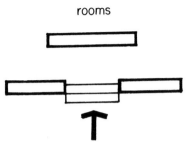

9. Diagram of the doorstep privacy pattern

Privacy when the front door is open.

If: The front door of any dwelling.

Then: Walls inside the main door so placed that a person standing on the doorstep, with the door open, cannot see into any room, especially the living room or kitchen, nor to any passage connecting rooms. The area immediately inside the door must be a dead end. (If there is a window near the front door, the pattern applies also to the areas visible through this window from the doorstep.)

The problem is that people want the inside of the house to be private when they open the front door.

The following tendencies conflict:
1. Politeness demands that when someone comes to the door, the door be opened wide. If the occupant goes back to get something, the door must be left open.
2. People seek privacy for the inside of their houses. In particular, they try to prevent callers from seeing an untidy house.
3. The family, sitting, talking, or at table, do not want to feel disturbed or intruded upon when someone comes to the door.
4. At various times of the day the members of the family may wander around inside the house incompletely dressed.
5. People in the house do not want their movements seen from outside.

Arrangements that cause this conflict are a door that opens directly into any living room, or a door that opens in such a way that a person standing on the step can see into any room whose door is open.

The first part of the pattern is immediate. The argument for the second part is that it may be desirable to have a window opening onto the front doorstep. However, if this window is badly placed it will be curtained and its function destroyed. The window must be placed in such a way that people feel comfortable to leave it uncovered.[10]

10. People are reluctant to use clear glass in doors. See Albert Haberer, *Doors and Gates*, pp. 8–12. When clear glass is provided, if the inside rooms or movement are visible, curtains are put over the glass. For a dramatic example consider a recent house by Edward Barnes. Although the living room seems to be screened from the entrance, in fact the glass at the entrance does give onto the sides of the living room, and the path from the bedroom to the kitchen passes right past the glass. Inevitably the architect was forced to put curtains in as soon as the building went into use. See *Architectural Record*, January 1957, p. 208.

34 Engineering Research and Design in Socioeconomic Systems

Gerald Nadler

Department of Industrial Engineering
University of Wisconsin
Madison, Wisconsin

Gerald Nadler is Professor of Industrial Engineering at the University of Wisconsin and Chairman of the Planning Committee of the Wisconsin Regional Medical Program. He received his Ph.D. in industrial engineering from Purdue University in 1949. He has had extensive industrial and managerial experience and has written widely about industrial engineering research. He was Chairman of the Human and Organizational Factors Area at Washington University, St. Louis, and later Chairman of the Industrial Engineering Division at Wisconsin. His most recent book is *Work Systems Design: The IDEALS Concept*. This paper is reprinted with permission from Arnold Reisman, ed., *Engineering: A Look Inward and a Reach Outward*.

This paper is about the role of systems engineering methods in the planning and design of physical and socioeconomic systems. The aims of research are seen to be different from the aims of design, but the conventional method or strategy of design is identical with the research strategy. In order to develop a comprehensive design method consistent with the aims of design, the nature of all systems encountered in design is analyzed and a universal definition of system given. A sufficient description of a system is offered in terms of a design matrix, the cells of which are filled by means of operational models. However, knowledge of the models is not sufficient to define a comprehensive design method; strategy is also critical. The conventional strategy of problem identification—subdivision into smaller units, analysis of the units, and making changes and implementing them—is criticized, and examples of its use are given. An alternative strategy, the IDEALS concept, is recommended. This is a design strategy and organized program through which is formulated by the ideal system concept the most effective system for achieving necessary functions. Levels of ideal systems from theoretically ideal to technologically workable are discussed, and solutions recommended. Steps in this strategy are outlined. Some examples from physical planning, design, and organizational planning are given to illustrate the argument and recommended strategy.

As technical problems become more complex and as systems engineering is more and more involved with society's problems, this branch of engineering is developing a sense of its history and an international awareness. It is beginning consciously to study previously off-limits concepts. This paper is about the role of systems engineering in the planning and design of the physical environment.

Methodology in Engineering is Critical

We do not yet have a systematization of design or an understanding of what design is all about, as we have a systematization and understanding of scientific research. Science involves a rationale and philosophy as well as a plan of attack to achieve its results. Research, usually critical and exhaustive investigation or experimentation having for its aim the establishment of general laws, is the methodology or strategy of science. Design, the act or art of making plans, schemes, patterns, models, is the way useful results are obtained in engineering, architecture, and planning. The end is not to generalize but to reach a specific solution. Yet when a design strategy is stated explicitly, it is almost identical to research strategy. How could two such diverse purposes have the same strategies? And why is it that research on strategies is so recent?

Strategy must involve concepts of creativity, systems definition, optimization, and a program of implementation. All these facets are tied together in a step-by-step attack on a particular problem.

Perhaps some illustrations are in order. In each of the particular problems listed here, you should imagine how you would seek a solution. As you do this, you will be using a strategy that in almost all cases is based on the research strategy. The broad engineering question I am addressing is what strategy should be used in designing an optimal system to achieve a particular result.

1. Traffic flow in a city. This problem obviously involves many components with complex interrelationships. Yet there is a particular objective to be achieved. How would you go about trying to solve a traffic flow problem? What would you do first? What steps would you follow? Almost all people would immediately respond with an analytical approach, the research approach. Analysis will be used in my proposed method, as later discussions will show, but at a much more appropriate time.

2. Loading dock in a warehouse. An engineer suggested a $25,000 expenditure for a piece of equipment which would almost automate a section of the loading dock. The rate of return was quite good, payback in much less than one year. It was approved by three levels of management before the vice president asked two staff men to review the request. What strategy or plan of attack should be used to investigate the necessity for and rationale of this particular expenditure?

3. Development of a design methodology curriculum for a department of engineering, architecture, or planning. Notice that the desired result, as in all the other illustrations, is a specific solution or "system" to achieve a specific purpose in a specific setting. What plan of attack would you follow in designing such a system?

4. Gasoline tank cover. This cover has to be designed to admit air when the tank is above water but exclude water when the tank is underwater. (The vehicle is an Army tank.) What strategy would you follow in designing the specifications for the cover?

5. Regional medical program for heart diseases, stroke, and cancer. The problem is to design health systems for delivering the best heart, stroke, and cancer care to the citizens of the Wisconsin region. What strategy would you follow for this problem?[1]

I could give additional illustrations, but this broad spectrum, including several socioeconomic problems, will suffice to show that some strategy is involved in seeking solutions. In the broad sense, each of these projects is a systems engineering problem. I will refer again to these illustrations to show how the appropriate strategy produced excellent results, better than any conventional strategy.

Importance of Investigating Strategies

The problems I have presented are critical in our society, and the way solutions are sought is likewise critical. There are several reasons why this is so.
1. We cannot afford many errors in proposing a solution. Time is often critical, and an error pushes the problem into even greater complexities because of the lost time.
2. Society needs to maximize the utilization of the scarcest national resource of all, human beings. We engineers have done little to maximize the utilization of human resources compared to what we did for natural resources such as coal, oil, and iron.
3. Better education of engineers, and others, can be achieved by emphasis

---

1. This example is discussed in Paul C. Nutt, David H. Gustafson, and Gerald Nadler, "Systems Engineering as Applied to Planning Processes: An Example from the Wisconsin Regional Medical Program," in this volume.

on the proper design strategy. Why should we teach an approach to design which is not correct and hope that the student will intuitively find a better one? Creative geniuses use a strategy different from that of research. Why not teach the correct strategy?

Today's systems engineer needs to obtain the best of two worlds: the knowledge developed by the sciences on which engineering relies and the problem and design orientation that has classically been the role of engineering.

With this background, I want (1) to show how a universal definition of system permits all the illustrative projects I presented earlier to be viewed in the same system context, and (2) to describe a design strategy that permits any system, regardless of size, scope, or technology, to be approached with the same plan of attack to assure the best possible design for immediate use.

Universal Definition of System

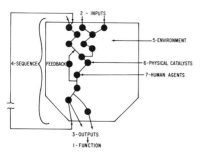

1. Model of any system

I suppose if I asked all of you to define "system," we would get as many answers as there are people. For example, people often define systems in terms of size: a system will be anything that involves 25 or more people. Or in terms of cost: a system must cost $100,000 or more. Or in terms of complexity: a system has to have many interrelating factors. Or by putting an adjective in front of the word system: computer system, building system, or transportation system. System ought to be defined instead in terms of its seven basic elements which are applicable in design settings regardless of the kind of project or of the technology involved.

Figure 1 illustrates the seven elements. It represents a system as a hopper. A large hopper means a bigger system and a little hopper a smaller system. It is even possible to put a hopper around any one of the circles and the same seven system elements describe that small system.

1. Function. If there is one mistake made in system design today, it is to forget the fact that a system must have a function. What is the system supposed to be accomplishing, not how will it accomplish this?

2. Inputs. Inputs can be physical (a coil of steel to be processed), informational (verbal or written matter, holes in a card, a magnetic tape), or human. "Feedback" input of any of these three types refers to previous output which entered the outside world and returns to the system again as inputs.

3. Outputs. Outputs are the end result of converting the inputs. Notice the important difference between outputs and function. These are not the same; one of the biggest mistakes in systems design is to assume that the output is the same as the function. For example, take a common mechanical pencil. What is the function of the system of manufacturing these pencils? Most people say the function is to make pencils at a profit. In reality, the function of the system is to produce an instrument to record information. The output, on the other hand, is this particular mechanical pencil. There is a great difference; just ask the manufacturers of pencils at about the time ballpoint pens were introduced. Ballpoint pens have the same function, but the output is different.

4. Sequence. Sequence is the order of steps for converting inputs into outputs. Yet sequence alone is frequently considered a system. In my definition it is only one of seven elements.

5. Environment. Environment can be physical or it can be attitudinal; for example, the managerial atmosphere. Is it a permissive organization or an autocratic organization? Important in the systems idea is the concept that the environment in many ways can be designed along with the other elements.

6. Physical catalysts. Physical catalysts are any physical items that help convert inputs into outputs but do not become part of the output.

7. Human agents. The people and the methods used to aid in converting inputs into outputs but do not become part of that output. Therefore, human agents, like physical catalysts, differ from inputs. For example, through one door of a hospital may come a person who enters that hospital as a patient. Through the same door may come a nurse. By my definition the nurse, as a human agent who aids in converting inputs to outputs, is distinguished from the patient, an input.

This seven-point definition of a system applies to any one of the illustrative projects I mentioned and all others you can think of. It is universally applicable. It represents the elements an engineer should consider as he designs a system. When the elements are placed, with "dimensions," in a design matrix, shown in Figure 2, the engineer has a convenient aid. The design matrix defines the cells of information which should be reviewed and filled in to prepare a complete design for that system. The design matrix uses the seven system elements as the rows and the physical, rate, control, and state dimensions as columns. When each element row is completed, the system we have in mind is fully designed.

Dimensions

A word should be said about the "dimensions" of the matrix. The *physical* dimension is the tangible or real-life part of the system. The physical dimension of output for the mechanical pencil specifies ¼ inch diameter, 5½ inches long, white top, black plastic base.

DIMENSIONS

	PHYSICAL	RATE	CONTROL	STATE
FUNCTION				
INPUTS				
OUTPUTS				
SEQUENCE				
ENVIRONMENT				
PHYSICAL CATALYSTS				
HUMAN AGENTS				

SYSTEM ELEMENTS

2. Design matrix

The *rate* dimension represents some measure of the physical dimension per unit of time. For example one output rate dimension might be 1000 pencils an hour. A sequence rate dimension might be processing 3000 pencil barrels per hour. The environment rate dimension might involve the number of times per hour the air is completely circulated.

The *control* dimension pertains to the way one or more of the other dimensions is to be measured as the system operates, compared through feedback information to desired specifications and confidence limits, and corrected if necessary to maintain the desired specifications.

The *state* dimension refers to the anticipated state of physical rate, and/or control dimension at some point in the future. We cannot say that the physical, rate, and control dimensions for the traffic flow problem, for example, will remain the same as today. The state dimension provides for continuing orderly change; we should not design a system unless we design into it the dimensions for change.

A system is considered designed when all necessary information, usually in the form of models, is placed in each cell of the design matrix. The information describes how the whole system is to operate. Thus the design matrix is a convenient summary by which an engineer, architect, or planner can review any kind of project. If each cell can not be filled in, the engineer or designer must review it to determine if information is necessary. But if a designer gives me all 28 cells of information for a particular system, I should be able to go any place in the world and, given the resources there, establish that system exactly as it might be set up here.

The Concept of Strategies

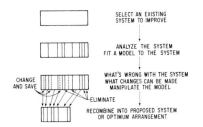

SELECT AN EXISTING SYSTEM TO IMPROVE

ANALYZE THE SYSTEM FIT A MODEL TO THE SYSTEM

WHAT'S WRONG WITH THE SYSTEM WHAT CHANGES CAN BE MADE MANIPULATE THE MODEL

CHANGE AND SAVE

ELIMINATE

RECOMBINE INTO PROPOSED SYSTEM OR OPTIMUM ARRANGEMENT

3. Schematic of the conventional process

All of us use a strategy in seeking a solution to a problem. Figure 3 illustrates the conventional design strategy, the one most often followed. The first step is to identify a problem or existing system, illustrated by the first rectangle. The second step is to subdivide the system into components or analyze the existing system and break it into smaller units. The third step is to manipulate the analysis, reviewing the various components to find what is wrong with them. The fourth step then is to make the changes and install the recommendations.

As an illustration of how pervasive this strategy is, consider the problem of designing an industrial engineering curriculum. When evaluating the curriclum at the University of Puerto Rico, the chairman of the department told me they had analyzed all their existing courses by detailing the outlines, listing all the problems and exercises, and identifying all the textbooks. He suggested we start by reviewing all this analysis, course by course, and I could then criticize what had been done. In effect, the chairman of the department had identified the curriculum as the existing system (step 1), broken it into components (step 2), and then asked me to help them review the analysis and subdivision to find how the system might be modified or changed (step 3). It is obvious that what I suggested we do follows the design strategy I will describe in a moment, rather than his strategy, but you should recognize that the conventional strategy is followed almost all the time.

It is interesting to note that most engineers follow the same strategy even though they might be designing a *new* system. For example, what would be your probable first reaction if I were to ask any of you who had never designed a plant for manufacturing mechanical pencils to now assume the responsibility for such a system design project? Following the conventional strategy, it would be, "Let's find out what is done in other pencil manufacturing systems." You would go to some other facilities to learn what is happening now. This is analyzing the system, then checking it to see what might be changed to arrive at a system you could call your own.

In other words, the conventional strategy is almost identical to research strategy, a strategy used to identify general laws, theories, or principles. It should be apparent that research for developing laws is much different than design for detailing a specific system solution for a specific set of circumstances. The first is inductive; it seeks a generalization to unify a series of facts. Design, on the other hand, is deductive; it seeks a specific answer deduced from generalizations or theories.

The two strategies do intermix. For example, we were designing a data-processing system for physicians' orders in a hospital. One specific solution for a specific set of circumstances was sought. As we proceeded with the design strategy, we found that a particular generalization was not available, namely, the characteristics and distributions of physicians' orders. At that point, we stopped and did research with the research strategy. We gathered and analyzed existing information to give us a useful generalization, for example, a negative exponential distribution relating the frequency of orders with the types of orders. The research strategy was used to find this generalization within the design strategy for the whole project.

I think it is unfortunate that the conventional strategy is used for design. It gives a solution which is very limited. It puts blinders on the eyes of the designer, involving him in what is wrong instead of in what should be done. It forces designers to adopt a technique orientation, that is, finding where a technique can be applied rather than what problem needs solving. And it causes people in organizations to defend the present methods just because so much about the systems in which they work is presented in an unfavorable light.

The IDEALS Concept

The design methodology or strategy I recommend is the IDEALS concept (Ideal Design of Effective And Logical Systems). I will present solutions to some of the problems I mentioned earlier, point out how the results using the IDEALS strategy are better than those from the conventional strategy, and discuss how this kind of empirical work is developing a more useful strategy and providing better solutions for new socioeconomic problems as well as for more usual problems.

The IDEALS concept is a design strategy and organized program applicable to contemplated and present systems in which is formulated, through an ideal systems concept, the most effective systems for achieving necessary functions. Let me explain this definition.

"Design strategy" merely says that a step-by-step approach or plan of attack will be used for design. It will be orderly, but it will not necessarily be based on the research strategy. The phrase "contemplated and present systems" means that the strategy is not restricted to those systems now in existence. The same strategy can be adopted for a system not yet existent, for one that does exist but in difficulty, or for one that exists in a satisfactorily operating state.

"Most effective systems" introduces the idea that efficiency is not the sole criterion for systems design; how well the function is achieved (effectiveness) is more important. Efficiency is included in effectiveness but effectiveness means more than efficiency.

"For achieving necessary functions" is one of the most important parts of this concept. There is nothing more disconcerting than to find an elegant and efficient system for an unnecessary function. For example, consider the system I saw for removing paper and glue from the front of chrome-plated stainless steel sheets. It was a beautiful layout, efficient in its flow. I asked what was the function of the system. After consideration, my host said that they, the fabricator, assumed that the vendor put on the paper and glue to protect the front of the sheet in shipment so it would not get scratched. The vendor, on the other hand, assumed that the fabricator wanted the paper and glue to protect the front of the sheet as it was being punched and stamped through the fabrication process. It turned out that neither vendor nor operator wanted the paper.

For a second example, consider the warehouse I mentioned earlier. The engineer at the warehouse recommended a new piece of automation equipment for the loading dock. The equipment would cost $25,000 with payback period of less than one year, thus providing a very good rate of return. It was approved by the supervisor of the warehouse, the manager of the warehouses, and the director of distribution. When the request reached the vice president, it was given for evaluation to a group using the IDEALS concept strategy. Their recommendation was to sell the warehouse. In its place, the solution they found was a transportation system for distributing goods from manufacturing plants to retailers which did not require warehousing and necessitated only a slightly increased amount of inventory at the plants. The $25,000 worth of equipment for the old warehouse would have technically returned the cost in less than a year, but the better solution was found by focusing on the function of the total system and identifying a necessary function level.

The phrase "through the ideal systems concept" is the last we need to consider. I have already put the basic idea, that instead of analyzing the existing system, you design the *best* system possible, and then use that information as a guide in developing a recommended solution. It is a very simple idea. It is obviously a lot more difficult to execute, and it must be implemented *now*, not later. That is the role of systems designers. But the critical difference of using the information derived from designing the ideal system provides much better recommended solutions.

Imagine, for example, how you would design a system to manufacture pencils. The conditions would be far more ideal for the design if there were unlimited distribution, unlimited resources, and only one model of pencil to design the system for. These represent a set of conditions we call ideal. We design the system for that set of conditions, and then, and only then, make it compatible with the fact that we need 14 different colors and 53 different styles of pencils. This is what happens in the IDEALS Concept. The strategy is to develop the best or ideal system for the conditions considered ideal and then make it compatible with real life.

Levels of Ideal Systems

The triangle in Figure 4 illustrates what is meant by ideal systems. Let the distance between the legs of the triangle be equivalent to cost per unit. Every

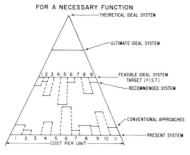

THEORETICAL IDEAL SYSTEM

ULTIMATE IDEAL SYSTEM

1 2 3 4 5 6 7 8 9
FEASIBLE IDEAL SYSTEM
TARGET (FIST)
RECOMMENDED SYSTEM

CONVENTIONAL APPROACHES

PRESENT SYSTEM

1 2 3 4 5 6 7 8 9 10 11
COST PER UNIT

4. Levels of ideal systems

system has a unit output whether the unit is a service, product, or type of information. A cost for that unit output can also be identified. Other criteria such as time or energy can also be used, but cost is the most general and the one most of us understand.

The apex of the triangle represents no cost per unit and this level is identified as the *theoretical ideal system.* But one never designs theoretical ideal systems just as one does not count to infinity. The theoretical ideal system fulfills the same role in the IDEALS concept that infinity fulfills in mathematics. It is a limit value. If someone asks me how far can I go in designing a system, the answer is to the no-cost-per-unit limit. It would be difficult to have a good design strategy without a theoretical ideal system or limit value toward which everyone moves in design activities.

The *ultimate ideal system* is a level actually designed. The ultimate ideal system is one that cannot be used today because further research and development is necessary before it can be made practical. For example, in manufacturing washing machines and dryers, one of the ultimate ideal systems is to have clothes that do not get dirty. If anyone develops this feature, the company might as well do it. True, it will gradually put them out of the business of making washing machines and dryers, but it will put them into the business of making clothes that do not get dirty.

A *feasible ideal system* (FIS) is a system that is technologically workable for the ideal conditions. Everyone, I am sure, agrees that it is possible to design a completely automatic system for manufacturing a particular mechanical pencil which represents one ideal condition. But one may not be able to install a FIS because other conditions and restrictions of the real-life situation must now be incorporated. Customers want colors in pencils other than black and white. They like 14 different colors and a variety of styles. Therefore, each component of the FIS is reviewed to develop alternatives to the ideal system components that are as close as possible to the *feasible ideal system target* or FIST. Thus the recommended solution comes as close as possible to the feasible ideal.

Three important advantages accrue to engineers and designers who are using the IDEALS strategy. The first advantage is that a better system is designed. This has been shown by many comparisons between the results of two groups of professionals designing the same system, one group using the conventional strategy and the other group using the IDEALS concept. For example, recall the warehouse system presented earlier. The engineer at the warehouse used the conventional strategy. He recommended one solution, whereas the solution recommended by the group using the IDEALS strategy was to sell the warehouse. Saving the total cost of the warehouse is a much better solution than spending $25,000 for an activity in the nonessential warehouse.

The second advantage is that it takes less time to design the better system. This might surprise you because you thought that designing an ideal system requires a great deal of time. It does not. Much time in conventional strategies is spent analyzing the existing system, and this the IDEALS concept greatly reduces. In addition, analysis of the existing system never gives a clue about what information is needed. You probably have had the experience of asking your boss, or of having someone ask you, what information should be gathered for a particular project. A shrug of the shoulders is the usual answer, along with "I don't know, you might as well get it all." A great deal of information-gathering then takes place, and most of it is never used. By developing the ideal system first, a clear specification of the necessary information is available, and only that information is gathered.

The third advantage is just as important as the first two, but is especially important if you do not believe the first two. When the recommended system is installed, built-in change is also installed because the changes that can be expected are already designed. The installation of a system derived by a conventional strategy seldom includes any idea of what changes might be made in that system. As a matter of fact, the conventional strategy makes the designers so glad to be able to install any system that they forget the fact the system can be made even better at some future point in time. This need is essential regardless of the type of project, and it is just as important as any other benefit of the IDEALS concept.

Steps in the IDEALS Concept Strategy

The design strategy in the IDEALS concept involves ten steps, five of which are presented in some detail.

1. Function determination. This step means more than just the function of the system that starts the project; it means identifying the function of the system that should be designed. In most cases, the selected function is different than that for the originating system. This step thus ascertains the necessity of the system. Is the system really necessary, or, conversely, is the system being designed for a necessary function?

2. Ideal systems development. Develop several ideal systems from which the best guide, called the feasible ideal system target (FIST), can be selected.

3. Information gathering. Of the many questions that arise, answer only the pertinent ones. Research is also often performed in this step. It should be clear that this IDEALS concept strategy enables systems designers to identify what information is essential and deal only with that research or information. Sometimes this reduces data collection as much as 95 percent.

4. Alternative suggestions. Some of the gathered information may point out that a component or two in the FIST are not usable. It is thus necessary to develop alternatives to incorporate the exceptions. The pencils, for example, are needed in 14 colors instead of one.

5. Select the workable system. Which of the many alternatives should be combined into the whole real-life system for the particular situation is a question that involves tradeoffs among the various criteria for evaluating the systems.

The next five steps are: (6) formulate and optimize the details of the system, (7) review the system details, (8) test the system or some components, (9) install the system, and (10) establish performance measures. The last step enables an orderly transfer of the system design to an operator, controller, or manager who will operate the system.

Throughout steps 3 through 10, the FIST or ideal system target is used as a continual reference to keep the actual system as close as possible to the ideal system. In addition, all steps are iterative, rather than being followed in monolithic fashion one step at a time.

Conclusion

The systems engineer of today is progressing both in technical developments and in engineering design strategy. He applies design strategies to diverse fields, to environmental design and planning, education, government, the building industry, regional medical programs, and others I have mentioned. It seems fortunate that engineers are broadening their interest in terms of applications, doing the research to provide themselves with new knowledge in undertaking new types of projects, and educating themselves in a broader range of disciplines in the preparation for this work.

The involvement of engineers in today's and tomorrow's socioeconomic and environmental problems is taking place on a much higher level than the crude attempts at social engineering in the early 1900s. The engineer is a member of a team, he utilizes disciplines other than his own, he has much better techniques and tools, and he is greatly interested.

I have tried to present only two major items from the whole list of research and design advances that engineers are making:[2] a definition of system and a design strategy. The major points, therefore, that summarize my paper are:

1. There is a definition of system, four dimensions of seven elements, that is universally applicable to old and new areas of engineering applications.

2. There is a design strategy, the IDEALS concept, markedly different from the conventional or research strategy and which gives much better results in systems design.

2. For other examples within the context of design and planning methodology, see Morris Asimow, *Introduction to Design*; John R. Dixon, *Design Engineering: Inventiveness, Analysis, and Decision*; Sidney A. Gregory, ed., *The Design Method*; and Edward V. Krick, *An Introduction to Engineering and Engineering Design.*

35 A Design Process Model: Theory and Application to Transportation Planning

Marvin L. Manheim

Department of Civil Engineering
Massachusetts Institute of
Technology
Cambridge, Massachusetts

Marvin L. Manheim is Associate Professor
of Civil Engineering at M.I.T. He received
an S.B. in civil engineering in 1959 and a
Ph.D. in transportation and urban planning in 1964, both from M.I.T. As a Captain
in the Transportation Corps, U.S. Army, he
received the Army Commendation Medal
for developing Project STRATMAS, applying computer systems to strategic mobility
analyses. Since 1966 he has been responsible for the academic and research programs of the Transportation Systems
Division at M.I.T. He is a regional editor
of *Transportation Research,* academic
vice-president of the Transportation Research Forum, a member of the Long-
range Planning Committee of the Highway
Research Board, and Chairman of the
Editorial Advisory Board of the Design
Methods Group. This research was supported by the U.S. Department of Transportation, Office of Systems Analysis; the
General Motors Grant for Highway Transportation Research; the Special Assistant
to the Joint Chiefs of Staff for Strategic
Mobility, Department of Defense; and the
Ford Foundation through a grant to the
Urban Systems Laboratory of M.I.T.

The objective of this paper is to outline a
theoretical model of the design process
and show its operational implications. To
motivate this discussion, the essential
features of transportation planning are
summarized as an example of a class of
design problems. In the next section a
popular model of the design process, the
rational model, is reviewed and its limitations discussed. A more complete model
of the design process, the PSP (problem-
solving process) model, is then presented
and its implications explored. In the
fourth section the applicability of the
PSP model to transportation planning is
demonstrated, and systematic analyses
of transportation alternatives are illustrated. Specific operational techniques
which have been developed to implement
or extend the PSP model, in the light of
issues raised by the prototype analysis,
are described in conclusion.

Before entering the central discussion of a general design process model,
the essential features of one class of design problems, transportation systems
analysis and planning, will be summarized.

The Problem of Transportation Planning

Describing the transportation systems problem requires identification of the
options, the potential impacts of the options on the environment, the procedures for prediction of impacts, and the issues of "search and choice."

Options

There are five main aspects of a transportation system which can be varied:
1. Technology: development and/or implementation of new combinations
of transportation components which enable transportation services to be
offered in ways which were not previously available; for example, containers,
and new urban mass transportation concepts.[1]
2. Networks: the general configuration of the network as well as the approximate geographic location of the network links.
3. Link characteristics: capacity, speed, etc., in connection with highways,
airways, and rail lines.

---

1. For new urban mass transportation concepts, see Mark Hanson, ed., *Project ME-
TRAN,* and the Department of Housing and Urban Development, *Tomorrow's Transportation.*

4. Vehicles: number of vehicles in the system, and their characteristics.
5. Operating policies: how the transportation system is operated, routes and schedules of the vehicles, types of service including passenger meal services, diversion and reconsignment privileges for freight, and prices to be charged.

This set of transportation options fully defines the space of possible transportation plans and policies. However, these options are not exercised in a vacuum but in the context of a system of social and economic activities. These transactions, both actual and potential, determine the demand for transportation, and in turn the levels of spatial patterns of these interactions are affected in part by the transportation services provided.

Therefore, in addition to the options about the transportation system itself, we must clearly identify those options in the activity system which will be expressed as the demands on the system.
1. Travel: the decisions by every potential user of the transportation system whether to take a trip at all, where to make it, when, and by what mode and route. The aggregate result of all the individual decisions about travel is expressed as the demand for transportation.
2. Activity system: each of the social, economic, and political actors in the activity system has a wide range of options about how, when, and where to conduct its activities. Over the long term, these options profoundly influence the demand for transportation. For example, forces within the economy external to the transportation system, such as housing subsidies or mortgage policy, may impact on the spatial pattern of activity and thus affect the demand for transportation.

These options are in the hands of a large variety of public and private decision-makers. Whether controllable or not, the full set of transportation and activity system options must be considered in any analysis.

Impacts

When evaluating alternative transportation systems, one would like to consider all relevant impacts. Any change in the transportation system can potentially affect a large variety of individuals and interests, grouped as follows:
1. Users: by location within the region, by trip purpose, and by socioeconomic groups; for example, suburban residents commuting to central city jobs, and low-income non-car-owning residents of the central city traveling to clinics or other health facilities.
2. Operators: by mode, by link; for example, air carrier or toll highway operator.
3. Physical: by type of impact, by link; for example, families, jobs, taxable values displaced by new construction, pollution of immediate environment through noise, fumes, air pollution, and ground water changes.
4. Functional: by location within region, by type; for example, changes in retail sales areas of shopping center.
5. Governmental: by location, by level; for example, local, state, and national representatives.

Prediction

Any proposed change in a transportation system (or a completely new system) can be expressed in terms of the options identified above. The problem of prediction is to anticipate the impacts associated with any set of options. In transportation, as illustrated in Figure 1, the impacts depend upon the pattern of flows in the network, and this will result from the particular set of options. The approach to predicting these flows is that of network supply-demand equilibrium analysis.[2]

While conceptually simple, network equilibrium analysis is generally difficult and expensive. The major, but by no means only, difficulty is the role of the network in constraining the equilibrium flow pattern. In order to implement fully this analysis approach, a system of five major types of models is re-

---

2. See Manheim, Kiran Bhatt, and Earl R. Ruiter, *Search and Choice in Transport Systems Planning: An Overview.*

quired: supply, demand, resource, network equilibrium, and demand shift models.

The Problems of Search and Choice

The framework of equilibrium analysis provides a basis for prediction of the impacts associated with a particular set of options. However, there still remain major issues:

1. The problem of search: how to generate alternative transportation systems worth "testing" in the complex system of prediction models.

2. The problem of choice: given the predicted impacts of several alternative specifications of options, how to evaluate the impacts and choose among the alternatives. The difficulties in choice arise in part because an essential characteristic of transportation is the differential incidence of its impacts; some groups will gain from any transportation system change, others may lose.

Transportation choices are essentially sociopolitical choices; the interests of different groups must be balanced.[3] The development of a real-world, implementable transportation plan or policy requires more than just the prediction of impacts of one or two alternatives. Feasible, desirable solutions can be developed only through a sensitive analysis, in a systematic way, of a variety of alternatives and their impacts.

Systematic analysis in transportation planning requires that a wide variety of alternative options be explored and their differential impacts traced out explicitly, as in Figures 2 and 3, where systematic exploration of the full range of options for each transportation link is shown. For example, changes in a particular link by introducing a new mass transit technology or changing the fare over the route will impact differentially on various user groups, the operator of this particular facility, the operators of all other facilities, and the physical and functional components. Figure 3 shows how changes in the options for this particular link, as reflected solely in speed over the link, might impact differentially on the various groups. (This is hypothetical; the actual variations would be a property of the network at hand.) Because of the complexity of the supply-demand interactions in the network, prediction of the change in impacts for any change in options requires the full set of prediction models.

Thus, the task is systematically to search out and choose among transportation systems alternatives, with careful consideration of the differential impacts on different groups. Inevitably, the hard realities of alternative transportation technologies and complex computer models lead into the "soft," subtle differences of impacts: who gets better service with a prospective change, who gets worse service, who pays, and how do the users change the way they work, live, and relax as a result.

The Rational Analysis Process

Underlying the discussion of transportation systems was a concern with how this substantive problem should be analyzed. In order to understand how to conduct systematic analyses of transportation policy, we must step back from the substantive problem of transportation and focus on the general process of analysis.

This section discusses the analysis process in transportation by first pointing out some of the major issues and reviewing the rational model and its limitations. In the next section, a new conceptual model will be outlined.

The Rational Model and Its Limitations

The essence of the rational model of decision-making is expressed in the common prescription of "systems analysis": (1) Define objectives and formulate a utility function; (2) enumerate all the possible alternative actions; (3) identify the consequences of each action; (4) evaluate the consequences

---

3. This does not mean that negative impacts of a system on some group are inevitable. It may well be possible, particularly with complementary programs such as relocation subsidies and industrial development to develop a concerted strategy such that no single group is hurt unduly. But to do this requires sensitive analysis of the transportation and nontransportation options.

1. The prediction problem

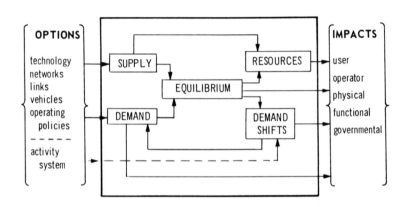

2. Changes in a network

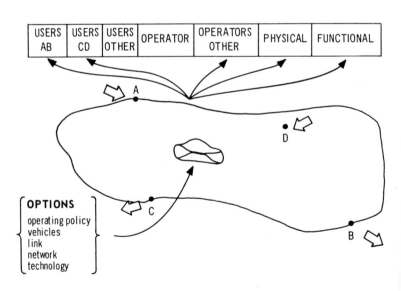

3. Differential impacts

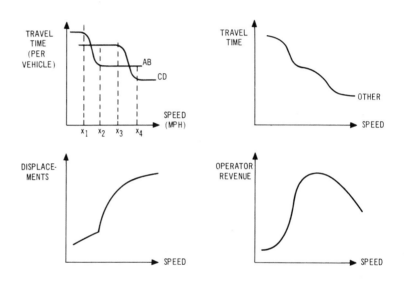

4. Basic search and choice cycle

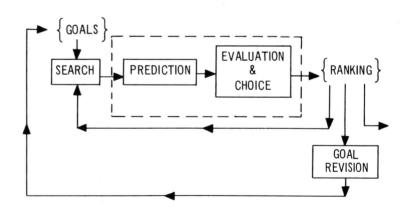

in terms of the objectives via the utility function; and (5) choose that action which best achieves the objectives.[4]

This "synoptic" model[5] has only limited application to complex policy questions such as transportation, for many reasons:

1. We can never know completely all the alternatives.

2. We can never define all the relevant objectives, consistently and completely. First, there are too many points of view, "actors," to get agreement on objectives, and second, objectives are difficult to formulate in the abstract and will be substantially revised and clarified through examination of the consequences of specific alternatives.[6]

3. We can never completely identify the relative values of all possible combinations of the various objectives (i.e., we can never get a fully defined utility function). We prefer to examine alternatives explicitly and to evaluate the incremental differences between them.[7]

4. There will always be uncertainty in the prediction of consequences. Many relevant consequences will be left out, and there will be unanticipated consequences.[8]

5. The costliness of analysis is a severe constraint.

6. Analysis is dynamic. Problems are never solved completely. Massive changes in a system such as the transportation system generally take time for implementation, and as specific changes are implemented, the context of the problem changes. Within the analysis process itself, initial statements of objectives will be revised as successive alternative actions are generated and examined, and examination of previous alternatives will suggest new ones for analysis.

Perhaps the best way of summarizing the limitations of the rational model is that "in the face of man's limited capacities, it offers simply a prescription: Be comprehensive!"[9] The comprehensive ideal fails to accept the realities of policy analysis: the costs of analysis, and the inability to be comprehensive, because of cost and cognitive reasons. This does not mean, as some would argue, that systematic analysis must be discarded altogether; rather, the simple five-step model of the analysis process must be replaced by a more subtle structure.

PSP: A Dynamic Model of Decision-Making

As a partial answer to the limitations of the rational model described, a more complete model of decision-making is necessary. Such a model has been formulated, the PSP model. Only a few of its major characteristics will be summarized here.[10]

The first important characteristic of the problem-solving process model is the role of time. To develop, evaluate, and choose among alternatives takes time. Further, the analysis process is itself imbedded in the larger evolutionary process of the real-world system of interest; the actions selected by analysis are implemented, their results observed, and new analyses lead to new, revised actions—also taking time.

---

4. See, for example, Sidney Schoeffler, "Toward a General Theory of Rational Action"; Arthur D. Hall, *A Methodology for Systems Engineering;* Charles J. Hitch and Roland N. McKean, *The Economics of Defense in the Nuclear Age;* William J. Baumol, *Economic Theory and Operations Analysis;* and Russel L. Ackoff, *Scientific Method: Optimizing Applied Research Decisions.* See also Section 7, Applications of Systems Engineering, in this volume.

5. David Braybrooke and Charles E. Lindblom, *A Strategy of Decision*; and Lindblom, *The Intelligence of Democracy.* Although drawing heavily on their insights, I have modified them substantially. See also W. Steger and T. Lakshmanan, "Plan Evaluation Methodologies: Some Aspects of Decision Requirements and Analytical Response."

6. Lindblom, *Intelligence of Democracy,* pp. 140–142.

7. *Ibid.*

8. Martin Meyerson and Edward C. Banfield, *Politics, Planning and the Public Interest,* p. 319.

9. Lindblom, *Intelligence of Democracy,* p. 139.

10. For complete treatment, see Manheim, *Problem-Solving Processes in Planning & Design* and Manheim, Kenneth G. Follansbee, and Ronald Walter, *Modelling the Evolutionary Nature of Problem-Solving.*

The second important characteristic of the PSP model is the distinction between generating actions and choosing among them. We emphasize this distinction by defining search and selection as the procedures which perform these functions. *Search* designates any procedure used to produce one or more alternative actions. Search may be intuitive, as in the sense of "design," or it may be formalized, as in a linear programming model. *Selection* designates the process of choosing among several alternative actions. The input to selection is a set of alternative actions. The output of selection is a "preference ordering," or ranking of the actions by desirability.

To accomplish selection, three basically different kinds of procedures are required. *Prediction* models are used to anticipate the consequences an action would have if implemented in the real world. For example, a model could be used to predict volume of travel on a particular transportation link. *Evaluation* procedures operate upon the predicted consequences to yield statements of the valuations or relative desirabilities of those consequences, for example, the values of user costs and benefits associated with a particular flow volume on a link, or the relative desirability of a particular regional growth pattern. Since all predicted consequences cannot be represented adequately by a single measure of value, or valuation, we do not assume that evaluation summarizes all the valuations into such a single measure. For example, we do not assume that construction dollars, loss of recreation land, and regional development patterns can all be lumped into a single measure of value, such as dollars or some overall utility measure. Therefore, after evaluation there must be *choice* procedures in which each action is compared on the basis of its set of valuations—dollar costs, recreation land acreages, quality of regional pattern, etc.—and a decision made about the rankings of the actions. Choice is difficult, but necessary.[11]

The third important characteristic is a distinction between the state of the analysis process at any particular time, and the procedures which may be used to change that state. The state of the process expresses the analyst's current view of the problem. The problem-solving system contains a variety of procedures, to be used in the problem-solving process when and as appropriate. Each time a procedure is used, it changes the state of the process as it changes the analyst's view of the problem.

From the point of view of our present discussion, the major variables describing the state of the process are the actions, A, the goals, G, and the current ranking of the actions, R. The major procedures for changing the state are search, selection, and goal formulation and revision.[12] Both search and selection involve some reference to the current set of goals G.

The basic view of the problem-solving process which this implies is shown in Figure 4. Alternative actions are generated and a preference ordering is established over those alternatives. If the most desirable alternative is sufficiently attractive, then the problem-solving process ceases and that most desirable action is implemented in the real world. If not, then search is repeated and new actions are generated. The sequence is repeated, until finally there is one action sufficiently attractive for implementation in the real world.

This image of a "trial-and-error" process, basic to the PSP concept, is completely contrary to the image of a problem for which the optimal solution is obtained directly by "solving" a mathematical (or other) model. Such "optimizing" methods do have an important role in the broader PSP, but such real

---

11. At this point we shall not distinguish between choice executed by the analytical staff, and choice executed by a small group of decision-makers or by the larger political process.
12. Additional state variables include: consequences, valuations, raw information and probability distributions over uncertain variables. Additional procedures include information analysis, model construction and revision, decomposition and restructuring procedures, and metaprocedures. See Manheim, *Problem-Solving Processes in Planning and Design.*

problems as transport-systems planning are too complex for such techniques to carry the whole burden. A particular optimizing method corresponds to *one* search-and-selection sequence, but many kinds of search and selection procedures are required in addressing the total problem.

Evolution of Actions and Goals

The focus of a PSP is on actions. Because search and selection procedures concern the basic generation and selection of actions, these procedures are at the heart of the PSP. There are a variety of other activities which must occur in a PSP to allow search and selection to operate, but except for those concerned with goals, these are not discussed here.[13]

The purpose of goal formulation and revision procedures is just that: to formulate and revise the statement of goals, G, as new actions are generated and their consequences examined. That is, each cycle of search and selection potentially may trigger goal revision. This can be summarized as follows:
1. An initial statement of goals is formulated.
2. The search procedures are executed, one or several times, producing one or more alternative actions.
3. The selection procedures are executed, identifying and evaluating the consequences of the actions, and their performance with respect to the goals. The result is a ranking of the alternatives.
4. In the basic cycle, steps 2 and 3 may be repeated a number of times, until an action sufficiently desirable for implementation has been found, or until analysis resources have been exhausted.
5. The mutability of goals must be recognized, however, and so step 3 or even step 2 may be followed by goal revision.

Goal revision may follow search immediately, particularly when the results of search are either very disappointing (when it proves difficult to generate actions that achieve the goals) or very successful (the goals are set so low it is not at all difficult to achieve them). By this simple model, the analysis process is typified by continued and parallel evolution of the set of actions A and the set of goals G. The ranking of the alternative actions will change, not only by addition of new actions to the set but also by revision of the goals G.

Search and choice interact heavily in the sociopolitical arena. To account for this interaction, a more subtle model of the analysis process than the static, "rational," model is required. The evolution of goals as well as actions is an important facet of the more complete model.

Implications of the PSP Model

In this brief exposition we have touched only quickly upon the characteristics of a more general model of the problem-solving process. Let us now explore some of its implications. Once we shift from a static conception of the analysis process to an evolutionary one in which actions and goals change over time, our perception of the interaction of search and choice changes in fundamental ways.

For one thing, we need no longer search desperately for a utility, or social welfare, function. Such functions are used to reduce a multidimensional set of goals to a single dimension (for example, benefit-cost ratio). In an evolutionary process we can accept a less structured set of goals because all that we require at any time is sufficient information about goals to reach a choice over alternatives, not a function over all conceivable combinations. (In fact, we may not need to have a completely consistent goal structure to produce agreement over alternatives; as Lindblom points out, actors may reach agreement on actions even though they are striving for different objectives.) Thus, a much looser, more flexible structure of goals is appropriate and useful. The concept of a "goal fabric" has been proposed to serve this purpose. This will be discussed later.

13. See Manheim, *Problem-Solving Processes* and Manheim, Follansbee, and Walter, *Evolutionary Nature of Problem-Solving.*

A second important implication is that alternatives need not be single massive system proposals but can and should be formulated as staged strategies over time. The typical urban transportation study chooses among a small number of alternative transportation system plans for a target year (1985, say). Instead, there should be a much richer number of smaller actions, each one being the building of a specific part of the network in a particular year (or other options such as buying additional transit cars). Then the major alternative 1985 plans could be composites of a number of the specific time-staged facility actions. However, the whole approach to analysis would be different. Instead of choosing among single packages, the emphasis would be upon choosing among sequences of actions staged over time. In this way there would be a great deal of flexibility for revision of both actions and goals as each stage of the system selected is implemented. Furthermore, the decision about appropriate facilities to construct at each successive time period could be revised as changes in the real world are observed, and the goals or the available actions can be revised as new technologies are developed. Models for searching out and choosing among sequential decisions in transportation planning are under development.[14]

A third implication concerns more emphasis on the value of information. That is, instead of collecting all the information necessary for constructing demand models and the other analysis models in one single survey, there can be a much more efficient use of resources through continuous sampling over time, with a flexible readjustment of data acquisition as new issues are identified for study. This is an important consequence of the time-staged strategy approach. Further, this implies that there should be an economic analysis of the value of information in its relevance to the search and choice issues at hand; as the actions and goals change over time, the value of different types of information will also change. Models for optimal information collection strategies in networks are under development.[15]

Finally, and perhaps most important, the evolutionary image of the analysis leads to a major new perspective for the relationship between the analysis team and the political environment.

The evolution of actions and goals takes place at several different levels. First of all, consider the technical analysis team actually working on transportation systems and related studies for a particular area. Within this team the sets of actions and goals will evolve fairly rapidly: the team is engaged in day-to-day development and testing of alternatives, and as it learns more about the problem it will almost continuously be revising its assumed goals. At a second level, this analysis team will interact periodically with the political decision-makers or other responsible public or private officials for whom the analysis team is acting as staff. As a result of these more or less frequent interactions, the actions and particularly the goals will be further refined and revised. These decision-makers, in turn, will interact with the body politic: the individuals and interest groups who are affected by transportation systems alternatives. As a result of their interactions with the body politic, the decision-makers will revise their conceptions of actions and more particularly goals, and will pass these revised conceptions on to the analysis team. But also the results of the analysis team, as communicated through the decision-makers to the public at large, will help to change and broaden the perceptions of the decision-makers and of the body politic.

The interactions in search and choice among analysis teams, decision-makers, and polity should be exploited explicitly. Perhaps the most important role of technical analysis is to clarify public objectives, even more than to develop and implement specific actions. For example, one of the major contributions of the federal highway transportation program may have been to

---

14. Wayne M. Pecknold, Doctoral dissertation in preparation, Department of Civil Engineering, M.I.T.
15. William F. Johnson, Doctoral dissertation in preparation, Department of Civil Engineering, M.I.T.

create a public awareness of the choices that need to be addressed in the core of the metropolitan area. By threatening highways through the centers of cities, the program has set political forces in motion and has helped to raise serious discussion about the competing objectives of groups in the metropolitan area. In so doing, the search for new transportation technologies has been stimulated, as well as new methods of highway planning.

Example: The Prototype Analysis

The scope of a comprehensive systematic analysis of transportation and a theoretical model of the analysis process have been outlined. The feasibility and utility of these ideas have been demonstrated by conducting a prototype analysis of passenger transportation in the Northeast Corridor of the United States. To the maximum extent feasible, realistic data was used. The result demonstrates how analytical approaches and techniques can be applied to improve policy decisions. However, the result is not of sufficient detail or comprehensiveness to be used for policy decisions without further calibration and modifications of the models and substantial additional data.

TRANSET II, a Laboratory

To do this prototype analysis it was necessary to develop a set of models. These models, in the form of computer programs, provided a "laboratory" for experiments in systematic analysis of transportation. This laboratory is TRANSET II, a new subsystem of ICES, the Integrated Civil Engineering System.[16] TRANSET II is a problem-oriented command-structured language for transportation system analyses, designed for analysts without computer training. For example, to create a new regional transportation network by adding a link to a network previously stored in the computer, the analyst might give the computer this problem-oriented language command:

MODIFY NETWORK 'BASE' FORMING 'NEWRAIL' ADD LINK FROM 56 TO 97, DISTANCE 37.2, LANES 6, VOLUME/DELAY 4

In this example, BASE is the previously-stored network, NEWRAIL the name to be given to the new network. The modification consists of a link from node 56 to 97, with the indicated length, number of lanes, and supply function (volume/delay curve number 4). Such problem-oriented language enables the analyst to use the computer models in a much more flexible and efficient manner than with more traditional forms of programs.

As a system of computer models, TRANSET II provides the capability to analyze transportation problems by predicting supply and demand equilibrium in a multimodal transportation network. Some of its particular features are: (1) the capability to express transportation policy options through technology choices, network configuration, link characteristics, fares, frequency of service, subsidy, and tax policy; (2) the use of the Baumol-Quandt abstract mode demand model; (3) incremental assignment techniques as an approach to calculating equilibrium; and (4) explicit evaluation routines for tracing out impacts on different groups.

With the cooperation of the Northeast Corridor Project of the U.S. Department of Transportation, data were obtained through which the Northeast Corridor network was modeled in both a five-district and a twenty-nine district version, with the networks modeled at corresponding levels of abstraction. The resulting models then served as the basis for a number of analyses. Using the TRANSET II model system as a laboratory, numerous experiments have been conducted using the five-district data. These experiments demonstrate the feasibility of developing a supply-demand equilibrium model for transportation analysis, the difference between equilibrium and nonequilibrium approaches to the problem, and how different options and impacts can be included in a single model so that their interactions can be explored systematically. It is also possible to explore tradeoffs between options, to trace out impacts among different actors as the options are

16. Earl R. Ruiter, *ICES TRANSET I: Transportation Network Analysis Engineering Users' Manual*. The development of TRANSET II is based upon additions and changes to TRANSET I; see Daniel Roos, *ICES System Design*.

varied, and to analyze sensitivity and effects of alternate time-staging of actions.

The major points to be discussed in the following sections will be the applicability of the PSP model as illustrated by TRANSET II, and the systematic analysis of options and impacts.[17]

Applicability of PSP Model

To see how the PSP model can be applied to transportation systems analysis, we can refer to the specific problem-oriented language of TRANSET II.

Search. No explicit search procedure is provided in TRANSET II at this time, although several are under development. At present, the analyst must generate a policy alternative, that is, he must execute search, through his own judgment. He may generate a completely new action or use parts of one or more previously generated actions as stored in the computer files (i.e., on disk). If he stored components of an action, he may modify them if he wishes. One particularly powerful capability of TRANSET II is the ability to name data files. Thus the analyst may store several transportation networks under such arbitrary names as 1956–1, RAIL–2, HWAY, etc.

To generate a completely new transportation system alternative (or new components of an alternative), to save portions or all of an alternative in computer storage, and/or to create a new alternative through modification of a previously-stored component, he uses these commands as in the analysis set out earlier:

Transportation Options:

READ NETWORK, for general network characteristics.
LINKS, for network connectivity and link characteristics.
READ VOLUME DELAY SET, for generalized supply functions.
INPUT MODAL SERVICE DATA, for interzonal fares and frequencies for each mode.
INPUT MODAL COST DATA, for cost parameters for each mode.

Activity System Options:

INPUT DISTRICT DATA, for population, incomes, and holding capacities, for each zone.
INPUT MODAL SPLIT PARAMETERS, for demand model parameters.

In addition to specifying a completely new alternative, it is also possible to generate an action by using portions of another action previously stored in the computer:

MODIFY NETWORK (plus name of network to be changed)
ADD LINK
DELETE LINK (plus specification of changes)
CHANGE LINK
REVISE MODAL DATA (plus name of data to be changed)
MODE COST
MODE FREQUENCY (plus specification of changes)
REVISE DISTRICT DATA (plus name of data to be changed)
DISTRICT (plus specification of changes)

Prediction. The prediction procedures of TRANSET II are based upon the supply-demand equilibrium concept. The commands for a specific alternative are:

PREDICT POTENTIAL TRIPS, generate estimated trip demands.
PREDICT ACTUAL TRIPS, predict actual network equilibrium flows.

---

17. Other experiments, too lengthy to be summarized here, are contained in Earl R. Ruiter, *A Prototype Analysis.*

PREDICT DISTRICT DATA, predict future population and income for each zone based upon predicted network flows.

Evaluation. The evaluation components of TRANSET II are relatively simple. For any particular alternative action, its predicted consequences can be displayed in a variety of ways for intuitive evaluation by the analyst. User, operator, and government costs can be computed and aggregated in a variety of ways, through the EVALUATE COSTS commands. Accessibilities can also be evaluated, as measures of functional impacts (i.e., potential changes in the activity system). There are no capabilities at this stage for predicting physical or governmental impacts explicitly.

Display Flow Pattern Consequences:

REQUEST FINAL
LINK DATA
MINIMUM PATHS
TRAVEL TIMES
SYSTEM TRAVEL
DISTRIBUTION
INTERZONAL TRIPS

PRINT TRIP MATRIX

EVALUATE COSTS
EVALUATE ACCESSIBILITY

Choice. Choice involves the comparison of alternatives. In TRANSET II no automatic choice capability is provided. However, a simple but powerful set of commands provides the analyst information which is extremely useful in his decision between alternatives. These commands do a pairwise comparison of two alternatives, displaying the differences between them. Then the analyst can examine the incremental differences between the two alternatives as well as the absolute levels of the impacts.

COMPARE TRIPS, for summary of the differences in flow volumes between two alternatives.
COMPARE SURPLUSES, for differences in user benefits, as provided by consumer surplus measures.
COMPARE ACCESSIBILITIES, for differences in functional impacts.

The problem-oriented language capability is particularly useful in such commands as: COMPARE TRIPS, ALTERNATIVES AIR AND RAIL.

Utility Commands. There are also available in TRANSET II a variety of utility commands for editing data, obtaining intermediate results during the course of the computations, or filing data on computer disk storage.

Systematic Exploration of Options and Impacts. Often, in using computers for problem-solving, far too much emphasis is placed upon getting the computer model running, and not enough attention is given to how the model is to be used once it is running. A major objective of the prototype analysis was to demonstrate how prediction models should be used in transportation systems analysis.

The basic issues are these: What different combinations of options can achieve the same impacts? What different combinations of impacts can be achieved by any combination of options? Using TRANSET II as a laboratory, a number of experiments were conducted to trace out such tradeoffs. These are illustrated in Figures 5 through 8. The relationships in Figures 5, 6, and 7 were derived from data produced by a series of computer runs in which three levels of fare and three levels of frequency were explored, resulting in nine combinations. In Figure 8 a third option, level of investment in the network, was added.

Figure 5 shows how, as frequency of service between two points is increased, fare must also be increased to maintain the same volume of trips in the system (e.g., 1.10 = 1,100,000 trips per day). Thus, this figure shows how two options, fare and frequency over one single route, must be manipulated together to achieve a constant level of one impact, that is, total trips. In Figure 6, this same approach is extended to consideration of several different impacts simultaneously: total trips in the system, total trips to or from Philadelphia, average trip time, and net benefit to the region as a whole.

In Figure 7 the impacts are shown on the axes. Thus, the same data is now shown as tradeoffs between operator profit and average trip time (a user impact). All other things being equal (they are not), the point most to the upper left would be most desirable. Evaluation and choice deal with such tradeoffs among impacts, whereas tradeoffs among options are needed for search.

In Figure 8 level of investment in the network is added. There are now twenty-seven data points: three different levels of network, and nine combinations of fare and frequency for each. From this sample we can now infer the locus of the most desirable alternatives, as indicated by the dotted line (again, everything else assumed equal!).

These examples illustrate how a number of runs of the computer models can be used to generate information. In this way tradeoffs among options and among impacts can be systematically analyzed, yielding information useful for both search and choice. As systematic relations among the options are perceived, search procedures can concentrate on generating alternatives in the most interesting areas of the space of possible options. As achievable tradeoffs among impacts are identified, the key issues of choice become clearer. It may be relatively easy to find options that produce desirable impacts for each of one group of actors, but there may be unavoidable conflict in the impacts achievable between two other groups of actors. For example, it may be that decreased travel time for suburban residents can only be achieved by displacing families from central city homes by freeway construction. It is precisely these differential impacts which must be traced out.

Conclusions from the Prototype Analysis

The prototype analysis demonstrated the feasibility of network equilibrium analysis and the applicability of the PSP model, and it illustrated the systematic exploration of options and impacts. However, it also emphasized a number of problems:
1. Systematic analysis generates, and requires, a large volume of information from a number of computer runs. How can the analyst deal with and understand this model-generated information to infer such relationships as are illustrated in the figures?
2. If differential impacts among a variety of groups are to be considered explicitly, how can evaluation and choice be carried out without aggregating all the impacts indiscriminately?
3. What kinds of procedures can be developed to assist in search?
4. Each run of the computer models costs time, money, and other resources. Must all search and selection cycles be at the same level of detail? If not, what errors are introduced?

Extensions of the PSP Model

While showing the feasibility of systematic analysis, the prototype analysis also raised a number of issues about the difficulties in performing such an analysis. Techniques and approaches are now under development to handle these problems.

DODO: A PSP Oriented System

A large volume of information is produced in a systematic analysis of transportation alternatives. If only twenty different actions have been generated and compared, the analyst has real difficulty understanding the differences and similarities among the actions: (1) which actions are basically different in their impacts, which are similar, and (2) what the feasible tradeoffs in impacts are and which actions produce the most desirable combinations.

5. Trips—total system

6. Differential impacts

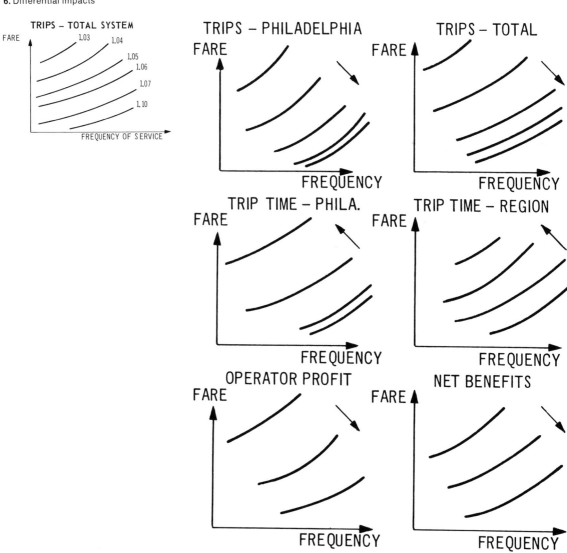

7. Tradeoffs among impacts

8. Dominating tradeoffs

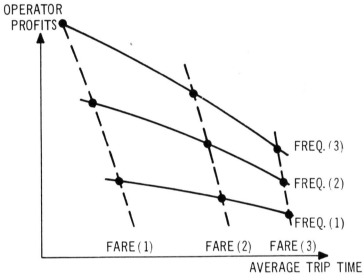

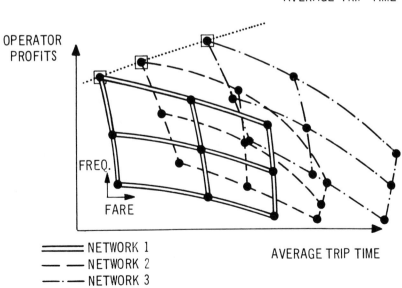

9. The goal fabric concept

GOAL FABRIC

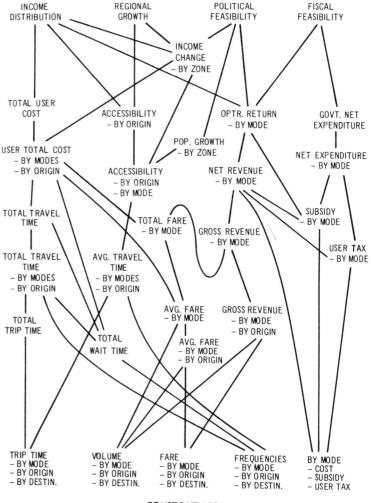

INCOME
DISTRIBUTION

REGIONAL
GROWTH

POLITICAL
FEASIBILITY

FISCAL
FEASIBILITY

INCOME
CHANGE
– BY ZONE

TOTAL USER
COST

ACCESSIBILITY
– BY ORIGIN

OPTR. RETURN
– BY MODE

GOVT. NET
EXPENDITURE

USER TOTAL COST
– BY MODES
– BY ORIGIN

POP. GROWTH
– BY ZONE

NET EXPENDITURE
– BY MODE

ACCESSIBILITY
– BY ORIGIN
– BY MODE

NET REVENUE
– BY MODE

TOTAL TRAVEL
TIME

TOTAL FARE
– BY MODE

GROSS REVENUE
– BY MODE

SUBSIDY
– BY MODE

USER TAX
– BY MODE

TOTAL TRAVEL
TIME
– BY MODES
– BY ORIGIN

AVG. TRAVEL
TIME
– BY MODES
– BY ORIGIN

TOTAL
TRIP TIME

AVG. FARE
– BY MODE

GROSS REVENUE
– BY MODE
– BY ORIGIN

TOTAL
WAIT TIME

AVG. FARE
– BY MODE
– BY ORIGIN

TRIP TIME
– BY MODE
– BY ORIGIN
– BY DESTIN.

VOLUME
– BY MODE
– BY ORIGIN
– BY DESTIN.

FARE
– BY MODE
– BY ORIGIN
– BY DESTIN.

FREQUENCIES
– BY MODE
– BY ORIGIN
– BY DESTIN.

BY MODE
– COST
– SUBSIDY
– USER TAX

CONSEQUENCES

What is needed is a way of storing all the relevant information generated in a series of model runs, so that questions meaningful to the decision problem can be asked of the data. Some of these questions can be identified a priori and so built into the system, but many significant questions will occur to the analyst only as he examines the specific data of a series of runs. Therefore, the information system must be designed for interactive use with flexible query capabilities.

DODO (decision-oriented data organizer) is such an information system, intended to provide the decision-maker and analyst with the capability to analyze and structure the large amount of data that may be generated in the analysis of a complex problem.[18] The design of DODO is based upon the PSP model. An initial operational version of DODO has been developed in the context of the TRANSET II subsystem of ICES. Later versions of DODO will be more general, applicable to many other design problems as well as transportation planning.

The Goal Fabric Concept

The impacts of transportation alternatives are many. We can distinguish these impacts by their nature, the groups which are affected, and the time at which they occur. We could assume that all impacts are given weights and that some total score is computed to enable us to choose among alternatives. Standard economic criteria such as total annual cost, net present worth, or benefit-cost ratio are variants of this scheme. However, as shown in the discussion of the "rational" model, a total score is unsatisfactory, particularly because in a sociopolitical context such as transportation it is essential to examine the differential incidence. One alternative may score high on the goal variables important to group A but low on those important to group B, and therefore the total score hides the essential issue of choice. Recognizing the difficulties of the "scoring scheme" approach, a looser, more subtle, more flexible approach to evaluating and choosing among alternatives was developed. It is termed the "goal fabric."[19]

The goal fabric used in the prototype analysis is shown in Figure 9. This figure indicates how many different goal variables the analyst may wish to examine, and the complex structure of their interrelations.

Search

A variety of search techniques is available in transportation system analysis. If we simplify in the problem, we can apply such powerful techniques as mathematical optimization, including linear programming, integer programming, dynamic programming, and other techniques based on calculus. Alternatively, direct search or other hill-climbing approaches may be used, as well as heuristic search techniques such as pattern recognition and network aggregation. Another important family of search techniques is to provide an effective on-line computer environment with graphic display, enabling the analyst to operate efficiently in rapidly searching out and evaluating a large number of alternatives.

A rich variety of search techniques of different types will probably prove more efficient as a system than any single technique used alone. Furthermore, the judgment of the analyst can and should play a strong role throughout the search process. Therefore it is appropriate to develop a variety of different search techniques as well as a flexible environment in which they can be used. Work is proceeding in both directions.

Multilevel Problem Solving: Network Aggregation

In human problem-solving we rarely analyze real problems at only one level. It is a natural approach to problem-solving to operate at several levels of analysis. In some contexts, this corresponds to first doing "preliminary design," then "detailed." When an analysis process deals with several levels, we say it is hierarchically structured.

---

18. See Manheim, Follansbee, and Walter, *Evolutionary Nature of Problem-Solving*.
19. Marvin L. Manheim and Fred L. Hall, *Abstract Representation of Goals*.

A model of hierarchically-structured problem-solving processes has been developed, hinging on the concept of inclusion among actions.[20] The complexity of the transportation systems problem suggests we may find it efficient to structure it as a multilevel process, as was proposed for the Northeast Corridor study.[21]

To develop this approach, experiments are being conducted in aggregation of transportation networks.[22] The basic idea is that each link of an "aggregate" network corresponds to a set of links in the true network. The usefulness of aggregation in a transportation planning environment is reflected in the ability to analyze a larger number of alternative transportation systems for a given budget than would be possible if aggregation techniques were not employed.

Conclusion

We began with a brief description of the problem of transportation systems analysis, emphasizing the number and variety of options and impacts, the complexity of the systems of predictive models, and the need to trace out differential impacts systematically. After review of the rational model, we described a more general model of the design process, PSP, and its implications. To show the just position of these two themes, we next discussed a prototype analysis of the Northeast Corridor passenger transportation system. We showed the PSP structure in the computer language developed for transportation analysis, and we illustrated the systematic analyses which could be performed. In the last section we described extensions to the PSP model in the form of specific operational techniques to address these issues: DODO, Goal Fabric, Search, and Network Aggregation. Work continues in testing, refining, and making more operational the overall PSP model of the design process.

20. Marvin L. Manheim, *Hierarchical Structure: A Model of Design and Planning Processes.*
21. Henry W. Bruck, Marvin L. Manheim, and Paul W. Shuldiner, *Transport Systems Planning as a Process: The Northeast Corridor Example.*
22. Yu-Po Chan, Kenneth Follansbee, Marvin L. Manheim, and John R. Mumford, *Network Aggregation: An Application of Hierarchical Structure.*

36 Is It Possible to Describe General Problem-Solving Processes?

Comments on the paper by Marvin L. Manheim

Aaron Fleisher

Laboratory for Environmental Studies, Department of Urban Studies and Planning, Massachusetts Institute of Technology
Cambridge, Massachusetts

Aaron Fleisher is Professor of Urban and Regional Studies at M.I.T. and a member of the Harvard-M.I.T. Joint Center for Urban Studies. He has been involved with various aspects of quantitative methods and research in planning and design and has written and lectured extensively on these topics.

It is Marvin Manheim's purpose to describe a procedure for designing what he calls the "problem-solving process." He contrasts it with "systems analysis," which he charges with the disadvantages of requiring depths of rationality and ranges of comprehensiveness that are beyond the scale of human capabilities. Any procedure that makes life lighter and gayer without appreciably compromising its quality is an advantage. But heuristics are not his concern. His description of the transportation problem yields to none in detail and complexity, and his problem-solving process requires no less knowledge and understanding than does systems analysis. It is, like systems analysis, a very general checklist of all the steps that the complete problem-solver must take. It is a rather more elaborate checklist than one usually finds among the descriptions of systems analysis. But checklist it is, and inabilities to execute items on the list are no more fatal to the systems analyst than to the processor of problems. In one way or another both make a living.

There is some emphasis in the rhetoric of the "problem-solving process" on the groping, fumbling nature of design and problem-solving and the necessity of keeping in mind that solutions are at best tentative. This emphasis is summed up in the substitution of "process" for "analysis." The point is well worth making and it is made well.

Another sense of process is even more important. Describing a solution removes only part of the problem. Getting there is the rest and is the only sufficient test of feasibility. But feasibility is not a matter for a priori processing. It can follow only from the nature and content of the problem. Therefore the problem-solving process can do little else than exhort the problem-solver to be feasible.

Manheim does not argue that the problem-solving process is a problem-solving process now. But he does think that it can become one, and offers TRANSET as an example of how it might look. TRANSET is a repertory of manipulations that operate on networks. Having it would certainly ease the solution of transportation problems. But is its contribution to problem-solving any different from some machinery that does sums and products? A toolbox does not design chairs nor does the U.S. Pharmacopoeia write prescriptions.

Is it possible that a general problem-solving process for the environmental sciences can eventually be developed? I doubt it. Nothing like it exists anywhere even for limited ranges of problems. The physical sciences have isolated the logic of the solution for only some classes of problems, and mathematicians have persuaded themselves, in the form of Godel's theorem, that a general mathematical problem-solving process is impossible. It seems hardly likely that the future of problem-solving in any of the social sciences can be rounder and rosier.

The attempt at a general problem-solver is an exercise in utopian optimism. It is not therefore useless. Quite the contrary. Every well-balanced research organization should have one utopian. Speculating on a best of all possible worlds can clarify the potentials. Parts may be attainable, and with sufficient restrictions perhaps a general process is also possible. Therefore Manheim's paper becomes most valuable when he limits his attention to the design of transportation systems. It is in the analysis of this complex problem that he makes his principal contribution. The synthesis of a solution is much more difficult, for it requires a fine judgment of what is important and a delicate hand that can cut the complex into simpler, separable parts. Problem-solving is a selective, not an exhaustive activity. I think Manheim (and most others) see that clearly. We differ on making the selection procedural.

10 Reflections

In conclusion, this section contains three papers which diverge from the research theme of the rest of the volume. The first paper addresses the education of students wishing to enter the field, and the second and third pose questions for the field to consider.

There comes a time in the development of any new field when there are sufficient students wishing to enter it that a few of the leaders must devote part of their time to the critical problem of devising a program of training that will provide both a deep feeling for the practical and theoretical problems of the field and the necessary foundations for conducting research. One of the first such programs was introduced in 1963 by Christopher Jones at the University of Manchester Institute of Science and Technology. As a review of this program could be of assistance to educators with similar intentions, the Program Committee invited him to comment on it.

It may be noted that the methods presented in this volume, with one or two exceptions, assume implementation of proposals from above, that is, assume that the environmental designer or planner in conjunction with builders, city officials, or government agencies will determine a plan best suited to the interests of the users and will, through whatever channels necessary, implement that plan. Several authors take this view of fulfilling user needs and values more seriously than others. However, almost no one involves the user in the generation of his own environment. The environment, no matter how good, is imposed from "above." If the user is to be more than just considered, if he is to be *involved* in the design and planning process, as many blacks are demanding in the United States, can the new methods still be used to advantage? We asked a group of experts, all actively involved in advocacy and social planning, to discuss this issue, and to discuss whether design and planning in the context of the urban crisis can be conducted at all by abstract methods, or must all environmental change be conducted in the arena of community participation and political process? An edited transcription of this panel discussion is presented in this section.

And finally, John Eberhard, then the Director of the Institute for Applied Technology of the United States National Bureau of Standards and now the first Dean of the new School of Architecture and Environmental Design at the State University of New York, Buffalo, was invited to present the closing address, a reflection on the conference and some of its more serious undertones. His address concludes the volume.

37 An Experiment in Education for Planning and Design

J. Christopher Jones

Design Research Laboratory
Department of Building
University of Manchester
Institute of Science & Technology
Manchester, England

J. Christopher Jones is Senior Lecturer
in Industrial Design Technology at the
University of Manchester Institute of
Science and Technology, where, with
Professor Denis Harper, he instituted one
of the first educational programs in
design methodology and design research.

The experiment described in this paper is an attempt to extend the education of architects, engineers, and others to include the new applied sciences that are increasingly relevant to designing and planning the physical environment but are not yet included in the conventional training of professional designers and planners. These new sciences, of which the best known are computing, ergonomics (human factors engineering), operations research, systems engineering, and systematic design methods, have been blended together under the title "design technology," to form courses for the Master of Science degree and for the University Diploma in Technical Science at the University of Manchester Institute of Science and Technology.

The purpose of this experiment in design education is to find ways of removing the barriers between arts and sciences and between the many professions that are increasingly relevant to design problems. The working principle is to give each student enough experience of the seemingly conflicting methods of science and of design to enable him to resolve the differences within himself. It is argued that the barriers between disciplines and professions are much more easily crossed by persons who understand both sides than by attempts to communicate between persons each of whom knows only one side. The practical aim is to train people for work in inter-disciplinary and interprofessional planning and development teams.

Syllabus

Both programs begin with six months of formal teaching from October to March, followed by a comprehensive examination in May and a minor research project thereafter, diploma projects until the end of June, and M.Sc. projects until the following September or longer.

Principles

The formal teaching is more concerned with principles and methods than with particular design problems. Projects are likewise more concerned with gathering information on which to base design decisions than with making design decisions, i.e., the program is concerned with design research rather than actual designing. The main emphasis, in both teaching and practice, is on the ability to deal formally and precisely with the many uncertainties that present themselves at the start of a design problem.

Practice

Students spend most of their time carrying out observations, opinion surveys, controlled experiments or calculations, and preparing and discussing written reports. They are chiefly concerned with the objective expression of the thinking that designers traditionally keep to themselves and with the formulation of group design strategies. The subjects chosen for design research are always those that are too big, or too new, to be dealt with by experience alone and those for which some degree of prior research is essential, e.g., jointing problems in industrialized building.

Formal Teaching

Each week of formal teaching includes about ten hours of lectures and ten hours of practical periods, seminar discussions, and tutorials allocated approximately as shown here. The content is outlined in Appendix A. Additional time is spent on individual and group assignments, preparing reports and summaries, and performing exercises in design methods, computing, and statistics.

	Lectures	Practical tutorials and discussions
Design methods	1	5
Statistics and computing	3	2
Ergonomics	2	3
History of technology and design	2	–
Systems engineering	1	–
Information handling	1	–
Total	10 hours	10 hours

Examinations

As will be seen from Appendix B, examination questions require the candidate to exercise judgment in dealing with ambiguity and lack of information. There are a few compulsory questions of a mathematical kind, but the emphasis is on the ability to identify variables and to impose some degree of pattern upon a situation in which too little is known to be certain of a correct result. Candidates are expected to demonstrate knowledge of the principles underlying the subjects taught. They have to be able to calculate accurately, to choose appropriate mathematical tools, and to write with the precision expected of researchers.

Results

Admissions and Previous Qualifications

The number of students applying for the program has been quite large and has encompassed a great variety of previous qualifications, including building technology, mathematics, and economics. The students not in design appear to be better at design research than are the design professionals. This seems to be because the nondesigners are trained to take an unbiased view of what already exists (rather than what might exist) and have some experience of committing their thoughts to paper and criticism. Designers, on the other hand, have some unlearning to do; they are not trained to explore a design situation without the accompaniment of a vision of how it might be changed. This ability is a disadvantage in carrying out design research, but it is an advantage in deciding, of the many questions that could be researched, which would substantially benefit the field.

Teaching Design Methods

The teaching of design methods, as opposed to methods of gathering and evaluating design information, takes only a small part of the time. The practical part of it has not yet progressed far beyond such simple methods as morphology, brainstorming, synectics, and elementary examples of mathematical programming and simulation. The intentions are, first, to acquaint students with the literature on the subject and, second, to give them experience of using some of the simpler methods, both as individuals and as members of interprofessional design teams. The new methods are presented as aids to the general problems of selecting and controlling design strategy and of relating the thinking of a group of experts to a novel design problem. Design methods teaching is based either on case histories of industrial projects in which the staff are currently involved or on design exercises devised to give rapid experience of one or more techniques. For example, students may be asked to explore the possibilities of designing lecture theaters to accommodate educational TV and other new teaching methods. At this stage the students produce only preliminary reports.

Design Research Projects

The design research projects which the students carry out after the examination are usually preliminary investigations of design questions of general interest not yet subjected to much research.[1] The goal is to give each student the experience of carrying out applied research intended to reach a publishable standard. The subjects are chosen by research supervisors and are restricted to areas in which supervisors are interested and experienced. The main difficulty in these research projects is that of enabling the student to understand and become involved in the problem area sufficiently quickly to complete the research in a few months. This difficulty has been lessened by the recent practice of preceding the research project by a "group pilot study." Two students, plus their supervisor and experienced research advisers, form a group that has the task of planning two overlapping research projects within a loosely-defined subject area. The pilot study lasts for a few weeks and enables all concerned to make rapid reviews of the relevant literature and to conduct some rough experiments or surveys to find out which questions are worth pursuing and are likely to be answered within the available time. The two research projects that emerge may be of far less scope than the broad studies envisaged at the start but they are less likely to flounder for want of understanding of objectives and of feasibility. The main difficulty, which the group pilot study is intended to avoid, is that the student researcher may take far too long to get started and the supervisor may be obliged to give advice for which the student does not appreciate the reasons. The idea that research is a form of self-expression aimed at being "original" seems to conflict with the idea that design research must always answer an urgent question in which many people are directly concerned. A major aim of both the research projects and the program as a whole is to harness all available intelligence, not just that of the researcher, to the posing and answering of design questions.

Conclusions

Several of the writer's opinions and conclusions have already been expressed.[2] These and other conclusions derived from five years' experience with the program are summarized here.
1. It is assumed that there is a need for a new kind of design technologist who is trained to work in interprofessional and interdisciplinary design teams.
2. It is further assumed that the best way of training people for this work is to expose them to the principles and methods of both sciences and arts so that the apparent conflicts between disciplines and professions can be resolved *within* persons rather than *between* persons.
3. It is believed that the emphasis in such training should be on design research rather than on detailed designing.
4. The main objectives of the practical parts of this program in Design Technology are to provide experience of working in groups on preliminary studies of novel design problems and in carrying out design research projects.

1. Details of these projects are available in the annual *Design Research Reports* from the Design Research Laboratory, University of Manchester Institute of Science and Technology.
2. "The State-of-the-Art in Design Methods," Part 1 of this volume.

5. The main difficulty that has emerged is that the students find it hard to relate the subjects studied, and their own research projects, to the crucial aspects of a particular design problem in which the major variables have yet to be identified. Group pilot studies, with staff and students jointly exploring a real design situation in order to identify objectives, appear to be of some help. The assumption of many students that research is a form of self-expression, to be done in private, conflicts with the principle of applying all available intelligence to the exploration and solution of design problems.

6. The studies described here go only part of the way toward training people for interdisciplinary design research but they certainly widen the horizons of those who have suffered from the narrowness of undergraduate and professional training. As the scope of designing widens so does the educational (as opposed to the vocational) aspects of design teaching.

Appendix A
Lecture Courses, Practicals, and Seminars in Design Technology

1. History of Technology and Design
History of Innovation. The advance of science, scientific thought, and technology from the Greeks to the end of the 19th century.
Design Methods. Review of traditional and modern methods, concentrating on the characteristics and implications of craftwork, mechanization, and automation.
Design Methods (practical). Examination of some current approaches to systematic design.

2. Ergonomics Technology
Ergonomics I. Man-machine systems, the senses, perception, decision-making, and measurement of human performance.
Ergonomics II. Research methods, display of information, controls, learning of skills, training, speed of work, vigilance tasks, and fatigue.
Ergonomics Laboratory. Experiments concurrent with Ergonomics I.
Statistics. Descriptive statistics, theoretical distributions, statistical inference, parametric and nonparametric tests.
Statistics Laboratory. Experimental verification of theoretical distributions.

3. Information Technology
Computer Technology. Four courses: (1) History of computers and computation, development of hardware and software; (2) Computation: Atlas Autocode and examples; (3) Optimization: treatment of boundaries, nonlinear optimization methods, created-response surface technique, and quadratic convergence; and (4) Simulation: Monte Carlo methods, simulation languages, and statistical behavior.
Information Handling. Critical path analysis, scheduling, and resource allocation.
Reliability and Testing. Definition of reliability, calculation of system and subsystem reliabilities, random failure, Poisson distribution, specifications, and environmental testing.
Flow Systems. Continuous and discrete time, flow diagrams, signal flow, stability, sampling, logical paths, and elementary theory of queues.

4. Seminars
A series of seminars given by students in the program: Information Theory, Management and Technology, Simulation of Voice Recognition Machines, Review of the Papers Presented in the 1962 Design Methods Conference, Garden Cities, Tools of Social Science, Case Histories of Two Chair Designs, Signal Flow Graphs, Comprehension of Engineering Drawings, Critical Incident Technique, Understanding Media, Artificial Intelligence, Sensory Motor Performance, Creativity, Human Operators in Complex Systems, Comfort, Value Analysis, Computers in Architecture, Uses of Information Centers.

Appendix B
Typical Questions from M.Sc. Examination Papers[3]

Paper 1: History of Technology and Design
1. *Either* write an essay on the "tabu of the natural" in the ancient and early

---

3. Reproduced by permission of the University of Manchester.

medieval worlds, *or* discuss, with examples, the stages whereby Europeans became inventive technologists before 1500.

2. You are the leader of a team that is planning the integration of road and rail traffic in the United Kingdom. The plan is to be put into effect during the period 1970 to 1980. How would you enable your team to identify the critical variables?

Paper 2: Ergonomics Technology

1. The following data are from a survey to assess wastage of student nurses during their training period.

	Hospital types		
	A	B	C
Students who completed course	197	65	140
Students who did not complete course	122	46	118

Would you say that hospital types have some effect on the wastage of student nurses? Give reasons for your choice of statistical test.

2. Write the word "Ergonomics" under the following conditions: (a) with your accustomed hand and with your eyes open, (b) with your accustomed hand and with your eyes closed, (c) with your unaccustomed hand and with your eyes open, (d) with your unaccustomed hand and with your eyes closed. Describe the main differences between these four examples of your handwriting. In what ways do these differences illustrate the important characteristics of skilled performance?

Paper 3: Information Technology

1. (a) What is the significance of constraints in optimization problems? Explain the use of the "Graded Response Technique" for handling bounded nonlinear optimization problems. (b) Describe the "simple simplex method" of nonlinear optimization and explain how the true optimum solution is detected in unbounded problems. What is "evolutionary operation" and when might it arise? How can the simple simplex method be used to obtain and maintain optimum conditions?

2. (a) What is meant by "utility data" in relation to the compression of activity duration in arrow networks? What do you consider are the problems involved in arriving at utility data values? (b) The table below refers to a sequence of operations for which the normal durations and their estimated direct cost are given, together with the permissible crashed duration for each operation and the additional cost per day for the additional resources required to achieve the shorter durations. You are required to determine the most economical period for the sequence, and the minimum period to which the sequence can be crashed if the overall cost is not to exceed £7100.

i.j.	Duration in days normal	Max crash	Estimated normal direct cost £	Utility data £/day
1.2	7	4	560	80
1.3	12	9	1200	100
2.3	6	4	420	70
2.4	6	3	480	80
2.5	4	2	280	70
3.4	–	–	–	–
3.6	5	3	500	100
4.6	–	–	–	–
4.7	8	5	640	80
5.7	4	2	280	70
6.7	3	2	300	100

Total Estimated Direct Cost £4660

3. Discuss the application of Systems Engineering ideas to the provision of a reservoir water supply for a proposed new town. Make any necessary assumptions and state them clearly.

38 Design and Planning: Abstract Methods or Political Process?

A Panel Discussion:

Participants

Bernard Frieden, Department of City and Regional Planning, M.I.T.

Barry Jackson, Fisher–Jackson Associates, New York and Berkeley

James Morey, Urban Planning Aid, Cambridge, Massachusetts

Lisa Peattie, Department of City and Regional Planning, M.I.T.

Moderator

Marvin Manheim, Chairman of the Editorial Advisory Board, Design Methods Group

Bernard Frieden is an Associate Professor of City and Regional Planning at M.I.T. and a member of the Harvard-M.I.T. Joint Center for Urban Studies. He received a Ph.D. in city planning from M.I.T. in 1962, was editor of the *Journal of the American Institute of Planners,* and is the author of several books and articles on urban planning and social policy. Barry Jackson is an advocate planner, principal in Fisher–Jackson Associates, Architecture and Urban Design, and a member of Housing Action System in Harlem. He received an M. Arch. from Berkeley in 1965 and is presently working on a Model Cities plan for Harlem. James Morey is director of Urban Planning Aid, an advocacy planning group in Cambridge and Boston. He received a Ph.D. in psychology from Harvard in 1953. After many years as a systems analyst and operations research scientist with the RAND Corporation, System Development Corporation, and the MITRE Corporation, he resigned over intended military uses of projects he was directing. Lisa Peattie is an Associate Professor of Urban Anthropology at M.I.T. and a member of the Joint Center for Urban Studies. She received a Ph.D. in social anthropology from the University of Chicago in 1968 and has done extensive field work and advocacy planning. She is the author of a book and several articles on social and political aspects of planning. Marvin Manheim is an Associate Professor of Transportation Systems Planning at M.I.T. Kenneth Geiser, Jr., of the Department of City and Regional Planning at M.I.T., organized the panel and prepared this summary.

Lisa Peattie

I feel that I am in a perfect frame of mind for this, because although I wasn't here this morning, I was listening to some design students going over what they had been doing this past year. They were addressing themselves to the problem of low-income housing. They started out by applying a sort of a rational systems analysis to the problem. They looked into the way General Electric designed a better light bulb, and they tried to apply somewhat the same approach. They set up a list of criteria. They did a lot of information-gathering on client needs, user wants, and this kind of thing. They made a flowchart of all this information, and they found out that some 360 decisions had to be made; by no means were these on a single scale.

This particular experience illustrates one of the reasons why I think rational decision-making is very questionable. There are just too many factors. Basically, I think that the students were on a dead end, and I think that designers and planners run in this wrong direction all the time.

You can't take such a simple-minded approach because it is practically impossible, and it is psychologically misleading. That is to say, because of the desire of people to identify with, to manipulate, to control, to make something their own, they resent having things designed for them, however suitably the product may be designed.

In the kind of a process I was listening to this morning, for instance, you get very easily into the question of whether you should have a dining room plus living room or a larger living room. But in this way of designing it is impossible to raise the question of whether you have a dining room or an automobile; a dining room or a trip to Florida. There are too many tradeoffs possible, and the designer, in fact, by trying to rationalize the problem has to narrow his choice field down to a point which prejudges the options of the people to a degree which I would consider to be intolerable.

So for all of these reasons, I think that this morning's example is not a very good way to proceed, and I submit that what designers ought to be spending their time on is trying to design a product which can be decentralized, which can be marketed, which is some set of components among which people can pick and choose, manipulate, reassort, do things to, with, or on top of, and all at a price which they can afford. I would suggest that designing in such a decentralized manner is the only way we'll be able to allow for decisions which are relevant to people.

Marv Manheim   Barry, you have been actively involved in planning in Harlem; do you agree with Lisa's position?

Barry Jackson   Well, I think we can look at it from the other end of the scale. Let us assume that we can have a rational design or planning method. Let us assume that we can use any of the processes which people have discussed during the conference. The problem, I think, is implementing the plan; how do you get it built? If we begin to see it from this point of view, design methods begin to fall apart, and we get caught up in the revolving relationship between political structure and community situation.

I think in the old way that the game was played the planner and the politician were allies working oblivious to the community. In the new situation the community was supposed to have a voice in the planning. The planner was going to act as referee between these two protagonists. I found out rapidly that the community doesn't see it this way. The community looks at the designer as an ally, and the client becomes the community. So we begin to get a different view of the entire designer-community scene.

Our firm is really confronted with this. We are in the middle of a planning project where we are supposed to be dealing directly with the community and we really haven't been able to deal with the community at all. The community isn't structured in any way like a client with whom we can communicate.

Marv Manheim   Jim, on the basis of your experiences in Cambridge, how can the planner or designer work with the community?

Jim Morey   I do want to go back to something Lisa said, and then get into this question of how the planner fits in relation with the community.

I think that some of the things Lisa said concerning essentially trying to feature decentralization and modularity in design so that there would be a high degree of individual choice were fine. Certainly it makes quite a bit of sense in some fields, and housing, I would think, is one. In other fields it is harder to see how we would carry out this approach. Transportation planning is one field which contrasts rather sharply, and I think it is a good one to discuss. There are obvious factors like traffic flow involved, and the interesting thing is that these factors have led to a rather highly developed abstract methodology. On this abstract side we do have many elaborate computer simulation models that allow us to manipulate traffic volumes and to assign different transportation networks and modes, while taking into account all kinds of things in simulating the choice that people will make. Within this type of model we can come up with certain kinds of "hard measures" having to do with traffic volumes and transportation costs, *if* we make certain assumptions about freeways saving people's time and people's time being worth so much money and so on.

Now first of all, I think that at any time we look at these models it is perfectly clear that they themselves have many built-in biases. Just as one example, the models I have noted which are concerned with saving the driver's time—that is, saving time coming in from the suburbs—are not concerned about cross traffic and the loss of time of pedestrians who have to walk four blocks to get to an overpass in their own neighborhood. This could be quantified just as easily in terms of time savings; presumably these residents' time is worth the same amount as suburban resident's time. Now the other side of it is the broad social impacts, such as building a freeway and sealing off an area that then becomes a hard-core ghetto. How do we weigh the impact on the people of a whole city of having made a major step in creating this kind of a situation?

It seems to me that in trying to relate this kind of problem to how you plan with the political process and community involved, we may have to deal with it in two pieces. First, we must recognize that the official planning agency and the community do not have the same objectives or values. Second, there is of course, the difficulty of how to take the abstracted quantitative factors that have something to do with the overall problem and interrelate them to more intangible, more important factors which often relate to only a small part of the community.

Marv Manheim

Bernie, you have been involved in the more legislative aspects of these same problems. How would you view Jim's comments?

Bernie Frieden

The issue that I see emerging here is really an issue of how to manage a decision-making process. In this case it happens to be a design process or a planning process. I think that this is the issue much more than how to design a better product. I think we see increasing weight given to the processes by which decisions are made. There are glimmerings in this direction at the federal level in the form of requirements for citizen participation and provisions for separate funding so that elected neighborhood boards can hire their own planning and design staff and not be dependent solely on the city's technical staff. The Model Cities program goes the farthest in recognizing local decision-making processes. What this means is that the issues which will become important are not so much the issues of what kind of house will be built but who influences the decision, whose plan is in and whose plan is out, who has a say in what is going to emerge.

I certainly agree with the attractiveness of the solution that Lisa Peattie proposed. Decentralizing the decision-making in the design process would allow individuals to make as many decisions for themselves as possible. But as Jim has pointed out, it isn't always possible to do that, for there still do remain all sorts of collective decisions and not everyone will be able to make these decisions in a totally decentralized way. I think our job is to figure out ways to make those decisions which do have to be made collectively while giving as much representation as possible to things that have been traditionally left out of the process of design and planning.

Marv Manheim

Then the real question is this: Assuming in fact we want to plan with people, not for people, how can we do this effectively? I mean not only at the scale of housing but also at the level of massive public investments, like transportation systems?

Lisa Peattie

I think that that is a hard one to lick, because the larger the scale the harder it is to get meaningful community involvement. In fact, what you often get is interfactional fights, even among the planners.

Barry Jackson	I think that the solution to planning *with* people requires tradeoffs. It isn't clear how we make these tradeoffs, but I think that the political structure knows how to make those tradeoffs. The reason we have political bosses in the city is that bosses know how to get in the back room with their cigars and trade things off. They know how to trade a park in one borough for street paving in another. All this model-making—it almost gets to be nonsense because we can't talk to the people of the community about things like that. Community people understand tradeoffs, but they don't understand all the logic of our systematic approaches. I think that really is the problem. I think we need a new language, the language of the guys out there in the streets, so we can talk with them and see it exactly how they see it.
Marv Manheim	I guess we really have a sense of how politicians trade off among themselves, but can't such tradeoffs be built into the planning and design process?
Jim Morey	It seems to me that at the moment, there *is* a process of tradeoffs, but it's not the best one by any means. The way it seems to work out in so many cases is that you start out with an official plan that is developed by an official planning agency with little or no interaction with the people who will be living in the areas that will be directly affected. The communities then attempt to fight that plan and keep it from happening until the official agencies are willing to modify it in certain ways. There is the tradeoff. How much difficulty can a community organization create to the point that the official agency feels it must compromise on certain aspects in order to keep its appropriations? Some tradeoffs are achieved in this manner. The trouble is, all of the tradeoffs must take place within the framework originally defined in the official plan. This often makes some tradeoffs impossible.
Bernie Frieden	Well, I sense that we all are getting to be good at stating this problem. The next stage is to solve it. Recent trends in city programs are worth noting. One is giving up the idea that the mayor speaks for everyone in the city. A great deal of work is going on at the neighborhood level now, and this makes the job considerably easier. This is achieving a better sense of what people's priorities are and getting local people into positions where they can be effective. Second, we are getting better, more sensitive, programs to work with. Past programs have not had the objective of doing much for the people who are affected; the object was just to clear the land. Third, more effort is being made to listen to local groups, to try to determine just what people's priorities are.
Questions from the Audience	What kind of vocabulary do you need to speak directly to the community? *Barry Jackson:* Just go into the community and listen to the way people speak and speak to them in the language that they are using. It is a difficult task; it's like going to France and not knowing French.
	Are there specific instances that you know of where a community has actually beaten the system? *Jim Morey:* The only victories of communities that I know about are cases where tremendous efforts on the part of particular communities have managed to create a situation which isn't quite as bad as it might otherwise have been. But I think if you look at urban renewal, as an example, there are *no* victories if you mean real improvement.
	Here we are faced with the hottest issue on the program over the past three days, and I have sat here and heard minor statements about problems of getting communities involved. As I read the issue—Design and Planning: Abstract Methodology or Political Process?—we've never confronted that issue. What about this idea of abstract methodology? We all gathered here to speak about these methodologies, yet when we confront real-life situations, all we can discuss is problems of the political process. Is political process the only way to get things done? *Jim Morey:* Well I don't think that there is a spokesman on the panel that

says that design and planning isn't abstract methodology *and* political process.

Comment by Christopher Jones

I would say something on a larger time scale. I think that it is useful to consider the end of the century or beyond as the real arena for our design methodologies. What kinds of things in the present situation are going to suffice by the end of the century? Is it the analytical models we have heard about over the past three days or is it the existing political situation in the communities we are now talking about? We can see that only the first, these models and languages, are going to survive, for the political structures are in constant transformation. Let us look at the international scene. There are some marvelous examples of abstract methodology being employed quite successfully without regard to any of the national political structures. On the international scene there is no supernational political agency governing air line transportation, the international television, the international cable, the international postal system. Yet all of these work far better than most national systems. Why is this? Partly because there are overriding methodologies which are matched to the kinds of political situations all by themselves. Internationally and over long periods of time, I think we have a much better record with methodologies than we do under short-range local situations.

39 We Ought to Know the Difference

Closing Address:

John P. Eberhard

Dean, School of Architecture
and Environmental Design
State University of New York
Buffalo, New York

John Eberhard is the first Dean of the new
School of Architecture and Environmental
Design at Buffalo. He received a B.S. in
architectural design from the University of
Illinois in 1952 and an S.M. in industrial
management from M.I.T. in 1959. He practiced as an architect, was one of the in-
corporators, later president of Creative
Buildings, Inc., a prefabricated building
design and manufacturing firm, and lectured at the Sloan School of Industrial
Management. From 1959 to 1963 he was
Director of Research for the Sheraton
Corporation of America. Then he joined
the federal government, first as Consultant to the Assistant Secretary for Science
and Technology of the Department of
Commerce (later Deputy Director), and in
1964 as Director of the Institute for Applied Technology of the National Bureau
of Standards. He is the author of *Systems
Design and Urban Places*.

I was asked to reflect on what has happened in this conference and the implications of current problems of the man-made physical environment on our future research. It has been my experience in making speeches that if I can deal with one problem I am lucky. Therefore, rather than problems, I want to talk about one problem which I think is a generic one for all designers and especially for all of us engaged in improving the design process, one which has grave if not easily seen consequences for the future of design methods research.

The statement of the problem comes from Alexis de Tocqueville, who observed what was occurring in America in 1830. He was concerned at that point about the disparity between what happened to life in a democracy and what happened to life in an aristocracy.

In democracies there is always a multitude of persons whose wants are above their means and who are very willing to take up with imperfect satisfaction rather than abandon the object of their desires altogether. The artisan readily understands these passions for he himself partakes in them. In an aristocracy he would seek to sell his workmanship at a high price to the few; he now conceives that the more expeditious way of getting rich is to sell them at a low price to all. But there are only two ways of lowering the price of commodities.

The first is to discover some better, shorter, and more ingenious method of producing them; the second is to manufacture a large quantity of goods, nearly similar, but of less value. Among a democratic population all the intellectual faculties of the workman are directed to these two objects; he strives to invent methods that may enable him not only to work better, but more quickly and more cheaply; or if he cannot succeed in that, to diminish the intrinsic quality of the thing he makes, without rendering it wholly unfit for the use for which it is intended. When none but the wealthy had watches they were almost all very good ones; few are now made that are worth much, but everybody has one in his pocket. Thus, the democratic principle not only tends to direct the human mind to the useful arts, but it induces the artisan to produce with great rapidity many imperfect commodities, and the consumer to content himself with these commodities.

That is our concern. That's our concern with the design process. That's our concern as designers, and it seems to me that it pervades our whole society, all the way from watches to automobiles to houses to cities. We have tried in this country to do something about making the product cheap enough and somehow or other preserving its qualities so that everybody could have one, or at least have equal access to one—and we have failed. We have failed pretty miserably when it comes to housing, as we've heard many times.

Uncertainties and Anxieties

Now is the time to do something about the other alternative: to discover some better, shorter, and more ingenious methods of producing the things of our lives. And that's an orientation towards process design, not product design. Designers in practice as contrasted with designers in theory have to produce solutions. These solutions will probably always have to be developed in the face of uncertainties. Uncertainty about a sufficient problem statement, that is, how can we identify what the user's needs really are? Uncertainty about the sufficient development of alternative solutions: the big idea versus the better idea. If we're convinced that we have the "big idea," then we no longer have to develop and explore alternatives. Or we may be uncertain about the sufficiency and elegance of the tools for evaluating these alternatives. A good deal of this has been discussed during the past three days. Or we may be uncertain about the sufficiency of the skills of the workmen and the processes available to produce the product as conceived. Or we may be uncertain about the sufficiency of the feedback from previous experience. As I have suggested many times, after three thousand years of building technology, if we still build buildings that leak, we do not have very good feedback in the design process.

These uncertainties, it seems to me, divide the design world into three camps. First, those who are blithely ignorant of the uncertainties. I presume none of these are present. Second, those who recognize the uncertainties but haven't the time to do anything about them; they've got to get on with the job, "We don't have time to fool with analysis, we want action." And third are those who are attempting to shed light on the design process and on methods for realistically handling these uncertainties. (I like to believe most of the people at this conference and reading this book are in this class.) To use the metaphor that Tony Ward used earlier in the conference: we should learn to move the lightpost from where it is to where we dropped the coin, rather than doing what many scientists do, which is to look where the light falls and not where they dropped the coin. If we are really concerned about shedding light, as people have been saying for three days, we still have some major obstacles to overcome. Our design methods are filled with anxieties. From the conference five sorts of anxieties emerge clearly. I would like to discuss them now.

The Hierarchical Nature of Complexity

One anxiety inherent in design methods is the hierarchical nature of complexity. This anxiety moves in two directions, escalation and infinite regression. I will use a story, "The Warning of the Doorknob," to illustrate the principles of escalation.

This has been my experience in Washington when I had money to give away. If I gave a contract to a designer and said, "The doorknob to my office really doesn't have much imagination, much design content. Will you design me a new doorknob?" He would say "Yes," and after we establish a price he goes away. A week later he comes back and says, "Mr. Eberhard, I've been thinking about that doorknob. First, we ought to ask ourselves whether a doorknob is the best way of opening and closing a door." I say, "Fine. I believe in imagination, go to it." He comes back later and says, "You know, I've been thinking about your problem, and the only reason that we have to worry about doorknobs is that you presume you want a door to your office. Are you *sure* that a door is the best way of controlling egress, exit, and privacy?" "No, not at all." "Well, I want to worry about that problem." He comes back a week later and he says, "The only reason we have to worry about the aperture problem is that you insist upon having four walls around your office. Are you sure that is the best way of organizing this space for the kind of work you are doing as a bureaucrat?" I say, "No, I'm not sure at all." Well, this escalates until (and this has literally happened in two contracts, although not through this exact process) our physical designer comes back and he says with a very serious face, "Mr. Eberhard, we have to decide whether capitalistic democracy is the best way to organize our country before I can *possibly* attack your problem."

On the other hand is the problem of infinite regression: If this man faced with the design of the doorknob had said, "Wait. Before I worry about the doorknob, I want to study the shape of man's hand and what man is capable of doing with it," I would say, "Fine." He would come back and would say, "The more I thought about it, there's a *fit* problem. What I want to study first is how metal is formed, what the technologies are for making things with metal in order that I can know what the real parameters are for fitting within the hand." "Fine." But then he says, "You know, I've been looking at metal-forming and it all depends on metallurgical properties. I really want to spend another three or four months looking at metallurgy so that I can understand the problem better." "Fine." After three months he'll come back and say, "Mr. Eberhard, the more I look at metallurgy, the more I realize that it is atomic structure that's really at the heart of this problem." And so, our physical designer is in atomic physics from the doorknob. That is one of our anxieties, the hierarchical nature of complexity.

The Inclusiveness of Methodology

The second sort of anxiety I see is the inclusiveness of methodology. Have we really got all the variables within our analysis that we ought to be concerned about? And if we dare to ask the question then it becomes clear that we haven't considered everything because somebody will always say, "You haven't thought about *this* or *that* or some ramification thereof; it's not included." Therefore there is a tendency to list more variables, to develop more branches, more algorithms, in order to make the approach look complex enough to seem to have included everything that should have been considered. As somebody who is about to try to educate designers, I am a little concerned that this is perhaps an emphasis on methodology for its own sake, an anxiety about the quality of our matrix geometry rather than the quality of our problem solution.

Optimization

The third anxiety I see is one of optimization. We must optimize even if we end up having to minimize, even if we have to eliminate all goals except one, even if we have to attack only small problems because we can't optimize large problems. I had a rule of thumb in my job in Washington for the people around me: They were not to use the words "optimize" or "optimum" unless they could list all the variables and alternatives. If it is possible to say what all of the alternatives are then it may be possible to find the optimum among those alternatives. But if it is a question of housing for the poor or even a question of doorknobs, I do not think that it is possible to state all of the alternatives, and therefore I'm not concerned about optimizing. I *am* concerned with selecting workable alternatives.

The Futility of Individuality and Publish but Not Perish

The fourth sort of anxiety that I have heard throughout the conference is the futility of individuality. The problems are bigger than any of us, so let's link up, let's hook up in order to get turned on, tuned in with another discipline, with thirteen or fourteen other bright young men. And that's not really how you feel, at least most of you, because you're arrogant in the statements you make. I think the arrogance is a reflection of your wanting to express your individuality.

The anxiety of the futility of individuality is inexorably tied to the fifth anxiety, one I hope this group doesn't get trapped in, the anxiety to publish and not perish, but publish or not have your own thing. And your own thing has to have its own acronym even if its words like CHEAP, QUICK, or even JUNK. Let's not get hooked on that. Let's not be concerned about the futility of individuality in such a way as to feel that in order to maintain individual expression we have to publish *our* thing and can't build on anybody else's work. Some of us *should* be building on the shoulders of others.

What Is It We Mean by Man

Anxieties I think also have a beneficial effect. The necessity to omit or to minimize incidents of anxiety can cause us to be creative and to build on our own previous experiences. We should use our involvement together and with the environment as a system in which we achieve positive benefits from our anxieties. If it's true that the self-system rises and becomes visible and dominant because we accumulate and organize our educational experiences in such a way as to omit or minimize anxieties, then I would hope that as a group we will recognize the five anxieties I have expressed not as negative things but as positive forces, positive forces out of which our education and collective experiences will begin to give us the confidence and the ability to do something about designing for others. This is not to say that all of us need to design directly for others; I don't think that's what has come out in the past three days. We can afford to have, we need to have, and I want to have people who propose design processes and design methods for others to use. The design professional who is dealing directly with clients should be backed by other professionals who are expanding the knowledge base and methods of analysis available to him.

What I would be concerned about, however, for all of us who are involved with man as a measure, whether we are designers who work directly with users or designers who prepare design methods, is that we are very clear what it is we mean by "man." There are two quotations that represent what I consider to be disparate, but both useful views. One is Buckminster Fuller's description of man:

A self-balancing, 28-jointed adapter-base biped; an electrochemical reduction plant, integral with segregated storages of special energy extracts in storage batteries for subsequent actuation of thousands of hydraulic and pneumatic pumps with motors attached; 62,000 miles of capillaries. . . .

Millions of warning signal, railroad and conveyor systems; crushers and cranes (of which the arms are magnificent 23-jointed affairs with self-surfacing and lubricating systems) and a universally distributed telephone system needing no service for 70 years, if well managed. . . .

The whole, extraordinary complex mechanism guided with exquisite precision from a turret in which are located telescopic and microscopic self-registering and recording range finders, a spectroscope, etc.; the turret control being closely allied with an air-conditioning intake-and-exhaust and a main fuel intake. . . .

Within the few cubic inches housing the turret mechanisms, there is room also for two sound-wave and sound-direction-finder recording diaphragms, a filing and instant reference system, and an expertly devised analytical laboratory large enough not only to contain minute records of every last and continual event of up to 70 years' experience, or more, but to extend, by computation and abstract fabrication, this experience with relative accuracy into all corners of the observed universe . . .

'A man,' indeed Dismissed with the appellation, 'Mr. Jones.'

The other man is described by Robert Louis Stevenson:

What a monstrous spectre is this man, the disease of the agglutinated dust, lifting alternate feet or lying drugged with slumber; killing, feeding, growing, bringing forth small copies of himself; grown upon with like grass, fitted with eyes that move and glitter in his face; a thing to set children screaming. —and yet, looked at nearlier, known as his fellows know him, how surprising are his attributes! Poor soul, here for so little, cast among so many hardships, filled with so many desires so incommensurate and so inconsistent, savagely surrounded, savagely descended, irremediably condemned to prey upon his fellow lives; who would have blamed him had he been at peace with his destiny and a being merely barbarous?

And we look and behold him instead filled with imperfect virtues; infinitely childish, often admirably valiant, often touchingly kind; sitting down amidst his momentary life, to debate of right and wrong and the attributes of the deity; rising up to do battle for an egg or die for an idea; singling out his friends and his mate with cordial affection; bringing forth in pain, rearing with long-suffering solicitude, his young.

To touch the heart of his mystery, we find in him one thought, strange to the point of lunacy; the thought of *duty*; the thought of something owing to himself, to his neighbor, to his God; and ideal of decency to which he would rise if it were possible; a limit of shame below which, if it be possible, he will not stoop. . . .

. . . Of all earth's meteors, here at least is the most strange and consoling; that this ennobled lemur, this hair-crowned bubble of the dust, this inheritor of a few years and sorrow, should yet deny himself his rare delights, and add to his frequent pains and life for an *ideal* however misconceived. . . .

We ought to know the difference; we really ought to.

A Selected Cross-Classified Bibliography of the Literature of Environmental Design and Planning Methodology

Cross-Classification Index

All entries from the bibliography are cross-classified into thirty-one categories. An index is represented by a capital letter, a numeral, and in most cases a small letter. The capital letter indicates one of the three main divisions—current research, background theory, or application—and the numeral and lower-case letter indicate further subdivisions as detailed below.

1954, 1961; Sartre 1966; Scheerer 1963; Simon 1957; Taylor 1964; Taylor and Barron 1963; Vinacke 1952; Werner 1961; Werner and Kaplan 1963; Wertheimer 1959; Wulf 1938.

A3. Computer-Aided Design
A3a. Computer-aided design systems.

Barnette 1965; Berkeley 1968; Bernholtz and Bierstone 1967; Carnegie-Mellon University 1968; Casciato and Case 1962; Clark and Souder 1964; Coons 1963, 1967; Cogswell 1967; Cowan 1965; Fenves, Logcher, and Mauch 1965; Fenves, Logcher, Mauch and Reinschmidt 1964; Herzog 1967; Holstein 1964; Hershdorfer 1968; Jacks 1964, 1967; Jacks et al. 1964; Jones 1967a; Logcher, Flachsbart, Hall, Power, and Wells 1967; Mattox et al. 1967; Miller, C. L. 1963; Milne 1969; Negroponte in press; Negroponte and Groisser 1967; Newell and Simon 1963; Pask 1963; Ross 1967; Ross and Rodriguez 1963; Sturman 1967; Wells 1967.

A3b. Computer graphics, information systems.

Abzug 1965; Appel 1968; Ball 1965; Bergstrom 1967; Cralle and Michael 1967; Fetter 1965, 1967; Fisher 1964; Greenfield, Portnoy, and Wallace 1964; Grey 1967; Housing and Home Finance Agency 1963; Jacobs and Way 1968; Johnson 1963; Knowlton 1967; Krampen and Seitz 1967; Lindheim 1965; Mezei in press; Milne 1969; Newman, W. M. 1968; Noll 1965a, 1965b, 1967a, 1967b, 1967c; Seitz 1967; Sutherland 1963; Wurman and Killinger 1967; Wylie, Romney, Evans, and Erdahl 1968.

A3c. Related literature on computer simulation, artificial intelligence, and cybernetics.

Anderson 1964; Ashby 1956; Brody and Lindgren 1967; Carter 1965; Chomsky 1957, 1965; Dreyfus, H. 1967; Englebart 1962; Feigenbaum and Feldman 1963; Feldman and Gries 1968; Fogel, Owens, and Walsh 1966; Galernter 1963; Hovland 1960; Kleinmuntz 1966; Miller, G. A. 1956; Minsky 1963a, 1963b, 1966; Newell 1966; Newell and Simon 1964; Newman, A. D. 1966; Pask 1961; Quillian 1967; Reitman 1964, 1965; Sass and Wilkinson 1965; Shelly and Bryan 1964; Simon 1957, 1967, in press; Simon and Newell 1968; Simon and Simon 1962; Von Newmann 1965; Whitfield, Easterby and Whitfield 1967; Wiener 1954, 1961.

A4. Identification of Problem Structure
A4a. Computer decomposition models.

Alexander 1963d; Alexander and Manheim 1962b; Ball 1965; Bierstone and Bernholtz 1967; Brams 1968; Davis, C. 1967; Davis and Kennedy 1969; Frew 1967; Herbert 1964; Owen in press.

A4b. Case studies in problem formulation.

Alexander and Manheim 1962a, 1962c; Brams 1966; Koenig et al. 1966; Koenig, Rusch, Moore, et al. 1965; Milne, Matteson, et al. 1966; Milne and Rusch 1968; Owen in press.

A5. Building Layout Models
Including location and allocation models, building computer systems.

Archer 1963; Beaumont 1967; Brooks, Smith, Stone, and Tutte 1940; Buffa, Armour, and Vollman 1964; Bullock, Dickins, and Steadman 1968; Burnette 1968; Campion 1968; Carter, Colker and Leib 1968; Casalaina and Rittel 1967; Cooper 1964; Grey 1967; Gruman 1966–67; Hiller 1963; Hutchinson 1967; Judy and Levine 1965; Kiskunes and Peckenpaugh 1967; Kiviat and Colker 1964; Krejcirik 1968; Levin 1964; Mosley 1963; Moucka 1968; Murphy 1967; Nugent, Vollman, and Ruml 1968; Oakford, Allen, and Chatterson 1966–67, Parsons 1967; Souder, Clark, Elkinel, and Brown 1964; Teague 1968; Teague and Hershdorfer 1967; Tutte 1966; Whitehead and Elders 1964, 1965.

A6. Evaluation Systems
A6a. Evaluation of existing environments, user requirements, performance.

Alexander 1964; Brill 1968b, 1968c; Brill and Blake 1968; Davis, A. R. 1968; Department of Housing and Urban Development 1968; Duffy 1968; Ellis, R. H. 1968; Falk 1968; Jones 1963; Metropolitan Toronto School Board 1968; Poyner 1966; Rittel 1968; Sanoff 1968; Studer 1966; Wachs 1968.

A6b. Evaluation of alternatives.

Archer in press; Boyce and Goldstone 1966; Brill 1968d; Corney 1966; Crandall 1968; Cripp and Foot 1968; Gibbons 1968; Hay, Morlok, and Charnes 1966; Hill, M. 1967, 1968; Hutchinson 1967; Irwin 1966; Jessiman, Brand, Tumminia, and Brussee 1967; Lichfield 1960; Little 1963; Lowry 1964; Manheim 1967b; Manheim et al. 1968; Manning n.d.; Markus 1967; Meyerson and Banfield 1955; Platt 1966; Pleydell-Pearce 1966; Roberts 1966; Steger and Lakshmanan 1968; Steinitz and Rogers 1968; Wilson 1967; Wilson and Ernst 1967.

A7. Applications of Systems Engineering
A7a. Techniques of systems analysis and systems engineering.

Ackoff 1962; Baumol 1965; Bodack 1967; Chestnut 1965; Dixon 1966; Fabian 1968; Forrester 1969; Flagle, Huggins, and Roy 1960; Gosling 1962; Hall, A. D. 1962; Hitch and McKeen 1965; Hoos 1967; Krick 1965; Machol 1968; McKeen 1958; McMillan and Gonzales 1965; Nadler 1967a, in press; Roy 1960; Schoeffler 1954; Steinmetz 1968; Wildavsky 1966; Zwick 1963.

A7b. Case studies

Bernard Johnson 1968; Brill 1968a; Dalton-Dalton 1968; Daniel, Mann, Johnson, and Mendenhall 1968; Gibbs and Hill 1968; Kennedy 1968; Little 1963; M.I.T. Students 1968; Rust Engineering Co. 1968; Shamir and Howard 1968; Steinmetz 1968; Van Ginkel 1968.

A8. Approaches to the Form/Behavior Relationship
A8a. Techniques and methods.

Alexander 1964, 1965c, 1966a, 1966b, 1966c; Alexander, Ishikawa and Silverstein 1968; Chermayeff and Alexander 1963; Daley in press; Duffy 1969; Ellis, R. H. 1968; Jackson 1967; Koenig et al. 1966; Michelson 1968; Poyner in press; Studer in press; Van der Ryn and Silverstein 1967; Von Forester 1962.

A8b. Related literature from the behavioral sciences.

Amsel and Hancock 1957; Atkinson and Litwin 1960; Berlyne 1966; Cratty and Williams 1966; Davey 1958; Dembar and Earl 1957; Festinger 1964; Fogel 1963; Gans 1962; Hall, E. T. 1966; Heckhausen 1967; Hunt, J. McV. 1944; Kristol 1966; Lévi-Strauss 1967a, 1967b; Lewin 1941, 1966; Lewis 1961, 1968; Malinowski 1960; Merton 1965; Moore and

Christie 1963; Piaget 1950, 1951, 1954; Polanyi, K. 1944; Porter 1964; Rogers, C. R. 1961; Rosensweig 1944; Sartre 1966; Weiss and Bouterline 1962; Werner 1961; Wilkins 1964; Yates 1962.

A8c. Case studies.

Alexander 1963a, 1964, 1965a, 1965c, 1966a, 1966d; Alexander, Ishikawa, and Silverstein 1968; Alexander, King, Baker, and Ishikawa 1966; Chermayeff and Alexander 1963; Duffy 1969; Field et al. 1966; Goldberg 1968; Koenig et al. 1966; Koenig, Rusch, Moore et al. 1965; Longbone in press; Maki, Ohtaka, and Goldberg 1964; Milne, Matteson, et al. 1966; National Building Agency 1967; Poyner in press; Van der Ryn and Adams 1967; Van der Ryn and Silverstein 1967; Walkey 1967; Ward 1967; Wurster 1963.

A9. Major Theories of Design and Planning Methodology

Alexander 1964; Alexander, Ishikawa, and Silverstein 1968; Archer 1965, and in press; Asimow 1962; Banfield 1959; Bowen 1964; Braybrooke and Lindblom 1963; Churchman 1968; Davidoff 1965; Friedmann 1966; Godschalk 1968; Harris 1965; Isard 1960; Isard, Smith, Isard, Tung, and Dacey in press; Jones 1963, in press b; Jones and Thornley 1963; Levin 1966a, 1966b; Manheim 1967a; Manheim et al. 1968; Markus 1967; Meier 1965; Meyerson 1956; Meyerson and Banfield 1955; Nadler 1967a, 1967b, in press; Norberg-Schultz 1965; Perloff 1968; Pidgeon 1968; RIBA 1963; Rittel 1966; Robinson 1965; Smithson 1968; Starr 1963; Steinmetz 1968; Webber 1965.

A10. Action-Oriented and Political Processes
Including advocacy planning and social planning.

Alinsky 1962; Davidoff 1965; Davidoff and Reiner 1962; Frieden 1965, 1967; Frieden and Morris 1968; Peattie 1968a, 1968b, 1968c; Pidgeon 1968; Rowan 1968.

B. Theoretical Foundations
B1. Science and Research
B1a. Philosophy of Science.

Bergson 1942, 1944; Bertalanffy 1950; Boulding 1956; Cassirer 1932, 1953–57; Churchman 1968; Craik 1967; Croce 1922; Derry and Williams 1960; Helevy 1955; Jewkes, Sawers, and Stillerman 1962; Kaplan, A. 1964; Kuhn 1962; Langer 1953, 1963; Maslow 1946; McLuhan 1964; Mesarovic 1964; Mumford 1962; Polanyi, M. 1959, 1964; Popper 1959; Reid 1961; Scheffler 1963; Scriven 1959; Toulmin 1953, 1963; Wiener 1954.

B1b. Research methods.

Ackoff 1953, 1962; Adams and Messick 1958; Bakan 1967; Campbell and Stanley 1963; Chapanis 1959, 1967; Coombs 1950; Festinger and Katz 1953; Hays 1964; Madge 1963; Maroney 1951; Nadler 1963; Platt 1966; Stevens 1946, 1963.

B2. Decision Theory, Mathematical Programming, and Operations Research
B2a. Basic concepts of mathematics, symbolic logic, and economics.

Adler 1958; Arnold, B. H. 1962; Beckenbach 1964; Bergé 1962; Boulding 1962; Busacher and Saaty 1965; Feller 1957; Fox 1950; Halmos 1960; Hitch 1967; Kemeny, Snell, and Thompson 1966; Langer 1967a; Ore 1963; Prest and Turvey 1965; Schlaifer 1959; Tybout 1965; Wildavsky 1966.

B2b. Decision theory.

Arrow 1951; Bendixin 1967; Bross 1953; Braybrooke and Lindblom 1963; Churchman 1961b; Edwards and Tversky 1967; Fishburn 1964; Kaufmann 1968; Lindblom 1965; Luce and Raiffa 1957; Polya 1957; Schnelle 1967; Schoeffler 1954; Starr 1963; Thrall, Coombs, and Davis 1957; Tavistock Institute 1966; Willner 1960; Zwicky and Wilson 1967.

B2c. Mathematical programming and operations research.

Ackoff 1961a, 1961b, 1962; Ashby 1956; Battersby 1964; Baumol 1965; Beer 1959; Bellman and Brock 1960; Buffa 1965; Burns and Stalker 1961; Churchman 1961a; Churchman, Ackoff, and Arnoff 1957; Dantzig 1963; Dreyfus, S. 1961, 1965; Duckworth 1962; Elmaghraby 1964; Flagle, Huggins, and Roy 1960; Forrester 1961; Gass 1968; Hadley 1962, 1964; Hanika 1965; Hitch 1953, 1957; Hitch and McKean 1965; Jordon 1967; Koopman 1957; Koopmans 1951; Lavi and Vogl 1966; Lockyer 1964; Marglin 1967; McDonough 1963; Miller and Starr 1960; Morse 1967; National Economic Development Council 1967; Pask 1961; Roos 1967a, 1967b; Shaffer, Rutter, and Meyer 1965; Shannon and Weaver 1949; Trakhtenbrot 1963; Vajda 1960, 1961; Weigartner 1963; Wilde 1963; Wilde and Brightler 1967.

B2d. Gaming and simulation theory.

Greenberger 1968; Luce and Raiffa 1957; Naylor, Balinfy, Burdick, and Chu 1966; Teichroew and Lubin 1966; Vajda 1960, 1961; Von Newmann and Morgenstern 1953.

C. Applications to Environmental Design and Planning
C1. Industrial Design and Engineering.

Alexander 1964; Archer 1962, 1965, in press; Asimow 1962; Bodack 1967; Bowen 1964; Dixon 1966; Gregory 1966a, in press; Herzog 1967; Holstein 1964; Jacks 1964, 1967; Jacks et al. 1964; Jones 1958, 1959, 1963, in press b; Jones, Talbot, and Goodwin 1967; Jones and Thornley 1963; Krampen and Seitz 1967; Krick 1965; Matchett 1965; Matchett and Briggs 1966; Maver 1965, 1966; McCrory 1963; McCrory, Wilkinson, and Frink 1963; Mezei in press; Nadler 1963; Noll 1967b, 1967c; Norris 1963; Pask 1963; Rittel 1966; Roos 1967a, 1967b; Seitz 1967; Siddell 1966; Starr 1963; Terry 1968; Ward and Broadbent in press; Woodson 1966.

C2. Architecture and Building Design
Including structural engineering, landscape architecture, urban design.

Alexander 1961, 1964, 1965c, 1966a, 1966b; Alexander, Ishikawa, and Silverstein 1968; Alexander, King, Baker, and Ishikawa 1966; Archer 1963, in press; Architectural Association 1967; Architectural Engineering Department, Pennsylvania State University 1966; Beaumont 1967; Berkeley 1968; Bernholtz and Bierstone 1967; Birrell n.d.; Brill 1968a, 1968c; Brill and Blake 1968; Bullock, Dickins, and Steadman 1968; Burnette 1968; Campion 1968; Carter, Colker, and Leib 1968; Casalaina and Rittel 1967; Chermayeff and Alexander 1963; Cogswell 1967; Crandall 1968; Cripp and Foot 1968; Davis, A. R. 1968; Department of Housing and Urban Development 1968; Duffy 1969; Falk 1968; Field et al. 1966; Gibbons 1968; Goldberg 1968; Greenfield, Portnoy and Wallace 1964; Heath 1968, in press; Hutchinson 1967; Jacobs and Way 1968; Jeanes n.d.; Jones 1963,

1965, in press b; Jones, Talbot, and Goodwin 1967; Jones and Thornley 1963; Judy and Levine 1965; Kishkunes and Peckenpaugh 1967; Kliment 1963, 1968; Koenig et al. 1966; Koenig, Rusch, Moore, et al. 1965; Krampen and Seitz 1967; Krejcirik 1968; Levin 1964, 1966a, 1966b; Longbone in press; Manning n.d.; Markus 1967; Mattox et al. 1967; Maver and Carson 1966; Metropolitan Toronto School Board 1968; Milne 1969; Milne, Matteson et al. 1966; Mosley 1963; Moucka 1968; Murphy 1967; Nadler 1967a, in press; National Building Agency 1967; Negroponte in press; Negroponte and Groisser 1967; Norberg-Schultz 1965; Nuttall n.d.; O'Brian 1965; Owen in press; Parsons 1967; Pidgeon 1968; Poyner 1966, in press; RIBA 1963; Rittel 1966, 1968; Rowan 1967, 1968; Seitz 1967; Smith 1968; Smithson 1968; Souder, Clark, Elkinel, and Brown 1964; Studer 1966, in press; Sturman 1967; Van Ginkel 1968; Vigier 1965; Van der Ryn and Adams 1967; Van der Ryn and Silverstein 1967; Ward 1967; Ward and Broadbent in press; Wells 1967; Whitehead and Elders 1964, 1965; Zwicky 1948.

C3. Urban and Regional Planning
C3a. General Theory.

Alexander 1966b; Alonso 1968; Altshuler 1965; Banfield 1959; Braybrooke and Lindblom 1963; Churchman and Webber n.d.; Creighton 1968; Davidoff 1965; Davidoff and Reiner 1962; Duke 1961; Dyckman 1961, 1967; Frieden 1966, 1968; Frieden and Morris 1968; Frieden and Nash 1968; Friedmann 1966; Friedmann and Alonso 1964; Godschalk 1968; Harris, B. 1965; Hausler 1968; Hoffman 1966; Isard 1960; Isard, Smith, Isard, Tung, and Dacey in press; Jay 1963; Kennedy 1968; Kilbridge, O'Block, and Teplitz in press; Levin 1966b; Lowry 1964; Lynch 1966; Meier and Duke 1966; Meyerson 1956; Nadler 1967a, 1967b, in press; Perloff 1968; Pidgeon 1968; Rapoport and Drews 1962; Robinson 1965; Steger and Lakshmanan 1968; Steinitz and Rogers 1968; Steinmetz 1968; Sturman 1968; Tyrwhitt 1968; Webber 1965; Wheaton 1963; Wood 1968; Young 1966; Zwick 1963.

C3b. Urban Development.
Including housing, renewal, economic activity.

Alexander 1963a; Alonso 1964; Berry 1961; Chapin 1964, 1965a, 1965b; Chapin and Weiss 1962; Chermayeff and Alexander 1963; Dalton-Dalton 1968; Daniel, Mann, Johnson, and Mendenhall 1968; Department of Housing and Urban Development 1968; Fisher 1964; Forrester 1969; Garin 1966; Goddard 1968; Harris, B. 1965; Harris, C. C. 1968; Herbert 1964; Hill, D. M. 1965; Housing and Home Finance Agency 1963; Isard 1956, 1960; Isard and Smith 1967; Kaiser and Weiss 1967; Kresge 1965; Lathrop 1965; Lichfield 1960; Little 1963; Mao 1966; McManmon 1959; Meier 1962, 1965; Meyerson and Banfield 1955; Michelson 1968; Pfouts 1960; Ratcliff 1952; Robinson, Wolfe, and Barringer 1965; Rogers, A. 1966; Schlager 1965; Silvers and Sloan 1965; Sternlieb 1967; Steger 1965a, 1965b; Stone 1964; Tryon 1955; Voorhees 1959.

C3c. Transportation.

Alexander 1966d; Alexander and Manheim 1962a, 1962c; Boyce and Goldstone 1966; Bruck, Manheim, and Shuldiner 1967; Casciato and Case 1962; Chan, Follansbee, Manheim, and Mumford 1968; Ellis, R. H. 1968; Falk 1968; Gakenheimer 1968; Garrison 1965; Gibbs and Hill 1968; Goldberg 1968; Hill, M. 1967, 1968; Homburger 1967; Irwin Jessiman, Brand, Tumminia and Brussee 1967; Jones in press a; Manheim 1961, 1966a, 1966b, 1967a, 1967b; Manheim et al. 1968; Manheim, Follansby, and Walter 1968; Manheim and Hall, 1968; Meyer, Kain, and Wohl 1966; Martin, Memmott, and Bone 1965; Roberts 1966; Roberts and Suhrbier 1966; Ruiter 1968a, 1968b; Schofer and Levin 1967; Schriever and Seifert 1968; Voorhees 1959; Walkey 1967.

C3d. Applications of gaming and simulation.

Boyce and Goldstone 1966; Chapin 1965a; Forrester 1969; Hamilton et al. 1968; Kresge 1965; Little 1963; Lowry 1964; Meier and Duke 1966; Robinson, Wolfe and Barringer 1965; Steger 1965b; Taylor and Madison 1968; Wolfe and Ernst 1967.

Bibliography

The entries below are given in conventional form except for the addition of a list of indexes following each entry. Brief descriptions and the full collection of works which fall under each index are given in the preceding section.

Abzug, I

(1965), "Graphic data processing," *Datamation*, Vol. 11, January, pp. 35–37. A3b.

Ackoff, R. L.

(1953), *Design of Social Research*. Chicago: University of Chicago Press. B1b.

ed. (1961a), *Progress in Operations Research*. New York: Wiley. B2c.

(1961b), "The meaning, scope, and methods of operations research," in *Progress in Operations Research*, Vol. 1. New York: Wiley, pp. 1–34. B2c.

(1962), *Scientific Method: Optimizing Applied Research Decisions*. New York: Wiley. A7a, B1b, B2c.

Adams, E., and S. Messick

(1958), "An axiomatic formulation and generalization of successive interval scaling, *Psychometrika*, Vol. 23, pp. 355–368. B1b.

Adler, I.

(1958), *The New Mathematics*. London: John Day. New York: Signet, 1968. B2a.

Alexander, C.

(1961), "Information and an organized process of design," *Proceedings of the Building Research Institute*, Spring, pp. 115–124. C2.

(1963a), "Determination of the components for an Indian village," in J. C. Jones and D. G. Thornley, eds., *Conference on Design Methods*. London: Pergamon and New York: Macmillan, pp. 83–114. A8c, C3b.

375

Alexander, C.

(1963b), *HIDECS 3: Four Computer Programs for the Hierarchical Decomposition of Systems which have an Associated Linear Graph.* Cambridge: Civil Engineering Systems Laboratory, M.I.T. A4a.

(1964), *Notes on the Synthesis of Form.* Cambridge: Harvard University Press, and London: Oxford University Press. A6a, A8a, A8c, A9, C1, C2.

(1965a), "The city is not a tree," *Architectural Forum,* Part I, April, pp. 58–62, and Part II, May, pp. 58–61; reprinted in *Design,* February 1966, pp. 46–55. A8c.

(1965b), "The question of computers in design," *Landscape,* Spring, pp. 6–8. A1.

(1965c), "The theory and invention of form," *Architectural Record,* Vol. 139, April, pp. 177–186. A8a, A8c, C2.

(1966a), "The city as a mechanism for sustaining human contact," *Transactions of the Bartlett Society,* Vol. 4, pp. 93–136. Also in W. R. Ewald, Jr., ed., *Environment for Man: The Next Fifty Years.* Bloomington, Ind.: Indiana University Press, 1967, pp. 60–102. A8a, A8c, C2.

(1966b), *The Coordination of the Urban Rule System.* Berkeley: Center for Planning and Development Research, University of California, published in *Regio Basiliensis Proceedings* (Basle, Switzerland), 1966. A8a, C2, C3a.

(1966c), "From a set of forces to a form," in G. Kepes, ed., *The Man Made Object.* New York: Braziller, pp. 96–107. A8a.

(1966d), "The pattern of streets," *Journal of the American Institute of Planners,* Vol. 32, pp. 273–278; reprinted in *Architectural Design,* Vol. 37, 1967, pp. 529–531; comments and rejoinder, *Journal of the American Institute of Planners,* Vol. 33, November 1967, pp. 409–417. A8c, C3c.

S. Ishikawa, and M. Silverstein (1968), *A Pattern Language Which Generates Multi-Service Centers.* Berkeley: Center for Environmental Structure. A8a, A8c, A9, C2.

V. M. King, M. Baker, and S. Ishikawa (1966), "Relational complexes in architecture," *Architectural Record,* Vol. 140, September, pp. 185–190. A8c, C2.

and M. L. Manheim (1962a), *The Design of Highway Interchanges: An Example of a General Method for Analyzing Engineering Design Problems.* Cambridge: Civil Engineering Systems Laboratory, M.I.T. A4b, C3c.

(1962b), *HIDECS 2: A Computer Program for the Hierarchical Decomposition of a Set with an Associated Linear Graph.* Cambridge: Civil Engineering Systems Laboratory, M.I.T., A4a.

(1962c), *The Use of Diagrams in Highway Route Location.* Cambridge: Civil Engineering Systems Laboratory, M.I.T. A4b, C3c.

C. Wilson, L. March, C. Norberg-Schultz, and M. Browne (1967), "Design innovation: An exchange of ideas," *Progressive Architecture,* Vol. 48, November, pp. 126–131. A1.

Alger, J. R., and C. V. Hays

(1964), *Creative Synthesis in Design.* Englewood Cliffs, N.J.: Prentice-Hall. A2a.

Alinsky, S.

(1962), *Citizen Participation and Community Organization in Planning and Urban Renewal.* Chicago: Industrial Areas Foundation. A10.

Alonso, W.

(1964), *Location and Land Use: Toward a General Theory of Land Rent.* Cambridge: Harvard University Press. C3b.

(1968), "Predicting best with imperfect data," *Journal of the American Institute of Planners,* Vol. 34, pp. 248–255. C3a.

Altshuler, A. A.

(1965), *The City Planning Process: A Political Analysis.* Ithaca, N.Y.: Cornell University Press. C3a.

Amsel, A., and W. Hancock

(1957), "Motivation properties of frustration, III: Relation of frustration effect to antecedent goal factors," *Journal of Experimental Psychology,* Vol. 53, pp. 126–131. A8b.

Anderson, A. R., ed.

(1964), *Minds and Machines.* Englewood Cliffs, N.J.: Prentice-Hall. A3c.

Appel, A.

(1968), "Some techniques for shading machine renderings of solids," *Proceedings Spring Joint Computer Conference,* Vol. 32, pp. 37–45. A3b.

Archer, L. B.

(1956), "Intuition versus mathematics," *Design,* No. 90, June, pp. 12–19. A1.

(1962), *Studies in the Function and Design of Non-Surgical Hospital Equipment.* London: Royal College of Art. C1.

Archer, L. B.	(1963), "Planning accommodation for hospitals and the transportation problem technique," *Architects' Journal*, Vol. 138, pp. 139–142. A5, C2.
	(1965), *Systematic Method for Designers*. London: Council of Industrial Design, reprinted from *Design*, No. 172–188, April 1963 to August 1964. A9, C1.
	(in press), *The Structure of Design Processes*. London: Longmans. A6b, A9, C1, C2.
Architectural Association	(1967), *Reporting Back Attingham Park: The Teaching of Design—Design Method in Architecture*. London: Architectural Association. C2.
Architectural Engineering Department, Pennsylvania State University	(1966), *Emerging Techniques of Architectural Practice*. Washington: American Institute of Architects. A1, C2.
Arnold, B. H.	(1962), *Intuitive Concepts in Elementary Topology*. Englewood Cliffs, N.J.: Prentice-Hall. B2a.
Arnold, J. E.	(1962), "Useful creative techniques," in S. J. Parnes and H. F. Harding, eds., *A Source Book for Creative Thinking*. New York: Scribners, pp. 252–268. A2b.
Arrow, K.	(1951), *Social Choice and Individual Values*. New York: Wiley. B2b.
Ashby, W. R.	(1956), *An Introduction to Cybernetics*. New York: Wiley, and London: Methuen, 1965. A3c, B2c.
Asimow, M.	(1962), *Introduction to Design*. Englewood Cliffs, N.J.: Prentice-Hall. A9, C1.
Atkinson, J. W., and G. H. Litwin	(1960), "Achievement motivation and test anxiety concerned as motive to approach success and motive to avoid failure," *Journal of Abnormal Psychology*, Vol. 60, pp. 52–63. A8b.
Bakan, D.	(1967), *On Method: Toward a Reconstruction of Psychological Investigation*. San Francisco: Jossey-Boss. B1b.
Ball, G. H.	(1965), "Data analysis in the social sciences: What about the details?" *Proceedings Fall Joint Computer Conference*, Vol. 27, pp. 533–559. A3b, A4a.
Banfield, E. C.	(1959), "Ends and means in planning," *UNESCO International Social Science Journal*, Vol. 11, pp. 365–368. A9, C3a.
Barnette, J.	(1965), "Computer aided design and automated working drawings," *Architectural Record*, Vol. 138, October, pp. 143–150. A3a.
	(1968), "Glass box and black box: Or can artificial intelligence help solve design problems?" *Architectural Record*, Vol. 144, July, pp. 137–138. A1.
Bartlett, F. C.	(1961), *Remembering*. London: Cambridge University Press. A2b.
Battersby, A.	(1964), *Network Analysis for Planning and Scheduling*. New York: Macmillan. B2c.
Baumol, W. J.	(1965), *Economic Theory and Operations Analysis*, 2nd ed. Englewood Cliffs, N.J.: Prentice-Hall. A7a, B2c.
Beaumont, M. J.	(1967), "Computer aided techniques for synthesis of layout and form with respect to circulation," unpublished doctoral dissertation, University of Bristol. A5, C2.
Beckenbach, E. F., ed.	(1964), *Applied Combinatorial Mathematics*. New York: Wiley. B2a.
Beer, S.	(1959), *Cybernetics and Management*. London: Universities Press. B2c.
Bellman, R., and P. Brock	(1960), "On the concepts of a problem and problem solving," *American Mathematics Monthly*, Vol. 67, pp. 119–133. B2c.
Bendixen, P.	(1967), "The complexity of decision-making situations," *Kommunikation*, Vol. 3, pp. 103–114. B2b.
Benet, J., *et al.*	(1967), *SCSD: The Project and the Schools*. New York: Educational Facilities Laboratories, C2.
Bergé, C.	(1962), *Theory of Graphs and their Applications*. London: Methuen, and New York: Wiley. B2a.
Bergson, H.	(1942), *Introduction to Metaphysics*. New York: Bobbs-Merrill. B1a.
	(1944), *Creative Evolution*. New York: Random House. B1a.
Bergstrom, L. A.	(1967), *An Annotated Bibliography in Computer Graphics*. Seattle: Urban Data Center, University of Washington. A3b.

Berkeley, E. P.

(1968), "Computers for design and design for the computer," *Architectural Forum,* Vol. 128, March, pp. 60–65. A3a, C2.

Berlyne, D. E.

(1966), "Conflict and arousal," *Scientific American,* Vol. 215, August, pp. 82–88. A8b.

Bernard Johnson Engineers, Inc.

(1968), "A proposal for a systems engineering study of water pollution abatement," *Consulting Engineer,* Vol. 30, March, pp. 185–189. A7b.

Bernholtz, A., and E. Bierstone

(1967), Computer-augmented design: A case history in architecture, *Design Quarterly,* No. 66/67, pp. 41–51. Also in M. Krampen and P. Seitz, eds., *Design and Planning 2.* New York: Hastings House, 1967, pp. 41–51. A3a, C2.

Berry, B. J.

(1961), "A method for deriving multi-factor uniform regions," *Polish Geographical Journal* (Warsaw), Vol. 33, pp. 263–279. C3b.

Bertalanffy, L. von

(1950), "An outline of general systems theory." *British Journal of the Philosophy of Science,* Vol. 1, pp. 134–165. B1a.

Bierstone, E., and A. Bernholtz

(1967), *HIDECS-RECOMP Procedure.* Cambridge: Department of Civil Engineering, M.I.T. A4a.

Birrell, G. S.

(n.d.), *Data Processing for Building Control: An Integrated Concept.* Edinburgh: University of Edinburgh. C2.

Bodack, K. D.

(1967), "A model of the conceptual phase of the engineering design process," unpublished master's thesis, University of California, Berkeley. A7a, C1.

Bolan, R. S.

(1967), "Emerging views of planning," *Journal of the American Institute of Planners,* Vol. 33, pp. 233–245. A1.

Bonsiepe, G.

(1967), "Arabesques of rationality: Notes on the methodology of design," *Kommunikation,* Vol. 3, pp. 142–161. A1.

Boole, G.

(1951), *An Investigation of the Laws of Thought.* New York: Dover. A2b.

Boulding, K. E.

(1956), "General systems theory: The skeleton of science," *Management Science,* Vol. 2, pp. 197–208. B1a.

(1962), *A Reconstruction of Economics.* New York: Science Editions. B2a.

Bouterline, S., and R. Weiss

The Seattle World's Fair. Cambridge: IBM Cambridge Scientific Center.

Bowen, H. M.

(1964), "Rational design," *Industrial Design,* Vol. 11, February–August. A9, C1.

Boyce, D. E., and S. E. Goldstone

(1966), "A regional economic simulation model for urban transportation planning," *Highway Research Record,* No. 149, pp. 29–41. A6, C3c, C3d.

Brams, S. J.

(1966), "Transaction flows in international systems," *American Political Science Review,* Vol. 60, pp. 880–898. A4b.

(1968), "DECOMP: A program for the condensation of a directed graph and the hierarchical ordering of its strong components," *Behavioral Science,* Vol. 13, pp. 344–345. A4a.

Braybrooke, D., and C. Lindblom

(1963), *A Strategy of Decision.* New York: Free Press. A9, B2b, C3a.

Brill, M.

(1968a), "Architecture and planning: Using the systems approach," *Report of the Building Systems Section.* Washington: Institute for Applied Technology, National Bureau of Standards. A7, C2.

(1968b), "Performance evaluation techniques as developed in Federal Government building programs," Institute for Applied Technology, National Bureau of Standards, Washington (unpublished). A6a.

(1968c), "Performance requirements for housing," in Department of Housing and Urban Development, *The Performance Concept: A Study of its Application to Housing.* Washington: Department of Housing and Urban Development. A6a, C2.

(1968d), "Rank ordering techniques," in Department of Housing and Urban Development, *The Performance Concept: A Study of its Application to Housing.* Washington: Department of Housing and Urban Development. A6b.

and R. W. Blake (1968), "Systems, performance, and the office building," *Building Research,* Vol. 5, July–September, pp. 40–47. A6a, C2.

Broadbent, G. H.

(1966a), "Creativity," in S. A. Gregory, ed., *The Design Method.* London: Butterworths, and New York: Plenum Press, pp. 111–119. A2a.

Broadbent, G. H.

(1966b), "Design method in architecture," *Architect's Journal,* Vol. 144, pp. 679–685. Reprinted in A. Ward and G. Broadbent, ed., *Design Methods in Architecture.* London: Lund Humphries, and New York: Wittenborn (in press). A1.

(1968), "A plain man's guide to systematic design methods," *Royal Institute of British Architects Journal,* Vol. 5, May, pp. 223–227. A1.

Brodey, W. M., and N. J. Lindgren

(1967), "Human enhancement through evolutionary technology," *IEEE Spectrum,* Vol. 4, September, pp. 87–97. A3c.

Brooks, R. L., C. A. Smith, A. H. Stone, and W. T. Tutte

(1940), "The dissection of rectangles into squares," *Duke Mathematical Journal,* Vol. 7, pp. 312–340. A5.

Bross, I. D.

(1953), *Design for Decision.* New York: Macmillan. B2b.

Brown, D. S.

(1967), "Team 10, Perspecta 10, and the present state of architectural theory," *Journal of the American Institute of Planners,* Vol. 33, pp. 42–50. A1.

Bruck, H. W., M. L. Manheim, and P. W. Shuldiner

(1967), "Transport systems planning as a process: the Northeast Corridor example," *Transportation Research Forum,* pp. 67–98. C3c.

Bruner, J. S., J. J. Goodnow, and G. A. Austin

(1956), *A Study of Thinking.* New York: Wiley. A2b.

Buffa, E. S.

(1965), *Modern Production Management.* New York: Wiley. B2c.

G. C. Armour, and T. E. Vollman (1964), "Allocating facilities with CRAFT," *Harvard Business Review,* Vol. 42, March–April, pp. 272–290. A5.

Bullock, N., P. Dickins, and P. Steadman

(1968), "University planning: a theoretical model," *Official Architecture and Planning,* Vol. 31, April, pp. 505–512. A5, C2.

Burnette, C. H.

(1968), *The ARC Septem: A Functional Organization for Buildings.* Philadelphia: Institute for Environmental Studies, University of Pennsylvania. C2.

Burns, T., and G. M. Stalker

(1961), *The Management of Innovation.* London: Tavistock. B2c.

Busacker, R. G., and T. L. Saaty

(1965), *Finite Graphs and Their Networks.* New York: McGraw-Hill. B2a.

Campbell, D. T., and J. C. Stanley

(1963), *Experimental and Quasi-Experimental Designs for Research,* Chicago: Rand McNally. B1b.

Campion, D.

(1968), *Computers in Architectural Design.* London and New York: Elsevier. A1, A5, C2.

Carnegie-Mellon University

(1968), *Computer Augmented Design Bibliography.* Pittsburgh: Department of Computer Science, Carnegie-Mellon University. A3a.

Carter, D. A., A. A. Colker, and J. S. Leib

(1968), "Simulation model for vocational educational facility planning," *Journal of Industrial Engineering,* Vol. 19, pp. 68–75. A5, C2.

Carter, E. S.

(1965), "Experimental heuristics as an approach to problem solving," in M. A. Sass and W. D. Wilkenson, eds., *Computer Augmentation of Human Reasoning.* New York: Sparton and London: Macmillan, pp. 13–23. A3c.

Carver, W. W.

(1964), "Creativity in architectural design: The ACSA reports," *Journal of Architectural Education,* Vol. 19, pp. 19–22. A2a.

Casalaina, V., and H. Rittel

(1967), "Generating floor plans from adjacency matrices," paper presented to the NBS Conference on Computer-aided Building Design, M.I.T., Cambridge (unpublished). A5, C2.

Casciato, L., and S. Case

(1962), "Pilot study of the automatic control of traffic signals by a general purpose electronic computer," *Highway Research Board Bulletin,* Vol. 338, pp. 28–39. A3a, C3c.

Cassirer, E.

(1932), *The Philosophy of the Enlightenment.* Mohr: Berlin, and Boston: Beacon, 1962. B1a.

(1953–1957), *Philosophy of Symbolic Forms,* 3 Vols. New Haven: Yale University Press. A2b, B1a.

Chan, Y.-P., K. Follansbee, M. L. Manheim, and J. R. Mumford

(1968), *Network Aggregation: An Application of Hierarchical Structure.* Cambridge: Department of Civil Engineering, M.I.T. C3c.

Chapanis, A.

(1959), *Research Techniques in Human Engineering.* Baltimore: Johns Hopkins. B1b.

(1967), "The relevance of laboratory studies to practical situations," *Ergonomics,* Vol. 10, pp. 557–577. B1b.

Chapin, F. S.

(1964), "Selected theories of urban growth and structure," *Journal of the American Institute of Planners,* Vol. 30, pp. 51–58. C3b.

(1965a), "A model for simulating residential development," *Journal of the American Institute of Planners,* Vol. 31, pp. 120–125. C3b, C3d.

(1965b), *Urban Land Use Planning,* 2nd ed. Urbana: University of Illinois Press. C3b.

and S. F. Weiss (1962), *Factors Influencing Land Development: Evaluation of Inputs for a Forecast Model.* Chapel Hill: Institute for Research in Social Science, University of North Carolina. C3b.

Chermayeff, S., and C. Alexander

(1963), *Community and Privacy: Toward a New Architecture of Humanism.* Garden City, N.Y.: Doubleday. A8a, A8c, C2, C3b.

Chestnut, H.

(1965), *Systems Engineering Tools.* New York: Wiley. A7a.

Chomsky, N.

(1957), *Syntactic Structures.* The Hague: Mouton, and New York: Humanities. A3c.

(1965), *Aspects of the Theory of Syntax.* Cambridge: M.I.T. Press. A3c.

Churchman, C. W.

(1961a), "Direction and value theory," in R. L. Ackoff, ed., *Progress in Operations Research,* Vol. 1. New York: Wiley, pp. 35–64. B2c.

(1961b), *Prediction and Optimal Decision.* Englewood Cliffs, N.J.: Prentice-Hall. B2b.

(1968), *Challenge to Reason.* Berkeley: University of California Press. A9, B1a.

R. L. Ackoff, and E. L. Arnoff (1957), *Introduction to Operations Research.* New York: Wiley. B2c.

and M. W. Webber (n.d.), *Technology and Urban Management.* Berkeley: Space Sciences Laboratory, University of California. C3a.

Clark, W. E., and J. J. Souder

(1964), "Man and computer in the planning process," in S. R. Greenfield, H. P. Portnoy, and D. D. Wallace, eds., *Architecture and the Computer.* Boston: Boston Architectural Center, pp. 29–33. A3a.

Cogswell, A. R.

(1967), "Housing, the computer, and the architectural process," *Law and Contemporary Problems,* Vol. 32, Spring, pp. 274–285. A3a, C2.

Coombs, C. H.

(1950), "Psychological scaling without a unit of measurement," *Psychological Review,* Vol. 57, pp. 145–158. B1b.

Coons, S. A.

(1963), "An outline of the requirements for a computer-aided design system," *Proceedings Spring Joint Computer Conference,* Vol. 23, pp. 299–304. A3a.

(1967), "Computer-aided design," *Design Quarterly,* No. 66/67, pp. 7–13. Also in M. Krampen and P. Seitz, eds., *Design and Planning 2.* New York: Hastings House, pp. 7–13. A3a.

Cooper, L.

(1964), "Heuristic methods for location-allocation problems," *SIAM Review* (Society for Industrial and Applied Mathematics), January, Vol. 6, pp. 37–53. A5.

Corney, C. T.

(1966), "Reliability and maintenance," in S. A. Gregory, ed., *The Design Method.* London: Butterworths, and New York: Plenum Press, pp. 219–233. A6b.

Cowan, J. D.

(1965), "Some principles underlying the mechanization of thought processes," *Arena, Architectural Association Journal,* Vol. 80, March, pp. 251–257. A3a.

Craik, K. J.

(1967), *The Nature of Explanation.* London: Cambridge University Press. B1a.

Cralle, R. K., and G. A. Michael

(1967), "A survey of graphic data processing equipment for computers," in M. Krampen and P. Seitz, eds., *Design and Planning 2.* New York: Hastings House, pp. 155–176. A3b.

Crandall, R. H.

(1968), *Cost-Benefit Analysis in a University Setting: The Housing of Students.* Ann Arbor: University Microfilms. A6b, C2.

Cratty, B. J., and H. G. Williams

(1966), *Perceptual Thresholds and Non-Visual Locomotion.* Berkeley: University of California Press. A8b.

Creighton, R. L.

(1968), "Measurements and the regional planning process," *Highway Research Record,* No. 229, pp. 1–20. C3a.

Cripp, E. L., and D. H. Foot

(1968), "Evaluating alternative strategies," *Official Architecture and Planning,* Vol. 31, pp. 928–944. A6b, C2.

Croce, B.

(1922), *Aesthetics,* New York: Noonday. B1a.

Daley, J.   (in press), "A philosophical critique of behaviourism in architectural design," Paper 1 "Whither behaviourism" and Paper 2 "Relational theory," in A. Ward and G. Broadbent, eds., *Design Methods in Architecture*. London: Lund Humphries and New York: Wittenborn. A8a.

Dalton-Dalton Associates, Inc.   (1968), "A systems concept for urban revival," *Consulting Engineer*, Vol. 30, March, pp. 156–163. A7b, C3b.

Daniel, Mann, Johnson, and Mendenhall   (1968), "A proposal for a systems engineering study of the route to rural redevelopment," *Consulting Engineer*, Vol. 30, March, pp. 207-ff. A7b, C3b.

Dantzig, G.   (1963), *Linear Programming and Extensions*. Princeton: Princeton University Press. B2c.

Davey, J. B.   (1958), "The vision of a group of drivers," *British Journal of Physical Optics*, April. A8b.

Davidoff, P.   (1965), "Advocacy and pluralism in planning," *Journal of the American Institute of Planners*, Vol. 31, pp. 331–338. A9, A10, C3a.

and T. A. Reiner (1962), "A choice theory of planning," *Journal of the American Institute of Planners*, Vol. 28, pp. 103–115. A10, C3a.

Davis, A. R., ed.   (1968), "User requirement studies," *Official Architecture and Planning*, Vol. 31, pp. 774–791. A6a, C2.

Davis, C.   (1967), *EVAPROBST3*. Lexington, Ky.: School of Architecture, University of Kentucky. A4a.

and M. Kennedy (1969), *EPS: Program Documentation*. Lexington, Ky.: School of Architecture, University of Kentucky. A4a.

Deese, J.   (1965), *The Structure of Associations in Language and Thought*. Baltimore: Johns Hopkins. A2b.

De Groot, A. D.   (1965), *Thought and Choice in Chess*. The Hague: Mouton. A2b.

(1966), "Perception and memory versus thought," in B. Kleinmuntz, ed., *Problem Solving: Research, Method, and Theory*. New York: Wiley, pp. 19–50. A2b.

Dembar, W. N., and R. W. Earl   (1957), "Analysis of exploratory, manipulative, and curiosity behavior," *Psychological Review*, Vol. 64, pp. 91–96. A8b.

Department of Housing and Urban Development   (1968), *The Performance Concept: A Study of its Application to Housing*. Washington: Department of Housing and Urban Development. A6a, C2, C3b.

Derry, T. K., and T. I. Williams   (1960), *A Short History of Technology*. Oxford: Clarendon Press. B1a.

Dixon, J. R.   (1966), *Design Engineering: Inventiveness, Analysis, and Decision*. New York: McGraw-Hill. A7a, C1.

Dreyfus, H.   (1967), *Philosophic Issues in Artificial Intelligence*. Cambridge: M.I.T. Publications in the Humanities, No. 80. A3c.

Dreyfus, S.   (1961), "Dynamic programming," in R. L. Ackoff, ed., *Progress in Operations Research*, Vol. 1. New York: Wiley, pp. 211–243. B2c.

(1965), *Dynamic Programming and the Calculus of Variations*. New York: Academic Press. B2c.

Duckworth, E.   (1962), *A Guide to Operational Research*. London: Methuen. B2c.

Duffy, F.   (1968), "The user and the office building," *Building Research*, Vol. 5, July–September, pp. 31–37. A6a, C2.

(1969), "Work, organization, behavior, and office buildings: Some proposals for analysis and design," unpublished master's thesis, University of California, Berkeley. A8a, A8c, C2.

Duke, R. D., ed.   (1961), *Automatic Data Processing: Its Application to Urban Planning*. East Lansing: University of Michigan Press. C3a.

Durkin, H. E.   (1937), "Trial-and-error, gradual analysis and sudden reorganization," *Archives of Psychology*, Vol. 30, Whole No. 210. A2b.

Dyckman, J. W.   (1961), "Planning and decision theory," *Journal of the American Institute of Planners*, Vol. 27, pp. 335–345. C3a.

(1967), "City planning and the treasury of science," in W. R. Ewald, Jr., ed., *Environ-*

ment for Man: The Next 50 Years. Bloomington, Ind.: Indiana University Press, pp. 11–59. C3a.

Eastman, C. M.
(1968), *Explorations in the Cognitive Processes of Design*. Pittsburgh: Carnegie-Mellon University. A2a.

(in press), "Cognitive processes and ill-defined problems: A case study from design," *Proceedings First Joint International Conference on Artificial Intelligence*. A2a.

Eberhard, J. P.
(1962), "A computer based building process: Its potential for architecture." *Architectural and Engineering News*, Vol. 4, December, pp. 16–18. A1.

(1968), "A humanist case for the systems approach," *American Institute of Architects Journal*, Vol. 50, July, pp. 34–38. A1.

(1969), "Systems and the city: Hardware and software" (synopsis), *Boston Systems Group, Society for General Systems Research Bulletin*, Vol. 8, January. A1.

Educational Facilities Laboratory
(1967), *SCSD: The Project and the Schools*. New York: Educational Facilities Laboratories. C2.

Edwards, W., and A. Tversky
(1967), *Decision Making: Selected Readings*. London and Baltimore: Penguin. A2b, B2b.

Ellis, R. H.
(1968), "Toward measurement of the community consequences of urban freeways," *Highway Research Record*, No. 229, pp. 38–52. A6a, A8a, C3c.

Ellis, W. D., ed.
(1938), *A Source Book of Gestalt Psychology*. London: Routledge & Kegan Paul, and New York: Humanities. A2b.

Elmaghraby, S. E.
(1964), "An algebra for the analysis of generalized activity networks," *Management Science*, Vol. 10, pp. 494–514. B2c.

Englebart, D. C.
(1962), *Augmenting Human Intellect: A Conceptual Framework*. Palo Alto: Engineering Sciences Division, Stanford Research Institute. A3c.

Fabian, T.
(1968), "Systems techniques," *Consulting Engineer*, Vol. 30, March, pp. 140–145. A7a.

Falk, E. L.
(1968), "Measurement of community values: The Spokane experiment," *Highway Research Record*, No. 229, pp. 53–64. A6a, C2, C3c.

Feigenbaum, E. A., and J. Feldman, eds.
(1963), *Computers and Thought*. New York: McGraw-Hill. A3c.

Feldman, J., and D. Gries
(1968), "Translator writing systems," *Communications of the ACM*, Vol. 11, February, pp. 77–113. A3c.

Feller, W.
(1957), *An Introduction to Probability Theory and Its Application*, 2nd ed. New York: Wiley. B2a.

Fenves, S. J., R. D. Logcher, and S. P. Mauch
(1965), *STRESS: A Reference Manual—A Problem Oriented Computer Language for Structural Engineering*. Cambridge: M.I.T. Press. A3a.

and K. F. Reinschmidt (1964), *STRESS: A User's Manual—A Problem Oriented Computer Language for Structural Engineering*. Cambridge: M.I.T. Press. A3a.

Festinger, L., ed.
(1964), *Conflict, Decision, and Dissonance*. London: Tavistock. A8b.

and D. Katz, eds. (1953), *Research Methods in the Behavioral Sciences*. New York: Dryden Press. B1b.

Fetter, W. A.
(1965), *Computer Graphics in Communication*. New York: McGraw-Hill. A3b.

(1967), "Computer graphics," in M. Krampen and P. Seitz, eds., *Design and Planning 2*. New York: Hastings House, pp. 15–23. A3b.

Field, H., et al.
(1966), *Problems of Pediatric Hospital Design*. Washington: U.S. Public Health Service. A8c, C2.

Fishburn, P.
(1964), *Decision and Value Theory*. New York: Wiley. B2b.

Fisher, H.
(1964), "A technique for processing complex statistical data into meaningful graphic form," in S. R. Greenfield, H. P. Portnoy, and D. D. Wallace, eds., *Architecture and the Computer*. Boston: Boston Architectural Center, pp. 13–18. A3b, C3b.

Flagle, C. D., W. H. Huggins, and R. R. Roy, eds.
(1960), *Operations Research and Systems Engineering*. Baltimore: Johns Hopkins. A7a, B2c.

Fogel, L. J.
(1963), *Biotechnology: Concepts and Applications*. Englewood Cliffs, N.J.: Prentice-Hall. A8b.

Fogel, L. J.

A. J. Owens, and M. J. Walsh (1966), *Artificial Intelligence Through Simulated Evolution*. New York: Wiley. A3c.

Forrester, J. W.

(1961), *Industrial Dynamics*. Cambridge: M.I.T. Press. B2c.

(1969), *Urban Dynamics*. Cambridge: M.I.T. Press. A7a, C3b, C3d.

Fox, C.

(1950), *An Introduction to the Calculus of Variations*. London: Oxford University Press. B2a.

Frieden, B. J.

(1965), "Toward equality of urban opportunity," *Journal of the American Institute of Planners*, Vol. 31, pp. 320–330. Reprinted in H. W. Eldredge, ed., *Taming Megalopolis*. Garden City, N.Y.: Anchor Books, 1967, pp. 507–535. A10.

(1966), *Metropolitan America: Challenge to Federalism*. Washington: Advisory Commission on Intergovernmental Relations. C3a.

(1967), "The changing prospects for social planning," *Journal of the American Institute of Planners*, Vol. 33, pp. 311–323. A10.

(1968), "Housing and national urban goals: Old policies and new realities," in J. Q. Wilson, ed., *The Metropolitan Enigma: Inquiries into the Nature and Dimensions of America's Urban Crisis*. Cambridge: Harvard University Press, pp. 159–204. C3a.

and R. Morris, eds. (1968), *Urban Planning and Social Policy*. New York: Basic Books. A10, C3a.

and W. Nash, eds. (1968), *Shaping an Urban Future: Essays in Memory of Catherine Bauer Wurster*. Cambridge: M.I.T. Press. C3a.

Friedmann, J.

(1966), "Planning as innovation: The Chilean case," *Journal of the American Institute of Planners*, Vol. 32, pp. 194–204. A9, C3a.

and W. Alonso, eds. (1964), *Regional Development and Planning: A Reader*. Cambridge: M.I.T. Press. C3a.

Frew, R. S.

(1967), *An Introduction to Systems Architecture*, unpublished master's thesis, University of Waterloo, Waterloo, Canada. A4a.

Gakenheimer, R. A.

(1968), "Social factors in planning urban transportation," *High Speed Ground Transportation Journal*, Vol. 2, September, pp. 400–409. C3c.

Galernter, H.

(1963), "Realization of a geometry theorem proving machine," in E. A. Feigenbaum and J. Feldman, eds., *Computers and Thought*. New York: McGraw-Hill, pp. 134–152. A3c.

Gans, H.

(1962), *The Urban Villagers*. New York: Free Press. A8b.

Garin, R. A.

(1966), "A matrix formulation of the Lowry model for intrametropolitan activity allocation," with a note by A. Rogers, *Journal of the American Institute of Planners*, Vol. 32, pp. 361–366. C3b.

Garrison, W. L.

(1965), "Urban transportation planning models in 1985," *Journal of the American Institute of Planners*, Vol. 31, pp. 156–158. C3c.

Garvin, W. L.

(1962), "Creativity and the design process," *Journal of Architectural Education*, Vol. 17, December, pp. 96–97. A2a.

Gass, S.

(1958), *Linear Programming*. New York: McGraw-Hill. B2c.

Ghiselin, B., ed.

(1952), *The Creative Process*. Berkeley: University of California Press. A2b.

Gibbons, J. E.

(1968), "Apartment feasibility studies," *Appraisal Journal*, Vol. 36, pp. 325–332. A6b, C2.

Gibbs & Hill, Inc.

(1968), "A proposal for a systems engineering study of metropolitan area transportation," *Consulting Engineer*, Vol. 30, March, pp. 168–179. A7b, C3c.

Goddard, J.

(1968), "Multivariate analysis of office location patterns in the city centre: A London example," *Regional Studies*, September. C3b.

Godschalk, D. R., ed.

(1968), "Planning strategies in developing countries," *Journal of the American Institute of Planners*, Special Issue, Vol. 34, November. A9, C3a.

Goldberg, T.

(1968), "Design for a teenage center," unpublished master's thesis, University of California, Berkeley. A8c, C2, C3c.

Gombrich, E. H.

(1956), *Art and Illusion: A Study of the Psychology of Pictorial Representation*. London: Phaidon, and New York: Pantheon, 1965. A2b.

Gordon, W. J. J.   (1961), *Synectics: The Development of Creative Capacity*. New York: Harper & Row. A2b.

Gosling, W.   (1962), *The Design of Engineering Systems*. London: Heywood. A7a.

Green, P. M., and R. H. Cheney   (1968), "Urban planning and urban revolt: A case study," *Progressive Architecture*, Vol. 49, January, pp. 135–156. A10.

Greenberger, M., ed.   (1962), *Computers and the World of the Future*. Cambridge: M.I.T. Press. A1.

(1968), "Simulation methodology," in J. M. Beshers, ed., *Computer Methods in the Analysis of Large Scale Social Systems*. Cambridge: M.I.T. Press, pp. 190–196. B2d.

Greenfield, S. R., H. P. Portnoy, and D. D. Wallace, eds.   (1964), *Architecture and the Computer*. Boston: Boston Architectural Center. A3b, C2.

Gregory, S. A., ed.,   (1966a), *The Design Method*. London: Butterworths, and New York: Plenum Press. A1, C1.

(1966b), "Design science," in *The Design Method*. London: Butterworths, and New York: Plenum Press, pp. 323–330. A1.

(in press), "Morphological analysis: Some simple explanations," in A. Ward and G. Broadbent, eds., *Design Methods in Architecture*. London: Lund Humphries, and New York: Wittenborn. C1.

Grey, J. C.   (1967), "Compound data structure for computer aided design, a survey," *Proceedings ACM 22nd National Conference*, p. 355. A3b, A5.

Gruber, H. E., G. Terrell, and M. Wertheimer, eds.   (1964), *Contemporary Approaches to Creative Thinking*. New York: Atherton. A2b.

Gruman, A. J.,   (1966–67), "A comparison of computer programs for the assignment of students to classes: Report of an experimental study," *Journal of Educational Data Processing*, Vol. 4, pp. 7–15. A5.

Guilford, J. P.   (1967), *The Nature of Human Intelligence*. New York: McGraw-Hill. A2b.

Hadamard, J.   (1945), *An Essay on the Psychology of Invention in the Mathematical Field*. Princeton: Princeton University Press. A2b.

Hadley, G.   (1962), *Linear Programming*. Reading, Mass.: Addison-Wesley. B2c.

(1964), *Non-Linear and Dynamic Programming*. Reading, Mass.: Addison-Wesley. B2c.

Halevy, E.   (1955), *The Growth of Philosophical Radicalism*. Boston: Beacon. B1a.

Hall, A. D.   (1962), *A Methodology for Systems Engineering*. Princeton: Van Nostrand. A7a.

Hall, E. T.   (1966), *The Hidden Dimension*. New York: Doubleday. A8b.

Halmos, P. R.   (1960), *Naive Set Theory*. New York: Science Editions. B2a.

Hamilton, H. R., et al.   (1968), *Systems Simulations for Regional Analysis*. Cambridge: M.I.T. Press. C3d.

Hanika, F. de P.   (1965), *New Thinking in Management*. London: Hutchinson. B2c.

Harlow, H. F.   (1949), "The foundation of learning sets," *Psychological Review*, Vol. 56, pp. 551–565. A2b.

Harris, B.   (1960), "Plan or projection," *Journal of the American Institute of Planners*, Vol. 26, pp. 265–272. A1.

ed. (1965), "Urban development models: New tools for planning," *Journal of the American Institute of Planners*, Special Issue, Vol. 31, May, A9, C3a, C3b.

(1967), "The limits of science and humanism in planning," *Journal of the American Institute of Planners*, Vol. 33, pp. 324–335. A1.

Harris, C. C.   (1968), "A stochastic process model of residential development," *Journal of Regional Science*, Vol. 8, pp. 29–39. C3b.

Hausler, J.   (1968), "Planning: A way of shaping the future," *Management International Review*, Vol. 8, pp. 12–24. C3a.

Hay, G. A., E. K. Morlok, and A. Charnes   (1966), "Toward optimal planning of a two-mode urban transportation system: A linear programming formulation," *Highway Research Record*, No. 148, pp. 20–48. A6b, C3c.

Hayakawa, S. I.   (1963), "The fully functioning personality," in *Symbol, Status, and Personality*. New York: Harcourt Brace & World, pp. 51–69. A2b.

Hays, W. L.	(1964), *Statistics for Psychologists*. New York: Holt, Rinehart & Winston. B1b.
Heath, T. F.	(1968), "Problems of measurement in environmental aesthetics," *Architectural Science Review,* Vol. 11, March, pp. 17–28. C2.
	(in press), *Experimental Aesthetics and Architecture*. New York: American Elsevier, C2.
Hebb, D. O.	(1949), *The Organization of Behavior*. New York: Wiley. A2b.
Heckhausen, H.	(1967), *The Anatomy of Achievement Motivation*. New York: Academic Press. A8b.
Herbert, J. D.	(1964), *A Procedure for the Articulation of Complex Development Programming Problems*. Ann Arbor: University Microfilms, A4a, C3b.
Hershdorfer, A. M.	(1968), "Hardware, software," *Architectural and Engineering News,* Vol. 10, March, pp. 3–6. A3a.
Herzog, B.	(1967), "Engineering, design, and the computer," in M. Krampen and P. Seitz, eds., *Design and Planning 2.* New York: Hastings House, pp. 129–137. A3a, C1.
Hill. D. M.	(1965), "A growth allocation model for the Boston region," *Journal of the American Institute of Planners,* Vol. 31, pp. 111–120. C3b.
Hill, M.	(1967), "A method for the evaluation of transportation plans," *Highway Research Record,* No. 180, pp. 21–34. A6b, C3c.
	(1968), "A goals-achievement matrix for evaluating alternative plans," *Journal of the American Institute of Planners,* Vol. 34, pp. 19–29, A6b, C3c.
Hiller, F. S.	(1963), "Quantitative tools for plant layout analysis," *Journal of Industrial Engineering,* Vol. 14, pp. 33–40. A5.
Hitch, C. J.	(1953), "Sub-optimization in operations research," *Operations Research,* Vol. 1, pp. 87–99. B2c.
	(1957), "Operations research and national planning: A dissent," *Operations Research,* Vol. 5, pp. 718–723. B2c.
	(1967), "Program budgeting," *Datamation,* Vol. 13, September. B2c.
	and R. N. McKean (1965), *The Economics of Defense in the Nuclear Age.* New York: Atheneum. A7a, B2c.
Hoffman, R. B.	(1966), "The transfer of space and computer technology to urban security," *Proceedings Fall Joint Computer Conference,* Vol. 29, pp. 523–529. C3a.
Holstein, D.	(1964), "Automated design engineering," *Datamation,* Vol. 10, June, pp. 28–34. A3a, C1.
Homburger, W. S., ed.	(1967), *Urban Mass Transit Planning.* Berkeley: Institute of Transportation and Traffic Engineering, University of California. C3c.
Hoos, I. R.	(1967), *A Critique of the Application of Systems Analysis to Social Problems.* Berkeley: Space Sciences Laboratory, University of California. A7a.
Housing and Home Finance Agency	(1963), *Using Computer Graphics in Community Renewal.* Washington: U.S. Government Printing Office. A3b, C3b.
Hovland, C. I.	(1960), "Computer simulation of thinking," *American Psychologist,* Vol. 15, pp. 687–693. A2b, A3c.
Humphrey, G.	(1951), *Thinking: An Introduction to Its Experimental Psychology.* London: Methuen, also New York: Wiley, 1963. A2b.
Hunt, E. B.	(1962), *Concept Learning: An Information Processing Problem.* New York: Wiley. A2b.
Hunt, J. McV., ed.	(1944), *Personality and Behavior Disorders.* New York: Ronald Press. A8b.
Hutchinson, B. G.	(1967), "Simulation of exhibition visitor circulation on a digital computer," in M. Krampen and P. Seitz, eds., *Design and Planning 2.* New York: Hastings House, pp. 139–143. A5, A6b, C2.
Irwin, N. A.	(1966), "Criteria for evaluating alternative transportation systems," *Highway Research Record,* No. 148, pp. 9–19. A6b, C3c.
Isard, W.	(1956), *Location and Space Economy.* Cambridge: M.I.T. Press. C3b.
	(1960), *Methods of Regional Analysis: An Introduction to Regional Science.* Cambridge: M.I.T. Press. A1, A9, C3a, C3b.

Isard, W.   and T. E. Smith (1967), "Coalition location games: Paper 3," *Papers, Regional Science Association: European Congress,* Vol. 20, pp. 95–107. C3b.

P. Isard, T. H. Tung, and M. Dacey (in press), *General Social and Regional Theory.* Cambridge: M.I.T. Press. A9, C3a.

Jacks, E. L.   (1964), "A laboratory for the study of man-machine communications," *Proceedings Fall Joint Computer Conference,* Vol. 25, pp. 343–350. A3a, C1.

(1967), "Design augmented by computers," in M. Krampen and P. Seitz, eds., *Design and Planning 2.* New York: Hastings House, pp. 25–30. A3a, C1.

et al. (1964), *The GM DAC-I System: Design Augmented by Computers.* Warren, Mich.: Computer Technology Department, General Motors Corporation. A3a, C1.

Jackson, B.   (1967), "The relationships between needs and the elements of form," *Zodiac* (Ivrea, Italy), April, pp. 210–214. A8a.

Jacobs, P., and D. Way   (1968), *Visual Analysis of Landscape Development.* Cambridge: Graduate School of Design, Harvard University. A3b, C2.

Jay, L. S.   (1963), "A systematic approach to the problems of town and regional planning," in J. C. Jones and D. G. Thornley, eds., *Conference on Design Methods.* London: Pergamon, and New York: Macmillan, pp. 11–21. C3a.

Jeanes, R. G.   (n.d.), *CPM Applied to the Overall Process of Building.* Watford, Herts., England: Building Research Station. C2.

Jessiman, W., D. Brand, A. Tumminia, and C. R. Brussee   (1967), "A rational decision-making technique for transportation planning," *Highway Research Record,* No. 180, pp. 71–80. A6b, C3c.

Jewkes, J., D. Sawers, and R. Stillerman   (1962), *The Sources of Invention.* London: Macmillan. B1a.

Johnson, T. E.   (1963), "Sketchpad III: A computer program for drawing in three dimensions," *Proceedings Spring Joint Computer Conference,* Vol. 23, pp. 347–353. A3b.

Jones, J. C.   (1957–1958), "Automation and design," *Design,* Nos. 103, 104, 106, 108, 110. C1.

(1959), "A systematic design method," *Design,* No. 124, pp. 49–51. C1.

(1963), "A method of systematic design," in J. C. Jones and D. G. Thornley, eds., *Conference on Design Methods.* London: Pergamon, and New York: Macmillan, pp. 53–73. A6a, A9, C1, C2.

(1965), "Systematic design methods and the building design process," *Proceedings CIB Congress: Towards Industrialised Building.* London: Elsevier. Reprinted in *Architects' Journal,* Vol. 145, 1965. A1, C2.

(1966a), "Design methods compared: 1. strategies, 2. tactics," *Design,* Part 1, No. 212, August, pp. 32–35, Part 2, No. 213, September, pp. 46–52. A1.

(1966b), "Design methods reviewed," in S. A. Gregory, ed., *The Design Method.* London: Butterworths, and New York: Plenum Press, pp. 295–309. A1.

(1967a), "The designing of man-machine systems," in W. T. Whitfield, R. S. Easterby, and D. C. Whitfield, eds., *The Human Operator in Complex Systems.* London: Taylor & Francis. Reprinted in *Ergonomics,* Vol. 10, A3a.

(1967b), "Traditional and modern design methods," *Ark* (Royal College of Art, London), Summer. A1.

(in press a), "A credible future for urban traffic," *Proceedings European Conference on Technological Forecasting.* Edinburgh: Edinburgh University Press. C3c.

(in press b), *Design Methods.* New York: Wiley, A1, A9, C1, C2.

R. J. Talbot, and C. A. Goodwin, eds. (1967), *Design Research Reports.* Manchester: Department of Building, Manchester Institute of Science and Technology. C1, C2.

and D. G. Thornley, eds. (1963), *Conference on Design Methods.* London: Pergamon, and New York: Macmillan. A1, A9, C1, C2.

Jordon, J., ed.   (1967), *ICES: Programmers' Reference Manual.* Cambridge: Department of Civil Engineering, M.I.T. B2c.

Judelson, D.   (1968), "The Design Methods Group conference: Logical decisions on arbitrary problems," *Connection* (Harvard School of Design), Summer, pp. 36–41. A1.

Judy, R. W., and J. B. Levine   (1965), *A New Tool for Educational Administration: Educational Efficiency Through Simulation Analysis.* Toronto: University of Toronto Press. A5, C2.

Kaiser, E. J., and S. F. Weiss   (1967), "Local public policy and the residential development process," *Law and Contemporary Problems,* Vol. 32, Spring, pp. 232–249. C3b.

Kaplan, A.   (1964), *The Conduct of Inquiry.* San Francisco: Chandler. B1a.

Kaplan, B., and S. Wapner. eds.   (1960), *Perspectives in Psychological Theory.* New York: International Universities Press. A2b.

and R. Bibace (in press), *A Developmental Approach to Psychopathology.* New York: McGraw-Hill. A2b.

Kaufmann, A.   (1968), *The Science of Decision-Making: An Introduction to Praxeology.* New York: McGraw-Hill. B2b.

Kemeny, J. G., J. L. Snell, and   (1966), *Introduction to Finite Mathematics,* 2nd. ed. Englewood Cliffs, N.J.: Prentice-
G. L. Thompson   Hall, B2a.

Kennedy, R. F.   (1968), "A way to save our cities," *Consulting Engineer,* Vol. 30, March, pp. 150–155. A7b, C3a.

Kilbridge, M. D., R. P. O'Block, and   (in press), "A conceptual framework for urban planning models," *Management Science.*
P. V. Teplitz   A1, C3a.

Kishkunes, L. J., and D. H. Peckenpaugh   (1967), *A Comprehensive Concept for Vocational Educational Facilities.* Pittsburgh: Board of Public Education. A5, C2.

Kiviat, P. J., and A. Colker   (1964), *GASP: A General Activity Simulation Program.* Santa Monica, Calif.: RAND Corporation. A5.

Kleinmuntz, B., ed.   (1966), *Problem Solving: Research, Method, and Theory.* New York: Wiley. A2b, A3c.

Kliment, S. J., ed.   (1963), "Automation in architecture," *Architectural and Engineering News,* Special Issue, March. C2.

(1968), "The computer in architecture," *Architectural and Engineering News,* Special Issue, March. A1, C2.

Klüver, H.   (1933), "Behavior mechanisms in monkeys," *University of Chicago Press Publications,* Whole No. 387. A2b.

Knowlton, K. C.   (1967), "Computer-generated movies, designs, and diagrams," in M. Krampen and P. Seitz, eds., *Design and Planning 2.* New York: Hastings House, pp. 59–63. A3b.

Koenig, D., et al.   (1966), *Educational Facilities for the Visually Handicapped.* Berkeley: Design Research Laboratory, University of California. A4b, A8a, A8c, C2.

C. Rusch, G. T. Moore, et al. (1965), *Design for Mental Health Services at the Community Level.* Berkeley: Design Research Laboratory, University of California. A4b, A8c, C2.

Koestler, A.   (1964), *The Act of Creation.* New York: Macmillan. A2b.

Koffka, K.   (1963), *Principles of Gestalt Psychology.* New York: Harbinger. A2b.

Köhler, W.   (1964), *Gestalt Psychology.* New York: Mentor. A2b.

Koopman, B. O.   (1957), "The theory of search, III. The optimum distribution of searching effort," *Operations Research,* Vol. 5, pp. 613–627. B2c.

Koopmans, T. C., ed.   (1951), *Activity Analysis of Production and Allocation.* New York: Wiley. B2c.

Krampen, M., ed.   (1965), *Design and Planning.* Waterloo, Canada: University of Waterloo Press. A1.

and P. Seitz, eds. (1967), *Design and Planning 2: Computers in Design and Communication.* New York: Hastings House. A1, A3b, C1, C2.

Krejcirik, M.   (1968), *Computer-Aided Building Layout.* Prague, Czechoslovakia: Research Institute for Building and Architecture, Letenska 3. A5, C2.

Kresge, D.   (1965), "A simulation model for development planning." Cambridge: Harvard Transport and Economic Development Seminar, Discussion Paper No. 32, November. C3b, C3d.

Krauss, R. I., and J. R. Myer   (1968), *Design: A Case History/A Designer's Specifications for a Computer System.* Cambridge: Center for Building Research, M.I.T. A2a.

Krick, E. V.   (1965), *An Introduction to Engineering and Engineering Design.* New York: Wiley, A7a, C1.

Kristol, I.   (1966), "The Negro today is like the immigrant yesterday," *New York Times Magazine,* September 11, pp. 50, 124–142. A8b.

Kuhn, T. S.   (1962), *The Structure of Scientific Revolutions.* Chicago: University of Chicago Press. B1a.

Kusysgyn, I., and A. Paivio   (1966), "Transition probability, word order, and noun abstractions in the learning of adjective-noun paired associates," *Journal of Experimental Psychology,* Vol. 71, pp. 800–805. A2b.

Laing, R. D.   (1959), *The Divided Self.* London: Tavistock, and Baltimore: Penguin. A8b.

(1967), *The Politics of Experience* (with *The Bird of Paradise*). London: Pelican, and New York: Ballantine. A8b.

Langer, S. K.   (1953), *Feeling and Form.* New York: Scribners. B1a.

(1963), *Philosophy in a New Key.* New York: Mentor. B1a.

(1967a), *An Introduction to Symbolic Logic.* New York: Dover. B2a.

(1967b), *Mind: An Essay on Human Feeling.* Baltimore: Johns Hopkins. A2b.

Lathrop, G. T., and J. R. Homburg   (1965), "An opportunity-accessibility model for allocating regional growth," *Journal of the American Institute of Planners,* Vol. 31, pp. 95–103. C3b.

Lavi, A., and T. Vogl, eds.   (1966), *Recent Advances in Optimization Techniques.* New York: Wiley. B2c.

Le Corbusier,   (1946), *Vers une Architecture,* 3d Ed. Paris: Editions Grès, 1923, translated by F. Etchells, *Towards a New Architecture.* London: Architectural Press, and New York: Praeger, 1946. A9.

Lévi-Strauss, C.   (1967a), *Structural Anthropology.* New York: Anchor. A8b.

(1967b), *Tristes Tropiques.* New York: Atheneum. A8b.

Levin, P. H.   (1964), "Use of graphs to decide the optimum layout of buildings," *Architects' Journal,* Vol. 140, pp. 809–815. A5, C2.

(1966a), "Decision-making in urban design," *Building Research Station Current Papers,* Ser. 49. A9, C2.

(1966b), "Design process in planning," *Town Planning Review,* Vol. 37, April, pp. 5–20. A9, C2, C3a.

Lewin, K.   (1941), "Frustration and regression: An experiment with young children," *University of Iowa Studies in Child Welfare,* Vol. 18, pp. 58–59. A8b.

(1966), *Principles of Topological Psychology.* New York: McGraw-Hill. A8b.

Lewis. O.   (1961), *The Children of Sánchez.* New York: Vintage. A8b.

(1968), *La Vida.* New York: Vintage. A8b.

Lichfield, N.   (1960), "Cost-budget analysis in city planning," *Journal of the American Institute of Planners,* Vol. 26, pp. 273–279. A6b, C3b.

Lindblom, C. E.   (1965), *The Intelligence of Democracy.* New York: Macmillan. B2b.

Lindheim, R.   (1965), "Computers and architecture," *Landscape,* Spring, pp. 8–11. A3b.

Little, Arthur D., Inc.   (1963), *San Francisco Community Renewal Program: Purpose, Scope, and Methodology.* San Francisco: Arthur D. Little, Inc. A6b, A7b, C3b, C3d.

Lockyer, K.   (1964), *Critical Path Analysis.* London: Pitman. B2c.

Logcher, R. D., B. B. Flachsbart, E. J. Hall, C. M. Power, and R. A. Wells   (1967), *ICES STRUDL I: Engineering User's Manual.* Cambridge: Department of Civil Engineering, M.I.T. A3a.

Longbone, N.   (in press), "The physical organization of sheltered workshops for the blind," in A. Ward and G. Broadbent, eds., *Design Methods in Architecture.* London: Lund Humphries, and New York: Wittenborn. A8c, C2.

Lowry, I. S.   (1964), *A Model of Metropolis.* Santa Monica, Calif. RAND Corporation. A6b, C3a, C3d.

(1965), "A short course in model design," *Journal of the American Institute of Planners,* Vol. 31, pp. 158–166. A1.

Luce, R. D., and H. Raiffa   (1957), *Games and Decisions.* New York: Wiley. B2b, B2d.

Lynch, K. (1966), "Quality in city design," in L. B. Holland, ed., *Who Designs America*. New York: Anchor Books, pp. 120–171. C3a.

Machol, R. (1968), "Systems tools," *Consulting Engineer*, Vol. 30, March, pp. 146–149. A7a.

MacKinnon, D. W. (1960). "Genus architectus creator varietas Americanus," *American Institute of Architects' Journal*, Vol. 34, September, pp. 31–35. A2a.

(1961), "The personality correlates of creativity: A study of American architects," in S. Coopersmith, ed., *Personality Research*, Vol. 2. Copenhagen: Munksgaard, A2a.

(1962), "The nature and nurture of creative talent," *American Psychologist*, Vol. 17, pp. 484–495. Reprinted in A. Anastasi, ed., *Individual Differences*. New York: Wiley, 1965, pp. 282–295. A2a.

Mackworth, N.H. (1964), "Originality," *American Psychologist*, Vol. 20, pp. 51–66. A2b.

Madge, J. (1963), *The Tools of Social Science*. London: Longmans. B1b.

Maier, N. R. F. (1945), "Reasoning in humans III: The mechanisms of equivalent stimuli and of reasoning," *Journal of Experimental Psychology*, Vol. 35, pp. 349–360. A2b.

Maki, F., M. Ontaka, and J. Goldberg (1964), *Investigations in Collective Form*. St. Louis: Washington University Press. A8c.

Maldonado, T., and G. Bonsiepe (1964), "Science and design," *Ulm*, (Hochschule für Gestaltung), No. 10/11, May. A1.

Malinowski, B. (1960), *A Scientific Theory of Culture*. London and New York: Oxford University Press. A8b.

Maltzman, I. (1960), "On the training of originality," *Psychological Review*, Vol. 67, pp. 229–242. A2b.

Manheim, M. L. (1961), "Data accuracy in route location," *Traffic Quarterly*, Vol. 15, January, pp. 153–178. C3c.

(1966a), *Hierarchical Structure: A Model of Design and Planning Processes*. Cambridge: M.I.T. Press. C3c.

(1966b), "Transportation, problem solving, and the effective use of computers," *Highway Research Record*, No. 148, pp. 49–58. C3c.

(1967a), *Problem Solving Processes in Planning and Design*. Cambridge: Department of Civil Engineering, M.I.T. Abridged in *Design Quarterly*, No. 66/67, 1967, pp. 31–39, and in M. Krampen and P. Seitz, eds., *Design and Planning 2*. New York: Hastings House, 1967, pp. 31–39. A9, C3c.

ed. (1967b), "Transportation systems analysis and the evaluation of alternative plans," *Highway Research Record*, Special Issue, No. 180. A6b, C3c.

et al. (1968), *Search and Choice in Transport Systems Planning*, 8 Vols. Cambridge: Department of Civil Engineering, M.I.T. A6b, A9, C3c.

K. G. Follansbee, and R. Walter (1968), *Modeling the Evolutionary Nature of Problem-Solving*. Cambridge: Department of Civil Engineering, M.I.T. C3c.

and F. L. Hall (1968), *Abstract Representation of Goals*. Cambridge: Department of Civil Engineering, M.I.T. Published in *Transportation: A Service*. New York: N.Y. Academy of Science, 1968. C3c.

Manning, P. (n.d.), *Appraisals of Building Performance and their Use in Design*. Ottawa, Canada: York University. A6b, C2.

Mao, J. C. T. (1966), "Efficiency in public urban renewal expenditures through benefit-cost analysis," *Journal of the American Institute of Planners*, Vol. 32, 1966, pp. 95–107; letters and rejoinders, Vol. 32, 1966, pp. 297–299 and Vol. 33, 1967, pp. 181–183. C3b.

Marglin, S. A. (1967), *Public Investment Criteria*. Cambridge: M.I.T. Press. B2c.

Markus, T. A. (1967), "The role of building performance measurement and appraisal in design method," *Architects' Journal*, Vol. 146, pp. 1567–1573. Reprinted in A. Ward and G. Broadbent, eds., *Design Methods in Architecture*. London: Lund Humphries, and New York: Wittenborn (in press). A6b, A9, C2.

Maroney, M. J. (1951), *Facts from Figures*. London and Baltimore: Penguin. B1b.

Maslow, A. H. (1964), "Problem-centering vs. means-centering in science," *Philosophy of Science*, Vol. 13, pp. 326–331. B1a.

(1959), "Creativity in self-actualizing people," in H. H. Anderson, ed., *Creativity and its*

Cultivation. New York: Harper, pp. 83–95. Reprinted in Maslow, *Toward a Psychology of Being*. Princeton: Van Nostrand, 1962, pp. 127–137. A2b.

Matchett, E.   (1965), "The controlled evolution of engineering design," *Engineering Designer*, February, pp. 1–9. C1.

(1968), "Control of thought in creative work," *Chartered Mechanical Engineer,* Vol. 15, April, pp. 163–166. A2a.

and A. H. Briggs (1966), "Practical design based on method (Fundamental design method)," in S. A. Gregory, ed., *The Design Method*. London: Butterworths, and New York: Plenum Press, pp. 183–199. C1.

Mattox, R. F., et al.   (1967), *Computer Aided Campus Planning for Colleges and Universities*. Houston: Caudill Rowlett Scott. A3a, C2.

Maver, T. W.   (1965), "The design of storage calorifiers: A case study," *Operational Research Quarterly*, Vol. 16, March, pp. 77–88. C1.

(1966), "Some techniques of operational research illustrated by their application to hot and cold water plant sizing," *Journal of Institution of Heating and Ventilating Engineers,* Vol. 33, January, pp. 301–313. C1.

and W. Carson (1966), "Cost-effectiveness and the engineering services in hospitals," *Problems and Progress in Medical Care: Essays on Current Research*. London: Nuffield Provincial Hospital Trust. C2.

McCrory, R. J.   (1963), "The design method: A scientific approach to valid designs," Paper 63-MD-4, American Society of Mechanical Engineers. A1, C1.

W. H. Wilkinson, and D. W. Frink (1963), "Synthesis of concepts in the design method," Paper 63-MD-37, American Society of Mechanical Engineers. C1.

McDonough, A. M.   (1963), *Information Economics and Management Systems*. New York: McGraw-Hill. B2c.

McKeen, R.   (1958), *Efficiency in Government Through Systems Analysis*. Santa Monica, Calif: RAND Corporation. A7a.

McLuhan, M.   (1964), *Understanding Media*. New York: McGraw-Hill; also London: Routledge & Kegan Paul, 1966. B1a.

McManmon, G. M.   (1959), *A Survey of the Literature on Industrial Location*. Syracuse: Business Research Center, University of Syracuse. C3b.

McMillan, C., and R. F. Gonzales   (1965), *Systems Analysis: A Computer Approach to Decision Models*. Homewood, Ill.: R. D. Irwin. A7a.

Meier, R. L.   (1962), *A Communications Theory of Urban Growth*. Cambridge: M.I.T. Press. C3b.

Meier, R. L.   (1965), *Development Planning*. New York: McGraw-Hill, A9, C3b.

and R. D. Duke (1966), "Gaming simulation for urban planning," *Journal of the American Institute of Planners*, Vol. 32, pp. 3–17. C3a, C3d.

Merleau-Ponty, M.   (1951), *The Structure of Behavior*. Boston: Beacon, A2b.

(1962), *Phenomenology of Perception*. London: Routledge & Kegan Paul, and New York: Humanities Press. A2b.

Merton, R. K.   (1965), *Social Theory and Social Structure*. New York: Free Press. A8b.

Mesarovic, M. D., ed.   (1964), *Views on General Systems Theory*. New York: Wiley. B1a.

(1965), "Toward a formal theory of problem solving," in M. A. Sass and W. D. Wilkenson, eds., *Computer Augmentation of Human Reasoning*. New York: Spartan, and London: Macmillan, pp. 37–64. A2b.

Metropolitan Toronto School Board   (1968), *Educational Specifications and User Requirements for Elementary (K-6) Schools*. Toronto: Ryerson Press. A6a, C2.

Meyer, J. R., J. F. Kain, and M. Wohl   (1966), *The Urban Transportation Problem*. Cambridge: Harvard University Press. C3c.

Myerson, M   (1956), "Building the middle-range bridge for comprehensive planning," *Journal of the American Institute of Planners*, Vol. 22, pp. 58–64. A9, C3a.

and E. C. Banfield (1955), *Politics, Planning, and the Public Interest: The Case of Public Housing in Chicago*. Glencoe, Ill.: Free Press, and London: Macmillan. A6b, A9, C3b.

Mezei, L.   (1966), "The electronic computer: A tool for the visual arts," *Proceedings Computing and Data Processing Society of Canada.* A3b, C1.

(in press). "The electronic computer: a tool for the visual arts," *Proceedings Computing and Data Processing Society of Canada.* A3b, C1.

Michelson, W.   (1968), "Urban sociology as an aid to urban physical development: Some research strategies," *Journal of the American Institute of Planners,* Vol. 34, pp. 105–108. A8a, C3b.

Miller, C. L.   (1963), "Man-machine communications in civil engineering," *Journal of the Structural Division ASCE,* Vol. 89, August, pp. 5–29. A3a.

Miller, D. W., and M. K. Starr   (1960), *Executive Decisions and Operations Research.* Englewood Cliffs, N.J.: Prentice-Hall. B2c.

Miller, G. A.   (1951), *Language and Communication.* New York: McGraw-Hill. A2b.

(1956), "The magic number seven, plus or minus two: Some limits on our capacity for processing information," *Psychological Review,* Vol. 63, pp. 81–97. A3c.

and N. Chomsky (1957), *Pattern Conception.* Cambridge: IBM Cambridge Scientific Center. A2b.

E. Galanter, and K. Pribram (1960), *Plans and the Structure of Behavior.* New York: Holt. A2b.

Milne, M. A.   (1965), "The design process," unpublished master's thesis, University of California, Berkeley. A2a.

ed. (1969), *Computer Graphics in Architecture and Design.* New Haven: School of Art and Architecture, Yale University. A1, A3a, A3b, C2.

J. L. Matteson, et al. (1966), *Computer Aided Design: An Experiment with a Design Process as Applied to the Problem of Undergraduate Study.* Eugene, Ore.: University of Oregon Press. A4b, A8c, C2.

and C. W. Rusch (1968), "The death of the Beaux Arts: The Cal-Oregon experiment in design education," *Journal of Architectural Education,* Vol. 22, March, pp. 22–27. A4b.

Minsky, M.   (1963a), "A selected descriptor-indexed bibliography to the literature on artificial intelligence," in E. A. Feigenbaum and J. Feldman, eds., *Computers and Thought.* New York: McGraw-Hill, pp. 453–523. A3c.

(1963b), "Steps towards artificial intelligence," in E. A. Feigenbaum and J. Feldman, eds., *Computers and Thought.* New York: McGraw-Hill, pp. 406–450. A3c.

(1966), "Artificial intelligence," *Scientific American,* Vol. 215, September, pp. 246–252. A3c.

M.I.T. Students   (1968), *Project Romulus: MIT Students System Project.* Cambridge: M.I.T. Press. A7b.

Moore, G. T.   (1970), "Creativity and the prediction of success in architecture," *Journal of Architectural Education,* Vol. 24, March. A2a.

and L. M. Gay (1967), *Creative Problem Solving in Architecture.* Berkeley: Design Research Laboratory, University of California. A2a.

Moore, R. L., and A. W. Christie   (1963), "Research on traffic signs," *Engineering for Traffic Conference.* London: Road Research Laboratory, pp. 113–114. A8b.

Morse, P. M., ed.   (1967), *Operations Research for Public Systems.* Cambridge: M.I.T. Press. B2c.

Mortin, B. V., F. W. Memmott, and A. J. Bone   (1965), *Principles and Techniques of Predicting Future Demand for Urban Area Transportation.* Cambridge: M.I.T. Press. C3c.

Mosley, L.   (1963), "A rational design theory for planning buildings based on the analysis and solution of circulation problems," *Architects' Journal,* Vol. 138, pp. 525–537. A5, C2.

Moucka, J.   (1968), "Decision making in the initial phase of design," *SIGSPAC Bulletin,* Vol. 2, November, pp. 5–12. A5, C2.

Mumford, L.   (1962), *Technics and Civilization.* London: Routledge & Kegan Paul. B1a.

Murphy, J.   (1967), *School Scheduling by Computer: The Story of GASP.* New York: Educational Facilities Laboratories. A5, C2.

Nadler, G.   (1963), *Work Design*. Homewood,Ill.: R. D. Irwin. B1b, C1.

(1967a), *Work Systems Design: The IDEALS Concept*. Homewood, Ill.: Irwin. A7a, A9, C2, C3a.

(1967b), "An investigation of design methodology," *Management Science,* Vol. 13, June, pp. B642–B655. A9, C3a.

(in press), *Work Design: A Systems Design Strategy,* rev. ed. Homewood, Ill.: Irwin. A7a, A9, C2, C3a.

National Building Agency   (1967), *Generic Plans*. London: National Building Agency. A8c, C2.

National Economic Development Council   (1967), *Investment Appraisal,* London: Her Majesty's Stationery Office. B2c.

Naylor, T. H., J. L. Balinfy, D. F. Burdick, and K. Chu   (1966), *Computer Simulation Techniques*. New York: Wiley. B2d.

Negroponte, N.   (1970), *The Architecture Machine*. Cambridge: M.I.T. Press. A3a, C2.

and L. Groisser (1967), *URBAN5: An On-Line Urban Design Partner*. Cambridge: IBM Scientific Center Report 320–2012. Abridged in *Ekistics,* Vol. 24, 1967, pp. 289–291. A3a, C2.

Neisser, U.   (1957), *Cognitive Psychology*. New York: Appleton-Century-Crofts. A2b.

Newell, A.   (1966), *On the Analysis of Human Problem Solving Protocols*. Pittsburgh: Carnegie Institute of Technology, ARPA Report. A2b, A3c.

J. Shaw, and H. A. Simon (1964), "The processes of creative thinking," in H. E. Gruber, G. Terrell, and M. Wertheimer, eds., *Contemporary Approaches to Creative Thinking*. New York: Atherton, pp. 63–119. A2b.

and H. A. Simon (1963), "GPS: A program that simulates human thought," in E. A. Feigenbaum and J. Feldman, eds., *Computers and Thought*. New York: McGraw-Hill, pp. 279–293. A3a.

(1964), "Problem-solving machines," *International Science and Technology,* Vol. 12, pp. 48–49, 53–62. A3c.

Newman, A. D.   (1966), "Patterns," in S. A. Gregory, ed., *The Design Method*. London: Butterworths, and New York: Plenum Press, pp. 105–109. A3c.

Newman, W. M.   (1968), "A system for interactive graphical programming," *Proceedings Spring Joint Computer Conference,* Vol. 32, pp. 47–54. A3b.

Noll, A. M.   (1965a), "Computer-generated three-dimensional movies," *Computers and Automation,* Vol. 14, November, pp. 20–23. A3b.

(1965b), "Stereographic projections by digital computer," *Computers and Automation,* Vol. 14, May, pp. 32–34. A3b.

(1967a), "A computer technique for displaying *n*-dimensional hyperobjects," *Communications of the ACM,* Vol. 10, pp. 469–473. A3b.

(1967b), "Computers and the visual arts," in M. Krampen and P. Seitz, eds., *Design and Planning 2*. New York: Hastings House, pp. 65–79. A3b, C1.

(1967c), "The digital computer as a creative medium" *IEEE Spectrum,* Vol. 4, October, pp. 89–95. A3b, C1.

Norberg-Schultz, C.   (1965), *Intentions in Architecture*. Cambridge: M.I.T. Press. A9, C2.

Norris, K. W.   (1963), "The morphological approach to engineering design," in J. C. Jones and D. G. Thornley, eds., *Conference on Design Methods*. London: Pergamon, and New York: Macmillan, pp. 115–140. C1.

Nugent, C. E., T. E. Vollman, and J. Ruml,   (1968), "An experimental comparison of techniques for the assignment of facilities to locations," *Journal of the Operations Research Society of America,* Vol. 18, pp. 150–173. A5.

Nuttall, J. F.   (n.d.), *Operational Research in Building in Europe*. Watford, Herts., England: Building Research Station. C2.

Oakford, R. V., D. W. Allen, and L. A. Chatterton   (1966–1967), "School scheduling: Practice theory," *Journal of Education Data Processing.* Vol. 4, pp. 16–50. A5.

O'Brian, J. J.   (1965), *CPM in Construction Management: Scheduling by the Critical Path Method*. New York: McGraw-Hill. C2.

Ore, O.	(1963), *Graphs and Their Uses*. New York: Random House. B2a.
Osborn, A. F.	(1957), *Applied Imagination: Principles and Procedures of Creative Problem Solving*. New York: Scribners. A2b.
Owen, C. L.	(in press), *Case Studies in Design Methods*. New York: Reinhold. A4a, A4b, C2.
Parnes, S. J. and Harding, H. F., eds.	(1962), *A Source Book for Creative Thinking*. New York: Scribner's, 1962. A2b.
Parsons, D.	(1967), "Planning by the numbers," *Progressive Architecture*, August, pp. 111–112. A5, C2.
Pask, G.	(1961) *An Approach to Cybernetics*. London: Hutchinson; also New York: Harper & Row, 1962. A3c, B2c.
	(1963), "The conception of a shape and the evolution of a design," in J. C. Jones and D. G. Thornley, eds., *Conference on Design Methods*. London: Pergamon, and New York: Macmillan, pp. 153–167. A3a, C1.
Peattie, L. R.	(1968a), "Reflections on advocacy planning," *Journal of the American Institute of Planners*, Vol. 34, pp. 80–88. A10.
	(1968b), "The dilemma: Architecture in an affluent society," *Architectural Design*, Vol. 38, August, pp. 361–364. A10.
	(1968c), *The View from the Barrio*. Ann Arbor: University of Michigan Press. A10.
Perloff, H. S.	(1968), "Key features of regional planning," *Journal of the American Institute of Planners*, Vol. 34, pp. 153–159. A9, C3a.
Pfouts, R. W., ed.	(1960), *The Techniques of Urban Economic Analysis*. West Trenton, N.J.: Chandler-Davis. C3b.
Piaget, J.	(1950), *The Psychology of Intelligence*. London: Routledge & Kegan Paul; also Paterson, N.J.: Littlefield Adams, 1963. A2b, A8b.
	(1951), "Introduction: Problems and methods," *The Child's Conception of the World*. London: Routledge & Kegan Paul; also Paterson, N.J.: Littlefield Adams, 1967, pp. 1–32. A8b.
	(1954), *The Construction of Reality in the Child*, New York: Basic Books; also London: Routledge & Kegan Paul, 1955. A8b.
Picasso, P.	(1949), *Picasso, Lithographe*. Monte Carlo: A Sauret. A2b.
Pidgeon, M., ed.	(1968), "The architecture of democracy," *Architectural Design*, Special Issue, Vol. 38, August. A9, A10, C2, C3.
Platt, J. R.	(1966), "Strong inference," in *The Step to Man*. New York: Wiley, pp. 19–36. A6b, B1b.
Pleydell-Pearce, A. G.	(1966), "Choosing and evaluating," in S. A. Gregory, ed., *The Design Method*. London: Butterworths, and New York: Plenum Press, pp. 121–129. A6b.
Polanyi, K.	(1944), *The Great Transformation*. New York: Rinehart. A8b.
Polanyi, M.	(1959), *The Study of Man*. London: Routledge & Kegan Paul; also Chicago: University of Chicago Press, 1962. B1a.
	(1964), *Personal Knowledge: Towards a Post-Critical Philosophy*. Chicago: University of Chicago Press. B1a.
Polya, G.	(1957), *How To Solve It*. Garden City, N.Y.: Doubleday Anchor. B2b.
Popper, K. R.	(1959), *The Logic of Scientific Discovery*. London: Hutchinson; also New York: Harper & Row, 1965. B1a.
Porter, T.	(1964), "A study of path choosing behavior," unpublished master's thesis, University of California, Berkeley. A8b.
Poyner, B.	(1966), *Activity Data Method: R. & D. Bulletin*. London: Her Majesty's Stationery Office. A6b, C2.
	(in press), "The evolution of environmental structure," in A. Ward and G. Broadbent, eds., *Design Methods in Architecture*. London: Lund Humphries, and New York: Wittenborn. A8a, A8c, C2.
Prest, A. R., and R. Turvey	(1965), "Cost-benefit analysis: A survey," *Economic Journal*, Vol. 75, December, pp. 683–735. B2a.

Pye, D. (1964), *The Nature of Design*. London: Studio Vista Ltd. A1.

Quillian, M. R. (1967), "Word concepts: A theory and simulation of some basic semantic capabilities," *Behavioral Science*, Vol. 12, pp. 410–430. A3c.

Rapoport, A. (in press), "Facts and models," in A. Ward and G. Broadbent, eds., *Design Methods in Architecture*. London: Lund Humphries, and New York: Wittenborn. A1.

Rapoport, L., and W. P. Drews (1962), "Mathematical approach to long-range planning," *Harvard Business Review*, Vol. 40, May-June, pp. 75–87. C3a.

Rappaport, D., ed. (1951), *The Organization and Pathology of Thought*. New York: Columbia University Press. A2b.

Ratcliff, R. U. (1952), "Housing standards and housing research," *Land Economics*, Vol. 28, November, pp. 328–331. Reprinted in W. L. C. Wheaton, G. Miligram, and M. E. Meyerson, eds., *Urban Housing*. New York: Free Press, 1966, pp. 391–394. C3b.

Reid, L. A. (1961), *Ways of Knowledge and Experience*. London: George Allen & Unwin. B1a.

Reitman, W. R. (1964), "Heuristic decisions procedures, open constraints, and the structure of ill-defined problems," in M. W. Shelly and G. L. Bryan, eds., *Human Judgments and Optimality*. New York: Wiley, pp. 282–315. A2b, A3c.

(1965), *Cognition and Thought*. New York: Wiley. A2b, A3c.

RIBA (1963), *Handbook of Architectural Practice and Management*. London: Royal Institute of British Architects. A9, C2.

Rittel, H. (1966), *The Universe of Design*. Berkeley: Institute of Urban and Regional Development, University of California. A9, C1, C2.

(1968), *Measuring the Performance of Building*. Washington: Institute for Applied Technology, National Bureau of Standards. A6a, C2.

Roberts, P. O. (1966), "Multi-viewpoint evaluation of transportation projects and systems," *Transportation Research Forum*, pp. 169–183. A6b, C3c.

and J. H. Suhrbier (1966), *Highway Location Analysis: An Example Problem*. Cambridge: M.I.T. Press. C3c.

Robinson, I. M. (1965), "Beyond the middle-range planning bridge," *Journal of the American Institute of Planners*, Vol. 31, pp. 304–312. A9, C3a.

H. B. Wolfe, and R. L. Barringer (1965), "A simulation model for renewal programming," *Journal of the American Institute of Planners*, Vol. 31, pp. 126–134. C3b, C3d.

Roe, P. H., G. S. Soulis, and V. K. Handa (1965), *The Discipline of Design*. Waterloo, Canada: University of Waterloo Press. A1.

Rogers, A. (1966), *Matrix Analysis of Interregional Population Growth and Distribution*. Berkeley: Center for Planning and Development Research, University of California. C3b.

Rogers, C. R. (1957), "Toward a theory of creativity," *ETC: A Review of General Semantics*, Vol. 11, pp. 249–260. Reprinted in Rogers, *On Becoming a Person*. Boston: Houghton Mifflin, 1961, pp. 347–359. A2b.

(1961), *On Becoming a Person*. Boston: Houghton Mifflin. A2b, A8b.

Roos, D., ed. (1967a), *ICES System: General Description*. Cambridge: Department of Civil Engineering, M.I.T. B2c, C1.

(1967b), *ICES System Design*. Cambridge: M.I.T. Press. B2c, C1.

Rosenzweig, S. (1944), "An outline of frustration theory," in J. McV. Hunt, ed., *Personality and Behavior Disorders*. New York: Ronald Press, pp. 379–388. A8b.

Ross, D. T. (1967), "The AED approach to generalized computer-aided design," *Proceedings ACM 22nd National Conference*, pp. 367–385. A3a.

and J. E. Rodriguez (1963), "Theoretical foundations for the computer-aided design system," *Proceedings Spring Joint Computer Conference*, Vol. 23, pp. 305–322. A3a.

Rowan, J., ed. (1967), "Performance design," *Progressive Architecture*, Special Issue, Vol. 48, August. A1, C2.

(1968), "Advocacy planning: What it is, how it works," *Progressive Architecture*, Vol. 49, September, pp. 102–115. A10, C2.

Roy, R. H.

(1960), "The development and future of operations research and systems engineering," in C. D. Flagle, W. A. Huggins, and R. H. Roy, eds., *Operations Research and Systems Engineering*. Baltimore: Johns Hopkins, pp. 8–27. A7a.

Ruiter, E. R.

(1968a), *ICES TRANSET I: Transportation Network Analysis—Engineering Users' Manual,* Cambridge: Department of Civil Engineering. M.I.T. C3c.

(1968b), *A Prototype Analysis.* Cambridge: Department of Civil Engineering, M.I.T. C3c.

Rusch, C. W.

(1965), "The psychological basis for an incremental approach to architecture," unpublished master's thesis, University of California, Berkeley. A2a.

Rust Engineering Company and Applied Science Division of Litton Industries

(1968), "A proposal for a systems engineering study of metropolitan air pollution control," *Consulting Engineer,* Vol. 30, March, pp. 195–199. A7b.

Sanoff, H.

(1968), *Techniques of Evaluation for Designers.* Raleigh, N.C.: School of Design, North Carolina State University. A6a.

Sartre, J.-P.

(1966), *The Psychology of the Imagination.* New York: Washington Square Press. A2b, A8b.

Sass, M. A., and W. D. Wilkinson

(1965), *Computer Augmentation of Human Reasoning.* Washington: Spartan, and London: Macmillan. A3c.

Scheerer, M.

(1963), "Problem solving," *Scientific American,* Vol. 208, April, pp. 118–128. A2b.

Scheffler, I.

(1963), *The Anatomy of Inquiry.* New York: Knopf. B1a.

Schlager, K. J.

(1965), "A land use plan design model," *Journal of the American Institute of Planners,* Vol. 31, pp. 103–111. C3b.

Schlaifer, R.

(1959), *Probability and Statistics for Business Decisions.* New York: McGraw-Hill. B2a.

Schnelle, E.

(1967), "Methods for solving complex decision-making situations," *Kommunikation,* Vol. 3, pp. 115–129. B2b.

Schofer, R. E., and B. M. Levin

(1967), "The urban transportation planning process," *Socio-Economic Planning Sciences,* Vol. 2, December, pp. 185–196. C3c.

Schoeffler, S.

(1954), "Toward a general theory of rational action," *Kyklos,* Vol. 7, pp. 245–271. A7a, B2b.

Schriever, B. A., and W. W. Seifert

(1968), *Air Transportation 1975 and Beyond: A Systems Approach.* Cambridge: M.I.T. Press. C3c.

Scriven, M.

(1959), "The logic of criteria," *Journal of Philosophy,* Vol. 56, pp. 857–868. B1a.

Seitz, P., ed.

(1967), "Design and the Computer," *Design Quarterly,* Special Issue, No. 66/67. A1, A3b, C1, C2.

Shaffer, L. R., J. Rutter, and W. L. Meyer

(1965), *Critical Path Method.* New York: McGraw-Hill. B2c.

Shamir, U., and C. D. Howard

(1968), "Water distribution systems analysis," *Journal of the Hydraulics Division ASCE,* Vol. 94, January, pp. 219–233. A7b.

Shannon, C., and W. Weaver

(1949), *The Mathematical Theory of Communication.* Urbana, Ill.: University of Illinois Press. B2c.

Shelly, M. W., and G. L. Bryan, eds.

(1964), *Human Judgments and Optimality.* New York: Wiley. A3c.

Siddell, J. N.

(1966), "Decision theory in design," *Product Design and Value Engineering,* October, pp. 47–52. C1.

Silvers, A. L., and A. K. Sloan

(1965), "A model framework for comprehensive planning in New York City," *Journal of the American Institute of Planners,* Vol. 31, pp. 246–251. Comment and rejoinder, Vol. 32, 1966, pp. 107–114. C3b.

Simon, H. A.

(1957), *Models of Man.* New York: Wiley. A2b, A3c.

(1967), "The logic of heuristic decision making," in N. Rescher, ed., *Logic of Decision and Action.* Pittsburgh, Pa.: Pittsburgh University Press. A3c.

(1969), *The Sciences of the Artificial.* Cambridge: M.I.T. Press. A3c.

and A. Newell (1958), "Heuristic problem solving: The next advance in operations research," *Operations Research,* Vol. 6, pp. 1–10. A3c.

Simon, H. A.

and P. A. Simon (1962), "Trial and error search in solving difficult problems: Evidence from the game of chess," *Behavioral Science,* Vol. 7, pp. 425–429. A3c.

Smith, P. R.

(1968), "Programming a building addition to minimise inconvenience to the occupier," *Architectural Science Review,* Vol. 11, June, pp. 58–60. C2.

Smithson, A., ed.

(1968), *Team 10 Primer.* Cambridge: M.I.T. Press. A9, C2.

Souder, J. J., W. E. Clark, J. J. Elkinel, and M. B. Brown

(1964), *Planning for Hospitals: A Systems Approach Using Computer-Aided Techniques.* Chicago: American Hospital Association. A5, C2.

Stanlieb, G.

(1967), "Slum housing: A functional analysis," *Law and Contemporary Problems,* Vol. 32, Spring, pp. 349–356. C3b.

Starr, M. K.

(1963), *Product Design and Decision Theory.* Englewood Cliffs, N.J.: Prentice-Hall. A9, B2b, C1.

Steger, W. A.

(1965a), "Review of analytic techniques for the CRP," *Journal of the American Institute of Planners,* Vol. 31, pp. 166–172. C3b, C3d.

(1965b), "The Pittsburgh urban renewal simulation model," *Journal of the American Institute of Planners,* Vol. 31, pp. 144–150. C3b.

and T. Lakshmanan (1968), "Plan evaluation methodologies: Some aspects of decision requirements and analytical response," *Urban Development Models.* Washington: Highway Research Board. A6b, C3a.

Steinitz, C., and P. Rogers

(1968), *A Systems Analysis Model of Urbanization and Change.* Cambridge: Department of Landscape Architecture, Harvard University. A6b, C3a.

Steinmetz, A. M., ed.

(1968), "Systems engineering as applied to five major social problems of our time," *Consulting Engineer,* Special Issue, Vol. 30, March. A7a, A7b, A9, C3a.

Stevens, S. S.

(1946), "On the theory of scales of measurement," *Science,* Vol. 103, pp. 677–680. B1b.

ed. (1963), *Handbook of Experimental Psychology.* New York: Wiley. B1b.

Stone, P. A.

(1964), "Decision techniques for town development," *Operational Research Quarterly,* Vol. 15, pp. 185–205. C3b.

Studer, R. G.

(1966), "On environmental programming," *Arena, Architectural Association Journal,* Vol. 81, pp. 290–296. A6a, C2.

(in press), "The dynamics of behavior-contingent physical systems," in A. Ward and G. Broadbent, eds., *Design Methods in Architecture.* London: Lund Humphries, and New York: Wittenborn. A8a, C2.

Sturman, G. M., ed.

(1967), "A review of the NBS Conference on computer-aided building design," *SICCAP Bulletin,* Vol. 1, April, pp. 7–16. A3a, C2.

(1968), "Second annual ACM urban symposium," *SICCAPUS Bulletin,* Vol. 2, January, pp. 8–17. C3a.

Sutherland, I. E.

(1963), "Sketchpad: A man-machine graphic communication system," *Proceedings Spring Joint Computer Conference,* Vol. 23, pp. 329–346. A3b.

Tavistock Institute

(1966), *Interdependence and Uncertainty.* London: Tavistock. B2b.

Taylor, C. W., ed.

(1964), *Widening Horizons of Creativity.* New York: Wiley. A2b.

and F. Barron, eds. (1963), *Scientific Creativity: Its Recognition and Development.* New York: Wiley. A2b.

Taylor, J. L., and R. N. Madison

(1968), "A land use gaming situation: The design of a model for study of urban phenomena," *Urban Affairs Quarterly,* Vol. 3, June, pp. 37–51. C3d.

Teague, L. C., Jr.

(1968), "The representation of spatial relationships in a computer system for building design," unpublished doctoral dissertation, M.I.T. A5.

and A. M. Hershdorfer (1967), "BUILD: An integrated system for building design," paper presented at the ASCE Structural Engineering Conference, Seattle, May, Conference Preprint No. 500. A5, C2.

Teicholz, E. D.

(1968), "Architecture and the computer," *Architectural Forum,* Vol. 129, September, pp. 58–61. A1.

Teichroew, D., and J. F. Lubin

(1966), "Computer simulation: Discussion of the technique and comparison of languages," *Communications of the ACM,* Vol. 9, October, pp. 723–741. B2d.

Terry, G. J.

(1968), "A chart system to help designers," *Chartered Mechanical Engineer,* Vol. 15, February, pp. 56–59. C1.

Thrall, R. M., C. H. Coombs, and R. L. Davis, eds.

(1957), *Decision Processes.* New York: Wiley. B2b.

Toulmin, S.

(1953), *The Philosophy of Science.* London: Hutchinson; also New York: Harper Torchbooks, 1960. B1a.

(1963), *Foresight and Understanding.* New York: Harper Torchbooks. B1a.

Trakhtenbrot, B. A.

(1963), *Algorithms and Automatic Computing Machines.* Boston: D. C. Heath. B2c.

Tryon, R. C.

(1955), *Identification of Social Areas by Cluster Analysis.* Berkeley: University of California Press. C3b.

Tutte, W. T.

(1966), "Squared rectangles," *Proceedings IBM Scientific Computing Symposium on Combinatorial Problems.* White Plains, N.Y.: IBM Data Processing Division, pp. 3–9. A5.

Tybout, R. A., ed.

(1965), *Economics of Research and Development.* Columbus: Ohio State University Press. B2a.

Tyrwhitt, J.

(1968), "The IDEA Method: A new development in regional planning methodology," *Ekistics,* Vol. 26, pp. 185–195. C3a.

Vajda, S.

(1960), *An Introduction to Linear Programming and the Theory of Games.* London: Methuen. B2c, B2d.

(1961), *The Theory of Games & Linear Programming.* New York: Wiley. B2c, B2d.

Van der Ryn, S., and S. Adams, eds.

(1967), *Three Proposals for Innovative Correctional Facilities.* Berkeley: Department of Architecture, University of California. A8c, C2.

and M. Silverstein (1967), *Dorms at Berkeley: An Environmental Analysis.* Berkeley: Center for Planning and Developmental Research, University of California. A8a, A8c, C2.

Van Ginkel, H. P. D.

(1968), "The systems approach: A working tool for airport design," *Architectural Record,* Vol. 144, August, pp. 128–131. A7b, C2.

Vigier, F.

(1965), "An experimental approach to urban design," *Journal of the American Institute of Planners,* Vol. 31, pp. 21–31. C2.

Vinacke, W. E.

(1952), *The Psychology of Thinking.* New York: McGraw-Hill. A2b.

Von Forester, H.

(1962), "Logical structure of the environment and its internal representation," *International Design Conference,* Aspen, Colo., pp. 27–38. A8a.

Von Neumann, J.

(1963), *The Computer and the Brain.* New Haven: Yale University Press. A3c.

and O. Morgenstern (1953), *Theory of Games and Economic Behavior.* Princeton: Princeton University Press. B2d.

Voorhees, A. M., ed.

(1959), "Land use and traffic models: A progress report," *Journal of the American Institute of Planners,* Special Issue, Vol. 25, September. C3b, C3c.

Wachs, M.

(1968), "A survey of citizens' opinions of the effectiveness, needs, and techniques of urban transportation planning," *Highway Research Record,* No. 229, pp. 65–76. A6a.

Walkey, R.

(1967), "A transportation network for cities," unpublished master's thesis, University of California, Berkeley. A8c, C3c.

Ward, A.

(1967), *The Organization of Prison Workshops: Report for the Penal Establishments Group MPBW.* London: Ministry of Public Buildings and Works. A8c, C2.

and G. Broadbent, eds. (in press), *Design Methods in Architecture.* London: Lund Humphries, and New York: Wittenborn. A1, C1, C2.

Webber, M. M.

(1965), "The roles of intelligence systems in urban-systems planning," *Journal of the American Institute of Planners,* Vol. 31, pp. 289–296. A9, C3a.

Weingartner, M.

(1963), *Mathematical Programming and the Analysis of Capital Budgeting Problems.* Englewood Cliffs, N.J.: Prentice-Hall. B2c.

Weiss, R. S., and S. Bouterline

(1962), *Fairs, Pavilions, and their Audiences.* Cambridge: IBM Communications Research. A8b.

Wells, R. A.

(1967), *ICES STRUDL I: The Uses of ICES STRUDL I.* Cambridge: Department of Civil Engineering, M.I.T. A3a, C2.

Werner, H.   (1961), *Comparative Psychology of Mental Development*. New York: Science Editions. A2b, A8b.

and B. Kaplan (1963), *Symbol Formation: An Organismic-Developmental Approach to Language and the Expression of Thought*. New York: Wiley. A2b.

Wertheimer, M.   (1959), *Productive Thinking*. New York: Harper & Row. A2b.

Wheaton, W. L. C.   (1963), "Operations research for metropolitan planning," *Journal of the American Institute of Planners,* Vol. 24, pp. 250–259. C3a.

Whitehead, B., and M. Z. Elders   (1964), "An approach to the optimum layout of single-story buildings," *Architect's Journal,* Vol. 139, pp. 1373–1380. A5, C2.

(1965), "The planning of single-story layouts," *Building Science,* Vol. 1, September, pp. 127–139. A5, C2.

Whitfield, W. T., R. S. Easterby, and D. Whitfield, eds.   (1967), *The Human Operator in Complex Systems*. London: Taylor & Francis. A3c.

Wiener, N.   (1954), *The Human Use of Human Beings: Cybernetics and Society*. Garden City, N.Y.: Doubleday Anchor. A3c, B1a.

(1961), *Cybernetics: Or Control and Communication in the Animal and Machine*. Cambridge: M.I.T. Press. A3c, B1a.

Wildavsky, A.   (1966), "The political economy of efficiency: Cost-benefit analysis, systems analysis, and program budgeting," *Public Administration Review,* Vol. 26, pp. 292–310. A7a, B2a.

Wilde, D. J.   (1963), *Optimum-Seeking Methods*. Englewood Cliffs, N.J.: Prentice-Hall. B2c.

and C. S. Brightler (1967), *Foundation of Optimization*. Englewood Cliffs, N.J.: Prentice-Hall. B2c.

Wilkins, L. T.   (1964), *Social Deviance*. London: Tavistock. A8b.

Williamson, H. H.   (1969), "Psychological influences on architectural education," *Progressive Architecture,* Vol. 50, March, pp. 148–149. A2a.

Willner, D., ed.   (1960), *Decisions, Values, and Groups*. Oxford: Pergamon. B2b.

Wilson, A. G.   (1967), "Morphology and modularity," in F. Zwicky and A. G. Wilson, eds., *New Methods of Thought and Procedure: Contributions to the Symposium on Methodologies*. New York: Springer-Verlag. A6b.

Wolfe, H. B., and M. L. Ernst   (1967), "Simulation models and urban planning," in P. M. Morse, ed., *Operations Research for Public Systems*. Cambridge: M.I.T. Press, pp. 49–81. A6b, C3d.

Wood, R. C.   (1968), "Application of computers to the problems of urban society," *Socio-Economic Planning Sciences,* Vol. 1, pp. 209–213. C3a.

Woodson, T. T.   (1966), *Introduction to Engineering Design*. New York: McGraw-Hill. C1.

Wülf, F.   (1938), "Tendencies in figural variation," in W. D. Ellis, ed., *A Source Book of Gestalt Psychology*. London: Routledge & Kegan Paul, and New York: Humanities, pp. 136–148. A2b.

Wurman, R. S., and S. W. Killinger   (1967), "Visual information systems," *Architecture Canada,* Vol. 44, March, pp. 37–56. A3b.

Wurster, C. B.   (1963), "The form and structure of the future urban complex," in L. Wingo, ed., *Cities and Space: The Future Use of Urban Land*. Baltimore: Johns Hopkins, pp. 92–101. A8c.

Wylie, C., G. Romney, D. Evans, and A. Erdahl   (1968), "Half-tone perspective drawings by computer," *Proceedings Fall Joint Computer Conference,* Vol. 32, pp. 37–45. A3b.

Yates, A.   (1962), *Frustration and Conflict*. London: Methuen. A8b.

Young, R. C.   (1966), "Goals and goal-setting," *Journal of the American Institute of Planners,* Vol. 32, pp. 76–85. C3a.

Zwick, C. J.   (1963), *Systems Analysis and Urban Planning*. Santa Monica, Calif.: RAND Corporation. A7a, C3a.

Zwicky, F.   (1948), "A morphological method of analysis and construction," *Studies and Essays* (Courant Anniv. Volume). New York: Interscience. C2.

and A. G. Wilson, eds. (1967), *New Methods of Thought and Procedure: Contributions to the Symposium on Methodologies*. New York: Springer-Verlag. B2b.

Index